The
Witch Studies
Reader

The Witch Studies Reader

SOMA CHAUDHURI AND JANE WARD · *editors*

DUKE UNIVERSITY PRESS *Durham and London* 2025

© 2025 DUKE UNIVERSITY PRESS
All rights reserved
Project Editor: Bird Williams
Designed by Matt Tauch
Typeset in Arno Pro, Quadraat Sans, Tangerine and Origami
by Westchester Publishing Services

Library of Congress Cataloging-in-Publication Data
Names: Chaudhuri, Soma, [date]- editor. | Ward, Elizabeth
Jane, editor.
Title: The witch studies reader / Soma Chaudhuri and
Jane Ward, editors.
Description: Durham : Duke University Press, 2025. | Includes
bibliographical references and index.
Identifiers: LCCN 2024025715 (print)
LCCN 2024025716 (ebook)
ISBN 9781478031352 (paperback)
ISBN 9781478028130 (hardcover)
ISBN 9781478060369 (ebook)
Subjects: LCSH: Witchcraft. | Witches. | Feminist spirituality.
| Occultism—Social aspects.
Classification: LCC BF1566 . W7375 2025 (print)
LCC BF1566 (ebook)
DDC 133.4/3—dc23/eng/20241121
LC record available at https:// lccn.loc.gov/2024025715
LC ebook record available at https:// lccn.loc.gov
/2024025716

Cover art: Matt Tauch

To witches everywhere

Contents

xi   *Acknowledgments*

1   Introduction: Manifesting Witch Studies
SOMA CHAUDHURI AND JANE WARD

I   THE COLONIAL ENCOUNTER

23   ONE · Witchcraft in My Community: Healing Sex and Sexuality
TUSHABE WA TUSHABE, PATRICIA HUMURA, AND RUTH ASIIMWE

34   TWO · "What Is a Witch?": *Tituba*'s Subjunctive Challenge
NATHAN SNAZA

46   THREE · Irish Feminist Witches: Using Witchcraft and Activism to Heal from Violence and Trauma
SHANNON HUGHES SPENCE

60   FOUR · Whose Craft?: Contentions on Open and Closed Practice in Contemporary Witchcraft(s)
APOORVAA JOSHI AND ETHEL BROOKS

II   LINEAGES OF HEALING

75   FIVE · "You Deserve, Baby!": Spiritual Co-creation, Black Witches, and Feminism
MARCELITTE FAILLA

90   SIX · Resurrecting Granny: A Brief Excavation of Appalachian Folk Magic
BRANDY RENEE MCCANN

105	SEVEN · "Some Decks May Be Stacked against Us but This Deck Is Ours": Justice-Centered Tarot in and against the New Age
	KRYSTAL CLEARY
118	EIGHT · Ecstatic Desires: Queerness and the Witch's Body
	SIMON CLAY AND EMMA QUILTY
131	NINE · Deitsch Magic Past and Future
	ERIC STEINHART
144	TEN · "We Are Here with Our Rebellious Joy": Witches and Witchcraft in Turkey
	AYÇA KURTOĞLU
158	ELEVEN · Fortune-Telling, Women's Friendship, and Divination Commodification in Contemporary Italy
	MORENA TARTARI

III KILLING THE WITCH

175	TWELVE · A Feminist Theory of Witch Hunts
	GOVIND KELKAR AND DEV NATHAN
190	THIRTEEN · Occult Violence and the Savage Slot: Understanding Tanzanian Witch-Killings in Historical and Ethnographic Context
	AMY NICHOLS-BELO
205	FOURTEEN · Going All the Way: From Village to Supreme Court for a Witch-Killing in Central India
	HELEN MACDONALD
219	FIFTEEN · Contemporary Trends in Witch-Hunting in India
	SHASHANK SHEKHAR SINHA
233	SIXTEEN · Bewitching Gender History
	ADRIANNA L. ERNSTBERGER

IV ART, AESTHETICS, AND CULTURAL PRODUCTION

249 SEVENTEEN · Mista Boo: Portrait of a Drag Witch
ISABEL MACHADO

262 EIGHTEEN · Witching Sound in the Anthropocene (and Occultcene)
D FERRETT

275 NINETEEN · A Witch's Guide to the Underground: Sixties Counterculture, Dianic Wicca, and the Cultural Trope of the "Witchy Diva"
SHELINA BROWN

289 TWENTY · A Queer Critical Analysis of Contemporary Representations of the *Churail* in Hindi Film
SAIRA CHHIBBER

304 TWENTY-ONE · Pakistan's *Churails*: Young Feminists Choosing "Witch" Way Is Forward
MARIA AMIR

318 TWENTY-TWO · From "Born This Witch" to "Bad Bitch Witch": A History of Witch Representation in Western Pop Culture
JAIME HARTLESS AND GABRIELLA V. SMITH

331 TWENTY-THREE · "I Put a Spell on You and Now You're Mine": A Vulvacentric Reading of Witchcraft
ANNA ROGEL

V PROTEST AND RECLAIMING

347 TWENTY-FOUR · Hexing the Patriarchy: The Revolutionary Aesthetics of W.I.T.C.H.
CAROLYN CHERNOFF

361 TWENTY-FIVE · Witch-Ins and Other Feminist Acts
TINA ESCAJA AND LAURIE ESSIG

372	TWENTY-SIX ·	Disappearing Acts: Attending "Witch School" in Brooklyn, New York
		JACQUELYN MARIE SHANNON
388	TWENTY-SEVEN ·	We Are All Witches: My Pagan Journey
		BERNADETTE BARTON

VI WITCH EPISTEMOLOGIES

401	TWENTY-EIGHT ·	Witching the Institution: Academia and Feminist Witchcraft
		RUTH CHARNOCK AND KAREN SCHALLER
420	TWENTY-NINE ·	A Ruderal Witchcraft Manifesto
		MARGARETHA HAUGHWOUT AND OLIVER KELLHAMMER
436	THIRTY ·	Feminism as a Demon, or, The Difference Witches Make: Chiara Fumai with Carla Lonzi
		NICOLE TRIGG
449	THIRTY-ONE ·	Religion and Magic through Feminist Lenses
		MARY JO NEITZ AND MARION S. GOLDMAN
464	THIRTY-TWO ·	Crafting against Capitalism: Queer Longings for Witch Futures
		KATIE VON WALD AND AP PIERCE

475	*Contributors*
489	*Index*

Acknowledgments

We would both like to thank our editor, Elizabeth Ault, the fabulous editorial team at Duke University Press, the anonymous reviewers who provided thoughtful comments at various stages of the manuscript, and our dedicated authors who have managed to produce critical pieces of feminist scholarship while navigating the challenges of a global pandemic. We are grateful for the generous financial support provided by the Humanities and Arts Research Program (HARP) and by the Department of Sociology at Michigan State University toward production costs for the project. Finally, this reader would not have been possible without the labor and resilience of the witches whose stories appear in this book, or without the guidance of feminist scholars who came before us.

Jane would like to thank her colleagues and comrades in the witchy Department of Feminist Studies at UC Santa Barbara for their embrace of her wildness. Thank you to Grandmother Rainbow, who once lived in a trailer in the hills of Santa Barbara and taught a young Jane how to howl at the moon. Deep gratitude to Starhawk for the love spell she offered in Los Angeles in 2004, which led Jane to her wife, Kat. A debt of gratitude is owed to UC Riverside, and to Sherine Hafez, for making it possible for Jane to teach a course on witches and witchcraft. Thank you to Shirley Ward, for always being willing to dress up like the witches we are. Thank you to Stephanie Brill for all of the healing. Thank you to Wild Terra in Los Angeles for the raw ingredients. And to Fancypants, the potbelly pig, thank you for being such a challenging familiar. Above all, eternal gratitude to the woods of Seawitch, where Jane and her family find magic and respite.

Soma would like to thank Gary Jensen, Emeritus Professor of Sociology at Vanderbilt University, who encouraged her travel with him a very long time ago, tracing the path of the devil through tempests in teapots. To her dear feminist friends, Paromita Sanyal, Jaita Talukdar, stef shuster, Stephanie Nawyn, and Sandy Marquart-Pyatt, words are never enough to express Soma's gratitude toward their unwavering faith in her over the years. For now, a mere *thank you* will have to suffice. To her parents, Susanta and Sukriti Chaudhuri, *pronam* for the magic of giving life to her, for always supporting her, and for tolerating her nonsense. To Sumit, whose fascination with *churails*, *bhoots*, and *dainis* is legendary in the family, thank you for introducing Soma to the horror genre of the Ramsay brothers on cable TV. Soma continues to cringe at the movies. To Ahona (Rumi) and Sahana (Raya), Soma's very own kitty witches, life has become magical, sparkly, and filled with happy potions. Finally, a note of gratitude to Arijit, Soma's husband and partner in all things witchy and witchcraft.

Introduction · SOMA CHAUDHURI AND JANE WARD

Manifesting Witch Studies

You could say that we are both obsessed with witches, but for quite different reasons; and it is through our vastly different journeys that a vision for a global reader that would reimagine the study of witches, witchcraft, and witch hunts was born. Stories about witches, found in nearly every corner of the world, are by their nature stories about the most basic and profound of human experiences—healing, sex, violence, tragedies, aging, death, and encountering the mystery and magic of the unknown. It is no surprise, then, that witches loom large across the span of our cultural imaginations. Almost everyone is intrigued by the power of witches; their simultaneous allure and danger are now well documented in centuries of folklore and have been popularized on TV and in film, fiction, and social media. In academia, there are anthropological subdisciplines devoted to the study of witches; yet they all too often view their subject through the well-worn gaze of the colonizer or outsider rather than from the perspectives emerging from scholars who are themselves witches and/or embedded in communities of witchcraft practitioners. This reader stems from our longing not just to place witches' voices alongside feminist academic examinations of witchcraft but to make clear that scholars and witches are sometimes the same people. From a decolonial feminist perspective, this overlap makes sense, as witches are keepers of suppressed knowledges, manifesters of new futures, exemplars of praxis, and theorists in their own right. Just as importantly, we envisioned a reader that would trace points of departure and convergence as we followed the witch across the globe, looking for new understandings that upend the white supremacist, colonial, and patriarchal knowledge regimes that have informed many previous writings. And, thus, the global witch studies reader was launched as an effort to call into existence a new interdisciplinary field of feminist witch studies.

OUR STORIES

Soma spent more than a decade in the 2000s studying how witchcraft accusations are leveraged to legitimize violence against women. Documenting the rise of witch hunts among some *adivasi* tea plantation labor communities in northern Bengal, India, she found a complex set of gendered and political-economic factors tied to the colonial roots of the plantation economy that led to women becoming credible targets during witch hunts. Growing up with urban class and caste privileges, Soma imagined tea plantations as sites of luxurious vacations among the lovely tea bushes, sprinkled with sights of tea-leaf pickers with their bamboo baskets and afternoons spent sipping the first flush tea while relaxing on rattan furniture at the planter's bungalow-turned-tourist hotel—perfect for holiday postcards of yesteryear or for selfies in Instagram posts in today's world. This is the popular image promised by the "tea resorts," where city dwellers get to enjoy proximity to nature, have adventures in the forests, and feast on local and colonial era–inspired delicacies. Welcome to the glamour of plantation life, where witches, or *dain* in the local Sadri language, are erased from the carefully reconstructed pictures.

Instead, Soma's first trip to the field site gave her a glimpse of the oppressive labor, dismal work conditions, and abject poverty that are part of tea plantation life. At the bottom of the plantation class hierarchy are the *adivasi*, a community of laborers lured to the area with the promise of better lives when the colonial plantations were originally set up almost 150 years ago. Isolated through the oppressive and violent policies that undergird the plantations, today the tea estates are an image of an "ailing industry." While the brown upper-caste planters have replaced the white owners, frequent closure of the plantations, inconsistent wages, starvation, and malnutrition are the material realities that visitors encounter if they ever cross from the paths of the colonial bungalows toward the labor lines, the areas where the workers live. *Adivasi* women suffer the most due to their intersectional identities (as women, migrant workers, and members of the Indigenous groups occupying the lowest paying jobs in the plantation economy), and they become targets of their community's anger and frustrations. As Soma's 2013 book, *Tempest in a Teapot*, closely examines, this scapegoating of women takes the form of witch hunts that often end with the women's violent public deaths. Violence against women, both metaphorical and physical, is present everywhere on the plantation, where women are raped, tortured, and murdered, all in the name of being labeled a *daini*, a wild, evil, sexually perverted, ugly woman who must be controlled and killed to end the community's suffering. Plantation management and the local police have largely ignored these killings as something that the incurable *adivasi* engage in as their favorite pastime.[1] Witch hunts are not good for tourism.

Thus, for Soma, the witch became a symbol of a devastating curse, a stigma that has destroyed many women and their families. It became almost impossible for her to envision an alternative to the label, where the identity of a witch and the practice of witchcraft could be reclaimed through feminist empowerment and healing that is both visible and mainstream. It is important to note here, that in India, there *is* a small witchy world that not only exists but also is celebrated. Coming from urban, English-language-preferred and privileged backgrounds (artists, performers, writers, and social workers), the members of this community are often the safekeepers of the colonial charm. These witches identify as Wiccans and are led by a self-declared high priestess trained in the West, who gives lessons on Wiccan life and healing in old country clubs and luxury hotels. Speaking in carefully anglicized English accents, dressed in mostly Western clothing, this exclusive group of Indian witches and their followers come with the baggage of homophobia and elitist class exclusiveness;[2] in addition, they are strikingly disconnected from the precarity facing *adivasi* women accused of witchcraft. Between the emotional overwhelm of studying the extreme violence perpetrated against migrant women laborers accused of witchcraft and the disgust elicited by the anglicized pagan witches, who promised empowered healing through a mix of crystal gazing accompanied by a "healthy" dose of homophobia, Soma was pretty much done with witches.

But then Jane reached out. Jane, a white American professor of feminist and queer studies, became enchanted with pagan forms of witchcraft in the late 2010s as part of a search for healing and spiritual practices not anchored in white people's racist appropriation of Indigenous and Global South traditions.[3] Driven by a desire to relate differently to the natural world and to her own anxiety—both a lifelong anxiety disorder and a newer sense of existential crisis animated by rising fascism and environmental crisis—she dove into her ancestral records and began studying the seasonal rituals and plant-based medicinal practices that structured life for centuries in the parts of Northern Europe where her ancestors had lived. She learned about the stories, symbols, foods, crafts, and planting and harvesting activities associated with the pagan holidays. She took classes in herbal medicine and made teas from the mugwort, yarrow, nettle, and calendula she grew in her backyard. For Jane, this return to ancestral healing was not initially about witchcraft at all; it was an expression of white anti-racist values, a refusal of the kind of sage-burning and mantra-chanting that many white people take up in order to connect with nature or spirit. But she soon discovered that many of the best resources on European paganism and herbalism were produced by women who identified as witches and who understood their work as witchcraft.

Silvia Federici's classic *Caliban and the Witch* provides the historical foundation for the European connection between women's healing or nature-based practices and witchcraft. As women became the scapegoats for the violent clash between feudal land privatization and peasant revolt in medieval Europe, their essential roles in their communities as healers, farmers, land stewards, and public laborers became criminalized through the catch-all accusation of witchcraft. One legacy of the European witch hunts is that, in the Global North, to be a woman who grows her own herbs to use as medicine, or who lives alone in the woods, or who appears to be more connected to animals than humans, is to be perceived as a "witchy" woman. For Jane—living as a white woman settler in the United States and having long been drawn to the nebulous queerness of Hollywood's vengeful crones, wicked stepsisters, and black-clad spinsters—to be a witch carried little risk. Jane hit her mid-forties and embraced her silver hair, dreamed of a house deep in the woods with a potbelly pig as her animal familiar.[4] To be an aging and perverse witch felt, in this context, like a "fuck you" to patriarchy, like a reclaiming of the way the world already viewed queer feminist women. But this defiance was, of course, a chosen identification forged in many kinds of privilege and not an accusation that carried the risks of rape and death that are faced by the *adivasi* women at the heart of Soma's research. Jane's embrace of witchcraft, as for many white women in the Global North drawn to reconnecting with traditional healing practices, was haunted by histories of horrific violence against women of European descent; but it was also enabled by the colonial, white supremacist, and patriarchal histories that undergird all commodified "freedoms" in the United States.

In 2018, Jane began teaching a course at UC Riverside on gender and witchcraft that had originally been created by her colleague Sherine Hafez. It was this course that led her to pull together, as best she could, a decolonial feminist witchcraft studies syllabus that decentered European-derived paganism and traced the relationship between witchcraft, the transatlantic slave trade, and settler colonial violence across the Global South and North. In sections on witchcraft in the Americas, the course shifted attention away from the white feminist witchcraft practices that have traditionally received ample coverage in the mainstream media and focused instead on Black witches and brujas engaged in African-derived and Indigenous spiritual practices inseparable from healing the violent histories of colonization. The course also included feminist research, like Soma's, on contemporary anti-witch violence, witch camps, and witch-hunting laws in South Asia and Africa, leading the students in the course, mostly women and queer and trans people of color, to ask why they previously had no idea that women accused of witchcraft were *currently* targets of mass violence. These conversations, along with Jane's Instagram feed filled with high-profile white, Black, and Latinx witches (mostly from the United States)—who commonly referenced historical violence but who never discussed the witch hunts happening in the present—led Jane to reach out to Soma to ask how she made sense of this striking gap in knowledge.

Jane's questions intrigued Soma, who was familiar with some Global North academics' reactions of horror and disbelief toward witch hunts that were still taking place in some parts of the world but who had not been tracking the uptick of witch identification in the United States or its cultural expressions on social media. While the field of anthropology initially popularized the study of witchcraft, the problematic racial undertones by mostly white men academics studying Indigenous communities and their practices had isolated the study of witches to a small field within the discipline. This led to a decline in its academic popularity in recent years, leading perhaps to a false assumption that incidents of witch-hunting were historical problems even as, or perhaps especially as, the popular witchcraft-as-feminist-empowerment trend was again on the rise in the Global North.

In the Global North, the phenomenal financial success of the *Harry Potter* franchise (a story of young wizards and witches triumphing over evil), the explosion of witchcraft-themed content on TikTok and Instagram, and the ubiquitous witchcraft book display at chain bookstores like Barnes & Noble made unmistakably clear that witchcraft had gone about as mainstream as lattes and yoga. From 2018 to 2020, US-based news outlets like the *Guardian*, the *New York Times*, and the *Atlantic* asked, respectively: "Why are witches so popular?" "Why did everybody become a witch?" and "Why is witchcraft on the rise?"[5] The answer, they all explained, was not only that interest in spirituality and the occult increased during periods of political upheaval and uncertainty—as trust in mainstream institutions waned—but that witchcraft, in particular, appealed to young feminists during times of patriarchal backlash, symbolizing women's power to change their circumstances using alternative methods (ritual, spellcasting, divination, herbalism, goddess/nature worship). Witchcraft was, again, offering feminist and queer ways of life aimed at using "magical activism" to reimagine political systems, healthcare practices, natural environments, and collective futures.

Unlike the feminist witchcraft movement of the 1980s, Black witches, brujas/brujxs, and queer and trans witches were at the helm of the COVID-era witch resistance, and public hexes on the patriarchy and on white supremacy were among this era's witches' most popular spells. Collective, public performances of witchcraft popped up in a range of contexts: witches convened at Catland Books in New York to place a hex on Brett Kavanaugh in 2018; witches across the United States (acting together as "the Magical Resistance") cast a binding spell against Donald Trump during each waning crescent moon of his presidency; a collective of Mexican feminists protested femicide in 2020 under the name *Brujas del Mar*, or "Witches of the Sea"; three dozen witches rallied at the state capitol to protest against Michigan Republican Party chair Ron Weiser in 2021; an army of Argentinian witches came together to cast spells to protect the golden boy Messi, the star Argentinian footballer, at the 2022 World Cup Finals.[6] Beginning around 2015, a steady flow of new books about how to practice witchcraft moved from the occult section at the back of the bookstore to prominent displays where the latest how-to guides and tarot decks sat next to essential oil potions and candles for casting assorted spells. Witchcraft also took its place inside queer and feminist movement spaces, with feminist influencers proudly blending identities of feminist, anti-racist, abolitionist, organizer, witch. Tarot and astrology experienced renewed popularity among social justice activists, who reconceptualized them as tools for surviving the steady drumbeat of soul-killing news about state violence, ongoing climate disasters, and the devastating COVID-19 pandemic.

Looking at the resurgence of witchcraft in the United States might lead one to imagine that it is a good time to be a witch or that, finally, "witches are having their hour," to quote another 2019 essay from the *New York Times*.[7] And yet, we must ask whether the commodified embrace of youth-oriented and self-help–driven "witchy vibes" in the Global North has led to a greater respect for aging women or women's labor in Europe and the United States—perhaps the truest test of whether witches in these regions are having their hour. This book arises, then, not only from a need to address the Global North's erasure of women in the Global South, for whom the label of witch remains dangerous and devastating, but also from a need to illuminate the Global North's continued patriarchal erasure of the crone from public life and its persistent colonial paranoia about magic, spirit possession, and other spiritual practices associated with the Global South. Thus, we envision a reimagining of witch studies as a practice of decolonial feminist theorizing as well as intersectional healing and solidarity that flows multidirectionally, from South to North, and North to South.

GATHERING THE GLOBAL COVEN: AN INTERSECTIONAL AND DECOLONIAL APPROACH TO WRITING ABOUT WITCHES

Bringing a decolonial feminist lens to witch studies requires that we grapple with the reasons that contemporary witch hunts have been omitted from Global North accounts of witches and witchcraft. It also requires that we trace the connections between the Global North and the Global South, noting the ways that colonial, patriarchal, and white supremacist logics enable the exploitation and control of aging women's bodies, labor, and resources in every corner of the globe—with witchcraft accusations being but one method used to exercise this control of women. Tens of thousands of poor women, Indigenous women, and/or aging women across the Global South in Asia (India, Indonesia, Nepal, and Papua New Guinea) and sub-Saharan Africa (Kenya, Ghana, Tanzania, Cameroon, Uganda, Zambia, Mozambique, Nigeria, South Africa, Angola, and the Congo) have been murdered for their association—real or imagined—with witchcraft in the past eighty or more years, and this violence is ongoing. As Maile Arvin, Eve Tuck, and Angie Morrill explain in their groundbreaking essay "Decolonizing Feminism," witch hunts, like colonialism and state-sanctioned slavery, are often presumed to be located "at an historical point in time away from which our society has progressed."[8] Feminist researchers of contemporary witchcraft-related murders upend that presumption, documenting how the forces of patriarchy, global capitalism, and land displacement continue to intersect to make women vulnerable to scapegoating during times of economic crisis.[9]

Today's witchcraft accusations in the Global South frequently revolve around limited access to, or loss of, scarce resources—land, drinking water, food, adequate sanitation, employment—with women positioned as easy targets of blame for the profound inequities wrought by settler colonialism and global capital. Widows who own landed property are accused of witchcraft by their relatives. Women elders who accrue financial wealth over the course of their lifetime are targets of jealousy and resentment. Women who are too old to bear children are blamed for being a drain on scarce resources. Women who are farmers or traders are viewed as threats to men who perceive them as competition. Women who are healthy when others fall ill are suspected of malicious supernatural activity. For all these reasons, women have been tortured, shamed, hanged, stoned, cut open, burned, and buried alive in recent decades, while few have been able to seek refuge in precarious shelters. In India alone, it is estimated that more than 25,000 witch-killings occurred between 1987 and 2003, while many more incidents remain unreported. In stark contrast with the feminist reclaiming of witchcraft in the United States and parts of Europe and Latin America, women's repudiation of witchcraft is a matter of life or death in many countries. The differences are staggering.

And yet, when we approach witches from a global perspective, our attention is also drawn to the many ideas about witches that span cultures and continents. Not disconnected from real-life views about women, folklore about witches offers a window onto the way that different communities imagine women and sex, money, aging, and nature. Some of the commonalities are staggering, too. The wildly specific notion, for instance, that witches are female shapeshifters who appear to men as young, beautiful seductresses until they reveal their hideous, barren, aging, bony, distorted bodies, often part animal and part human, and either devour their male targets or drive them mad, is a theme present in folklore about the aswangs of the Philippines, La Siguanaba of El Salvador, Lamia of ancient Greece, and the *churails* of India. In another transnational theme, witches are seen as cannibals with a particular taste for children. The witch Baba Yaga, of Russian origin, is but one of many witches who lives in the forest and eats fetuses and children; keeping her in good company are real-life brujas of Mexico who have been accused of sucking the blood of children,[10] the Boo Hag of American folklore who steals the breath and skin of children, and the nineteenth-century German witch, from *Grimm's Fairy Tales*, who attempts to eat Hansel before his sister Gretel rescues him. Many of these child-eating witches live in the deep, dark woods, like one of Jane's personal favorites, the stick-sculpture-making, child-killing witch from the 1999 film *The Blair Witch Project*. Yet another global theme is the association of witches with plant- and animal-based magic and the brewing of powerful potions in cauldrons. The obeah witch of the African diaspora is known to create evil potions in her kettle or pot, as are many witches of European origin, such as the Celtic goddess-hag Cailleach or the witches of Medieval England, their cauldrons made famous by William Shakespeare for boiling "eye of newt and toe of frog" in Macbeth. La Llorona of Mexico, like Bloody Mary of the United States and Hanako-san of Japan, inhabits the space between ghost and witch, striking fear in children with her mournful wailing and vengeance for the pains of womanhood (the loss of children, cheating husbands, the shame of menstruation, surviving abuse). La Llorona, like many witches, roams the night and can be found near fog-shrouded water (in her case, wearing a tattered wedding dress). Bloody Mary and Hanako-san both haunt girls' bathrooms, evoking the terrible rituals of being witnessed in puberty (Jane is thinking here about the deeply formative "plug it up!" locker room scene—somehow one of her queer roots—from the 1976 horror film Carrie).

Mapping these similarities casts light on the witch's symbolic function vis-à-vis the gender binary. The very qualities of beauty, fertility, and maternalism that constitute the female side of the mythical gender binary are themselves transient; femininity ultimately shrivels, hardens, and decays. The witch—once goddess and then crone, a youthful beauty morphed into the grotesque hag—is arguably a memento mori, a personified reminder of the inevitability of aging and death. Of course, the hag is not just an old person but an old woman, specifically, whose discernment and infertility pose a threat to heteropatriarchy and the narrow space it reserves for girls and women. Both in folklore and in justifications of real-life witch-killings, the witch is the anti-feminine; she is excess, no longer useful to men, a drain on resources, without beauty or fecundity to contribute in return. In this way, the witch sits at the nexus of gender and horror, her terrifying impact rooted in a kind of hetero-erotic bait-and-switch where youthful femininity is suddenly replaced with embodied cronehood. We see this theme in one of the most frightening scenes in the 1980 Stanley Kubrick film The Shining, in which a young and sexy woman lures Jack Nicholson toward her as she emerges naked from a bathtub, only to transform into a cackling, decaying hag. We see the seductress-hag, again, in the 2015 film The Witch, when an adolescent boy, Caleb, is wandering in the woods and encounters a young woman emerging from a moss-covered, brambly hut wearing a red cloak, showing abundant cleavage and an eager smile. As she leans in to embrace and kiss Caleb, her arm is revealed to be that of an old woman. The horror!

"Dark magic" witches and vengeful women spirits not only haunt us for gendered reasons but also appear as justifications for, and as punishers of, colonial and white supremacist projects. La Llorona, for instance, is often described as the terrifying ghost of a jealous Indigenous woman who killed the children she bore from a Spanish man after finding him with another woman. In this oft-told version of the tale, La Llorona is akin to La Malinche, a traitor to her people who assists the Spanish in their conquest of the Aztec and Maya empires. But other accounts rewrite this relationship between the Indigenous woman and the colonizer, such as the 2019 Guatemalan film *La Llorona*, in which the weeping woman is crying not with jealousy over a lover, but with rage at the injustice of colonization and the genocide against the Mayan people.

A central tension in this volume, and in feminist thinking about witches more broadly, is how to make sense of the countless ways that people have understood witches and witchcraft across time and place. There are many paths to the witch. For instance, we can approach the witch primarily as a patriarchal and colonial construction, as a scapegoat used to justify profound theft of land and life, one so entrenched in violent legacies that it/she must be disavowed or wholly reimagined once and for all. Or we can view the witch as a supernatural force, a sorceress, a goddess, or a healer found in forests and amid dense fogs not because she was placed there by the patriarchal imagination but because this is where the plants and animals live and where her work is done. In another variation on these themes, we can understand the witch as a spectacularly powerful and generative symbol of what men, owning classes, and colonizing nations fear most about women's collective knowledge—of nature, childbirth, healing, sex, and death—a symbol with enduring power to mobilize feminist action and to imagine the future otherwise. We can also offer up the witch as history's best example of misogyny in its most basic form, a testament to the fact that simply being an aging woman, an outspoken woman, a skilled woman, a sexual woman, and so on, has resulted in the most brutal forms of torture and death.

Ultimately, can the label of the witch transition into something that is powerful in a way that not only resists the patriarchal attacks on women but also becomes meaningful for survivors of violence and for women everywhere? Almost a decade and a half ago, Ramani, an *adivasi* woman, was accused by villagers of practicing witchcraft and causing harm to neighborhood children. Ramani survived the horrific witch hunt and later, with the help of local women's groups in her community, became an advocate

FIGURE I.1 Ramani, a witch-hunt survivor, a nurturer, and a witch, 2005. Photograph by author.

of anti–witch hunt campaigns. An important part of her advocacy lay in retelling stories of how she acquired the label of *daini*, a label that she both disavowed and embraced as a survivor of violence. It is in her role as survivor, protector, activist, and nurturer that Ramani displays her feminist agency at the fullest: devoid of fear from labels and empowered with the knowledge of survival. Ramani uses the label of the witch as a counternarrative during community meetings for anti–witch hunts to stop future violence against community women: "You say I am a witch?! I am a witch. I can eat you, cut you into pieces . . . just test me. See what happens to you if you make one more accusation against another sister." Ramani is always accompanied by another woman, Shamita, at these meetings. Shamita had given Ramani, a single childless woman, shelter after the hunt and employed her to look after Shamita's children. Shamita sometimes brings her now adult children to the meetings as evidence that Ramani is not evil and that her children remained unharmed and well protected under her care.

Ramani is among a small handful of women in India who have embraced the label of witch in defiance, as a form of grassroots protest against patriarchal trauma (evoking many other examples of reclaiming identities rendered abject by the patriarchy, such as *queer, fag, joto, slut, whore, cunt,*

INTRODUCTION 11

pussy, and so on). Women in the Global South continue to be harassed, tortured, and killed based simply on accusations (real or perceived) of practicing witchcraft. In this context, in communities where the label "witch" carries the risk of terrible violence, can Indigenous women afford to embrace this identity, let alone re-envision it as a source of empowerment? Inspired by Ramani, this book imagines the spaces of possibility for global solidarities and healing; it offers a multitude of ways in which the label "witch" can be defied, embraced, and reinterpreted using a queer decolonial framework that refuses the racist and colonial legacy of studies in witches and witchcraft.

> Ramani's Hex:
> I am a witch.
> I can eat you, cut you into pieces
> just test me.
> See what happens to you
> if you make one more accusation.

EPISTEMOLOGIES OF THE SCHOLAR-WITCH

This reader would not be possible if not for the pathbreaking writing of interdisciplinary feminist scholars who have already troubled the boundary between scholarship and spirituality, researcher and practitioner, knowledge and memory. In her foundational book *Pedagogies of Crossing*, Afro-Caribbean feminist anthropologist M. Jacqui Alexander writes about an experience of writers' block that became "unblocked" only by opening herself up to the haunting presence of her research subject, Kitsimba, an enslaved woman who was captured in Central Africa, survived the Middle Passage, and was then accused of sorcery/witchcraft and put on trial. Alexander describes her attempt to study Kitsimba using conventional research methods; she examined documents in archives but simply could not put words to the page and the project stalled out. Being Trinidadian and raised with Yoruba influence in her family's religious practices, Alexander then met with a Yoruba priestess and explained the problems she was having with the research. The priestess helped Alexander channel the spirit of Kitsimba, who turned out to be a very mischievous, contrary, and playful spirit who had been haunting Alexander, resisting Alexander's "fancy" academic ways of trying to research her. Kitsimba told Alexander that she wanted to be accessed in a different way, a way that allowed her to speak about her experience of the Middle Passage in great detail, and that allowed Alexander to integrate her feminist ways of knowing with the sacred.

Feminist scholars like M. Jacqui Alexander, Avery Gordon in *Ghostly Matters*, and Saidiya Hartman in *Wayward Lives, Beautiful Experiments*, are not centrally concerned with witches, but their work has mapped the ways that the collective experience of unfathomable horror and violence produces a collective memory that is deposited everywhere—in the rocks that still surround us, the trees, the ground, the buildings, the photographs. When profound human suffering occurs, we are haunted. The apparatus of the academy cannot detect or integrate the traces of this kind of information about the human experience; but turning our attention to certain figures—the witches, the spirits, the ghosts, the ancestors—is a first step in pushing us (feminist scholars) to grapple with the limits of Enlightenment paradigms and to set aside our "fancy" ways of knowing when they do not actually serve us.

Writing by Indigenous feminist scholars like Robin Wall Kimmerer, of Potawatomi heritage, also inspires the project at hand by describing ways of knowing that are both grounded and sacred and that challenge settlers to inhabit the earth as if we care about it and plan to stay. In *Braiding Sweetgrass*, Kimmerer describes the settler experience of species loneliness—a kind of melancholy that humans experience when we ignore, or think we are superior to, the plants and animals who inhabited the earth long before us. This human arrogance and ignorance—this failure to become a fully integrated member of the multispecies communities in which we live by knowing about its nonhuman inhabitants—is the lens through which many Native activists have described the destruction and dysfunction of settler ways of life. Witchcraft, often a practice of returning to the ancient healing practices and nature-based knowledge of one's ancestors, is for many practicing witches a set of tools for the care and healing of oneself, one's community—of plants, animals, and humans—and the earth (the soil, the air, the water). Witchcraft requires receptivity to multiple (human and nonhuman) voices, and so too does the academic study of witchcraft. As scholar of Caribbean and Black diaspora studies Omise'eke Natasha Tinsley articulates in *Ezili's Mirrors*—a brilliant book that reads like a love letter to the Haitian Vodou spirits of sexuality, femininity, water, fluidity, and pleasure that go by the name Ezili—to write about spirituality is to "tune into another vocabulary" that is the prism through which gender, power, pleasure, and justice are often experienced, and that might hold explanations as powerful and generative as those found in the academy.[11]

> *Spell for accessing knowledge:*
> *May we shed our attachments to disciplined ways of knowing and listen with humility*

THE CHAPTERS TO FOLLOW

Taken together, the chapters in this book are in dialogue with, and also radically expand upon, what has been written about witches and witchcraft to date. Some bring us into the lifeworld of the witch as a real person embedded in community and in intimate relationships or as a healer vital to her community's ability to survive the future. Others approach the witch as a formidable cultural and political symbol, as a nimble epistemological position, or as a historical construct imbued with centuries of far-flung, traveling, and comingled ideas about gender, race, and power. As such, the book is organized into six parts that reflect clusters of ideas and overlapping themes in the chapters: part I, "The Colonial Encounter"; part II, "Lineages of Healing"; part III, "Killing the Witch"; part IV, "Art, Aesthetics, and Cultural Production"; part V, "Protest and Reclaiming"; and part VI, "Witch Epistemologies." These are not discrete themes but rather interconnected pathways that lead toward what we hope is a capacious field of anticolonial and feminist witch studies.

The chapters in the book's first part, "The Colonial Encounter," elucidate that we cannot understand the witch outside of the varied feudal and colonial contexts that named her and against which she has struggled to survive. This means that "witchcraft" itself is an unwieldy and fraught concept, one that struggles to capture a vast, locally variable, syncretic, and ever-shifting set of practices anchored in relationships of violence and resistance. One of the intractable tensions in witchcraft studies is that witches are never only subjects but also points of encounter, contested relationships that emerge from spaces of colonial, white supremacist, and patriarchal power and the social transformations they engender.

Illuminating many of these themes, Tushabe wa Tushabe, Patrica Humura, and Ruth Asiimwe argue that colonization and Christianity in Uganda have worked to recast important healing and community-based practices, often centered in sexual pleasure and other gendered intimacies, into a stigmatized "African witchcraft" imaginary so embedded in colonial violence and misinterpretation that the concept itself may not be recuperable. Nathan Snaza's chapter also attends to themes of encounter and misrecognition through a decolonial feminist reading of Maryse Condé's *I, Tituba*. Snaza conceptualizes the witch as a dynamic and relational creation—a concept that emerged in and from points of contact between colonizer and colonized—as well as a means of resisting the colonizer's misrecognition of local practices.

Part I also highlights one of the paradoxes of witchcraft: the local witch (and the patriarchal and white supremacist terror she incites) may be the outcome of the colonial gaze, but she is also a source of healing from the pain caused by this misrecognition. Grounding us in an example of this duality, Shannon Hughes Spence documents the ways that Irish witches use their craft to heal intergenerational trauma wrought by Irish colonization at the hands of England, the Catholic Church, and the Irish state. Similarly focused on decolonial praxis, Apoorvaa Joshi and Ethel Brooks mine the complexities of racialized witchcraft practices declared "closed" to outsiders so as to preserve healing practices threatened by colonization and targeted by the state. They invite us to envision this protective boundary-making as a form of what Chela Sandoval has called "decolonial love."

The book's second part, "Lineages of Healing," traces the lineages that have kept witchcraft alive despite centuries of efforts to destroy witches and their knowledge. In folklore, witches often live and enact their magic in isolation, but the lived experience of witchcraft practitioners is one of deep embeddedness in communities where healing traditions are passed down through generations, most often from older women to girls, and where community members rely on traditional and feminized methods of care and healing. The chapters in this part document that witchcraft is not only a practice but a lineage—a blended, co-created, multigenerational bricolage of ideas and methods for care and healing when dominant systems (capitalism, Western medicine, organized religion, science) fail us—as they do.

In her chapter on Black witches and manifestation, Marcelitte Failla develops the concept of spiritual co-creation to give name to shared beliefs—informed by Black feminist and Africana religious philosophies—that blend a structural critique of capitalism with an investment in the healing and well-being of Black women and femmes. Extending our attention to the blending of different cosmologies, Brandy Renee McCann examines the multigenerational role of the granny witch of Appalachia. The granny witch is a healer and keeper of cultural knowledge who blends magic with Christianity and a position that McCann herself is intended to inhabit as she ages. In a chapter on justice-centered tarot, Krystal Cleary theorizes tarot produced by feminists of color as a survival and healing tool that contributes to the sustainability of movement work and that stirs the revolutionary imagination toward other possible futures. Turning to the queerness of witchcraft, Simon Clay and Emma Quilty illuminate the way that witches offer queer rituals to their communities that dissolve the boundary between the sacred and the obscene: sexual rites, altered states of consciousness (induced by plants, chanting, drumming, breathwork), ecstatic dance, BDSM as a spiritual practice, and more. And, building on themes of gender and healing, Eric Steinhart traces the influence of witchcraft enacted by the Deitsch, or Pennsylvania Germans, on Anglo-American witchcraft, with particular attention to relative salience of gender in Deitsch lore, symbolism, and rituals.

Another theme of part II is that the relational nature of witchcraft is often marked by homosocial intimacies among women that resist the heteronormative organization of women's lives. Drawing on interviews with Turkish fortune tellers and witches, Ayça Kurtoğlu distinguishes between the relational intimacy forged among women in private fortune-telling spaces and the political utility of the figure of the witch in protest spaces, both of which gesture to a "third space" of women's resistance to men's control of the public sphere. Morena Tatari looks to Italian women's engagement with the homosocial world of fortune-telling, wherein women are initiated into the practice by other women, provide their services to women clients, and create tight-knit networks with other women practitioners that offer a buffer against the stigma associated with supernatural belief.

Chapters in part III, "Killing the Witch," make the strong case that when we shift our analysis of witchcraft from the Global North to the Global South, we recognize witch hunts not as a medieval tragedy but as an ongoing, contemporary crisis. This part lays to rest, we hope, the singular and sometimes even romanticized feminist association of witch hunts with early modern Europe. Govind Kelkar and Dev Nathan offer a transnational theory of the three conditions that give rise to witch-killings across time and place: the devaluation of women's knowledge and labor, widely held cultural beliefs in the human use of supernatural powers to cause harm, and active economic and technological transformations that reorganize systems of production and accumulation. In her essay on witch-killings in Tanzania, Amy Nichols-Belo challenges white supremacist notions about African "occult" violence by spotlighting the resemblance between witch-killings and secular forms of mob violence. Helen Macdonald examines why and how laws designed to end witch-hunting in Central India, like the Chhattisgarh Witchcraft Atrocities Prevention Act, have brought only partial justice for the women accused of witchcraft. Shashank Shekhar Sinha demonstrates that witch hunts in India can be understood only through the lens of multiple and intersecting regional, spatial, ethnic, and economic conflicts and through the lens of patriarchal dynamics. And Adrianna L. Ernstberger shows us that previous efforts to develop a field of witch studies have resulted in an erasure of witches and witchcraft histories from the Global South; her chapter offers a step-by-step guide to teaching a truly global, decolonial course on witch hunts.

Part IV, "Art, Aesthetics, and Cultural Production," refocuses our lens on the witch as both a cultural worker and a film/television trope. Here the authors not only attend to the witch as an archetype widely taken up in performance to engage themes of haunting, revenge, rage, magic, and femme monstrosity; they also illuminate what it means for a sight or sound to bewitch us. Examining the career of the provocative Mexican drag queen Mista Boo, Isabel Machado maps the intersections between performance art and witchcraft, revealing anew that gender performances are their own form of ritualized magic. D Ferret considers the sonic world of the "doom metal" band Divide and Dissolve as a site from which to listen beyond the Anthropocene and to tune in to the sonic geology of the Occultcene. Extending this part's engagement with bewitching music, Shelina Brown investigates the witchy women musicians of 1960s rock counterculture, highlighting this period as the origin of many contemporary witch aesthetics and musical forms.

Part IV also critically explores popular representations of the witch, with particular emphasis on the ways these representations simultaneously threaten and entrance audiences. Saira Chhibber considers the *churail*'s representation in Bollywood film, tracing her evolution from Hindu cautionary figure to righteous freedom fighter. Maria Amir offers an incisive reading of Pakistan's television series *Churails*, drawing attention to the enduring nexus of feminist rage, revenge, and the witch's coven in the popular imagination. In their genealogy of witch representation in Global North popular culture, Jaime Hartless and Gabriella V. Smith identify new themes within the trope of the monstrous feminine, including the millennial feminist claim that witches are "born this way" and later, by contrast, "the bad bitch witch" who embodies the more agentic politics of Gen Z. Taking the cult classic *Hocus Pocus* as her case study, Anna Rogel uncovers the power of the "funny witch," a figure both alluring and repulsive and who, despite her cannibalism, inspires delight among audiences.

Part V, "Protest and Reclaiming," argues for the liberatory potential of witchcraft rituals and political solidarities formed under the broad and ever-shifting identity category of the witch. No discussion of "witch politics" would be complete without an analysis of the anonymous activist group W.I.T.C.H. (founded in the 1960s as the Women's International Terrorist Conspiracy from Hell), and Carolyn Chernoff offers precisely this analysis in her chapter on the group's revolutionary aesthetics, documenting the ways that twenty-first-century W.I.T.C.H. members deploy social media and the monstrous femme to disseminate confrontational graphic art. Taking a deep dive into the absurdist tactics of the Vermont-based grassroots organization Feminists Against Bullshit, Tina Escaja and Laurie Essig pay homage to the performative power of the witch, along with the hysteric and the failed mother, in feminist street protest. Mapping the relationship between grief and witchcraft-inspired protest, Jacquelyn Marie Shannon takes their experience as a student at the Catland Witch School to investigate how purification and protection rites created opportunities for action in response to loss and despair during the global COVID-19 pandemic. In an autobiographical essay, Bernadette Barton reclaims the centrality of pagan rituals to many of the taken-for-granted traditions of interconnectedness in American daily life, arguing for greater reverence for everyday magic and its liberatory potential.

Part VI, "Witch Epistemologies," invites us to view witchcraft as an epistemological project, one engaged in imagining the future differently: brewing, cultivating, transforming, manifesting, concocting, invoking, and otherwise taking action to bring new forms of consciousness into being. In a spellbinding essay about witchcraft in the academy, Ruth Charnock and Karen Schaller model how to build a witch's ritual archive and materialize an epistemology of the witch. Margaretha Haughwout and Oliver Kellhammer look to the resilience of ruderal ecologies, plants species that grow in spaces of disturbance and ruin, to conjure a witchcraft manifesto aimed at harnessing the power to thrive in "the wastelands of capitalism." Nicole Trigg takes feminist performance art engaged with possession and haunting as her point of departure for excavating the multiple, the unknowable, and unnameable. Mary Jo Neitz and Marion S. Goldman call upon scholars of religion to take magic-based spiritual practices more seriously, especially in light of the growing appeal of magical practices (astrology, tarot) during a time of ostensibly increased secularization. Bringing this part, and the book itself, to a galvanizing close, Katie Von Wald and AP Pierce blend Black feminist thought and queer theory to develop the concept of resistive witchcrafting as a relation that connects bodies through pleasure and care and that resists the mainstream consumerism of "witchy" self-identity and commodified magic.

> May each word to follow
> be an offering
> to the infinite altar that holds our collective brilliance,
> the place where every witch's heartbreak wail and freedom spell
> has claimed its little corner,
> there, waiting, for the next witches
> to carry on the work

NOTES

1. The upper caste/class gaze views the *adivasi* with racist prejudice; and *adivasi* women are fetishized as sexual commodities. *Adivasi* women's dance performances are a big tourist attraction. In popular Bollywood and regional films, *adivasi* women's bodies are treated as spaces of lust, while the men are emasculated, portrayed with childlike simplistic characteristics.
2. "A Response to Wiccan Ipsita Roy Chakraverti."
3. By the way, Jane's wife, Kat, comes from a long line of lesbians. Her great aunt, now in her eighties, refers to gay people as "the enchanted."
4. Even when she was young, Jane found the pretty, youthful witches from *Charmed* (1998–2006) and *Sabrina the Teenage Witch* (1996–2003) simply not hardcore enough.
5. Neil Armstrong, "Coven Ready: From Instagram to TV, Why Are Witches So Popular?," *Guardian*, September 15, 2018, https://www.theguardian.com/tv-and-radio/2018/sep/15/witches-occult-dramas-tv-chilling-adventures-of-sabrina-strange-angel; Jessica Bennet, "Why Did Everybody Become a Witch?," *New York Times*, October 24, 2019, https://www.nytimes.com/2019/10/24/books/peak-witch.html; Bianca Bosker, "Why Witchcraft Is on the Rise," *Atlantic*, March 2020, https://www.theatlantic.com/magazine/archive/2020/03/witchcraft-juliet-diaz-605518/.
6. Jack Nicas and Ana Lankes, "Behind Argentina's World Cup Magic, an Army of Witches," *New York Times*, December 17, 2022, https://www.nytimes.com/2022/12/17/world/americas/argentina-world-cup-witches.html.

7   Laura Holson, "Witches Are Having Their Hour," *New York Times*, October 11, 2019, https://www.nytimes.com/2019/10/11/style/pam-grossman-witch-feminism.html.
8   Arvin, Tuck, and Morrill, "Decolonizing Feminism."
9   Chaudhuri, *Witches*; Federici, "Caliban."
10 Fabrega and Nutini, "Witchcraft-Explained Childhood Tragedies."
11 See Omise'eke Tinsley, *Ezili's Mirrors*, 4.

BIBLIOGRAPHY

Arvin, Maile, Eve Tuck, and Angie Morrill. "Decolonializing Feminism: Challenging Connections between Settler Colonialism and Heteropatriarchy," *Feminist Formations* 25, no. 1 (Spring 2013): 8–34.

Chaudhuri, Soma. *Tempest in a Teapot: Witches, Tea Plantations, and Lives of Migrant Laborers in India*. Lanham, MD: Lexington Books, 2013.

Fabrega, H., and Nutini, H. "Witchcraft-Explained Childhood Tragedies in Tlaxcala, and Their Medical Sequelae." *Social Science and Medicine* 36, no. 6 (1993): 793–805.

Federici, Silvia. *Caliban and the Witch: Women, the Body and the Primitive Accumulation*. Brooklyn, NY: Autonomedia Press, 2004.

"A Response to Wiccan Ipsita Roy Chakraverti and Her Homophobia from a Practising Pagan." *Gaylaxy Magazine*, May 8, 2017. https://www.gaylaxymag.com/articles/queer-voices/%E2%80%8Ba-response-wiccan-ipsita-roy-chakraverti=homophobia-practising-pagan/.

Tinsley, Omise'eke Natasha. *Ezili's Mirrors: Imagining Black Queer Genders*. Durham, NC: Duke University Press, 2018.

THE COLONIAL ENCOUNTER

I

One · TUSHABE WA TUSHABE, PATRICIA HUMURA, AND RUTH ASIIMWE

Witchcraft in My Community: Healing Sex and Sexuality

Witchcraft was legislated as evil in colonial constitutions across Africa. In Uganda, the Witchcraft Act of the 1957 constitution, adopted five years before Uganda became independent from Britain, laid down punishment for those who practice witchcraft. The constitution categorized witchcraft as a religion and has since shaped debate, narratives, and counternarratives about witchcraft, which tend to begin and end with the framework of religion, especially Christianity. According to Justin Chapman, the court "later voided the sections about witchcraft from the constitution on the basis of their vague definitions."[1] The question of witchcraft is so incredibly convoluted that it has no definition, and to free it from negative connotations requires an orientation according to which the questions asked and answers sought must be framed outside the paradigms that identify the practice as witchcraft. Amid portrayals of some traditional and cultural practices as witchcraft—and some herbalists and healers as witches or witch doctors—it is worth noting that witchcraft's endurance continues to elicit acceptance in some contexts and rejection in others. We want to share witchcraft stories from our experiences, from conversations with women and witch doctors as well as from speculations and interpretations as they circulate in our communities and shape our relations.

Stepping outside the paradigms that identify practices of healing as witchcraft is a necessary shift because, framed as a religion and as evil, perceptions of witchcraft present distortions, misconceptions, misinterpretations, and misclassifications of herbal healing and herbal medicine. Those who view witchcraft as a religion associate it with evil spirits;[2] with causing harm to another person and as being a source of trouble and misfortune;[3] with violence or magic;[4] and with practice by unchristian, unintelligent and uneducated "villagers."[5] A different worldview holds that witchcraft is a practice of healing set into contexts of meaning that enable people to make sense of life events and their experiences.[6] For example, John S. Mbiti explains that witchcraft is part of African spirituality and should not be considered a religion. Mbiti underscores the belief in witchcraft as "a force or power or energy in the universe which can be tapped by those who know how to do so."[7] Witchcraft (healing) is not a thing that people without intelligence do, as Chapman argues;[8] rather, it has an important communal significance and takes skill and careful fostering.

As it is part of community, spirituality, and a way of life, witchcraft shapes our worldviews. We come to this work as Tushabe and Humura from the Bakiga, and Asiimwe from the Batooro in Western Uganda. Having realized we were educated to sideline and denigrate our traditional practices of healing, we now share our stories. We are motivated by the need to heal ourselves from colonial shame and harm and to celebrate our self-knowledge outside of colonial constructions of us as Africans. We want to heal ourselves from the teaching and dogma that sees our cultures as worthless and our languages as incapable of creating knowledge; and we want to remove ourselves from the notion that we become human only when we are assimilated into Christian and Western worldviews. We want to heal from the whips and verbal humiliation and other punishments our teachers inflicted on us for speaking our mother tongues or in broken English on school campuses. In *Decolonizing the Mind*, Ngũgĩ wa Thing'o laments the numerous punishments he and his peers endured at school for speaking their language, Gikuyu. Our affirmation of witchcraft as healing is also a celebration of languages.

Language shapes our relationship to the lives, cultures, and practices of witchcraft as part of who we are. We celebrate witchcraft as healing practiced and experienced within spiritual, relational, and communal interdependencies.[9] We appreciate Lucida Domoko Manda's reflection on *isangoma* (traditional healers) in South Africa, for asserting that in African healing practices, "a holistic approach is key . . . healing methods involve not only a recovery from bodily ailments, but also a social, spiritual and psychological reintegration of the patient into the community of the living and the living-dead."[10] We come to this conversation with the understanding that what is dubbed witchcraft is healing of the whole person; it is herbal medicine and a process of strengthening relationships and keeping harmony in community.

Our relationship to herbal healing or witchcraft is rooted in the knowledge of practices of sex and sexuality that, according to the paradigms that define what is or is not witchcraft, are seen as witchcraft. It is imperative that we share our stories as they are based in our experiences and our conversations with women and witch doctors as well as our stories from speculations and interpretations as they circulate in our communities, because these stories shape and are shaped by our relations. We use first-person plural voice because we write ourselves with, from, and for our communities; and we write to share our lives with the world. In *Decolonizing Methodologies*, Linda Tuhiwai Smith reminds us that when reading research on the Aboriginal and Māori people she did not find *her* people. Smith highlights that "reading interpretations present problems when we do not see ourselves in the text. There are problems, too, when we do see ourselves but can barely recognize ourselves through the representation."[11] In a similar way, we find that we exist in most scholarship as textual constructions, and we would like to bring ourselves in the flesh to the text.

Because we have seen different things that we find categorized as the same under witchcraft, we will each tell our stories and conclude with brief thoughts. We take sex and sexuality to be inseparable from community and all things that make a person; our discussion, then, integrates community, sex, and sexuality at the same level of being. We retain the terms witch/witch doctor/witchcraft to humanize the people and practices. Witch/witch doctor references *omufumu*, or healer/herbalist, in both the Kiga and Tooro languages. In our sense, witchcraft refers to cultural practices and their practitioners of which Christianity does not approve. However, we relate to witchcraft as healing relationships, bodily ailments, spiritual imbalances, and sex and sexuality. While an analysis of why these practices of healing and their practitioners conjures up fear from those who follow Christian morality is important, our focus here is to claim, without shame, the presence and importance of witchcraft in our communities.

IDEAS OF WITCHCRAFT LEARNED IN COMMUNITY

Tushabe grew up in Kanungu, southwestern Uganda. The climate, topography, and vegetation favored sheep, and a variety of wildflowers hosted bees. Due to Christian influences, people who reared sheep, kept bees, or had cats for pets were suspected of practicing witchcraft. Women who chewed locally grown tobacco—unlike those who smoked factory-made cigarettes—were believed to practice witchcraft. Introverted men who did not socialize much with other men were thought to be possessed by *emandwa*, an evil spirit. Girls and boys who did not marry by age twenty-five were considered to be bewitched or held back by *emandwa* in their families. People who used vulgar language or cussed, people who were beset by misfortune, or people who had stained teeth or disabilities were thought to be bewitched, possessed by an evil spirit, or practitioners of witchcraft. The idea was that God makes perfect bodies and brings success to His people. Misfortune meant disfavor from God.

There was also common knowledge that intersex people, those sexually oriented toward people of the same sex or both sexes, and those who cross-dressed occupied a special place in community and possessed extra knowledge and experience inaccessible to the rest of the community. Apart from intersex people whose sexual orientation was not speculated upon by society, girls were taught by paternal aunties about sex and sexuality, including how to give and receive sexual pleasure and how to take care of their bodies and vulvas to maximize sexual pleasure. Girls would get together and share such knowledge learned from their aunties, which included building lasting friendships and pleasuring each other sexually.[12] Paternal uncles had a similar responsibility toward their nephews. However, the colonial education system tore this responsibility from cultural sex educators and entrusted it to schoolteachers. Homosocial spaces have since become suspect as stringent anti-homosexuality bills and acts have been debated or signed, most especially since the early 2000s.

The Bakiga are devoted to the spiritual charisma of Nyabingyi, a spiritual figure. The word *nyabingyi* means one who has multiple identities, multiple abilities, and can simultaneously be in multiple places and do multiple things. Nyabingyi is believed to have feminine energy but was neither woman/female nor man/male. Bakiga people practice the spirituality of Nyabingyi, whose values include but are not limited to community, *obuntu* (humanity, *obuntu*), unity, love, cooperation, good health, healing, and family. Spiritual rituals happen in many spaces, and some people choose to build shrines. Those who have shrines are initiated into *okubandwa*. The practice is called *okubanda*, also known as sorcery or soothsaying.[13] Whether or not one has a shrine, practitioners are healers and use herbal medicine.

Ideas of community, family, good health, and healing inform ways of dealing with sex and sexuality. In a conversation with Zikwenya about *omusisa*, a tree where *ebihindi* (intersex people) were said to gather at night,[14]

Kenyangyi, a twelve-year-old girl, approached us with her young brother, Betware, and walked in the direction of the shortcut path that passed through Katungyi's (a witch doctor) compound. Zikwenya scolded them, asking where they were going. Kenyangyi said they were going to Matama's, their mother's friend, who was Katungyi's neighbor. Zikwenya told them to take the long path because the shortcut passed through the witch doctor's compound. "Kyo, yamawe! yamawe! yamawe! imwe banamwe! Mutazayo okwo n'omubafumu."[15] *My goodness! Do not go there, that is a home of witch doctors.* From this exchange, I noticed that what used to be shared space now had rigid boundaries. Culturally, healers performed their craft in shrines, among crowds, in people's homes, in gardens, on paths, anywhere and everywhere, depending on the context for which the healing ritual or herbs were needed. People paid with animals, fowl, fruits, grains, alcohol, tobacco, bedding, or manual labor and even land.

Zikwenya did not shy from our conversation on *ebihindi* (intersex people). She knew how people in the community talked about seeing the fire at night at the *musisa* tree, but she also said the tree was burned and that intersex people were no longer in her community. "Ego. Abantu bakaba baragugambaho munonga. Kwonka manya hati abantu bakahweza. Omusisa bakagwosya gwagyenda n'e bihindi byagwo." In agreement, Keviini added, "Haza ebyo kubyahwireho abaheru batandika kutureetera obyobushambani bwa sitani." *Yes. People used to talk about it* [musisa tree]. *Nowadays people are enlightened. They burned down the tree and intersex people burned with it. However now outsiders* [Westerners] *brought us* LGBTQIA+, *which are evil.* Nonheterosexual sexualities are now condemned as evil in similar ways as is witchcraft. One of sexual practices that is equally condemned but that evades the inclusion in the same category is polygamy. Interestingly, Zikwenya did not want to talk about it.

HUMURA'S EXPERIENCE WITH WITCHCRAFT

As a Christian hailing from Muko, I learned that witchcraft has a negative meaning. It is believed that witches use spiritual means either to end someone's life or to cause harm to a family or community.[16] A person intending to cause harm visits a witch doctor, or *omufumu*, to perform rituals that initiate the action. Christian teaching warns against a number of bad habits including smoking, chewing, or selling local tobacco (but this prohibition does not apply to factory-made cigarettes or other tobacco products) and the use of alcohol, especially local brews (but again, factory-made liquor and spirits are excluded). Those who smoke, chew, or sell local tobacco are labeled witches. My grandmother smokes and runs a petty tobacco business of homegrown tobacco. People in the village say she has connections to witchcraft because she smokes and sells local tobacco. When I first learned about this, I thought people were maligning her for money. As I advanced in my studies, I realized two things: capitalism is at the heart of the denigration and devaluation of local products in favor of Western or foreign-made products. Even if the factories are located in the country, their products are favored over local products. The disassociation from local tobacco symbolizes civilization, modernity, and being a good Christian. That factory-made tobacco and other tobacco products do not hinder one from being a good Christian while locally grown tobacco does is simply incomprehensible.

Other things associated with witchcraft include eating mutton or rearing sheep; failure to go to church on days of worship; being friends with people said to practice witchcraft; being bedeviled by many problems in one's family, including frequent or consecutive deaths; accidents and illnesses in the family; infertility; still births; miscarriage; early pregnancies; and even selling sex for money. The relationship between witchcraft and sexuality is complicated. A girl's paternal aunt, *shwenkazi*, is entrusted with teaching her matters of sex and sexuality. It is believed that one's *shwenkazi* is spiritually strong and carries blessings, and that her words contribute to having a good sex life.[17] *Shwenkazi* used to teach female anatomy, focusing especially on parts that stimulate sexual pleasure. Sex education was to prepare people for marriage, to demystify the female body and its pleasures, to train young people to be comfortable with their bodies and to satisfy each other sexually. Girls from age fifteen would meet in secluded spaces in bushes and share lessons from their aunties; they would show each other their bodies, touch and stimulate each other sexually, teach each other how to moan, different sex positions, and kissing. Some choose to practice solo or in group masturbation, while others developed intimate relationships that lasted a while. Buhimba's first sexual experiences were with girls. While she enjoyed the experience, Buhimba says she cannot freely talk about it since Uganda's constitution outlaws same-sex sexuality. Most of all, Buhimba fears being labeled a witch because she loves women. Previously, shame and witchcraft were not associated with girl (and boy) spaces and sexual practices.

ASIIMWE'S ENCOUNTER WITH WITCHCRAFT

At seven years of age, I learned from conversations in community that Amooti, a woman in the village, had sex with Akiiki's husband, and Akiiki sent Kifaro, an evil spirit who travels at night, to Amooti. People believe they can recognize the spirit by its sound and other, visible signs.[18] Accordingly, Kifaro came and tormented Amooti throughout the night. Kifaro also left six snakes in her house. I remember the people in the village running to Amooti's house to see the fighting snakes. That was the first time I heard about witchcraft.

People described witchcraft as evil and a kind of black magic that involved casting spells and reading into the future. Witchcraft was said to involve dark forces and evil people who were feared and shunned. There were nearby villages that people did not visit and roads that people did not take for fear they might meet witches and get bewitched. They talked of other things associated with witchcraft, such as a swarm of ants invading your house or appearing after a burial.

In my culture, a rooster that crows between midnight and 5 o'clock in the morning will be slaughtered immediately. It is thought to be out of alignment and symbolizes bad luck. Similarly, an owl growling or barking near one's house every morning for three days is interpreted to be announcing death in that household. Sometimes people carry out rituals to deter death and cleanse themselves of the spirit of death. Whether coincidental or not, the contexts in which events occur generate meanings by which people generate beliefs.

Those who do witchcraft are called *abachwezi* (pl.; *omuchwezi*, sing.). According to my friend Araali, who learned from a *muchwezi*, placing a basin of water under the bed prevents spirits from coming to you in your sleep. Araali believes that when spirits come and drink the water, they feel pleased and go away. Araali still sleeps with a basin of water under the bed. For this chapter, I had a phone conversation with Mwebaza, who is a *muchwezi*, about water under the bed.

> *The work I do harmonizes the body, mind, and spirit. When people are burdened with problems, they may have trouble sleeping or become paranoid. So, I give them remedies to their problems. If someone gets some sleep, speaks with the neighbor or relative again, conceives a child, enjoys good sex with her husband, is that witchcraft?*[19]

I asked him why, if he believes that his work is good work, does he not register with the government, to which he replied, "Why would I allow the government to put its hand in my pocket? Why don't nurses and medical doctors pay to do their work?"[20] Besides conducting herbal healing, Mwebaza is a university graduate and an employee in local government.

IMPLICATIONS OF WITCHCRAFT IN COMMUNITY ADVANCEMENT

As people from these cultures, we realize there is work involved in learning and unlearning, with the goal of retaining practices that are more meaningful and affirming for our communities. While healers are shunned as witches, the *only* healers whose craft is not perceived as witchcraft are those who operate in public offices, who take money as the medium of exchange for their work, who package their herbs in containers with printed labels, who record their interpretations of patient illnesses in patient books, who are registered with and certified by the government, and who have clear signs and addresses to their offices and certificates hanging on their office walls. Their herbs and methods are similar to those of the people dubbed witches. They heal all kind of illnesses, including matters of sex and sexuality, such as infertility, dryness, low libido, and lack of sexual pleasure, for young people, single people, sexual partners, and married couples. While all healers do similar work, the scrutiny is reserved for witch doctors.

Whether portrayed negatively or not, witchcraft is still tolerated in communities. For example, despite being despised as witches, rainmakers' expertise is usually sought when people do not want rain to interfere with their activities, such as a government dignitary's rally, weddings, harvests, roofing a house, or the performance of certain rituals. In case of drought, a rainmaker might be blamed for "chasing away the rain."[21] Other practices of witchcraft that may be condemned in some situations yet accepted in others include contacting a healer to bring back the person who ran away from home under unexplained circumstances or healing those who have mental ill-health. According to Kemigisa, a mother of three, she "walked 20 km to a witch doctor to heal my son who had been homebound due to mental ill-health. People knew; they said the cause of the illness was my failure to fully ritualize my husband's burial,"[22] and they accepted Kemigisa's visit to the witch doctor. Witchcraft may be condemned as evil, but it is also practiced for the good of community by all sorts of people under different circumstances.

Although the education system forbids traditional sex educators such as aunties and uncles from doing their work, it remains one of those prohibited traditional practices that has survived colonial and Christian erasure and remains sought after. Regardless of religious affiliation, women may intentionally meet in women-identified spaces to share knowledge of sex and sexuality. There are herbs women bathe with to bring them good luck and fertility, to manage menopausal symptoms, or to motivate a partner to stay committed in a relationship. Herbs such as *marunga, kamunye,* and *kakuurra* are used to keep partners committed in a relationship. Such herbs are also believed to restore virginity, hydrate the body and the vulva, and stimulate sexual appetite. Because of the medicinal value, women are especially motivated to use herbs to keep their relationships lively. Other aids include animals or their products like *emana ya gonya* (literally, a crocodile's vagina). The vagina of a female crocodile is dried and ground, and the powder is inserted in a woman's vagina minutes before sex. This is supposed to seduce the partner to come back. *Eboha* (wolf's skin) is another animal product. It has spiritual significance and is believed to keep partners together for good. I, Asiimwe, asked, Jessica, a young deacon, why Christian women engage in witchcraft, and she explained, "Mukama njuna nagaawe otaireho. Tinkwemereza omutima; hakiri nyikare manyire arahikya agaruke."[23] *God protects those who protect themselves. Rather than live in anxiety and uncertainty, I would rather rest assured they will eventually return to me.* A Christian God is sometimes invoked in practices dubbed witchcraft. That is to say, a Christian like Kemigisa may pray to God to give power and insight to a witch doctor to heal her son. Because witchcraft is a spiritual practice and has endured despite colonial efforts at aimed its erasure, the line between Christianity and witchcraft is blurred, and a mix of the two is evident. What threatens witchcraft is the lack of freedom of communities to set clear guidelines for the practice, which discourages future practitioners from nurturing their interests and talents.

CONCLUSION

When herbal medicine is seen in its own right, used for healing and in repairing broken relations, the notion of witchcraft does not find entry into one's conscience. When we, as Africans, see ourselves as human beings in our own communities and with our own cultures—without the filters of colonial constructions and Christian teachings—we may be able to appreciate herbalists and their craft and embrace all parts of our *being*, of which sexuality is an integral part. It is up to us, as Africans, to revisit our practices and to reclaim, without shame, those parts of us that have been dehumanized or denigrated as witchcraft.

NOTES

1. Chapman, "Witchcraft Doctors and Con Artists," 31.
2. Chapman, "Witchcraft Doctors and Con Artists," 33–34.
3. Heald, "Witches and Thieves," 65–66.
4. Allen and Reid, "Justice at the Margins," 110.
5. Chapman, in "Witchcraft Doctors and Con Artists," claims that witchcraft is practiced by "unintelligent villagers," 31.
6. Manda, "Spiritual and Ethical Values," 126.
7. Mbiti, *Introduction to African Religion*, 19.
8. See Chapman, "Witchcraft Doctors and Con Artists."
9. Mbiti, *Introduction to African Religion*, 37.
10. Manda, "Spiritual and Ethical Values," 126.
11. Smith, *Decolonizing Methodologies*, 35.
12. See Akande, *Kunyaza*.
13. Taylor, *Runyankore-Rukiga-English Dictionary*, 99.
14. See, especially, Tushabe, "Decolonizing Homosexuality in Uganda," 113.
15. Nyakwezi, conversation with Tushabe wa Tushabe, October 3, 2021.
16. Mbiti, *Introduction to African Religion*, 19.
17. While paternal uncles taught boys, they were not associated with spiritual powers as aunties are.
18. Mbiti, *Introduction to African Religion*, 24–25.
19. Mwebaza, phone conversation with Ruth Asiimwe, January 29, 2022; see also Idowu, *African Traditional Religion*, 174.
20. Mwebaza, phone conversation.
21. See Mbiti, *Introduction to African Religion*, 12.
22. Kemigisa, conversation with Ruth Asiimwe, December 28, 2021.
23. Jessica, conversation with Ruth Asiimwe, January 6, 2022.

BIBLIOGRAPHY

Akande, Habeeb. *Kunyaza: The Secret to Female Pleasure*. London: Rabaah Publishers, 2018.

Allen, Tim, and Kyla Reid. "Justice at the Margins: Witches, Poisoners, and Social Accountability in Northern Uganda." *Medical Anthropology: Cross Cultural*

Studies in Health and Illness 34, no. 2 (2015): 106–23. https://doi.org/10.1080/01459740.2014.936060.

Chapman, Justin. "Witchcraft Doctors and Con Artists: A First-Hand Account of Witchcraft in Africa." *Skeptic* 18, no. 2 (2013): 31–34.

Heald, Suzette. "Witches and Thieves: Deviant Motivations in Gisu Society." *Royal Anthropological Institute of Great Britain and Ireland* 21, no. 1 (1986): 65–66.

Idowu, E. Bolaji. *African Traditional Religion: A Definition*. London: S.C.M. Press, 1973. https://archive.org/details/africantraditionooooidow_z4b7.

Manda, Lucinda Domoko. "Spiritual and Ethical Values of Traditional African Healthcare Practices." In *Persons in Community: African Ethics in a Global Culture*, edited by Ronald Nicholson. Scottsville: University of Kwazulu-Natal, 2008.

Mbiti, John S. *Introduction to African Religion*. Chicago: Heinemann, 1991.

Richardson, Naval R. "Reflections on Reconciliation and Ubuntu." In *Persons in Community: African Ethics in a Global Culture*, edited by Ronald Nicholson. Scottsville: University of Kwazulu-Natal, 2008.

Smith, Linda Tuhiwai. *Decolonizing Methodologies: Research and Indigenous Peoples*. London: Zed Books, 1999.

Taylor, C. *A Simplified Runyankore-Rukiga-English and English-Runyankore-Rukiga Dictionary*. Kampala: Fountain Publishers, 1959.

Tushabe, Caroline. "Decolonizing Homosexuality in Uganda." In *Women, Gender, and Sexualities in Africa*, edited by Toyin Falola and Nana Akua Amponsah, 147–54. Durham, NC: Carolina Academic Press, 2013.

Wa Thiong'o, Ngũgĩ. *Decolonizing the Mind: The Politics of Language in African Literature*. Nairobi: East African Educational Publishers, 1981.

Two · NATHAN SNAZA

"What Is a Witch?": *Tituba*'s Subjunctive Challenge

Maryse Condé's *Moi, Tituba, Sorcière... Noire de Salem* (1986) is a novel based on scant but extant historical references to Tituba, the single woman of color (possibly "Indian," possibly a slave of Afro-Caribbean descent[1]) in the Salem Witch Trials (1692–93). While a great deal is known about the white Congregationalist minister in Salem Village who enslaved her (Samuel Parris); the preachers, like Cotton Mather, whose writings played a key role in the hunt and trials; and many of the women (and at least one man) accused and executed as a result, most of what is known about Tituba is sketchy at best, more rumor than empirical fact. Tituba is thus paradoxically one of the most marginalized figures of the Salem Witch Trials even as she—and her affirmative answer (later recanted) to the charge of witchcraft, which sparked elaborate if vague descriptions of pacts with the devil—is central to the emplotment we have inherited.[2]

The kernel of known facts, beyond what is preserved of her incredible testimony, includes this, from *Salem Witchcraft Papers*: "Tituba, an Indian woman brought before us."[3] Condé (re)creates Tituba, a Caribbean woman conceived during a rape on a slave ship, whose presence in Salem is due to her having married an enslaved man named "John Indian." And Condé's novel fills in the historical paucity, weaving together the transatlantic slave trade, settler colonization of North America, and patriarchal violence in nuanced ways. Building on Sylvia Wynter's claim that in colonial modernity, a specific (imperialist, white, heteropatriarchal) version of the human—Man—violently "overrepresents" itself as if it were the *only* way of being human,[4] I am attentive to how claims about what "is" (what is real, what is true) work to settle scenes of possibility into hardened, indicative claims. I will argue that Condé's novel tries to unsettle such indicative claims by foregrounding the subjunctive mood where counterfactuals (what could be, might be, may be) hold open potential and possibility. In this chapter, I read *I, Tituba, Black Witch of Salem* as theory that turns to history in dubious or disputed ways but precisely in the service of promoting an understanding of "witchcraft" as a discursive concept that appears in *colonial* situations. In shifting from the indicative to the subjunctive, *I, Tituba* challenges us to feel otherwise worlds that might have been as they call us toward futures that might yet be.[5] While my claim is that the novel itself makes this move, my ability to notice that move and think about it as a crucial gesture in the "abolition of Man"[6] has been made possible by Black feminist theorists like M. Jacqui Alexander, Avery Gordon, Hortense Spillers, and Saidiya Hartman whose work has simultaneously analyzed antiblack grammars of worlding (what I call the indicative) and experimented with "subjunctive" historical thinking in order to "paint as full a picture . . . as possible" of the lives coloniality has violently erased.[7]

In Tituba's impossible, extratemporal narrative voice, the novel engages directly with the historical archive and its ongoing interpretation by (racist) historiographers. On her way to prison in Ipswitch during the Salem Witch Trials, Tituba feels a "future injustice that seemed more cruel than even death itself": being forgotten.[8] She thinks:

> It seemed that I was gradually being forgotten. I felt that I would be mentioned only in passing in these Salem witchcraft trials about which so much would be written later, trials that would arouse the curiosity and pity of generations to come as the greatest testimony of a superstitious and barbaric age. There would be mention here and there of "a slave originating from the West Indies and probably practicing 'Hoodoo.'" There would be no mention of my age or my personality. I would be ignored. As early as the end of the seventeenth centuries, petitions would be circulated, judgments made, rehabilitating the victims, restoring their honor, and returning their property to their descendants. I would never be included! Tituba would be condemned forever! There would never, ever, be a careful, sensitive biography recreating my life and its suffering.[9]

Not for the last time, the novel here ironically declares the historical impossibility of its very existence, since this last sentence is probably as good a summary as anyone could construct of *I, Tituba, Black Witch of Salem*. And the sentence also gestures at the novel's refusal of a clean distinction between history and fiction: biography is "re-creation." The details of Tituba's life in the historical archive are so sketchy that the editor of *The Witchcraft*

Sourcebook can write, introducing a transcript of her testimony that appears, almost verbatim, in Condé's novel: "Tituba remained in prison during the entire episode and might very well have been executed at the end of the trials, but she was released in the general pardon by the governor."[10] That is, while some of Tituba's testimony survives, and scholars generally agree that she was pardoned, it is not possible to reconstruct the judgment against her ("might very well have" is hardly a locution signaling established empirical fact; even "would have been" might suggest a stronger empirical claim).[11] In her "Historical Note" appended to the novel, Condé attributes the relative paucity of "facts" around Tituba (compared to the white Puritans) to racism:

> Around 1693 Tituba, our heroine, was sold for the price of her prison fees and the cost of her chains and shackles. To whom? Such is the intentional or unintentional racism of the historians that we shall never know. According to Anne Perry, a black American novelist who also became passionately interested in our heroine, Tituba was bought by a weaver and spent the rest of her days in Boston.
>
> A vague tradition says Tituba was sold to a slave dealer, who took her back to Barbados.
>
> I myself have given her an ending of my own choosing.[12]

As Angela Y. Davis, in her foreword to the first English translation of Condé's novel, writes: "As an African-American feminist, I offer my profound gratitude to Maryse Condé for having pursued and developed her vision of Tituba, Caribbean woman of African descent. Should a Native American Tituba be recreated, in scholarly or fictional terms, this would be true to the spirit of Condé's Tituba and her revenge. For in the final analysis, Tituba's revenge consists in reminding us all that the doors to our suppressed cultural histories are still ajar. . . . And sometimes there is magic behind those doors, sparkling clues about possibilities ahead."[13] The words "sometimes" and "ajar" remind us that we have to be careful *how* we approach and think about "our" suppressed histories, attentive to the violences of homogenization attending indicative thinking, and (at)tending the subjunctive possibilities of other worlds that haunt us subjunctively.

DISCOURSE IN THE CONTACT ZONE

Throughout the novel, Tituba continually poses the question, "What is a witch?" and then, instead of answering in the indicative, refers it to the conditions of the concept's enunciation: Who says "witch"? In what context? With what material supports for their discourse? My aim in this chapter is to draw out how Tituba herself teaches us that the answer is not a denotative, indicative statement but instead the patient unfurling of conditions of discourse appearing in what Stephan Palmié has called "Atlantic modernity": "What I take this concept to refer to is, in part, a set of structural linkages that, since the early sixteenth century, transformed the Atlantic Ocean into an integrated geohistorical unit: an expanding theater of human interaction defined by a vast and intricate web of political and economic relations objectively implicating actors and collectivities on three continents in each other's histories."[14] "The witch" is a part of the discursive construction and elaboration of Atlantic modernity, one that does—in different ways and at different times—a great deal of cultural work to reinforce the endurance of a colonialist, homogenizing world by generating its constitutive outsides. Uttered indicatively, "the witch" participates in enlightenment modes of homogenization, but in Tituba's narration its sense switches modes, referring instead to a collision of relational knowledge practices where the endurance of coloniality is *at stake*.

Local esoterisms that become "witchcraft" through homogenization tend "to be tied up with moral systems" that "have to be understood in [cultural/historical] context."[15] "Witchcraft" is almost always a linguistic translation of a local vernacular term, one bound with local cosmologies and more-than-human relations. The contributors to Luis Nicolau Parés and Roger Sansi's *Sorcery in the Black Atlantic*, a volume gathering a range of recent anthropological research, explore specific practices that are sometimes, even often (but seldom always), folded into a concept like witchcraft: *feitiçaraia*, fetishism, sorcery, Candomblé, *brujería*, magic, and so on. Not only are these potentially distinct systems of belief/practice; they are also tied in complex and contradictory ways to valuation: "white" versus "black" magic, for instance. Witchcrafts proliferate and evolve, and this happens in very specific conditions; but the indicative account of these practices still generally participates in conceptual homogenization, where "witchcraft" (or "sorcery" in the Francophone and Lusophone contexts) conceptually flattens practices that are "disqualified" by enlightenment rationality.[16]

All the linguistic and conceptual complexity attends to a very simple fact that emerges across *Sorcery in the Black Atlantic* and much of the anthropology that is adjacent to it. Rather than witchcraft being the name for premodern or sometimes Indigenous knowledges that are superseded by rational, enlightenment, scientific thought, it is a specific discursive space opened within the colonial contact zone. That is, it is a word that appears when imperialist enlightenment projects encounter knowledge practices that constitute alternatives—alternatives that are forced to change in response to colonial violence. Witchcraft, then, is not "outside" of modernity; it is a particle around which Atlantic modernity stabilizes and tries to expand its borders. João José Reis writes, drawing on the work of Rachel Harding: "Candomblé was not simply a slave religion, which is one primary reason why it is somewhat complicated to discuss it in terms of slave resistance. Candomblé would rather seem to be a set of beliefs and practices that implied resistance by different groups and individuals to predominantly Western values, in particular Catholic conventional doctrine, as well as medical and other allegedly scientific procedures."[17] Generalizing toward the reading I am about to give of Condé's novel, I want to suggest that witchcraft signals a confrontation—of highly unequal forces—between colonialist expansion and the knowledge practices associated with genres of being human that colonialism disqualifies by homogenizing them into "witchcraft." "Witchcraft" and its cognates appear only where autochthonic or vernacular knowledges (especially those associated with women and/or care practices) encounter colonialist force (as with Mama Yaya's knowledge in *I, Tituba*). Neither "Indigenous" nor "colonial," witchcraft is a concept that arises in confrontation between different tendings in colonial contact zones. The specifics of each colonial situation (and they were/are manifold) determine how "witch" as an appellation sticks in peculiar ways to people (mostly women), things, practices, phenomena. Condé's novel draws our attention away from a focus on this homogenizing concept toward how Tituba attends to and tends otherwise worlds that accompany colonial worlding as (at least) virtual or subjunctive possibilities.

"WHAT IS A WITCH?"

This question appears on page 17 of the first English translation of *I, Tituba, Black Witch of Salem*, and is raised often, directly or indirectly, throughout the novel. Near the end of the novel, when Tituba is involved with Christopher, a maroon on Barbados organizing a slave revolt, he asks her, "Are you a witch?" In response, Tituba sighs and says, "Everyone gives that word a different meaning. Everyone believes he can fashion a witch to his way of thinking so that she will satisfy his ambitions, dreams, and desires."[18] While Christopher does not have the "patience" "to stay here listening to you philosophize," what I want to do in this chapter is track precisely the way that in the novel this word becomes a refrain that allows Condé to insist on the inseparability of her esoteric practices and political projects animated by decolonial, feminist, abolitionist, and even queer desires. Thinking this inseparability through, then, may be called philosophy.

In its first iteration, the question appears in relation to a quip by Tituba's lover—an enslaved man named John Indian—who says, "What are you doing, little witch?" Tituba thinks: "He was joking, but it made me think. What is a witch? I noticed that when he said the word, it was marked with disapproval. Why should that be? Why? Isn't the ability to communicate with the invisible world, to keep constant links with the dead, to care for others and heal, a superior gift of nature that inspires respect, admiration, and gratitude?"[19] Tituba here registers the difficulty, if not impossibility, of separating claims about what things are (or that they are) and judgments about value. In order to think subjunctive understandings of what the "witch" *might* be, Tituba enlists the interrogative mood to pry apart what seems inseparable. This is most explosive in the barest sentence here ("Why?"), which is, grammatically, nothing but that interrogative force. Summoned here, this force makes legible how any indicative statement ("A witch is . . .") is one of many possible ways of indicating something about a world. In settling that potential into seemingly ontological claims, indicative statements mask the extent to which they arise *within* and as part of struggles over the existence of worlds. Condé underscores how ontology, conceptual language, and judgment are intra-active with another question, a question crucially in the subjunctive mood: "Consequently, shouldn't the witch (if that's what the person who has this gift is to be called) be cherished and revered rather than feared?"[20] When we use human language to talk about things (always but pointedly in cases where these things have an ontologically uncertain status) our relation to them is constitutively shaped by the conceptual labor of words and the ways that value judgments prime our perception of the world.

The paragraph ends with Tituba reflecting on her love for the man who just, and in jest, called her "little witch." She reflects: "I recalled my mother's lament: 'Why can't women do without men?' Yes why?"[21] There is something about the ontological/linguistic/evaluative cluster appearing around the word "witch" that leads Tituba quickly back to her own familial history and to another sentence amplifying the interrogative force, this time elongated only by a word ("yes") serving to join Tituba, through affirmation, to a prior interrogative utterance. Mother and daughter here speak, as it were, together, and citational or iterative practice creates a kind of collective speech across an "unreal" expanse of time. The force of the mother's question—which calls into question how sexuality and patriarchy have been linked—resounds into the present, where Tituba joins in with her own amplifying voice. And the paragraph's structure loops this (hetero)sexual question in with the prior question about what a witch is and her value. That is, the question, "What is a witch?" is brought into a circuit with the question of why women "can't do" without men.

Except, of course, they can. The novel does not do more than gesture in this direction, but a crucial pair of questions is sounded when Tituba, imprisoned in Salem, shares a cell with Hester Prynne from Nathaniel Hawthorne's *The Scarlet Letter*. The two women commiserate by sharing their experiences of patriarchal violence, although adultery (with a minister) and witchcraft constitute different crimes against the patriarchal/Christian state. Just before Tituba is released from prison following the Massachusetts governor's general pardon of those accused of witchcraft,[22] we read the following, which hovers somewhere between memory, fantasy, and haunting: "That night Hester lay down beside me, as she did sometimes. I laid my head on the quiet water lily of her cheek and held her tight. Surprisingly, a feeling of pleasure slowly flooded over me. Can you feel pleasure from hugging a body similar to your own? For me, pleasure had always been in the shape of another body whose hollows fitted my curves and whose swellings nestled in the tender flatlands of my flesh. Was Hester showing me another kind of bodily pleasure?"[23]

These questions (separated by a sentence that signals the kind of standpoint epistemology that we find called for in feminist theory after at least the Combahee River Collective Statement) suggest, without leaving the interrogative mood, a kind of answer to Tituba's mother's question. While we might underscore how sex here determines the shape of a body more than race, queer erotics—where "bodily pleasure" need not solely take the forms we are taught to recognize in "sexuality"—signal a possible, subjunctive line of flight away from the patriarchal state's carceral and dispossessive hold on feminine pleasures, bodies, and knowledges. This line of flight, or what Omise'eke Natasha Tinsley has called "thiefing sugar," is not represented in the novel's plot, which finds Tituba continually subjected to statal violence, almost all of it the result of Tituba's proximity to the state and caused by her sexual desire for men. But readerly attention can be turned away from the plot so that these questions' impact is not muted through disavowal or disinterest. Tituba's pleasure, at the very least, holds open the potential—stumbled upon not conceptually but in the erotics[24] of the situation of otherwise worlds.

Hester asks Tituba, "Why were they calling you a witch?" which leads Tituba to again reflect on how that word's particular modulation of ontological postulation and affect-laden valuation are tied to specific forms of (colonial) social life. She says, "Why in *this* society does one give the function of a witch an evil connotation? The witch, if we must use this word, rights wrongs, helps, consoles, heals . . ."[25] Tituba clearly here separates the *word* "witch" (she will say a bit later: "Here I was again, up against that epithet"[26]) from the *function* of a witch. She also separates both the function and the word from "connotation" as something given. This pithy meditation on the complexities of signification could be read, in one way, as a symptom of the novel's postmodernity, whereby a mise-en-abyme is set up to affectively disorient readers not only at this moment but at every moment they encounter words, both while reading the novel and in any other context. But more than a shift to some kind of semiotic free play, this passage attunes us to a political and historical, which is to say a *colonial*, grammar governing significatory operations, thus revealing the extent to which postmodern affirmations of play largely remain(ed) within coloniality.

Condé's ellipsis trailing after Tituba's list of practices attributable to "the witch" sets up an interruption by Hester in the form of laughter: "She interrupted me with a burst of laughter. 'Then you haven't read Cotton Mather!'"[27] Cotton Mather's sermons played a crucial role in the events in Salem, and yet unlike the novel's presentation of Tituba's testimony before the court,[28] which is taken nearly verbatim from historical records,[29] Condé introduces Mather's ideas by having Hester do a mocking impression: "She puffed herself up and solemnly declared: 'Witches do strange and evil things. They cannot perform true miracles; these can only be accomplished by the visible saints and emissaries of the Lord.'"[30] When Tituba asks, "Who is this Cotton Mather?" Hester "did not answer." For the novel, then, Mather—a preacher, like his father, Increase (the president of Harvard College at the time of the trials), whose surviving sermons are the basis of much of the historical work trying to understand the theological conditions of possibility for the "witch hunt" in Salem—is important as a historical quilting point, but refused any direct, nonsardonic citation. It is as if the ideas of Mather—a matrix of Puritan gravity, colonial ambition, patriarchal rage, and pedantic border policing—are simply not worth serious engagement, even as this refusal to cite also speaks to its force in shaping the discursive field of "witchcraft" (the novel's silence is a response to its omnipresence).

Across the next few pages, Hester coaches Tituba to "give names, give names!" when she is interrogated during the trial,[31] which leads to a reflection on patriarchal structures that cut across race. Hester says, "Life is too kind to men, whatever their color." This prompts Tituba as narrator to articulate something she does not say: "Something deep inside me told me she was telling the truth. The color of John Indian's skin had not caused him half the trouble mine had caused me. Some of the ladies, however Puritan they might be, had not denied themselves the pleasure of flirting with him."[32] Here again, we see a direct presentation of the intersecting operations of race, gender, and sexuality where (white) Puritan women, Black men, and Black women can all be differentially dehumanized relative to white men in ways that both conjoin their experiences and struggles and generate *relative* proximities to Man such that violence is not smoothly distributed, but uneven, asymmetrical, and contradictory; and this registers affectively.

I, Tituba offers proto-intersectional attention to how power and history shape the present. Tituba's shift from the indicative to the subjunctive (aided by the interrogative) amplifies how different people differently attune to the histories and the violences saturating the present. Condé invites us to feel how a word like "witch" appears only in contact zones where a set of material (and ideological, spiritual) conditions and habits attempt to orient life toward the sustaining of coloniality through the production of Man. But because the word arises precisely at the moment of contestation—where coloniality encounters the knowledges and (non-Man) genres of being human that it wants to violently erase or dissolve through incorporation—"the witch" also carries virtual, subjunctive possibilities that *may* be tapped into. *I, Tituba, Black Witch of Salem* helps us feel how "witchcraft"—as a discursive pattern emergent in colonial contact zones—can participate in the endurance of the colonial world even as Tituba's narration constantly unsettles that colonial endurance by feeling out the decolonial potential that always haunts the indicative.

NOTES

An earlier version of this chapter was published as chapter one in Nathan Snaza, *Tendings: Feminist Esoterisms and the Abolition of Man* (Durham, NC: Duke University Press, 2024).

1. Imani Perry writes, "Recent critics generally believe that Tituba was not African, as she is generally represented, but either Indigenous or both Indigenous and African. In any case, she was of a people who were outside of or, at best, ancillary to recognition in the legal regime where they resided." Perry, *Vexy Thing*, 27.
2. Glover, *Regarded Self*, 42.
3. Boyer and Nissenbaum, *Salem Witchcraft Papers*, 286.
4. Wynter, "Unsettling the Coloniality of Being."
5. Crawley, *Blackpentacostal Breath*.
6. Weheliye, *Habeas Viscus*.
7. Hartman, "Venus in Two Acts," 11. See also Alexander, *Pedagogies*; Gordon, *Ghostly Matters*; Spillers, *Black, White, and in Color*; and Hartman, *Scenes of Subjection*.
8. Condé, *I, Tituba*, 110.
9. Condé, *I, Tituba*, 110.
10. Levack, *Witchcraft Sourcebook*, 285.
11. Perry, however, states, "Tituba was ultimately executed." Perry, *Vexy Thing*, 28. Rather than take a side in an argument about facts, I note this simply to underscore just how little certainty there is in the indicative archive around Tituba.
12. Condé, *I, Tituba*, 183.
13. Angela Y. Davis, "Foreword," in Condé, *I, Tituba*, xi.
14. Palmié, *Wizards and Scientists*, 15.
15. Moore and Sanders, *Magical Interpretations*, 4.
16. Savransky writes: "In the wake of the tangled catastrophes of capitalism, colonialism, and extractivism, the mass disqualification of differences through which the modern world was born has radically devastated the conditions of livability of myriad human and more-than-human worlds in this world." Savransky, *Around the Day*, 4.
17. Reis, "Candomblé and Slave Resistance," 57.
18. Condé, *I, Tituba*, 146.
19. Condé, *I, Tituba*, 17.
20. Condé, *I, Tituba*, 17.
21. Condé, *I, Tituba*, 17.
22. Condé, *I, Tituba*, 119.
23. Condé, *I, Tituba*, 122.
24. Lorde, "Uses of the Erotic," in *Sister Outsider*.
25. Condé, *I, Tituba*, 96. Ellipsis in original.

26 Condé, *I, Tituba*, 135.
27 Condé, *I, Tituba*, 96.
28 Condé, *I, Tituba*, 104–6.
29 Levack, *Witchcraft Sourcebook*, 286–89.
30 Condé, *I, Tituba*, 96.
31 Condé, *I, Tituba*, 100.
32 Condé, *I, Tituba*, 101.

BIBLIOGRAPHY

Alexander, M. Jacqui. *Pedagogies of Crossing*. Durham, NC: Duke University Press, 2005.

Boyer, Paul S., and Stephen Nissenbaum. *The Salem Witchcraft Papers: Verbatim Transcripts of the Legal Documents of the Salem Witchcraft Outbreak of 1692*. New York: Da Capo Press, 1977.

Condé, Maryse. *I, Tituba, Black Witch of Salem*. Translated by Richard Philcox. New York: Ballantine Books, 1983.

Crawley, Ashon. *Blackpentacostal Breath*. New York: Fordham University Press, 2017.

Da Silva, Denise Ferreira. *Toward a Global Idea of Race*. Minneapolis: University of Minnesota Press, 2007.

Glover, Kaiama. *A Regarded Self: Caribbean Womanhood and the Ethics of Disorderly Being*. Durham, NC: Duke University Press, 2021.

Gordon, Avery. *Ghostly Matters: Haunting and the Sociological Imagination*. Minneapolis: University of Minnesota Press, 1997.

Hartman, Saidiya V. *Scenes of Subjection: Terror, Slavery, and Self-Making in Nineteenth-Century America*. Oxford: Oxford University Press, 1997.

Hartman, Saidiya V. "Venus in Two Acts." *Small Axe* 26 (2008): 10–14.

Levack, Brian, ed. *The Witchcraft Sourcebook*. New York: Routledge, 2015.

Lorde, Audre. *Sister Outsider: Essays and Speeches*. 1984. Reprint, Berkeley: Crossing Press, 2007.

Moore, Henrietta, and Todd Sanders, eds. *Magical Interpretations, Material Realities: Modernity, Witchcraft, and the Occult in Postcolonial Africa*. New York: Routledge, 2001.

Palmié, Stephan. *Wizards and Scientists: Explorations in Afro-Cuban Modernity and Tradition*. Durham, NC: Duke University Press, 2002.

Parés, Luis Nicolau, and Roger Sansi, eds. *Sorcery in the Black Atlantic*. Chicago: University of Chicago Press, 2011.

Perry, Imani. *Vexy Thing: On Gender and Liberation*. Durham, NC: Duke University Press, 2018.

Reis, João José. "Candomblé and Slave Resistance in Nineteenth-Century Bahia." In *Sorcery in the Black Atlantic*, edited by Luis Nicolau Parés and Roger Sansi, 55–74. Chicago: University of Chicago Press, 2011.

Savransky, Martin. *Around the Day in Eighty Worlds: Politics of the Pluriverse*. Durham, NC: Duke University Press, 2021.

Snaza, Nathan. *Tendings: Feminist Esoterisms and the Abolition of Man*. Durham, NC: Duke University Press, 2024.

Spillers, Hortense. *Black, White, and in Color*. Chicago: University of Chicago Press, 2003.

Tinsley, Omise'eke Natasha. *Thiefing Sugar: Eroticism between Women in Caribbean Literature*. Durham, NC: Duke University Press, 2010.

Weheliye, Alexander. *Habeas Viscus: Racializing Assemblages, Biopolitics, and Black Feminist Theories of the Human*. Durham, NC: Duke University Press, 2014.

Wynter, Sylvia. "Unsettling the Coloniality of Being/Power/Truth/Freedom: Towards the Human, after Man, Its Overrepresentation—An Argument." CR: The New Centennial Review 3, no. 3 (2003): 257–337.

Three · SHANNON HUGHES SPENCE

Irish Feminist Witches: Using Witchcraft and Activism to Heal from Violence and Trauma

WHO ARE IRISH FEMINIST WITCHES?

A feminist witch can be defined as someone who utilizes "myths and symbols both to shape a framework of meaning that reinterprets the relationship between the spiritual and the material, and attempts to redefine power, authority, sexuality and social relations."[1] Feminist witches are individuals who engage in the spiritual practice of witchcraft and/or the political practice of utilizing the image of the witch. By engaging in the practice of witchcraft, feminist witches use magical workings to create, alter, and shape the reality of their lives. Their witchcraft practice may include the worshipping of deities, or it may not. By utilizing the image of the witch in their political practices, feminist witches lend the weight of history, misogyny, and mythology to their activism.[2] The persecution of witches throughout history and the newly packaged image of the witch wrapped in feminist values has attracted many young women who identify with the witch for both political and spiritual reasons, as shown within my own research and in other studies.

Wendy Griffin has highlighted how feminist witches and women in the American Goddess movement feel empowered through reading, assignments, and discussions that utilized a feminist analysis of gender and power. Many of the feminist witches within the American Goddess movement have frequently engaged with activities in the community, such as volunteering at rape crisis centers, family planning centers, and resource centers.[3] Kristen Aune has found that feminist spirituality has been de-churched, a term that does not often appear in the sociology of religion, although, she argues, it is more accurate than de-institutionalized as the latter term obscures the fact that it is the Christian Church and generally not another religious institution that these feminists have distanced themselves from. Aune goes on to highlight the increase in holistic spiritualities among feminists.[4] This finding is mirrored within the findings of my own study, with several Irish feminist witches having shared that they renounced their Catholic identity before turning to witchcraft, which will be further explored in this chapter.

Although there have been studies on feminist witches in other countries, there is a lack of data on feminist witches within Ireland. Therefore, this study answers the question: Why do a number of people living in Ireland identify as feminist witches in the twenty-first century? To answer this question, I conducted five individual semistructured Zoom interviews, each lasting from twenty to sixty minutes, with Irish feminist witches. The participants came from a range of counties in Ireland, and from both rural and urban settings. Each of the participants had previously been involved in social movements that utilized the image of the witch and/or had publicly made their spiritual identity as a witch known, thus openly classifying themselves as feminist witches. Positionality refers to the way that social positions and power shape a person's identities in society. Social and political contexts in society influence identities in terms of both fixed positionalities (such as race, skin color, and nationality), while some aspects of positionality are seen as more fluid (such as gender, class, and sexuality).[5] However, "all parts of our identities are shaped by socially constructed positions and memberships to which we belong" and which are "embedded in our society as a system."[6] Although I did not seek out a homogenous participant sample group, the homogeneity of my participant sample is evident in that each of the five participants is a white, Irish, cisgender woman under the age of forty-five; four of the five belong to the LGBTQ+ community. We must also consider that the experiences of Irish feminist witches who fall outside of the positionality of this sample group may have differing experiences.

THE LIVED EXPERIENCES OF IRISH FEMINIST WITCHES

The witch trials of the 1400–1600s never truly gripped Ireland as they did Europe, the United Kingdom, or the colonies of New England in the

United States.[7] Despite this, the Irish feminist witches whom I interviewed relate to the persecution of witches on a deep level, having experienced or witnessed violence or trauma suffered by Irish women at the hands of family members, the Catholic Church, and the Irish Free State. The experience of Irish feminist witches presents a unique perspective due to the complex relationship Ireland has with colonialism and with Catholicism in a postcolonial state. In my interviews with the five participants, I wanted to discover how they were introduced to the concepts of witchcraft and feminism, how their political and spiritual values and practices overlapped, and what they perceived the role of the Irish feminist witch to be in resisting patriarchal power structures.

The Gateway to Feminism and Witchcraft

All participants recalled how they first encountered both feminism and witchcraft. The most common gateway to both was through university, social media, and attempts to find a connection or sense of belonging in a world where they felt different from or frustrated by the injustices they were experiencing.

Double, Double Toil and Trouble: Discovering Feminism

Cleo, a member of the LGBTQ+ community, was first led to feminism when she began to experience inequalities within her own life. Cleo feels a sense of duty to stand up for what she believes in, sharing that "as a woman and as someone who is LGBTQ+, I feel like it's my job just to stand up and make a statement. I just feel like I can't really sit back and let injustice happen." Similarly, Erin was first introduced to feminism from a young age, looking for a community where she—"growing up in the '80s as a bi kid in Ireland"—would be accepted. As two outspoken members of the LGBTQ+ community, Cleo and Erin express their innate sense of duty to stand on the side of human rights and justice. Despite homosexuality having been decriminalized in Ireland in 1993,[8] and Ireland having been the first country in the world to legalize same-sex marriage in 2015 by popular vote,[9] 76 percent of LGBTQ+ young people feel unsafe at school, and 69 percent have received homophobic remarks from other students.[10] Moreover, reported hate crimes have increased by 30 percent in Ireland since 2022, with LGBTQ+ people being the second-most-targeted cohort for hate crimes (with racist attacks being number one).[11] Such statistics reinforce why the participants feel so strongly about standing up to injustices and why their identity as feminists is so important to them.

Maggie was first explicitly introduced to feminism and women's issues when she began university. During her time at university, she witnessed overt displays of sexism while simultaneously witnessing a grassroots activist movement forming to repeal the eighth amendment of the Irish constitution, which banned abortion. Maggie had friends who previously had to travel abroad to the United Kingdom to access the healthcare they were denied in Ireland. Similarly, Sally was introduced to feminism through the "Repeal the 8th" movement and through being "involved in the feminist society in college for two to three years." The Repeal the 8th movement saw abortion become legalized in Ireland through popular vote in 2018.[12] However, this was not before decades of harrowing stories coming from women and families who had lived in a culture of shame, purity, and control and who had been denied abortions under the Irish State.

One such infamous story is that of Ann Lovett. Ann Lovett was a fifteen-year-old schoolgirl who gave birth in secret and alone in a grotto dedicated to the Virgin Mary on a cold January afternoon in 1984. Neither Ann Lovett nor her child survived.[13]

In December 1991 a fourteen-year-old girl was raped by a man who was known to her and her family. She became pregnant as a result. The rape was reported to the police in January 1992. The girl and her family decided to travel to the UK to undergo an abortion. The family informed the police of this decision to ensure that the fetal remains could be tested to prove the paternity in the rape case. However, the police, the director of Public Prosecutions, and the attorney general stopped the teenager and her family from leaving the country to undergo the abortion, maintaining that the unborn fetus had the same legal right to life as the mother. In the end, the girl miscarried.[14]

In 2014, a clinically brain-dead woman was kept alive on life support—against her family's wishes—because she was eighteen weeks' pregnant. Doctors were fearful that they could be prosecuted for turning off the life-support machine due to Ireland's strict abortion laws. Eventually, a High Court ruling allowed for the life-support machine to be turned off.[15] Unfortunately, these stories are not unique. Many similar stories compounded with the nine women a day who left Ireland to travel to the UK to access abortions undoubtedly had an impact on all my study participants and their strong feminist values of agency and bodily autonomy.

Megan could not pinpoint an exact moment when she began identifying as a feminist. She explains, "It was a combination of things that [she] was seeing and reading and being angry about not being able to walk places or being able to go places after dark. And always having to be so vigilant and so aware of everything." Megan's frustration regarding being unable to walk freely and without fear, or go to places after sunset, reflects the statistic that in Ireland, 61 percent of women ages fifteen and older avoid public spaces for fear of being physically or sexually assaulted.[16] Moreover in 2022, Ireland reported the highest rate of femicide in the last ten years, with fifteen women in total having been murdered.[17]

It is evident that from my participants' responses that feelings of anger exist among women in Ireland, alongside a sense of duty to fight against injustices. This is due to Ireland's history and current levels of harm and violence toward women. Each of these branches of harm—LGBTQ+ hate crimes, harrowing stories of women being denied healthcare, and alarming statistics of violence against women—is rooted in a culture that has cast women in a subordinate role since the establishment of the Irish State. After Ireland's eight hundred years of colonization by the British Empire ended in the early 1920s, the Irish Free State joined forces with the Catholic Church. Developing a close relationship with the Catholic Church, the Irish Free State believed, was the most effective way to establish itself and create a sense of national identity. However, this relationship only exacerbated the already marginalized status of women. As the next decade progressed, the Irish government began to incorporate several Catholic principles into legislation, allowing right-wing traditional values to dominate the 1937 Irish Constitution.[18] The newly independent Catholic Ireland quickly began to define and confine women (and the feminine) as mother/homemaker/subordinate, the effects of which are still prevalent today, as reflected by the study participants.

Something Wicked This Way Comes: Unearthing Witchcraft

When seeking to understand how the study participants were introduced to witchcraft, it became clear that both Sally and Cleo were introduced to witchcraft through social media, whereas Maggie was first exposed to magic through her family, with her Catholic grandmother and aunts often telling her stories "that had really large Pagan undertones like the Bean Sí and all that stuff. Real not Christian stuff." On a similar note, Megan was first drawn to witchcraft due to its "connection with the Earth," and specifically "that kind of emancipation of women and connecting to old Celtic and feminine roots."

Again, the participants subtly attributed their interest in both feminism and witchcraft to aspects of Irish history. British colonizers viewed the Irish population as superstitious and primitive idolaters, attributing their misfortunes to spirits who originated from a supernatural race, known as the Aos Sí.[19] Ireland has a long history that is rich in mythology and beliefs surrounding the supernatural. Throughout British discourse, Ireland and the people were regarded as "feminine," a damsel in distress who longed to be saved by a strong masculine entity, in this case, Britain.[20] From being seen as a form of weakness by the British Empire to the ideal constructed by the Catholic Church and Irish State—defining the feminine in restrictive gender essentialist terms and confining women to the domestic sphere and the role of wife and mother—the feminine within Ireland has a complex history. By framing femininity as solely soft and delicate (which it can be), a disservice is done to all, as stories and experiences of radical resistance in the face of oppressive patriarchal forces can often be overlooked. For Irish feminist witches, however, the feminine does not necessarily mean female from a gender essentialist view. It is instead the power of connection, solidarity, collective action, and healing and the valuing of the earth, nature, and its resources.

The ancient Celtic and pagan heritage of Ireland, coupled with the de-churching of young people and their disillusionment with the Catholic Church, has resulted in a great interest in paganism and witchcraft among people in Ireland, particularly among young women. However, not all the study participants were quick to accept the enchanting aspects of witchcraft and feminism. Erin explained her initial hesitation to approach witchcraft and magic.

Erin described herself as a "person who would have previously rejected this kind of talk around witchcraft and magic until fifteen years ago" when she began therapy and found that it was "literally magic because, there is real magic around human connection." This profound experience had such an impact on Erin that she trained as a psychotherapist, and she now has "no doubt it's [magic] there. I feel it and I use it. In the language of psychotherapy, it's around connection and healing and there's energy there and that was my route into this stuff [witchcraft]."

Despite the differing routes each participant took to encounter feminism and witchcraft, each of the women felt an innate affinity to both the feminist and witchcraft community and what each represents: empowerment, resistance, and connection. The study participants saw the Catholic Church as a dominant power structure opposed to change. However, atheism was not necessarily the answer. The participants searched for meaning "beyond the mundane, the artificial, and the dogmatic. But it had to be new, even if by way of the very old."[21] The Irish feminist witches rejected the dominant religion in Ireland that saw the institutionalization of thousands of unmarried mothers,[22] clerical abuse cover-ups,[23] and the general oppression of women for a spiritual practice that centered around traditional Irish occult practices and beliefs. Although there remains a degree of conflict over the authenticity around the historical legitimacy of pagan and Celtic traditions as they are celebrated today,[24] there is undoubtedly a revival of occult-based workings practiced by young Irish women who believe that they are reconnecting to a greater power that is the anthesis to the patriarchal Catholic Church.

Fire Burn and Cauldron Bubble: The Overlap of Political and Spiritual Practices

Participants' engagement with witchcraft as a form of spiritual practice and how that influenced their political identity was a key finding within my research. This finding also shines a light on the unique experience of Irish feminist witches in healing their own trauma and the intergenerational trauma experienced by Irish women at the hands of the Catholic Church and the Irish State. Throughout the interviews, it became evident that the participants' political and spiritual values overlapped, culminating in individuals who deeply appreciated themes of agency, empowerment, resistance, and healing.

Cleo, like all participants, stressed that her spiritual practice of witchcraft was not like the type of witchcraft depicted in films and on television. Cleo shared that her spiritual practice centers around "a lot of meditation with different crystals and herbs, incense, and oils." As someone "who is dealing with mental illnesses and past traumas," Cleo enjoys having "that time alone, and that in itself is healing." Cleo's political practice sees her attending "rallies and protests for abortion referendums, awareness campaigns for domestic abuse and sexual abuse and assault . . . not so much as a witch, but as a woman." Although Cleo briefly mentioned that she experienced traumas in the past, she did not go into detail. However, she explained that her witchcraft practice acts as a form of self-care after engaging in political demonstrations regarding sexual violence and domestic abuse. Campaigning in such areas requires a significant amount of physical, mental, and emotional energy. Cleo's spiritual practice is therefore not only a form of self-care but a form of protection and fuel to keep fighting injustices.

Maggie's spiritual and political practices center around the protection and agency of women, from engaging in protest to ensure human rights to using witchcraft as a tool of resistance against an oppressive figure in her former household. Maggie openly shared her experience with abuse. Maggie described how she and her mother lived with her abusive stepfather for over a decade. Domestic abuse is not uncommon in Ireland. In Ireland one in four women (26 percent) have experienced physical and/or sexual violence by a partner or nonpartner, while 31 percent experienced psychological violence by a partner.[25] Now Maggie and her mother live together without an oppressive force, and they have "been doing a lot of stuff [witchcraft] in our house now, like cleansing it and saining [blessing] the house and everything, writing down our intentions and burning them and stuff." Maggie discussed how her mother now feels empowered by engaging in witchcraft practices. Maggie stated, "We've started to do spell jars before the court cases against him and stuff and it really calms her down and makes her feel like things are going to go her way. . . . And you feel like a weight has been lifted off your shoulders and like we're taking the power back into our own hands." In conjunction with court procedures to separate herself and her mother from the abusive stepfather, through witchcraft, Maggie and her mother have found much-needed solace and a reclamation of power to heal themselves from their past experiences with violence.

Similarly, Megan's political and spiritual witchcraft practices revolve around the concepts of empowerment and agency. Megan's political and spiritual values overlap. She states that she "strives to be very trans-inclusive," and she does not "like this air of witchcraft that says you need to have a vagina to be a witch." Megan holds space for inclusivity of the trans community within witchcraft while simultaneously acknowledging "the demonization of women, periods, childbirth, and women's body parts."

Once again, this is a subtle reference to Ireland's disturbing past. With the Irish Free State being heavily influenced by the Catholic Church, purity became a fundamental aspect of Irish identity; and it was primarily a woman's responsibility.[26] Sexual deviancy was perceived as a threat to national identity. A discourse of purity and shame toward women permeated society. With such conservative social norms and expectations of women to remain "pure," a social climate was created where institutions that punished individuals who deviated from the norm were tolerated. The Magdalene laundries/Magdalene asylums/Mother and Baby Homes have been described as dark stains upon Ireland's recent history. Unmarried pregnant women were institutionalized in Magdalene laundries by their families due to the shame unwed mothers brought to their families.[27] Within the last few years, many of the victims from the Magdalene laundries have shared their harrowing accounts of their time inside, recalling the physical, psychological, and sexual abuse they were exposed to.[28]

Erin's spiritual and political practice also centered around the healing of marginalized groups. After her involvement in the Repeal the 8th campaign, Erin has continued to campaign for Safety Access Zones outside of hospitals that provide abortion services, to prevent antichoice demonstrators from protesting outside with graphic images and hateful language. However, Erin shared, "When I'm out and about, I do not use the language of coven or magic, but for me that's what it is, women supporting women and the profound power of solidarity. It is magic and it's powerful." Although the participants within this study are technically solitary witches who engage in their spiritual practices alone, as opposed to within a coven, the collective impact the individual feminist witches have is evident as they engage in social movements that aim to positively influence people's lives in transformational and healing ways.

Sally reinforced how her political and spiritual values overlap, stating, "Witchcraft is a practice that helps you find your own inner power ... anyone can be a witch regardless of age, sex, gender. I think it's about reclaiming, especially as women, what was taken from us by the patriarchy, and particularly in Ireland, the Catholic Church. We were so put down by the church and it's about reclaiming that power and stepping away from those patriarchal institutions." The persecution of Irish women was a major influence in all participants' identities as feminist witches, with many of the participants of my research empathizing with survivors of Church and state abuse.

Outrage at the myriad of injustices within Ireland was highlighted by the participants as well, whether outrage with the institutionalization of unmarried mothers, the ban on abortion, or being unable to walk alone at night. Although Ireland has a limited history when it comes to the persecution of witches, the small country has a deep and dark history of persecuting women. It is this history of persecution and Ireland's perceived connection to a magical and ancient land that has given rise to such a strong affinity between Irish feminists, the image of the witch, and witchcraft itself. This allows for the overlap between the fire of passion that burns within each Irish feminist witch and the cauldron that bubbles.

The Witching Hour: The Future and the Role of Irish Feminist Witches

The study participants believe that the role of Irish feminist witches should focus on combating current injustices, facilitating support to victims of inequalities, and remembering the power of human connection.

Cleo believes that Irish feminist witches should focus on "helping people who have suffered at the hands of oppressors. Providing healing and comfort for those people." Maggie similarly views the role of Irish feminist witches as "speaking more because this country is very judgmental to anyone who is different." On the same note, Megan believes Irish feminist witches could focus on "changing one person's perspective or mind. That's a victory. It's about talking and about highlighting what your personal experiences are, what you've been through."

Erin thinks it is particularly inspiring to see "that there [are] a lot of women who are now strongly rejecting anything to do with the Catholic ethos with a visceral intensity, and of course the witch is the anthesis of that." Erin shared that she would love to see even more people "identifying with witches as potentially a rejection of the Catholic Church and Catholic ethos and the repression that we would have felt growing up, particularly around sexuality and gender, ethnicity." Sally also believes that "having those conversations and explaining why you practice could cause a bit of a shift in the views on religion in the country and the views around women as well and the Church, because it still has quite a hold on society. I think talking. Not necessarily just getting onto the streets and protesting, but just talking to those around you can be really powerful because it creates a ripple effect. I practice witchcraft because I find it very powerful as a woman. Ireland can be very closed-minded; you're either Catholic or you're not."

The participants collectively recognize the power of collective action, having all been involved in previous social movements that campaigned against the teachings and beliefs of the Catholic Church, most notably the Repeal the 8th campaign to legalize abortion in Ireland. However, they also highlight how important human interaction and connection can be in bringing about a more tolerant and inclusive society. Despite each having suffered or witnessed suffering to varying degrees, the Irish feminist witches believe that due to the overlap of their political and spiritual identities, they have an important role, as both witches and women, in resisting the norms of a patriarchal Irish society that has caused harm to generations of women.

CONCLUSION

The experience of Irish feminist witches is rather unique. Whether it is because they come from a land that has always been associated with ancient links to Celtic paganism or because they live in a country that sacrificed the progress and lives of women in order to establish itself as an independent state by joining forces with the Catholic Church, Irish feminist witches can appreciate the complexity of possessing a history from precolonial times, colonialism, and a postcolonial state.

The findings of this research show that Irish feminist witches have rebelled against the patriarchal society and Church that have vilified them for being born female. To regain power and control over their own bodies and to be empowered as women, the participants have returned to a worldview that sees feminine energy as a source of power and magic that can be tapped into and utilized in order to realize the potential and power within oneself. Moreover, when collectively harnessed, it has the capacity to bring about transformational societal impact. It is therefore evident where the spiritual and political affinities of the witch overlap. With the experience of growing up in a country that demonized them because of their sex and gender, treating them as mere vessels, it is unsurprising that several Irish feminists found comfort not only in the symbol of the witch but in the practice of witchcraft, the very practice that the Catholic Church found to be the epitome of evil and rebellion.

With the realization of the neglect of the role of women within Irish history, the uncovering of the multitude of abuses suffered by thousands of women at the hands of the Catholic Church and the Irish State, the cover-ups of mass graves at previous Magdalene laundries,[29] and current challenges regarding violence against women, there are generations of rage and trauma fueling Irish women. Irish feminist witches are engaging in political demonstrations in public and powerful manifestation rituals in private, both actions an attempt to heal the suffering and trauma of their fellow women.

NOTES

1. Griffin, "Embodied Goddess," 35.
2. Sollee, *Witches, Sluts, Feminists*, 54.
3. Griffin, "Embodied Goddess," 35.
4. Aune, "Feminist Spirituality."

5   Chiseri-Strater, "Turning In upon Ourselves."
6   Misawa, "Queer Race Pedagogy," 26.
7   Sneddon, *Possessed by the Devil*; and Sneddon, *Witchcraft and Magic*.
8   Walshe, O'Searcaigh, and Fitzmaurice, "Sexing the Shamrock."
9   Kerrigan, "After Marriage."
10 Pizmony-Levy and To, *National School Survey*.
11 LGBT Ireland, "Sectoral Response to Hate Crime."
12 O'Shaughnessy, "Triumph and Concession."
13 O'Toole, "I Wish Ann Lovett Were Out."
14 O'Carroll, "Twenty Years On."
15 McDonald, "Brain-Dead Pregnant Woman's Life Support."
16 Doyle, Ashe, and Lawler, "Addressing Domestic Violence," 2.
17 Safe Ireland, "2022 Deadliest Year."
18 Rockett, "Film Censorship and the State."
19 Sneddon, *Witchcraft and Magic*.
20 Stevens, Brown, and Maclaran, "Gender, Nationality and Cultural Representations."
21 Bebergal, *Season of the Witch*, 74.
22 Barry, "The Lost Children."
23 Donnelly, "Sins of the Father."
24 Butler, "Remembrance of the Ancestors."; Santino, "Halloween in America."
25 Doyle, Ashe, and Lawler, "Addressing Domestic Violence," 2.
26 Meaney, *Sex and Nation*.
27 Inglis, "Origins and Legacies of Irish Prudery."
28 Fischer, "Gender, Nation, and the Politics of Shame," 826.
29 Barry, "The Lost Children."

BIBLIOGRAPHY

Aune, Kristen. "Feminist Spirituality as Lived Religion: How UK Feminists Forge Religio-spiritual Lives." *Gender and Society* 29, no. 1 (2015): 122–45.

Barry, Dan. "The Lost Children of Tuam." *New York Times*, October 28, 2017.

Bebergal, Peter. *Season of the Witch: How the Occult Saved Rock and Roll*. New York: Penguin, 2015.

Butler, Jenny. "Remembrance of the Ancestors in Contemporary Paganism: Lineage, Identity, and Cultural Belonging in the Irish Context." *Journal of the Irish Society for the Academic Study of Religions* 2, no. 1 (2015): 94–118.

Chiseri-Strater, Elizabeth. "Turning In upon Ourselves: Positionality, Subjectivity, and Reflexivity in Case Study and Ethnographic Research." In *Ethics and Responsibility in Qualitative Studies of Literacy*, edited by Peter Mortensen and Gesa E. Kirsch, 115–33. Urbana, IL: National Council of Teachers of English, 1996.

Donnelly, Susie. "Sins of the Father: Unravelling Moral Authority in the Irish Catholic Church." *Irish Journal of Sociology* 24, no. 3 (2016): 315–39. https://doi.org/10.7227/IJS.0009.

Doyle, Jessica, Sinead Ashe, and Lauren Lawler. "Addressing Domestic, Sexual and Gender-Based Violence. Part One: Overview." House of the Oireachtais, November 10, 2021. https://data.oireachtas.ie/ie/oireachtas/libraryResearch/2021/2021-11-15_l-rs-note-addressing-domestic-sexual-and-gender-based-violence-part-one-overview_en.pdf.

Fischer, Clara. "Gender, Nation, and the Politics of Shame: Magdalen Laundries and the Institutionalization of Feminine Transgression in Modern Ireland." *Journal of Women in Culture and Society* 41, no. 4 (2016): 821–43. https://doi.org/10.1086/685117.

Griffen, Wendy. "The Embodied Goddess: Feminist Witchcraft and Female Divinity." *Sociology of Religion* 56, no. 1 (1995): 35–48. https://doi.org/10.2307/3712037.

Inglis, Tom. "Origins and Legacies of Irish Prudery: Sexuality and Social Control in Modern Ireland." *Irish American Cultural Institute* 40, nos. 3–4 (2005): 9–37. https://doi.org/10.1353/eir.2005.0022.

Kerrigan, Páraic. "After Marriage: The Assimilation, Representation, and Diversification of LGBTQ Lives on Irish Television." *Television and New Media* 22, no. 1 (2021): 47–64. https://doi.org/10.1177/1527476420976122.

LGBT Ireland. "LGBTQI+ Sectoral Response to Garda Hate Crime Statistics Published Today." March 22, 2023. https://lgbt.ie/lgbtqi-sectoral-response-to-garda-hate-crime-statistics-published-today/.

McDonald, Henry. "Brain-Dead Pregnant Woman's Life Support Can Be Switched Off, Irish Court Rules." *Guardian*, December 26, 2014. https://www.theguardian.com/world/2014/dec/26/ireland-court-rules-brain-dead-pregnant-womans-life-support-switched-off.

Meaney, Gerardine. *Sex and Nation: Women in Irish Culture and Politics*. Dublin: Attic Press, 1991.

Misawa, Mitsunori. "Queer Race Pedagogy for Educators in Higher Education: Dealing with Power Dynamics and Positionality of LGBTQ Students of Color." *International Journal of Critical Pedagogy* 3, no. 1 (2010): 26–35.

O'Carroll, Sinead. "Twenty Years On: A Timeline of the X Case." *The Journal*, February 6, 2012. https://www.thejournal.ie/twenty-years-on-a-timeline-of-the-x-case-347359-Feb2012/.

O'Shaughnessy, Aideen Catherine. "Triumph and Concession? The Moral and Emotional Construction of Ireland's Campaign for Abortion Rights." *European Journal of Women's Studies* 29, no. 2 (2022): 233–49. https://doi.org/10.1177/13505068211040999.

O'Toole, Emer. "I Wish Ann Lovett Were Out Buying a Swimsuit for Lanzarote." Paper Visual Art, May 24, 2018. https://papervisualart.com/2018/05/24/i-wish-ann-lovett-were-out-buying-a-swimsuit-for-lanzarote/.

Pizmony-Levy, O., and Belong To. *The 2022 Irish National School Climate Survey Report*. Global Observatory of LGBTQ+ Education and Advocacy. Dublin: Belong To; New York: Teachers College, Columbia University, 2022.

Rockett, Kevin. "Film Censorship and the State." *Film Directions* 3, no. 9 (1980): 11–125.

Safe Ireland. "2022 Deadliest Year of the Decade for Women and Children." 2022. https://www.safeireland.ie/2022-deadliest-year-of-the-decade-for-women-and-children/.

Santino, Jack. "Halloween in America: Contemporary Customs and Performances." *Western Folklore* 42, no. 1 (1983): 1–20. https://doi.org/10.2307/1499461.

Sneddon, Andrew. *Possessed by the Devil*. Dublin: History Press Ireland, 2013.

Sneddon, Andrew. *Witchcraft and Magic in Ireland*. London: Palgrave Macmillan, 2015.

Sollee, Kristen. *Witches, Sluts, Feminists: Conjuring the Sex Positive*. Chicago: ThreeL Media, 2017.

Stevens, Lorna, Stephen Brown, and Pauline Maclaran. "Gender, Nationality and Cultural Representations of Ireland: An Irish Woman's Place?" *European Journal of Women's Studies* 7, no. 4 (2000): 405–21. https://doi.org/10.1177/135050680000700412.

Walshe, E., Cathal O'Searcaigh, and G. Fitzmaurice. "Sexing the Shamrock." *Critical Survey* 8, no. 2 (1996): 159–67. https://www.jstor.org/stable/41555996.

Four · APOORVAA JOSHI AND ETHEL BROOKS

Whose Craft?: Contentions on Open and Closed Practice in Contemporary Witchcraft(s)

Witches have haunted the cultural imagination of the West, from Homer's Circe to cool teen-witch figures like *Sabrina the Teenage Witch* in contemporary popular culture.[1] Over the years, what it means to be a "witch" has become highly contested; contemporary witchcraft remains a decentralized and diverse group of systems of belief and practice. Ranging from highly commodified "witchy" aesthetics on social media to hereditary and syncretic religions such as Voodoo, the original cultural symbol of the Witch has been reclaimed, subverted, and exploited by various groups toward different ends. The landscape between these various camps of witchcraft is fractured by boundaries that shift and are negotiated actively by practitioners, often along racialized lines.

One such contested boundary, and the focus of this chapter, is the discussion around "open" and "closed" practices in contemporary witchcraft. Closed practices refer to those that are restricted to in-group members and often considered inappropriate, immoral, or even *impossible* for outsiders to perform. The boundaries around these practices highlight the racialization of certain witchcraft lineages—perhaps, *witchcrafts*—and underscore implicit power dynamics among practitioners based on race and ethnicity. Debates have erupted, especially in online spaces, among practitioners about whether practices developed by BIPOC people or those who remain under the umbrella of racialized systems should be practiced by nonmembers (especially white witches) or whether they should remain closed. These discussions embody concepts such as cultural belonging, appropriation, and purity. Fundamentally, contemporary witchcraft encompasses syncretic systems whose origins pull from several religions and spiritualities, merging them into new cultural configurations, and this troubles the very idea of practices "belonging" to only one group. However, the capture of witchcraft practices and objects for mass commodification demonstrates the power of hegemonic global structures to encroach upon the sacred and the marginal and turn them into vehicles for capital. Additionally, this shows how closing practices is protective; it may turn those crafts into spaces of resistance against white supremacy, capitalism, and patriarchy. This chapter illustrates the key contentions in contemporary social discourse about open/closed practice and how they may or may not provide avenues for decolonizing witchcraft.

This chapter focuses on debates about open and closed practices that have been playing out dynamically online, particularly on the social media platform TikTok. Witches as a subject matter remain a popular topic on social media. For example, as of July 2022, Instagram lists about 14.9 million posts tagged with the hashtag #witch, and 7.5 million posts use the tag #witchcraft. For context, #christian logs 17.1 million posts. What it means to be a witch and to practice witchcraft are continually re-defined in these online spaces. Digital methods, with regard to qualitative sampling from social media, are evolving. In order to construct a useful dataset of content for this chapter, we opted to sample *conceptually* across all TikTok content related to open/closed practice in witchcraft.[2] As Waseem Ahmed notes, all TikTok data across "the forms of video, text, likes, comments, and views can be analysed for academic insight."[3] Therefore, we reviewed TikTok posts' for audio, visual, and text content, as well as limited metadata like number of comments on a video, self-categorization through hashtags, and the use of trending audio samples in their content (this is supposed to boost engagement). Additionally, the volatile nature of social media landscapes highlights how deletion and quiet suppression of posts (colloquially known as "shadowbanning") can pose issues to analysis after data collection is complete. For example, the two years or so that elapsed between the initial analysis for this chapter and publication saw several changes to TikTok's content guidelines and censorship policies, which in turn led to the deletion, hiding, and re-creation of both user accounts and posts.[4] Thus, it is difficult to glean stable data on users at any given moment in time from the application (which also does not have an official API as of this chapter's writing).[5] Therefore, we have had to rely on witchcraft practitioners with public accounts who weigh in on the discussion about open/closed practice and self-identify their credentials.

Additionally, the platform's proprietary algorithm guides the content we are shown, necessarily influencing data collection and analysis. TikTok is especially noted for its sophisticated algorithm, wherein user activity on certain videos predicts other videos of interest to queue in an attempt to keep the user engaged.[6] Rather than frame this as a detraction from sample validity, we have leaned into this function of the platform to help us find relevant data to analyze. Given the constraints and developing norms around these data, and our focus on open/closed practice in witchcraft, we are intentionally presenting a small, conceptual sample of content from a larger pool curated by the platform algorithm, creating what we are calling an "algorithmic snowball sample."[7]

OPEN AND CLOSED PRACTICES: DEBATES ON BOUNDARIES IN CONTEMPORARY WITCHCRAFT

"Here's the thing: if you have a problem with the word 'closed practice,' you probably have boundary issues and you should work on that. They're closed for a reason." TikTok creator Anastasia (@anastasiamoongirl) recounted into the camera in a November 2021 video. The creator, whose account bio identified her as a "Mixed Rootworker," focused on various traditions of witchcraft, including Haitian Voodoo, drawing on her heritage. The comments on the post (nearly 200 at the time) included a number of concurring sentiments, including from user "Asparagus" (@aquaichor): "closed practice are a commitment for life baby, not as long as you're entertained." The video and its comments were posted in response to a brewing debate over the concept of open and closed practices within witchcraft; indeed, it serves as a microcosm of the dynamics among witchcraft practitioners in the broader culture. Specifically, practitioners on the platform debated through a series of video responses to one another whether it is appropriative for nonmembers to perform "closed" practices. Syncretism in folk practice, including several lineages of witchcraft, is generally accepted— and yet, these systems of practice are all still negotiating boundaries in real time, resulting in disagreements on what should and should not be permitted by the witchcraft community. The related practice of *gatekeeping*, or policing the boundaries around closed practice, is often discussed. Gatekeeping interventions range from discussing the impossibility (and actual danger) of closed practices working for out-group members to simply refusing to share information about such practices. Gatekeeping is a behavior that highlights the relationship between imagination, practice, and resistance to hegemony.

Contemporary witchcraft is a contested space, due partially to the inclusion of belief-practice systems whose origins reside in oppressed and marginalized cultures. These religions and spiritualities were transformed into *witchcraft* or *devil worshipping* through colonization; this was a criminalized concept that traveled back to mainland Europe and was established as a capital offense primarily targeting women and marginal groups during the witch "craze," or the height of the early modern European witch trials.[8] Developing out of the disempowerment of Black and Indigenous peoples, various forms of magic and witchcraft were practiced both as ways of remembering lost heritage and as acts of agency and often protection. Fundamentally, closed practice is associated with origins in cultures that have been systematically othered and oppressed by the state: for example, Jewish kabbalistic magic, Hoodoo and Voodoo (from Black descendants of slaves), Romani fortune-telling and divination, several Indigenous American spiritual systems, and individual European folk magics (especially those that are attributed to proletariat and serf/peasant origins, such as Slavic heritage practices).

The notion that many witchcrafts find their origins in low culture or folk religion (and therefore stem from oppressed categories of society) is one perspective that offers an argument with which to blur the boundary around closing practices. That is, many practitioners acknowledge the natural diffusion of beliefs and practices across cultural contexts, especially when the groups sharing them come from similar social positions of marginality. The similarities between cultural appropriation (using a closed practice when you are not a member of the closed group) and the cultural syncretism of many witchcraft systems obscures neat distinctions between open and closed systems. It seems, then, the idea that we cannot draw boundaries around *any* practice—and that there is no "pure origin" of any system—can take hold. The decontextualization of closed practices, however, is key to their appropriation: one (usually dominant) culture absorbs a (marginal) practice or custom *without* acknowledging its origins or context. Closing practices today can thus be seen as a protective measure against the ability of hegemonic power structures (like white supremacy and capitalism) to capture, homogenize, and strip them of these origins and of, according to some practitioners, their revolutionary power.

And so, the syncretic usage of shared content from various cultural sources within witchcraft becomes a question of power: Are these stolen practices, or are oppressed peoples simply sharing their magic for everyone's benefit? One TikTok user, Frederick Butler (@drunk_on_decay), mused in a now-private video: "I had a thought today on cultural appropriation in occult and witchy communities.... I saw a discussion about the use of psalms and the use of talismans.... This began from what was presented as a Hoodoo practice of writing psalms to carry in your shoe—and I am obviously no expert on Hoodoo practice but I am Jewish and a student of Kabbalah where psalms are very important and talismans are written ... utilizing the words of psalms. I think it's important we recognize the difference between specific closed practices and *shared spiritual content*."

This question and the consideration of power in creating boundaries for closed practice often touches on the fact that witchcraft lineages span global history, including European cultures. Particularly the consideration of white-dominant systems of magic—those such as Wicca (a New Age syncretic religion drawing on professed European pagan practices) or Norse/"Viking" magic—as open practices elucidates how this discussion is related to how enclosure will or will not allow marginalized populations access to power. Kathryn Gottlieb outlines how debates on the blogging platform Tumblr regarding participation in these systems has been put into the broader context of power dynamics between white and nonwhite practitioners of witchcraft(s) and subsequently these practices' proximity to white supremacist beliefs.[9] Additionally, in a 2021 video, TikTok creator Lady Speech (@ladyspeechsankofa) celebrated the idea of white witches in the West looking back into their *own* ethnic heritages for forms of magic rather than participating in racialized lineages closed for BIPOC witches. In response to a question a commenter asked about researching voodoo as a European person, they said:

> Europe is the seat and the throne of so much colonization. Before a lot of European people colonized the rest of the world, they colonized *their fucking selves*! So here's the thing: the reason why so many of y'all are so connected to researching *our* shit is because there is a hidden call up under you. You have very magic ancestors who were colonized, who have a magic that is native indigenous *to you*.... Why would you waste [time researching BIPOC closed practices] when you can research your own shit and practice your own native motherfuckin' magic that can help heal you and help dismantle white supremacy.

In addition to contentions on whether one *should* use closed practices, notions about the limits of those magics for white folks—or *can* one use closed practices?—present interesting implications for understanding shared conceptions of *possibility*. Another TikTok creator, Alejo Do Lodo (@itsalexsiwa), references ethical (and spiritual) consequences for appropriating Black witchcraft practices. In a series of (now deleted) videos explaining Hoodoo he said:

> Hoodoo is specifically Black. It's a specifically Black cultural practice ... it's more like an ethno-religion comparable to Judaism ... [and similarly,] you can be ethnically Hoodoo and not practice. And that's because Hoodoo *is* Black culture. It's the basis of everything that is Black in the United States.... You don't get Hoodoo without Blackness and you don't get Blackness without a Black experience [yourself].... A lot of parts of Hoodoo are just too fucking dangerous for you to do if you are not a Black person.

In a follow-up video he stated, "Hoodoo is an [African Traditional Religion]. And ... ATR's can be very, very dangerous. Some of the Hoodoo Saints we call upon in our workings *did not fuck with white people*. I'm talking Nat Turner, Gullah Jack, High John the Conqueror.... Hoodoo love workings are so effective because of the suffering of Black women.... Hoodoo has cultural context, that's all I'm saying."

However, in another (now deleted) video delineating the differences between Hoodoo and Voodoo, creator Omilana (@divinepriestess), defined Hoodoo as *cultural* practices and Voodoo as an initiate-only African diasporic *religion*. This conversation touches on the notion of *which* magic is *possible* and for whom. She said, "Hoodoo is everywhere.... Hoodoo is in the food that you cook, [it's] in the way you clean your house ... those specific prayers [from the Bible] you say at night.... When you practice Voodoo, you have to be initiated ... and the Spirits will let you know if they will allow you to initiate.... Do not get Hoodoo and Voodoo confused.... You can be initiated in Voodoo and practice Hoodoo but [not vice versa]." The enclosing of Voodoo and framing it as a calling by the *loa* (spirits) further exemplifies how the notions of possibility are related to these boundaries around practices, specifically if they are open/closed, and to what degree, or for whom.

The decontextualization of witchcraft practices and their related objects is fundamentally a study in power. The ability of hegemonic whiteness and capital to frame magical objects steeped in histories of oppression as newly discovered ideas/practices and then repackage them for mass consumption illustrates how revolutionary potential can be stripped from marginal cultures and can sometimes also endanger those practices. For example, the widespread use of crystals in New Age and popularized spiritualities (the origin of which is much disputed and found across cultures—ranging from Tibetan Buddhist, Hindu, and several Indigenous peoples) has resulted in open-pit and strip-mining operations in the Global South that have caused vast environmental and labor abuses in order to meet the demand for the crystals in the Global North.[10] "The revival of magical beliefs is possible today because it no longer represents a social threat," writes Silvia Federici, echoing this sentiment of a divorcing of modern witchcraft from its potential social power.[11]

Recalling that the origins of witchcraft lie in systems that gave marginalized people access to power in a social order that otherwise forbade it connects the concept of contemporary witchcraft to the cultural symbol of "the Witch," indeed the most salient social construction of witchcraft practice in the shared imagination of the West. The Witch, portrayed as a malevolent female entity whose existence threatens the social order (normalized to the point that she seemed to disturb God's *natural world* itself), was a figure forged in the crucible of sweeping social change during the centuries of the European witch trials (roughly from the fourteenth to seventeenth centuries), at a time of emergent colonization, capitalism, and the rise of religious-patriarchal power over bodies.[12] The Witch haunted a social order that was defined by a ruling class invested in capitalist-colonial expansion and its patriarchal underpinnings. She remained a serious threat in her ability to introduce other ways of living (especially those that recalled feminine power, communal resources, and reverence of folk knowledges) in the imaginations of laypeople. By decontextualizing closed practices from their relationship to the Witch, we enact a process of removing them from their roots: challenging the power of white male masters—a fundamental role of witchcraft since its inception.

CLOSING PRACTICES AS DECOLONIAL LOVE: MASS COMMODIFICATION AND WITCHCRAFT

History, culture, and global capitalism fundamentally structure the creation, dissemination, and meaning of cultural objects.[13] The meaning of the Witch, too, was mediated by the rise of capitalism. Federici, particularly, asserts that the Witch of early modern Europe drew on the revolutionary potential of the antifeudal movement (often spearheaded by women) and its role as the main antecedent to an anticapitalist movement in early modern Europe: "Capitalism was the response of the feudal lords, the patrician merchants, the bishops and popes, to a centuries-long social conflict that, in the end, shook their power.... Capitalism was the counter-revolution that destroyed the possibilities that had emerged from the anti-feudal struggle—*possibilities* which, if realized, might have spared us the immense destruction of lives and the natural environment that has marked the advance of capitalist relations worldwide."[14] The development of capitalism necessitated the delineation of private property, the disciplining of bodies into rigid social-moral categories, and the disavowal of magic as a viable possibility (and the destruction of systems of meaning related to magic). The violence of the public witch trials sought to crush the possibility of the Witch: a symbol of the fast-disappearing Commons when in the form of a destitute woman reliant on (private) charity instead of social goods; a reminder of lost healing knowledges women were now precluded from learning, including abortions; and a supernatural intermediary to a bygone time when the world remained Enchanted and alternate possibilities of the present still existed.[15]

Given this context of the Witch as a symbolic antagonist to colonial-capitalism, the role of commodification in shaping the creation, dissemination, and interpretation of witchcraft-related cultural objects—including objects used within ritual—becomes an important facet in understanding the debate around open/closed practices. For example, the use of palo santo wood, often utilized in several Indigenous Latin American and mestizo spiritualities, has generally been enclosed by heritage witchcraft practitioners, marking a shift away from the wood's use in New Age and majority-white spaces.[16] Voices from within communities whose use of palo santo stretches back for generations have challenged the use of the incense, stating that burning palo santo was a sacred practice reserved only for those born into the native cultures.

Another witchcraft TikTok creator and commentator, "Witchfoot" (@witchfoot_incorporated), posted a video in February 2022 challenging this enclosure, stating that through a poll on a previous post, commentors from the same Indigenous cultures responded that the *use* of palo santo was not closed, but they raised concerns about the mass commodification and unsustainable harvesting of the material. Alongside questions about whether or not burning palo santo was closed, a more popular debate raged online centered on concerns about harvesting and commodification.[17]

Additionally, the growing popularity of the neologism "witchy"—which appears to reference a common understanding of what a witch *looks like*—has its own categorical tag on social media platforms including Instagram, TikTok, and Twitter. The popularity of *witchiness* (if not actually being a witch or practicing witchcraft) has been capitalized upon by large companies. For example, now-infamous "starter witch-kits" were sold by beauty brand Pinrose at trendy outlets like Sephora and Urban Outfitters; these sets included crystals, white sage for burning, tarot cards, and perfumes from the company. The kits were poorly received by self-identified witches and finally pulled from the shelves in light of backlash from witches. Pam Grossman, author of the memoir-cum-guidebook to witchcraft culture *Waking the Witch*, captures the complexity of attributing these commodified objects to witchcraft, and that in itself reflects the complexity of the witch: "But let's be clear: plenty of other mainstream stores sell all kinds of witchcraft items . . . and I am certain that not every single one has been produced or vetted by actual practitioners. And that's where things get confusing, and it can seem like the goalposts for what a 'real witch' is are constantly moving."[18] Practitioners, many of whom are small-scale producers of magical objects on platforms such as Etsy or local witch markets, remain the nexus around which the debates about commodification, appropriation, and dissemination of witchcraft practices revolve. While the hard boundary around closed practice may act as a way of staving off the appropriation of protected practices, the witchcraft community may have to remain vigilant against the annexation of sacred objects by capital.

In conclusion, we posit another way to understand witchcraft through a deeper recognition of its racialized and gendered origins, on the one hand, and through a deliberate commitment to *decolonial love*, on the other. Magic has been racialized and, of course, gendered from the beginning of the colonial project. Romani people were persecuted for being holders of magic; they were hunted and expelled for their "outlandish" ways;[19] and they were labeled "untouchable," racializing Romani people's relation to magic from the beginning.[20] This scaffolding undergirded European colonial violence, war, slavery, and occupation across centuries and across geographies. Recognition of these histories—of Voodoo and Hoodoo, of Candomblé and Santería, of Indigenous spiritual practices, of Romani fortune-telling and divination—and their formations against coloniality, moves from debates around boundedness, enclosure, and open/closed practices into a space of what Chela Sandoval calls "decolonial love." She argues for "differential consciousness and social movement [as] crucial for shaping effective and ongoing oppositional struggle."[21] If we engage witchcraft as a practice of decolonial love, as an agent of social movement that moves toward liberation, we can open up possibilities for manifold formations of witchcraft that move beyond cultural appropriation and the violence of capitalism and whiteness into a space of decoloniality, differential consciousness, and recognition for its multiple lineages.

NOTES

1. Roper, *The Witch in the Western Imagination*; Johnston and Aloi, *The New Generation Witches*.
2. Zerubavel, *Generally Speaking*.
3. Ahmed, *How to Conduct Research on TikTok*, 2.
4. As alluded to by TikTok Community Guidelines in 2024 (https://www.tiktok.com/community-guidelines/en).
5. Ahmed writes that "no 'official' API or other ways to access data from TikTok [exists] in order for academics to analyse and study content on the platform. Similar to earlier methods of studying online platforms, such as Web-forums and closed social media platforms, academics must utilise more creative methods to capture and analyse data from TikTok" (Ahmed, *How to Conduct Research on TikTok*, 3).
6. Bhandari and Bimo, "Why's Everyone on TikTok Now?"
7. Discussions of commodification, appropriation, and coloniality in witchcraft greatly mirror the concept of "data colonialism" developed by Nick Couldry and Ulises A. Mejias in their 2018 article. The intentionality of our approach to acknowledging TikTok's algorithm and appropriation of user data for purposes which reify colonial relations attempts to "hack" the algorithm to amplify suppressed subjectivities and voices as much as is possible as lay-users of the platform.
8. Federici, *Caliban and the Witch*; Silverblatt, *Moon, Sun, and Witches*.
9. Gottlieb, "Cultural Appropriation in Contemporary Neopaganism and Witchcraft."
10. McClure, "Dark Crystals."
11. Federici, *Caliban and the Witch*, 272.
12. Ben-Yehuda, "The European Witch Craze"; Barstow, *Witchcraze*.
13. Capitalism functions as a myth in the Barthesian sense; it naturalizes its ideology as (necessarily) part of human society, and therefore as the only *possibility* for the social world. Mark Fisher writes in *Capitalist Realism*: "We are inevitably reminded of the phrase attributed to Fredric Jameson and Slavoj Žižek, that it is *easier to imagine the end of the world than it is to*

imagine the end of capitalism. That slogan captures precisely what I mean by 'capitalist realism': the widespread sense that not only is capitalism the only viable political and economic system, but also *that it is now impossible even to imagine a coherent alternative to it.*"

14   Federici, *Caliban and the Witch*, 21–22 (emphasis added).
15   Federici, *Caliban and the Witch*.
16   The term *New Age* is perhaps intuitively grasped by many readers, but is itself a nebulous concept: an amalgamation of belief systems and practices, ranging from yoga and Eastern philosophies to tarot cards, "alternative" medicine, and astrology, all with varying levels of decontextualization and capture by capital. "The first line of criticism is that the term 'New Age' covers too great a variety of concepts to be of use" (Chryssides, *Defining the New Age*, 10). Steven Sutcliffe (*Children of the New Age*, 11) writes, "'New Age' is not a distinctive empirical formation but a (now rather stale) codeword for the heterogeneity of 'alternative' spirituality, best classified as a sub-type of 'popular religion.'"
17   Martin, "Is Palo Santo Endangered?"
18   Grossman, *Waking the Witch*, 259.
19   The Egyptians Act of 1530 (22 *Henry 8, c. 10*, https://statutes.org.uk/site/the-statutes/sixteenth-century/1530-22-henry-8-c-10-the-egyptians-act/), referring to Romani people, ordered the expulsion from the realm of "outlandish people calling themselves Egyptians."
20   The G-slur is derived from the Greek term *athiganoi*, referring to the magic for which Romani people were known. See European Roma Rights Center (ERR) v. Greece (Complaint No. 15/2003), November 3, 2004, https://rm.coe.int/no-15-2003-european-roma-rights-centre-errc-v-greece-case-document-no-/168073e91f. See also Iulia Hau, "Roma Slavery in Romania: A History," *European* (blog), July 7, 2021, https://www.europeana.eu/en/blog/roma-slavery-in-romania-a-history.
21   Sandoval, *Methodology of the Oppressed*, 45.

BIBLIOGRAPHY

Ahmed, Wasim. *How to Conduct Research on TikTok*. Sage Research Methods: Doing Research Online, SAGE Publications, Ltd., 2022. How-to Guide. https://doi.org/10.4135/9781529607437.

Barstow, Anne Llewellyn. *Witchcraze: A New History of the European Witch Hunts*. San Francisco: Pandora, 1995.

Ben-Yehuda, Nachman. "The European Witch Craze of the 14th to 17th Centuries: A Sociologist's Perspective." *American Journal of Sociology* 86, no. 1 (1980): 1–31.

Bhandari, Aparajita, and Sara Bimo. "Why's Everyone on TikTok Now? The Algorithmized Self and the Future of Self-Making on Social Media."

Social Media + Society 8, no. 1 (2022): 1–11. https://doi.org/10.1177/20563051221086241.

Chryssides, George D., "Defining the New Age." In *Handbook of New Age*, edited by Daren Kemp and James R. Lewis, 5–24. Leiden: Brill, 2007.

Couldry, N., and Ulises A. Mejias. "Data Colonialism: Rethinking Big Data's Relation to the Contemporary Subject." *Television and New Media* 20, no. 4 (2019): 336–49. https://doi-org.proxy.libraries.rutgers.edu/10.1177/1527476418796632.

Federici, Silvia. *Caliban and the Witch: Women, the Body and Primitive Accumulation*. New York: Autonomedia, 2014.

Fisher, Mark. *Capitalist Realism: Is There No Alternative?* Hants, UK: O Books, 2009.

Gottlieb, Kathryn. "Cultural Appropriation in Contemporary Neopaganism and Witchcraft." Honors thesis, University of Maine, 2017.

Grossman, Pam. *Waking the Witch: Reflections on Women, Magic, and Power*. New York: Gallery Books, 2019.

Johnston, H. E., and Peg Aloi, eds. *The New Generation Witches: Teenage Witchcraft in Contemporary Culture*. New York: Routledge, 2007.

Martin, Crystal. "Is Palo Santo Endangered?" *New York Times*, December 16, 2019.

McClure, Tess. "Dark Crystals: The Brutal Reality behind a Booming Wellness Craze." *Guardian*, September 17, 2019.

Roper, Lyndal. *The Witch in the Western Imagination*. Charlottesville: University of Virginia Press, 2012.

Sandoval, Chela. *Methodology of the Oppressed*. Minneapolis: University of Minnesota Press, 2000.

Silverblatt, Irene Marsha. *Moon, Sun, and Witches: Gender Ideologies and Class in Inca and Colonial Peru*. Princeton, NJ: Princeton University Press, 2002.

Sutcliffe, Steven. *Children of the New Age: A History of Spiritual Practices*. London: Routledge, 2003.

Zerubavel, Eviatar. *The Fine Line: Making Distinctions in Everyday Life*. Chicago: University of Chicago Press, 1993.

Zerubavel, Eviatar. *Generally Speaking: An Invitation to Concept-Driven Sociology*. New York: Oxford University Press, 2021.

TIKTOK REFERENCES

1   Alejo Do Lodo (@itsalexsiwa). "[Series on Hoodoo] (part 2)." TikTok, accessed December 2021. https://www.tiktok.com/foryou?is_copy_url=1&is_from_webapp=v1&item_id=6954874030071565574&q=itsalexsiwa%20hoodoo&t=1647324059729#/@itsalexsiwa/video/6954874030071565574.

2   Alejo Do Lodo (@itsalexsiwa). "[Series on Hoodoo] (part 3)." TikTok, accessed December 2021. https://www.tiktok.com/@itsalexsiwa/video/6954874355029495046?is_copy_url=1&is_from_webapp=v1.

3   Anastasia (@anastasiamoongirl). "The way I keep getting sent ppl not caring about closed practice. At this point mess around n find out lol #witchtip #closedpractice." TikTok, November 27, 2021. https://www.tiktok.com/@anastasiamoongirl/video/7035278577645980933?is_from_webapp=1&sender_device=pc&web_id7072518151062849070.

4   "Asparagus" (@aquaichor). Comment on Anastasia (@anastasiamoongirl) post "The way I keep getting sent ppl not caring about closed practice. At this point mess around n find out lol #witchtip #closedpractice." TikTok, November 27, 2021. https://www.tiktok.com/@anastasiamoongirl/video/7035278577645980933?is_from_webapp=1&sender_device=pc&web_id7072518151062849070.

5   Butler, Frederick (@drunk_on_decay). "let's not gatekeep the book of psalms ok? details of use vs textual connection to source etc. #occultok #witchtok." TikTok, December 10, 2021, accessed January 2022. https://www.tiktok.com/@drunk_on_decay/video/7040257387630021935?is_copy_url=1&is_from_webapp=v1&lang=en.

6   Lady Speech (@ladyspeechsankofa). "Answer to @skylerdugan06 #Hello #Goodbye #LadySpeech #WastingTime #realTalk #TheQuestions #ClosedPractice #WitchTok #SpiritualTok #WiseWords." TikTok, June 16, 2021. https://www.tiktok.com/@ladyspeechsankofa/video/6974145930849307909?is_copy_url=1&is_from_webapp=v1&q=closed%20practice%20ladysankofa&t=1647323961496.

7   "Omilana" (@divinepriestess). "[Video on Hoodoo versus Voodoo]." TikTok, accessed January 2022. https://vm.tiktok.com/ZTdyGUyXN/?k=1.

8   "Witchfoot" (@witchfoot_incorporated). "#palosanto #closedpractice #notclosed." TikTok, February 14, 2022. https://www.tiktok.com/@witchfoot_incorporated/video/7064438453597130031?is_copy_url=1&is_from_webapp=v1.

LINEAGES OF HEALING

Five · MARCELITTE FAILLA

"You Deserve, Baby!": Spiritual Co-creation, Black Witches, and Feminism

In *Sisters of the Yam: Black Women and Self Recovery*, bell hooks asks, "What would it mean for black people to collectively believe that despite racism and other forces of domination, we can find everything that we need to live well in the universe, including the strength to engage in the kind of political resistance that can transform domination?"[1] Through interviews with influential Black witches, this chapter explores how they do just that.[2] The term *Black witch* is the nomenclature I am using to define a vast network of Black women and femmes[3] spread across the United States who vary in age, region, and economic and educational demographics. Although Black witch, as defined by many practitioners, is not gender-specific, the overwhelming majority are women and individuals identifying as femme. Most are also practitioners of African-heritage religions like Yoruba Ifá, African American Hoodoo, and Haitian Vodou.[4] Some are seekers who are only just becoming acquainted with their spiritual abilities, while others have undergone an initiatory rite into various religions and will often serve as mentors to younger or more novice practitioners. Black witch networks are experiencing exponential growth due to an increased interest in African-heritage religions and a desire to connect to spiritual abilities.[5] They are highly visible on Instagram accounts like @thehoodwitch (curated by Bri Luna and boasting 475,000 followers) and in Facebook groups like Magically Spiritual Black Women (which has drawn a crowd of over 107,000 members). Social media platforms are crucial virtual locations that Black witches use to build communities, share rituals, and develop collective spiritual and political beliefs. Practicing Black witches also gather at in-person and online conferences (such as the annual Dawtas of the Moon convention,[6] usually held in Baltimore, Maryland) to further nurture the community.

Based on about four years of ethnographic research,[7] I have concluded that Black witch networks produce shared beliefs concerning what is popularly known as manifestation discourse; in other words, these are beliefs about engaging the spiritual realm to affect a desired result. I claim that by merging an Africana religious orientation with a Black feminist critique, Black witches are constructing a notion of what I call *spiritual co-creation*. Spiritual co-creation is an interpretation of material manifestation discourse that challenges the prosperity gospel and aspirational New Age thought, which are frequently entangled with exploitative capitalism or individualism. It also challenges the false promise that one can shift all economic or social circumstances with a positive mindset alone. Instead, it is important to understand Black witch spiritual co-creation as inseparable from a contemporary Black feminist anti-capitalist critique, as invested in an equal distribution of resources while remaining rooted in a legacy of African-descended people using the available spiritual tools—such as herbs employed in magical remedies—to survive, thrive, and heal from anti-Blackness.

Based on a Black feminist and Africana religious orientation, four core components shape spiritual co-creation: an emphasis on healing, a critique of capitalism, a commitment to mutual aid, and a sense of deservedness. It is neither a religion nor a ritualistic tool (like tarot) but a set of beliefs that impact practitioners' engagement with their spiritual practice and subsequent communities. In this co-creative process, combining a spiritual petition with tangible strategic actions is essential to the Black witch developing an internalized faith that provides them with the belief that their spiritual practice can literally provide (or manifest) the resources necessary to meet their material, emotional, and social needs. As a result, spiritual co-creation shifts internalized notions of inferiority derived from repeated denials of basic needs such as housing, financial security, or family and marriage stability into long-term self-belief and worth.

Within the context of spiritual discourse, capitalism and its many exploitative features take on the shape of the prosperity gospel. The prosperity gospel is a collection of beliefs that a God/spirit/universe wants to help believers acquire material wealth and physical health. Iterations include right-wing preachers in Southern evangelical churches, liberal African American groups, and New Age rhetoric. However, each form espouses similar messages of optimism, positive thought, a commitment to virtuosity, and a belief that the more you give, the more blessings God will bestow. The concern associated with prosperity gospel messaging—whether vaguely spiritual or Christian—is that it omits structural inequality, blaming instead the individual for their lack of material and social access. Many versions propose that the path toward upward mobility lies with the individual, thus obscuring the need for governmental social support such as Medicaid and Medicare or public housing and education.[8]

As a new wave of interest in African-heritage religions expands, many seek spiritual services from expert practitioners while retaining a get-rich-quick mentality derived from the prosperity gospel. Prosperity gospel rhetoric typically seeps into larger Africana spiritual discourse through two discrete avenues. First, many seekers grew up in Black churches like that of T. D. Jakes, where prosperity gospel messaging is prominent.[9] They then leave these churches for African-heritage religions, but occasionally, regardless of whether intentionally or unintentionally, retain some of their ideology. Alternatively, they learn prosperity gospel thinking through New Age popular media.[10] The influence of this messaging on Black witch communities becomes evident when clients demonstrate a feeling of entitlement when interacting with Black spiritual service providers. Hess Love, cofounder of the Chesapeake Conjure Society, based in Baltimore, Maryland, spoke with me about how whiteness, capitalism, and exploitation have affected Hoodoo and Black witch communities. They observed the following:

> Many people underestimate how insidious whiteness is and how it can live in your spirit in certain ways, such as through the microwave mentality where everybody wants something quick. It's a form of entitlement and hyper-consumerism. I am also thinking of people making a business out of Hoodoo. As opposed to other diasporic faiths, Hoodoo is often the trinket you sell out front. It's becoming reduced to merely the mojo bag or candle you sell to make money. But other philosophies are important to Hoodoo that are not reflected in this thinking.[11]

Hess Love also spoke about clients taking advantage of spiritual service providers due to a lack of respect for their work. Entitlement is a considerable problem within Black witch networks. Many of my respondents spoke of clients being unwilling to pay for spell work, calling late at night for divination requests when in crisis, or neglecting to inject effort into the material realm and then blaming the witch when their desire fails to actualize.

Because Hoodoo is a tradition that was intentionally created to meet the needs of Black people surviving chattel slavery and later Jim Crow segregation, many rituals aim to ensure financial prosperity, safety, security in romantic relationships, and health. It was also—and still is—essential for practitioners to have a ritual protocol and material supplies readily accessible and known. However, accessibility puts Hoodoo at risk of exploitative practices that separate it from its philosophical beliefs and cosmological orientations, thus effectively, as Hess Love notes, reducing the tradition to mere "trinkets" that can be sold to meet a desired result. Moreover, because most spiritual service providers are women and femmes, their work—like other mostly femme labor such as childcare or housework—is undervalued in a patriarchal and capitalist society. The entitlement to Black women's and femmes' time and labor, coupled with disrespect for Hoodoo, is profoundly anti-Black and feeds into the exploitative capitalist mentality propagated by many prosperity gospel adherents.

To counter an exploitative system, many expert Black witches have integrated their Black feminist analysis into beliefs about manifestation to create a discourse of spiritual co-creation. They have derived their insights from the works of Black feminists such as Angela Davis, Audre Lorde, and bell hooks who have a long-standing commitment to the issues of social and political justice, especially concerning Black women's aspirations for and capacity to lead a free and prosperous life.[12] Arguing for the integration of theory and praxis, Patricia Hill Collins asserts, "Knowledge for knowledge's sake is not enough—Black feminist thought must both be tied to Black women's lived experiences and aim to better those experiences in some fashion."[13] Black witches recognize an immense need for material well-being but also note that without a critique of capitalism and a desire to provide for *all* Black people, manifestation discourse can quickly dissolve into the prosperity gospel. In *All about Love*, bell hooks, critical of a capitalist tendency in New Age commentary, notes, "I am often struck by the dangerous narcissism fostered by spiritual rhetoric that pays so much attention to individual self-improvement and so little to the practice of love within the context of community."[14]

Instead, predicated on a more extensive Black feminist critique, Black witches understand abundant life as being based on Black feminist desire, specifically the desire for all people to have access to necessary materials and social resources for actualizing their full potential.[15] Members of the Combahee River Collective stated, "We realize that the liberation of all oppressed peoples necessitates the destruction of the political-economic systems of capitalism and imperialism as well as patriarchy.... Material resources must be equally distributed among those who create these resources."[16] This statement highlights the revolutionary approach to resource distribution—a sentiment and approach to capitalism increasingly evident in the growing Black witch movement.

Ultimately, a Black feminist analysis integrates with an Africana religious orientation to produce an approach that counters the prosperity gospel, creating instead what I am calling spiritual co-creation. This concept is not a ritual practice unto itself; instead, it should be viewed as a set of beliefs about how to engage the spiritual realm and one's community in ways that combine Africana religious beliefs with a structural critique of capitalism and an investment in the well-being of Black women and femmes. There are four areas of spiritual discourse through which spiritual co-creation is particularly evident: a focus on healing, a critique of capitalism, a commitment to mutual aid, and, finally, a sense of deservedness cultivated within the practitioners themselves. I will begin with healing.

Emotional and psychological healing is often missing from prosperity gospel and New Age rhetoric. In popular books, such as Joel Osteen's *I Declare! 31 Promises to Speak Over Your Life* and Shakti Gawain's *Creative Visualization*, the authors go no further than providing a superficial treatment of internal well-being.[17] Instead of addressing structural or ancestral issues, their analyses merely ensure that one thinks positively. Although many Black witches have echoed and reinforced the need for positive thinking, they have also emphasized that it is nearly impossible to believe in possibility without healing generations of ancestral trauma. They recognize that issues such as depression, substance abuse, anxiety, or repeated toxic relationships result from generations of structural inequality and racially motivated violence. Thus, one must elevate the ancestors targeted by such violence in order to heal its subsequent mental health effects. At the first annual Detroit Hoodoo Festival (in Detroit, Michigan), I sat down with spiritual life coach and antiviolence facilitator Alexis Douglass, who uses astrology and ancestor mediumship to help clients heal generational trauma, as she explained:

> I had a client who had a deceased mother who did sex work, but not by her choosing, more because it was a colonized island and Indigenous women were forced into this position. Because she did sex work on a colonized island, her baby can't connect, she can't soften to her man who loves her, and she grew defensive like she had to be an independent woman. And this

wasn't coming from her need for survival but more because her mother had been violated more than one time and had to shut off a certain part of herself because it was unsafe. So I worked with this client to unravel that and elevate that ancestor.[18]

Alexis concluded, "When you finally let go of the trauma that is not yours, you get to have a wider range of positive experiences and create a life based on what you believe is possible."[19] In other words, it is nearly impossible to create the life one desires when ancestral trauma—such as codependency, shame, or intimacy issues—blocks its actualization. In effect, what is established are cycles of relived and recreated trauma. Here, Alexis refers to ancestor veneration, a West and West-Central African religious belief, but also contextualizes her client's experience within a history of colonialism. She emphasizes that spiritual intervention is necessary for her client to co-create her desired life.

Black witches have similarly integrated an Africana religious orientation into an analysis of capitalism. Black witches offer an approach that differs from Black feminist thought of the late twentieth century, where most texts that critique capitalism tended to remain secular.[20] Osunfunmilola, who lives in Baltimore, Maryland, and is popularly known as Juju Bae (figure 5.1), hosts *A Little Juju Podcast* and shared how her Africana spiritual practice informs her Black feminist analysis concerning money:

> The more I immerse myself in spiritual work with my *ile* [Ifá temple], godparents, and Hoodoo, my politics have changed. For example, although I'm still anti-capitalist in conversations around money, there was a disconnect in how I saw money as just being completely evil.
>
> I can't say money's supposed to be eradicated when I'm looking at someone in a divinatory reading and be like, "Baby, you're supposed to be rich." Or I see them walking with the spirits of money. Like I can't take away that destiny. Instead, can we rethink what we mean when we say anti-capitalism? How can we use money not rooted in capitalism or in people having to die or not getting paid for their labor, but also recognize that money isn't quite the issue?[21]

Juju Bae emphasizes that when separated from a spiritual connection, movement work or any political analysis will lack a nuanced scope. Purely secular approaches to political change offer only models primarily developed in response to Christian supremacy and the need for a separation between church and state. Moreover, when Juju Bae's nuanced approach to

FIGURE 5.1 A photograph of Juju Bae from her website.

money is adopted, two frequently opposing beliefs can exist concurrently: a desire to have abundant resources *and* a wish to live in a world without the exploitation of Black and Brown people to acquire those resources.

One way that Black witches actualize the latter desire is through mutual aid programs—an approach to resource distribution that aims to dismantle systems of oppression while meeting the immediate needs of individuals. Daizy October Latifah, a Hoodoo expert and Black witch from Los Angeles, California, implements this method through the *Blitch* Fund, a mutual aid program that gives money to mostly low-income Black women. She shared,

> I grew up pretty poor in South Central Los Angeles. I've had many situations in my life where I'm like, "I wish an angel would pop out of the sky and pay for my plane ticket up to college or else I'm not gonna be able to go to school. That kind of appearance where you don't have to beg or work for it. *It's just something you deserve that comes to you.* So as soon as I had the opportunity to set something up like that, I did.[22]

She continued,

> The *Blitch* Fund is a permanent community mutual aid fund where contributions are collected from anybody who wants to contribute and are

given to people in need. And the only qualifiers are that the person must be Black and a practitioner of African spiritual traditions. We've probably given about $60,000 to people in the U.S., the Caribbean, and Africa. You don't have to apply. You don't need merit. All you must do is send a message. And only the ancestors decide who gets it. Names are chosen through divination because, to me, that feels fair. The ancestors have the bird's eye view about what's necessary, who needs it, and their intentions. Once it's decided, the person receives their portion of the pot for that month, no questions asked.[23]

Daizy's *Blitch* Fund exemplifies spiritual co-creation both through its emphasis on African-heritage religions—that the recipient must be a practitioner and deciding on the fund's recipients through the use of divination—as well as through her anti-capitalist mutual aid structure that differs from typical philanthropy. Scholar and activist Dean Spade identifies several differences between charity work and mutual aid. Specifically, Spade notes that the characteristics of charity and governmental social service organizations are as follows: "1) They offer 'help' to the 'underprivileged' absent of a context of injustice or strategy for transforming the conditions ... 2) they follow government regulations about how the work needs to happen 3) they impose eligibility criteria for services that divide people into 'deserving' and 'undeserving.'"[24] Alternatively, mutual aid groups show themselves to be political through "1) efforts to support people facing the most dire conditions, 2) use people power to resist any efforts by the government to regulate or shut down activities, and 3) they value self-determination for people impacted or targeted by harmful social conditions."[25] The *Blitch* Fund reflects principles of mutual aid. There are no lengthy dehumanizing applications characteristic of governmental institutions; nor are examples of exceptionalism or merit typical within higher education required; nor are there moral guidelines or a required devotion to a leader. Daizy omits these requirements because she recognizes—based on her lived experiences and her broader Black feminist thought—that structural inequality impedes access to basic needs for Black people in the United States and the larger African diaspora.

Last, what an integrated political and religious discourse produces for Black women and femmes is a notion of the deservedness of an abundant life and an ability to shape one's destiny. In *Sisters of the Yam*, bell hooks observes, "Many black people see themselves solely as victims with no capacity to shape and determine their own destiny. Despite powerful anti-racist struggle in this society, expressed in the sixties' civil rights and black power movements, internalized racism manifested by ongoing self-hate and low self-esteem has intensified."[26] A devastating effect of internalized racism has been an inability to cultivate feelings of worth, not just pertaining to material success but regarding the resources needed to live fully actualized.

Juju Bae spoke about internalized racism and worth when I asked her about manifestation work:

> The big part of manifestation work is that you really must know that you deserve something to manifest it. If you don't think that you deserve money, a nice house, comfortable clothes, how can you properly do manifestation work to bring that thing in when you're struggling with even being a person who feels like they deserve to live? Particularly for Black people. I think we're behind on what we think we should have because people have told us we don't deserve sh*t.
>
> I remember I went on a date with this guy from Baltimore. . . . I asked him, "If you could have anything that you wanted without money being a concern, what would you have?" And he said, "I don't know. There's no point in even dreaming that because I will never have it."
>
> That was heartbreaking to me. How are we supposed to manifest if we think there's no point cause [we'll] never have it? We can't. That's what manifestation work is for me. It's building the foundation of *"you deserve, baby."* You got to know that first, then let's get to the candles or the spells.[27]

Juju Bae's account demonstrates a belief that a community, a safe and comfortable home, a romantic partnership, or a fulfilling career are impossible to co-create with the spiritual realm without first establishing a sense of worthiness. Juju Bae's spiritually co-creative philosophy suggests that one's ancestors or venerated deities are not able to respond to requests for support without Black people—Black women and femmes, especially—adopting an understanding of *"you deserve, baby."* hooks adds to our understanding, offering, "We are not raised to believe that living well is our birthright. Yet, it is. We have to claim this birthright. Doing so automatically creates a change in perspective that can act as an intervention on the stress in our lives."[28] This notion of deservedness is crucial to Black people's imagining of what is possible not only in our personal lives but also in our collective future. Once the vision becomes clear, the path—and the action—is also illuminated.

Iyalosa Osunyemi Akalatunde is an initiate to the Orisa Osun in the Yoruba Ifá tradition and a spiritual leader who has mentored Black women through her YouTube channel for more than eleven years. Through a Yoruba-originated religious approach, she echoes the need for an entitlement among Black women and femmes through a framework of divine inheritance; the *ori*, or one's personal guiding deity; and the agreement one's spirit makes with the supreme creator, Olodumare, before descending to earth. She explains:

> Before you were born, you laid out a life for yourself. You don't have to worry if you deserve it. You already gave it to yourself before you got here. So, getting it is a matter of remembering that it's yours. Not thinking, "People who look like me don't get to have this." The *odu* says no one can bless you without the consent of your *ori*. We be blocking ourselves. But when you stop, you realize there's a life that you knew you were supposed to have.
>
> When I had my first child, my mother told me, "It is only your prayers that will feed and house this child. Don't let anyone make you think that it's your husband, your job, or the money that you receive." She said, "Whenever you're down to your last and don't know what you're supposed to do, then pray, and it will come to you. And truly, like magic, it will be there."
>
> What we owe to the universe is the fulfillment of this destiny. But to do that, our needs must be met. I got to live by the beach. I can't fulfill it nowhere else. But we're scared to say that. And once you say that, the universe is like, "You right. That was our agreement. Here you go, the house by the ocean." But too often, we wait for somebody else's approval when they don't have anything to do with it.[29]

Iyalosa Osunyemi espouses an Africana theological belief that by divine right, Black people, and indeed all people, deserve access to the resources that equip them to actualize their destiny. One need not subscribe to the belief that fulfilling one's desires depends on external factors. On the contrary, a spiritually co-creative orientation dictates that one necessarily believe otherwise: by focusing on divine intervention and inherent self-power. According to this belief, while limiting racist, sexist, classist, homophobic, transphobic, or ableist institutions might exist, Black witch magic requires rejecting the internalization of these oppressive systems to affirm instead a Black feminist, anti-capitalist approach to resource redistribution.

Iyalosa Osunyemi, Juju Bae, Hess Love, and Daizy reflect a growing movement where the political meets the religious and where Black feminism is integrated into an Africana religious orientation that helps meet practitioners' immediate needs.[30] When an Africana religious philosophy is combined with Black feminist intent, a collective discourse of spiritual co-creation develops. It challenges the individualistic consumerism of the prosperity gospel, often apparent in seekers' interactions with spiritual service providers. The merging of the political and religious through spiritual co-creation is evident in notions concerning the relationship between healing and manifestation, nuanced beliefs about capitalism and desire for money, and collective efforts toward mutual aid. Finally, beliefs in destiny and the ancestors' capacity to provide support produce a faith in the idea that one's material, social, and economic needs will be met. It is a faith of *"you deserve, baby,"* where anti-Blackness and its pervasive denial of the capacity of Black people is obliterated. Thus, a new vision develops where it is not only possible but necessary.

NOTES

I received verbal permission to record and publish the identities and stories of my interviewees. The Emory University Institutional Review Board approved this study and the request to receive verbal consent from participants. This approval was granted on March 16, 2021, by Sam Roberts, Research Protocol Analyst at Emory University.

1. hooks, *Sisters of the Yam*, 75–76.
2. This chapter represents a condensed version of an extensive body of work that is presently being developed into a book manuscript.
3. I use *femme* as a queer term for anyone who identifies their gender expression with a feminine aesthetic, behavior, or political orientation and who does not identify as a woman.
4. Black witches and Black witchcraft should not be confused with the African religions themselves. This differentiation is crucial because—while witchcraft has been a subject of academic inquiry over the past century—the use of the term *witch* bears the weight of a fraught past, particularly among practitioners of African-heritage religions. In the early to mid-twentieth century, most anthropological studies of the witch focused on sub-Saharan Africa, where scholars applied European-derived terms and concepts to cultures with distinct traditions and worldviews. By the 1970s, anthropologists and religionists began to argue for frameworks native to the practitioners being discussed. They recognized that terms were intentionally incorrectly applied to African religious traditions to reduce complex practices and beliefs into mere magic, characterizing an already racialized people as a group without the skills or intelligence to develop religions worthy of respect. Yoruba scholar Teresa N. Washington argues that African-traditional religions are not witchcraft. Washington, *The Architects of Existence*, 8–13.

See also Hutton, *The Witch*, 3–10; Ardener, "The New Anthropology and Its Critics"; Geertz, "An Anthropology of Religion and Magic, I." For more discussion on the racialized stereotyping of Africana religions, see Long, "Primitive/Civilized"; Herskovits, *The Myth of the Negro Past*, 1–32; Lofton, "The Perpetual Primitive."

5 See Nadra, "'We're Reclaiming These Traditions'"; Samuel, "The Witches of Baltimore"; VICE Life, "Why Some Black Women Are Turning to Witchcraft."

6 See Dawtas of the Moon, "Black Witch, Hoodoo, Rootworker"; Luna, "Hoodwitch."

7 My conclusions are based on four years of research on Black witch networks. I chose Black witches over other growing spiritual communities because they veer Black religious discourse into Black feminist and Africana-orientated notions of spiritual practice. I visited cities with sizable Black witch populations—including New York City, Detroit, and New Orleans—and spoke with thirty Black witches who actively contribute to Black witch discourse through social media, the authorship of books on Africana religions, and the organization of conferences. My position as a Black witch who practices Ifá and Hoodoo also contributed to a more comfortable exchange between myself and my interviewees.

8 See Bowler, *Blessed*.

9 See Lee, "Prosperity Theology."

10 Byrne, *The Secret*.

11 Hess Love, in discussion with author, April 23, 2021.

12 See Davis, *Women, Race and Class*; Lorde, *Sister Outsider*; hooks, *Ain't I a Woman*.

13 Hill Collins, *Black Feminist Thought*, 35.

14 hooks, *All about Love*, 76.

15 In addition to Black feminist praxis, many attribute a notion of equitable resource distribution as a means for actualization to early theories of Blackfoot Native Americans. See Ravilochan, "Could the Blackfoot Wisdom That Inspired Maslow Guide Us Now?"

16 Taylor, *How We Get Free*, 15–27.

17 See Osteen, *I Declare*; Gawain, *Creative Visualization*.

18 Alexis Douglas, in discussion with author, April 18, 2021.

19 Alexis Douglas, in discussion with author, April 18, 2021.

20 Alice Walker's term *womanism* is a caveat to this statement. She coined the term to account for the interplay of spirituality, culture, Blackness, and feminism in Black women's experiences and collective outlook. The term gained traction among Black women theologians in the 1980s and 1990s with popular works by Jacqueline Grant and Delores Williams, among many others. These theologians, however, were Christian-centered, unlike contemporary Black witch discourse. See Walker, *In Search of Our Mothers' Gardens*.

21   Osunfunmilola Juju Bae, in discussion with author, May 10, 2021.
22   Daizy October Latifah, in discussion with author, October 1, 2021.
23   Daizy October Latifah, in discussion with author, October 1, 2021.
24   Spade, "Mutual Aid Chart."
25   Spade, "Mutual Aid Chart." Dean Spade also notes that these categories are fluid, and many organizations blur the lines while still centering a revolutionary approach to organizing.
26   hooks, *Sisters of the Yam*, 20.
27   Osunfunmilola Juju Bae, in discussion with author, May 10, 2021.
28   hooks, *Sisters of the Yam*, 73.
29   Iyalosa Osunyemi Akalatunde, in discussion with author, July 30, 2021.
30   Please visit these Black witches' work: Daizy October Latifah at https://www.theafromystic.com/; Iyalosa Osunyemi Akalatunde at https://www.got2boshun.org/; Hess Love at https://hoodoosociety.com/community; and Osunfunmilola aka Juju Bae at https://www.jujubae.com/.

BIBLIOGRAPHY

Ardener, Edwin. "The New Anthropology and Its Critics." *Man* 6, no. 3 (1971): 449–67. https://doi.org/10.2307/2799031.

Awolalu, J. Omosade. "Yoruba Sacrificial Practice." *Journal of Religion in Africa* 5, no. 2 (1973): 81–93. https://doi.org/10.2307/1594756.

Bowler, Kate. *Blessed: A History of the American Prosperity Gospel*. New York: Oxford University Press, 2013.

Byrne, Rhonda. *The Secret*. New York: Atria Books, 2006.

Chesapeake Conjure Society. "Hoodoo Society." Accessed January 5, 2022. https://hoodoosociety.com/community.

Chireau, Yvonne. *Black Magic: Religion and the African American Conjuring Tradition*. Berkeley: University of California Press, 2006.

Chopra, Deepak. *The Spontaneous Fulfillment of Desire: Harnessing the Infinite Power of Coincidence*. New York: Harmony Books, 2003.

Davis, Angela Y. *Women, Race and Class*. New York: Vintage Books, 1983. https://archive.org/details/WomenRaceClassAngelaDavis/page/n1/mode/2up.

Dawtas of the Moon. "Black Witch, Hoodoo, Rootworker." Accessed October 2023. https://dawtasofthemoon.org/.

Gawain, Shakti. *Creative Visualization: Use the Power of Your Imagination to Create What You Want in Your Life*. Rev. ed. Navato, CA: Nataraj Publishing, 2002.

Geertz, Hildred. "An Anthropology of Religion and Magic, I." *Journal of Interdisciplinary History* 6, no. 1 (1975): 71–89. https://doi.org/10.2307/202825.

Hazzard-Donald, Katrina. *Mojo Workin': The Old African American Hoodoo System*. Urbana: University of Illinois Press, 2013.

Herskovits, Melville J. *The Myth of the Negro Past*. Boston: Beacon Press, 1990.

Hill Collins, Patricia. *Black Feminist Thought: Knowledge, Consciousness, and the Politics of Empowerment*. 2nd ed. New York: Routledge, 2009.

hooks, bell. *Ain't I a Woman: Black Women and Feminism*. 2nd ed. New York: Routledge, Taylor and Francis Group, 2015.

hooks, bell. *All about Love: New Visions*. New York: William Morrow, 2018.

hooks, bell. *Sisters of the Yam: Black Women and Self-Recovery*. 3rd ed. New York: Routledge, Taylor and Francis Group, 2015.

Hutton, Ronald. *The Witch: A History of Fear, from Ancient Times to the Present*. New Haven, CT: Yale University Press. 2017.

Iyalosa Osunyemi Akalatunde. "Got2BOshun." Accessed September 30, 2021. https://www.got2boshun.org.

Juju Bae. *A Little Juju Podcast*. Accessed October 20, 2023. https://www.jujubae.com/a-little-juju.

Latifah, Daizy. "Blitch." The AfroMystic. Accessed January 20, 2022. http://www.theafromystic.com/blitch.

Latifah, Daizy. "The #Blitchfund." The AfroMystic. Accessed January 27, 2022. http://www.theafromystic.com/the-blitchfund.

Lee, Shayne. "Prosperity Theology: T. D. Jakes and the Gospel of the Almighty Dollar." *CrossCurrents* 57, no. 2 (2007): 227–36.

Lofton, Kathryn. "The Perpetual Primitive in African American Religious Historiography." In *The New Black Gods*, edited by Edward E. Curtis IV and Danielle Brune Sigler, 171–91. Bloomington: Indiana University Press, 2009.

Long, Charles H. "Primitive/Civilized: The Locus of a Problem." *History of Religions* 20 (1980): 43–61. https://doi.org/10.1086/462861.

Lorde, Audre. *Sister Outsider: Essays and Speeches*. Berkeley, CA: Crossing Press, 2007.

Luna, Bri. "Hoodwitch." Accessed January 20, 2022. https://www.thehoodwitch.com.

Nadra, Nittle. "'We're Reclaiming These Traditions': Black Women Embrace the Spiritual Realm." NBC News, October 30, 2020. https://www.nbcnews.com/news/nbcblk/we-re-reclaiming-these-traditions-black-women-embrace-spiritual-realm-n1245488.

Osteen, Joel. *I Declare: 31 Promises to Speak Over Your Life*. New York: FaithWords/Hachette Book Group, 2013.

Ravilochan, Teju. "Could the Blackfoot Wisdom That Inspired Maslow Guide Us Now?" *Medium* (blog), August 18, 2021. https://gatherfor.medium.com/maslow-got-it-wrong-ae45d6217a8c.

Samuel, Sigal. "The Witches of Baltimore." *The Atlantic*, November 5, 2018. https://www.theatlantic.com/international/archive/2018/11/black-millennials-african-witchcraft-christianity/574393/.

Spade, Dean. "Mutual Aid Chart." December 4, 2019. http://www.deanspade.net/2019/12/04/mutual-aid-chart/.

Taylor, Keeanga-Yamahtta, ed. *How We Get Free: Black Feminism and the Combahee River Collective*. Chicago: Haymarket Books, 2017.

Thompson, Robert Farris. *Flash of the Spirit: African and Afro-American Art and Philosophy*. New York: Vintage Books, 1984.

VICE Life. "Why Some Black Women Are Turning to Witchcraft." YouTube, May 18, 2021. https://www.youtube.com/watch?v=5q0spq0cTw0.

Walker, Alice. *In Search of Our Mothers' Gardens: Womanist Prose*. Orlando: Harcourt, 2004.

Washington, Teresa N. *The Architects of Existence: Àjẹ̀ in Yoruba Cosmology, Ontology, and Orature*. Rev. ed. Orífín, Ilé Àjẹ́: Ọya's Tornado, 2014.

Six · BRANDY RENEE MCCANN

Resurrecting Granny: A Brief Excavation of Appalachian Folk Magic

I dig through the cupboard looking for the right jar—a jar to hold a special kind of magic. There are quart jars that once held my mom's canned green beans, curvy jars that held salsa, and pint jars from apple butter bought at the fall festival; there are pretty honey jars and jam jars. Something sweet is needed, and I choose a gilded jar that held grocery-store strawberry jam.

A young man I know has been gloomy lately, and I worry that he has fallen under some troubling influences; I want to do what I can to help him. I start planning a spell jar for protection. After choosing the jam jar, I take the next few days to meditate on my young friend's troubles, letting the right items come to mind: a dash of lemon balm is good for strengthening the heart, rosemary for protection; a small prayer cloth anointed with oil and prayed over at my mom's Pentecostal church; a feather from a baby bird for innocence; I add some other small items over the next few days and then set the jar outside to charge under a full moon. I say words of protection and love for my friend, recite the 23rd Psalm; and when the moon begins to noticeably wane, I bury the jar.

This bit of magic reflects many elements typical of Appalachian folk magic: lacking a formal system, making do with items at hand, believing in astrological influences, and engaging aspects of Christianity.

HISTORICAL CONTEXT

Understanding the dynamic nature of folk magic in Appalachia means understanding the history of Appalachia. The Appalachian region is a mountainous area in the eastern United States that stretches from Maine to Georgia; culturally the region reaches as far north as western New York; as far south as the northern counties of the states of Georgia, Alabama, and Mississippi; and as far west as the Ozark Mountains of Arkansas. However, colloquially in mainstream America, "Appalachia" is most often associated with the central coalfields and the southern highlands. Known for their deciduous, temperate rainforests and rich biodiversity, the mountains are the ancestral homelands of many Indigenous peoples, such as the Cherokee, Susquehannock, and Shawnee, among others.

It is important to understand that unlike other places in what would become the United States, before the arrival of the railroads in the nineteenth century and the subsequent explosion of extraction industries, much of the mountainous land was considered undesirable to many colonists because it was difficult land to farm and a considerable distance from growing urban centers.[1] In colonial days, the Appalachian Mountains were the western frontier, attracting increasing numbers of Europeans who settled in the so-called backcountry where Indigenous peoples had been hunting or living for millennia. While there was certainly conflict over land and resources in the Appalachian region, at the same time, much of the mountains were held in commons, where various groups hunted game and gathered herbs and roots for their own use and for trade.[2] Thus, during the seventeenth and early eighteenth centuries, the mountains were a place to which Indigenous people would have been confined rather than driven from as they were in the nineteenth century.[3]

European settlers in this (at the time) western frontier region—largely Ulster Scots, English, Welsh, and German—came because they were poor or had been indentured servants, or because they sought the freedom and opportunities available in the backcountry. Both free and enslaved people of African origin/ancestry also made homes in the mountains during colonial times. The backcountry was a rugged and diverse place; and despite differences in cultural heritages and episodic violence among and between peoples in the region, they often depended on each other for trade and survival, sharing knowledge of medicinal plants, religious beliefs, and spiritual practices.[4]

Stereotypes of rural Appalachian people as indolent, superstitious, and ignorant are based on travel writing from as early as the eighteenth century by writers visiting the southern highlands and central coalfields (e.g., William Byrd's travel journals); these stereotypes solidified during the late nineteenth century in which "local color" writing "othered" poor

Whites in the region as "hillbillies" and often erased American Indians, African Americans, and other ethnic groups living in Appalachia, a practice that continued through the twentieth century.[5] Stereotypes about southern mountaineers, in particular, were well-developed by the nineteenth century. These "others" were shaped by the mountainous geography (i.e., limited access to urban centers, heavy reliance on subsistence agriculture, and exploitation, in the early days, by extraction industries such as timber and coal). Although scholars have demonstrated that Appalachia was never as isolated or ethnically hegemonic as the local color writing suggests, many people in rural Appalachia were relatively limited in their contact with middle and urban America and held on longer to ancestral folk beliefs.[6] One area in which this was especially true, and remains true today, is in the provision of healthcare.[7]

Enter the granny woman.

A granny woman was an older woman who helped deliver babies and provided other basic medical care. Ethnographic studies of granny women and healthcare practices in southern Appalachia demonstrate that through the mid-twentieth century, older, knowledgeable women (and sometimes men) took on the role of a granny woman or root doctor, to fill gaps in health services.[8] Although midwifery seems to have constituted the granny woman's most common practice, it waned as hospitals became more accessible to rural residents; but those granny women with botanical and spiritual knowledge were still called on as healers.

In popular culture, the granny woman or granny witch became a well-worn archetype of an Appalachian woman. She is cited over and again as a stereotypical portrayal of a knowledgeable, older Appalachian woman—but in her representation she is both Granny Clampett's superstitious crone and Ellie Mae's hypersexualized maiden. It is this representation that Appalachian women must wrestle with, especially those of us who are artists and feminists: I do not want to perpetuate stereotypes that have been harmful to my region, yet so much of my experience as an Appalachian person resonates with tropes from local color portrayals. I am a descendant of the Hatfields (of the infamous Hatfield-McCoy feuds); I married very young and have been divorced four times; and I have a thick Central Appalachian dialect that marks me every time I speak. Carole Ganim writes, "Embedded within the literature written by women about the Appalachian mountains is this kind of identification of body and mind, of nature and spirit. . . . A woman born in the closely-clustered hills . . . is surrounded, if not almost suffocated, by symbols of herself from birth."[9] In literary and visual culture portraying Appalachia in the twentieth century, the granny woman took on mythic and nostalgic proportions. This granny lives in the consciousness of many Appalachian women, especially if we had similar women in our families—women who may have gone north to work in factories as young women yet returned home to become matriarchs in their families.

The other side of the granny coin in popular culture is the hypersexualized young hillbilly woman—the granny woman's younger self. Carissa Massey argues that in popular culture "the hillbilly woman [such as Daisy Duke] is sexually deviant, aggressive, overly fecund, and masculine," a foil to the stereotype of Appalachian men who are often portrayed as being drunk and lazy.[10] Like the mythic grannies they will become, these younger women wield an unnatural power in their sexual aggression, typified by displays of exaggerated femininity such as wearing short shorts with bare feet or high heels.

Ultimately, it is the supposed power that Appalachian women possess that provides the fodder for stereotypes in mainstream media. Appalachian poet Rebecca Gayle Howell's poem "The Granny Woman's Note" recalls the idea that, traditionally, a granny was a woman who stood as an intermediary between life and death. She was a midwife, a healer, and a wake sitter. Her position and power, her presence at the openings and closings of life, also made her vulnerable to criticism and critique by mainstream culture for her perversion of conventional womanhood.

They buzz at me like horseflies. "Where are you from, Ellie Mae?" they ask, noting my peculiar way of speaking. When I say, "West Virginia," they float away. Except the ones who claim to have been bewitched; they stay despite their own good sense. They want to tame me, to break me, to transform me into a well-behaved wife. But I am becoming granny; I'm not her yet, but I am aware of the mysteries unfolding along my Valley of the Shadow of Doubt. And so I study the old ways: how to plant by the signs, how to stop bleeding with a Bible verse, how to talk to crows.

KEY TRADITIONAL PRACTICES

In addition to the terms *granny woman* or *granny witch*, folk magic traditions in Appalachia are referred to as *conjure, hillbilly hoodoo, root work, work, doctoring,* and *cunning,* among other terms. These other terms take a granny's practice beyond that of providing help with physical problems (e.g., knowledge of home remedies) and denote a more purposeful move in providing help with spiritual troubles, whether a streak of bad luck or a suspected curse from a baneful "witch."[11] A baneful witch might be an outsider or a vulnerable woman in the community, but she could simply be a matriarch in another family, or a woman hired by anyone with whom the supposed victim did not get along.[12] In that way, theoretically, any woman could be subjected to accusations of witchcraft. However, due to the ruralness of the communities and close kin networks, such accusations were more likely to lead to a feud than to an indictment from local authorities.

Despite the possibilities of magical feuds, mostly granny magic is just ordinary making do. Some practices are unique to Southern and Central Appalachia where the folk traditions of the European colonizers (particularly Irish, Scottish, Welsh, and German) mixed with African traditions (e.g., hoodoo) from enslaved and freed people as well as with Indigenous practices.[13] What follows are common traditions in Appalachia folk magic, with commentary on the origins of these practices.

PLANTING BY THE SIGNS · *Recently a lady I'd grown up around in church made a request on Facebook. She hadn't been able to find a Ramon's calendar and wanted to know what the signs would be in later in the week. She wanted to get her spring peas in the ground but didn't want to plant them if the signs were going to be bad. I replied with information from my Ramon's calendar, and another person said she had some extra Brownie calendars if the friend wanted to come get one.*

Planting by the signs refers to using astrological knowledge as a guide for gardening. Most almanac calendars can be used, but the iconic red and white paper calendar, commonly called a Ramon's calendar (named for the first company who used it as an advertising piece, Ramon's Brownie Pills), was a freebie given out by small businesses across the region since the late nineteenth century. The calendars have largely been replaced with calendars that boast scenic photographs of far-off places accompanied by inspirational Bible verses. Few young people in the region have time to garden or know how to plant by the signs, something their ancestors took for granted; but the practice is regaining popularity among self-described green witches (i.e., witches who work with plants).

Almanac calendars have been used for centuries in Europe and America and rely on the Western zodiac to recommend the best days for planting, fishing, animal husbandry, and other activities important to those dependent on subsistence farming.[14] Even the dominant group of rather conservative

Christians (of various denominations) use the stars as a guide to help them become better gardeners. The seeming contradiction is resolved by references throughout the Christian Bible to God speaking to humans via signs and omens. And two verses in particular reference agriculture: "To every thing there is a season, and a time to every purpose under the heaven: A time to be born, and a time to die; a time to plant, and a time to pluck that which has been planted."[15] The chapter goes on to discuss the divine mysteries and that the purpose of humankind is to surrender to those mysteries. These explicit instructions to look for signs and omens in nature as a message from the divine allows even the strictest Christians to practice this bit of folk magic.

The practice has recently gained popularity with those us of in the pagan community who have witnessed our older family members using this method. For example, Jake Richards includes a brief overview of planting by the signs in his book on *Backwoods Witchcraft*, as does Rebecca Beyer in her book *Wild Witchcraft*.

BIBLICAL CHARMS · *My mom tells me her grandpa knew how to stop a nosebleed or any kind of bleeding. He'd lay hands on the person and recite some Bible verse. I can't remember which one, she says. Another relative tells me about his granny's Bible: "She knew how to do all that with the Bible. She could stop a bleed, cure a toothache or a headache, all kinds of things. There's some special verses you got to use depending on what's afflicted."*

Referencing the Bible to justify using astrology for agricultural purposes is just one aspect of how people in Appalachia have historically used the Bible and "Bible talk," that is, Middle English as used in the King James version of the Bible,[16] as a magical tool. It is not clear exactly how this practice originated, as it is commonly used among those of European origins as well as among those practicing African American hoodoo traditions. Likely the resonance between what is termed "magic" and more mainstream spiritual practices, such as prayer, meant that extra-textual uses of the Bible were an easy slide for those who practiced folk magic. Among lay folk, Bible verses and Bible talk were acceptable for invoking help and protection; among conjure and cunning folk, including grannies, using the Bible made their workings more palatable by framing them in Judeo-Christian terms.[17]

Bible verses, accompanied by the laying on of hands and praying, are still recited during healing ceremonies, for protection, for guidance, for speaking power. These charms are adjacent to special healing services in evangelical churches where the laying on of hands and anointing of oil are performed while congregants pray for intercession for an afflicted person. For example, a congregant with a medical problem goes to the front of the church to be prayed over. Sometimes a cloth is anointed with special oil and given to the afflicted person as a reminder of God's healing power. Importantly, these practices are performed in conjunction with allopathic and conventional medicinal practices.

Outside the context of church such practices were also common. To stop bleeding, a healer or granny woman would recite Ezekiel 16:6: "When I passed by thee and saw thee polluted in thine own blood, I said unto thee when thou was in thine blood, Live, yea, I said unto thee when thou was in thy blood, Live." Notably, this verse is rhythmic in structure repeating a version of "in thy blood" three times, with commands to "live" twice, making it especially potent as an incantation. Similarly, a granny might be called upon for a Bible charm for help with a particularly bad toothache, the thrush, burns, and other maladies, or for a Bible charm as a divination tool to help someone make an important decision. Thus, these grannies were arguably protofeminists who held power adjacent to the patriarchal social structures common in rural Appalachian communities.

USE OF HERBS · *I've been stalking a patch of mayapple for two years, watching it in different seasons, letting it speak to me. Its medicine is complicated, and I'm not sure if I should be harvesting any or not. So I watch and listen. For decades my daddy has roamed the hills collecting ginseng ("sangin" in Appalachian speak), yellow root, and mayapple root. He watches and listens. He's not a root doctor; but he sells the precious medicines to supplement our family's income. Nevertheless, he has taught me to take only a little, and only from a vigorous patch. "If there's berries, let the berries fall. Sometimes I even knock a little dirt over them," he says. As a granny in the making, I am mindful of my daddy's respect for the plants he forages.*

Medicinal plants have a long history with all the different peoples who inhabited the Appalachian region. As noted above, healers from all traditions in Appalachia would have had a working knowledge of medicinal plants. Indigenous healers would have been the most familiar with native plants and undoubtably taught early settlers how to recognize, harvest, and use medicinal plants;[18] in addition to native plants, European and African American people brought useful plants and seeds with them to the "new" world.[19] Some of these nonnative species have had a benign effect in the mountains, while others have overrun old gardens and have come to be known as invasive species, choking out native plants in the region.[20]

Following Robin Wall Kimmerer and other Indigenous activists and scientists, many contemporary practitioners of Appalachian folk magic have incorporated "wild tending" as part of their magical practice. Wild tending refers to the practice of cultivating wild spaces, with a particular emphasis on the health of native plants, and it often includes responsible harvesting and other human interventions long enacted by Indigenous populations. Independent scholar, witch, and wild tending practitioner Rebecca Beyer—who is based out of western North Carolina but who, like many regional homesteaders, is not originally from the southern Appalachia—represents a growing movement intent on acknowledging and incorporating Indigenous practices in Appalachian folk magic and medicine.

In addition to healing uses, plant matter can be used for magical purposes, particularly in container spells such as sweet jars and witch bottles, mojo bags, spirit middens, charms, and amulets as well as for the consecration of spaces, as in the practice of burning herbs: smudging (using smoke from burning sage, per some Indigenous groups), or saining (using smoke from juniper or rosemary, per Scottish tradition). Container spells, conceived as talismans or wards, have a long history in both African and European folk traditions.[21] Container spells often include herbs or roots, stones, bones, and other meaningful materials that are either sewn into a bag made of natural materials or placed in a pottery or glass jar.

HOLIDAYS · *While mainstream America celebrates Memorial Day by picnicking and sporting red, white, and blue, many of us in Appalachia gather with our families to decorate the graves of our ancestors, the recently departed, or our progeny who've gone too soon. The old women carry big bags of colorful flowers to the graveyard and distribute them among the children. The old men talk and point out headstones, telling stories about loved ones gone on.*

Celebrations around graveyards, often held on Memorial Day in contemporary Appalachia, have a varied history. First, many families held family reunions, or homecomings called "dinner-on-the-grounds," which meant a gathering and meal on the grounds of a churchyard or family cemetery. Affrilachian writer Crystal Wilkinson discusses her experiences with dinner-on-the-grounds in her books, noting that people would come back home from all over for this special event. In other families, these homecomings coincided with Decoration Day: begun after the Civil

FIGURE 6.1 Kitchen altar. Photograph by Brandy Renee McCann.

War, Decoration Day was a day set aside to clear and decorate the graves of those who died in the war.[22] As with dinner-on-the-grounds, Decoration Day was not on a set date originally, but it gradually became conflated with the national holiday, Memorial Day. Appalachian people also decorate more accessible cemeteries on other holidays such as Christmas, birthdays, and Easter. Importantly, these kinds of holidays are seen not as a type of ancestor veneration but as a demonstration of the ways in which we rural Appalachian people continue to relate to our dead and celebrate our extended kin. And for those who more intentionally practice magic, dinner-on-the-grounds or Decoration Day provides a good opportunity to scoop up some graveyard dirt for later spellwork.

Another important holiday with folk magic elements is Old Christmas. Stevenson and colleagues show how elements of Appalachian granny culture emerged from traditions imported to the mountains by Welsh immigrants.[23] For example, they note that Old Christmas (January 6, or Epiphany Day in some Christian denominations), a holiday celebrated in some Appalachian communities, is a traditional Welsh holiday, a holdover from before the change was made from the Julian to the Gregorian calendar in the mid-eighteenth century. The new Gregorian calendar lost eleven days, but some folks persisted in celebrating Christmas according to the old calendar; hence, Old Christmas. Old Christmas is not simply a celebration of the birth of Jesus, but a day associated with magic. On Old Christmas, animals may speak or pray, plants may bloom, and young women may be able to divine their fates.

OTHER PRACTICES · The practices described above highlight some of the ways in which people of the Appalachian region incorporate folk magic into our everyday lives. Appalachian folk magic practice also includes the use of dollies in conjure and cunning work; of personal items such as shoes, footprints, and hair (often in conjunction with container spells[24]); of water gathered from various sources;[25] of interpretations of signs and omens found in nature; and so forth.

These practices were typically incorporated into everyday life for many, but for more purposeful workings, such as protection, certain folks in a community were called upon to help. In some families, this help, or "doctoring" (whether as a "yarb"/herb doctor or root doctor), was something passed down from one generation to the next.

CONTEMPORARY PRACTITIONERS

Although stereotypes of Appalachian women can be problematic, the granny witch and her kinfolk are part of a bricolage of Appalachian identities that reconfigures those stereotypes, taking back and making new who and what we can be. Indeed, there is rich literary (e.g., folktales) and ethnographic data (e.g., the Foxfire series) about the granny witch in Appalachia. Rather than rejecting her as an unsavory stereotype, many contemporary witches and folk magic enthusiasts are empowered by her magical energies.

H. Byron Ballard's, Rebecca Beyer's, and Jake Richards's recent publications attest to the contemporary potency of Appalachian folk magic practices. Both Ballard and Richards are multigenerational Appalachians who originally learned mountain magic from the elders in their respective families. That is, they have each inherited their practice and continue to build on their knowledge, changing with the times. In their books, Ballard and Richards each acknowledge the deep connection with biblical verse used as spells and other ties to Protestant Christianity in early America. Perhaps unexpectedly, then, both Ballard and Richards have aligned themselves with the political and cultural left, overtly supporting Black Lives Matter and positioning themselves within LGBTQ+ communities.

Cunning folk, such as Ballard and Richards, represent one type of Appalachian witchcraft. Other contemporary practices such as covens and online groups on social media specifically for Appalachian witchcraft showcase wide-ranging interest in and practice of Appalachian folk magic. In at least three different private Facebook groups dedicated to the topic (at the time of this writing one has over 75,000 members; another has nearly 8,000 members; and third has over 5,000), women and men from around the world are drawn to topics related to Appalachia and magic. Some are merely curious; some identify as Christian witches; some have connections to Wicca or similar formal traditions; some follow family lineages; still others are solitary witches who enjoy commitment-free community on social media.

There are many opportunities for consciousness-raising among contemporary Appalachian witches. I see myself as a typical Appalachian practitioner—an outsider to the dominant Appalachian culture (i.e., consumerist, fundamentalist, nationalist), seeking connection to my heritage in a way that honors the "understory"[26] of the mountains, at once mindful of the legacies of colonization and of cultural appropriation.

Here I think of writer and feminist bell hooks,[27] who said feminism is its best when it is "feminist movement," that is, when it is dynamic and engaged and resisting definition. Not unlike the boundaries of Appalachia, feminist witchcraft in Appalachia, or anywhere, is at its best when it is open to change and fluid in its practice, even if it feels messy and contested at times. Ongoing conversations about cultural appropriation, for example, may be uncomfortable, but it is also necessary. Likewise, people seem to be drawn to Appalachian folk practices because they *seem* more authentic than some more formal traditions such as Wicca or various goddess-focused practices. But as a feminist, I question this desire for "authenticity," which can become a consumerist and ego-driven quest to be the most authentic, especially by privileged folk who have the time and money to buy lots of books, attend workshops, and so on. While it is important to do one's homework and to be respectful regarding practices whose origins are clearly outside our own traditions,[28] it is also important to hold space for how our class backgrounds, for example, inform our practice.

Thus, for me, breathing life into granny means a magical practice that is socially embedded, spiritually renewing, and politically active—keeping in mind that what these practices look like will vary over our life course and are dependent on our individual and community resources. At this time in my life when I'm a working single mother, my *socially embedded* practice means that I connect to my communities in a real way by listening to local Indigenous voices regarding land stewardship, by supporting local agriculture when I can, and by volunteering my time for community projects that benefit our most vulnerable. For me, *spiritually renewing* practice is focused on making my magical practice sustainable: here I really pull on my Appalachian granny roots by making do rather than consuming. Though I buy as many candles as the next witch, I challenge myself to think about ways I can work magic that feels productive and creative—writing my own spells, or painting an old tea tin to use as a witch jar, or using the leftover beeswax from a candle to make a salve. I feel spiritually renewed when I immerse myself in the work of making and doing rather than only consuming. Finally, my practice is *politically active* when I instill in my sons a feminist consciousness, when I advocate for reproductive justice, and when I challenge myself to investigate the ways in which my own beliefs and choices may contribute the oppression of others. Rather than be spiritually complacent, I want my magical practice to be characterized by feminist movement.

Contemporary Appalachian folk magic can be its best when, like a homemade, patchwork quilt made by our granny, it is a testament to making do and ultimately being useful in our communities.

NOTES

Many thanks to my partner, Karl Precoda, for his editorial wizardry, as well as his love and support.

1. Williams, *Appalachia*.
2. Manget, *Ginseng Diggers*.
3. See Carroll, *Roots of Our Renewal*, for a discussion of the development of nation-building processes among the Cherokee beginning with pressures toward assimilation by colonists. Also, the first chapter in Williams, *Appalachia*, gives a detailed history of how colonialization and treaty making-and-breaking affected various American Indian groups from the sixteenth through the nineteenth centuries.
4. Carroll, *Roots of Our Renewal*; Hazzard-Donald, *Mojo Workin'*; Lucas, "Empowered Objects." See also Steinhart, this volume (chapter 9).
5. Masterson, "William Byrd in Lubberland"; Lewis and Billings, "Appalachian Culture and Economic Development"; B. E. Smith, "De-gradations of Whiteness."

6. Engelhardt, "Trying to Get Appalachia Less Wrong"; Eisenstadt, "Almanacs and the Disenchantment of Early America."
7. A. Smith, "The Rural Health Physician Narrative."
8. Wigginton, *Foxfire Book*.
9. Ganim, "Herself," 258.
10. Massey, "Appalachian Stereotypes," 126.
11. Jones, "Practitioners of Folk Medicine."
12. Steinhart, this volume (chapter 9); Richards, *Backwoods Witchcraft*.
13. Lucas, "Empowered Objects"; Manget, *Ginseng Diggers*.
14. Eisenstadt, "Almanacs and the Disenchantment of Early America."
15. Ecclesiastes 3:1–2.
16. Foxwood, *Mountain Conjure and Southern Rootwork*.
17. Chireau, "Conjure and Christianity"; Easton, "Four Spiritual Middens."
18. Birch, "A Comparative Analysis of Nineteenth Century Pharmacopoeias."
19. Beyer, *Wild Witchcraft*.; Carney, "Seeds of Memory."
20. Kimmerer, *Braiding Sweetgrass*.
21. Bird, *Sticks, Stones, Roots, and Bones*; Augé, "Embedded Implication of Cultural Worldviews"; Roolf, "Healing Objects."
22. *Affrilachian* is an adjective used to describe an African American person who is from or who has made a home in the Appalachian region; but it is primarily used by writers and artists who identify as both Black and Appalachian; Jabbour and Jabbour, *Decoration Day in the Mountains*.
23. Stevenson et al., "Curers, Charms, and Curses."
24. Manning, "The Material Culture of Ritual Concealments."
25. Ballard, *Roots, Branches, and Spirits*.
26. "Understory" has been used in recent years by artists, activists, and academics to describe marginalized populations and stories within Appalachian culture.
27. bell hooks was raised in eastern Kentucky and wrote extensively about her connections to the Appalachian region.
28. For example, controversies around the burning of white sage—a practice originating within particular Indigenous communities. Not only is this a clear case of cultural appropriation, especially when it ends up being sold by major retailers, but white sage's popularity has led to its being a threatened species if not technically endangered.

BIBLIOGRAPHY

Augé, C. Riley. "Embedded Implication of Cultural Worldviews in the Use and Pattern of Magical Material Culture." *Historical Archaeology* 48, no. 3 (2014): 166–78. http://www.jstor.org/stable/43491314.

Ballard, H. Byron. *Roots, Branches, and Spirits: The Folkways and Witchery of Appalachia*. Woodbury, MN: Llewellyn, 2021.

Bennett, Bradley C. "Doctrine of Signatures: An Explanation of Medicinal Plant Discovery or Dissemination of Knowledge?" *Economic Botany* 61, no. 33 (2007): 246–55. https://doi.org/10.1663/0013-0001(2007)61[246:DOSAEO]2.0.CO;2.

Beyer, Rebecca. *Wild Witchcraft: Folk Herbalism, Garden Magic, and Foraging for Spells, Rituals, and Remedies*. New York: Simon Element, 2022

Birch, Joanne L. "A Comparative Analysis of Nineteenth Century Pharmacopoeias in the Southern United States: A Case Study Based on the Gideon Lincecum Herbarium." *Economic Botany* 63, no. 4 (2009): 427–40.

Bird, Stephanie Rose. *Sticks, Stones, Roots, and Bones: Hoodoo Mojo and Conjuring with Herbs*. Woodbury, MN: Llewellyn, 2004

Carney, Judith. "Seeds of Memory: Botanical Legacies of the African Diaspora." In *African Ethnobotany in the Americas*, edited by Robert A. Voeks and John Rashford, 13–33. New York: Springer, 2013. https://doi.org/10.1007/978-1-4614-0836-9.

Carroll, Clint. *Roots of Our Renewal: Ethnobotany and Cherokee Environmental Governance*. Minneapolis: University of Minnesota Press, 2015.

Chireau, Yvonne. "Conjure and Christianity in the Nineteenth Century: Religious Elements in African American Magic." *Religion and American Culture: A Journal of Interpretation* 7, no. 2 (1997): 225–46. https://doi.org/10.2307/1123979.

Easton, Timothy. "Four Spiritual Middens in Mid Suffolk, England, ca. 1650 to 1850." *Historical Archaeology* 48, no. 3 (2014): 10–34. http://www.jstor.org/stable/43491307.

Eisenstadt, Peter. "Almanacs and the Disenchantment of Early America." *Pennsylvania History: A Journal of Mid-Atlantic Studies* 65, no. 2 (1998): 143–69. http://www.jstor.org/stable/27774098.

Engelhardt, Elizabeth S. D. "Trying to Get Appalachia Less Wrong: A Modest Approach." *Southern Cultures* 23, no. 1 (2017): 4–9. https://www.jstor.org/stable/26391674.

Foxwood, Orion. *Mountain Conjure and Southern Root Work*. Newburyport, MA: Red Wheel/Weiser, 2021.

Ganim, Carole. "Herself: Woman and Place in Appalachian Literature." *Appalachian Journal* 13, no. 3 (1986): 258–74. http://www.jstor.org/stable/40932788.

Hazzard-Donald, Katrina. *Mojo Workin': The Old African American Hoodoo System*. Urbana: University of Illinois Press, 2012.

Howell, Rebecca Gayle. "The Granny Woman's Note, and: The Basketmaker's Note, and: The Stone Carver's Note." *Appalachian Heritage* 46, no. 2 (2018): 44–47. https://doi.org/10.1353/aph.2018.0092.

Jabbour, Alan, and Karen Singer Jabbour. *Decoration Day in the Mountains: Traditions of Cemetery Decoration in the Southern Appalachians*. Chapel Hill: University of North Carolina Press, 2010.

Jones, Louis C. "Practitioners of Folk Medicine." *Bulletin of the History of Medicine* 23, no. 5 (1949): 480–93. http://www.jstor.org/stable/44442274.

Kimmerer, Robin Wall. *Braiding Sweetgrass: Indigenous Wisdom, Scientific Knowledge, and the Teachings of Plants.* Minneapolis, MN: Milkweed Editions, 2013.

Lewis, Ronald L., and Dwight B. Billings. "Appalachian Culture and Economic Development: A Retrospective View on the Theory and Literature." *Journal of Appalachian Studies* 3, no. 1 (1997): 3–42. http://www.jstor.org/stable/43664361.

Lucas, Michael T. "Empowered Objects: Material Expressions of Spiritual Beliefs in the Colonial Chesapeake Region." *Historical Archaeology* 48, no. 3 (2014): 106–24. http://www.jstor.org/stable/43491311.

Manget, Luke. *Ginseng Diggers: A History of Root and Herb Gathering in Appalachia.* Berea: University Press of Kentucky. 2022

Manning, M. Chris. "The Material Culture of Ritual Concealments in the United States." *Historical Archaeology* 48, no. 3 (2014): 52–83. http://www.jstor.org/stable/43491309.

Massey, Carissa. "Appalachian Stereotypes: Cultural History, Gender, and Sexual Rhetoric." *Journal of Appalachian Studies* 13, nos. 1–2 (2007): 124–36. http://www.jstor.org/stable/41446780.

Masterson, James R. "William Byrd in Lubberland." *American Literature* 9, no. 2 (1937): 153–70. https://doi.org/10.2307/2920039.

Richards, Jake. *Backwoods Witchcraft: Conjure and Folk Magic from Appalachia.* Newburyport, MA: Red Wheel/Weiser, 2019.

Roolf, Becka. "Healing Objects in Welsh Folk Medicine." *Proceedings of the Harvard Celtic Colloquium* 16–17 (1996): 106–15. http://www.jstor.org/stable/20557317.

Smith, Ashley. "The Rural Health Physician Narrative: A New Historic Analysis of Appalachian Representation in Twentieth-Century Rural Physician Narratives." Master's thesis, East Tennessee State University, 2019. https://dc.etsu.edu/etd/3604.

Smith, Barbara Ellen. "De-gradations of Whiteness: Appalachia and the Complexities of Race." *Journal of Appalachian Studies* 10, nos. 1–2 (2004): 38–57. http://www.jstor.org/stable/41446605.

Snyder, Bob. "Image and Identity in Appalachia." *Appalachian Journal* 9, nos. 2–3 (1982): 124–33. http://www.jstor.org/stable/40932479.

Stevenson, Peter, Zoe Childerley, Veronika Derkova, Ruth Jên Evans, Maria Hayes, Valériane Leblond, and Jacob Whittaker. "Curers, Charms, and Curses Meddygon, Swynion, a Melltithion: Celebrating the Shared Folk Cultures of Appalachia and Wales." *Southern Cultures* 25, no. 4 (2019): 82–97. https://www.jstor.org/stable/26844568.

Wiggington, Eliot, ed. *The Foxfire Book: Hog Dressing; Log Cabin Building; Mountain Crafts and Foods; Planting by the Signs; Snake Lore, Hunting Tales, Faith Healing; Moonshining; and Other Affairs of Plain Living.* New York: Anchor Books/Doubleday, 1972.

Williams, John Alexander. *Appalachia: A History.* Chapel Hill: University of North Carolina Press, 2002.

Seven · KRYSTAL CLEARY

"Some Decks May Be Stacked against Us but This Deck Is Ours": Justice-Centered Tarot in and against the New Age

Riffing off Zoe Leonard's 1992 poem "I Want a President," nonbinary tarot reader Tess Giberson queers tarot's traditional archetypes in a poem shared in a 2018 email newsletter: "i want a dyke for Magician, i want a person with AIDS for High Priestess, and i want a fag for Empress."[1] Giberson continues through the first thirteen cards, lyrically hailing a justice-centered approach that wrings the cis heteronormativity, ableism, white supremacy, and capitalist neocolonialism out of the tarot tradition. They conclude, "i want to know why we started learning that somewhere down the line that tarot is always good vibes only, always your vibes attracting your tribe, always colonizing and never intersectional," thus rhetorically questioning tarot's complicity with oppressive logics. Giberson articulates a sentiment widely expressed by marginalized tarot practitioners, one that seeds an ever-growing crop of independently published decks produced by feminists, queers, and people of color that decenter tarot's historic white cis heteronormativity. I refer to these decks as justice-centered (rather than Queer, Trans, Black, Indigenous, People of Color [QTBIPOC], or inclusive) to underscore their application of social justice frameworks to recast tarot's traditional imagery, interpretations, and uses. The expanding roster of justice-centered decks includes Next World Tarot (2017), Our Tarot (2018), and many others.

This chapter is informed by my investments as a scholar and a tarot reader. As a tarot insider, I bring experiential expertise to my examination of tarot tradition and how it is reimagined by contemporary tarotists.[2] Tarot is at once a physical cultural artifact and a networked discursive terrain, necessitating an interdisciplinary approach that tends to its materiality, digital culture, and tarotists' interpretive paradigms and practices. I bring media studies and intersectional feminist studies to bear on an examination of the history and contemporary upswell of justice-centered tarot decks, their politics of representation, and corresponding digital discourses. This approach enables me to frame tarot as a *medium* of meaning-making that spans the material and digital as well as the spiritual and political.

My analysis of contemporary justice-centered tarot is situated in a genealogical account of its emergence. I first provide an overview of tarot history and its imbrication in the neoliberal New Age industry, followed by a discussion of early feminist decks' politicization of tarot. I then elucidate the three facets of justice-centered tarot work: (1) critiquing tarot tradition through the creation of culturally accessible decks, (2) framing tarot as self-care through a healing justice framework, and (3) engaging tarot as an emergent strategy for activating political imaginaries in the service of conjuring a just future. These three interventions constellate a tarot praxis that blends movement theory with tarot work. Justice-centered tarot is not simply revolutionary for the tarot world but points to creative practices within and against New Age culture for enduring oppression and envisioning a world beyond it.

TAROT AND THE NEOLIBERAL NEW AGE

The tarot is a deck of seventy-eight cards broken into two categories, the Major Arcana and the Minor Arcana.[3] The Major Arcana comprises twenty-two cards, each depicting a symbolic figure or scene and bearing a unique name (e.g., The Empress, The Moon). The Minor Arcana is divided into four suits, each consisting of fourteen cards, numbered ace through ten plus four court cards (Page, Knight, Queen, and King). It is generally accepted that tarot originated in mid-fifteenth-century Europe as a card game. By the late eighteenth century, this simple pack of playing cards had been revised by Western occultists for divination.[4] Not all tarotists identify as occultists or as witches, and tarot reading is not witchcraft. Even so, witches and other magical practitioners frequently use tarot to strengthen intuition, aid spellwork, and prompt self-reflection. A swift survey of witchcraft books on the market reveals that a tarot deck is often regarded as an essential item in the witch's toolkit.

Tarot has been massively mainstreamed as part of New Age culture's imbrication in the self-help industry. In her analysis of white women's participation in New Age culture, Karlyn Crowley capaciously defines it as "diverse spiritual, social, and political beliefs and practices that promote personal and societal change through spiritual transformation."[5] New Age culture has exploded since the 1990s, as evidenced by the proliferation of metaphysical shops and the popularization of an array of spiritual practices, most of which co-opt Indigenous lifeways the world over. As the New Age becomes increasingly commercial, the focus on social (r)evolution has been largely supplanted by what Brenda R. Weber calls spiritual neoliberalism, or "the establishment of spiritualized goals—such as salvation, peace, and fulfillment—as best (or only) achievable through neoliberal methods requiring individual choice and 'free' markets."[6] The New Age industry inflects the neoliberal discourse of self-help with a mystical promise: personal development facilitated by commercial consumption—like acquiring the latest tarot deck—will unlock one's potential as an enlightened, self-actualized individual. While some employ tarot for cartomancy, it is increasingly common for practitioners to use it for psychospiritual therapeutics of the self.

Counter to New Age culture's original investment in social transformation, the commercialization of tarot has reified what has always been true: tarot is mainstream insofar as it has internalized dominant logics along the lines of race, gender, sexuality, class, and ability. The Rider-Waite-Smith Tarot (1909), inarguably the most iconic deck, is replete with Christian imagery and hierarchal figures of European monarchy that have been replicated in most every deck on the market. It is also vital to note that some Romani people argue that tarot is a closed practice, one for which Romani people continue to be persecuted.[7] Mainstreaming tarot has thus served to increase its accessibility and relatability to those who have always seen themselves reflected in tarot and dominant culture. Tarot is therefore not inherently subversive, despite its association with the occult.

THE FIRST FEMINIST TAROT DECKS

Scholarship on the New Age focuses largely on its problematic aspects. Yet we must take the New Age seriously, Crowley asserts, not least because some women turn to it to find empowerment in a society that strips them of it.[8] The Motherpeace Tarot (1981) and Daughters of the Moon Tarot (1984) are products of women's engagement with New Age culture to resist patriarchal domination. Alongside others born of 1970s and 1980s American feminism, these independently produced decks revised tarot's androcentric imagery to document feminist spiritual culture. Daughters of the Moon excised men from its representational archive almost entirely and included two Lovers cards—one depicting a lesbian couple and the other a heterosexual pair—from which the querent could choose. Both decks are best known for their atypical round shape. Most tarot cards are rectangular and are read upright or reversed, each engendering a distinct meaning. The round shape of these decks was a strategic design choice intended to disrupt "dualities or oppositions, a concept developed by the patriarchal either/or mind" and to encourage interpretative nuance instead.[9]

These two decks' feminist remix was not merely a diversification of tarot's visual landscape; it was also a shift in its intended use. Widening tarot's traditionally narrow focus on the individual querent to systemic power, the creators conceived of the decks as tools for dislodging internalized patriarchal beliefs. According to co-creator Ffiona Morgan, Daughters of the Moon Tarot was "created by a circle of womyn who were frustrated with using patriarchal tarot decks which did not serve our needs as an oracle.... Recording our present womyn's culture and writing of the old goddess cultures is a way of creating new images in our minds, thereby greatly influencing our belief system. Changing our ingrained basic beliefs is possibly the most important step in our liberation."[10] Likewise, Karen Vogel, co-creator of the Motherpeace Tarot, asserts that the cards "became more than a divination tool for us; they were, and are, a fundamental healing process for reaching beyond the limitation of the gender roles in our society."[11]

With over 300,000 copies sold, the Motherpeace's public presence has surged in the past few years. Its imagery was reproduced on textiles in a 2018 Dior collection, while contemporary tarotists grapple with its cultural appropriation. After the deck was published, Vogel learned that the images she replicated on two cards depict clitoridectomy rituals of the Ngere tribe.[12] The deck's decontextualized reproduction of imagery at cross-purposes with its feminist ethos has prompted many tarotists to reject it. Though deserving of critique, the Motherpeace and Daughters of the Moon are significant because they explicitly politicized tarot, a project that is ongoing among contemporary justice-centered tarotists.

CONTEMPORARY JUSTICE-CENTERED TAROT

A rapid upswell of independently produced tarot decks created by and for marginalized people emerged starting in 2016, a watershed moment in New Age culture. The double entendre on the tuckbox of Our Tarot crystallizes contemporary justice-centered tarot's extension of earlier feminist decks' politicization of tarot within and against the New Age: "Some decks may be stacked against us but this deck is ours." In what follows, I detail the recent proliferation of justice-centered tarot and, by invoking only a few illustrative decks due to space, I outline its three overlapping modes of intervention.

Redrawing the Tarot: Cultural Accessibility and Visual Critique

As a kind of media, justice-centered tarot decks are designed to be culturally accessible to marginalized tarotists. Media scholar Elizabeth Ellcessor explains that accessibility is not just technical; it "may also be cultural, referring to the active inclusion of culturally relevant disabled perspectives. Cultural accessibility entails reimagining disability and the norms of media production and representation."[13] My application of cultural accessibility is not a decentering of disability. Instead, cultural accessibility widens the analytical lens beyond a preoccupation with the mere presence of diversity in tarot imagery to emphasize the production of culturally relevant tarot representation by and for marginalized tarotists.

Justice-centered decks broaden the visual archive of tarot to include more culturally accessible imagery. Dust II Onyx (2018), which features stunningly textured portraits of Black figures set against cosmic backgrounds, was created by Black queer artist Courtney Alexander, after struggling to find a deck that did not exclude or exoticize Blackness, "to be a resistance against the idea that spiritual beings and realms can only be imagined through a Eurocentric and westernized lens."[14] Our Tarot—a nod to the 1971 feminist tome *Our Bodies, Ourselves*—follows in the footsteps of earlier feminist decks by replacing traditional tarot archetypes with figures from women's history. White creator Sarah Shipman made a point to include "Black American women who were/are abolitionists, activists, and champions of civil rights. I do not seek to throw a veil over the violence of American history, but instead call much-needed attention to it, by honoring the lives of these women."[15] In doing so, Our Tarot is animated by a commitment to antiracist representation not seen in the first feminist decks.

Slow Holler Tarot (2016) and Slutist Tarot (2017) craft cultural accessibility by troubling tarot's androcentric, hierarchal structure. Slow Holler, a collaboration between thirty queer and/or Southern artists, "move[s] away from the white, patriarchal, old European focus of traditional tarot decks ... to create a deck that queer folks, people of color, and folks with varied gendered identities can more readily feel at home with and can more easily see themselves in."[16] Its new titles upend tarot's gender binary and hierarchal structure. For example, The Emperor becomes The Navigator, and the court cards—Pages, Knights, Queens, and Kings—are renamed Students, Travelers, Visionaries, and Architects. Whereas the tarot traditionally asks the querent to identify with the male archetype of The Fool, Morgan Sirene's Slutist Tarot inverts this androcentrism, replacing The Fool with The Maiden. The deck is deeply invested in sexual reclamation: not only does it work to redefine the archetype "slut"; it also retains the hierarchal titles of Princess, Prince, Queen, and King to honor the way they are embraced in LGBTQIA+ and kink communities.

A critical consideration of tarot's Eurocentric legacy is brewing in the digital cauldron, a discourse that fuels the creation of justice-centered decks. For instance, in a 2017 YouTube video, white tarot reader Tom Benjamin states, "Whenever we ask someone to look at cards we are laying out for them and we are using an entirely white deck, we are saying implicitly, please put aside your experience and allow me to interpret your experience through these white images."[17] Some of this discourse has circulated with the hashtag #tarotsowhite, created by white tarot reader Kelly-Ann Maddox in a 2016 YouTube video that, as of this writing, has been viewed upward of seven thousand times.[18] The video spurred wide debate in the online tarot community, and in a response post, Asian American tarot author Benebell Wen adds that the whiteness of tarot renders the casual inclusion of racial diversity (rather than stereotypes) a distraction to intuitive work. Wen implores tarotists to use their buying power to shift the New Age industry: "If no one buys tarot and oracle decks featuring ordinary people of color (and by extension, tarot readers get used to seeing—and liking—decks that feature ordinary people of color), then deck creators and publishers won't be inclined to feature ordinary people of color, and so we will never get to that point where the Asianness of an Asian High Priestess or the Blackness of a Black Emperor won't distract us. . . . Social progress in the tarot world will only happen if it's profitable for deck publishers."[19] As Wen predicted, many popular independent justice-centered decks have been picked up by mainstream publishers for distribution.

"Making Space for Unwellness": Tarot and Healing Justice

As with other mediums, the tarot's politics of representation are fraught. Justice-centered decks diversify the visual archive of tarot, but—as scholars of race, gender, sexuality, and media have long argued—visibility is not tantamount to systemic change. In her analysis of Black popular culture, Racquel J. Gates asserts that representations, whether deemed positive or negative, "do not do the work by themselves, and, to take it a step further, they may not even do the work that we presume them to do."[20] Tarot decks do not do anything on their own, no matter how inclusive their imagery and titles: "positive" (i.e., more diverse or nonstereotypical) cards do not linearly lead to new interpretations or new utilizations of the tarot.

Though the revolutionary potentialities of diversified tarot representation are not a given, many justice-centered decks explicitly guide users to rewrite existing interpretive paradigms and to embrace tarot as a tool for both self-care and collective care. In other words, justice-centered tarot praxis adopts a healing justice framework. Healing justice "identifies how we can holistically respond to and intervene on generational trauma and violence and to bring collective practices that can impact and transform the consequences of oppression on our bodies, hearts and minds."[21] Attentive to the concern that investment in personal wellness mires one in individualism that collapses movement work, healing justice is anchored in a critique of inequitable access to healthcare and an insistence that social transformation is unsustainable if activists are burned out. Loretta Pyles understands healing justice as "both a paradigm and a set of practices that invites practitioners to heal themselves at the same time that they heal the world," asserting that "the ability to cultivate relationships by tapping into their intuition and collective resilience is as critical as ever and must be reclaimed."[22]

The Asian American Tarot is a salient example of a healing justice reclamation of intuition that intercedes on structural conditions of unwellness. The deck is one of five materials included in the *Asian American Literary Review*'s 2016 Open in Emergency special issue on mental health in Asian American communities. Open in Emergency is a multidisciplinary survival kit of book art tools for those already living in states of emergency. As guest editor and deck curator Mimi Khúc explains, "If you look at communities of color, and other marginalized communities, we are always in crisis, it's always an emergency, because we're always dealing with historical and cultural structures that are harming us ... you should have already been engaging these kinds of art tools for your and your community's wellness."[23] The included deck is framed as a decolonized mental wellness tool that critiques the white supremacy of the medical-industrial complex and tarot tradition alike for Asian Americans who experience both as culturally inaccessible and/or violent. The collaboratively produced deck abandons all traditional tarot archetypes for figures resonant with Asian American cultural memory and contemporary life, like The Adoptee, Migrant, and Ancestor. Driven by Khúc's desire to "make space for unwellness," the Asian American Tarot engages tarotists in asking, "How do we find new languages to capture what hurts, to capture all the ways that we are unwell, beyond the kind of limitations of psychological and psychiatric discourse?"[24]

Inspired by the Asian American Tarot, Piper Serra and Lani Nguyen created These Small Mysteries, a deck of six cards designed to mediate difficult conversations about rape culture. The deck is a product of Tulane University's 2018 academic course Project IX: Student Design to End Sexual Assault, which tasked students with generating creative interventions into campus sexual violence after a university climate survey evidenced strikingly higher rates than the national average. Each card offers an illustration, discussion question, and quote as avenues into vulnerable and collaborative meaning-making. Serra and Nguyen erected an interactive tarot tent to present These Small Mysteries alongside other projects at a campus showcase. Attendees were invited to work with the deck in the tent, to "make space for unwellness." No copies were made of the original deck and the tent was a one-off experience. However, its ephemerality underscores that tarot is not solely a commodity: through a healing justice framework, it can facilitate opportunities for individual and collective healing.

"We Are Forever": Tarot as Emergent Strategy

Justice-centered tarotists also wield the tarot to stimulate the political imagination toward a world otherwise. This intervention does not reject the tarot practice of forecasting the future but *multiplies* it: in justice-centered tarot, the future is a terrain of infinite possibilities and an iterative project of world-building. As Charlie Claire Burgess, nonbinary creator of the Fifth Spirit Tarot (2020) writes, tarot is "about *creating* the future."[25] Said otherwise, these decks and their attendant discourses engage tarot as a tool for emergent strategy, which adrienne maree brown theorizes as "how we intentionally change in ways that grow our capacity to embody the just and liberated worlds we long for."[26] Emergent strategy emphasizes critical connections over critical mass in its focus on practicing just relationships that we seek to replicate on a macro level. And, like revolution, tarot is "science fiction behavior," the emergent strategy of *imagining* the next world into being.[27]

Next World Tarot exemplifies the reframing of tarot as a tool for arousing the radical imaginary to divine alternative futures. The postapocalyptic visual landscape of Cristy C. Road's Next World Tarot is populated by mostly queer people of color dismantling oppressive institutions and building a more just and compassionate future. The Tower card—which traditionally signals a profound personal upheaval—is renamed Revolution and depicts activists protesting an oil drilling site engulfed in flames. Road's artistic rendering of The Tower broadens its myopic focus on the individual to highlight the political contexts that shape our lives. The guidebook's interpretation of Revolution reminds us that "while we can't overthrow entire systems in one sitting, we can still rebuild our own lives."[28] A querent who pulls this card might approach it as a prompt to bring awareness to the ways oppressive logics have structured their relationships, or consider what small actions they can take in service of liberation. At once terrifying and beautiful, Revolution captures Next World Tarot's commitment to not only redefining tarot but also, as a political-spiritual tool, supporting marginalized people living in systems of oppression and fighting for liberation.

The apocalyptic future of some people's nightmares is many marginalized communities' present: as the Asian American Tarot underscores, futurity and emergency are differentially constructed by structural violence. In this vein, the Society of Disabled Oracles positions disabled people as *oracular*, as dispatching crip wisdom across constructions of time to divine alternative futures. Created by Aimi Hamraie, Jen White-Johnson, and Alice Wong, the online project is a digital disabled oracle deck comprising twelve images, each accompanied by a series of questions to prompt the submission of written, audio, video, and graphic "telegrams" for feature on its website. The Society of Disabled Oracles yokes a disability justice framework to tarot/oracle divination to gather the prescient brilliance of the disabled community for thriving in this world and the next.[29] Countering the explicitly and latently eugenic violence of systemic ableism, the Society's oracle project affirms: "We are the past. We are the present. We are the future. We are forever."[30]

This mode of justice-centered tarot praxis loops back to the first: creating culturally accessible tarot decks that depict potential futures incrementally materializes those futures and provides a tool for expanding our capacity to sustain them. While emergent strategy draws our attention to the smallest units of society, brown insists that "this doesn't mean to get lost in the self, but rather to see our own lives and work and relationships as the front line, a first place we can practice justice, liberation, and alignment with each other and the planet."[31] In this way, the solitary and interpersonal intimacy of tarot reading is far from a self-indulgent distraction from movement work when practiced through a justice-centered lens but instead a practice that energizes activism and expands our notion of where and how social transformation is incited.

CONCLUSION

"New Age sensibility is identified as a feminized sensibility" by critics who leverage misogyny to discredit it as narcissistic, consumptive, and irrational.[32] These critiques are also espoused by activist communities on the left that denigrate New Age and self-care practices as depoliticized navel-gazing that diverts attention from movement work. Yet tarot has also been publicly embraced by prominent organizers and thought leaders like Leah Lakshmi Piepzna-Samarasinha and adrienne maree brown. Why are the critically conscious and politically active picking up tarot? Xine Yao argues, "Tarot's appeal to queer of color spiritual practices comes from viewing its dubious history and false universality as potential for reappropriation rather than grounds for dismissal. From this angle, tarot is a dynamic cultural site for ways of reading and storytelling that inspires queers of colors to remake that Western occult tradition in their own image."[33] To build on Yao, tarot privileges "nonrational" epistemologies that challenge who can be a knower, what can be known, how, and to what end. Like intersectional feminist standpoint theories, justice-centered tarot frames lived experience as generative grounds for knowledge production about the mechanisms of power.

In *Living a Feminist Life*, Sara Ahmed advises feminists to curate killjoy survival kits, conceptual and tangible collections of resources that sustain our work of disrupting joy when that joy rests on a bedrock of oppression. Ahmed offers this caveat: "To think of a killjoy survival kit as self-care might seem to be a neoliberal agenda, a way of making feminism about the resilience of individuals."[34] Anchoring into Audre Lorde's now-iconic quote, "Caring for myself is not self-indulgence, it is self-preservation, and that is an act of political warfare," Ahmed clarifies that feminist self-care is not motivated by one's own happiness but by "finding ways to exist in a world that makes it difficult to exist."[35] Important to any killjoy survival kit are tools, the ones we make and the ones we use in ways we are not supposed to.[36] Tarot is one such tool. From the Motherpeace to Next World Tarot, creators of justice-centered tarot decks are producing seventy-eight interactive pieces of art that imagine the world otherwise. People are using them in the privacy of their bedrooms as they grapple with how to access pleasure after trauma, in communities to thwart burnout and inform activist work, with friends at the kitchen table to support individual (un)wellness and collective care networks when access to mental healthcare is limited. Perhaps tarot is or once was one of the master's tools, to conjure Lorde again, but justice-centered tarotists work to refashion this tool in an effort to collectively heal from the master's rule, chip away at the master's house, and envision the house anew.[37]

NOTES

1. Giberson, "November Monthly Missive."
2. The term *tarotists* refers to tarot creators and readers.
3. *Arcana* is Latin for mysteries.
4. For more tarot history, see Farley, *Cultural History of Tarot*.
5. Crowley, *Feminism's New Age*, 2.
6. Weber, "Epistemology of the (Televised, Polygamous) Closet," 380.
7. A closed practice is only for members of a cultural/ancestral lineage or those initiated into its traditions. In a now-deleted post, the authors argue that, athough tarot does not originate solely in Romani culture, Romani people were the first to use it for divination and are the only group stigmatized for doing so. Romani Members of SLYSCA, "Your Tarot Card Practice Is Romani Appropriation."
8. Crowley, *Feminism's New Age*.
9. Morgan, *Daughters of the Moon Tarot*, 8.
10. Morgan, *Daughters of the Moon Tarot*, 7.
11. Vogel, *Motherpeace Tarot Guidebook*, 3.
12. Vogel acknowledges yet sidesteps this discovery: "It seems a contradiction to have the power of the High Priestess and Temperance cards framed in a ritual that includes female genital mutilation. . . . Still I am inspired by the extraordinary dance, music, and regalia, which I hope will live on in powerful rituals without female genital mutilation." Vogel, *Motherpeace Tarot Guidebook*, 27.
13. Ellcessor, *Restricted Access*, 34.

14 Alexander, *Dust II Onyx*, ix.
15 Shipman, *Our Tarot Guidebook*, 9.
16 *Slow Holler*, 186.
17 Benjamin, "Diversity and Inclusion in Tarot."
18 Maddox, "307. Cardslinger: Reversals, Mini Decks."
19 Wen, "My Perspective and #TarotsoWhite."
20 Gates, *Double Negative*, 14.
21 Incite!, "Reflections from Detroit."
22 Pyles, *Healing Justice*, 9, xix.
23 Khúc and Young, "Dr. Mimi Khúc on Claiming Unwellness."
24 Khúc and Young, "Dr. Mimi Khúc on Claiming Unwellness."
25 Burgess, *Fifth Spirit Tarot Guide*, 1.
26 brown, *Emergent Strategy*, 3.
27 brown, *Emergent Strategy*, 16.
28 Road, *Next World Tarot*, 24.
29 Tarot and oracle are both card-based divination tools, but oracle decks do not adhere to tarot's structure.
30 Society of Disabled Oracles, "About the Project."
31 brown, *Emergent Strategy*, 53.
32 Crowley, *Feminism's New Age*, 26.
33 Yao, "The Craft," 366.
34 Ahmed, *Living a Feminist Life*, 236
35 Lorde, *Burst of Light*, 130; Ahmed, *Living a Feminist Life*, 239.
36 Ahmed, *Living a Feminist Life*, 241.
37 Lorde, "Master's Tools."

BIBLIOGRAPHY

Ahmed, Sara. *Living a Feminist Life*. Durham, NC: Duke University Press, 2017.

Alexander, Courtney. *Dust II Onyx: A Melanated Tarot*. Tampa: Black and Sage Press, 2018.

Benjamin, Tom. "Diversity and Inclusion in Tarot." YouTube, June 3, 2017. https://youtu.be/TPMp63Gqjno.

brown, adrienne maree. *Emergent Strategy: Shaping Change, Changing Worlds*. Chico, CA: AK Press, 2017.

Burgess, Charlie Claire. *The Fifth Spirit Tarot Guide*. Portland: Self-published, 2020.

Crowley, Karlyn. *Feminism's New Age: Gender, Appropriation, and the Afterlife of Essentialism*. Albany: SUNY Press, 2011.

Ellcessor, Elizabeth. *Restricted Access: Media, Disability, and the Politics of Participation*. New York: NYU Press, 2016.

Gates, Racquel J. *Double Negative: The Black Image and Popular Culture*. Durham, NC: Duke University Press, 2018.

Giberson, Tess. "November Monthly Missive." Email newsletter, October 28, 2018.

Farley, Helen. *A Cultural History of Tarot: From Entertainment to Esotericism*. London: I. B. Tauris, 2009.

Incite!. "Reflections from Detroit: Reflections after the 4th Annual INCITE! Track at the AMC." August 25, 2010. https://incite-national.org/category/reflections-from-detroit/.

Khúc, Mimi, and Ayana Young. "Dr. Mimi Khúc on Claiming Unwellness/304." *For the Wild* (podcast), September 14, 2022. https://forthewild.world/listen/dr-mimi-khuc-on-claiming-unwellness-304.

Lorde, Audre. *A Burst of Light and Other Essays*. Mineola, NY: Ixia Press, 2017.

Lorde, Audre. "The Master's Tools Will Never Dismantle the Master's House." In *Sister Outsider: Essays and Speeches*, 110–13. Berkeley, CA: Crossing Press, 1984.

Maddox, Kelly-Ann. "307. Cardslinger: Reversals, Mini Decks and Complaining about Whiteness." YouTube, April 21, 2016. https://youtu.be/5Pqbo30NzAo.

Morgan, Ffiona. *Daughters of the Moon Tarot*. Willitis, CA: Daughters of the Moon, 1984.

mystif, Alanis, Corina Dross, Destiny Hemphill, and JB Brager (editor.) *Slow Holler Tarot Guidebook*. Self-published, 2016.

Pyles, Loretta. *Healing Justice: Holistic Self-Care for Change Makers*. New York: Oxford University Press, 2018.

Road, Cristy C. *Next World Tarot*. New York: CROADCORE, 2017.

Romani Members of SLYSCA. "Your Tarot Card Practice Is Romani Appropriation." February 15, 2021. https://www.patreon.com/posts/your-tarot-card-47577597.

Shipman, Sarah. *Our Tarot Guidebook*. Self-published, 2018.

Society of Disabled Oracles. "About the Project." Accessed September 24, 2022. https://societyofdisabledoracles.com/About-the-Project.

Vogel, Karen. *Motherpeace Tarot Guidebook*. Stamford, CT: U.S. Games Systems, Inc., 1995.

Weber, Brenda R. "The Epistemology of the (Televised, Polygamous) Closet: Progressive Polygamy, Spiritual Neoliberalism, and the Will to Visibility." *Television and New Media* 17, no. 5 (2016): 375–391. https://doi.org/10.1177/15274764156251.

Wen, Benebell. "My Perspective and #TarotsoWhite." April 22, 2016, https://benebellwen.com/2016/04/22/my-perspective-and-tarotsowhite/.

Yao, Xine. "The Craft: QTBIPOC Tarot in Mariko Tamaki and Jillian Tamaki's Skim." In *Q&A: Voices from Queer Asian North America*, edited by Martin F. Manalansan IV, Alice Y. Hom, and Kale Bantigue, 364–72. Philadelphia: Temple University Press, 2021.

Eight · SIMON CLAY AND EMMA QUILTY

Ecstatic Desires: Queerness and the Witch's Body

Witchcraft is power and possesses this in ekstasis, sex and ordeal. Witchcraft is unbridled sexuality. —PETER GREY

INTRODUCTION

The witch is a slippery and beguiling figure. She has taken on countless forms over the centuries, but the image of the witch as a seductive, child-snatching woman who roams the night and trucks with demonic forces dates back to ancient Mesopotamia and Assyria.[1] Today's Witches are a far cry from the diabolical caricatures of the early modern period. However, the notion that Witches represent an active threat to the integrity of heteropatriarchal structures, engage in deviant sexual practices, and transgress gender roles remains firmly intact.[2] This chapter explores the inherent queerness of the Witch's body and how witchcraft techniques of *ekstasis*, including BDSM and "flying ointments," queer the body. We focus on the methods Witches use to unsettle normative constructions of the body that dictate where it ends and the other-than-human begins. We also examine how these ecstatic practices can be considered both forms of radical resistance against systemic marginalization and acts of feminist defiance.

Witches have always been queer creatures. In early modern Europe, much of the fear around them stemmed from a belief in their ability to wield *wyrd*[3] forms of power that could force the hand of fate, manifest change, and uncover the secrets of the universe. Witches eluded systems of control and did not fit within the category of "human." Women accused of witchcraft during this period in European history were imagined to be able to transform from human to animal in a breath. They could fly to the heavens on nothing more than an oven fork or stalk of straw and let their spirits slip from their bodies to dance with the gods.[4] The otherness projected onto them by their communities rendered them alien figures that stalked the outskirts of towns.[5] Sarah Johnston contends that witches, like demons, have historically represented a mirror image of Western society's heteropatriarchal norms and structures: they engage in behaviors seen as the inverse of what is acceptable and expected of civilized women and therefore become classified as nonhuman.[6]

The witch's body was portrayed in the early modern period as highly sexed and disordered. Witches had misplaced nipples secreted near their anus or vulva for imps to sup upon and would ardently receive anilingus and cunnilingus from demons or their animal familiars. They would also exchange "abominable kisses" with the Devil to seal their dreadful pact.[7] The vagina, anus, and mouth became interchangeable orifices. Because the witch was a perversion of the maternal (a "monstrous mother"[8]), it was believed she would steal babies and feed them poisonous milk from her withered breasts.[9] In their notorious anti-witchcraft text, the *Malleus Maleficarum*, Jacob Sprenger and Heinrich Kramer write about how women are drawn to witchcraft because of their essential licentiousness. Their uncontainable sexual desires push them to fly through the night, looking to drain sleeping men of their semen and steal their penises for sorcerous purposes.[10] Witches were abject and the epitome of transgression; they represented everything that threatened the functionality of heteronormative society.

European women's primary role and destiny in the early modern period was to procreate and to nurture children into adulthood. They were expected to suppress their excessive sexual desires, engage in marital sex only, remain passive and obedient, and tend to the home.[11] Women who appeared to challenge these misogynistic norms by not marrying or by breaking out of their designated domestic and maternal roles were often declared to be witches.[12] Their refusal to marry and/or their defiance of men's authority was considered an attack on society. Moreover, women perceived as dyspeptic were often accused of being witches because they had committed some social wrongdoing, such as letting their cow eat a neighbor's hay, and showed no shame about it.[13] These "witches," it was believed, would go on to procure abortions, murder children, steal husbands, and blight communities.[14] However, these accused witches were just ordinary women whose skills, social connections, political power, community leadership, and/or other forms of social and economic capital simply challenged the power structures of the European church and state.[15]

Even though efforts to locate witches at the nexus of the erotic and the grotesque were animated by misogyny, many contemporary spiritual practitioners have found queer forms of freedom in this nexus. Mey Rude is one such Witch. She recounts her first one-night stand and describes how she felt like she was "flying" and "entering a religious fervour" that exorcised much of the shame she felt about sex and her own sexual desires. She writes: "I finally became my true self... I realised that I'm a slut and I love being a slut and I'm powerful when I'm a slut. That is who I am... I won't let anyone dictate my sexuality except for me. I'm made of magic, motherfucker."[16]

QUEER BODIES

Many queer scholars have demonstrated how bodies and identities come into being through symbols and social structures and do not simply exist as pre-discursive facts or as essential biological qualities. Our feeling bodies partially construct social reality and are relationally co-created with surrounding bodies.[17] There can be queer bodies as well as experiences, practices, or emotions that make way for queer forms of embodiment. A queer body is one that does not fit into normative ideals of how a body "should" look and/or function. This could be a "cripped" body that cannot be "cured" and refuses to function "properly,"[18] or it could be a body that transgresses the gender-sexuality binaries of woman/man, female/male, feminine/masculine. Some consider the fat body to be queer because it deviates from what is considered to be a "normal" and "healthy" body.[19] The fleshiness of the fat body also blurs gender legibility: fat feminizes the masculine body with larger hips and breasts and masculinizes the feminine body by burying the womanly "hourglass" figure.[20] Bodies that have been "biohacked" with digital technology or undergone other modifications that contest the body's "natural" limits can also be classified as queer.[21] Overwhelming sensations like pain, grief, or disgust can queer the way we experience our body, rendering it "an estranged, alien, 'thing-like' presence."[22]

In this chapter, we see queerness as an intensity of strange affects and peculiar feelings. It is a dis/orientation and way of relating to the world that challenges norms and upsets rubrics of classification.[23] Queerness is also a political sentiment that can be mobilized in the form of protest and in striking back at systems of oppression that seek to destroy those who are often pushed to the margins of society.[24] We understand queer identity as any expression/embodiment of identity that resists more normative ideas of how to move through the world and that embraces alternative forms of desire and eroticism.

FLYING HIGH: BDSM MAGIC AND ECSTATIC PRACTICES

The pursuit of altered states of consciousness to contact the divine and enter spiritual realms has been a quintessential part of many magical traditions over the ages. There is a substantial range of instructional texts available to Witches and other spiritual practitioners who wish to use ecstatic techniques to channel and communicate with the other-than-human and twist the threads of fate.[25] Some of these techniques include drumming, chanting, dance, breath work, and engaging in repetitive movements like rocking. These techniques manipulate the body so that it becomes a semi-detached entity. Individuals are then able to partially "leave" their bodies and enter alternative realities where they can more actively engage with the other-than-human.

Ecstatic practices regularly occur in group ritual settings. Starhawk advises that every ritual should be ecstatic and improvisational. A ritual should contain an ensemble of different roles divided among its attendants, feel inspired, and have an organic flow.[26] When these elements come together alongside methods of ekstasis like dancing, drumming, and singing, the group is able to raise currents of power that ripple through each member of the circle. The edges where one body ends and the other begins gradually blur and disintegrate. Through this ecstatic sense of oneness, the group becomes an independent entity that can hold and send out magic and allow the participants' consciousness to travel elsewhere.[27]

Sex and the utilization of erotic desire are two ecstatic practices with a long magical history. In the early to mid-twentieth century, sex magic underwent a renaissance. Figures like Aleister Crowley and Rosaleen Norton, who were known for their sex magic practices, highlighted the sacrality of carnal pleasure and sex/sexuality. They also emphasized how these forces can be harnessed as potent forms of power. Members of the modern Reclaiming Witchcraft tradition are strong advocates for mobilizing sex and erotic desire in magical and spiritual ways. Described as "an anarchist and ecofeminist-informed tradition,"[28] Reclaiming Witchcraft was founded at the height of the Goddess movement in 1979 by Starhawk and Diane Baker.

These two women formed a community of feminist Witches and began teaching this community about the Goddess and her rituals. Reclaiming Witchcraft's rapid popularity was partly due to its unique approach of using sex and eroticism as powerful sources of magic. It also attracted a great deal of women because its feminist orientation and values opened new avenues of spirituality that were not governed by the hegemonic discourses of the then-male-dominated occult world. This tradition celebrates the sensual body in all its forms, particularly female/feminine bodies that have historically been denigrated as abject. Reclaiming Witchcraft uses sex and erotic desire as techniques of magic and ways of repairing the violence inflicted by heteropatriarchy. Kink and BDSM practices are also prominent features of the Reclaiming Witchcraft community (as well as of many other feminist Witchcraft traditions). Performances of queer, transgressive sex in ritual settings are considered sacred and radical acts of resistance; ritual space is where bodily fluids and fluid sexualities become magical instruments.[29]

As part of her doctoral project, Emma Quilty conducted a series of interviews with Reclaiming Witchcraft Witches in a number of Australian cities and "WitchCamps"[30] to explore how this feminist approach to Witchcraft is put into action.[31] Tiff,[32] a young woman and Witch living in Brisbane, Queensland, reflected on her experience attending a workshop titled "Consensual Violence." The workshop was run as an education session on how kink and pleasurable pain can create transcendent experiences when combined with Witchy rituals. Tiff reflected on the use of kink techniques to achieve a state of transcendence: "There was lots of talk in that workshop of using self-inflicted pain almost like a shamanic tool to leave your body and have a transcendent experience."

As Tiff describes, BDSM can be a deeply spiritual practice for some. There is the ritualistic preparation of materials and the creation of sacred space; personal and bodily boundaries are manipulated to open pathways into different realities where the divine can be felt in potent ways.[33] Kinksters often experience a sense of empowered erotic surrender by submitting to pain and relinquishing their power to another. This surrendering combined with the dynamics between players, atmosphere, and state of mind gives way to transcendent experiences. The ecstasy that kink practitioners describe once they pass across this threshold can range from feeling like a trance state to total rapture. It can also be accompanied by a brisance of spiritual, psychic, and erotic release that reveals the numinous and divine.[34] Jonathan Cahana notes how queer BDSM practices can be remarkably similar to the ancient Gnostic rituals practiced by early Christians.[35]

Queer BDSM and ancient Gnostic rituals aim to both create a visceral intimacy with the divine and other bodies and establish a sense of being simultaneously within and outside of one's body. They also focus on subverting traditional sex/gender structures. The Gnostics believed a tyrannical god created gender and biological sex to hide the truth of existence from humans, and therefore must be dismantled.[36] Queer BDSM practitioners have a similar approach. They embrace "'exuberant intimacies'... that reject reason, moderation, mediocrity... [and] celebrate difference, tension, intensity... as well as becoming something beyond the human."[37]

The aim of using BDSM and "consensual violence" as spiritual practices is to establish states of in-betweenness and nonreality. A vast repertoire of techniques is used in BDSM rituals to create sensory extremes that facilitate the production of these ephemeral states of transcendence. The smart from the snap of a riding crop, the intensifying ache from stress positions, and the exquisite burn of hot wax can loosen perceptions of time and blur the boundaries of "reality" to create a unique, temporally suspended space. In her landmark study on Witchcraft in Australia, Lynne Hume describes the range of sensory and embodied techniques Witches use to create a liminal space to facilitate their transformative experiences. "In play," she writes, "there is a freedom from normative constraints; one steps out of one time into another and enters an enclave within which it seems anything may happen."[38] These ecstatic techniques allow Witches to enter unstable states of in-betweenness where they can send out magic and more actively interact with other-than-human forces.

The imperative to disrupt systems of societal injustice is one of the key tenets of the Reclaiming Witchcraft community. Followers believe Witchcraft has the potential to transfigure society and undo systems of marginalization, and sex can be one way of doing this. Witchy rituals have a similar energetic flow to sex: there is a rise (casting a circle/foreplay), an ecstatic peak (ritual climax/orgasm), and a gradual fall (closing a circle/afterplay). There are dedicated rituals and sacred spaces at Reclaiming Witchcraft WitchCamps, like the Bower,[39] that are specially crafted so individuals can reclaim and transform sexuality into something magical. Matt,[40] a participant from Quilty's study, described a "chocolate ritual" he attended at California WitchCamp. This ritual involved people eating chocolate-dipped fruit off one another and engaging in various sexual activities as a way of embracing the joy and beauty of sex: "Some WitchCamps, like the California WitchCamp, have a chocolate night-ritual with an open play-space. As the night progresses, it ends up with people making out on the floor and stuff. I suppose [outsiders might] view an orgy as a depraved sexual experience, whereas [the chocolate ritual] is more of a sensual [experience] ... and sexual celebration. It's about consenting adults engaging in consensual acts of love and pleasure."

The chocolate ritual at the California WitchCamp presents sexual intimacy as a way to access the sacred rather than as something that should be denied or shamed and is a way of enhancing community intimacy. It is "a sacrament, an outward sign of an inward grace."[41] Sexuality performs a dual role in this sense. On a material level, sexual connections pertain to the physical relationships of overlapping and intersecting corporality that exist between humans in an everyday sense. On an immaterial or ephemeral level, the sacred energy of the cosmos becomes an erotic energy.[42] The popularity of alternative forms of sex within certain Witchcraft traditions and the way carnal pleasure is harnessed as a magical technology gives insight into the inherent queerness of Witchcraft. Here, gender roles are reversed and abandoned in group rituals, queer expressions of eroticism are celebrated, and sexual desire becomes an electric current that enhances the potency of a ritual. These Witches are playing with the boundaries of the body and states of consciousness and using pleasurable pain to connect with the divine.

The use of "flying ointments" is another ecstatic practice long associated with witches. Witches' salves were a key feature of the early modern European witch trials and appeared in many confessions of accused witches. Inquisitors and witch-hunters were obsessed with the idea of a demonic entity gifting a magical salve to a witch. This diabolical ointment would give her the power to fly (physically and/or spiritually), to curse or murder people from afar, to summon demons, and to transform into an animal. By coercing an accused witch to confess that she possessed such an ointment, inquisitors could easily demonstrate her guilt and sentence her to death.[43] It has been hotly contested whether flying ointments actually existed during this period. The general consensus is that they were a fiction created by witch-hunters, inquisitors, and physicians to support their accusations.[44]

Flying ointments enjoy a broad popularity today. Many Witches sell homemade magic balms on the online marketplace Etsy, stating that they can facilitate communication with particular deities and land spirits, enhance psychic abilities, and allow one to fly to the witches' sabbath. It is also relatively easy to find recipes for flying ointment in Witchcraft blogs, contemporary grimoires, and herbal Witchcraft guides.[45] These unguents typically contain a blend of extracts from various psychotropic and tropane-rich plants or "witch herbs." A typical flying ointment will contain some combination of highly toxic herbs like mandrake, datura, deadly nightshade, and/or henbane alongside less potent ones, such as wormwood, mugwort, damiana, and/or clary sage. These plants are blended in ritual settings and charged with power. Flying ointments are typically used in conjunction with trance-inducing techniques like rocking and breath work. They are applied to areas of the body where the skin is thinnest, such as the armpits, groin, neck, and wrists. This is primarily to enable faster absorption of the balm's entheogens, but it can also be read as an act of defiance against early modern witch-hunters. Inquisitors would often strip suspected witches naked and scour the "secret" parts of their bodies for tell-tale blemishes or marks. By applying witch ointments to these hidden, erogenous areas, modern Witches are engaging with the sensuality of ritual and showing that the witch-hunters were right, in a way: these are sites of devilry and witchcraft, just not in the way they believed. Today's Witches are carrying on this tradition of connecting erotic areas of the body with Witchcraft.

The power of flying ointments is two-fold. Not only do the entheogenic properties of these plants enable individuals to slip more easily into a trance state and experience unsettling sensations, but using these ointments is also a unique form of nature worship and a way of working with plants on a magical and practical level. These balms blur the body's boundaries, enmeshing the body with the surrounding environment. This enables the user to extend rhizomes of connections with the spirit realm and other-than-human forces.

These salves are a potent symbol of feminist empowerment and pride. Some Witches use flying ointments to connect to the "old ways," or the early modern European folkloric traditions and practices women engaged in and were subsequently persecuted for. These women often knew how to prepare particular herbs and plants to relieve different health problems. It was common for women to go foraging for plants to make antiseptic balms for the household, which were often then seized by inquisitors as evidence of witchcraft.[46] By applying a balm containing a blend of similar herbs used by women during the early modern period, contemporary Witches can feel a feminist intimacy with these healing women who were murdered by the state; it is a way of honoring them and recognizing and celebrating the important role women had in those communities.

Just like kink and BDSM, ecstatic practices that involve flying ointments and trance-inducing techniques are deeply queer in that they blur the edges of the body and enable practitioners to enter different states of consciousness and connect with the other-than-human. This queer process of dissolving and becoming other-than-human ruptures the socially ingrained binaries of self/other, nature/society, corporeal/incorporeal. Furthermore, many

Witchcraft practices and ecstatic techniques embrace the fluidity and instability of reality. These practices counter the coercive systems of normalization and social control perpetuated by psychiatry and biomedical science, which categorize different states of consciousness and experiences of the world as either "normal" or "pathological."[47] Witches and other spiritual practitioners also pursue queer affective states by manipulating their bodies so they can temporarily "leave" them and travel to other worlds. By hyperventilating, applying specially crafted unguents, rocking their bodies, and dancing till they are exhausted, these practitioners are embracing strange and unusual sensations that render the body a semi-alien being; they become both attached and detached from their bodies and expand further into the other-than-human world.

CONCLUSION

Witchcraft and queerness intersect in many ways. The witch's body was depicted as a bizarre and distorted object in the early modern period, as something that only an evil being could inhabit, much like the modified queer body today. Queer and trans individuals who exceed the threshold of acceptable body modification are deemed to be outsiders with "ruined" or freakish bodies. We have shown how ecstatic practices designed to induce peculiar sensations and altered states of consciousness are a fundamental aspect of Witchcraft and are used by Witches to connect with the other-than-human. These ecstatic practices demonstrate there is no clear self/other, human/nature split but rather a constellation of consciousnesses that can be experienced in myriad ways. Witches slide in and out of their bodies with ease. They show us there is so much more to the world than meets the human eye. The Witch, like queerness, can never be pinned down.

NOTES

1. Bloom, *Jewish Mysticism and Magic*, 170–72.
2. I capitalize *Witch* when referring to modern-day feminist witches. My lowercase *witch* refers to historic descriptions of witches.
3. The *wyrd* relates to the concept of fate and destiny and is the Old English root of "weird." It draws from the image of the Moirae, or the three Fates of Greek mythology, and is a term regularly used by contemporary witches.
4. Tuczay, "Witches and Devil's Magic," 31–32; Kachuba, "Shapeshifters," 38.

5   Zika, "Towards an Alien Community," 207.
6   Johnston, "Defining the Dreadful," 363–64.
7   Millar, "Over-Familiar Spirits," 181; Millar, "Sleeping with Devils," 217–18.
8   Kosmina, *Feminist Afterlives of the Witch*, 105–25.
9   Roper, *Oedipus and the Devil*, 25, 208.
10 Mackay, *The Hammer of Witches*, 187, 328.
11 Coontz, "Marriage, a History," 142, 170–71.
12 Goodare, *The European Witch-Hunt*, 91–92, 292.
13 Goodare, *The European Witch-Hunt*, 91–92, 292.
14 Kivelson, "So They Will Love Me and Pine for Me," 119–21; Roper, *Oedipus and the Devil*, 1; Goodare, *The European Witch-Hunt*, 91–92, 292.
15 Federici, *Caliban and the Witch*, 12–13.
16 Rude, "My Witch's Sabbath," 130–31.
17 Butler, *Bodies That Matter*, 1–3; Grosz, *Volatile Bodies*, 19–24.
18 Kafer, *Feminist, Queer, Crip*, 15–17.
19 LeBesco, "Queering Fat Bodies/Politics," 74–75.
20 White, "Fat/Trans," 89–90.
21 Malatino, "Biohacking Gender," 179–80.
22 Williams, "Bodily Dys-order," 61.
23 Ahmed, *Queer Phenomenology*, 5–9.
24 Baroque, "Introduction," 9.
25 See, for example, Parma, *Ecstatic Witchcraft*.
26 Salomonsen, *Enchanted Feminism*, 39.
27 Salomonsen, *Enchanted Feminism*, 138–40, 195–97.
28 Morgain, "Sacred Materialism," 175.
29 Telford-Keogh, "Queering Feminist Witchcraft," 53–54.
30 WitchCamp is an annual retreat run by the Reclaiming Witchcraft community, where participants can learn and further develop a range of spiritual tools and engage in large group rituals.
31 Quilty, "Letting the Juices Flow," 95–109.
32 A pseudonym.
33 Carlström, "Spiritual Experiences," 756–62; Westerfelhaus, "The Spirituality of Sex," 268–72.
34 Baker, "Sacred Kink," 444–50.
35 Cahana, "Dismantling Gender," 67–72.
36 Cahana, "Dismantling Gender," 67–72.
37 Bauer, *Queer BDSM Intimacies*, 4.
38 Hume, *Witchcraft and Paganism in Australia*, 7.
39 The Bower is a space dedicated to free sexual activity and reversing the shame surrounding sexuality. More generally, the term "bower" is often used by pagans to describe where the Witch Goddess resides during spring and summer: having revived nature from the death of winter, she brings warmth, joy, and fecundity to the lands from her verdant bower.
40 A pseudonym.

41 Starhawk, *The Spiral Dance*, 123.
42 Starhawk, *Dreaming the Dark*, 136–38.
43 Clifton, "Witches Still Fly," 229, 233–34; Ostling, "Babyfat and Belladonna," 52–53, 62–70.
44 Clifton, "Witches Still Fly," 224; Ostling, "Babyfat and Belladonna," 45–47. Ayelet Even-Ezra, however, offers some compelling counterclaims to this. See Even-Ezra, "Cursus," 314–30.
45 Schulke, *Viridarium Umbris*, 261–68; Roth, *The Witching Herbs*, 135–36.
46 Clifton, "Witches Still Fly," 233–234; Ostling, "Babyfat and Belladonna," 51–52.
47 Greenwood and Goodwyn, *Magical Consciousness*, 1–2.

BIBLIOGRAPHY

Ahmed, Sarah. *Queer Phenomenology: Orientations, Objects, Others*. Durham, NC: Duke University Press, 2006.

Baker, Alexzandria. "Sacred Kink: Finding Psychological Meaning at the Intersection of BDSM and Spiritual Experience." *Sexual and Relationship Therapy* 33, no. 4 (2018): 440–53.

Baroque, Fray. "Introduction." In *Queer Ultra Violence: Bash Back! Anthology*, edited by Fray Baroque and Tegan Eanelli, 9–31. Berkeley, CA: Ardent Press, 2011.

Bauer, Robin. *Queer BDSM Intimacies: Critical Consent and Pushing Boundaries*. London: Palgrave Macmillan, 2014.

Bloom, Maureen. *Jewish Mysticism and Magic: An Anthropological Perspective*. London: Routledge, 2007.

Butler, Judith. *Bodies That Matter: On the Discursive Limits of "Sex."* New York: Routledge, 1993.

Cahana, Jonathan. "Dismantling Gender: Between Ancient Gnostic Ritual and Modern Queer BDSM." *Theology and Sexuality* 18, no. 1 (2012): 60–75.

Carlström, Charlotta. "Spiritual Experiences and Altered States of Consciousness: Parallels between BDSM and Christianity." *Sexualities* 24, nos. 5–6 (2021): 749–66.

Clifton, Chas. "Witches Still Fly: Or Do They? Traditional Witches, Wiccans, and Flying Ointment." In *Magic and Witchery in the Modern West: Celebrating the Twentieth Anniversary of "The Triumph of the Moon,"* edited by Shai Ferraro and Ethan White, 223–44. Cham, Switzerland: Palgrave Macmillan, 2019.

Coontz, Stephanie. *Marriage, a History: How Love Conquered Marriage*. London: Penguin Books, 2005.

Even-Ezra, Ayelet. "Cursus: An Early Thirteenth-Century Source for Nocturnal Flights and Ointments in the Work of Roland of Cremona." *Magic, Ritual, and Witchcraft* 12, no. 3 (2017): 314–30.

Federici, Silvia. *Caliban and the Witch: Women, the Body and Primitive Accumulation*. 2004. Brooklyn: Autonomedia, 2009.

Goodare, Julian. *The European Witch-Hunt*. London: Routledge, 2016.

Greenwood, Susan, and Erik Goodwyn. *Magical Consciousness: An Anthropological and Neurobiological Approach*. New York: Routledge, 2016.

Grosz, Elizabeth. *Volatile Bodies: Toward a Corporeal Feminism*. Bloomington: Indiana University Press, 1994.

Hume, Lynne. *Witchcraft and Paganism in Australia*. Melbourne: Melbourne University Press, 1997.

Johnston, Sarah. "Defining the Dreadful: Remarks on the Greek Child-Killing Demon." In *Ancient Magic and Ritual Power*, edited by Marvin Meyer and Paul Mirecki, 361–90. Leiden, Netherlands: Brill, 2011.

Kachuba, John. *Shapeshifters: A History*. London: Reaktion Books, 2019.

Kafer, Alison. *Feminist, Queer, Crip*. Bloomington: Indiana University Press, 2013.

Kivelson, Valerie. "'So They Will Love Me and Pine for Me': Intimacy and Distance in Early Modern Russian Magic." In *Emotions in the History of Witchcraft*, edited by Laura Kounine and Michael Ostling, 117–36. London: Palgrave Macmillan, 2016.

Kosmina, Brydie. *Feminist Afterlives of the Witch: Popular Culture, Memory, Activism*. Cham, Switzerland: Palgrave Macmillan, 2023.

LeBesco, Kathleen. "Queering Fat Bodies/Politics." In *Bodies Out of Bounds: Fatness and Transgression*, edited by Jana Braziel and Kathleen LeBesco, 74–87. Berkeley: University of California Press, 2001.

Mackay, Christopher. *The Hammer of Witches: A Complete Translation of the "Malleus Maleficarum."* Cambridge: Cambridge University Press, 2009.

Malatino, Hilary. "Biohacking Gender: Cyborgs, Coloniality, and the Pharmacopornographic Era." *Angelaki* 22, no. 2 (2017): 179–90.

Millar, Charlotte-Rose. "Over-Familiar Spirits: The Bonds between English Witches and Their Devils." In *Emotions in the History of Witchcraft*, edited by Laura Kounine and Michael Ostling, 173–89. London: Palgrave Macmillan, 2016.

Millar, Charlotte-Rose. "Sleeping with Devils: The Sexual Witch in Seventeenth-Century England." In *Supernatural and Secular Power in Early Modern England*, edited by Marcus Harmes and Victoria Bladen, 207–32. Farnham, UK: Ashgate, 2015.

Morgain, Rachel. "Sacred Materialism: Things and Relations in a US Pagan Community." *Australian Journal of Anthropology* 26, no. 2 (2015): 174–95.

Ostling, Michael. "Babyfat and Belladonna: Witches' Ointment and the Contestation of Reality." *Magic, Ritual, and Witchcraft* 11, no. 1 (2016): 30–72.

Parma, Gede. *Ecstatic Witchcraft: Magick, Philosophy and Trance in the Shamanic Craft*. Woodbury, MN: Llewellyn Publishing, 2012.

Quilty, Emma. "Letting the Juices Flow." In *Embodying Religion, Gender and Sexuality*, edited by Sarah-Jane Page and Katy Pilcher, 95–109. London: Routledge, 2020.

Roper, Lyndal. *Oedipus and the Devil: Witchcraft, Sexuality and Religion in Early Modern Europe*. 1994. London: Routledge, 2005.

Roth, Harold. *The Witching Herbs: 13 Plants for Your Witch Garden*. Newburyport, MA: Weiser Books, 2017.

Rude, Mey. "My Witch's Sabbath of Short Skirts, Long Kisses, and BDSM." In *Becoming Dangerous: Witchy Femmes, Queer Conjurers, and Magical Rebels on Summoning the Power to Resist*, edited by Katie West and Jasmine Elliott, 130–39. Sandy, UK: Fiction and Feeling, 2018.

Salomonsen, Jone. *Enchanted Feminism: Ritual, Gender and Divinity among the Reclaiming Witches of San Francisco*. London: Routledge, 2002.

Schulke, Daniel. *Viridarium Umbris: The Pleasure Garden of Shadow*. Chelmsford, UK: Xoanon Press, 2005.

Starhawk. *Dreaming the Dark: Magic, Sex and Politics*. 1982. Boston: Beacon Press, 1988.

Starhawk. *The Spiral Dance: A Rebirth of the Ancient Religion of the Goddess: 20th Anniversary Edition*. 1979. New York: HarperCollins, 1999.

Telford-Keogh, Catherine. "Queering Feminist Witchcraft." In *Feminist Spirituality: The Next Generation*, edited by Chris Klassen, 33–62. Lanham, MD: Lexington Books, 2009.

Tuczay, Crista. "Witches and Devil's Magic in Austrian Demonological Legends." In *Cultures of Witchcraft in Europe from the Middles Ages to the Present*, edited by John Barry, Owen Davies, and Cornelie Usborne, 23–52. Cham, Switzerland: Palgrave Macmillan, 2018.

Westerfelhaus, Robert. "The Spirituality of Sex and the Sexuality of the Spirit—BDSM Erotic Play as Soulwork and Social Critique." In *Sexualities and Communication in Everyday Life: A Reader*, edited by Karen E. Lovaas and Mercilee M. Jenkins, 265–76. London: Sage Publications, 2006.

White, Francis. "Fat/Trans: Queering the Activist Body." *Fat Studies* 3, no. 2 (2014): 86–100.

Williams, Simon. "Bodily Dys-order: Desire, Excess and the Transgression of Corporeal Boundaries." *Body and Society* 4, no. 2 (1998): 59–82.

Zika, Charles. "Towards an Alien Community of Dancing Witches in Early Seventeenth-Century Europe." In *Feeling Exclusion: Religious Conflict, Exile, and Emotions in Early Modern Europe*, edited by Giovanni Tarantino and Charles Zika, 207–32. Abingdon, UK: Routledge, 2019.

Nine · ERIC STEINHART

Deitsch Magic Past and Future

INTRODUCTION

One of the largest and oldest European American magical traditions begins with the Pennsylvania Germans (the *Deitsch*). The Deitsch are not Dutch, and very few Deitsch are Amish. As an example of Deitsch influence, consider the slogan "Hex the patriarchy." The word *hex*, along with other magical concepts, entered Anglo-American culture from Deitsch. As will become clear, my interest in Deitsch magic is not merely academic: I am Deitsch, I was immersed Deitsch magical culture during my childhood in the 1960s and 1970s, and I am eager to understand its past and to shape its future.

I begin with the German mystic Jacob Boehme (1575–1624). Boehme describes the emergence, from the abyss of primal nothingness, of the male God and the female Virgin of Wisdom. Wisdom (Sophia) is a powerful divine figure.[1] Through Sophia, magic enters nature. Boehm has an elaborate theory of magic.[2] Magic is a divine power that can be used for good or evil.[3] Boehme does not call Sophia a goddess, though he does refer to the moon and sun as goddesses.[4] Boehme greatly influenced the radical German pietists as well as dissenting Protestants in England, such as the Quakers.

The Quaker leader William Penn brought German pietists to Pennsylvania.[5] Conrad Beissel, who was inspired by Boehme, traveled from Germany to Pennsylvania in 1732 to found the Ephrata Cloister. Beissel affirmed an androgynous primal deity, which split into a male God and the divine female, Sophia.[6] In his *Dissertation on Man's Fall*, Beissel refers to Sophia as a "God-femalety." Beissel affirmed both good and evil magic.[7] Also inspired by Boehme, a German group called the Harmony Society referred to Sophia as a goddess.[8] They moved to Pennsylvania in the mid-1700s. Around that time, the Moravians moved from Germany to Pennsylvania.

They had absorbed many pietist ideas, including that of divine androgyny.[9] They moved toward greater equality between men and women, and tried to replace the nuclear family with communal (but sexually segregated) living arrangements. They conceived of phallic-vaginal coitus as a holy sacrament.

All these German groups, and many others, became the Pennsylvania Deitsch. The theological innovations introduced by Boehme and his followers allowed many old heathen ideas to enter Deitsch culture. The Deitsch were probably the first Americans to break from masculinist Christianity by introducing a goddess. Likewise, the Deitsch broke from older family living arrangements to try to create new intentional communities. Moreover, while Anglo cultures condemned magic, Deitsch cultures encouraged it. From the early 1700s through the mid-1900s, Deitsch magic thrived in Pennsylvania.

SOME MAGICAL POWERS OF FEMALE BODIES

Although Deitsch magical culture properly begins with the arrival of the German pietists in Pennsylvania, the Deitsch brought with them many themes and motifs from pre-Christian Norse and Viking heathenry.[10] A central theme, which will be relevant for the future of Deitsch magic, involves the roles of women in social conflict. Archaeology reveals a high degree of gender equality among heathens.[11] This equality permits women and men to play similar roles in war. The historical literature repeatedly attests to female Viking warriors, and archaeology makes it very difficult to doubt their existence.[12]

Human female warriors are closely connected in heathenry to divine women known as *idisi*, who often appear as a triad. The three *idisi* are often simply referred to as the three women. Their deeper roots may lie in the Roman-Germanic triple goddesses known as the Matres or Matronae (or in even older triple goddesses).[13] They appear as the three Norns from Norse mythology and are closely linked with the three valkyries from the Volund poem in the *Poetic Edda*. They appear as three valkyries in the heathen First Merseburg Charm. As *idisi*, they have the magical power to bind or unbind both humans and deities. Charms involving the three women occur in the early modern German grimoire known as *The Egyptian Secrets: White and Black Art for Man and Beast*, which was used by the Deitsch.[14] A female trinity charm occurs in the Deitsch grimoire called the

Secrets of Sympathy.[15] Edwin Fogel cites many Deitsch spells involving the three women motif.[16] Several spells from the Deitsch grimoires resemble the First Merseburg Charm. It is not implausible to see the Deitsch Sophia as manifesting herself in a trinity of *idisi*. The *idisi* provide the Deitsch with a concept of female magical power not found in Anglo cultures.

For the Deitsch, the bodies of human women have distinctive magical powers. On the one hand, they have some negative magical powers. The presence of a woman interferes with making soap. Pregnant or menstruating women should stay away from vinegar barrels. Pregnant women should not cut children's hair. On the other hand, female bodies have some positive magical powers. Women should set hens and carry eggs for hatching. The names of three women should be invoked when starting yeast or making vinegar. If pregnant women plant or shake fruit trees, they will bear much fruit.[17]

The Deitsch scholar Patrick Donmoyer discusses spells used by women to control male drunkenness and domestic violence.[18] For example, a woman could take a man's strength by cutting his hair.[19] Some of the magical sayings give women control over the traditionally male activities of hunting and fishing.[20] By performing simple ritual actions (e.g., with their aprons), women could ruin hunting and fishing expeditions. Belief in the power of these spells was apparently strong enough to cause hunters to go home. Donmoyer suggests that these were ways women prevented men from poaching on their family landholdings.[21] Yet women hunted, too, and could bring good luck to hunting parties.

RITUAL SPECIALISTS: BRAUCHERS AND HEXERS

While many Deitsch spells and magical procedures could be used by almost anybody and without much training, others required special training and equipment. Ritual specialists used grimoires like John Hohman's *The Long Lost Friend*, the aforementioned *Egyptian Secrets*, Dr. Helfenstein's *Secrets of Sympathy*, and the anonymous *The Sixth and Seventh Books of Moses*.[22] Besides verbal spells, Deitsch magic involves written spells and charms (with occult symbols). It involves drawings and diagrams. It uses many tools (amulets, canes, divinatory wands, dolls, etc.). It uses many herbs, and substances taken from the earth or animals. Ritual specialists need to be trained by established ritual specialists in a wide variety of magical operations. Deitsch magic is usually passed from male teachers to female students, or from female teachers to male students. However, within families, magical power and training can flow along same-sex lines.

Ritual specialists now divide along ethical lines. On the one hand, *braucherei* is benevolent or helpful magic, practiced by *brauchers*. English speakers refer to *braucherei* as *powwow*, but I will use the Deitsch term. *Brauchers* often use Bible texts as incantations, and they use the Bible as a talisman. They invoke the trinity and channel divine power to help others. Yet they also use non-Christian sources. On the other hand, *hexerei* is harmful magic and is practiced by *hexers*. Some malevolent spells are found in *The Egyptian Secrets*, but hexers often use *The Sixth and Seventh Books of Moses*. Taboos urge *brauchers* to avoid doing harm.[23] *Brauchers* respond to harmful agents with spells intended to break curses cast by hexers, to bind harmful agents so they cannot act further, and to banish harmful wills or intentions. But *brauchers* do not aim to harm hexers.

Deitsch ritual specialization is egalitarian with respect to gender. *Brauchers* can be either male or female. David Kriebel shows that the gender ratios of *brauchers* are very close to equal.[24] While illnesses specific to each sex were traditionally handled by *brauchers* of the same sex, male and female *brauchers* otherwise functioned equally. Successful *brauchers* often became regionally famous and commanded great respect. For women, *braucherei* was an opportunity to escape from the constraints of private domesticity and to gain high public authority and social power. Indeed, the most famous *brauchers* were women.[25] These included Sophia (Leininger) Bailer and the legendary Mountain Mary (Anna Maria Jung). Hexers can also be male or female. Since *hexerei* was practiced secretly, it is difficult to know the gender ratio of hexers. The fact that *braucherei* was practiced equally by males and females suggests that the same holds true for *hexerei*. Donmoyer discusses famous hexers, both male and female.[26] The male hexer Nelson Rehmeyer was murdered in York County, Pennsylvania, in 1928 by another male hexer at the behest of a female hexer. Spells against hexers were modified depending on the gender of their target.

The Deitsch believed that *hexerei* was widely practiced and could cause serious harm. However, in contrast to Puritan Salem, politically organized action against hexers was neither theologically nor practically required. Theologically, at least for Deitsch pietists inspired by Boehme, magic ultimately came from God. Although it could be turned toward evil, it was not intrinsically satanic. Practically, the Deitsch had magical remedies against hexers. For example, when unseen hexers trapped Jake Strauss in darkness and brambles, he escaped by ritually offering them tobacco.[27] The Deitsch regularly practiced breaking, binding, and banishing against hexers.[28]

BRAUCHERS AND VALKYRIES

Neither *brauchers* nor hexers fit neatly into demographic binaries. They may be women or men, young or old, married or single, and so on. Yet, consider the stereotype that includes women who are willful, cross, nonconformist, haggard, disfigured, elderly, and so on. Within Anglo-American culture, this stereotype is strongly correlated with *hexerei*. However, within Deitsch culture, this stereotype includes both hexers and *brauchers*. For instance, while Mountain Mary exactly fits the Anglo stereotype of the willful spell-working hag, she was not a hexer. On the contrary, she was revered as a great *braucher*, a saint, or a holy woman. Pilgrimages to her grave have been held at least through 2009 (she died in 1819). She was portrayed in 2021 as a heroic Deitsch-pagan shaman.[29] As a cultural hero, she is an *idisi*. Again, the *idisi* provide the Deitsch with an alternative concept of female magical power not available in Anglo cultures.

To highlight the differences between Deitsch and Anglo conceptions of female magical power, some history can help. Pre-Christian North Sea cultures, including old English and Germanic cultures, shared many terms for magic-workers.[30] These included *wychez, warlocks, varlets,* and *valkyries*. During Christianization, most of these terms disappeared from English. A medieval distinction emerged between malevolent witches and benevolent cunning folk.[31] Well into the twentieth century, Deitsch *brauchers* map most closely onto the cunning folk, while Deitsch hexers map most closely onto witches. During the mid-twentieth century, Gerald Gardner (along with others) invented a pseudo-history of the Anglo witch.[32] This pseudo-history became normative in America. When neo-pagan feminists sought a symbol for female magical power, they had only the witch. The new Anglo witch uses magic to implement a progressive social and political agenda.[33] She uses magic to overcome sexual, racial, economic, and ecological injustices. While the old Anglo witch was a hexer, the new Anglo witch is a *braucher*.

Confronting new forms of Christo-fascism after the 2016 US presidential elections, many progressive Anglo witches cast spells to break, bind, banish, and heal.[34] They behaved like *brauchers* rather than *hexers*. Rountree argues that much goddess spirituality, including feminist witchcraft, aims at "healing the 'wounds of the patriarchy.'"[35] This again is *braucherei*. As part of the "magical resistance" to Christo-fascism, these Anglo witches used the slogan "Hex the patriarchy."[36] From a progressive Deitsch perspective, this is incorrect. It is the patriarchy itself which is the hex. Christo-fascism is the malevolent spell that must be broken; its agents must be bound, and their evil intentions banished. From this Deitsch perspective, the correct slogan is "*Brauch* the patriarchy."

Here the Deitsch will justifiably point out that current Anglo magical terminology is impoverished. Besides hexers, the Deitsch have *brauchers*, *idisi*, and valkyries. Of course, late Norse literature domesticated the valkyries. Yet they serve neither Odin nor Freya. Ellis Davidson shows how earlier heathenry portrays them as terrifying *idisi*, autonomous divine female warriors.[37] The *Njals Saga* portrays them weaving the fates of male warriors on a bloody loom, whose strings are their entrails, and whose weights are their severed heads. They had the power to bind (binding even Odin to his death at Ragnarok) and to unbind (as in the First Merseburg Charm). As warrior-women, binding men and gods to their fates, the valkyries combine both male and female features. Kathleen Self argues that the valkyrie breaks the man-woman binary to create a third gender.[38] The Deitsch do not share the Anglo view that the powerful magic-working woman is a witch. For the Deitsch, the powerful magic-working woman who establishes her own independence as a heathen female warrior is an *idisi*, a valkyrie in the ancient sense, a destroyer of worlds.

POSSIBLE FUTURES FOR DEITSCH MAGIC

Deitsch magical culture started to fade after World War II. During my childhood, in the 1960s and early 1970s, in Lancaster County, Pennsylvania, it was still present. I was immersed in Deitsch magic as a child. I had two cowlicks in my hair, indicating inborn magical talents.[39] But this magical culture mostly disappeared as my grandparents' generation passed in the 1980s and 1990s.[40] Many Deitsch people, including myself, are interested in reviving old family magical traditions and integrating them into contemporary life. Hence my interest is both academic and personal. So, I will now turn to my own views on some possible futures for Deitsch magical culture.

According to the way of persistence, we might try to practice Deitsch magic in the twenty-first century much as the old-timers did.[41] Here Deitsch magic aligns with extremely conservative Protestantism. Unfortunately, such Christianity suffers from many ethical defects. It is patriarchal and homophobic; it has politically allied itself with white supremacism and Christian nationalism. Since I seek futures guided by progressive values, I reject this way. Moreover, it is arguable that Boehme's work points to new forms of post-Christian paganism. I believe the pagan elements in Deitsch culture led me away from Christianity. Since I am not a Christian, I am not interested in any Christian ways to continue Deitsch magic. Of course, many other Deitsch have also left Christianity. They may also be interested in non-Christian ways to continue Deitsch culture.

Another way to continue Deitsch magic involves neo-heathenry. Thus, *Urglaawe* (original faith) blends Deitsch practices with the contemporary Germanic neo-pagan movement known as Ásatrú.[42] Yet Ásatrú has little in common with Deitsch traditions, and much neo-heathenry is fascistic. Although the *Urglaawe* rejects fascism, the affinities between neo-heathenry and fascism run deep. I am skeptical of neo-paganisms that seek to reconstruct the ways of "our ancestors." Such ethnic revivals risk devolving into tribalism, bloodline purity, and racial hatred. I am interested in new forms of Germanic paganism that look to the future rather than to the past. German thinkers are known for building abstract systems. Thus, I seek to move from concrete ethnic particulars to abstract pagan universals. Some people are trying to integrate Deitsch magic with contemporary occult practices.[43] However, from the Thule Society to the Order of Nine Angles, the occult has long overlapped with fascism. Many occult cultures are post-truth cultures, which reject shared norms of truth and turn instead to conspirituality and authoritarianism. Since I seek futures guided by progressive ethical and political values, I reject the occult.

A more promising way to continue Deitsch magic involves Wicca, founded by Gerald Gardner in England in the 1940s. Gardner influenced the English Wiccan Sybil Leek, who visited Pennsylvania in 1967. Three Pennsylvania groups soon combined Deitsch magic with ideas derived from Wicca. Leek helped found the first two groups, namely, the Catta Coven and the Wolfa Coven.[44] A third group is the Black Forest Clan, founded by the controversial Wiccan writer Silver RavenWolf.[45] However, the Deitsch scholar David Kriebel sharply criticizes RavenWolf's writing as fakelore.[46] He says that anyone who integrates Wicca and Deitsch magic will not share in "the Pennsylvania Dutch worldview."[47] However, Kriebel's criticism goes too far. These three groups have already done good work combining Wiccan and Deitsch ideas.

Deitsch magic and Wicca have many similarities. Both take ideas from Boehme. Boehme greatly influenced Franz Hartmann, whose book *The Life and Doctrines of Jacob Boehme* (1891) is probably the most important book on Boehme in English. Hartmann helped found the occult group known as the Ordo Templi Orientis around 1900. In 1947, Gardner joined the Ordo and quickly became one of its leaders. Hence there are lines from Boehme to Wicca. Even if they are indirect and weak, they do exist.

Deitsch theology has some similarities with Wiccan theology. Both traditions have goddesses. Starhawk's creation story resembles Boehme's.[48] Both stories contain an abyss, a mirror, self-relationality, and a divine creative female. Scott Cunningham's Wiccan theology resembles the Sophianic theologies of Conrad Beissel and the Harmony Society.[49] In these theologies, a gender-neutral or androgynous deity unfolds into a divine male-female couple. The Deitsch three divine women (*idisi*) resemble the Wiccan Triple Goddess. And there are practical parallels. Moravian sacramental sex has a counterpart in the sacramental sex of the Wiccan Great Rite. The Deitsch had "sleeping preachers," who spoke from trances (perhaps recalling heathen *seidr* trances).[50] These Deitsch trance practices resemble the Wiccan rituals of "Drawing Down the Moon" and "Drawing Down the Sun." Of course, these similarities should not be pressed too far.

On the basis of all these ideas, I propose extending Deitsch magic according to what I will call the *Way of Sophia*. This way incorporates ideas from traditional Deitsch magic, old heathenry, and Wicca. It transforms them and integrate them into a new synthesis. It welcomes *brauchers* both male and female. It practices drawing down the *idisi*, enabling women to theurgically bear the weapons of the valkyries. Given the importance of signs in Boehme's work, and in magic generally, I will refer to this type of Sophianic magic as *Deitsch signcraft*. As a future-oriented practice, Deitsch signcraft has little interest in the agrarian spells from the old Deitsch grimoires. It adapts ideas from contemporary witchcraft. Yet Deitsch magic includes more than spells. While the Deitsch did not use the Wiccan wheel of the year, they used annual astrological cycles and were intimately attuned to the seasons.[51] Jayme Moye describes a magical path (close to green witchcraft) based on mindful experience of the changing seasons.[52] This path fits well into Deitsch signcraft. The Deitsch were expert herbalists. Deitsch signcraft expands this herbalism to include all physiologically active molecules. You can cast spells on your body by taking curcumin and cannabis, or by taking ibuprofen and mirtazapine.

Boehme was regarded by G. W. F. Hegel as the first German philosopher. His work inspired the German idealists, who were known as rationalists. They built great metaphysical systems with extremely abstract concepts. The early Deitsch distinguished themselves through their focus on Sophia as Divine Wisdom. Since Sophia inspires philosophy, Deitsch signcraft will base itself on a systematic metaphysics. Deitsch magicians will strive to work out the philosophical foundations of signcraft. Women are not excluded from rationality; they can "do" philosophy as well as men. After all, like Isis and Athena, Sophia is a goddess. Lance Gharavi shows how failure to engage with philosophy transforms apparently feminist witchcraft into a merely capitalist commodity.[53] As a philosophical movement, Deitsch signcraft will stress shared norms of truth. It will work against those post-truth cultures that lead to conspirituality, authoritarianism, and fascism.

Boehme influenced F. W. J. Schelling, who influenced Charles Sanders Peirce. Peirce has an evolutionary cosmology. Following Boehme, his cosmology begins with the self-negation of nothingness. This self-negation produces an explosion of creative energy, which self-organizes into an infinity of possible worlds. From Peirce a direct line runs to David Lewis, who worked out the logic of possible worlds. Alternative versions of ourselves dwell in other worlds. Lewis says we can vicariously (that is, mentally) enter into other worlds by simulating our counterparts in those worlds. We can enter other worlds through ritual. Diane Stein and Kathryn Rountree describe ways that feminist witches carry out world-building and self-building by entering other worlds in their rituals.[54] Deitsch signcraft incorporates these ideas into a philosophical theory of magic.

Following the way of Sophia, Deitsch magic can help to create a better future cultural world. It will be a post-Christian world. It will be a new form of Germanic paganism, distinct from ethnic paganisms like Ásatrú. It will bring Wiccan motifs and Deitsch motifs together into a new synthesis. It will use ideas from Boehme and his philosophical descendants, both German and American, to fit these motifs into a rational framework. It will provide clear meanings for its concepts and will justify them using logical arguments. It will strive for shared norms of truth and will avoid the post-truth elements of magical cultures that tend toward fascism. It will use its philosophical tools to build a pagan ethics that strives for progressive values and social justice.

NOTES

1. Boehme, *Forty Questions on the Soul.*
2. Boehme, *Mysterium Pansophicum*; and Boehme, *Six Mystical Points.*
3. Boehme, *Six Mystical Points*, 5.19.
4. Boehme, *Aurora*, 16.126, 20.39, 21.4; Boehme, *Three Principles*, 8.12, 8.22.
5. Hessayon, "Jacob Boehme."
6. Everham, "The Recovery of the Feminine."
7. Bach, *Voices of the Turtledoves*, ch. 5.
8. Kring, "Religious Symbols," 59.
9. Atwood, "Sleeping in the Arms of Christ"; Fogleman, "Jesus Is Female."
10. Fogel, *Beliefs and Superstitions*, 8–17.
11. Buckwalter and Baten, "Valkyries."
12. Price et al., "Viking Warrior Women?"
13. Tommasi, "Matres/Matronae."
14. Magnus, *Egyptian Secrets*, 9, 12, 110.
15. Donmoyer, *Powwowing in Pennsylvania*, 293.
16. Fogel, *Beliefs and Superstitions*, #906, 908, 921, 923, 924.
17. The spells from Fogel, *Beliefs and Superstitions*, are as follows: negative magical powers #399, 423, 459; making soap #644; vinegar barrels #927, 928; cutting hair #84; hens and eggs #889, 900; three women #906, 908, 921, 923, 924; throw blankets #957; shake fruit trees #1047, 1063, 1067, 1068.
18. Donmoyer, *Powwowing in Pennsylvania*, 276–78.
19. Fogel, *Beliefs and Superstitions*, #1831.
20. Fogel, *Beliefs and Superstitions*, #482, 486, 1376, 1378.
21. Donmoyer, *Powwowing in Pennsylvania*, 276.
22. Hohman, *Long Lost Friend*; Magnus, *Egyptian Secrets*; Dr. Helfenstein, *Secrets of Sympathy*, in Donmoyer, *Powwowing in Pennsylvania*, 284–306.
23. Donmoyer, *Powwowing in Pennsylvania*, 186.
24. Kriebel, *Powwowing among the Pennsylvania Dutch*, 31.
25. Donmoyer, *Powwowing in Pennsylvania*, 50–57.
26. Donmoyer, *Powwowing in Pennsylvania*, ch. 6.
27. Hoffman, "Folk-Lore."
28. Fogel, *Beliefs and Superstitions*, #625–654; Donmoyer, *Powwowing in Pennsylvania*, ch. 6.
29. "Mountain Mary."
30. Mitchell, "Warlocks, Valkyries, and Varlets."
31. Davies, "Cunning-Folk"; Hutton, "Witchcraft and Modernity."
32. Purkiss, "Getting It Wrong."
33. Greenwood, "Feminist Witchcraft."
34. Magliocco, "Witchcraft as Political Resistance."
35. Rountree, "Goddess Pilgrims," 486.
36. Magliocco, "Witchcraft as Political Resistance."

37 Ellis Davidson, *Gods and Myths*.
38 Self, "The Valkyrie's Gender."
39 Fogel, *Beliefs and Superstitions*, #24.
40 Kriebel, *Powwowing among the Pennsylvania Dutch*, ch. 1.
41 Bilardi, *The Red Church*.
42 Schreiwer, *First Book of Urglaawe Myths*.
43 Stavish and Yoder, *Pietism*.
44 Hoke, *Coven of the Catta*; Nightwind, "Faith-Healing."
45 RavenWolf, *HexCraft* and *Silver's Spells*.
46 Kriebel, *Powwowing among the Pennsylvania Dutch*, 145–46, 151, 216–20.
47 Kriebel, *Powwowing among the Pennsylvania Dutch*, 217.
48 Starhawk, *Spiral Dance*, 41.
49 Cunningham, *Wicca*, 123.
50 Hiller, "The Sleeping Preachers."
51 Winkler, "Pennsylvania German Astrology" series. *Pennsylvania Folklife* covered Winkler's topic across sixteen issues (21.3–28.2) from 1972 to 1979.
52 Moye, "How Studying Witchcraft Changed."
53 Gharavi, "Hex and the City."
54 Stein, *Casting the Circle*, 7; Rountree, "How Magic Works."

BIBLIOGRAPHY

Atwood, Craig. "Sleeping in the Arms of Christ: Sanctifying Sexuality in the Eighteenth-Century Moravian Church." *Journal of the History of Sexuality* 8, no. 1 (1997): 25–51.

Bach, Jeff. *Voices of the Turtledoves: The Sacred World of Ephrata*. University Park: Pennsylvania State University Press, 2005.

Bilardi, C. *The Red Church, or The Art of Pennsylvania German Braucherei*. Los Angeles: Pendraig Publishing, 2009.

Boehme, Jacob. *The Aurora*. Translated by John Sparrow. London: John M. Watkins, 1960.

Boehme, Jacob. *The Forty Questions on the Soul*. Translated by John Sparrow. Whitefish, MT: Kessinger Publishing, 1992.

Boehme, Jacob. *Mysterium Pansophicum*. Translated by John Rolleston Earle. New York: Knopf, 1920.

Boehme, Jacob. *A Short Explanation of Six Mystical Points*. Translated by John Rolleston Earle. New York: Knopf, 1920.

Boehme, Jacob. *The Three Principles of Divine Essence*. Translated by John Sparrow. Detroit: Kraus House, 2016.

Buckwalter, Laura, and Joerg Baten. "Valkyries: Was Gender Equality High in the Scandinavian Periphery since Viking Times? Evidence from Enamel Hypoplasia and Height Ratios." *Economics and Human Biology* 34 (2019): 181–93.

Cunningham, Scott. *Wicca: A Guide for the Solitary Practitioner.* St. Paul, MN: Llewellyn Publications, 2004.

Davies, Owen. "Cunning-Folk in England and Wales during the Eighteenth and Nineteenth Centuries." *Rural History* 8, no. 1 (2009): 91–107.

Donmoyer, Patrick. *Powwowing in Pennsylvania: Braucherei and the Ritual of Everyday Life.* Morgantown, PA: Masthof Press, 2017.

Ellis Davidson, Hilda. *Gods and Myths of Northern Europe.* New York: Penguin, 1964.

Everham, Wendy. "The Recovery of the Feminine in an Early American Pietist Community: The Interpretive Challenge of the Theology of Conrad Beissel." *Pennsylvania Folklife* 39, no. 2 (1989): 50–56.

Fogel, Edwin. *Beliefs and Superstitions of the Pennsylvania Germans.* Philadelphia: American Germanica Press, 1915.

Fogleman, Aaron. "Jesus Is Female: The Moravian Challenge in the German Communities of British North America." *William and Mary Quarterly* 60, no. 2 (2003): 295–332.

Gharavi, Lance. "*Hex and the City*: Spells for Late Capitalism." PAJ: *A Journal of Performance and Art* 28, no. 3 (2006): 114–23.

Greenwood, Susan. "Feminist Witchcraft: A Transformatory Politics." In *Practicing Feminism: Identity, Difference, Power*, edited by N. Charles and F. Hughes-Freeland, 109–34. New York: Routledge, 1996.

Hessayon, Ariel. "Jacob Boehme and the Early Quakers." *Journal of the Friends Historical Society* 60, no. 3 (2005): 191–223.

Hiller, Harry. "The Sleeping Preachers: An Historical Study of the Role of Charisma in Amish Society." *Pennsylvania Folklife* 18, no. 2 (1968): 19–31.

Hoffman, W. "Folk-Lore of the Pennsylvania Germans III." *Journal of American Folklore* 2, no. 6 (1889): 191–202.

Hohman, John. *The Long Lost Friend.* 1820. University Park: Pennsylvania State University Press, 2008.

Hoke, Gary. *Coven of the Catta: Elders and History; Unique Ritual Practices and Spells.* N.p.: Lulu.com, 2011.

Hutton, Ronald. "Witchcraft and Modernity." In *Writing Witch-Hunt Histories*, edited by M. Nenonen and R. Toivo, 191–211. New York: Brill, 2013.

Kriebel, David. *Powwowing among the Pennsylvania Dutch.* University Park: Pennsylvania State University Press, 2007.

Kring, Hilda. "Religious Symbols in a Symbol-less Society." *Pennsylvania Folklife* 33, no. 2 (1984): 57–60. https://digitalcommons.ursinus.edu/pafolklifemag/103/.

Magliocco, Sabina. "Witchcraft as Political Resistance." *Nova Religio* 23, no. 4 (2020): 43–68.

Magnus, Albertus [pseud.]. *Egyptian Secrets: White and Black Art for Man and Beast.* Chicago: De Laurence, 1919. https://archive.org/details/albertus-magnus-egyptian-secrets-of-white-and-black-art-for-man-and-beast/page/1/mode/2up.

Mitchell, Stephen. "Warlocks, Valkyries, and Varlets: A Prolegomenon to the Study of North Sea Witchcraft Terminology." *Cosmos* 17 (2001): 59–81.

"Mountain Mary: Contemporary Visions of the Sainted Healer." Pennsylvania German Cultural Heritage Center. Accessed August 3, 2022. https://www.pagerman.org/heritage-center-collections-highlights/mountain-mary/.

Moye, Jayme. "How Studying Witchcraft Changed My Relationship with the Outdoors." *Outside*, October 31, 2021. https://www.outsideonline.com/outdoor-adventure/snow-sports/witch-witchcraft-wicca-nature/.

Nightwind, Thorn. "Faith-Healing, Pow-Wow and Hexerei in Pennsylvania." Wolfa Coven, March 13, 2021. https://covenofthewolfa.wordpress.com/2021/03/13/faith-healing-pow-wow-witchcraft-in-pennsylvania/.

Price, Neil, Charlotte Hedenstierna-Jonson, Torun Zachrisson, Anna Kjellström, Jan Storå, Torsten Günther, Verónica Sobrado, Mattias Jakobsson, and Anders Götherström. "Viking Warrior Women? Reassessing Birka Chamber Grave Bj.581." *Antiquity* 93, no. 367 (2019): 181–98. https://doi.org/10.15184/aqy.2018.258.

Purkiss, Diane. "Getting It Wrong: The Problems with Reinventing the Past." *Pomegranate* 21, no. 2 (2019): 256–77.

RavenWolf, Silver. *HexCraft: Dutch Country Magick*. Woodbury, MN: Llewellyn, 1997.

RavenWolf, Silver. *Silver's Spells: Magick for Love, Protection, and Abundance*. Woodbury, MN: Llewellyn, 2018.

Rountree, Kathryn. "Goddess Pilgrims as Tourists: Inscribing the Body through Sacred Travel." *Sociology of Religion* 63, no. 4 (2002): 475–96.

Rountree, Kathryn. "How Magic Works: New Zealand Feminist Witches' Theories of Ritual Action." *Anthropology of Consciousness* 13, no. 1 (2002): 42–59.

Schreiwer, Robert. *The First Book of Urglaawe Myths*. Bristol, PA: Deitscherei.com, 2014.

Self, Kathleen. "The Valkyrie's Gender: Old Norse Shield-Maidens and Valkyries as a Third Gender." *Feminist Formations* 26, no. 1 (2014): 143–77.

Starhawk. *The Spiral Dance: A Rebirth of the Ancient Religion of the Great Goddess*. New York: HarperCollins, 1979.

Stavish, Mark, and Russell Yoder. *Pietism, Pow-Wow, and the Magical Revival*. Self-published, CreateSpace, 2018.

Stein, Diane. *Casting the Circle: A Women's Book of Ritual*. Freedom, CA: Crossing Press, 1990.

Tommasi, Chiara. "Matres/Matronae." In *The Encyclopedia of Ancient History*, edited by A. Erskine, D. Hollander, and A. Papaconstantinou. New York: John Wiley, 2021.

Winkler, Louis. "Series on Pennsylvania German Astrology in Sixteen Parts." *Pennsylvania Folklife* 21, no. 3 (1972)–28, no. 2 (1979). https://digitalcommons.ursinus.edu/pafolklifemag/index.5.html.

Ten · AYÇA KURTOĞLU

"We Are Here with Our Rebellious Joy": Witches and Witchcraft in Turkey

"Freedom for Human, Animal, Nature and the Earth"
"Femicide Is Not Coincidence. It Is POLITICAL"
"I March for My Mother's Dreams That You Have Stolen"
"Respect Our Existence or Respect Our Resistance"
"The Female Bird Unmakes the Family, My Dear"

The slogans above are from the nineteenth night march held on International Women's Day (March 8) in Istanbul in 2022.[1] The feminist night marches were inaugurated in 2003 to voice feminist demands and to show that women will not abandon the streets at night.[2] Voicing women's anti-war (in Iraq) stance was the main theme of the first night march. As the first night march attracted nonfeminists from other civil organizations, the main theme of the march was adjusted to "feminist rebel" in 2004.[3]

Regarding the subject of this study, another turning point for the night marches was the year 2013—for two reasons. First, the Gezi Park protests in Istanbul in May 2013, which attracted a wide range of diverse and oppositional people, spread across Turkey in a short time span before they finally calmed down in autumn of that year. The previously tolerated March 8 feminist night marches were subsequently banned by the Ministry of Interior after 2013. Since then, the march has taken place despite barricades, pepper gas, and arrests. Some women were even charged with jumping to the rhythm of the slogans, such as "Jump! Jump! One not jumping is Tayyip [the President]."[4] Second, Kampüs Cadıları (Campus Witches), a network of feminist university students and prominent participants in the night marches since 2014, came to life during and in the aftermath of the Gezi Park movement. The movement was a reaction to a continuum of violence and cultivated cosmopolitan/universal norms "in defense of rights and freedoms by politicizing previously apolitical ordinary citizens. . . . [It] also deepened and broaden[ed] the struggle for democratization using a language that resonate[d] all over the world."[5]

Feminists marching at night were challenging and resisting at least five things: (1) the international destructive masculinist orders as seen in anti-war or pro-environment stances; (2) the Law on Demonstrations and Marches (Art. 7), which states that a march can begin after sunrise;[6] (3) the government's anxiety about oppositional collective action as reflected in the Ministry's ban on demonstrations around Taksim Square, the scene of the Bloody May Day of 1977 and the Gezi Park movement;[7] (4) other civil society organizations sneaking into the feminist agenda; and (5) traditional values that assign women to the private sphere and conservative social codes that consider cheer to be a sign of being a bad girl/woman. Campus Witches resist these things both by creatively demonizing themselves and by maintaining the Gezi Park spirit.

Campus Witches are a distinct group within the feminist movement in Turkey because they are the first and only group to fully identify with witches. Although their recent formation is not surprising, given the absence of witch hunts in Turkey's history,[8] I claim in this study that their appearance as a group within the feminist movement is a product of the history of the feminist movement; of how witches, witchcraft, and witchiness are culturally and politically constructed; and of the ways in which women have been incorporating witchcraft and witch-ness in a broader sense into their everyday practices. Accordingly, this study is divided into two parts. The first part narrates the development from spellcasting to Campus Witches. The second part deals with how everyday practices of womanly resistance to masculine domination facilitated the adoption of witch identities by young feminists.

FROM SPELLCASTING TO #IHAVEFEMINISTREBELLIONINME

In her novel the *Witches of Smyrna*, Mara Meimaridi (2015) narrates the story of an Ottoman Greek mother and her daughter.[9] They migrate from an inner Anatolian town to Smyrna, the-then-Ottoman port city on the Aegean coast of Anatolia from which they intend to migrate further, to an island of Greece at the turn of the twentieth century. On their way to Greece, the two dispossessed women remove all barriers, like thorny daily relations, financial problems, or procedural difficulties, by using their hereditary skill of spellcasting, and safely reach Greece.

Witchcraft for the two women in the novel symbolizes a means of empowerment in a world where they are structurally powerless, given their rural background, lower class, and gender. They were also rendered vulnerable under the Ottoman state in its dissolution from a traditional lifeworld to modern capitalist lifeworld divided into nation-states. In these insecure, uncertain, and conflict-ridden conditions, the two women transgress all kinds of borders and masculinist patterns of power in womanly ways. To maintain the fiction, it is possible to imagine that they functioned as healers in their hometowns and were wise enough to foresee the upcoming dissolution of the Ottoman Empire by the end of the World War I, the liberation war of Turkey (1919–23), and the establishment of a nation-state (1923), resulting in the exchange of population (1923–26) between Greece and Turkey to create "correct" citizens according to the state-sanctioned faiths adopted by these states. In Meimaridi's story, witchcraft facilitates continuous moves between ordinary and extraordinary life and provides the qualities of fluid and hybrid presence. These qualities attributed to witches enable the two women to survive the ongoing processes of change and to live in between spaces. But the questions remain: What if "all that is solid melts into air?" as expressed by Marshall Berman;[10] or, What if the sense of insecurity and uncertainty and the conflict-ridden conditions are permanent for those who are made secondary?; and, What if fluidity and hybridity become the general features of their social lives? The first question can describe spaces constructed through a masculine gaze in modernity that women carve out for themselves by their everyday resistances, and the remaining other questions can describe conditions, feelings, and manners of modernity that women experience deeper as they are formed according to male norms.

At the time when the witches of Smyrna moved to Greece, women living in the Ottoman Empire, Istanbul, were already organized and demanding civil and political rights.[11] Women applied for the establishment of a political party, namely, the Women's People Party, immediately after Turkey's foundation as a nation-state in 1923, even though women did not have political rights at the time. Their application was rejected on the ground that women's political representation was not possible according to the election law of 1909.[12] Upon the rejection of their application, the group formed an organization, named the Women's Union, in 1924, and would publish a journal, *Women's Path* (in 1925). The Women's Union complied with the limits of the law by removing the demand for equal rights from their program, but they joined the International Women's Suffrage Alliance and the International Women's Union in 1924. However, the group was integrated into government circles after the recognition of equal political rights in the 1930s, and the journal was discontinued after two years.[13]

The period between the 1930s and 1950s in Turkey's history is called radical modernity because of the reforms aimed at effecting full-scale changes in the country's political, social, and cultural systems.[14] At the beginning of this period, several legal changes were made to eliminate traditional elements and to disseminate modernity in people's political and social lives. A central component of this attempt—which included replacing tradition and myth with rationality and science, and replacing traditional institutions with legal-rational institutions—was the corpus of the Republican Laws, which are laws that cannot be removed or amended. The Law on the Abolishment of Lodges, Zawiyahs [small Islamic monasteries] and [sacramental] Tombs, and the Prohibition of Tomb Keeping and Certain Titles abolished all places run by religious orders that performed the function of modern institutions like education or health, and banned both all titles forming estate-like hierarchies, such as grandfathership, discipleship, sainthood, or emirate, and all activities performed by those people such as spellcasting or fortune-telling. The penalty for involvement in such activities was three months in prison and a fine. While women had wanted legal equality, the so-called state feminism of the 1930s to 1950s recognized equal rights in the form of uniform equality in the public and private spheres. Moreover, state intellectuals promoted their notion of a "new woman": a good mother and wife who lived for others' well-being and who served as guardian of the reforms, modernization, and Enlightenment.[15] The new woman began living in a family based on a secular, heteronormative marriage contract and was treated equally in inheritance.[16] But, according to the Turkish Civil Code of 1926, women had to renounce the following rights: equal representation in the family; individual decisions about work, contracts, and loans; and claims to property acquired during the marriage. Women obtained the right to make individual decisions about work in 1996, and the Civil Code was fully amended to grant women full equality within the family only in 2002. Familism remained the constitutional foundation of social, political, and welfare policies in Turkey since the 1960s.[17] Until the mid-1970s, this left little personal space for women beyond charity and professional organizations in the public sphere, and joyous magic-seeking or desperate spellcasting in the private sphere.[18]

The picture above started changing radically as of the mid-1970s. The Turkish Communist Party encouraged its women members to form a women's organization on the eve of the first UN World Women's Congress. Thus, the Progressive Women's Association (PWA) was founded; the PWA organized the first public celebration of International Women's Day in 1975. The PWA had 33 branches, 35 representative offices, and nearly 15,000 members; and its newspaper, *Women's Voice*, had a circulation of 30,000 when it was shut down by martial law in 1979.[19]

After the military coup in 1980, all political organizations, including those of women, were suspended, and many academics and civil servants were dismissed.[20] While the coup facilitated Turkey's sudden shift to a neoliberal economy by dissolving the opposition, women participating in liberation movements started to reflect on their experiences. As narrated in the documentary *Eylül'ün Kadın Yüzleri* [Women's faces of September] (2014), they were in youth organizations of various leftist groups and on the streets like their male friends, but they were treated as secondary in the organizations before the coup.[21] They were insulted and oppressed because of their own or their family members' political activities after the coup. Identifying common experiences and learning from feminists in the West, academic and nonacademic women mostly from leftist backgrounds revived the women's movement in the 1980s under the guise of second-wave feminism. The feminist opposition was concerned with forming women's own organizations and demanding women's rights and the politicization of the body and the home. The very first act of feminists after the military coup of 1980 was upon Turkey's ratification of the Committee on the Elimination of Discrimination against Women (CEDAW) in 1985. As the then government did not take any further action after the ratification, feminists organized a petition to demand that the government implement the CEDAW in 1986. The second act was the campaign "Solidarity Against Beating" held in 1987.[22]

In this atmosphere of the feminist revival, Flying Broom was founded in 1996. Flying Broom was the very first feminist group in Turkey that identified itself with witchcraft. Halime Güner was a member of PWA before 1980 and one of the founders of Flying Broom. When I interviewed her, she said they had a long list of things to do, mostly centered on organizing women and demanding things from the state. Maybe inspired by *Bewitched*, a woman in the group said, "A flying broom could do all these things."²³ Then the name was adopted by the entire group. Flying Broom is famous for its film festival. Hence, its witch-ness relates more to what it has been doing to fight against women's oppression and for its contributions to feminist movement that are conventionally seen in movements aimed at disrupting society.

The witch as a theme appeared for the second time when *Kitchen Witches*, a bulletin of the Socialist Feminist Collective (SFC), was published between 2008 and 2016, when the SFC was dissolved. The SFC was launched with "a two-fold aim: to develop an analysis of patriarchal capitalism, with the category of women's labor at its core, and to create a solid basis for not only socialist but all anti-systemic feminists to organize and become a 'collective political subject' pursuing their independent agenda."²⁴

Kitchen Witches never covered a concern or a sign related to witches. When finalizing the SFC, they questioned the form of their holistic policy, centralized organizing, and links to the feminist movement. They asked if a network-type organization model would be more appropriate to cover the differences in dispositions and abilities and varieties of private sphere–related positions among women as they had members across Turkey and borders; and topics like body, peace, women's works, or violence.

While *Kitchen Witches* printed its very last issue in 2014, Campus Witches was formed in the same year. Campus Witches narrated their story to Işıl Kurnaz (2016) as follows:

> When we came together as young university women, we pondered for a long time what our name would be. We looked at the history of the struggle for women's liberation and came across "witches." There is a period in the Middle Ages when women, who were midwives, doctors, pharmacists, rebellious, disobedient, resisted the male-dominated politics of the church monarchy, were burned and murdered for being "witches" or "sorcerers." "Witchcraft" is an adjective associated with disobedient women, who do not accept their taught roles as women, who rebel and are rebellious. . . .
>
> . . . [This] matched exactly with what we wanted to do on campus. We said we're going to be witches and we decided to call ourselves as Campus Witches. Our concern is not to make witchcraft sympathetic but to restore it to its true meaning. Women who resist male domination continue to live on in every age. We are the grandchildren of the witches they couldn't burn.²⁵

In short, young women wanted to form a feminist group, so they reviewed the literature, just as they had learned to do in gender courses or women studies programs at their universities. They were searching for something like Flying Broom or *Kitchen Witches*. They came across Silvia Federici's, Margaret Atwood's, and others' works.[26] They also navigated through libraries and linked themselves with feminists of the world.

Campus Witches pursue a transversal politics.[27] They organize locally and online without leadership, and they are locally and transnationally networked. Their culture is cosmopolitan. For instance, Campus Witches, inspired by Atwood's *Handmaid's Tale* and by witches in Poland, dressed in red to protest against femicides shortly after Turkey announced its withdrawal from the Istanbul Convention in 2021. Their activism is well reflected in the hashtag #IHaveFeministRebellionInMe developed in 2022.

ALL THAT WE HOPE FOR HELP: FORTUNE-TELLING, MAGIC, ETC.

Witches and witchcraft do not appear only in activism but also among women and in between women's interactive relationships/communications. This section focuses on interactions among women facilitating the adoption of a witch identity by other women. The title of this section is inspired by a podcast session, called "Modern Witches," run by two young feminist women in their thirties.[28] In this podcast, the women talk about the tools they hope to use will help, including astrology, tarot card reading, or coffee cup reading. As the dialogue goes on, they accept that they not only hope for the help of those tools but also believe in some of them, like the evil eye. One of the women talks about how she envied her friend's gorgeous dress during a ball, and then her friend had an unexpected accident with her dress. Hence, her evil eye messed up her friend's dress.

I would like to interpret the tools that the women hope to use will help as themes in the repertoire of everyday resistance. Resistance to conditions where women are exploited, marginalized, rendered powerless, or subjected to various types of violence. As the magical tools require the presence of at least two people in communication, I argue a third sight appears between them, a new way of seeing things through the exchange of ideas and feelings between two people. John Berger claims that women as subordinates of men have two ways of seeing: their own and that of the dominant viewer, namely men.[29] Through interaction over a coffee cup, something is made meaningful, shared, and acted upon, but the meaning can be different for each of the parties in the interaction. This can also be thought of as a third space or a space where meanings and symbols of culture have no primordial unity or fixity but are hybrid, ambivalent, temporal, creating a capacity for progression of ideas and critical reflection.[30]

In 2007, I conducted semistructured interviews on coffee cup reading with fifteen women between the ages of thirty and fifty who worked in professional occupations (engineers, social workers, and accountants). Three of the fifteen were also coffee cup readers. The others were getting their coffee cups read for them. When I conducted the interviews, my intention was to explore well-educated women's everyday resistance to a world that is rationally and scientifically designed and ordered by the state according to hegemonic masculinist norms.

I chose coffee cup reading for three reasons: First, drinking Turkish coffee is a significant and ceremonial part of everyday life. Each cup of coffee is individually prepared over slow heat to get froth at the top of the pot; it is served in a single espresso-sized cup with a treat and a glass of water; and it is sipped over a longish time and over a conversation. The next step, especially for women, is usually reading the coffee cup. Hence, it symbolizes deference, friendship, peace, favor, kindness, and so on. Second, it was a facilitator of the formation of public space through coffee houses.[31] Third, drinking Turkish coffee was about a commonality between a picture of my mother in my childhood memories and my feminist friends. My mother, like many other middle-class housewives of her age, rushed to finish her morning chores so that she could have Turkish coffee with a friend before noon. Almost every time, the coffee drinking was followed by a coffee cup reading session and long chats about what was in the coffee cup reading and beyond. This was also my friends' ritual, especially in the presence of a woman who could read coffee cups.

All the women I interviewed expressed three positive aspects of coffee cup reading. First, and creatively pragmatic, coffee cup reading shortens the time needed to develop friendships/networks/closeness when one is (new) in a social environment, like a workplace. This is also a way of countering the homosocial male fraternal relationships in the anonymous, ordered public sphere by creating a fluid, hybrid, and loosely ordered feminized space. Second, and creatively social, it gives one courage. It enables one to reveal things or to tell the untellable over a coffee cup reading/fortune-telling. Thus, it can take the form of either an informal counseling session or a confession. This is the aspect that Rollo May called social courage.[32] Third, as a corollary to the second, it is the diffusion of determination, strength, and hope that triggers effervescence within oneself and between the two parties, especially when the reader is a friend.[33]

The aspects mentioned above are in line with Burçak Yıldız's words in an interview with a journalist. Yıldız is educated as a public-relations professional and works as a coffee cup reader. For her, there are three types of people who go for reading: those who do not believe in it, those who need it, and those who love to be read. She says, "Many people I know say that they have never believed in fortune-telling. However, they still enjoy it because they are very excited about what the fortune-teller says. At the same time, they like the feeling of satisfaction."[34] Satisfaction in her words refers to social courage in my translation. She goes on to describe those who love to be read: "people who drink coffee and send photos to fortune-telling apps daily. What you say to them doesn't really matter.... They probably have stable lives. They need another suggestion that comes from fortune-telling."[35]

The coffee cup readers I interviewed also mentioned the same issues, but two more aspects can be added. First, they were not only coffee cup readers, they were also readers of human beings. After the reading of my coffee cup, I asked one of them, whom I did not know previously, what led her to pinpoint my emotions or personality traits. Her answer was that my posture, my communication style, and so on, said much about me. While saying the same thing, Burçak refers to individuals' energy space. This is what Pierre Bourdieu calls habitus.[36] The second can be considered magicians' power. According to Susan Greenwood, the space of rituals is seen as a space of resistance to the wider rational culture.[37] She describes this from the perspective of the magician, who has the upper hand in the ritual. However, this is not Burçak's view: "The party with authority is the one that goes to the fortune-teller because the subjects are them and their lives. In this process the fortune-teller is only a guide. The communication process takes shape according to tips from the other side.... Although the one having the upper hand looks like the fortune-teller from the outside, the person who goes to the fortune-teller is the one managing the process."[38] In a male-dominated society where gender is based on a two-sex model and socio-political life is organized around the public-private divide, women in the public sphere are on alien terrain and are often socialized into roles as observing beings in both spheres. In my relationship with the coffee cup reader, she was the one with two sights: her way of seeing me and how she was seen by me. I was the one who had only one sight: the sight of reason. Looking back, I was in the position to initiate the development of a third sight, but I did not. Inspired by my personal conversations with two healers and an in-depth interview with another healer, I can argue that the interaction between the parties in coffee cup reading can open the formation of a third space. A space in which a coffee cup reader guides and encourages the other party, a person who could come from a different class and personal background. The other party discloses their emotional, ideational, and material lives for the reader's consumption. Even if it happens temporarily, the reader mentally fixes insecurities or uncertainties. The other party can become a kind of explorer, traveling to the reader's territories. On the one hand, this relationship conforms to the neoliberal conception of the individual who "valorizes autonomy and the ethic of self-interest and personal responsibility."[39] On the other hand, there is a potential for collective action, especially when the parties are friends or have similar concerns. However, the answer to the question of where the direction of the action can be is "wherever the solidarity goes," depending on their creativities in meeting each other's needs.

One direction can be toward spellcasting. In everyday life, a spell is used to meet individual needs and desires such as by canceling sorcery, binding or generating a person's sexual power, keeping children alive, or finding lost objects.[40] According to Ayhan Kerem Çakın, sorcery/spellcasting appears most often in divorce lawsuits.[41] In such cases, the woman casting a spell is considered at fault; the husband's violence and the wife's spell are counted as equal faults; and sorcery is considered sufficient reason for divorce. However, these decisions are not made on the grounds of the violation of the Republican Laws, but as a sign of a broken bond of trust, an indicator of the shaken foundation of the marriage union. Equally interesting, when sued, those who make money from magic, sorcery, or by casting spells are punished not on the grounds of the violation of the Republican Laws but on the grounds of aggravated fraud. Moreover, people who advertise themselves as magicians or the like are not prosecuted. I interpret this as a sign that witchcraft is not viewed politically by the legal authorities as long as it is confined to the private sphere; and it is tolerated as long as it is used as a solution to private problems. This is in accordance with the familism and the neoliberal policies as well as with the treatment of witches during trials.[42] This is why feminists demonstrating at night have been barricaded, sprayed with pepper gas, and even charged for jumping to the rhythm of the slogans.

CONCLUSION

In the absence of witch hunts in the history of Turkey, the phenomena relating to the witch, witchcraft, and witch hunt are popularly associated with the West. Hence, these words are often used metaphorically. Yet, feminists in the past twenty years have increasingly adopted witch-related identities. Rather than seeing their appearance as a group in the feminist movement as a product of media images and globalization, this study has tried to show that the presence of witches in the feminist movement is a product of the history of the movement itself as well as of how witches, witchcraft, and witch-ness are culturally and politically constructed and the ways in which women have been incorporating witchcraft and witchness in a broader sense in their everyday practices. While dealing with insecure, uncertain, and conflict-ridden conditions in a masculinist order, women interacting with each other through activities that fall outside of the dominant order—such as casting an evil eye, spellcasting, witch crafting, tarot, or coffee cup reading—can give rise to a hybrid and fluid third sight (depending, of course, on the subordinated subjects in interaction and their relations). This can also give rise to creative empowerment and solidarity among the participants in these practices. This may be why Campus Witches, the very first feminists who fully adopted the witch identity, remind each other: When you are scared, remember that you are a witch.

NOTES

1. Hamsici, "8 Mart Yürüyüşü."
2. Büyükgöze, "Feminist Gece Yürüyüşü."
3. Büyükgöze, "Feminist Gece Yürüyüşü."
4. Feministgeceyuruyusu, "Hepimiz Oradaydık."
5. Arat, "Violence, Resistance, and Gezi Park."
6. Law on Demonstrations and Marches, October 8, 1983.
7. Baykan and Hatuka, "Politics and Culture in the Making of Public Space"; Göle, "Gezi—Anatomy of a Public Square Movement."
8. Cohn, *Europe's Inner Demons*, 253.
9. Meimaridi, *İzmir Büyücüleri*.
10. Berman, *All That Is Solid Melts into Air*.
11. Çakır, *Osmanlı Kadın Hareketi*.
12. Zihnioğlu, *Kadınsız İnkılap*, 147.
13. Zihnioğlu, *Kadınsız İnkılap*, 147.

14 Tekeli, "Kent Tarihi Yazımı Konusunda Yeni Bir Paradigma Önerisi," 156.
15 Durakbaşa, "Kemalism as Identity Politics in Turkey," 142.
16 Arat, "Women's Rights and Islam in Turkish Politics."
17 Buğra, *Kapitalizm, Yoksulluk ve Türkiye'de Sosyal Politika*.
18 Kandiyoti, "End of Empire," 43; Ecevit, "Women's Rights, Women's Organizations, and the State."
19 Pervan, *İlerici Kadınlar Derneği*, 528.
20 Özcan, "Neoliberalism, National Security."
21 Altunç, *Eylül'ün Kadın Yüzleri* [Women's faces of September].
22 Özdemir, "1980'ler Türkiye Feminist Hareketinde," 13–76.
23 Güner, interview by the author, January 30, 2022 (Zoom).
24 Çağatay, "Challenging Conservative Neoliberalism in Turkey."
25 Kurnaz, "'Kadının Yazısız Tarihi Bir Mücadele Tarihidir!'"
26 Federici, *Caliban and the Witch*; Atwood, *The Handmaid's Tale*.
27 Yuval-Davis, "What Is 'Transversal Politics'?"
28 Modern Cadılar, "Medet Umduğumuz Şeyler."
29 Berger, *Ways of Seeing*, 47.
30 Bhabha, *The Location of Culture*, 53–54.
31 Özkoçak, "Coffeehouses."
32 May, *The Courage to Create*, 20.
33 Durkheim, *The Elementary Forms*, 213.
34 Bitiren, "Bir Falcının Ağzından ve Bilimin Gözünden."
35 Bitiren, "Bir Falcının Ağzından ve Bilimin Gözünden."
36 Bourdieu, *Outline of a Theory of Practice*.
37 Greenwood, *Magic, Witchcraft and the Otherworld*, 2, 121.
38 Bitiren, "Bir Falcının Ağzından ve Bilimin Gözünden."
39 Wrenn and Waller, "Care and the Neoliberal Individual," 500.
40 Ordu, "Kütahya'da Büyü ve Büyü Ile Ilgili Uygulamalar," 60–130.
41 Çakın, "Türk Hukukunda Büyü."
42 Cohn, *Europe's Inner Demons*.

BIBLIOGRAPHY

Altunç, A. Ayben, dir. *Eylül'ün Kadın Yüzleri* [Women's faces of September]. Günebakan Film, 2014. Documentary.

Arat, Yeşim. "Violence, Resistance, and Gezi Park." *International Journal of Middle East Studies* 45, no. 4 (2013): 807–9. https://doi.org/10.1080/02665430903421734.

Arat, Yeşim. "Women's Rights and Islam in Turkish Politics: The Civil Code Amendment." *Middle East Journal* 64, no. 2 (2010): 235–51. https://doi.org/10.3751/64.2.14.

Atwood, Margaret. *The Handmaid's Tale*. London: Vintage, 2016 [1986].

Baykan, Ayşegül, and Tali Hatuka. "Politics and Culture in the Making of Public Space: Taksim Square, 1 May 1977 Istanbul." *Planning Perspectives* 25, no. 1 (2010): 49–68. https://doi.org/10.1080/02665430903421734.

Berger, John. *Ways of Seeing*. London: Penguin, 1971.

Berman, Marshall. *All That Is Solid Melts into Air: The Experience of Modernity*. London: Verso, 1982.

Bhabha, Homi K. *The Location of Culture*. London: Routledge, 1994.

Bitiren, Gökhan. "Bir Falcının Ağzından ve Bilimin Gözünden: Fal Nedir? Kişi Üzerindeki Etkisi Nedir?" *Listelist*, July 31, 2020. https://listelist.com/fal-nedir-gercek-midir/.

Bourdieu, Pierre. *Outline of a Theory of Practice*. Translated by Richard Nice. Cambridge, UK: Cambridge University Press, 1977.

Buğra, Ayşe. *Kapitalizm, Yoksulluk ve Türkiye'de Sosyal Politika*. Istanbul: İletişim Yayınları, 2008. https://archive.org/details/ayse-bugra-kapitalizm-yoksulluk-ve-turkiyede-sosyal-politika/mode/2up.

Büyükgöze, Saime. "Feminist Gece Yürüyüşü." *Feminist Bellek*, January 15, 2021. https://feministbellek.org/feminist-gece-yuruyusu/.

Çağatay, Selin. "Challenging Conservative Neoliberalism in Turkey: The Socialist Feminist Collective." *Sosyalist Feminist Kolektif*, May 24, 2014. http://www.sosyalistfeministkolektif.org/english/challenging-conservative-neoliberalism-in-turkey-the-socialist-feminist-collective/.

Çakın, Ayhan Kerem. "Türk Hukukunda Büyü." *Hukuki Haber*, May 6, 2019. https://www.hukukihaber.net/turk-hukukunda-buyu-makale,6697.html.

Çakır, Serpil. *Osmanlı Kadın Hareketi*. Istanbul: Metis Yayınevi, 1996.

Cohn, Norman. *Europe's Inner Demons: An Enquiry Inspired by the Great Witch-Hunt*. Brighton: Sussex University Press, 1975.

Durakbaşa, Ayşe. "Kemalism as Identity Politics in Turkey." In *Deconstructing Images of "the Turkish Woman,"* edited by Zehra F. Kabasakal Arat, 39–156. New York: St. Martin's Press, 1998.

Durkheim, Emile. *The Elementary Forms of Religious Life*. Translated by Karen E. Fields. New York: The Free Press, 1995 [1912].

Ecevit, Yıldız. "Women's Rights, Women's Organizations, and the State." In *Human Rights in Turkey*, edited by Zehra F. Kabasakal Arat, 187–201. Philadelphia: University of Pennsylvania Press, 2007.

Federici, Silvia. *Caliban and the Witch: Women, the Body and Primitive Accumulation*. New York: Autonomedia, 2004.

Feministgeceyuruyusu (@<8 MART FEMINIST GECE YÜRÜYÜŞÜ >). "Hepimiz Oradaydık." Instagram, March 21, 2021. https://www.instagram.com/p/CMSDdLmg0yE/.

Göle, Nilüfer. "Gezi—Anatomy of a Public Square Movement." *Insight Turkey* 15, no. 3 (2013): 7–14. https://www.insightturkey.com/commentaries/gezi-anatomy-of-a-public-square-movement.

Greenwood, Susan. *Magic, Witchcraft and the Otherworld: An Anthropology*. London: Routledge, 2020.

Hamsici, Mahmut. "8 Mart Yürüyüşü: Polisin Engellemesine Rağmen Kadınlar Cihangir'de Bir Araya Geldi." BBC News Türkçe, March 9, 2022. https://www.bbc.com/turkce/haberler-turkiye-60669033.

Kandiyoti, Deniz. "End of Empire: Islam, Nationalism, and Women in Turkey." In *Women, Islam, and the State*, edited by Deniz Kandiyoti, 22–47. Philadelphia: Temple University Press, 1991.

Kurnaz, Işıl. "Kadının Yazısız Tarihi Bir Mücadele Tarihidir!" *Amargi: Feminist Dergi*, April 16, 2016. http://www.amargidergi.com/yeni/?tag=soylesi/

Law on Demonstrations and Marches. T. C. *Resmî Gazete* [Official gazette of the Republic of Turkey], No. 18185 (October 8, 1983), 1–10. https://www.resmigazete.gov.tr/arsiv/18185.pdf.

May, Rollo. *The Courage to Create*. New York: Bantam, 1985.

Meimaridi, Mara. *İzmir Büyücüleri [Witches of Smyrna]*. Translated by Şebnem Aslan Christakopoulos. Istanbul: Literatür Yayıncılık, 2015.

Modern Cadılar. "Medet Umduğumuz Şeyler." Listen Notes (podcasts), February 2, 2020. https://www.listennotes.com/podcasts/modern-cad%C4%B1lar/medet-umdu%C4%9Fumuz-%C5%9Feyler-niow-aBHC14/.

Ordu, Bilal. "Kütahya'da Büyü ve Büyü Ile Ilgili Uygulamalar." Master's thesis, Kütahya Dumlupınar University, 2020.

Özcan, Gülden. "Neoliberalism, National Security and Academic Knowledge Production in Turkey." In *The University and Social Justice: Struggles across the Globe*, edited by Aziz Choudry and Salim Vally, 60–77. London: Pluto Press, 2020.

Özdemir, Esen. "1980'ler Türkiye Feminist Hareketinde Örgütlenme Tartışmalarına Karşılaştırmalı Bir Bakış: Feminist ve Kaktüs Dergi Örnekleri." Master's thesis, Yıldız Technical University, 2020.

Özkoçak, Selma Akyazici. "Coffeehouses: Rethinking the Public and Private in Early Modern Istanbul." *Journal of Urban History* 33, no. 6 (2007): 965–86. https://doi.org/10.1177/0096144207304018,

Pervan, Muazzez. *İlerici Kadınlar Derneği (1975–1980): Kırmızı Çatkılı Kadınlar'ın Tarihi*. Ankara: Tarih Vakfı Yurt Yayınları, 2013.

Tekeli, İlhan. "Kent Tarihi Yazımı Konusunda Yeni Bir Paradigma Önerisi." In *Özcan Altaban'a Armağan: Cumhuriyet'in Ankara'sı*, edited by Tansı Şenyapılı, 2–21. Ankara: ODTÜ Yayıncılık, 2005.

Wrenn, Mary V., and William Waller. "Care and the Neoliberal Individual." *Journal of Economic Issues* 51, no. 2 (2017): 495–502. https://doi.org/10.1080/00213624.2017.1321438.

Yuval-Davis, Nira. "What Is 'Transversal Politics'?" *Soundings* 12 (1999): 88–93.

Zihnioğlu, Yaprak. *Kadınsız İnkılap: Nezihe Muhiddin, Kadınlar Halk Fırkası, Kadın Birliği*. Istanbul: Metis Yayınevi, 2003.

Eleven · MORENA TARTARI

Fortune-Telling, Women's Friendship, and Divination Commodification in Contemporary Italy

SITUATING THE STUDY

This chapter explores from a sociological perspective the practice of fortune-telling among female friends in contemporary Italy. Divination and its specific practices express the need for social order in a society located in a particular place and time.[1] However, few contributions address fortune-telling, intersectional issues, and everyday life in contemporary Western and European societies.[2] Kris Kissman explores women's friendship circles and divination practices in Iceland and highlights the function of divination to reproduce traditional gender roles and bonds with the family, but she also points out the function of social support that such practices offer to those women.[3] Tarot reading is even seen as a technology of care and a device that supports female self-care, awareness, and empowerment against patriarchal structures and expectations.[4] In Italy, the study of divination practices in domestic spaces and within the intimate sphere of friendship is mostly neglected. The attention is more on the commodification of such practices.[5]

This chapter addresses these uncommodified informal practices. My study involves six white Italian women who were born between the 1960s and the 1970s and who have practiced fortune-telling (through tarot and playing cards) and some forms of propitiatory witchcraft and protection rituals for about forty years.[6] They practice fortune-telling during their free time, and earn no significant income from this activity.

These practices are indigenous to Italy, as the origin of tarot cards is located in Italy in the fifteenth century.[7] However, recently, new practices and products from non-Italian traditions (e.g., channeling, meditation, investigation of past lives) have been introduced to the participants' experiences. These are often commodified and costly experiences with professionals who are outsiders to the friendship circle. As the literature suggests,[8] in these emergent commercial activities, the boundary between esoteric and holistic practices (centered on psychophysical well-being) is less and less traceable. The individualized well-being of the clients is at the center of these emergent practices and is achieved through the creation of new needs for these women who become customers of the individualized service that substitutes for their "older" informal and friendship networks. Participants are divided into those who view the introduction of these new practices with skepticism and those who welcome them with enthusiasm.

While expanding the scope of feminist knowledge into underinvestigated practices of divination, this chapter is engaged with and contributes to the growing literature on patriarchy, women's (self-)care practices, and the commodification of intimacies in the Global North, with attention on the role of global factors.[9] The challenge is to investigate how these new and old practices are affected by patriarchal structures of oppression and knowledge, and how these women negotiate with or resist the dominant discourse that rules gender roles and relations.

FRAMING THE STUDY

This research study is inspired by the feminist sociology of Dorothy Smith and utilizes biographical interviews and ethnographic accounts collected during participant observation.[10]

Participants belong to the middle class and upper middle class and have different levels of education. Two of them are married but in a condition of de facto separation, and the other women are single. Two of them are professionals; the others are unemployed or with precarious jobs. They live in a rural area of the northeast part of Italy, where there is a low rate of immigration and economic development; there are few possibilities for women to study and work outside of the home. People from this area emphasize traditional gender roles and relations; the presence of the Catholic religion is prevalent, and there has been a shift toward conservative political parties during the last twenty years. The women are in reciprocal connection with one another and have been sharing both friendship and esoteric practices for two decades of their adulthood.

The biographical accounts collected describe how these women began practicing, how their identities as fortune-tellers—that is, *cartomancers*[11]—and their trajectories as women were constructed in interaction with their clients (i.e., *querents*, who are mainly friends, relatives, friends of friends and, rarely, relatives, neighbors, or colleagues), the devices of divination, and the sociocultural and economic-political frames from the 1980s to the present.

Often these women are both "clients" and "practitioners," engaging in a circle of mutual exchange and care for each other. They use mainly tarot and local playing cards to answer clients' questions concerning love-related problems, work and money-related issues, and health issues. Each consultation can last from thirty minutes to hours and aims to describe the current life situation of the client, the future evolution in specific fields, and/or to answer specific questions. Clients are Italian, white, middle-class, middle-aged women with different educational backgrounds.

My participation in this study is multipositional because I acted as a practitioner and as a querent in many situations, participating in hundreds of sessions for about thirty-five years. This has allowed me to collect autoethnographic accounts and accumulate a deep knowledge of the practice and social relations and interactions involved in it. My aim as a researcher is not to legitimate the practice in the public sphere but to highlight the social relations and cultural processes entailed in such practice.

HOW TO BECOME A FORTUNE-TELLER

The first element that emerged from the analysis concerns the relationship between these women and the societal expectations of their gender roles and relations. These societal expectations shape the women's personal needs and their clients' needs for occult practices to direct the uncertainty of their futures toward the affirmation of a romantic heterosexual engagement and marriage. After all, they act in a patriarchal social context characterized by the marginalization of women's employment, which valorizes traditional gender roles and relations.

In this section, I explore how the patriarchal institutions' discourse on gender roles has been elaborated and incorporated differently over the years. The women's accounts allow for an understanding of how they have performed their selves, identities, and gender roles and, thus, elaborated their subjectivities in response to the societal dominant discourse. Their accounts show a tension between different versions of their selves over the years.

All participants encountered divination practices for the first time during their adolescence or youth, when they felt the need to govern the uncertainty in their own lives—in particular concerning their search for romantic heterosexual love, and during the period of adolescence in which the construction and affirmation of an individualized self is perceived as particularly urgent—and as the expression of their creative potential.

Participants learned divination rites from other women who were older friends or adult relatives and started practicing by themselves, often in secret. There were no particular rites of passage to become a fortune-teller aside from progressive socialization among women[12] and the construction of a self—in interaction with experienced consultants and new and old querents—that accepts explanations about everyday life that are different from the explanations offered by the dominant discourse about the relationship between humans and gods. Therefore, tarot (or, often, playing cards used as a divinatory device) became the alternative text through which the reality could be read and ruled the everyday relations and interpretations of their experience. The official, or orthodox, discourse about reality—the taken-for-granted relationship with a Christian god shared by the community in which these women have lived their entire lives—was thus questioned by and challenged with and through an alternative interpretation since the early years of their practice. The moral boundaries set by the Catholic religion that banishes any form of divination or spiritism were continuously challenged during these women's adolescence and youth, but often without in-depth knowledge or awareness of religious prescriptions and bans. Later, during their adulthood, these boundaries became more evident and conscious but were still cornered through a system of justifications (e.g., "the practice is nonmalevolent," "fortune-telling is *white* witchery") and/or mimicry (e.g., "some practices are private and do not need to be known by all people you know").

Their first clients were girls and women—friends, relatives, and acquaintances—who always asked to know their future regarding love and marriage. Rachele—a fifty-year-old practitioner—explained that between her twenties and thirties, romantic love was for her and her clients a kind of obsession and the fundament on which a woman was judged in terms of self-affirmation, desirability, and social status. Her accounts describe processes similar to the social and cultural processes described by Eva Illouz in her analysis of the Western romantic love and marriage market and, earlier, by Julio Baroja, on the processes of socialization among women—through magic rituals—to the world of romantic relationships, mothering, and economic survival.[13]

Rachele explained that women cannot reveal publicly that they are looking for advice from a fortune-teller because this would be considered a weakness and a breach of the "reality" discourse. Furthermore, women's need to rule the uncertainty of the marriage market seems to be related to the local context. Many of the participants live in rural areas with low rates of employment and few career prospects for women. Therefore, finding a partner was and is still a matter of surviving with greater ease and fewer economic problems. However, women's inquiries about their future in the marriage market is something that concerns not only economic capital but also how romantic love is culturally emphasized and prescribed, and how traditional gender relations are seen as a form of stability for local societies that try to resist to societal and family transformations.[14]

An inquiry into the texts that ruled the participants' youth allows for an understanding of the discourse on heterosexual romantic love and marriage market that permeated their experiences and their struggles for self-affirmation and that affected their trajectories, first as students, then as professionals or employees, and then as mothers and women later in their lives.[15] Their everyday lives since childhood had been exposed to a large amount of mass media content that presented romantic love and marriage as the primary aspiration for women. Moreover, religion reinforced the representation of the woman as a mother and carer who sacrifices her work for love. Therefore, the explanations offered by Illouz on how the discourse on romantic love affects the lives of Western women allow also for an understanding of how this discourse affects their practices of scrutinizing the future.

Rachele provided insightful accounts about the practice of fortune-telling itself and how the discourse of romantic love affects it. When she was in her twenties, she used playing cards, not tarot cards, to predict the future. Playing cards—she describes a specific regional variety—gave her the freedom to experiment with the connection with the "unknown" without the complexity of the well-codified texts of the tarot: "Playing cards follow me and do not need a complex system of symbols to be interpreted. They are close to me, there is a particular connection, a natural connection, I can't explain, but it is not a codified universe like for tarot. Tarot are always perceived as dangerous by beginners. Something to be not awakened. While playing cards are something closer to your everyday life, your natural simplicity."

Yet, playing cards left her focusing on the specific theme of romantic love and marriage without connecting with more articulated dimensions of life, as tarot does. Only in her thirties did she start learning how to read tarot, as did others among her friends. One of the explanations provided is that tarot needs to be governed by the reader with greater skills because it is a more complex system of meanings and outcomes to be ruled, one that, in turn, rules the teller and the client's life. In other words, Rachele and her friends postponed to a more mature age the acceptance and the use of a codified system that could rule their lives as a discourse alternative to the dominant discourse about reality. Playing cards left her room to express her connection with the unknown and her talent as a "reader" and as an interpreter, by focusing directly on the issue of love and marriage within a system of meanings more readable and understandable and that she perceived as her own system of meanings. These ideas about the naturalness and the expression of freedom established by interrogating and interpreting the future have been often shared by other participants.

Participants explained that during the course of their lives, the prominence of the love discourse has decreased, and other themes have became more central for them as readers as well as for their "clients": health, work, friendship, and their children's future. Some of them incorporated small acts of witchcraft mainly for their own use and not for their "clients," like rituals that aim to protect them from "negativity" received by reading cards—a kind of supernatural backlash for infringing the boundary between them, the client, and the unknown entities who guide their reading practices.

However, only after their forties did there emerge a kind of awareness about the societally dominant discourse concerning love and marriage; and some of the women acted by conveying to their querents this awareness. They started showing forms of resistance and a critical attitude toward gendered societal expectations and developing forms of mutual care.

KEEP TELLING: HOW TO MANAGE STIGMA AND PROFESSIONAL LIFE

Participants' accounts show how fortune-telling has always been heavily stigmatized for both practitioners and clients. The societal discourse about what is and is not to be taken for granted labels their practices and beliefs as mental illness that—if discovered—could result in stigma and marginalization.[16]

To try to avoid stigmatization and its effects on their lives, since the beginning of their practice, participants adopted some forms of "protection": they restricted their practice to small circles of acquaintances, friends, and relatives, or to other women who had previous experiences with fortune-telling and occultism and who were inclined to keep the secret.

To keep practicing after a young age means coordinating different social selves and undertaking a certain degree of "labor" in managing emotions and relations and in choosing proper forms of communication. In particular, when a woman's traditional professional career and status overlap with the practice of fortune-telling, the effort required in negotiating different discourses on "reality" becomes more evident and the conflict between roles more difficult to manage.

Rachele explained that before her graduation she practiced fortune-telling outside her friends' circles, asking only for "symbolic" fees in return. After her graduation, when she started working as a professional, these practices conflicted with her main role. Therefore, these activities were left for the free time spent with friends and were often suspended for long periods to avoid being judged negatively about the link between her professional self and these secret activities.

Even Romina, a fifty-nine-year-old lawyer, offered different explanations to her clients to justify her practice, and she elaborated strategies she used to cover her identity by managing different versions of reality and by avoiding talking about her practice outside her circle of friends.

Furthermore, Rachele explained her concern about her role as a separated mother and how her fortune-telling practice would have put her in a difficult situation with child custody if relatives or acquaintances were to discover that she adheres to a different set of beliefs concerning supernatural identities or if she were to reveal being prone to a certain kind of suggestibility that is represented and judged in terms of a personality disorder or hysterical or narcissist traits.

Therefore, a tension between overt and covert identities forged these women's selves to practice forms of social mimicry and to engage in hidden fortune-telling activities in informal networks of friends, acquaintances, and relatives—and only rarely with outsiders as querents.

Patricia—a sixty-year-old housewife—explained that the practice is much more tolerated when practitioners have no conflicts between roles or when people have no university degrees. In other words, she argued, a housewife has fewer interior conflicts than a professional who acts for courts, and fewer conflicts with the scientific discourse that labels divinatory practices as something used by people with mental issues.[17]

Over the years, with the affirmation of professional careers and jobs, the moral boundaries between informal practitioners and commercial practitioners have become more consistent and meaningful. Rachele explained: "You can't stay on the border. If you like to act as an official fortune-teller you have to choose between your career and that career; otherwise, your practice should be reserved only for friends and trusted acquaintances."

At the same time over the course of life, the participants have developed particular bonds with one another, a kind of sisterhood of mutual care. Their practice is restricted to their women-only meetings, dinners, and after-dinners among friends who share the same beliefs and who are aware of the fact that outside of that living room, the world labels their activities as the product of mental issues or as fraud. However, even if restricted to the living room on Friday or Saturday evening, their meetings are a form of mutual care in which they support each other in everyday life by finding responses and solutions through their connection with the supernatural. Donna—a fifty-nine-year-old housewife—explained:

> I developed forms of friendship and reciprocal support that I have never imagined before. But this has arrived with age. When I was younger, I was completely unable to see the relations with my friends in this way. We trust each other and we know that scientific thought has no sufficient explanations for what we see and foresee. I have been practicing for forty years and I have collected so much proof about the reliability of this practice, but I can't show evidence for this outside my group of friends. I keep practicing and asking questions and questioning the goodness of this practice. Every time I look for confirmation that the practice is reliable, that my response is accurate and reliable. Every time. I am not just a believer. I practice because this helps my friends. It reassures them, supports them, and makes their life journey less uncomfortable. . . . They have troubled stories of love and loss. They have never reached peace in their love relationships or their family. Me too. . . . Practicing makes me feel helpful, it is something . . . that I am really able to do, and that I have completely learned, understood, and constructed by myself, without exams, expectations, or judgments from other people. Even if a marriage ends, a job is

lost, or a son leaves, this skill, this world, this connection, and its infinite potentialities are always present and yours.

The construction of a stable self that is detached from traditional social expectations concerning marriage and work seems to be a rewarding achievement for many of these participants.

However, even if participants show forms of resistance and a critical attitude toward gendered societal expectations, they find it difficult to express the same criticisms and resistance outside their circle of friends; and some of them reproduce elements of the dominant discourse even within the circle. Reinterpreting and contesting their role in society is something that should be kept within the circle; dyscrasias between different selves should be managed constantly.

DIVINATION DEVICES, THE COMMODIFICATION OF INTIMACIES, AND THE EFFECTS OF GLOBALIZATION

Some participants described how globalization has progressively determined the monetization of some practices and the commodification of intimate relations. This change has affected their practice and the relationships among the women as friends.

How to avoid this kind of monetization and the exploitation of intimate issues has been a constant presence since the beginning of their experience as practitioners. Over the years, consultations for friends, relatives, and acquaintances have always been kept free of charge through a form of mutual agreement among participants. Even today, when the querents are outsiders, the common practice is to act free of charge, to ask for a symbolic donation, or to ask for a small amount of money in payment for a consultation. However, over the last two decades the pressure to commodify intimate and spiritual dimensions has increased.

> You have to know this. I have observed this during the last . . . I think, fifteen years. Two of my friends started buying books and new decks of cards and tarots. For each holiday, a new deck, a souvenir. Then, weird books. I mean, many books on how to read cards, with new techniques, new methods of inquiry. It makes me laugh. I mean, you are an experienced teller, you're a reader, an interpreter with thirty years of experience, you have a special connection, a gift from . . . I do not know from where . . . but you have it and you do not need anything else. . . . And then, they started with

new experiences, and new practices: channeling with angels, hypnosis to know past lives, spiritisms ... and new books, new materials, new groups of people, seminars, and conferences.... If you ask them, they explain that there is a need for new experiences, new explanations, and new keys to understanding the connection with the "beyond," to pacify themselves with death, and to find new meanings.... For instance, there is ... this channeler from the US who organizes seminars in Italy and sells thousands of copies of his books about past lives, channeling, and earns thousands of euros with these seminars. I think they look for something new and exciting to propose to friends and acquaintances.

Besides the fertile business developed with books, decks, and so on, another business has developed: it is the intimate relations between the querents and the fortune-tellers that can be exploited by the creation of the need for new "experiences," by both the practitioners themselves and their clients. It is the healing function of the ritual that is commodified,[18] its potential to improve women's well-being and support. About this aspect, Donna explains:

> I am almost sixty. And fortune-telling is not enough. Knowing that it works and that an entity, or entities, or something else allows this practice and makes it reliable is not enough. I needed more. I needed to reconcile with life and death, with my losses, my failures. I needed new frames to interpret my experience. Through exploring past lives, I have become in contact with parts of myself that were there, unexplored, untouched, but were there. Reasons, explanations, for example, about the death of my father, the behavior of my mother, the illness of my sister ... I needed them. I found them. I met these angels, I talked with them, and this reconciles me with losses, failures, and betrayals. I need this because death is approaching.... Then, ... I need to learn new ways to intrigue [people], to keep them involved and curious.

In the cultural cauldron produced by globalization, with the urgent need to heal herself, Donna welcomes a mixture of elements from different continents and cultural traditions. This is an alternative to classical ways of psychological healing, and it replaces the mutual support given by the circle of friends.

Until now their rituals have been kept for the Friday evenings at the house of one of the circle's members to reconfirm the role and relations that women have within the family and domestic spaces. However, the creation of new needs and roles brings this intimate dimension outside their domestic space to the room of a spiritual practitioner. If until now fortune-telling could be considered as a healing system through friendship and a form of Indigenous support,[19] it is now being reinterpreted as a commodified system that promotes a more individualized relation between a woman in need of support and a practitioner.

Even if some of these women show forms of masked racism and conservativism, they accepted and negotiated these new meanings and incorporated into their practices new elements from different cultural traditions (e.g., guided meditation, yoga, reiki, shamanism, coffee divination, tarot or decks from other cultures). However, the introduction of these new practices and symbolic meanings into the circle caused antagonism and skepticism from some of the members.

Participants described three different responses to the introduction of globalized contents and monetization: (1) rejection in order to preserve traditional values and practices, (2) incorporation of only those new elements compatible with a preexistent system of beliefs, and (3) acceptance of change as an expression of evolution. Women who have chosen to incorporate these new practices are judged as weak and seduced by consumption by those who choose to follow and maintain the traditional practice (i.e., Italian traditional tarot and playing cards). Those who have kept traditions alive highlight the need to be more focused on their abilities to listen, hear, learn, and tell. In other words, they emphasize their prosocial skills to dialogue with the others. They argue they must be able to maintain a sort of detachment from the ordinary world and its mundane affections in order to develop a form of spirituality. However, from a materialist perspective, after analyzing the class and income levels of the informants, those with higher income (independent from class) are the women who often use these new monetized forms of consultation, while those with lower income usually reject them. To summarize, women with lower income use these strategies of resignification as a form of resistance against the ruling relations that monetize and commodify their gendered domestic space and intimate relations.

BEYOND FUTURE-TELLING

This chapter tries to summarize complicated connections between systems of beliefs, ruling discourse on gender roles and relations, hidden patriarchy, spirituality, and individualization at the beginning of the twenty-first century. It does not aim to develop a more articulate interpretation of the ruling (and codified) textual discourses that affect fortune-telling practices and fortune-tellers' life trajectories.

Due to the dominance of the scientific discourse in Western countries, practices like divination or fortune-telling are marginalized, and so, too, are the people who practice them.[20] Thus, the opportunity to study fortune-tellers from a sociological perspective is considered marginal, even though this would allow for an understanding of the sociocultural processes of negotiation of beliefs and forms of resistance to or reproduction of the dominant discourse on traditional gender roles and hidden patriarchy.

Beyond the monetization and commodification aspects of the late capitalism discussed above, the reconfiguration of the relationship between the querent and the practitioner seems to support the development of neo-spiritual practices in a more codified way.[21]

Given that the relation between the actors is ruled by an *other-than-human* entity in the informal practice between friends and in the more individualized practice between a querent and a practitioner, this last practice appears to envision the *other-than-human* presence in a more formal and codified system of knowledge and beliefs that mixes elements from Catholicism and Paganism.[22] This seems to be, on the one hand, the result of bringing these practices outside the private sphere of the informal circles of friends and domestic space and, on the other hand, the result of the need of the practitioners to offer a coherent system of beliefs and, in this way, ensure the continuation of an activity that provides an income. However, these and other aspects need further investigation.

NOTES

1. Sosteric, "A Sociology of Tarot," 381.
2. See, for example, Farley, *A Cultural History of the Tarot*; see also Sosteric, "A Sociology of Tarot"; and Lavin, "On Spiritualist Workers."
3. Kissman, "The Role of Fortune Telling"; Laird, "Sorcerers, Shamans and Social Workers"; see also Baldwin, "Reading Tarot."
4. Lustig and Wu, "Tarot as a Technology of Care"; Reeves, "Make Room for Magic."
5. See, for example, Codacons, *Italia, otto miliardi per maghi e fattucchiere*.
6. See also Puca, "The Tradition of Segnature."
7. Dummet, "Six XV-Century Tarot Cards," 17.

8   Glendinning and Bruce, "New Ways of Believing or Belonging"; see also Palmisano and Pannofino, *Religione sotto spirito*.
9   Hochschild, *The Commercialization of Intimate Life*; see also Zelizer, *The Purchase of Intimacy*.
10 Smith, *Institutional Ethnography*.
11 Lavin, "On Spiritualist Workers."
12 For a comparison, see Baroja, *The World of Witches*.
13 Illouz, *Why Love Hurts*; Baroja, *The World of Witches*; see also Kissman, "The Role of Fortune Telling," 138.
14 For a comparison, see Federici, *Witches, Witch-Hunting, and Women*; and Ruspini, "Role and Perceptions of Women."
15 Illouz, *Why Love Hurts*.
16 Glendinning and Bruce, "New Ways of Believing or Belonging."
17 See Glendinning and Bruce, "New Ways of Believing or Belonging."
18 For a comparison, see Korkman, "Feeling Labor."
19 See, for example, Kissman, "The Role of Fortune Telling."
20 See also Jorgensen, "Divinatory Discourse"; and Tiryakian, "Toward the Sociology of Esoteric Culture."
21 See Muzzatti and Smith, "'The Spirits Tell Me That You're Seeking Help.'" See also Possamai, *In Search of New Age Spiritualities*.
22 See also Puca, "The Tradition of Segnature."

BIBLIOGRAPHY

Baldwin, Janet. "Reading Tarot: Telling Fortunes, Telling Friends, and Retelling Everyday Life." In *The Supernatural: In Society, Culture, and History*, edited by Dennis Waskul and Marc Eaton, 136–51. Philadelphia: Temple University Press, 2018.

Baroja, Julio C. *The World of Witches*. Chicago: University of Chicago Press, 1985.

Codacons. *Italia, otto miliardi per maghi e fattucchiere*. October 30, 2019. https://codacons.it/italia-otto-miliardi-per-maghi-e-fattucchiere/.

Dummet, Michael. "Six XV-Century Tarot Cards: Who Painted Them?" *Artibus et Historiae* 28, no. 56 (2007): 15–26.

Farley, Helen. *A Cultural History of the Tarot: From Entertainment to Esotericism*. London: Bloomsbury, 2009.

Federici, Silvia. *Witches, Witch-Hunting, and Women*. Oakland, CA: PM Press, 2018.

Glendinning, Tony, and Steve Bruce. "New Ways of Believing or Belonging: Is Religion Giving Way to Spirituality?" *British Journal of Sociology* 57, no. 3 (2006): 399–414.

Hochschild, Arlie Russell. *The Commercialization of Intimate Life: Notes from Home and Work*. Berkeley: University of California Press, 2003.

Illouz, Eva. *Why Love Hurts: A Sociological Explanation*. Cambridge: Polity, 2012.

Jorgensen, Danny L. "Divinatory Discourse." *Symbolic Interaction* 7, no. 2 (1984): 135–53.

Kissman, Kris. "The Role of Fortune Telling as a Supportive Function among Icelandic Women." *International Social Work* 33, no. 2 (1990): 137–44.

Korkman, Zeynep K. "Feeling Labor: Commercial Divination and Commodified Intimacy in Turkey." *Gender and Society* 29, no. 2 (2015): 195–218.

Laird, Joan. "Sorcerers, Shamans and Social Workers: The Use of Rituals in Social Work Practice." *Social Work* 29, no. 2 (1984): 123–28.

Lavin, Melissa F. "On Spiritualist Workers: Healing and Divining through Tarot and the Metaphysical." *Journal of Contemporary Ethnography* 50, no. 3 (2021): 317–40.

Lustig, Caitlin, and Hong-An Wu. "Tarot as a Technology of Care." *Interactions* 29, no. 4 (2022): 24–29.

Muzzatti, Stephen L., and Emma M. Smith. "'The Spirits Tell Me That You're Seeking Help': Fortune Telling in Late Capitalism." In *The Supernatural in Society, Culture, and History*, edited by Dennis Waskul and Marc Eaton, 116–35. Philadelphia: Temple University Press, 2018.

Palmisano, Stefania, and Nicola L. Pannofino. *Religione sotto spirito: Viaggio nelle nuove spiritualità*. Milano: Mondadori, 2021.

Possamai, Adam. *In Search of New Age Spiritualities*. London: Routledge, 2019.

Puca, Angela. "The Tradition of Segnature: Underground Indigenous Practices in Italy." *Journal of the Irish Society for the Academic Study of Religions* 7 (2019): 104–24.

Reeves, Laura. "Make Room for Magic." *Exclamat!on: An Interdisciplinary Journal* 6 (2022): 50–55.

Ruspini, Elisabetta. "Role and Perceptions of Women in Contemporary Italy." In *The Routledge Handbook of Contemporary Italy*, edited by Andrea Mammone, Ercole Giap Parini, and Giuseppe Veltri, 76–88. London: Routledge, 2015.

Smith, Dorothy E. *Institutional Ethnography: A Sociology for People*. Oxford: Altamira, 2005.

Sosteric, Mike. "A Sociology of Tarot." *Canadian Journal of Sociology/Cahiers canadiens de sociologie* 39, no. 3 (2014): 357–92.

Tiryakian, Edward A. "Toward the Sociology of Esoteric Culture." *American Journal of Sociology* 78, no. 3 (1972): 491–512.

Zelizer, Viviana A. *The Purchase of Intimacy*. Princeton, NJ: Princeton University Press, 2005.

KILLING THE WITCH

Twelve · GOVIND KELKAR AND DEV NATHAN

A Feminist Theory of Witch Hunts

In this chapter we seek to explain (1) why in some societies and at certain times women are primarily persecuted as supposed witches, and (2) why witch hunts have occurred and continue to occur in geographical locations that are as disparate in historical and socioeconomic terms as contemporary Africa, Indigenous Asia-Pacific, the Amazon, and early modern Europe. Our explanation utilizes three variables: patriarchy, culture, and structural transformation.[1]

We define patriarchy as an institution through which rights to ownership and control over resources—including knowledge, decision-making, and women's bodies—are allocated to men within the household and society. The subordination of women was established through the mechanism of witch hunts in some pre-state or proto-state Indigenous societies across regions of Asia and Africa, and patriarchy was redefined in early modern Europe through the mechanism of witch hunts. These gender struggles, however, occurred not just by themselves but in intersection with cultural beliefs and broader structural changes within their respective societies.

In brief, our theory is that given the cultural preconditions for witches (persons understood to practice witchcraft, that is, to utilize supernatural means to cause harm), witch hunts occur as part of gender struggles, which create or re-create patriarchy, a context in which women get defined as the persons who cause harm to others and are, therefore, witches. Further, this typically takes place in a society undergoing major structural transformation, as in the movement from subsistence to accumulative economies. In such societies in transition, witch hunts have occurred that mainly target woman and also, under certain special conditions, a few men.

Unlike many postmodern theorists who neglect the victims of witch hunts when they look at the witch phenomenon as only a reaction to modernity,[2] we start instead with the voices of the survivors of witch hunts, those whom we interviewed, over decades, across India, Southeast Asia, and China. Ours is a feminist approach that takes the standpoint of women,[3] who are the principal victims of witch hunts. Knowledge is socially situated, and in the particular relationship of witchcraft accusations and witch hunts, taking the standpoint of the victims allows us to develop a theory that can overcome witch hunts. Thus, our concentration is on witch hunts and not on the alleged use of witchcraft to cause harm to persons.

However, whether in early modern Europe, the countries of Africa we consider, or among the patrilineal Indigenous peoples in India, any woman in those communities could be accused of being a witch. Interestingly, such accusations were taken up against only specific categories of men, such as blacksmiths or shepherds in early modern Europe, who were thought to have been practicing some form of magic or to otherwise have been deviant men. "If you were a man [in early modern Europe] you could be confident that witches were other people; nobody would accuse you of witchcraft unless you fell within quite narrow categories. If you were a woman, you could not be sure; a witch could easily be you."[4]

PATRIARCHY: CREATION AND RE-CREATION

The subordination of women was established through the mechanism of witch hunts in some pre-state or proto-state Indigenous societies across regions of Asia and Africa. Witch hunts helped establish men's control over, access to, and use of spiritual knowledge, which was held to be necessary for the labor of production in early agriculturist societies. Spiritual knowledge helps set the timing of various agricultural operations, such as seeding, plowing, and transplanting. It is generally held that without the performance of these rituals, which are based on spiritual knowledge, production efforts will come to naught or not generate the expected results.

In several Indigenous societies in central India, women are prohibited from securing this spiritual knowledge. Women are not supposed to know the clan spirits or even enter the sacred groves where rituals are conducted. Such prohibition of women from specific forms of knowledge also occurs in Amazonian myths, where men are supposed to have stolen this knowledge from women and then prohibited women from reacquiring it.[5] Such stealing of special knowledge by men from women also arises among the Lua in central Thailand (as in the case of the use of salt in cooking[6]) and among the Rungus of Sabah, Malaysia, where the conduct of village affairs was taken away from the women priestesses, the Bobolizan.[7]

This exclusion of women from the socially regarded higher forms of spiritual knowledge has often been enforced through the practice of witchcraft accusations or the conduct of witch hunts against women who were thought to be trying to acquire this knowledge. In this division of knowledge in central Indian myths, for example, as among the Santhal, women are thought to be witches while men are considered witch-finders.[8]

In Africa, among the Ashanti of Ghana, it is not that women are denied access to some forms of knowledge; rather, the knowledge they do possess is denounced as being the source of evil. Among the Ashanti, both women and men ruled with their own areas of specialized knowledge. After a supposedly failed revolt by royal women, their spiritual knowledge was denounced as being evil and these women were labeled as witches.[9] Importantly, it was not just some women who became witches but "all women [who were] potentially witches."[10] With women's knowledge being denounced, we get the phenomenon of women being both wise and malevolent and, thus, doubly liable to be denounced as witches.

Witch hunts have been used not just to enforce women's exclusion from highly valued spiritual knowledge but also to establish patrilineal property regimes as part of patriarchy. In India we identified land as a factor in witch hunts,[11] and we have seen this again among the Dai in Yunnan, China, and in northern Thailand.[12] As one would expect, these witch accusations feature prominently in close family situations, particularly when patrilineal kin try to deprive unsupported women of their rights to land (for example, depriving widows of their husbands' land). Enforcing patrilineal descent with regard to the land then compounds the exclusion of women from key areas of social knowledge as factors resulting in witch hunts in the creation of patriarchy.

While the above deals with the denunciation of women as witches in the creation of patriarchy, what then of early modern Europe, which was already patriarchal?[13] Patriarchy, however, is not a fixed thing or a fixed set of relations. Men's dominance can take different forms in different socioeconomic formations. Thus, what we deal with in early modern Europe is the transformation of gender relations brought about through witch hunts.

In early modern Europe, women became legal subjects, something they were not during the Middle Ages. This would have led to an assertion of women's independence in many forms. In the Swedish region of Dalarna, high rates of male migration also led to the presence of a large number of independent women. Many of these women were persecuted as witches.[14] For Scotland, Cristina Larner pointed out, "The pursuit of witches could therefore be seen as a rearguard action against the emergence of women as independent adults. The women who were accused were those who had challenged the patriarchal view of the ideal woman."[15] Women not under direct male control, widows and older single women, could defy men's control.

Women who became legal subjects were subject to new forms of control, particularly through witch hunts. This was the case with midwives, whose knowledge of birth control was dangerous to the new-found mercantilist requirement of population growth following the decimation of Europe's population by the Great Plague around the mid-fourteenth century. The witch hunts directed at midwives, among others, were initiated "to suppress the traditional and highly sophisticated means of birth control . . . regarded as a serious obstacle to the repopulation of Europe."[16] After the early analysis of Barbara Ehrenreich and Dierdre English of witch hunts as an attack on midwives,[17] it has been pointed out that midwives constituted a small portion of women attacked as witches. But as the sixteenth century demonologist and economist theoretician of the Mercantile Doctrine of Accumulation, Jean Bodin, said, the intent was "to strike awe in some by the punishment of others."[18]

Patriarchy as a practice also includes the control of women's income or wealth, often manifested as jealousy. Jealousy of more prosperous or successful kin or neighbors has long been a factor in witch hunts, whether among Indigenous peoples in Asia, Africa, or early modern Europe. In the central Indian Indigenous societies, someone becoming well off is said to result in *hisinga*, which can be roughly translated as jealousy. This usually resulted in the better-off person having to feast off their minor accumulations through feasting the village. Such redistributive mechanisms, however, began to weaken with the increased possibilities opened by greater immersion in the market economy. This, as we saw in our fieldwork studying patrilineal and matrilineal societies in India, Southeast Asia, and China, often led to attacks on the better-off person, accusing them of having acquired their wealth using witchcraft; and the subsequent witch hunt resulted often in either killing or driving out the better-off individual and their family.

In Africa, this same phenomenon led to a new "witchcraft of wealth," whether in Cameroon or Ghana.[19] In Zambia, workers are said to dread retirement as they will be forced to share a lot of their retirement money.[20] In Papua New Guinea, those in urban jobs dread payday as they have to distribute much of their income among rural relatives. As summarized by Ralph Austen, "ascendant individuals are perceived to be witches."[21]

Women in early modern Europe were denied the right to own property. This made women who had a right to inherit land targets of witch hunts, as in colonial New England's infamous Salem witch hunts.[22] Women were confined to household or reproductive work. Some household crafts, such as brewing, baking, and cloth production, were commercialized, but women were excluded from the new (commercial) enterprises. When women tried to enter male-dominated fields, such as fishing in the Netherlands and Norway, they were denounced as witches, and, at times, all the women of whole villages were killed.[23]

Women who were "quarrelsome," meaning they demanded something or refused to be silenced, were often tried as witches. Women's particular methods of quarreling, which was to curse or scold, were cited as evidence of witchcraft. In Scotland, being argumentative was an offense during the period of the witch hunts, and those punished for scolding were women.[24] Keith Thomas put it succinctly: "When a bad-tongued woman shall curse a party, and death shall follow shortly, this is a shrewd token that she is a witch."[25] The point was to curb women's independent voice, as was manifested in being quarrelsome, scolding, or cursing.

Overall, witch hunts in early modern Europe relegated women to reproduction and obedience and men to production. Witch hunts targeted women who knew more, those who were midwives, and those who became or tried to become independent or who tried to assert their voices. As we see elsewhere, too, among Indigenous peoples in African countries, by punishing some women, other women too are silenced and intimidated into following patriarchal norms.

CULTURE

The aspect of culture we deal with is the belief about the role of humans in causing misfortune to others. The attribution of misfortune to the actions of witches was at one time labeled as the beliefs of a "primitive" type of mind with a cosmology of supposedly "prerational" people.[26] But the widespread existence of such beliefs among the supposedly rational people of early modern Europe and such beliefs' continuing existence in Africa among Indigenous Asian peoples and other societies exposes the prejudice of characterizing witchcraft beliefs as markers of so-called primitive minds. Even while we reject the idea that some people acquire and utilize supernatural powers, we must recognize the power that such existing beliefs can have in influencing human action.

We now give examples of the way beliefs about witchcraft are considered important in some of the different societies we are considering. Among Indigenous peoples in central India, illness and misfortune are understood not just as having natural causes, but also as being brought about by someone; and thus, an attempt is made to find out who is responsible. This belief in women's use of black magic is "deeply seated in the collective psyche of the settled Indigenous peoples of Jharkhand" (in central India).[27] This belief was so strong that in the nineteenth century, a leader of an Indigenous people's anti-British revolt was recorded by the Norwegian Missionary Skesfrud as saying, "The greatest trouble for the Santhals is witches."[28]

The Ralushai Commission, which was set up in South Africa to investigate and find ways to deal with the spate of witch hunts that took place after the end of apartheid rule, held that "our forefathers regarded witchcraft as an integral part of our lives."[29] The South African Law Commission also held that witchcraft "is considered a real threat and a cause of otherwise inexplicable misfortune, illness, or death."[30]

Similarly, in early modern Europe, the peasant world was one in which the supernatural "often seem[ed] indistinguishable from religion."[31] Thus, the supernatural was part of the explanation for everyday events that were unpredictable and uncontrollable, whether harvest failures or bad weather. Explanations were often found through Sabbath descriptions of the actions of witches in supposed nocturnal gatherings with dancing, feasting, and indiscriminate intercourse. As Carlo Ginzburg argues, the description of the Sabbath actions "document myths and not rituals."[32] While peasants accepted supernatural explanations, the clergy found the supposed magic of witches to come from their pacts with the devil, or diabolism.

Thus, whether it concerns Indigenous peoples in central and northeast India, people in Africa, or people in early modern Europe, there is an underlying belief that there are those who can cause harm with their supernatural powers. This is an important belief system underlying any witch hunt in which there is always the question: Who caused harm by using supernatural powers? A feature of witch accusations that Peter Geschiere pointed out is that they occur mostly within relatively closed communities of families or neighbors.[33] E. E. Evans-Pritchard held that hostilities and fears within these communities were crucial to witchcraft accusations.[34] We also saw that witch accusations occur within Indigenous societies, and usually within lineages, in India.[35] Even in Papua New Guinea where accusations of witchcraft used to occur between (and not within) communities, the communities interacted with one another and were not distant communities.[36] In Africa the witch accusations occurred within villages; and even in urban Africa, it is the "greedy neighbour" who does not share,[37] who is the target of witch accusations. In early modern Europe, accusations took place between neighbors, and in close surroundings, as is made explicit in the title of Robin Briggs's book *Witches and Neighbours*.

We have come across only one society, the matrilineal Khasi of India, where the accused person (usually a man) is a stranger and accused of trying to suck human blood from fingernails to feed Thlen, the mythical serpent, to acquire wealth. Matrilineal societies will likely require a separate analysis to see how they follow or differ from the patterns seen here. In any case, among the Khasi, too, there is the underlying cultural belief in harm caused by someone with supernatural powers. In addition, there is the factor of wealth acquired through mysterious or nontransparent means.

An explanation for misfortune as the result of actions of individuals from within families of close communities deflects attention from the social forces causing the misfortune or the inequality. For instance, in Niger, returning migrant workers are often attacked as witches. Those who have saved more are denounced, while the employers who employ the migrant workers for low wages escape attention. Austen points out that in African witch cases, the immediate targets are other Africans, while they "leave the European bases of power mystified to a point where they can only be avoided, not effectively invaded."[38]

STRUCTURAL TRANSFORMATION: FROM SUBSISTENCE TO ACCUMULATION

In the preceding pages we have dealt with Indigenous societies and African countries in their cultural and gendered aspects. These operated within the context of the economic and structural transformations that these societies were undergoing. In addition, these transformations were also taking place in the context of their connections to the rest of the world. Indigenous societies and African countries always remained in contact with societies outside their boundaries. In India, for instance, the Austro-Asiatic and Dravidian language-speaking Indigenous peoples interacted with the state formations around them, even as they were derided as being *mlechha*, or barbarians.[39] In China, the Indigenous peoples were also referred to as either White Barbarians or Black Barbarians.

For early modern Europe, obviously, the analysis of witch hunts has to engage the structural transformation that was underway. But regarding Indigenous peoples and Africa, it was with the postmodern turn of the 1990s that the connections with the structural transformation of colonial and postcolonial development were brought center stage.

Structural transformation includes a change in the nature of production, or in the key technology, as in the change from hoe to plow agriculture or livestock raising. Ester Boserup identified hoe agriculture as a female farming system and plow agriculture as a male farming system, based on their central roles in farming.[40] But along with the transformation of the production system, there was also the accompanying economic and social transformation from a subsistence economy of hoe agriculture to one with some regular surpluses in plow agriculture and livestock rearing. Regular surpluses allow for a greater extent of inequality compared with uncertain surpluses. It entails the change not just in production methods or technology but in how surpluses are used, distributed, or accumulated; and the changing patterns of consumption and inequality allow us to talk of structural transformation as being a comprehensive phenomenon, changing various social relations, including gender relations and the beginnings of patriarchy.

The nature of structural change is even more pronounced with the advent of capitalist transformation. Not only technologies but also the organization of production and the nature of accumulation changed. A largely subsistence economy was transformed by enshrining the principle of accumulation. With this, the moral economy of the earlier feudal or community-based production and distribution was transformed into one based on the single-minded logic of the market. This change in the moral economy and the socioeconomic process of primary accumulation, however, took place over many centuries and many struggles, including witch hunts.[41]

In this situation of the ascendant individual (and, thus, families), a distinction is made between those who share some of their wealth and those who do not. Jane Parish reports a woman from Ghana saying that because she shares with her relatives, she is perceived as a good woman.[42] Thus, the condemnation is not of the acquisition of wealth as such but of the way in which it is used. In early modern Europe too, it was how wealth was used that was targeted in witch attacks—the better-off person who accumulates and "does not give."[43]

What is important is that the "ones who did not give" were often men. In the Trier and Bamberg regions of Germany, most of those executed were men, all "wealthy and male."[44] In the Netherlands, there was the "profit-making witch," a label attached to whole patrilineages.[45] This factor of social transformation is what accounts for the special category of men accumulating wealth also becoming targets of witch hunts.

PROMOTING ACCUMULATION

Witch hunts were not only used to protect the old moral economy of sharing but also to promote the new economy of accumulation. Briggs calls this type of witch-hunting in England the "neighbour who asks," while Keith Thomas called it the charity refused model.[46] It may not have always been a refusal of charity but the denial of customary dues. In Rajasthan, India, we found such cases among those who wished to deny the customary dues to the lower caste women who perform their services (the woman who comes asking for the continuation of the customary relations). Upon being denied those customary dues, she then leaves, cursing, and is subsequently denounced as a witch.

Witch hunts have also been used to promote accumulation through dispossession, what Karl Marx termed primitive accumulation but what may be better termed primary accumulation. In central India, witch accusations have been used to seize lands from widows to promote the accumulation of resources in a patrilineal line. In Europe, single women who inherited land disrupted patrilineal succession.[47] Such witch accusations to seize land have also been reported from Malawi, Africa.[48]

The above analysis shows that witch hunts have occurred where society is undergoing a structural transformation from one set of norms (of a communitarian, sharing type) to an accumulative norm (of market-based transactions), that is, where an older moral economy is being replaced by new socioeconomic norms. A study of 2,433 households from 182 villages in Sierra Leone divided the villages into three types[49]—first, those where communitarian norms prevailed; second, those where both communitarian and market-based norms were in contention; and third, those where only market-based norms prevailed. The presence of witch accusations was highest in the second type of village, where there was a conflict between communitarian and accumulative norms. The number of accusations was lower in both the first and third types of villages. This would support our conclusion that witch hunts are more likely in areas where and during periods when there is a conflict between old and new norms. Where only old norms or only new norms prevail, there is a lower likelihood of witch hunts.

CONCLUDING THOUGHTS

As a necessary condition for the existence of witch hunts, we have identified a culture of belief in the existence of persons, chiefly women, with supernatural powers who use that power to cause misfortune. Whether in early modern Europe or whether among Indigenous peoples in Asia, Latin America, the Pacific, or Africa, we find the prevalence of such beliefs. It follows from this that in a culture where there is no such belief in the existence of humans with supernatural powers, there would be no witch hunts. This is a hypothesis to be investigated.

Another corollary is that, to eliminate witch hunts, it would be necessary to reject the belief in the existence of persons with supernatural powers who carry out witchcraft. In our discussions with witch hunt survivors and their communities, we often found that individuals accused as witches deny their use of witchcraft but do not reject the belief in the existence of witches. More recently, however, we found among Indigenous peoples in India the expression of a rejection of such beliefs. The accused women and others too denied that Indigeneity must necessarily include a belief in witches; they asked for proof of the use of supernatural powers. They denied the existence of persons who carry out evil practices using supernatural powers. Chhutni Devi, an accused witch and reputed fighter against witch hunts, said, "We cannot be accused of being witches without concrete evidence. If we are witches, then produce evidence of our use of evil practices."[50] A similar statement was made by Biru Bala Rabha of Assam.[51] This echoes the position of judges toward the end of the witchcraft trials in England; they began to ask for proof of the use of supernatural powers. In addition to such demands for proof, with the tensions in ongoing structural transformations from subsistence to accumulation, there is a need for social security systems, and for the secure and unmediated rights of women to productive resources that would enable societies to manage these transformations with dignity and equality in gender relations.

NOTES

1. Kelkar and Nathan, *Witch Hunts*.
2. See, for example, Comaroff and Comaroff, "Introduction"; and Ashforth, *Witchcraft*.
3. Harding and Hintikka, *Discovering Reality*; Hartsock, *Money, Sex, and Power*.
4. Goodare, *The European Witch-Hunt*, 311.
5. Bamberger, "The Myths of Matriarchy."
6. Satyawadhana, "Appropriation of Women's Indigenous Knowledge."
7. Porodong, "Bobolizan, Forests and Gender Relations."
8. Archer, "The Santal Treatment of Witchcraft."
9. McCaskie, "Anti-witchcraft Cults in Asante"; Akyeampong and Obeng, "Spirituality, Gender, and Power."
10. McCaskie, *State and Society in Pre-colonial Asante*, 408.
11. Kelkar and Nathan, *Gender and Tribe*.
12. Nathan, Kelkar, and Yu Xiaogang, "Women as Witches and Keepers of Demons."
13. Goodare, *The European Witch-Hunt*.
14. Hagen, "Witchcraft Criminality and Witchcraft Research."
15. Larner, *Enemies of God*, 102.
16. Heinsohn and Steiger, "Birth Control," 435–36.
17. Ehrenreich and English, *Witches, Midwives and Nurses*.
18. Bodin, "Witches and the Law," 214.
19. Geschiere, "Witchcraft as the Dark Side of Kinship," 201, 187.
20. Ntloedible-Kuswani and Seratwa, "Witchcraft as a Challenge to Botswana Ideas," 236.
21. Austen, "The Moral Economy of Witchcraft," 90.
22. Rowlands, "Witchcraft and Gender in Early Modern Europe."
23. De Blecourt, "The Making of the Female Witch"; Hagen, "Witchcraft Criminality and Witchcraft Research."
24. Goodare, *The European Witch-Hunt*.
25. Thomas, "The Relevance of Social Anthropology," 512.
26. Green, *Risk and Misfortune*, 197.
27. Bosu-Mullick, "Gender Relations and Witches," 120.
28. Archer, "The Santal Treatment of Witchcraft," 103.

29 Ralushai Commission, *Report*, 192.
30 Ralushai Commission, *Report*, 3, 31.
31 Clark, "Witchcraft and Magic," 110.
32 Ginzburg, *Ecstacies*, 9.
33 Geschiere, "Witchcraft as the Dark Side of Kinship."
34 Evans-Pritchard, *Witchcraft, Oracles, and Magic among the Azande*.
35 Kelkar and Nathan, *Witch Hunts*.
36 Godelier, *The Making of Great Men*.
37 Englund, "Witchcraft, Modernity, and the Person," 272.
38 Austen, "The Moral Economy of Witchcraft," 105.
39 Thapar, "The Image of the Barbarian."
40 Boserup, *Woman's Role in Economic Development*.
41 Thompson, "The Moral Economy"; Mies, *Patriarchy and Accumulation*; and Federici, *Caliban and the Witch*.
42 Parish, "The Dynamics of Witchcraft."
43 Briggs, *Witches and Neighbours*, 140.
44 Behringer, *Witches and Witch-Hunts*, 114.
45 De Blecourt, "The Making of the Female Witch."
46 Briggs, *Witches and Neighbours*, 149ff.; Thomas, "The Relevance of Social Anthropology."
47 Levack, *The Witch-Hunt in Early Modern Europe*; Godbeer, "Witchcraft in British America."
48 Hinfelaar, "Witch-Hunting in Zambia."
49 Grijspaarde et al., "Who Believes in Witches?"
50 Chhutni Devi, in conversation with Govind Kelkar, May 12, 2021.
51 Kelkar and Sharma, *Culture, Capital, and Witch Hunts in Assam*.

BIBLIOGRAPHY

Akyeampong, Emmanuel, and Pashington Obeng. "Spirituality, Gender, and Power in Asante History." *International Journal of African Historical Studies* 28, no. 3 (1995): 481–508.

Archer, William George. "The Santal Treatment of Witchcraft." *Man in India* 27, no. 2 (1947): 103–21.

Archer, William George. "The Santal Treatment of Witchcraft." In *The Santals*, vol. 1, edited by Joseph Troisi. New Delhi: Indian Social Institute, 1979.

Ashforth, Adam. *Witchcraft: Violence and Democracy in South Africa*. Chicago: University of Chicago Press, 2005.

Austen, Ralph. "The Moral Economy of Witchcraft: An Essay in Comparative History." In *Modernity and Its Malcontents: Ritual and Power in Postcolonial Africa*, edited by Jean Comaroff and John L. Comaroff, 89–110. Chicago: University of Chicago Press, 1993.

Bamberger, Joan. "The Myths of Matriarchy." In *Woman, Culture, and Society*, edited by Michelle Zimbalist Rosaldo and Louise Lamphere, 281–300. Stanford, CA: Stanford University Press, 1974.

Behringer, Wolfgang. *Witches and Witch-Hunts: A Global History*. Cambridge: Polity Press, 2004.

Bodin, Jean. "Witches and the Law" (1580). In *Witchcraft in Europe 1100–1700*, edited by Alan Kors and Edward Peters, 213–16. Philadelphia: University of Pennsylvania Press, 1973.

Boserup, Ester. *Woman's Role in Economic Development*. New York: St. Martin's Press, 1970.

Bosu-Mullick, Samar. "Gender Relations and Witches among the Indigenous Communities in Jharkhand, India." In *Gender Relations in Forest Societies in Asia: Patriarchy at Odds*, edited by Govind Kelkar, Dev Nathan, and Pierre Walter, 119–45. New Delhi: Sage Publications, 2003.

Briggs, Robin. *Witches and Neighbours: The Social and Cultural Context of European Witchcraft*. London: Penguin Books, 1998.

Clark, Stuart. "Witchcraft and Magic in Early Modern Culture." In *Witchcraft and Magic in Europe: The Period of the Witch Trials*, edited by Bengt Ankerloo and Stuart Clark, 97–186. Philadelphia: University of Pennsylvania Press, 2002.

Comaroff, Jean, and John L. Comaroff. "Introduction." In *Modernity and Its Malcontents: Ritual and Power in Postcolonial Africa*, edited by Jean Comaroff and John L. Comaroff, 11–37. Chicago: University of Chicago Press, 1993.

de Blecourt, Willem. "The Making of the Female Witch: Reflections on Witchcraft and Gender in the Early Modern Period." *Gender and History* 12, no. 2 (2000): 287–309.

Ehrenreich, Barbara, and Deirdre English. *Witches, Midwives and Nurses: A History of Women Healers*. New York: Feminist Press, 1983.

Englund, Harri. "Witchcraft, Modernity, and the Person: The Morality of Accumulation in Central Malawi." *Critique of Anthropology* 16, no. 3 (1996): 257–79.

Evans-Pritchard, E. E. *Witchcraft, Oracles, and Magic among the Azande*. 1935. London: Palgrave Macmillan, 1976.

Federici, Sylvia. *Caliban and the Witch: Women, the Body and Primitive Accumulation*. 2004. New Delhi: Phoneme Publications, 2013.

Geschiere, Peter. "Witchcraft as the Dark Side of Kinship." *Etnofor* 16, no. 3 (2013): 43–61.

Ginzburg, Carlo. *Ecstasies: Deciphering the Witch Sabbath*. New York: Penguin Books, 1991.

Godbeer, Richard. "Witchcraft in British America." In *The Oxford Handbook of Witchcraft in Early Modern Europe and Colonial America*, edited by Brian P. Levack, 393–411. New York: Oxford University Press, 2013.

Godelier, Maurice. *The Making of Great Men: Male Domination and Power among the New Guinea Baurya*. Cambridge: Cambridge University Press, 1982.

Goodare, Julian. *The European Witch-Hunt*. London: Routledge, 2016.

Goodare, Julian. "Women and the Witch-Hunt in Scotland." *Social History* 23, no. 3 (1998): 288–308.

Green, Judith. *Risk and Misfortune: The Social Construction of Accidents*. London: Routledge, 1997.

Grijspaarde, Huib van de, Maarten Voors, Erwin Bulte, and Paul Richards. "Who Believes in Witches? Institutional Flux in Sierra Leone." *African Affairs* 112, no. 446 (2013): 22–47.

Hagen, Rune Blix. "Witchcraft Criminality and Witchcraft Research in the Nordic Countries of Europe." In *The Oxford Handbook of Witchcraft in Early Modern Europe and Colonial America*, edited by Brian Levack, 375–92. New York: Oxford University Press, 2013.

Harding, Sandra, and Merrill Hintikka, eds. *Discovering Reality: Feminist Perspectives on Epistemology, Metaphysics, and the Philosophy of Science*. Dordrecht: D. Reidel, 1983.

Hartsock, Nancy. *Money, Sex, and Power: Toward a Feminist Historical Materialism*. Boston: Northeastern University Press, 1983.

Heinsohn, Gunnar, and Otto Steiger. "Birth Control: The Political-Economic Rationale behind Bodin's 'Demomanie.'" In *History of Political Economy* 31, no. 2 (1999): 423–48.

Hinfelaar, Hugo. "Witch-Hunting in Zambia and International Illegal Trade." In *Imagining Evil: Witchcraft Beliefs and Accusations in Contemporary Africa*, edited by Gerrie ter Haar, 229–46. Asmara: Africa World Press, 2007.

Kelkar, Govind, and Dev Nathan. *Gender and Tribe*. New Delhi: Kali for Women, 1991.

Kelkar, Govind, and Dev Nathan. *Witch Hunts: Culture, Patriarchy and Structural Transformation*. Cambridge: Cambridge University Press, 2020.

Kelkar, Govind, and Aparajita Sharma. *Culture, Capital, and Witch Hunts in Assam*. New Delhi: Council for Social Development and Rosa Luxemburg Stiftung, 2021.

Larner, Cristina. *Enemies of God: The Witch-Hunt in Scotland*. Baltimore, MD: Johns Hopkins University Press, 1981.

Levack, Brain P. *The Witch-Hunt in Early Modern Europe*. London: Routledge, 2006.

McCaskie, T. C. "Anti-witchcraft Cults in Asante: An Essay in the Social History of an African People." *History in Africa* 8 (1981): 124–54.

McCaskie, T. C. *State and Society in Pre-colonial Asante*. Cambridge: Cambridge University Press, 1995.

Mies, Maria. *Patriarchy and Accumulation on a World Scale: Women in the International Division of Labour*. Foreword by Silvia Federici. London: Zed Books, 2014.

Nathan, Dev, Govind Kelkar, and Yu Xiaogang. "Women as Witches and Keepers of Demons: Struggles to Change Gender Relations." *Economic and Political Weekly* 33, no. 44 (1998): 58–69.

Ntloedibe-Kuswani, Gomang Seratwa. "Witchcraft as a Challenge to Batswana Ideas of Community and Relationships." In *Imagining Evil: Witchcraft Beliefs and Accusations in Contemporary Africa*, edited by Gerrie ter Harr, 205–28. Asmara: Africa World Press, 2007.

Parish, Jane. "The Dynamics of Witchcraft and Indigenous Shrines among the Akan." *Africa* 69, no. 3 (1999): 426–47.

Porodong, Paul. "Bobolizan, Forests and Gender Relations in Sabah, Malaysia." In *Gender Relations in Forest Societies in Asia: Patriarchy at Odds*, edited by Govind Kelkar, Dev Nathan, and Pierre Walter, 97–118. New Delhi: Sage Publications, 2003.

Ralushai Commission. *Report of the Commission into Traditional Leadership Disputes and Claims in the Northern Province of South Africa*. Limpopo: The Commission, 1998.

Rowlands, Alison. "Witchcraft and Gender in Early Modern Europe." In *The Oxford Handbook of Witchcraft in Early Modern Europe and Colonial America*, edited by Brian P. Levack, 449–67. New York: Oxford University Press, 2013.

Satyawadhana, Cholthira. "Appropriation of Women's Indigenous Knowledge: The Case of the Matrilineal Lua in Northern Thailand." In *Gender Relations in Forest Societies in Asia: Patriarchy at Odds*, edited by Govind Kelkar, Dev Nathan, and Pierre Walter, 97–118. New Delhi: Sage Publications, 2003.

Thapar, Romila. "The Image of the Barbarian in Ancient India." In *Ancient Indian Social History: Some Interpretations*, 152–92. Delhi: Orient Longman, 1978.

Thomas, Keith. "The Relevance of Social Anthropology to the Historical Study of English Witchcraft." In *Witchcraft Confessions and Accusations*, edited by Mary Douglas, 47–81. London: Routledge, 1970.

Thompson, E. P. "The Moral Economy of the English Crowd in the Eighteenth Century." *Past & Present* 50, no. 1 (1971): 76–136.

Thirteen · AMY NICHOLS-BELO

Occult Violence and the Savage Slot: Understanding Tanzanian Witch-Killings in Historical and Ethnographic Context

Global and Tanzanian human rights advocates and journalists often describe Sukumaland (the home of the Sukuma, Tanzania's largest ethnic group) as witch-obsessed and steeped in occult violence.[1] While news outlets and scholars have recently focused on the murders of persons with albinism (PWA) for their "magical" body parts,[2] "witch-killings" defined Tanzanian and Western perceptions of the region and the Sukuma throughout the latter half of the twentieth century.[3] Tanzania's "witch-killings" are marked by vigilante violence against people—usually elderly, widowed women—accused of doing witchcraft. These murders typically take place at night and are carried out by hired vigilantes. Traditional healers have long been implicated in these killings since healers diagnose "witchcraft problems." Without discounting the very real violence experienced by PWA and elderly women (the primary victims of Tanzania's so-called witch-killings), it is important to recognize that stories of "occult violence" circulate within and outside of Tanzania, in part, because they reinforce ideas about African traditionalism, otherness, and savagery. In other words, these narratives fill "the savage slot" theorized by Michel-Rolph Trouillot.[4] Previous efforts to explain these murders offer functionalist explanations and fail to account for long-standing cultural and historical practices. In contrast, I argue that when removed from the larger frame of "occult violence," witch-killings are far more similar to other forms of vigilante violence (such as attacks on thieves) than other "witchcraft-related crimes."

After briefly describing what the terms "witch" (*mchawi*) and "witchcraft" (*uchawi*)[5] mean in Northwestern Tanzania and how these terms differ from "traditional healer" (*mganga*) and "traditional healing" (*uganga ya kienyeji*), I review previous analyses of anti-witchcraft violence. In response, I argue for a historicized perspective that demonstrates how continuity of belief can "prime" and "activate" violence.[6] In particular, I focus on how witch-killing resembles other forms of socially sanctioned vigilante violence, albeit with a gender inversion. At the same time, I suggest that the circulation of stories about witch-killing or, more recently, the murders of PWA, is a result of the Global North's fixation with Africa as a hotbed for the occult, an image reinforced by Tanzanian media, NGOs, and government authorities. My analysis is informed by ethnographic fieldwork and archival research carried out in Mwanza, Tanzania's second-largest city, over a period of more than sixteen months between 2004 and 2016. My research was approved by the Institutional Review Boards of the University of Virginia and Mercer University.

SLIPPAGES IN TERMINOLOGY

In Northwestern Tanzania, *uchawi* and *uganga* (healing, usually in the sense of non-Western healing and often involving anti-witchcraft practice) are often interpreted as having some overlap, especially by evangelical Christians, in legal proceedings and, more generally, by the state. Moreover, these two distinct terms are often conflated into a larger category of "occult practices," which are imagined as including everything from human rights violations (like the murders of elder women or sacrificial killings of PWA) to divination and ancestor propitiation.

Witchcraft is understood to be intentional and always malevolent, the cause of some relationship problems, physical and mental ailments, and even death. Witches are thought to attack or even kill kin and neighbors, though strangers sometimes accidentally encounter medicine meant for others. Koen Stroeken describes the Sukuma witch as an "absolute outsider within," who is thought to access victims through shared kinship ties or debts.[7] In theory, witches (like healers) can be male or female, but as in many other cultural contexts ranging from Europe to India, widowed elderly women are most typically accused, attacked, or even killed. Sukuma witches have red eyes thought to be a result of using medicines that produce night vision; in reality, these red eyes are often the result of a lifetime of gendered labor, cooking over charcoal or dung fires. Despite victims' economic marginality, Sukuma witches are imagined as jealous, asocial accumulators.

In contrast, *uganga* includes the use of a wide variety of practices including divination and the administration of medicines (*dawa*) orally, topically, and through steam. These practices may be used to treat common illnesses, to ameliorate relationship or financial woes, or to combat or prevent witchcraft affliction. Traditional healers obtain their knowledge in different ways; some claim authority from ancestors and dreams, while others root their expertise in Islamic healing. While most healers generally describe their work in benevolent terms, some are quite frank in explaining that one must have some knowledge of how witchcraft works in order to treat it.

The distinction between healer and witch has led to confusion since at least 1922,[8] when the British colonial government first implemented "An Ordinance to Provide for the Punishment of Persons Practicing or Making Use of So Called Witchcraft" (the "Ordinance effectively prohibiting the practice and accusation of witchcraft). The Ordinance was meant to prevent witchcraft accusations, poisonings, and other potentially criminal behavior and to shift the punishment of witchcraft from traditional leaders to colonial authorities who thought of themselves as less superstitious and more suited to adjudicating criminal cases.[9] Despite a clear framing of the Ordinance as one against "witchcraft," British colonial officials often conflated *uchawi* and *uganga* and prosecuted traditional healers for using divination or for administering treatments.[10] The Tanzanian government continues to use the postcolonial version of this law ("The Witchcraft Act") to arrest and prosecute traditional healers accused of facilitating occult violence. In a holdover from colonialism, English-speaking Tanzanians often call traditional healers "witchdoctors," a term that evokes the savage slot and reinforces the perceived overlap between the imagined evil witch and the charlatan healer. Between 2009 and 2020, at the height of the circulation of stories about violence against PWAS, the Tanzanian government prohibited *uganga* and subsequently argued for a re-imagining of traditional healing as formalized herbal medicine devoid of tacit healing knowledge and divination.[11] More recently, the Legal and Human Rights Centre (LHRC) reported the arrest of 504 people across the Great Lakes Zone, including traditional healers, who were accused of ordering the killings of thirty-two people whose genitals were removed for occult wealth generation.[12] While this example is profoundly troubling, most traditional healers do not, of course, use human body parts in their preparations.

WITCH-KILLING AS "OCCULT" PRACTICE

In Northwestern Tanzania, witchcraft is a source of anxiety and suffering, but it can be countered through a variety of anti-witchcraft practices. These practices include curative and protective medicine prepared by traditional healers, invoking Jesus's name to heal spiritually and cast out malevolent spirits in evangelical settings; prosecution by the state; and vigilante violence against the person thought to be using witchcraft. As my interlocutors, journalists, and other anthropologists have described them, contemporary witch-killings typically follow a similar process. The alleged victim of witchcraft receives a diagnosis from a healer who alludes to, but does not explicitly name, a possible culprit (typically an elderly widow). The *mganga* then facilitates an introduction to a band of witch-killers who may be hired for a significant sum.[13] Prior to their attack, the witch-killers are ritually purified and sometimes smoke hashish for self-fortification. They often dismember their victims' bodies, removing the "witch's" genitals and breasts, essentially eradicating her femininity and dehumanizing her body.[14]

Despite compelling evidence that such violence against accused witches occurred prior to, during, and immediately after colonialism, witch-killings began to be recognized as an escalating form of gender-based violence in the 1990s. Stories began to circulate in national and international media and human rights publications, the Tanzanian government conducted research, and NGOs such as Concern for the Elderly (COEL) emerged with the explicit goal of documenting and ending witch-killing. This form of violence was described as especially prevalent among the "witch-crazed" Sukuma and, thus, in Mwanza, Shinyanga, and Tabora (MST) Regions. COEL documented 6,680 killings between 1995 and 2004 in MST; astoundingly, 98.3 percent of the victims were women.[15] Three thousand murders of suspected witches (80 percent female) were identified across the nation by the Tanzanian Ministry of Home Affairs between 1994 and 1998,[16] while the government-run Mongela Commission found that 3,693 people (62 percent female) were killed between 1970 and 1984, with 65 percent of the incidents occurring in MST.[17] While female kin, including paternal aunts, co-wives, and stepmothers, are considered most vulnerable to accusations, neighbors were also blamed for witchcraft. One of my 2007 interviewees, an elder woman who lived with her sister and some young children expressed concerns that she might be accused of witchcraft because some bad things had happened to her neighbors. Many accused witches are marginal enough to be scapegoated in ways similar to victims of Indian witch hunts.[18]

As Tanzania's witch-killings began to appear in non-Tanzanian media, their meaning was transformed into a tangible and brutal example that filled the "savage slot."[19] When in January 2003, *Harper's Magazine* published its "index" of thought-provoking, quirky, and often disturbing statistics, it included the statement, "Estimated number of women killed as witches in Tanzania each year: 500"; this entry was meant to provoke a reaction—shock that such beliefs could exist in the twenty-first century, the shaking of heads, perhaps even laughter at the "backwardness" of Tanzanians. Terence Ranger has argued that Western media has a tendency to collapse everything from South African muti murders to the sale of human meat in London into "one sinister phenomenon."[20] While the *Harper's* "index" lacks any context and trades on shock value, the Tanzanian government, media, and NGOs have similarly attributed "occult superstition" and violence to African under-development and outdated beliefs.

According to the LHRC, reports to police of witchcraft-related killings—a much broader category of crimes that includes sacrificial killings, such as those of PWA or children[21]—have declined in recent years from 425 reports (nationwide) in 2015 to 112 in 2020 (with an average of 276 murders per year during the five-year period).[22] The LHRC attributes this decline in violence to increased policing and judicial action. In its 2020 and 2019 *Human Rights Reports*, the LHRC described a few cases of female witch-killings; however, these most recent reports no longer highlight Sukumaland as Tanzania's primary location for occult violence. Featured cases took place outside of the region and/or included sacrificial killings or male victims. While this means that, for now, witch murders are declining, it is still worthy of analysis.

EXPLAINING WITCH-KILLING

Witch hunts are a global phenomenon that need to be understood first and foremost as a form of violence against women, rooted in culturally specific forms of gender discrimination.[23] Federici argues that they are exacerbated by the profound economic consequences brought by neoliberalism and globalization.[24] More specifically, scholars have attributed Tanzanian witch-killings either to changes in land tenure that favor widows rather than patrilineal male descendants or to "income shock," produced by extreme rainfall.[25] While recognizing that witch-killing is a form of gender-based violence, I argue Sukuma witch-killing should not be treated as something new but as a historically and socially continuous form of violence that is "primed" and "activated" under certain conditions.[26]

In March 2007, I interviewed David, a resident of Mwanza City, who had recently returned from his paternal aunt Maria's funeral after a purported witch-killing. Her neighbors told him that an inheritance conflict might be the cause of the murder. Maria had been predeceased by a husband and two children, and she lived alone with her grandchildren. Neighbors speculated that Maria's brother-in-law (her husband's younger brother) wanted to inherit the property and had ordered her killing. After returning to Mwanza, David learned that Maria's brother-in-law and two other men had been taken to the police station and beaten until the brother-in-law admitted that he had hired men to kill her with machetes. David's anger at Maria's brother-in-law and the men who had "chopped her up like meat" was intense; while he believed in the existence of witchcraft, this was, in his opinion, "purely a problem of her brother-in-law not wanting a woman living alone to have property." He explained that "lots of people [in the community] . . . see an old woman and they think she is a witch, but sometimes she is not."

David's story illustrates the tension between new inheritance protections for women in Tanzania and customary law that recognizes patrilineal inheritance. Scholars have argued that liberalized inheritance laws allowing women to control property may act as an impetus for witch-killings.[27] This theory presumes that young men who "lose" their inheritances to elder kinswomen have them killed under the guise of witchcraft.

Writing on Tanzanian gender relations, Deborah Fahy Bryceson describes "the marriage contract," which has marked the change in "women's negotiating position vis-à-vis men . . . [from] that of 'slave' . . . [to] 'citizen.'"[28] While Bryceson notes improvements in women's access to the informal economy and urban job market, she also argues that privatization of property has solidified male access to property. While I support Peter Geschiere's much-cited assertion that "witchcraft is the dark side of kinship,"[29] the attribution of all witch-killing to female land inheritance fails to tell the whole story; seemingly, thousands of postcolonial witch-killings occurred prior to mid-1990s land reform. Moreover, women's access to land has increased over the last two decades, while witch-killings have declined. Additionally, land tenure disputes fail to account for cases of scapegoating not related to inheritance, as in the case described above of the elderly woman who was afraid of accusations by neighbors.

Edward Miguel's heavily cited econometric analysis—which uses rainfall data to link "income shock" to witch-killings in sixty-seven Meatu District villages and thus argues that there are "twice as many witch murders in years of extreme rainfall"[30]—is even more reductive. Using limited data, he concludes that poorer households are more vulnerable to witchcraft murders (but not to homicide generally), theorizing that witch-killing is a result of "income shock," not scapegoating. For Miguel, elderly women are a "net household economic liability" who could become "assets" if granted pensions.[31] This zero-sum thinking fails to account for the many ways that elderly women are *already* household assets who provide childcare, grow and prepare food, and perform other forms of domestic labor. It is worth noting that the high costs of hired witch-killers would be unaffordable for the households most prone to income shock.

Anthropologists have largely treated witchcraft accusations as a response to external stressors. Scholars in the mid-twentieth century believed that community imbalance[32] or urban crowding increased accusations.[33] More recently, many Africanist anthropologists have argued that a seeming increase in witchcraft belief, practice, and violence is a result of inequalities wrought by modernity, late-stage capitalism, structural adjustment policies, and migration.[34] Their analyses allow for the simultaneity of "modernity" and the "occult," and respond to previous scholars who believed that "development" would vanquish witchcraft beliefs. While postcolonial Tanzania has been shaped by postsocialist economic inequality (including changing ideas about land tenure), I believe that these analyses fail to recognize local continuities.

HISTORICAL AND CULTURAL PATTERNS

Instead, Sukuma witch hunts need to be interpreted within a larger pattern of occult and non-occult violence documented since the early days of independence and in concert with a broader array of anti-witchcraft practices.[35] British colonial anthropologist Hans Cory described how precolonial Sukuma chiefly courts punished murder and assault with fines, while cattle theft, treason, and serious cases of witchcraft were punishable by death. In cases where a sick or dying victim accused someone of using magic against them and a diviner confirmed the attack, then a case could be brought to the chief, who ordered either death or banishment. While Cory uses male pronouns and the gloss "sorcerer" when describing these cases, ethnographic and archival data suggest that witchcraft accusations were also levied at women, though perhaps not as disproportionately as in recent years.[36]

When British colonial authorities introduced the Witchcraft Ordinance, management of witchcraft accusations was removed from chiefly courts and administered by colonial authorities. Frustratingly for Tanzanians, proving witchcraft in colonial courts was notoriously difficult as a diviner's testimony was no longer acceptable evidence. People accused of witchcraft were fined or expelled from communities, often for their own safety. In spite of this, at least some witch-killings continued, albeit extralegally.

In September 1962, less than a year after independence, a series of attacks and murders of several women accused of witchcraft took place in Mwanza Region. Unlike the more recent secretive attacks or the legal process described by Cory, the 1962 murders took the form of vigilante mob violence with as many as 300 people responding to and participating in calls to attack and kill supposed witches. Ralph Tanner attributed these witch-killings to a power vacuum in the newly independent nation, arguing that "the Sukuma traditional system of government and religion has disappeared while leaving unchecked their belief in the practice of witchcraft."[37] More specifically, Tanner argued, witchcraft violence had been suppressed under colonialism, but "came to the surface as an expression of local tensions increased by the widening social and political distance between ruler and ruled."[38]

Whether or not Tanner's assertion that there was more "social and political distance" in the first years of Tanzanian statehood is accurate, a variety of forms of vigilantism emerged in the postcolonial era. The two main forms—spontaneous mob violence directed toward suspected thieves, murderers, and rapists and "justice" meted by Sungusungu groups—have been attributed to inadequate policing by the state.[39] Modeled on "traditional" Sukuma leadership and secret societies, the Sungusungu focused on matters of security and morality including "searching for thieves and witches"[40] and, for overzealous members, killing witches. Describing the case of Sado Luja, the presiding judge wrote that Sungusungu members confessed to killing the woman, "apparently thinking they had done a noble thing."[41]

For Tanzanian human rights activists, threats of "mob violence, extrajudicial killings, violence against law enforcement officers, witchcraft-related killings, attacks of PWAS, death penalty, road accidents, ... and gender-related jealousy motivated killings" are collectively viewed as affronts to the broader human rights framework of "right to life."[42] Yet the single category "witchcraft-related murders" obscures the larger meanings of both sacrificial violence and the murders of people believed to be witches (and thus socially deviant).[43] Indeed, this treatment fills the savage slot without contextualizing these distinct forms of violence.

Instead, I argue that witch-killing is a gender-inverted form of mob violence. Mob violence is shockingly pervasive in Tanzania, with an average of 640 reported cases per year (2015–19). Like witch-killing, mob violence violates human rights and due process, but stories of male thieves beaten to death by crowds do not circulate, even though the acts of violence may be equally stomach-turning. Stories about vigilante "justice" against male criminals do not fill the savage slot in the same ways as lynched elderly witches, who are both familiar and historically distant enough to evoke reaction and response in the Global North.[44] Despite recent condemnation by the LHRC and others, mob violence and witch-killings have historically been acceptable in Tanzania. In contrast, sacrificial murders and other forms of occult violence are denounced by virtually all Tanzanians, including traditional healers. My interlocutors regularly claimed that these practices were "imported" from Nigeria, South Africa, or Uganda, nations imagined as Tanzania's own version of the savage slot.

As the acceptability of witch-killing and mob violence wanes in response to changing social mores, better policing, and changing government policies and practices, it is worth pointing out that violence has always existed within a continuum of other responses. Tanzanians beat accused thieves *and* file formal charges at police stations; similarly, the majority of incidents thought to be caused by witchcraft are resolved without violence. Instead, people seek treatment from healers and evangelical ministers or file complaints with local authorities.

Witch-killing, then, is a kind of last resort that, like genocide, is a result of "priming" and "activation." According to Alexander Hinton, primes for genocides include socioeconomic or political upheaval as well as the instantiation of difference between groups, while activation triggers "the 'charge' that has been primed."[45] Witch-killing exists within a larger set of anti-witchcraft practices, but it is activated when biomedicine, traditional medicine, evangelical Christianity, or the state fail to cure illness or end other forms of suffering. It may be triggered by other social stressors including complex kinship relations, poor neighborly relations, economic marginalization, or urbanization. In other words, scholars and Mwanzans who call attention to matters of kinship, land tenure, and crowding are not wrong; rather, these experiences of social stress trigger a long, consistently primed charge that presupposes that women are, by their nature, more likely than men to be witches. As a former regional police authority told me, "contract murders have something [to do] with conflicts . . . [surrounding] property, a *shamba* (small farm), cattle, or problems arising from marriage. *Uchawi* can be a form of camouflage." This explanation need not be functionalist, but it can reflect this process of priming and activation.

While cases of witch-killing have declined, newer forms of violence have filled the savage slot. Despite the fact that fewer than one hundred cases have been documented (and none since 2015 according to the LHRC), and murders of PWA have been covered by the *Economist*, the *New York Times*, BBC, and *Al Jazeera*, these stories reinforce ideas about African savagery and, subsequently, produce new forms of witch hunts in Tanzania including increased state surveillance of traditional healers who are believed to engage in occult violence. In recent years, the state has moved to professionalize traditional healers by requiring them to complete formal education and licensure.[46] These efforts seem laudable but may result in another gendered witch-hunt, since female healers are less likely to complete secondary school and instead practice forms of traditional healing that are rooted in tacit and esoteric ways of knowing.

In this chapter, I have argued that narratives of occult violence circulate globally because they fill the savage slot, thus satisfying Western perceptions of Africa and Africans as barbaric, superstitious, and violent. I have focused on a particular form of gender-based violence—witch-killing—which is often lumped in with other forms of occult violence. Finally, I have argued for a historically continuous approach that analyzes witch-killing as a form of mob violence of last resort, produced in response to considerable social pressure, priming, and activation.

NOTES

1   Sukumaland is a cultural area that overlaps with Geita, Mwanza, Shinyanga, Simiyu, and Tabora Regions. A Region is a large administrative area. While Tanzania does not keep records of ethnicity, there are about 10 million

1. Sukuma people (roughly one-sixth of the national population or Tanzania's most numerous ethnic group). Importantly, these numbers do not translate to increased political power.
2. Brocco, "Albinism, Stigma, Subjectivity"; Bryceson, Jønsson, and Sherrington, "Miner's Magic"; Burke, "Media Framing of Violence"; Nichols-Belo, "'Witchdoctors in White Coats.'"
3. Mesaki, "Witchcraft and Witch-Killings"; Mesaki, "Witchcraft and the Law"; Tanner, *Witch Murders*.
4. Trouillot, "Anthropology and the Savage Slot." For Trouillot, this slot is how the West imagines and depicts imagines "the (savage) Other" in relation to reason and utopia.
5. Unless otherwise stated, all non-English words are Kiswahili and all individual's names are pseudonyms.
6. Hinton, *Why Did They Kill?*
7. Stroeken, *Moral Power*, 123.
8. The 1922 Ordinance made it illegal both to use witchcraft, defined to include "sorcery, enchantment, bewitching or the purported exercise of any supernatural power," "with malignant intent," or to accuse a person of witchcraft in the absence of a court, police, headman, or "other proper authority" (Tanganyika Territory No. 29 of 1922 as reproduced in Mesaki, "Witchcraft and Witch-Killings"). Re-titled as the Witchcraft Act, similar prohibitions live on in the Tanzanian Criminal Code.
9. Tanner, *Witch Murders*.
10. Mesaki, "Witchcraft and Witch-Killings"; Nichols-Belo, "Uchawi Upo."
11. Nichols-Belo, "'Witchdoctors in White Coats.'"
12. LHRC, *Tanzanian Human Rights Report 2020*, 22. They also report that traditional healers encouraged their clients to rape women in order to "become rich."
13. Approximately $100–300 in 2007.
14. In *Moral Power*, Stroeken argues that this dismemberment allows killers (and healers) to use these body parts as an important ingredient in protective medicine.
15. COEL's data was documented on handwritten charts in their Magu Office. See Nichols-Belo, "Uchawi Upo," for the full data.
16. Miller, *Encounters with Witchcraft*, 178.
17. Mesaki, "Witchcraft and Witch-Killings in Tanzania."
18. Chaudhuri, "Women as Easy Scapegoats."
19. Trouillot, "Anthropology and the Savage Slot."
20. Ranger, "Scotland Yard in the Bush," 274. Muti murders are a much-described South African phenomena in which individuals, often children, are murdered and dismembered so that their body parts can be made into muti (medicine).
21. LHRC, *Tanzanian Human Rights Report 2020*, reported no attacks on PWA in 2020, but described a series of child murders in Njombe District. The other

incidents took place in Rukwa (another witch-killing hotspot; see Machangu, "Vulnerability of Elderly Women") as well as in Kigoma, Katavi, Tanga, Mbeya, Njombe, and Lindi.

22 LHRC, *Tanzanian Human Rights Report 2020*, 20.
23 Chaudhuri, "Women as Easy Scapegoats"; Adinkrah, "Witchcraft Accusations."
24 Federici, "Witch-Hunting, Globalization, and Feminist Solidarity."
25 Masanja, "Some Notes of the Sungusungu"; Kibuga and Dianga, "Victimisation and Killing"; Miguel, "Poverty and Witch Killing."
26 Hinton, *Why Did They Kill?*
27 Masanja, "Some Notes of the Sungusungu"; Kibuga and Dianga, "Victimisation and Killing."
28 Bryceson, "Gender Relations in Rural Tanzania," 63.
29 Geschiere, *Modernity of Witchcraft*, 11.
30 Miguel, "Poverty and Witch Killing," 1153. Miguel's analyses are based on "0.2 murders per village-year on average, or roughly one per village every five years . . . with a total of 65 witch murders and 68 non-witch murders during the period" (1160), a shockingly small sample with which to establish a predictive relationship.
31 Miguel, "Poverty and Witch Killing," 1170.
32 Middleton and Winter, *Witchcraft and Sorcery in East Africa*; Marwick, *Witchcraft and Sorcery*.
33 Douglas, "Introduction."
34 Comaroff and Comaroff, *Modernity and Its Malcontents*; Geschiere, *Modernity of Witchcraft*; Moore and Sanders, *Magical Interpretations*; Meyer and Pels, *Magic and Modernity*.
35 Tanner, *Witch Murders*; Mesaki, "Witchcraft and Witch-Killings"; Miller, *Encounters with Witchcraft*.
36 Cory, *Indigenous Political System of the Sukuma*.
37 Tanner, *Witch Murders*, 39.
38 Tanner, *Witch Murders*, 41.
39 Abrahams, "Sungusungu"; Bukurura, "Sungusungu"; Paciotti and Mulder, "Sungusungu."
40 Song lyrics as quoted in Bukurura, "Sungusungu," 193.
41 Judge Mchome quoted in Mesaki, "Witchcraft and Witch-Killings," 204.
42 LHRC, *Tanzanian Human Rights Report 2020*, xix.
43 Ranger, "Scotland Yard in the Bush."
44 Stroeken argues that the problem of witch-killing has been overblown, explaining that the per capita witch-murder rate in Mwanza is roughly half that of Californian homicides. He concludes that international outrage is ethnocentric and "boils down to the fact the homicides occurring in Sukuma villages do not exhibit the Western age and gender division [of young male victims]" (Stroeken, *Moral Power*, 200).

45 Hinton, *Why Did They Kill?*, 280.
46 Nichols-Belo, "Witchdoctors in White Coats."

BIBLIOGRAPHY

Abrahams, Ray G. "Sungusungu: Village Vigilante Groups in Tanzania." *African Affairs* 86, no. 343 (1987): 179–96.

Adinkrah, Mensah. "Witchcraft Accusations and Female Homicide Victimization in Contemporary Ghana." *Violence against Women* 10, no. 4 (2004): 325–56.

Brocco, Giorgio. 2016. "Albinism, Stigma, Subjectivity and Global-Local Discourses in Tanzania." *Anthropology and Medicine* 23, no. 3 (2016): 229–43.

Bryceson, Deborah Fahy. "Gender Relations in Rural Tanzania: Power Politics of Cultural Consensus?" In *Gender, Family and Household in Tanzania*, edited by Colin Creighton and C. K. Omari, 37–69. Brookfield: Avebury, 1995.

Bryceson, Deborah Fahy, Jesper Bosse Jønsson, and Richard Sherrington. "Miner's Magic: Artisanal Mining, the Albino Fetish and Murder in Tanzania." *Journal of Modern African Studies* 48, no. 3 (2010): 353–82.

Bukurura, Sufian. "Sungusungu: Vigilantes in West-Central Tanzania." PhD diss., Cambridge University, 1994.

Burke, Jean. "Media Framing of Violence against Tanzanians with Albinism in the Great Lakes Region: A Matter of Culture, Crime, Poverty and Human Rights." *Australasian Review of African Studies* 34, no. 2 (2013): 57–77.

Chaudhuri, Soma. "Women as Easy Scapegoats: Witchcraft Accusations and Women as Targets in Tea Plantations of India." *Violence against Women* 18, no. 2 (2012): 1213–34.

Comaroff, Jean, and John L. Comaroff, eds. *Modernity and Its Malcontents: Ritual and Power in Postcolonial Africa*. Chicago: University of Chicago Press, 1993.

Cory, Hans. *The Indigenous Political System of the Sukuma and Proposals for Political Reform*. Nairobi: Eagle Press for the East African Institute of Social Research, 1954.

Douglas, Mary. "Introduction: Thirty Years after Witchcraft, Oracles, and Magic." In *Witchcraft Confessions and Accusations*, edited by Mary Douglas, xiii–xxviii. New York: Tavistock Publications, 1970.

Federici, Silvia. "Witch-Hunting, Globalization, and Feminist Solidarity in Africa Today." *Journal of International Women's Studies* 10, no. 1 (2008): Article 3. https://vc.bridgew.edu/jiws/vol10/iss1/3.

Geschiere, Peter. *The Modernity of Witchcraft: Politics and the Occult in Africa*. Charlottesville: University Press of Virginia, 1997.

Hinton, Alexander Laban. *Why Did They Kill?: Cambodia in the Shadow of Genocide*. Berkeley: University of California Press, 2005.

Kibuga, Kate Forrester, and Alex Dianga. "Victimisation and Killing of Older Women: Witchcraft in Magu District, Tanzania." *Southern African Journal of Gerontology* 9, no. 2 (2000): 29–32.

Legal and Human Rights Centre (LHRC). *Tanzanian Human Rights Report 2019: State of Human Rights in Tanzania Mainland: Key Issues and Highlights for the Year 2019*, 2020. https://www.humanrights.or.tz/en/post/resources-center/tanzania-human-rights-report-2019.

Legal and Human Rights Centre (LHRC). *Tanzania Human Rights Report 2020: Human Rights Protection and the Threat Posed by COVID19 in Tanzania*, 2021. https://www.humanrights.or.tz/en/post/resources-center/tanzania-human-rights-report-2020.

Machangu, Hamisi Mathias. "Vulnerability of Elderly Women to Witchcraft Accusations among the Fipa of Sumbawanga, 1961–2010." *Journal of International Women's Studies* 16, no. 2 (2015): 274–84. https://vc.bridgew.edu/jiws/vol16/iss2/17

Marwick, Max, ed. *Witchcraft and Sorcery: Selected Readings*. 2nd ed. New York: Viking Penguin, 1968.

Masanja, Patrick. "Some Notes of the Sungusungu Movement." In *The Tanzanian Peasantry: Economy in Crisis*, edited by Peter G. Forster and Sam Maghimbi, 203–15. Brookfield: Avebury, 1992.

Mesaki, Simeon. "Witchcraft and the Law in Tanzania." *International Journal of Sociology and Anthropology* 1, no. 8 (2009): 132–38. https://doi.org/10.5897/IJSA.9000106.

Mesaki, Simeon. "Witchcraft and Witch-Killings in Tanzania: Paradox and Dilemma." PhD diss., University of Minnesota, 1993.

Meyer, Birgit, and Peter Pels, eds. *Magic and Modernity: Interfaces of Revelation and Concealment*. Stanford, CA: Stanford University Press, 2003.

Middleton, John, and E. H. Winter, eds. *Witchcraft and Sorcery in East Africa*. London: Routledge, 1963.

Miguel, Edward. "Poverty and Witch Killing." *Review of Economic Studies* 72, no. 4 (2005): 1153–72.

Miller, Norman N. *Encounters with Witchcraft: Fieldnotes from Africa*. Albany: State University of New York Press, 2012.

Moore, Henrietta L., and Todd Sanders, eds. *Magical Interpretations, Material Realities: Modernity, Witchcraft, and the Occult in Postcolonial Africa*. New York: Routledge, 2001.

Nichols-Belo, Amy. "Uchawi Upo: Embodied Experience and Anti-witchcraft Practice in Mwanza, Tanzania." PhD diss., University of Virginia, 2014.

Nichols-Belo, Amy. "'Witchdoctors in White Coats': Politics and Healing Knowledge in Tanzania." *Medical Anthropology* 37, no. 8 (2018): 722–36.

Paciotti, Brian, and Monique Bogerhoff Mulder. "Sungusungu: The Role of Preexisting and Evolving Social Institutions among Tanzanian Vigilante Organizations." *Human Organization* 63, no. 1 (2004): 112–24.

Ranger, Terence. "Scotland Yard in the Bush: Medicine, Murders, Child Witches and the Construction of the Occult: A Literature Review." *Africa* 77, no. 2 (2007): 273–83.

Stroeken, Koen. *Moral Power: The Magic of Witchcraft*. New York: Berghahn Books, 2010.

Tanner, R. E. S. *The Witch Murders in Sukumaland: A Sociological Commentary*. Uppsala: Scandinavian Institute of African Studies, 1970.

Trouillot, Michel-Rolph. "Anthropology and the Savage Slot: The Poetics and Politics of Otherness." In *Recapturing Anthropology: Working in the Present*, edited by Richard G. Fox. Santa Fe, NM: SAR Press, 1991.

Fourteen · HELEN MACDONALD

Going All the Way: From Village to Supreme Court for a Witch-Killing in Central India

During the early hours of May 30, 1995, in a central Indian village, Kulwantin Bai Nishad was accused of being a *tonhī* (witch) and was murdered by a large group of men. The enraged mob banged on her door and accused her of instigating a large and scorching burn to a neighbor's leg that would not heal despite several months of medical care. Frightened, she sought refuge but found none. She was thrashed by the mob for two hours, stripped naked, and then beaten for another two hours. The village head and several village council members interceded but found themselves bullied by the threat of violence. The village head apprised the *kotvār* (village guard); the *kotvār*, however, showed little concern for the violence and went back to sleep, content to report Kulwantin Bai to the police the next morning as "missing." In the interim, assuming Kulwantin Bai was dead and hoping to hide her body, the mob fastened a large stone to her body and threw her into a well. She drowned. The following day, Chhattisgarh (then unbifurcated Madhya Pradesh) in central India awoke to headlines of her brutal murder.[1] The death of Kulmantin Bai, who was widowed, with two young children, and surviving on a paltry income, drew public outrage.

By the very nature of its being so public, Kulwantin Bai's murder involved family, community, healers, police, administration, courts of law, media, and the state. Once an accusation escapes the confines of the village, it typically falls first into the hands of the police. The Chhattisgarh police largely ensure that grievances concerning *tonhī* accusations are investigated and, when possible, placed before the courts.[2] However, police efficiency does not necessarily equate to efficacy in the wider sense of legal or social justice for persons accused as *ṭonhī*. Politicians and administrators derive short-term mileage by attaching themselves to public indignation. This energy and awareness, and that generated by the press, abruptly cease once a case enters the judicial system on the assumption that justice will be meted out to the perpetrators.

Crucially, this chapter tracks Kulwantin Bai's murder and its prosecution through all three tiers of the legal system, from 1995 to 2017, when it was heard by the Supreme Court of India. In a thought experiment, I juxtapose Kulwantin Bai's legal case with what might happen were she to be murdered today, in light of the Chhattisgarh Tonahi Pratadna Nivaran Adhiniyam, or Witchcraft Atrocities Prevention Act, which was passed in 2005. I explore the nebulous concepts of social and legal justice for women accused as witches (and for men, who make up 10 percent of these accusations), and the notion of a justice system as just that: a system. I argue that as a systemic tool, the Chhattisgarh Witchcraft Atrocities Prevention Act of 2005 (hereafter the Act), and the police enactment of it, would have had a positive impact on achieving both social and legal justice in Kulwantin Bai's case, as it does for other women accused as witches in today's legal world.

Methodologically, it is difficult to assess notions of (in)justice when information is largely unavailable from the Indian lower courts. India's legal system has, until recently, largely spurned the digital age, and as such, efforts to track criminal cases through the legal system have proved frustratingly difficult. For the moment, claims to legal justice, or the lack thereof, can be assessed only from High Court appeals. Much of this chapter's discussion draws on twenty-three years of ethnographic research on public accusations of witchcraft from Chhattisgarh, a predominantly *ādivāsī* (tribal) state of central India. I focus on 35 judgments, of which 28 are appeals from the appellant courts (both pre- and post-Act), and a further 33 bail and 5 withdrawal of bail hearings. Of the 33 bail hearings, 2 indicated that a compromise had been reached between the clashing parties. In addition, charges, acquittals, and sentencing from trial courts were reported in the media or during interviews, and many police stations kept updates of trial judgments. What is exceptional in Kulwantin Bai's case is the amount of information amassed between 1995 and 2017—multiple press reports, interviews with those involved (the accused, relatives, villagers, police, NGOs, and lawyers), medical records, photos of the leg injury that sparked the accusation, Kulwantin Bai's postmortem report, police records, a State Government Inquiry report, lower court transcripts and sentencing records, High Court bail hearings and appeal documents, and finally the Supreme Court ruling.

THE DROWNING OF KULWANTIN BAI NISHAD

Mannu Nishad's son, Dhruv, burned his leg helping to douse a mysterious fire at Kulwantin Bai's residence. When he returned home, he had a fever and aching limbs. He was administered an injection by a village doctor, but the injury became infected, filling with pus and rendering Dhruv disabled. Dhruv was sent by a local doctor to Raipur, where a chest X-ray and several pathology tests were performed, after which Dhruv was admitted to a small private medical center. After a week's treatment with no signs of improvement, the wound was surgically opened and drained. Dhruv remained under treatment for one and a half months, where a total of Rs40,000 (approximately Rs267,000 in 2023 terms) was spent on medication, doctor's fees, nursing home charges, X-rays, and pathology tests, all with no improvement to the wound evident.

Two months after the injury and amid the stalled recovery, Mannu Nishad and a large group of men thumped on Kulwantin Bai's door and threatened to kill her if she failed to cure Mannu's son. According to the lower court transcript of her daughter's testimony, Kulwantin Bai opened the door to her neighbors calling *"baujī, baujī* sister-in-law" (literally, brother's wife). Her two children, Vidya, then aged seven, and Harish, aged four, were restrained by other neighbors as they watched their mother being dragged outside. Against the odds, Kulwantin Bai broke free and ran away as quickly as she could, looking for safety. Running away is locally understood as a sign of guilt in witchcraft accusations.[3] "We only went to her house to pressure her into curing my son, but when she got scared and ran, this only confirmed our suspicions of her guilt, after all, 'Why is she running unless she is guilty?'" Mannu explained during an interview as he called his son to show me an extensive scar that ran from knee to ankle.

Kulwantin Bai's daughter, Vidya, knocked on neighbors' doors for help, but none was forthcoming. As described above, Kulwantin Bai was stripped naked and beaten for hours. Intervening village council members retreated when threatened with violence and instead woke the *kotvār*, so that he could report the events to the police. The *kotvār*, however, returned to bed, happy to report Kulwantin Bai as a "missing person" the next morning. Convinced Kulwantin Bai was dead, the mob transported her body by bicycle to a well, into which she was thrown, attached to a large rock to weigh down her body. Her body, later recovered from the well, was naked and bore marks of the beating. The postmortem noted "inflammation marks on the chest, head and thigh etc. of the body" and that Kulwantin Bai died from drowning.

The state and the public were outraged and convinced that Kulwantin Bai's murder could have been avoided if only the *kotvār* had gone to police rather than going back to sleep. Put simply in one newspaper article, "If the information about the incident was given to the police at night, it could have been possible to save Kulwantin." There was considerable media-provoked public empathy for the victim's widowhood and impoverishment and for her recently orphaned children. Kulwantin Bai's elder brother and his wife took the children to their village four kilometers away and two months later publicly disowned their village in the media. For the next month the children's unblinking eyes gazed out from the newspaper stalls, their photographs demanding that the public not forget their plight.[4]

For Kulwantin Bai's murder, the police were quick to arrest twenty-six people under various sections of the Indian Penal Code (IPC). An early court hearing on July 6, 1995, for Mannu Nishad and others promptly rejected bail for the defendants, and the case was brought before the court on July 24. It was quickly transferred by the Judicial Magistrate to the Sessions Court and registered on August 7, 1995.[5] In the 1990s, less serious charges around witchcraft accusations did not usually move beyond one of the Judicial Magistrate's courts, and those that did were quickly transferred to the district court. Typically, bail was granted. Unusually, for Hirau and Mannu, their bail was granted nine months later—and Amar was granted bail eleven months later.

In the Indian courts, positions for judges are often vacant, and there are close to thirty million cases pending in lower courts.[6] Four years after Kulwantin Bai's murder—on August 9, 1999—in *The State of Madhya Pradesh v. Dhirpal Nishad and 25 Others*, Judge R. K. Shrivastev gave his final judgment. In his ruling he stated that "all the accused pleaded innocent and said that they had been falsely implicated." The court dismissed eight witnesses and the *kotvār* after they "turned hostile," a common occurrence. The Madhya Pradesh Police Commission of 1965–66 stated that delays in trial cause witnesses to become hostile "on the repeated persuasions of the accused or they get tired of attending several hearings and become indifferent."[7]

Fortunately, six witnesses and the village head corroborated their original statements that the accused had beaten the victim. Kulwantin Bai's now ten-year-old daughter testified that her mother's accusers demanded that she cure Mannu's son or they would kill her. Another named witness testified that he had tried to stop two of the accused from proceeding with the beating and that he had attempted to "snatch the stick" from the hands of another. Another witness maintained he had prevented the owner of

TABLE 14.1 Timeline of Legal Actions for Mannu Nishad and Others in Kulwantin Bai Nishad's Murder

Date	Action
May 29, 1995	Kulwantin Bai murdered
May 30, 1995	*Kotvār* reports "missing person"
May 31, 1995	Police arrest 26 persons under Case No. 1058/95
July 6, 1995	Bail applications for Hirau, Mannu, and Amar rejected
July 24, 1995	Trial No. 701/95 placed before Magistrate's Court
August 4, 1995	Case transferred to Sessions Court
August 7, 1995	Trial No. 276/95 registered in Sessions Court
May 9, 1996	Hirau and Mannu granted bail
July 8, 1996	Amar granted bail
November 4, 1997	Kulwantin Bai's daughter, Vidya, gives evidence in court
August 9, 1999	Hirau Nishad, Bhangi Yadav, Mannu Nishad, and Amar Singh Nishad found guilty of murder and sentenced to life imprisonment. Others acquitted.
September 8, 1999	Criminal Appeal CRA No. 2369/1999. Madhya Pradesh High Court allows application to appeal in *Hirav and Others v. The State of Madhya Pradesh*
November 1, 2000	Transferred to Chhattisgarh High Court
March 2001	Released on bail
December 11, 2015	Appeal dismissed
October 3, 2017	CRLMP No: 8468/2017. Petition to the Supreme Court of India for special leave to appeal in *Bhangi and Another v. The State of Chhattisgarh*. Appeal dismissed.

the bicycle that was used for transporting Kulwantin Bai's body to the well from entering the incident site. The accused did not testify. The judgment concluded: "The accused did not refute these statements during their cross-examination. Therefore, it has been proved beyond doubt that the victim was severely beaten, who later died on the spot, on 29 May 1995 at night." Kulwantin Bai's death "was due to drowning, thus was not accidental but a criminal human murder." Judge Shrivastev acquitted twenty-two of the defendants, reasoning that the "case to relate them to the crime was not proved" and that their involvement "in the crime could not be proved beyond doubt":

> The accused Hirau, Bhangi, Amar and Mannu have been proved by prosecution, to be guilty of murder of Kulwantin Bai and of hiding the body to escape punishment and are sentenced under sections 147, 302/149 and 201 of IPC. As the charge of excesses inside the house has not been proved beyond doubt against them, they are acquitted of the charge under section 452.[8]

The four who were found guilty provided statements to the court "for consideration" in sentencing, arguing they were "under tension due to the incurable illness of Mannu's son. This criminal act happened as a result of spontaneous anger resulting from it." The court allowed "no exception to murder," that is, no leniency was shown, and Hirau Nishad, Amar Singh Nishad, Bhangi Yadav, and Mannu Nishad were sentenced to imprisonment for life. The four men lost no time in appealing the judgment to the Madhya Pradesh High Court; and upon state bifurcation, it was further transferred to the Chhattisgarh High Court. Each of the four appellants was released on bail of Rs10,000 in March 2001 (having served a total of eighteen months in jail). When I interviewed Mannu Nishad several months after his release, he was adamant that he had little to do with the whole incident: "I don't believe in *ṭonhī*, but because my son was sick, people and the courts are pinning all the blame on me." Mannu Nishad suggested that relations in the village had been "restored to normal. The case is not talked about among villagers." The village head agreed that relations with the arrested men were "almost normal," although their then-recent release from jail had sparked an interest in "what jail was like." Kulwantin Bai's brother, Mangan, did not have the money for legal fees to push the case any further. "I have good relations with the other village. I just want to *forget* things. After all, it is my moral duty to raise [Kulwantin Bai's] children." Whereas villagers were "starting to lose interest" in an implicit, gradual, and unmarked way, for Mannu and Mangan, forgetting was an explicit act of *not remembering*, or a "willed transformation of memory."⁹

In 2012, a government official made inquiries on my behalf to find out what had happened in Kulwantin Bai's case. I was informed that Amar Singh Nishad had died in 2009, and Hirau Nishad had been apprehended for unlicensed alcohol sales and was in and out of jail until he absconded for good in 2004. On December 11, 2015, the High Court dismissed the appeal in *Hirau and Others v. The State of Madhya Pradesh*. Kulwantin Bai's case was unique as her two remaining murderers took their appeal all the way to the top of India's judicial system. On October 3, 2017, the case made its way to the Supreme Court of India in *Bhangi and Another v. The State of Chhattisgarh*.¹⁰ Upon hearing the counsel, the highest court heard the petition and condoned the late appeal (condonation is used when a party has not complied with the time periods set by legislation). The court could find no grounds that the High Court's final judgment was impugned (a judgment under Indian law that is challenged as being illegal or defective) and dismissed the petition and any further petitions. Twenty-two years, four months, and four days after Kulwantin Bai was accused as a *ṭonhī* and murdered for causing Dhruv Nishad's injury, his father, Mannu, and fellow accomplice Bhangi Yadav had exhausted all legal options available to them. They are currently in Raipur's central jail serving life imprisonment.

My research shows that prior to the Act, the average time from committing the crime until sentencing was approximately 2 years and 5 months.¹¹ The longest trial lasted 13 years, 4 months, and 5 days.¹² It is worth noting that Kulwantin Bai's murder trial took 4 years, 4 months, and 12 days until sentencing—despite the considerable attention it attracted at the time of the crime. Once sentenced, those facing heavy sentences characteristically appeal to the High Court. When perpetrators (out on bail), victims, and their families live side by side, as is often the case, it is difficult to imagine justice in any form, whether legal or social, under this scenario.

A THOUGHT EXPERIMENT

A thought experiment is a mental assessment in which one imagines the practical outcome of a hypothesis when physical proof may not be available; it is what I prefer to call a device of the imagination. In this section, I imagine the kind of outcomes that Kulwantin Bai's case would produce if her murder had occurred after the enactment of the new law (the Chhattisgarh

Witchcraft Atrocities Prevention Act of 2005). This device allows me to explore the new law and its impact over the last eighteen years.

Kulwantin Bai's murder prompted the first calls for a new law, but it took a decade to introduce the Act. Radhika Coomaraswamy calls the decade of women's rights law "the triumph of a certain 'law and order feminism' which aims at punishing the perpetrator, using draconian provisions in the law," and this Act is no different.[13] She further argues that "law and order feminism" has led to unforgiving laws being enacted and that "though they provide an immediate sense of something being done, in the long run they pose serious dilemmas. In the end judges and juries just do not convict if they feel that the law is too harsh or unreasonable." In the United States, sociologist Elizabeth Bernstein has argued something similar, coining the phrase "carceral feminism" for a brand of feminism that advocates for harsher and longer prison sentences for gender-based crimes, believing they will help work toward solving these problems.[14] In both contexts these laws are seen as feminist victories. Specific to India, laws that "protect" women have included legislation addressing sex-selective abortions, dowry deaths, female trafficking, maintenance and welfare of elderly parents,[15] sexual harassment in the workplace, stalking, acid attacks, guaranteed employment, domestic violence, and so on. Unsurprisingly, when it was being crafted, the Chhattisgarh Act followed the pattern of other carceral feminist laws by acquiescing to societal pressures for significantly harsher penalties for such crimes.[16]

Before moving forward, it is important to note that Chhattisgarh is known to have a proactive stance in relation to other Indian States. By virtue of being a resident in Chhattisgarh, Kulwantin Bai's case was already less likely to be withdrawn, and charges were more likely to have been brought after the incident (and should there have been suspicions leading up to her murder, the police were more likely to have responded to such suspicions than the police in other Indian states). Research conducted by Partners for Law in Development collected eighty-five First Information Reports (FIRs) filed between 2010 and 2012 in Chhattisgarh, Jharkhand, and Bihar, all states with a high prevalence of witch-hunting.[17] Discernible state trends included that (a) all the offenses mentioned in the FIRs from Chhattisgarh were carried forward in the charge-sheets; (b) only Jharkhand showed evidence of "compromise"; (c) Chhattisgarh registered cases of indirect violence (abuse and threat) at an earlier stage than other states; and (d) only Chhattisgarh made use of section 294 of the IPC.

Residential advantage aside, a major difference with the new law is that sections 4 and 5 of the Act cover non-bailable offenses. For many women, their accusers would be released on bail; then the women would be living side-by-side with their accusers in the village, where pressure was subsequently placed on the women and their families to withdraw court cases and/or to "compromise." Under the new law, all accusers are arrested and jailed, and their first action is an appeal to the High Court, not the lower courts, for bail. From the thirty-three bail hearings I collected, 76 percent were allowed on the condition of a substantial bail bond. Where the crime date was indicated in the bail hearing, a quick calculation confirms that perpetrators spent an average of 159 days (a little more than five months) incarcerated before they were released on bail. The bail hearings ranged from a quick 17 days to a long 16 months. Immediately removing the offender from the victim and witnesses is no doubt the single most important action the new law allows. At a minimum, the new law involves incarceration of the accused, a longer time in jail, sizable bail bonds, and costly lawyers' fees to higher-level appeals courts.

And so, in this thought experiment, how would the new law have changed the outcome in Kulwantin Bai's case? From the above, we know the likelihood of the accused having their bail allowed was 76 percent; and hence, the accused may have served an average of five months in jail. They certainly would have spent significant amounts of money on High Court lawyers' fees. Overall, this does not sound promising. Where the new law makes the biggest impact is with the substantial reduction in time from the date of crime to sentencing. Prior to the new law, it took approximately 2.5 years from date of crime to sentencing in the lower courts (see table 14.2). Many of the individuals sentenced appealed their lower-court sentences to the High Court. Prior to the new law, the time elapsed from lower-court sentencing to the High Court appeal decision was on average over ten years, making the appeal process an incredibly attractive, if not costly, decade of freedom.[18] This is where the good news comes. The data show that since the introduction of the Act, the time elapsed from the date of crime to sentencing has been reduced by 33 percent (from 884 days to 594 days) (see table 14.2). Another astonishing reduction applies to having one's appeal heard: a reduction of 5 years and 4 months. And in the final sentencing from the date of crime to final appeal decision there is a reduction of 4–6 years.

It is not surprising that both Mannu Nishad and the village head felt that life was restored "to normal" because they spent over 17.5 years released on

TABLE 14.2 Average Time to Final Sentencing for Appeal Cases

	Crime date to sentencing	Sentencing to appeal judgment	Crime date to appeal judgment
PRIOR TO 2005 LAW	884 days ($n = 22$), or 2 years, 5 months, and 3 days	3,693 days ($n = 15$), or 10 years, 1 month, and 10 days	4,374 days ($n = 16$), or 11 years, 11 months, and 22 days
POST LAW	594 days ($n = 10$), or 1 year, 7 months, and 17 days	1,729 days ($n = 9$), or 4 years, 8 months, and 25 days	2,417 days ($n = 9$), or 6 years, 7 months, and 14 days
DIFFERENCE	Reduction of 291 days, or 9 months and 18 days	Reduction of 1,964 days, or 5 years, 4 months, and 18 days	Reduction of 2,227 days, or 6 years, 1 month, and 5 days

bail and only 18 months in jail (for a murder committed in 1995) before receiving their final judgment, *twenty years later*. Unwilling to accept the verdict, they appealed to the Supreme Court, which dismissed their case two years later. If we apply the reduced average time frames from the new law and the assumption that the accused would be granted bail (which I somehow doubt), then by the time the case was settled on October 9, 2001, the accused would have served ten months in jail. The difference is that the case would have been settled *fourteen years earlier* (see table 14.3), and it is worth considering that Amar, who died while out on bail, would instead have died in jail and that Hirau would not have been able to abscond.

CONCLUSIONS

I was once told that "India is the land of laws and no justice." This sentiment has been expressed at the highest level, where the utility of a proposed national law to ban witch-hunting was questioned: "This country has already got so many laws that there is a need to bring about a census of a per capita law in this country! It is very important . . . the governance system itself is becoming a matter of joke because we just pointlessly pass

TABLE 14.3 Application of Post-Law Averages to Kulwantin Bai's Case

	Actual dates	Time in jail in days	Possible dates under the new law averages	Time in jail in days
DATE OF CRIME	May 29, 1995		May 29, 1995	
POLICE ARRESTS	May 31, 1995		May 31, 1995	
BAIL ALLOWED	May 9, 1996		(if allowed, then an average of 159 days) November 6, 1995	
SENTENCING	August 9, 1999	344	(average 594 days) January 14, 1997	159
BAIL ALLOWED	March 1, 2001		(if allowed, then an average of 159 days) June 22, 1997	
APPEAL DISMISSED BY HIGH COURT	December 11, 2015	206	(average of 1,729 days) October 9, 2001	159
TOTAL DAYS IN JAIL		550		318

laws here and they never go down to the field level."[19] The Act does lead to increased protections for women accused of witchcraft, and it does offer more or less respite from violence. The Act has also severely closed down past discretionary practices once exercised by the police.[20] The police now bring cases before the courts utilizing both the IPC and the Act to ensure greater conviction rates. The accused are jailed and must appeal for bail directly to the High Court, a process that removes offenders from the victimized woman and is also quite costly. Sentencing delays have been significantly shortened, as have appeals to the High Court. Appeals for reduced sentencing succeed only under reasonable circumstances. When cases are dismissed, the State of Chhattisgarh has shown its determination to prosecute by appealing to the High Courts to have decisions reversed. Chhattisgarh has a significantly high success rate, with 67 percent of convictions sustained by the appellate courts, 8 percent having their charges reduced, and 25 percent being acquitted. The Act has had a positive impact on legal justice.

However, I also argue that what is sought from this legislation, in terms of imagined immediate justice, unfolds instead over time, as a continually refined process of social and legal justice. As Katharine Bartlett states regarding legislative change aimed at gender justice, "steps forward are often only partial or are co-opted by the system or watered down as entrenched interests absorb them."[21] Justice, as described above, points beyond the simple, straightforward principle of justice; instead, its advocates call for an actual material consideration of the circumstances of women accused as *ṭonhī*. The less tangible costs of a witchcraft accusation are considerable (and can extend to immediate family): physical and emotional wounding, loss of dignity and status, feelings of shame, social ostracism, confinement to specific domestic spheres by dread and anxiety, fear of future violence, ostracism from the entire community, and the list goes on. Here ethnography finds a place whereby stories can fill the gap between abstract legal principles and the actual experiences of women.

"Feminist scholars have had a very complicated relationship with the concept of equality," Bartlett maintains.[22] She further suggests that the decades of feminist legal theory in all their variations have been consistent in seeking equality and have exercised true reform. She argues that "it is possible to be disappointed with the results of the equality doctrine, while still being committed to the concept of equality."[23] However, this is unfinished business. No matter the reforms or the positive impacts described in this chapter, women cannot take for granted the right to feel safe and free from accusations of witchcraft, nor can the 2005 *Tonahi Pratadna Nivaran Adhiniyam*, or Witchcraft Atrocities Prevention Act, address the trauma and fear that witch accusations cause in women.

NOTES

1. Kulwantin Bai's death was covered by a series of articles published by *Deśbandhu*, June 1, 2, and 3, 1995; and July 7 and 21, 1995.

2   Macdonald, "Handled with Discretion"; Macdonald, *Witch Accusations from Central India*.
3   Macdonald, *Witch Accusations from Central India*.
4   This chapter focuses on legal responses. See Macdonald, *Witch Accusations from Central India*, 160–62, for descriptions of responses and interventions by the public, media, police, and state administration.
5   Sessions Trial No. 276/95, mphc.gov.in/ilr/docs/Full_bench_Digest_Final.pdf.
6   Mehra, "Indian Citizens Must Start Demanding a Better Policing System."
7   Government of Madhya Pradesh, Police Department, *Report of the Madhya Pradesh Police Commission*.
8   *The State of Madhya Pradesh v. Dhirpal Nishad and 25 Others*.
9   Battaglia, "The Body in the Gift," 14.
10 Supreme Court of India, Record of Proceedings, Petition for Special Leave to Appeal, CRLMP No: 8468/2017, *Bhangi and Another vs The State of Chhattisgarh*, October 3, 2017, https://indiankanoon.org/doc/46163716/.
11 These numbers are accurate to November 2021.
12 The quickest trial was 4 months and 16 days. Sessions Trial No. 57/2000—judgment dated May 2, 2000. See Criminal Case No. 597/1992; High Court of Chhattisgarh, Bilaspur, Criminal Revision No. 84/2004, *Ramratan @ Khadiya Satnami vs State of Chhattisgarh*, October 22, 2018, https://indiankanoon.org/doc/121912872/.
13 Coomaraswamy, "Human Security and Gender Violence," 4736.
14 Bernstein, "The Sexual Politics of the 'New Abolitionism.'"
15 Elder abuse is particularly directed toward widowed women.
16 See Macdonald, *Witch Accusations from Central India*, 237–38, for a detailed description of bringing the new law into being.
17 Agrawal, Mehra, and Partners for Law in Development, *Contemporary Practices of Witch Hunting*, 117.
18 I recently stumbled across a case where the accused, who threw acid on the face of a suspected witch on May 7, 1990, finally exhausted all legal avenues 28 years, 5 months, and 15 days later, on October 22, 2018. High Court of Chhattisgarh, Bilaspur, Criminal Revision No. 84/2004, *Ramratan @ Khadiya Satnami vs State of Chhattisgarh*. https://indiankanoon.org/doc/121912872/.
19 See Lok Sabha Debates, No. 49, "Further Discussion on the Motion for Consideration of the Ban on Witchcraft Bill, 2011, . . . ," August 9, 2012, https://indiankanoon.org/doc/194807885/.
20 Macdonald, *Witch Accusations from Central India*.
21 Bartlett, "Feminist Legal Scholarship," 428.
22 Bartlett, "Feminist Legal Scholarship," 428.
23 Bartlett, "Feminist Legal Scholarship," 428.

BIBLIOGRAPHY

Agrawal, Anuja, Madhu Mehra, and Partners in Law and Development. *Contemporary Practices of Witch Hunting: A Report on Social Trends and the Interface with Law*. New Delhi: Partners for Law in Development, 2014.

Bartlett, Katharine. "Feminist Legal Scholarship: A History through the Lens of the *California Law Review*." *California Law Review* 10, no. 2 (2012): 381–429.

Battaglia, Debbora. "The Body in the Gift: Memory and Forgetting in Sabarl Mortuary Exchange." *American Ethnologist* 19 (1992): 3–18.

Bernstein, Elizabeth. "The Sexual Politics of the 'New Abolitionism.'" *Differences* 18, no. 5 (2007): 128–51.

Coomaraswamy, Radhika. "Human Security and Gender Violence." *Economic and Political Weekly* 40, nos. 44–45 (2005): 4729–36.

Government of Madhya Pradesh, Police Department. *Report of the Madhya Pradesh Police Commission 1965–66*. Bhopal: Government Central Press, 1967.

Macdonald, Helen. "Handled with Discretion: Shaping Policing Practices through Witch Accusations." *Contributions to Indian Sociology*, n.s., 43, no. 2 (2009): 285–315.

Macdonald, Helen. *Witch Accusations from Central India: The Fragmented Urn*. Routledge: London, 2021.

Mehra, Ajay K. "Indian Citizens Must Start Demanding a Better Policing System." *The Wire*, October 9, 2017. https://thewire.in/185447/police-reform-demand-political-will/.

Fifteen · SHASHANK SHEKHAR SINHA

Contemporary Trends in Witch-Hunting in India

Even though witch-hunting is prevalent in more than one-third of the states in India, the subject remains a grossly underresearched academic terrain in the country. Broadly speaking, there are two kinds of assumptions or assertions in writing and discourses on witch hunts in contemporary India. Sometimes, the two intersect. The first approach, noticed more in official policy discourses and in the writing of administrators, development practitioners, and journalists, associates witch hunts with "superstitions" or "lack of education and health care." Some in this category also see witch-hunting as a "primitive" or "backward" practice exclusive to the tribes. The second approach, observed more in academic and activist writing available on the subject, relates witch-hunting predominantly or even exclusively to gender and patriarchy. Going beyond these two kinds of approaches, this chapter highlights the role of regional dynamics and locational contexts and shows how these intersect with the factors listed above to give new forms and meanings to witch hunts. Finally, the chapter examines aspects like social geography and the spectrum of violence to showcase the layered and complex character of witch hunts in India and to reassesses some popular stereotypes and assumptions connected with the practice.

INCIDENCE AND SPATIAL SPREAD

One of the big challenges facing researchers working on witch-hunting in India is the absence of an authoritative, comprehensive database. The figures that are quoted in most studies/reports are those taken from the National Crime Records Bureau (NCRB), a government organization compiling statistics related to different kinds of crimes in India. NCRB data deal exclusively with witch-killings, not with witch-hunting, which is far more pervasive and regular. It includes only those cases that were registered with the police and where the principal offense was registered as a murder motivated by witchcraft.

However, even if we go by the limited scope of the NCRB data, more than 3,000 people have been killed in India between 2001 and 2020 under the pretext of practicing witchcraft.[1] Within this period, cases of witch-killings have been consistently reported from more than ten of the twenty-eight states in India including Jharkhand, Bihar, Odisha (formerly Orissa), Assam, Chhattisgarh, Madhya Pradesh, Andhra Pradesh, Gujarat, Rajasthan, and Maharashtra. Though their respective numbers vary, these states have been reporting cases of witch-killings every year in the last ten to fifteen years, with only a few gaps in between. Between 2001 and 2020, according to the NCRB, Jharkhand reported a minimum of 564 witch-killings. The state of Odisha occupies a dubious second spot with at least 493 killings. In the same period, Andhra Pradesh reported at least 419 killings; Madhya Pradesh, 316; Chhattisgarh, 218; and Maharashtra, 127. The state of Haryana, not listed in the consistent "top ten," presents a curious case as it consistently reported witch-killings every year between 2005 and 2010. In 2010, it reported fifty-eight murders motivated by witchcraft, which was the highest figure among the states that year. After 2010, however, Haryana has reported only two to three cases in a few years. The state of West Bengal consistently reported witch-killings almost every year between 2001 and 2008, and then just one each in 2012 and 2014. In addition, cases have occasionally been reported from Karnataka (it recorded seventy-seven killings in 2011, which is the highest annual figure ever reported from any individual state), Uttar Pradesh, and West Bengal. The state of Telangana (which was carved out of the state of Andhra Pradesh in 2014) has consistently been reporting few killings; and in the last couple of years, few cases (one to two) have been reported from each of the states of Meghalaya, Manipur, and Himachal Pradesh.[2]

SOCIAL GEOGRAPHY, TRENDS, AND UNDERCURRENTS

Witch hunts are known for their randomness and uncertain trajectories. However, it is possible to discern some broad trends when one looks at their social geography in India.

First, most states or regions that now report cases of witch-killing or witch-hunting—the central Indian belt, also known as the hotspot of witch-hunting in India, along with its extended westward and northeastern projections—also reported such cases during the colonial period.[3]

Second, instances of witch-hunting are more prevalent among the marginalized communities such as the *adivasis* (literally, Indigenous inhabitants, but also a generic term used for Indigenous communities) who are described in official government documents as the Scheduled Tribes, the Scheduled Castes, and Other Backward Classes (OBCs; a term that includes castes that are educationally or socially disadvantaged), and Dalits (broadly speaking, the lowest stratum of the castes, or social groups). Very few cases of witch-hunting are reported from among the higher castes or dominant social groups. In general, most areas inhabited by such marginalized communities are lacking in resources and have a poor healthcare and education infrastructure. In some states in the central Indian hotspot—such as in mineral-rich Jharkhand, Odisha, and Chhattisgarh—the marginalized communities have undergone massive dispossession and displacement on account of development projects during both the colonial and the postcolonial periods. Others in states like Assam and Chhattisgarh have experienced displacement related to insurgency and counterinsurgency operations.

Third, women constitute the primary victims of witch-hunting within the affected communities and social groups. So, there is case of double marginalization—first, as members of marginalized communities, and second, as women belonging to such communities. The terms used for a witch in different parts of the country—*dayan, dakan, tonhi, bishahi, banamati*—are feminized as well.[4] The gendered nature of witchcraft accusations is clearly reflected in ethnographic and field research from the different regions.

Helen Macdonald's recent book on witch accusations in Chhattisgarh reveals that women are nine times more likely than men to be accused as witches. Her research indicates that, of the 84 accused witches in 63 public accusations, 90 percent were women.[5] Another recent study of 110 cases of witch persecutions and witch-hunting, spread across the states of Chhattisgarh, Jharkhand, Odisha, Rajasthan, and Telangana, estimates that women were the primary accused in 95 to 100 percent of the cases.[6] It must be clarified that within the category of women, it is not just the widows or single women who are accused of practicing witchcraft and then hunted. According to a report published in 2014, of the 48 cases reported from the districts of Bihar, Jharkhand, and Chhattisgarh, the majority of the targeted victims (35 of the 48 [or 70 percent]) belonged to the age group between 40 and 60. Further, most cases belonged to the age group between 30 and 60, which shows middle-aged and married women were more vulnerable to witch-hunting than both older and younger women.[7]

So how does one explain the persecution of men and children in cases of witch hunts? In majority of witch-hunt cases, men are found to be involved as secondary victims, as husbands or kin of the primary accused or, in a few cases, supportive neighbors. An estimate of cases of witch persecutions collected from five states over different time periods—Odisha (2007–16), Rajasthan (2000–2016), Jharkhand (2010–15), Chhattisgarh (2015–16), and Telangana (2015–16)—reveals that out of a total of 176 cases, only 2 men from Odisha, 11 from Jharkhand (who were co-accused with women), and 1 from Telangana were found to be accused of witchcraft.[8]

Fourth, in most cases of witch hunts, the accuser and the accused are related to each other through some ties including kinship (related through ties of family or marriage), community (social proximity), or neighborhood (physical proximity). Intimacy, everyday social interactions and shared belief systems play an important part in witch hunts, and most studies underscore that there is usually not much of a gap in the social and economic status of the accuser and the accused.[9]

Finally, witch hunts usually begin with accusations or labeling by someone from the kin group, neighborhood, or village. Provocations like illnesses, crop failures, and unnatural deaths (in both humans and animals) commonly provide the immediate context for the initiation of the witch hunts. In most cases, local witch doctors or sorcerers are involved in the "identification" or "verification" of the "witch." What follows is persecution or a series of persecutions, often sanctioned by the village authorities, the nature of which is not always pre-determined or predictable.

INTERSECTIONS OF CONTEXTS

While we observe some common underlying trends in the circumstances occasioning the witch hunts, in the gender of the primary victims, or in the treatment meted out to those accused of practicing witchcraft, regional dynamics and spatial contexts play an important part, too. They intersect with the socioeconomic and political configurations in different states or regions to give different meanings and forms to witch hunts. In most cases, multiple motivations are involved due to an interplay between various factors—structural, contextual, and individual. More often than not a combination of factors accruing from short-, medium-, or long-term tensions are at play in witch accusations. These can include those related to land grabbing, property disputes, patriarchal strains, village and social tensions, the region's history of witch-hunting, power relations, notions of protest, identity politics, socioeconomic dislocations and dispossessions, stereotyping and branding, sexual and social transgressions, the spurning of sexual advances, jealousies, and the scramble for resources in languishing economies. Available academic works and survey reports help us understand the intricacies associated with the locational contexts.

Instances of witch-hunting in Assam are seen mostly among three communities—the Bodos, the Rabhas, and the diverse migrant tribes called the *adivasis*. Of these, the Bodos and Rabhas are officially recognized as Indigenous communities in the state. In a situation of intense ethnic conflicts and identity politics that Assam has found itself in the last few decades, the Bodos have been asking for a separate state while the Rabhas are demanding greater political autonomy. The *adivasis*—inhabiting the tea plantations owned by Marwaris, Sindhis, Punjabis, multinationals, and Indian business houses—had originally migrated to these sites as indentured laborers during the colonial period. Unlike the Bodos and Rabhas, the *adivasi* tea garden laborers form a heterogeneous group and have been categorized as OBCs or MOBCs (More Other Backward Classes) by the state. Providing cheap labor, they have been living in very exploitative and backward conditions; they have also demanded a Scheduled Tribe status, a status accorded to them in the states they migrated from.[10]

A recent study by Debarshi Prasad Nath links the resurgence of witch hunts in Assam with identity politics and ethnic revivalism, which, he says, is a result of both the fallout of globalization and the associated process of cultural homogenization as well as the failure of the state to provide education and healthcare facilities.[11] Nath argues that witch-hunting cannot be seen just as a gender issue because women's questions are intricately connected to economic factors such as attempts to grab land and property. Breakdown of community ownership of land, fierce competition for resources, poor access to healthcare and education, and ethnic conflicts have created a climate of mutual resentment and suspicion and a fear of being marginalized. The problem gets further aggravated by conflict-induced displacement and by conflicting demands for greater political autonomy in an insurgency-ridden state. In such a situation, Nath underscores, ethnic revivalism and identity assertion not only showcase an important marker of difference but also provide a way of negotiating the threat of being marginalized. The belief in witchcraft, he points out, is a marker of unique and primordial ethnic identity. Witch-hunting therefore becomes a medium of identity assertion in a region and society fraught in the last few decades with insurgency, identity politics, and consumerism. It also constitutes a new language of protest for the disarticulated ethnic communities.[12]

As in Assam, the Indigenous-migrant dichotomy plays an important role in witch-hunting cases on the tea plantations of Jalpaiguri in West Bengal. Here Soma Chaudhuri's work offers interesting sociological insights. Unlike in Jharkhand, Chhattisgarh, and Bihar, where the *adivasis* officially constitute Indigenous communities, on the Jalpaiguri tea plantations, they are seen as migrant workers first (as opposed to Indigenous *bhumiputras*) and as *adivasis* second. This unique identity and positioning, Chaudhuri maintains, affect their rights and conditions of life on the plantations and finds manifestations in the state government's dealings with the conflict between plantation management and the workers.[13] Chaudhuri argues, however, that such accusations do not reflect exotic or primitive rituals of a "backward" community as has been commonly assumed. Rather, they constitute unusual expressions of social protest or periodic reaction by the alienated and oppressed *adivasi* migrant workers against their conditions of life and work. Witch hunts in Jalpaiguri therefore need to be situated in the context of ongoing conflicts between the management and the workers on the tea plantations.[14]

Unlike in Jalpaiguri in West Bengal, witch hunts are relatively more layered in the state of Jharkhand, earlier known as the Chotanagpur region. Shashank Shekhar Sinha's long-term study of Chotanagpur region/Jharkhand, which was carved out of Bihar as a "tribal" state, shows that witch hunts are rooted in the patriarchal and patrilineal structure of the settled agricultural tribes.[15] They have, however, evolved over a period of time and have acquired newer contexts and constituencies. Given the fact that under customary systems of land inheritance among the tribes only males can own land, instances of single women and widows in possession of land being hunted or killed as witches have grown significantly,[16] especially from 1980s onward, as land started becoming a scarcer resource in the post-"development" phase. One added complexity in the study of witch hunts in the mineral-rich areas like the Chotanagpur region, Chhattisgarh, and Odisha is the role of development-induced displacement. Chotanagpur region, for example, experienced massive development of capitalist enterprises, both government-owned and private, such as mines, industries, and other multipurpose projects in the decades following India's independence from the British (1947). This resulted in massive displacement of the *adivasi* inhabitants and their loss of land and livelihoods. The *adivasis* were then marginalized from the employment opportunities that emerged as most jobs, skilled and later even unskilled, went to the Bihari immigrants. All this happened in a context of shrinking access to forests (source of *adivasi* livelihoods and medicinal plants) because of restrictive Indian government policies. The strain generated by dispossession and deprivation fueled *adivasi* migration but also led to an intensification of the demand for a separate state of Jharkhand, a surge in anti-outsider agitation, a rise in Naxalism, and a resurgence of witch hunts. Land grabbing and intense competition for resources, alongside local power politics and village and social tensions, have given new meanings and forms to witch hunts in the decades following 1980s. Feeding of excreta, rapes, stripping and parading of the accused, and public humiliation have emerged as the new methods of intimidation or harassment besides killings and fines. Sinha also underscores how the social geography of the witch hunts has been enlarged. From their origin as an intratribal affair to involving other artisanal castes living in the neighborhood/village to becoming a village affair involving diverse tribes, castes, and communities, the witch hunts have acquired new constituencies.[17] In the last few decades, more cases are now being reported by Scheduled Castes, Muslims, and Dalits.[18] The survey report by Partners for Law in Development, *Contemporary Practices of Witch-Hunting*, also points out how the current witch hunts cut across religious affiliations and include cases of Muslims in Bihar and tribal Christians in Jharkhand.[19]

Helen Macdonald's recent publication on Chhattisgarh, by contrast, highlights the role of caste dynamics among other layers and complexities.[20] Her work underlines how the victim and the perpetrator involved in witch accusations are not necessarily from within the same caste. For example, whereas accusations against Rawat women are completely intercaste affairs, the Satnamis (a Dalit community that constitutes the largest group among the Scheduled Castes) tend to accuse exclusively within their community. Accusations among the *adivasis* or Gonds also occur overwhelmingly within the community and typically within the same lineage.[21] Macdonald also points out how women from castes who are engaged in exchange with other castes—like the herdsmen, water bearers, and milk vendors—are more likely to be accused of witchcraft than those belonging to the other castes.[22] As in Chhattisgarh, caste dynamics also characterize witch accusations in Rajasthan. Such accusations in Rajasthan sometimes emanate from tensions between the dominant Rajput or Gujjar castes and the service castes that are linked to the former through a traditional service of patron-client relationships called *jajmani*.[23] However, most incidents from Rajasthan are reported from the tribal belts of Bhilwara, Udaipur, Ajmer, Dungarpur, Banswara, and Pratapgarh. Ostracization and the desire to capture land or property are two strong undercurrents in witch hunts in the state.

In general, the social geography of witch hunts in India continues to be dominated by marginalized castes, communities, and tribes, sometimes with regional specificities. In the state of Madhya Pradesh, most cases of witch-hunting are reported from the western tribal belt of the Jhabua and Dhar districts inhabited by the Bhils. A recent report on witch hunts in Odisha by ActionAid India, however, states that such incidents are prevalent in twelve of the thirty districts of Odisha—especially Mayurbhanj, Keonjhar, Sundargarh, Malkangiri, Gajapati, and Ganjam—and that the primary victims include women from among the *adivasis*/Scheduled Tribes, Dalits, and OBCs.[24] Likewise, as the magazine *Fountain Ink* reported in a story on December 11, 2019, most cases of witch accusations in Gujarat are related to the *adivasi* tract in the districts of Dahod, Mahisagar, and Panchmahals, which are characterized by low land ownership, poverty, food insecurity, poor health facilities, and low literacy rates. One of the key underlying motivations behind witch accusations in this region is to silence women, mostly widows or single women claiming their rights over property. The state of Gujarat applies the Hindu Succession (Amendment) Act of 2005—legislation that recognizes that daughters and sons have an equal status in matters of succession—to *adivasi* women in inheritance matters. Most tribes, by contrast, do not recognize women's customary right to inherit land from parents or husbands. Naturally, many accusers are either potential co-heirs or members of the extended family.[25]

In Maharashtra, most instances of witch-hunting that have come to light reveal the practice as more prevalent among the tribes and rural poor of Amravati, Dhule, Nashik, Nandurbar, Thane, Chandrapur, Gondia, and Gadchiroli—regions with a high incidence of poverty and low levels of healthcare infrastructure and literacy. In Nandurbar, primarily an agrarian district with the largest population of tribal people in the state, ideas related to stoning the accused to death and social ostracization are very common.[26] Sometimes, one notices different trends in witch-hunting even in regions within the same state. A study of Warlis and *adivasis* of Thane district shows how loss of access to forests, which played a central role in their livelihoods, traditional medicine, and religion, exacerbated gender tensions and led to a renewed wave of witch-hunting.[27] By contrast, work related to the Gondia district of Maharashtra shows how an intensive presence of the police (to deal with the Naxalites in the region) restricted avenues for detecting and dealing with witches and the employment of sorcerers and witch diviners. This in turn led to a tremendous growth in the popularity of a Hindu devotional sect, the Mahanubhavpanth, which helped people cope with attacks of witchcraft and magic.[28]

SPECTRUM OF VIOLENCE

The violence associated with witch hunts has changed and evolved over time.[29] In more recent times, witch hunts have taken on a variety of forms that go beyond fines, banishment, and killing of the accused. These forms of persecution include social isolation, verbal abuse, sexual assault, public humiliation, mental and emotional stress, recurrent physical torture, loss of property, and disruption of livelihoods. And all or some these may happen together, or one after the other in no particular order.[30] The accused and their family members thus live in the constant fear of being attacked. What we discuss in the following paragraphs are some scattered examples of the violence associated with witch hunts, reported mainly in prominent national or international dailies in recent times. Again, this is not a completely representative or comprehensive picture, but it gives us some insights into a complex and multilayered phenomenon.

In June 2021, *The Telegraph*, an Indian newspaper, reported a case from Mayurbhanj district in Odisha where a tribal man beheaded his sixty-two-year-old aunt as he thought she was responsible for the death of his child. Later, he carried the severed head to a police station and surrendered.[31] Likewise, in another story carried by BBC News on July 22, 2015, a sixty-three-year-old woman, Purni Orang, was stripped naked and beheaded by villagers in Assam state, after she was blamed for illness in a tribal settlement in Sonitpur district.[32] Cases of beheading of suspected witches have also been reported from other states, including Jharkhand, Chhattisgarh, and Gujarat, in the recent past. In August 2013, according to a report by *India Today*, an Indian magazine, thirty-five-year-old Santu Bai was reportedly stoned to death in Hirapur, a tribal hamlet in Jhabua district of Madhya Pradesh, for practicing witchcraft. The reportage also mentions how, in other instances, tribal women have been beaten up, tortured, paraded naked, humiliated, and driven out of their villages by mobs in Jhabua and Dhar district of the same state.[33] In fact, it was the media and civil uproar around a similar case of witch-hunting in 2001 in Lachkera in the neighboring state that led to enactment of the Chhattisgarh Witchcraft Atrocities Prevention Act of 2005. The three women accused were reportedly paraded naked in Lachkera village and had the word "witch" etched onto their foreheads. When the accused asked for water, they were tied to an electric pole, and then some men urinated on them to send electric shocks through their bodies.[34]

Sometimes, witch hunts transcend ethnic or community boundaries and become extended village affairs. According to news carried by the *Times of India*, on February 7, 2010, in an incident in Patharghatia village in Deoghar district of Jharkhand, Sushila Devi along with four others (including a Muslim woman), mostly widows, were accused of being *dayans*. They were beaten, paraded naked through the village, and forced to eat excreta. Word had spread that the "*dayans* would be dancing" and there were at least 10,000 villagers watching when these women were beaten up.[35] Forced feeding of human excreta is particularly common in Jharkhand and Odisha. It is believed that excreta or dirty water or filth pollutes the body of the accused, forcing the possessing spirit to leave it. Similarly, feeding a person the sacrificial blood of an animal is believed to purge the body of evil spirits.

It needs to be clarified, however, that public humiliation and sexual assault are relatively recent additions to witch hunts and reflect the influences of caste societies. They are connected to the idea of violation of bodies of women, which, in caste societies, are seen as repositories of shame and honor. According to news reported by the *Hindustan Times* on June 24, 2011, thirty-six-year-old Karishma Gaur and her fifteen-year-old daughter, Naina, living in Monabarie Tea Estate in Assam's Sonitpur district, were raped and killed on the pretext of practicing witchcraft.[36] The *Hindustan Times* also carried another story on June 17, 2016, related to a case reported from Jharkhand's West Singhbhum district, in which a forty-five-year-old woman suspected of practicing witchcraft was allegedly stripped, beaten, and gang-raped by men.[37] But violence associated with witch hunts is not always so visible and apparent. Social ostracization, lifelong stigma associated with branding, and mental trauma and loss or disruption of livelihood are most common accompaniments of such hunts.

In January 2005, Bholi Devi of Bishnoi community—which is listed as an OBC in Rajasthan—was ostracized from Dariba village and forced to take shelter in Bhilwara, a city fourteen kilometers away. According to this news published in the *People's Archive of Rural India* (PARI), over the years, Bholi made repeated attempts to appease her fellow villagers by going on pilgrimages, participating in purifying rituals, and organizing multiple feasts on local festivals, but she could not get her social ostracization revoked. On August 14, 2016, Bholi's neighbor in Bhilwara, who had read about her accusation, alleged that she had caused her knee pains through black magic. Meanwhile, Bholis's daughter-in-law Hemlata was also called a witch in the Dariba village and had to face ostracism for twelve long years.[38] In 2011, Triveni Chanda, a Scheduled Caste woman from Gobar Landia village in Ganjam district of Odisha, was not only physically assaulted, stripped, and fed human excreta on suspicion of practicing witchcraft. She and her husband also lost all of their belongings, had to pay huge fines, and were deposed from their farming land. Following the incident, they had to work as daily laborers to earn their living.[39] Stereotyping of related communities is another phenomenon noticeable in cases of witch-hunting in contemporary India.

In January 2018, a report brought to light the extensive prevalence of the belief in witchcraft, or *dakan* customs, in at least twelve villages of Rajgarh and Shajapur districts inhabited by the Patidars, a landowning caste found mostly in Gujarat but also in some other states as well.[40] In such villages, a girl born to a woman labeled as a witch is also treated as one. Such girls experience dwindling of their marriage prospects, are not allowed to attend local village functions and weddings, and are even barred from eating spicy food.[41] A work by Sanjay Bosu Mullick also mentions the existence of similar villages in West Singhbhum district of Jharkhand, known as "poison villages" (*najom hatu*). Most women inhabitants of such poison villages are looked upon as witches, and they find it hard to get married to men outside the village. Also, visitors from outside prefer not to eat or drink anything during their stay in such a village.[42]

In conclusion, one can say that witch-hunting in India is geographically and socially more widespread than popularly assumed. The prevalence of such hunts among the Scheduled Castes, OBCs, Dalits, and Muslims contradicts the stereotypical belief that the practice is exclusive to *adivasis*. In addition, witch-hunting is more than just a practice connected with superstition and the lack of healthcare and education; nor is it exclusively a gender issue. Rather, diverse socioeconomic factors intersect with regional and spatial dynamics to give new meanings and forms to witch hunts. Finally, the emergence of sexual violence and public humiliation shows how the violence related to witch hunts is evolving and reflects the influence of caste societies and globalization.

NOTES

1. Compiled from annual NCRB figures; does not include figures for 2015. For details, see National Crime Records Bureau, "Crime in India," accessed September 28, 2022, Crime in India | National Crime Records Bureau (ncrb.gov.in), https://ncrb.gov.in/sites/default/files/CII-2021/CII%20Disclaimer%20 2021.pdf; accessed on September 28, 2022.
2. For data by year, see National Crime Records Bureau, ""Crime in India," accessed on September 28, 2022, Crime in India | National Crime Records Bureau (ncrb.gov.in).
3. For a broad idea of regional trends in witch-hunting during the colonial period, see Sinha, "Adivasis and Witchcraft in Chotanagpur."
4. Sinha, "Culture of Violence," 106.
5. Macdonald, *Witchcraft Accusations*, 101.
6. Kelkar and Nathan, *Witch Hunts*, 49. The research for this work was conducted between 2014 and 2016.
7. PLD, *Contemporary Practices of Witch Hunting*, 8–11.
8. Kelkar and Nathan, *Witch Hunts*, 49.
9. PLD, *Contemporary Practices of Witch Hunting*, 24–28.
10. PLD, *Witch Hunting in Assam*.
11. Nath, "Assam's Tale of Witch-Hunting," 54–60.
12. Nath, "Assam's Tale of Witch-Hunting," 59–60.
13. Chaudhuri, "Unusual Expressions of Social Protest," 24, 14, 15.
14. Chaudhuri, "Unusual Expressions of Social Protest."
15. Sinha, "Adivasis and Witchcraft in Chotanagpur."
16. Sinha, "Adivasis, Gender, and the Evil Eye," 128–29. Such customary systems of land inheritance could also be seen among other *adivasis* of central India.
17. Sinha, "Adivasis and Witchcraft in Chotanagpur."
18. For an idea of different kinds of cases involving different communities, see Mishra, *Casting the Evil Eye*; and Bosu Mullick, *Dayan Gatha*.
19. PLD, *Contemporary Practices of Witch Hunting*, 23.
20. Macdonald, *Witchcraft Accusations*, 121.
21. Macdonald, *Witchcraft Accusations*, 112–16.
22. Macdonald, *Witchcraft Accusations*, 121.
23. Kelkar and Nathan, *Witch Hunts*, 51.

24. ActionAid Association (India), *Witch Branding in Odisha: Violation of Women's Rights*, November 22, 2015, https://www.actionaidindia.org/publications/witch-branding-in-odisha-violation-of-womens-rights/.
25. Monica Jha, "The Witches of Dahod," *Fountain Ink*, December 11, 2019, https://fountainink.in/reportage/the-witches-of-dahod.
26. Jagtap, "Witch Practice (Dakin Pratha) in Adivasi Communities," 580–84.
27. Munshi, "Women and Forest."
28. Desai, "Anti-'Anti-witchcraft' and the Maoist Insurgency," 423–39.
29. For details on how the forms of violence have changed from colonial period onward, see Sinha, "Culture of Violence," 105–20.
30. Sinha, "Culture of Violence," 105–20.
31. Subhashish Mohanty, "Aunt 'Beheaded' on Witch Suspicion," Telegraph Online, June 15, 2020, https://www.telegraphindia.com/india/aunt-beheaded-on-witch-suspicion-in-odisha/cid/1781202.
32. BBC News, "India Arrests 16 for Beheading Woman for 'Witchcraft,'" July 22, 2015, https://www.bbc.com/news/world-asia-india-33605244.
33. *India Today*, "Mass Hysteria over Witchcraft Grips Madhya Prasdesh," August 13, 2013, https://www.indiatoday.in/magazine/special-report/story/19921215-mass-hysteria-over-witchcraft-grips-madhya-pradesh-767261-2012-12-21.
34. PLD, *Targeting of Women as Witches*, 15.
35. Saira Kurup, "When Women Become 'Witches,'" *Times of India*, February 7, 2010, https://timesofindia.indiatimes.com/when-women-become-witches/articleshow/5543904.cms.
36. Rahul Karmakar, "Rape behind Witch-Hunt Murders in Assam, 6 Held," *Hindustan times*, July 24, 2011, https://www.hindustantimes.com/india/rape-behind-witch-hunt-murders-in-assam-6-held/story-AfL7FNmWeRrLxE2IZxIimL.html.
37. Manoj Choudhary, "Labelled a Witch, Jharkhand Woman Stripped, Beaten Up, and Gang-Raped," *Hindustan Times*, June 17, 2016, https://www.hindustantimes.com/india-news/labelled-a-witch-jharkhand-woman-stripped-beaten-up-and-gang-raped/story-haHpZgIv2kb9PyiOtg8ceI.html.
38. Madhav Sharma, "In Dariba: Brand Them Witches, Grab Their Land," Rural India Online, February 25, 2020, https://ruralindiaonline.org/en/articles/in-dariba-brand-them-witches-grab-their-land/.
39. ActionAid Association (India), *Witch Branding in Odisha*, 20–21.
40. Shruti Tomar, "'Witches' No More: Women in MP's Patidar Villages Take on the Unfair Social Custom," *Hindustan Times*, January 26, 2018, https://www.hindustantimes.com/bhopal/branded-as-witches-women-of-mp-s-patidar-villages-fight-against-the-evil-practice/story-kFezv7rTU80103vyUWFljJ.html.
41. Tomar, "'Witches' No More."
42. Bosu Mullick, *Dayan Gatha*, 112–18.

BIBLIOGRAPHY

Act!onaid (India). "Witch Branding in Odisha: Violation of Women's Rights." https://www.actionaidindia.org/publications/witch-branding-in-odisha-violation-of-womens-rights/. Last updated November 22, 2015.

Bosu Mullick, Sanjay. *Dayan Gatha*. Ranchi: IDFG 2009.

Chaudhuri, Soma. "Unusual Expressions of Social Protest: Witchcraft Accusations in Jalpaiguri, India." CAS Working Paper Series, Centre for the Study of Social Systems, CAS/WP/14-5, Jawaharlal Nehru University, New Delhi, 2014.

Desai, Amit. "Anti-'Anti-witchcraft'" and the Maoist Insurgency in Rural Maharashtra, India." *Dialectical Anthropology* 33 (2009): 423–39.

Jagtap, Dilip Rambhau. "Witch Practice (Dakin Pratha) in Adivasi Communities: An Economic and Social Reality." *International Journal of Multidisciplinary Research and Development* 2, no. 11 (November 2015): 580–84.

Kelkar, Govind, and Nathan, Dev. *Witch Hunts: Culture, Patriarchy and Structural Transformation*. New Delhi: Cambridge University Press, 2020.

Macdonald, Helen. *Witchcraft Accusations from Central India: The Fragmented Urn*. Abingdon, UK: Routledge, 2021.

Mishra, Archana. *Casting the Evil Eye: Witch Trials in Tribal India*. Delhi: Roli Books, 2003.

Munshi, Indra. "Women and Forest: A Study of the Warlis of Western India." *Gender, Technology and Development* 5, no. 2 (2001): 177–98.

Nath, Debarshi Prasad Nath. "Assam's Tale of Witch-Hunting and Indigeneity." *Economic and Political Weekly* 49, no. 37 (2014): 54–60.

Partners for Law in Development (PLD). *Contemporary Practices of Witch Hunting: A Report on Social Trends and the Interface with Law*. New Delhi, 2014. https://papers.ssrn.com/sol3/papers.cfm?abstract_id=2660070.

Partners for Law in Development (PLD). *Targeting of Women as Witches: Trends, Prevalence and the Law in Northern, Western, Eastern and Northeastern Regions of India*, New Delhi, 2015.

Partners for Law in Development (PLD). *Witch Hunting in Assam: Individual, Structural and Legal Dimensions*. New Delhi, 2014. https://papers.ssrn.com/sol3/papers.cfm?abstract_id=2660709.

Sinha, Shashank S. "Adivasis, Gender, and the Evil Eye: The Construction(s) of Witches in Colonial Chotanagpur." In *Adivasis in Colonial India: Survival, Resistance and Negotiation*, edited by Biswamoy Pati, 128–29. New Delhi: Orient BlackSwan, 2011.

Sinha, Shashank Shekhar. "Adivasis and Witchcraft in Chotanagpur (1850–1950)." PhD diss., Department of History, University of Delhi, 2010.

Sinha, Shashank S. "Culture of Violence or Violence of Cultures? Adivasis and Witch-Hunting in Chotanagpur." *Anglistica AION* 19, no. 1 (2015): Article 106.

Sixteen · ADRIANNA L. ERNSTBERGER

Bewitching Gender History

A witch is born out of the true hungers of her time. —RAY BRADBURY, *Long after Midnight* (1976)

The history of witch hunts and the persecution of those accused of practicing witchcraft are fundamentally tied to gender, both historically and contemporarily. Witch hunts have occurred across the globe under the auspices of myriad religious and political tensions—tensions clearly tied to the disruption, or perceived disruption, of social gender norms. Extensive research exists on gender and witchcraft, especially on witch hunts in early modern Europe.[1] However, contributions that explore the history of witches and witchcraft globally, like those found in this anthology, are far too rare. Witch histories from the Global South are critical. They belong in the dominant narrative of witch studies, and without them we cannot get a truly global understanding of the connections between gender and the history of witches and witchcraft. It is that global perspective I am most interested in, both for the history itself and for how that history can help students explore larger systems of power.

To conclude her recent article, "Witchcraft and Gender," Raisa Maria Toivo, a historian of early modern European witchcraft, asserts that to effectively study the history of witches and witchcraft using gender as a category of analysis, "one must first decide whether one is examining witchcraft trials in order to learn more about early modern concepts of gender, or whether one is looking at gender to find an explanation for witchcraft trials."[2] Although my analysis and corresponding pedagogical application is more expansive, as it moves beyond early modern Europe, I agree with Toivo's call for specificity. In this chapter, I detail how a global comparative study of witch persecutions can be a lens through which students may study global gender history.

With such an enchanting subject matter, my approach results in a course that draws students from diverse majors; it also narrows down what could be an overwhelmingly broad subject matter—global gender history—into a manageable framework to enable comparative analysis and a theoretically rich focus. As a feminist historian, I focus my scholarship on comparative gender histories in the Global South with a keen interest in women's resistance to cultural and political oppression in the nineteenth and twentieth centuries. Using a global history of witch persecutions via secondary sources from leading subject experts and primary sources from diverse regional and temporal perspectives, my approach allows students to participate in a micro-level conversation about specific local histories while placing those regional histories into a macro-level comparative analysis. This broadens students' understanding of the history of witches and witchcraft beyond Salem and challenges their preconceived notions about the ways we study and understand gender history. Moreover, let's be honest: witch histories get students excited about history, especially when they discover that persecution of witches remains a dangerous reality to this day.

THEORETICAL UNDERPINNINGS

The work of María Lugones, the late Argentinian-born lesbian feminist philosopher, activist, and pioneer of decolonial feminism, has strongly influenced my conception of gender as central to understanding coloniality and decoloniality, hegemonic global capitalism, and the disproportionate weaponization of gender against women to maintain systems of inequality. Her synthesis of gender as a colonizing force in "The Coloniality of Gender" and her trailblazing essay "Toward a Decolonial Feminism" are central to my research on women's educational activism in the Global South, broadly, and to my use of witch persecutions as a lens for studying gender history, specifically.[3]

In "The Coloniality of Gender," Lugones expands on Aníbal Quijano's "coloniality of power" thesis, in which he uses world systems theory to explain the intersecting violence of European colonialism and capitalist expansion into the Americas as well as the resulting creation of racialized hierarchies.[4] Quijano posits that this emerging power structure relies on two equally important and inseparable axes: the coloniality of power and the coloniality of modernity, in which the nation-state centralizes all forms of power in the hands of the colonizer through domination, capitalist exploitation, race-based social hierarchies, and epistemological hegemony.[5] Lugones challenges the limitations of this "coloniality of power" because it lacks a nuanced analysis of the relationship between coloniality and gender; in so doing, she turns to contributions from feminists and critical race theorists from the Global South to develop her theory on gender and coloniality, what she calls the "colonial/modern gender system." Lugones argues that "coloniality does not just refer to 'racial' classification. It is an encompassing phenomenon . . . it permeates all control of sexual access, collective authority, labor, subjectivity/inter-subjectivity and the production of knowledge."[6] As such, institutionalized colonial, and arguably postcolonial, state power cannot be understood as separate from gender.

Providing yet another example of how gender is socially constructed and always situated in specific spaces and times, Lugones reminds us that gender has often been used as a form of colonial violence. She asserts that "as Eurocentered, global capitalism was constituted through colonization, gender differentials were introduced where there were none"; Lugones points to the work of Oyéronké Oyewùmí, who argues that "gender was not an organizing principle in Yoruba society prior to colonization by the West."[7] Lugones then looks to Paula Gunn Allen's research of Native Americans, among whom there was often a broad spectrum of gender identity that eschewed biological determinism.[8] And Lugones further complicates the relationship between coloniality and gender by highlighting the role of colonized men in the colonial/modern gender system through their acceptance of Western gender hierarchies that frame gender as a static binary of male/female and assign power and authority to gendered males. She posits that colluding with Western colonizers was central to the "inferiorization" of colonial women's power.[9] And, as we will see in many of the following case studies, it continues to be the precedent for many contemporary witch persecutions.

The imposition of Western gender norms on colonized bodies has its own robust body of literature; Lugones herself credits this literature as central to her ability to "affirm that gender *is* a colonial imposition."[10] As we investigate how gender is weaponized in witch persecutions, we must remember, as Lugones writes, that "turning the colonized against themselves was included in the civilizing mission's repertoire of justifications for abuse. Christian confession, sin, and the Manichean division between good and evil served to imprint female sexuality as evil, as colonized females were understood in relation to Satan, sometimes [even] as mounted by Satan."[11] Thus, it is not the revelation of gender as another form of colonial violence that marks Lugones's work as valuable to the study of witch persecutions but rather her focus on the ways the "coloniality of gender" resulted in the complicity of colonized men in subordinating colonized women. This complicity remains today and is evident in contemporary witch persecutions throughout the Global South in part because, "unlike colonization, the coloniality of gender is still with us; it is what lies at the intersection of gender/class/race as central constructs of the capitalist world system of power."[12]

As the case studies my students engage with repeatedly demonstrate, "The white colonizer constructed a powerful inside force as colonized men were co-opted into patriarchal roles."[13]

PEDAGOGICAL APPLICATION

What started as a "special topics" module embedded in one of my upper-division history electives quickly became a stand-alone course (History of Global Witch Hunts) taught on a regular rotation; it is one of my most popular classes. Gender, as a constructed identifier and collection of social expectations, has been, and continues to be, used to legitimate systemic power structures and to determine whose voices are valued and whose are relegated to society's margins. Certainly, gender is not the only category that contributes to systems of power or oppression; race, class, religion, sexual orientation, and coloniality are other central markers of identity that do not operate in a vacuum. However, designing the course around gender as the primary category of analysis helped meet the goal of using witch persecutions to understand comparative gender history.

Students need a clear outline of a course's aims; in this case, it is equally important to know what the course intentionally ignores. At the outset, I articulate our primary goal: to understand how gender manifests across time and place by studying the global history of witch persecutions. Though we focus on witches and witchcraft, I let students to know it is fundamentally a course on inquiry and argument, designed to help them learn strategies for asking analytical questions, conveying critical insights, articulating complex ideas, and practicing the historian's craft. I explain the intentionality and rationale behind the text selections, regional case studies, and specific theories we will unpack over the semester. We discuss what it means to "decolonize" the syllabus, which lays the groundwork for future conversations about legacies of racism and colonialism in the study of witches, witchcraft, and gender. Such conversations help students grapple with what it means for such legacies to still inform by whom, and from where, knowledge is produced and valued.

I situate myself as a feminist historian, which leads to conversation about, and clarification of, what feminism is, and how it pertains to me. I point out that I am a white, middle-class, cisgendered, American woman married to a man (and thus assumed to be heterosexual), and the product of a Catholic school education. I nudge students to consider their own intellectual and ideological position vis-à-vis the subject matter. This conversation introduces them to positionality and prepares them for the scope of our study. We will not debate the *existence* of witches and witchcraft specifically, nor the *reality* of magic, sorcery, or supernatural powers broadly. We will instead explore how gender is deployed through witch persecution.

Next, we spend the first couple weeks of the course reviewing relevant broad historiographies on witch persecutions in early modern Europe and the American colonies. Students are eager to relate new material to what is familiar. By starting with what they know, or think they know, and interrogating that material using theories about the connection between power and gender, students flex their analytical muscles. Following are some of the case studies that have effectively guided students through this work. With each regional and or/temporal case, I have included brief content summaries and examples of how the material can help students extrapolate patterns and points of difference in the use, and abuse, of gender. In presenting students with regionally and temporally diverse manifestations of witch persecutions, I challenge them to see gender not simply as a set of behaviors or expectations but as a constantly contested and often weaponized ordering principle that is foisted upon individuals as often as it is embraced.

Early Modern Europe: Late Fifteenth Century to Late Eighteenth Century

We first look at witch persecutions in Europe during the early modern period, something students know about, and we begin to tease out lessons about gender in this era. In "Witchcraft and Gender in Early Modern Europe," Alison Rowlands does not equivocate on the significance of gender in understanding the history of witches and witchcraft: "Gender shaped every aspect of early modern witchcraft and witch trials: beliefs about magic and witchcraft; social and psychological tensions from which accusation emerged; anxieties about their own gendered identities expressed by accusers and demonologists; the legal processes by which people were tried; and the degree of power that individual had to defend themselves from prosecution," she writes.[14]

Rowlands affirms the widely understood belief that women were the primary targets and victims of witch persecutions during this era, stating that "the idea that witches were predominantly female is confirmed by modern statistical analysis, which shows that overall, 70 to 80 percent of those tried for the crime of witchcraft in early modern Europe and New England were women."[15] Rowland rightly notes that not all accused witches were women, and that percentages change from region to region.

To balance our study, I present material about witch persecutions in Iceland, Russia, and Finland. Prior to the spread of Christianity and increased contact with Europeans, Icelandic views on magic and its practitioners were often positive. Magic was associated with authority, power, and knowledge, which often meant literacy, and men were its primary practitioners. When the witch hunts came to Iceland, relatively late, the witches who were accused, tried, and put to death were almost exclusively men. In his recent thesis on Icelandic witch persecutions during the seventeenth century, Dominick Zarillo notes that between 1625 and 1683, 170 people were accused of witchcraft, 130 trials were held, and 21 people were burned to death as convicted witches.[16] In contrast to the number of women accused of witchcraft in other parts of Europe during this time, of the 170 people accused, only 10 only were women, and only 1 was found guilty and executed.[17]

From Iceland we travel to Muscovy, Russia, an extremely hierarchical and patriarchal society in which the state severely regulated people's movement, access to education, and engagement in public spaces—via explicitly gendered regulations. Women had little access to education, were excluded from public engagements, and were expected to stay close to home. Conversely, men were more likely to be nomadic, landowning, and literate—all threats to the state. As Valerie Kivelson explains in her essay about witch persecution in Muscovy, Russia, "Because of the particular social anxieties of the time, Russian accusers and prosecutors identified members of certain social categories as the most prone to practicing magic. Since there were more men than women who filled these social roles, more men were accused."[18] Kivelson argues it is important to witch studies in general to look further into witch persecutions outside Western Europe, as "gender, when configured differently than in the West, could weaken the association between women and witchcraft and lessen the centrality of gender itself in the logic of witch belief."[19]

Finishing our early modern European Tour, we end in Finland, which offers students some complexity to consider in their analysis of gender and witch persecutions. According to Rune Blix Hagen, a historian of Nordic witch histories, Finland boasted one of Europe's highest percentages of men accused of witchcraft.[20] As Toivo demonstrates in "Witchcraft and Gender," though, gender distribution in Finland's witch persecution shifted three times between the sixteenth and eighteenth centuries![21] Between 1500 and 1660, and again from 1770 onward, the majority of those accused, tried, and executed for witchcraft in Finland were men. But during what Toivo calls the "most intensive" witch persecutions, between 1660 and 1770, the majority of witch persecutions targeted women.[22] Finnish history provides the perfect foil to simplistic summations about the gendered nature of witch persecutions and about gender as a static concept.

Supplementing these secondary histories, students examine primary sources from each of the regions, such as court records, folklore, art, and, of course, the infamous *Malleus Maleficarum*.[23] Taken together, students consistently pull out three critical elements. First, gender is a social construction tied to specific external factors, and it is assigned to specific bodies for specific purposes. Second, gender is neither fixed in definition nor in performance. Behavior seen as inherently masculine in 1640 Iceland, such as practicing magic and herbal-based healing arts; was classified as feminine in 1540 England; and again re-cast (pun intended) as masculine in 1720 Russia. Third, gendering is not a passive act. At its most benign, it is a conscious act directly tied to power; at its worst, it is an aggressive act that ascribes not only expectations but condemnations. My most recent group of students, undergraduate history majors and minors with minimal exposure to prior gender studies courses, impressed me in noting how the more sexualized and diabolical the concept of witchcraft became, the more likely a society was to make women the predominant target of witch accusations.

Colonial and Postcolonial Global South: Sixteenth Century to Present Day

As we move into the Global South, we shift to reading selected books in their entirety, which encourages students to engage more deeply with material in less familiar areas of the world and histories. After reviewing critical concepts like Global North/Global South, colonialism, postcolonialism, and transnationalism, we turn to Guatemala and read Martha Few's *Women Who Live Evil Lives*, an excellent study of gender and witch persecutions in seventeenth- and eighteenth-century Guatemala.

Few focuses on accounts of *mujeres de mal vivir*, women who live evil lives, a phrase repeated throughout colonial archives to describe "female sorcerers, witches, magical healers, and leaders of clandestine religious devotions."[24] Students become engrossed in the 1704 trial documents of Lorenza de Molina and María de Santa Inéz from Santiago de Guatemala, in which women are accused of using witchcraft to abuse a local priest. Using diverse primary sources, Few asserts that colonialism was in a state of constant contestation and that women's precolonial role as public figures in religious and community life made them ideal targets for persecution as witches. "Women's public roles in local religious culture left them vulnerable to accusations of sorcery and became opportunities for the Spanish state to re-inscribe colonial rule at the community level through institutions such as the Inquisition," she writes.[25] Supplemented with primary source activities related to the text, students become able to articulate the ways women's resistance to colonial rule was used to justify enforcement of state-determined normative gender roles as well as how rumor and gossip were tools of both colonized and colonizer.

After that excitement, we fast-forward to witch persecutions in the contemporary era, specifically in Ghana and India. Students continue to evaluate the role of colonialism/postcolonialism, state power structures, and violence in asserting and enforcing gender conformity in the twenty-first century. And now they must make sense of witch hunts as a contemporary reality. Published in 2017, the interdisciplinary *Witchcraft as a Social Diagnosis*, cowritten by Roxane Richter, Thomas Flowers, and Elias Kifon Bongmba, provides an accessible study of witch persecution in Ghana, focusing primarily on the largest of seven witch villages, Gnani, where more than 40,000 women and children live.[26] Using colonial and postindependence state records, public health reports, and extensive oral testimonies from women in Gnani, the authors "map the new social dynamics which characterize contemporary understandings of witchcraft" with a brief historical overview of witch persecution in the region that explains the role of social stigma and economic power.[27] According to reports from the Anti-Witchcraft Allegation Campaign Coalition–Ghana, although witch accusations were once levied at men and women who were believed to have used evil powers to cause crop failures, bring illness to their communities, or cause a family member's sudden death, contemporary witch persecutions target women: "Some 99.9 percent of condemned witches are exclusively women and children."[28]

In reading testimonies from widowed and older women condemned as witches and banished to Gnani, students learn that economic gain often motivates contemporary witch persecution in Ghana. Accusations of witchcraft and the resulting internment in Gnani are also used to punish behaviors that challenge the status of women as secondary to men in any way.[29] Classifying witch persecution as gender-based violence, the authors do not hold back in their condemnation of such practices: "Gender-based violence in Ghana gags its elderly widows, assertive business-women, liberated feminists, and childless brides like an antiquated muzzle: inciting fear, silencing public outcry, and eliciting manifest submission. It is an enduring stranglehold composed of intermingled fiscal, gender, cultural, religious, patriarchal, and social tourniquets."[30]

From the clear connection between witch persecution and gendered behaviors in Ghana, students move to the course's final regional case study, India. India is one of the world's most dangerous places for people, predominantly women, accused of witchcraft. According to the United Nations Human Rights Council, "In the last decade, there have been more than 20,000 registered human rights violations in 50 countries and six continents around the world" related to witch accusations and witch hunts; of those, more than 6,000 cases were in India.[31]

Students first read Govind Kelkar and Dev Nathan's *Witch Hunts*, which covers contemporary witch persecutions in India, precolonial perspectives on witches, and the ways a belief in witches and witchcraft has been imported and exported throughout South Asia. Providing theoretical analyses of patriarchy's role in witch hunts and policy-based arguments for ways to eradicate witch hunts globally, Kelkar and Nathan prepare students to do textual analysis of Indian legal codes for their final projects.

The purpose of India's first anti-witch-hunting act, The Prevention of Witch (Dain) Practices Act, 1999, was, first, to discourage the *practice* of witchcraft and, second, to discourage *assaults* on people accused of being witches. The act defines witches as specifically gendered females, equating womanhood and witches, by stating that a witch is a "woman who has been identified as a witch by someone else and having the power of intention of harming any person through the art of black magic, evil eyes, or 'Mantras' and it is deemed that she will allege harm any way to other person/persons or the community at large, in any manner."[32]

Between 1999 and 2019, seven regional acts against witch hunts were signed into law in multiple Indian states. Three of the seven maintain the defining feature of a witch as being a woman; the other four, which differ in their definitions of a witch, do not. The Karnataka Prevention and Eradication of Inhuman Evil Practices and Black Magic Act, 2017, contains by far the most expansive definition of who can be considered, and thus accused of being, a witch. A witch, it states, includes practitioners of "inhuman, evil practices and black magic by means of the commission of any act, specified in the schedule, by any person by himself or caused to be committed through or by instigating any other person"; it also contains a surprisingly expansive statement about personhood: "an Individual male, female, or a transgender, or a company or association or body of individual whether incorporated or not."[33]

By the time students finish reading these acts and engaging with the supplemental primary sources, they are able to complete a number of assignments that evaluate regional gender norms and speak to ways Indian witch persecutions are, as in Ghana, tied as much to land acquisition and economic control as they are to communal beliefs about people using black magic to cause harm.

CONCLUSION

Accusations of witchcraft and associated persecutions have occurred across the globe, and in various manifestations, throughout human history. These histories, especially ones that have been overlooked by mainstream witch studies—that is, those from the Global South—deserve our attention. However, to limit these witch histories to a singular content-based lens misses a valuable opportunity. Witch history is inherently beguiling. Students willingly, even gleefully, engage with theory and develop nuanced analyses informed by robust engagement with primary sources—work many would at best resist, and at worst, intentionally avoid, if not presented within such a spellbinding framework.

In a world where people are still hunted, burned, lynched, imprisoned, banished, and killed based on accusations of witchcraft—accusations that have grown increasingly feminized—a global comparative study of the history of witch persecutions provides an opportunity to explore power, identity, and gender. Exposed to the small but growing global historiography of witch studies, students get comfortable working with a diverse collection of historical sources from vastly different regions and time periods. They additionally become proficient in seeking out evidence-based explanations for the vacillating focus on women as witches, and in so doing, they begin to articulate a comparative understanding of global gender history.

At the same time, using the history of witch persecutions to study changes in the ways gender manifests across time and place shows students how gender norms have historically put both men *and* women at risk of witchcraft accusations. They come to understand the ways witchcraft accusations have been used as a state and/or religiously sanctioned tool to enforce gender norms in the name of social order, and they see the divergent ways that different cultural settings have allowed individuals to subvert those same gender norms.

As mentioned at the start of this chapter, witch studies scholars interested in the relationship between gender and the history of witches and witchcraft need to determine whether they are studying witches by way of gender, or gender by way of witches. Equal clarity and intentionality are necessary in pedagogy. Here, I have demonstrated the latter: how historians can teach global gender history by way of witches. My approach produces dynamic—dare I say bewitching—results. Students actively engage with the duality of agency and victimization, power and oppression, and the use of myth and rumor as agents of social order and disorder. Such engagement prepares them to formulate possible paths of resistance and postulate policy changes that could, finally, eradicate this specific weaponization of gender.

NOTES

1   See Opitz-Belakhal, "Witchcraft Studies," 90–99; Kounine, "Gendering of Witchcraft," 295–317; Toivo, "Gender, Sex and Cultures of Trouble," 87–108; Whitney, "The Witch 'She'/The Historian 'He,'" 77–101; and Levack, *New Perspectives of Witchcraft, Magic, and Demonology.*
2   Toivo, "Witchcraft and Gender," 228.
3   For additional work from Lugones relevant to this subject, see "Revisiting Gender," 29–39; and Lugones and Isasi-Diaz, "Methodological Notes Toward a Decolonial Feminism," 201.
4   Quijano, "Coloniality and Modernity/Rationality," 168–178.

5	Quijano, "Coloniality and Modernity/Rationality," 168–169.
6	Lugones, "The Coloniality of Gender," 1.
7	Lugones, "The Coloniality of Gender," 7.
8	Gunn Allen, *The Sacred Hoop*.
9	Lugones, "The Coloniality of Gender," 9.
10	Lugones, "Toward a Decolonial Feminism," 748. Emphasis added.
11	Lugones, "Toward a Decolonial Feminism," 745.
12	Lugones, "Toward a Decolonial Feminism," 747.
13	Lugones, "The Coloniality of Gender," 10.
14	Rowlands, "Witchcraft and Gender in Early Modern Europe," 466.
15	Rowlands, "Witchcraft and Gender in Early Modern Europe," 449.
16	Zarillo, "The Icelandic Witch Craze," 33.
17	Zarillo, "The Icelandic Witch Craze," 33.
18	Kievelson, "Male Witches and Gendered Categories," 606–607.
19	Kievelson, "Male Witches and Gendered Categories," 606.
20	Hagen, "Witchcraft Criminality and Research in the Nordic Countries," 381.
21	Toivo, "Witchcraft and Gender," 220.
22	Toivo, "Witchcraft and Gender," 220.
23	Kramer and Sprenger, *Malleus Maleficarum*.
24	Few, *Women Who Live Evil Lives*, ix.
25	Few, *Women Who Live Evil Lives*," 3.
26	Richter, Flowers, and Bongmba, *Witchcraft as a Social Diagnosis*, xiii.
27	Richter, Flowers, and Bongmba, *Witchcraft as a Social Diagnosis*, xvii–xviii.
28	Richter, Flowers, and Bongmba, *Witchcraft as a Social Diagnosis*, xiii.
29	Richter, Flowers, and Bongmba, *Witchcraft as a Social Diagnosis*, 29.
30	Richter, Flowers, and Bongmba, *Witchcraft as a Social Diagnosis*, 95.
31	Tembhekar, "UN Human Rights Body Asks States."
32	"Prevention of Witch Practices Act, 1999."
33	"Karnataka Prevention and Eradication of Inhuman Evil Practices and Black Magic Act, 2017."

BIBLIOGRAPHY

"Assam Witch Hunting (Prohibition, Prevention and Protection) Act, 2015." Government of Assam, accessed April 3, 2024. https://homeandpolitical.assam.gov.in/documents-detail/the-assam-witch-huntingprohibition-prevention-and-protection-act-2015.

"Chhattisgarh Tonahi Pratadna Nivaran Act, 2005." Bare Acts Live, accessed April 3, 2024. http://www.bareactslive.com/Ch/CG077.htm.

Few, Martha. *Women Who Live Evil Lives: Gender, Religion, and the Politics of Power in Colonial Guatemala*. Austin: University of Texas Press, 2002.

Gunn Allen, Paula. *The Sacred Hoop: Recovering the Feminine in American Indian Traditions*. Boston: Beacon Press, 1992.

Hagen, Rune Blix. "Witchcraft Criminality and Research in the Nordic Countries." In *The Oxford Handbook of Witchcraft in Early Modern Europe and Colonial America*, edited by Brian P. Levack, 375–92. New York: Oxford University Press, 2013.

"Karnataka Prevention and Eradication of Inhuman Evil Practices and Black Magic Act, 2017." Bare Acts Live, accessed April 3, 2024. http://www.bareactslive.com/KAR/kar087.htm.

Kelkar, Govind, and Dev Nathan. *Witch Hunts: Culture, Patriarchy, and Structural Transformation*. Cambridge: Cambridge University Press, 2020.

Kievelson, Valerie A. "Male Witches and Gendered Categories in Seventeenth-Century Russia." *Comparative Studies in Society and History* 45, no. 3 (2003): 606–31.

Kounine, Laura. "The Gendering of Witchcraft: Defence Strategies of Men and Women in German Witchcraft Trials." *German History* 31, no. 3 (2013): 295–317.

Kramer, Heinrich, and Jacob Sprenger. *Malleus Maleficarum*. Nurenberg: Anton Koberger, 1494.

Levack, Brian, ed. *New Perspectives of Witchcraft, Magic, and Demonology*. Vol. 4 of *Gender and Witchcraft*. New York: Routledge, 2001.

Lugones, María. "The Coloniality of Gender." *Worlds and Knowledges Otherwise* 2, no. 2 (2008). https://globalstudies.trinity.duke.edu/projects/wko-gender.

Lugones María. "Revisiting Gender: A Decolonial Approach." In *Theories of the Flesh: Latinx and Latin American Feminisms, Transformation, and Resistance*, edited by Andrea J. Pitts, Mariana Ortega, and José Medina, 29–39. New York: Oxford University Press, 2019.

Lugones, María. "Toward a Decolonial Feminism." *Hypatia* 25, no. 4 (2010): 742–59. http://www.jstor.org/stable/40928654.

Lugones, María, and Ada Maria Isasi-Diaz. "Methodological Notes toward a Decolonial Feminism." In *Decolonizing Epistemologies: Latina/o Theology and Philosophy*, edited by Ada Maria Isasi-Diaz and Eduardo Mendieta, 68–86. New York: Fordham University Press, 2011.

"Maharashtra Prevention and Eradication of Human Sacrifice and Other Inhuman, Evil and Aghori Practices and Black Magic Act, 2013." Bare Acts Live, accessed April 3, 2024. http://www.bareactslive.com/MAH/MH190.HTM#2.

"Odisha Prevention of Witch-Hunting Act, 2013." LegitQuest, accessed April 3, 2024. https://www.legitquest.com/act/odisha-prevention-of-witch-hunting-act-2013/8626.

Opitz-Belakhal, Claudia. "Witchcraft Studies from the Perspective of Women's and Gender History." *Magic, Ritual and Witchcraft* 4, no. 1 (2009): 90–99.

Oyewùmí, Oyéronké. *The Invention of Women: Making an African Sense of Western Gender Discourses*. Minneapolis: University of Minnesota Press, 1997.

Parida, Abash. "Odisha Accounts for 2nd Highest Witch Hunt Cases." *The Pioneer*, June 22, 2021. https://www.dailypioneer.com/2021/state-editions/odisha-accounts-for-2nd-highest-witch-hunt-cases.html.

"Prevention of Witch Practices Act, 1999." LegitQuest, accessed April 3, 2024. https://www.legitquest.com/act/prevention-of-witch-practices-act-1999/24EA.

Quijano, Aníbal. "Coloniality and Modernity/Rationality." *Cultural Studies* 21, nos. 2–3 (2007): 168–78.

"Rajasthan Prevention of Witch-Hunting Act, 2015." PRS Legislative Research, accessed April 3, 2024. https://lawsofindia.blinkvisa.com/pdf/rajasthan/2015/2015Rajasthan14.pdf.

Richter, Roxane, Thomas Flowers, and Elias Kifon Bongmba. *Witchcraft as a Social Diagnosis: Traditional Ghanaian Beliefs and Global Health*. Lanham, MD: Lexington Books, 2017.

Rowlands, Alison. "Witchcraft and Gender in Early Modern Europe." In *The Oxford Handbook of Witchcraft in Early Modern Europe and Colonial America*, edited by Brian P. Levack, 449–68. New York: Oxford University Press, 2013.

Tembhekar, Chittaranjan. "UN Human Rights Body Asks States to Take Steps to Eliminate Witchcraft." *Times of India*, August 7, 2021. https://timesofindia.indiatimes.com/city/mumbai/un-human-rights-body-asks-states-to-take-steps-to-eliminate-witchcraft/articleshowprint/85131316.cms.

Toivo, Raisa Maria. "Gender, Sex and Cultures of Trouble in Witchcraft Studies: European Historiography with Special Reference to Finland." In *Writing Witch-Hunt Histories: Challenging the Paradigm*, edited by Marko Nenonen and Raisa Maria Toivo, 87–108. Leiden: Brill, 2013.

Toivo, Raisa Maria. "Witchcraft and Gender." In *The Routledge History of Witchcraft*, edited by Johannes Dillinger, 219–32. London: Routledge, 2020.

Whitney, Elspeth. "The Witch 'She'/The Historian 'He': Gender and the Historiography of the European Witch-Hunts." *Journal of Women's History* 7, no. 3 (1995): 77–101.

Zarillo, Dominick. "The Icelandic Witch Craze of the Seventeenth Century." MA thesis, The College of New Jersey, 2018.

ART, AESTHETICS, AND CULTURAL PRODUCTION

Seventeen · ISABEL MACHADO

Mista Boo: Portrait of a Drag Witch

It is hard to summarize what the drag character embodied by artist and *brujo* Alejandro Garza (a.k.a. Alex Garza, or Mista Alex) represents. Mista Boo inspires unconditional adoration from her fans, the Boobulubus, but is also often involved in controversies and feuds in Mexico's drag scene, especially via social media. Adored and hated in almost equal proportions, it is impossible to be indifferent to her presence.[1]

Alejandro Before Mista Boo

> *There is a lot of speculation about my age. There are some people who do know how old I am, of course, but there are many who don't. They speculate my age or think that I am even older than I actually am. I like to leave this as an enigma. That has to do with all that I'm doing right now with drag. It's for the audience. So, my age is the age of my character, which is 500 years old. I'm centenarian.*[2]

Alejandro Garza was born in Reynosa, Tamaulipas, on the Mexico-US border. As he puts it, he had an "Americanized" childhood. He grew up watching cartoons and other TV shows in English on the US channels available in the area. Alex has also been in contact with the occult from an early age as his very Catholic mother read Tarot cards and had the sensitivity to feel a supernatural presence in one of his childhood homes. He used the word freedom several times to describe his childhood. He was free to go where he pleased and to play with whomever he wanted without strict adult supervision. That changed when he started to become aware of his queerness. He spent his preteen years in McAllen, Texas, and led a bilingual life between McAllen and Reynosa until he was fifteen years

FIGURE 17.1 Mista Boo, 2019. Portrait by Unosobrecuatro.

old. At that age, he started meeting other queer people. As he said, he was looking for a "tribe" with which to fit in. At first, his mother didn't seem too bothered by his "difference," which she interpreted as a "phase." But when it became clear that his nonconformance with heteronormativity would not just go away, things became more turbulent at home. Alex was also conflicted by the imposed gender roles he observed in gay men's relations in Reynosa:

> *There were jotos (faggots) or mayates. The mayate is a gay man who doesn't consider himself gay because he has sex with men but doesn't kiss them. He fucks them, or receives blow jobs from them but, to him, it is a kiss or being penetrated by another man that makes you gay. So if I hooked up with someone in Reynosa, I was the woman and he was the man, and he behaved like a man, and I had to behave like a woman with him. In other words, the aggression toward my gender came from a partner, right? That seemed normal there, but I said, "This can't be it, there has to be more." That was not what I wanted. The good thing is that I never wanted to stay in Reynosa.*

At the local gay club, Hip House, he found his tribe, and he began to hang out with them in the town square during the day. Yet, as he put it: "Small town: big hell. And the gossip began." When his mother heard that he was "hanging out with homosexuals," she interrogated him about his own sexuality. After he confirmed that he is gay, his family tried a series of tactics to make him "change." One of the strategies they employed to "fix" him was to send him to a military academy in Harlingen, Texas. His mother would also leave copies of *Nota Roja* (a violent, sensationalist tabloid) magazines on his bed so he would find headlines like "Satanic Narcos Kill Homosexual for Ritual" when he arrived home from school. At times she also left a Bible strategically open to the passages that directly condemned his "sins." Finally, she told him: "There is a doctor who gives you an injection that helps you change. Should I take you there or have you already changed?"

To appease his mother, he promised that he would change, even though he did not actually plan to. Yet these efforts to repress his identity and sexuality led to "philosophical and religious questions" that, in turn, led to even "deeper questions" about his life's mission and purpose as well as to suicide attempts. After his sixth failed suicide attempt, he decided that if he was still alive there must be a higher purpose for his existence. Still dealing with existential conflicts after finishing high school, he found solace, direction, and a calling in magic and witchcraft and decided to move to a bigger city.

> That's when I arrived at Wicca, magic, witchcraft, the exoteric. And it was very easy for me to do certain things. Like, I bought a Tarot deck and began to read it without any previous studies, and it turned out that everything I was saying was true. I started reading about it, but I didn't take a course or anything. I am self-taught. I started being interested in all that had to do with the religion of the Earth, Mother Nature, Father Sky, a goddess, a god who did not judge, who did not criticize. This idea that all the people on Earth are here because they have something to do, they have a mission. And that was when I decided to come to Monterrey to study.

While he shared with his mother the gift of card reading, he did not mention her as a direct inspiration for his practice. His discovery of a new spiritual belief system served as a means to counteract the harmful prejudices he encountered in his family's religion. When it comes to his journey toward becoming a witch, Alex describes himself as an autodidact. In US bookstores he found the teachings of other witches, like Scott Cunningham, Starhawk, Ann Moura, Robin Skelton, and T. Thorne Coyle, while the internet served as a means to find community and exchange information with fellow Wiccans.

As Sabina Magliocco notes, many LGBTQIA+ people "are drawn to Neo-Paganism because of its accepting attitude toward all sexual orientations, especially compared with the judgmental stance of most mainstream religions."[3] In *Witchcraft and Gay Counterculture* (1978), a foundational text for many queer witches, Arthur Evans writes: "The old religion was polytheistic. Its most important deity was a goddess who was worshipped as the great mother. Its second major deity was the horned god, associated with animals and sexuality, including homosexuality."[4] It is no wonder that Alex, like many other queer witches before and after him, would find his calling and purpose in and through Wicca after experiencing the rejection and repression of his identity and sexuality in the religion in which he was raised.

MAIDEN

Mista Boo was born two years ago, aaaaaand she hasn't killed me yet.

In Monterrey, Alex discovered a larger community of queer people and different possibilities for expressing and experiencing sexuality and affection that were not available in Reynosa. Located only three hours from the Mexico-US border, Monterrey is the largest and wealthiest city in Northern

Mexico. It attracts those looking for opportunities, from migrants on their way to the United States to LGBTQIA+ people from small towns all over the region:

> The majority here came from elsewhere, that's why there was so much freedom, because they were away from their towns, their families. When I went to a club and saw men holding hands, hugging each other, and showing each other love, I realized that this is was what was really missing. Affection. The sex was always there, but the affection, this connection, that's what was missing. So, when I get here and see all of that I don't want to ever go back to Reynosa.

Because of his thin frame and elegant feminine features, his new friends wanted him to compete in *travesti* (female celebrity impersonators) pageants; but he had already been exposed to other drag paradigms through US media. Instead, he brought his spiritual practices and training to alternative stages with esoteric performances in which he enacted the rituals he had learned. As he notes, these were still a long way from the shocking performances he would later create with his drag character: "But that is all part of the path, isn't it? This attraction to, this interest in the esoteric is also applied to my art." These experiences set the stage for the creation of the character who would indelibly change his life.

About thirteen years before Mista Boo was born, Alex experimented with drag for a photo shoot with a character called Vicious Baby, who represented vice incarnate. While he wanted to do performances as that character, he realized that Monterrey was still not ready for something like that. Not only was the city's mainstream culture too conservative for such performances, but its gay nightlife was dominated by *travesti* performers whose female celebrity impersonation shows graced audiences with polish, beauty, elegance, and perfection.[5] There did not seem to be room for the type of subversive performances he envisioned.

Alex continued dedicating himself professionally to Tarot reading sessions, spiritual consultations, and *límpias* (spiritual cleansings) until he decided to "create a drag character that is a very punk witch who doesn't give a fuck, and do some really badass, shocking performances. Performances that will make you think," as he put it. An early draft of the character manifested on Halloween 2016 and appeared again on Alex's birthday a few weeks later. Yet when a friend told him to enter a new drag contest, he hesitated, thinking about the social stigma and what his family would say if they found out. Despite his initial hesitations, after corresponding with the competition's "mother," Mama Bree (Carlos Briano), he decided to compete in the first season of *Regias del Drag*, a contest modeled in the format of reality shows such as *RuPaul's Drag Race* but performed live in a seedy local bear bar. On January 9, 2017, Mista Boo officially debuted on the stage of Brut33.

> *I entered Regias del Drag without knowing anything about makeup. I had an idea of what I wanted to do, but it wasn't inspired by something I saw in a video or a movie or by another performance. No, I wanted to do a performance where I used dialogue and songs to tell a story. That's what I did in the first episode and from that moment I captured everyone's attention. I did a really cool performance, which I think became a benchmark for the following competitors and for subsequent generations of Regias.*

The process of giving birth to Mista Boo for the competition happened in tandem with Alex's process of accepting and embracing his femininity. He found his voice as a *brujo* by studying the works of white women witches. When I asked him, "Who is Mista Boo?" he explained that she was born under the influence of "real witches" such as Laurie Cabot and Starhawk but with the "rebellious attitude of Punk." While his identity as a *brujo* (Alejandro/Mista Alex) and his *bruja* character (Mista Boo) were inspired by US and European witch archetypes, they are also in dialogue with local references and traditions, reflecting his/her/their borderland experiences. Both drag and professional witchcraft rely on communication with an "audience," understanding their environment and being able to provide references and speak in a language that is accessible to their interlocutors. As Mista Alex and as Mista Boo, Alejandro mastered the art of using elements from different sources to capture attention.

> *You see, everything has already been done. To copy something is to do it exactly the same, to reproduce exactly the same, yes? To be influenced by something is similar, but you adapt it, you appropriate it, you modify it to make it your own. So this phrase of the dark queen, the eternal queen of the night, comes from a series called Salem. Many phrases I use like, "I am the supreme, the Supreme Mista Boo," come from [American Horror Story] Coven, but that is something that I have to do to hook the audience. After Regias del Drag, my life ended as I knew it. I still have my esoteric, my witchcraft practices and all that, but I feel like Mista Boo absorbed a lot of my life.*

At the *Regias del Drag* Christmas extravaganza a few months after her crowning, Mista Boo expressed her appreciation for the audience with a ritualistic performance:

I took an audio from a Mexican Christmas movie where a girl says: "I don't want to be bad; I want to be good." They saw me as the soap opera villain of the competition, so it was like telling the public: "I'm not going to be bad anymore." I closed the show with Rihanna's umbrella song, but at the beginning I added the Coca-Cola peace song [from the 1970s commercial]. Then I shake a coke bottle and pfffff spray the audience. But then comes the intense part of the show. At the end, I take out a dagger and cut my hand and make a pact with the audience that I will always be with them, and I smear the blood on the stage. I was making a blood pact with them: "I will always be here." And I've remained faithful to that pact. Without the audience, there is no point in doing anything.

As Dracmorda, of the Boulet Brothers, notes: "Queerness and horror go hand in hand, and queer themes run deep through the origins of horror itself."[6] There are numerous iconic examples of queer artists who engage with witchcraft, the occult, and the horror genre. Kenneth Anger's film *Inauguration of the Pleasure Dome* (1959) was a manifestation of his involvement with Thelema and his fascination with Aleister Crowley. The Cockettes performed the Halloween horror spectacle *Les Ghouls* in San Francisco's Palace Theater in 1970, while the *The Rocky Horror Picture Show* (1975) took queer-horror-satire to broader audiences. The Hermanas Vampiro drag collective challenged the hegemony of the *travesti* beauty pageants and cabarets in mid-1990s Mexico City, but Monterrey would still have to wait almost two decades to have its first local dark queen.

In *Queering Drag*, Meredith Heller critiques "public knowledge about drag" as "narrow and premised on (and . . . limited by) a myopic vision of the genre," while showing the "many ways that drag performers construct, reproduce, bend, and challenge identity."[7] Mista Boo is part of a transnational movement of artists who apply the tools of horror, shock, and monstrosity to their drag performances as a means to upset these preconceived notions. April Seizemore-Barber's description of South African performer Stephen Cohen's message could just as well have been written about Mista Boo: "You think we are monstrous? We will be fabulous monstrosities and claim the marginal role you give us, in a tactical space to show you your own fears."[8]

I asked Alejandro about the spiritual aspect of drag, questioning how he perceives the fact that two people can inhabit his body. He replied:

Actually, it is not, it is not . . . The same happens in the spiritual realm. We are vehicles of souls, yes? But we are also a means through which other beings can speak. In rituals, for example, in a full moon ritual, we draw down the moon.

> *What does it mean to draw down the moon? It means you draw the spirit of the goddess into you so that she acts through you. It's personifying a goddess or personifying a god or a divine essence, that's what it is. It has never created a conflict in me. For the same reason that I have been telling you, everything that I have done has led me to this, or I could adapt to this.*

If, as Magliocco suggests, we understand magic and ritual as art, and, more importantly, as performance art, drag is the perfect vehicle for that convergence. Mista Boo blurs these lines when she performs real witchcraft rituals as part of her drag shows. Since the character became more popular, Alex also conducts private Tarot readings online as his drag persona. In those instances, not only is the line between the *brujo* Alejandro and the *bruja* Mista Boo dissolved but so is the line between fans and clients. Analyzing alternate states of consciousness and religious ecstasy in neo-pagan rituals, Magliocco writes: "In these states, individuals may feel they have become a different being. They may dance, fall to the floor, or move about in unexpected ways, performing actions that would be difficult under ordinary circumstances, taking on the role of the being they are impersonating."[9] What is a drag performance if not a moment of artistic ecstasy where the artists surrender their bodies to another entity that, many times, is quite different from their everyday personas?

MOTHER

> *The house started after I won the crown. My examples of drag houses had to do with voguing houses. Like in* Paris Is Burning. *It also has to do with the need for acceptance, for feeling like we belong to this tribe, to a clan, to a family. A feeling that you are a part of something. So, since I'm the crowned one, kids who want to start doing drag, or who started doing drag because of me, because they saw me and said, "This is what I want to do," begin to approach me. And they started asking me if I'm not going to start a house, if I don't want to be their mother.*

Regias del Drag and its dark queen irrevocably changed Monterrey's drag scene. Mista Boo's coronation consolidated the competition's clear departure from the polished beauty queens of previous pageants and contests.[10] Emerging victorious from *Regias*, she started her own drag/ballroom/voguing house and created one of the most subversive and inclusive horror/dark/alternative drag competitions in Latin America, gathering around her a coven of other like-minded queer folks for whom she became a maternal figure. It is interesting to note, however, that before creating a drag or ballroom house, Alejandro had already started a space of community in his former Barrio Antiguo home:

> But even before all this, there was already a house. It was Mista Alex's house where witches and wizards came to learn the Craft. I gave Tarot workshops, magic workshops, ritual workshops. I was teaching them everything. So I already had my own fraternity, my coven. When it comes to drag, it's the same. It turns out that some of the members of the house are also witches.

Mista Boo became a reference for those who saw in her as a local possibility model for doing alternative drag. While there were previous examples of horror drag in popular culture, from the season 4 (2012) winner of *RuPaul's Drag Race* Sharon Needles to the competition/reality show *Dragula* (2016–present), it is one thing to see these performances in a foreign TV show and quite another to experience it live.[11] The newly formed Haus of Boo immediately started planning *La Masacre*, which Mista described as:

> A competition to create a platform for horror drag, or for any drag that has no place in other competitions. We wanted to find and support alternative, horror, trashy, monster, dark drag artists. Or artists that have not been given the chance to perform anywhere else because they are not "pretty." In other words, we welcomed all of the rejects.

Organized along the same lines as reality shows, such as *RuPaul's Drag Race* and *Dragula*, and inspired by the local live competition *Regias del Drag*, *La Masacre* takes place in queer and alternative venues in Monterrey and creates a platform for new subversive drag talent. It has not only established and solidified Haus of Boo's image and reputation but also serves as a recruiting tool to find new members. On May 2022, Morgana Blavasky was the third monarch to win the *Masacre* crown, following Nita Kebo Nita (season 2) and Silvana Proietti (season 1).

Attending a *Masacre* show can be a visceral experience. As religion, and more specifically Catholicism, is often a fundamental source of oppression for people who defy gender and sexuality normativity in Latin America, it is not surprising that sacrilege and heresy are common themes in these performances. The Facebook event page for the semifinal episode of the second season of the "most sinister drag competition in Mexico" promised an unforgettable night of *vergüenza nacional* (national shame). The themes of the episode, which the competitors were tasked with embodying on stage, were sacrilege, blasphemy, and idolatry.[12] They were to show the audience why they were cast away from heaven and sent to the Haus of Boo drag inferno. And the performers delivered. One of the performers pulled a rosary out of her ass, while the queen who would go on to win the competition performed oral sex on a person embodying a crucified Jesus. The event ended with an orgiastic lip-synch battle. The spectacle evoked the black sabbath descriptions used by Inquisitors to persecute and kill witches in the past. Only this time it was queer folks ecstatically exorcising religious oppression on the stage to a mesmerized audience.

CRONE

> I have Saturn in my second house in my birth chart. That is the house of money, it is in Leo, and Saturn places time limitations. And an astrologer told me, "You are not going to . . ." How did she put it? . . . "You are only going to start making money, or you are only going to be successful on your job or your profession until you are older." Because of Saturn, because the time limitations it places.

At the end of our first interview on December 10, 2018, Alex acknowledged the symbolic relevance of us doing a recapitulation of his life on his birthday and joked that it might mean that he would die the following year. Little did we know when we conducted our last interview in January 2019 that one of the most exuberant chapters in Mista's trajectory was yet to be written. Less than a year later, with an iconic performance that included a golden shower, she entered the third installment of one of Mexico's most important drag competitions: *La Más Draga*. While her brilliance did not come across properly in the YouTube show (she did not win the crown), Mista Boo appropriated ageist insults and used the platform to solidify her place as a reference point for those who exist at the margins of an already marginalized community. The program's visibility expanded her influence to the rest of Mexico and other parts of Latin America's dark drag fandom, and the exposure meant exponential growth in her social media following. The larger platform brought fame and infamy, love and hate, and revealed to a much broader audience Mista Boo's incredible talent for transforming insult into art. As the oldest performer to compete in any of the show's seasons, the attacks often focused on her age. Yet she channeled ageist and classist comments into performances that embodied the third facet of the neo-pagan deity—the Crone—and was baptized Mexican drag's Weli (from *abuela*, or grandmother).

> Mista Boo was a lifeline for me. I thought that I had no direction anymore. Mista Boo is teaching me quite the opposite. She's telling me, "You don't have to get old." My mind is not going to tell me when I have to get old—I get to decide that, I control my mind. So, I am 2,000 years old. I like to play with my age. Everyone knows I'm old, but I'd like to see them at my age doing what I'm doing. I have always felt young; no one has taken my youth away from me. They say I suck the youth out of my daughters. I see my daughters; they are at a really cool age. Maybe I am already at the end of my path, right? And they are just starting. Just starting on their life journey. Who knows? I don't want to die anyway. I don't know how much longer I will be doing this, but I have a lot of passion for it. And because it's a passion, it gives me purpose. When you are depressed and you have no direction, it is because your life's purpose is over. But as long as you have a goal, as long as you have a purpose in life you don't die. In other words, there is no death. So why worry?

One of the most fascinating aspects of Alejandro's journey is how witchcraft keeps giving him new leases on life: First, when as a teenager he discovered in Wicca a reason to continue living. Several decades later, at an age when some drag performers are contemplating retirement, he started a new chapter by embodying the supreme dark witch, and subsequently reinvented himself yet again through a different platform.

There have been those who denounced Mista Boo's persona and performances as derogatory to witches, something that can be related to the broader question of whether drag is "degrading to women."[13] It can be argued that by modeling his character on the evil witch who consorts with the Devil and eats newborns, Alex is contributing to harmful stereotypes about women. When asked in a 2019 interview if feminists should embrace the image of the witch, Silvia Federici described "the image of the witch today" as "a sort of a battleground," and identified the two different camps disputing that image. On the one side are the feminists who reclaim the image of the witch in a positive way, as healers or women who possessed knowledge and wisdom. On the other side are the media representations that portray witches as "evil, evil women," reproducing images and discourses used in the witch hunts of the sixteenth and seventeenth centuries. Federici warns that these are not innocent initiatives and encourages young women to "picket" these movies "because they are waging a war against us."[14]

As both a real and a fictional witch, Mista Boo complicates this dichotomy, and if we understand "deviance as resistance" we can find queer and feminist empowerment even in his most controversial performances.[15] In *The Female Grotesque*, Mary J. Russo offers a counterpoint to the "normalization of feminism," or the "disarticulation of feminism from the strange, the risky, the minoritarian, the excessive, the outlawed, and the alien."[16] Russo also claims that "the 'female grotesque' does not guarantee the presence of women or exclude male bodies or male subjectivities," noting that the "category of the female grotesque is crucial to identity formation for both men and women as a space of risk and abjection."[17] Whether someone interprets Mista Boo as harmful or as empowering to witches reflects the perspective of the person who witnesses her shows. Or, as Alex would have it:

> *I know that I am not one person, I know that I am many people. Why? Because I have a perception of myself, but for you I am someone, for another person I am someone else, for all people, for everyone, I am different. I am never the same person.*

This chapter was written by a woman who derives immense joy, pleasure, and inspiration every time she has the privilege of experiencing Mista Boo on a stage.

NOTES

1. While Alejandro Garza identifies as a cisgender gay man, the character he embodies, Mista Boo, is a female witch, so I switch pronouns accordingly to respect these identities. When I am referring to both character and performer at the same time, I refer to them as they.
2. All quotes were extracted from two interviews conducted with Alejandro Garza in November 2018 and January 2019. The original interviews were conducted in Spanish as part of the "Queens of the South(s)" oral history project.
3. Magliocco, *Witching Culture*, 62.
4. Evans, *Witchcraft and Gay Counterculture*, 103.
5. The performers Verta Taylor and Leila J. Rupp documented in a Key West, Florida, drag cabaret in the late 1990s–early 2000s also pointed out the differences "between 'female impersonators' who generally do celebrity impersonation and keep the illusion of being women" and "drag queens who regularly break it in order to accentuate the inherently performative nature of gender and sexual meanings." Taylor and Rupp, "Chicks with Dicks," 115.
6. Simukulwa and Robledo, "Exclusive: The Boulet Brothers."
7. Heller, *Queering Drag*, 19.
8. Sizemore-Barber, *Prismatic Performances*, 35.
9. Magliocco, *Witching Culture*, 161.

10 For more on what *Regias del Drag* means for queer culture and worldmaking in Monterrey, see Alvarez, "Cementing."
11 I am borrowing the concept from trans actress/activist Laverne Cox (and others). See https://lavernecox.com/about/.
12 Haus of Boo, "La Masacre 2: Ángel Caído," Facebook event, October 26, 2019, https://web.facebook.com/events/2406473946347764/?acontext =%7B%22event_action_history%22%3A[%7B%22surface%22%3A%22page%22%7D]%7D.
13 Heller, *Queering Drag*.
14 TV Boitempo, "Should Feminists Embrace the Image of the Witch?," YouTube, July 13, 2020, https://www.youtube.com/watch?v=iO4rNi4WIIw.
15 Cohen, "Deviance as Resistance."
16 Russo, *The Female Grotesque*, vii.
17 Russo, *The Female Grotesque*, 12.

BIBLIOGRAPHY

Alvarez, Laura Patricia. "The Cementing of an Empire." *Journal of Festive Studies* 3 (2021): 236–55.

Cohen, Cathy J. "Deviance as Resistance: A New Research Agenda for the Study of Black Politics." *Du Bois Review: Social Science Research on Race* 1, no. 1 (2004): 27–45.

Evans, Arthur. *Witchcraft and the Gay Counterculture: A Radical View of Western Civilization and Some of the People It Has Tried to Destroy*. Boston: Fag Rag Books, 1978.

Heller, Meredith. *Queering Drag: Redefining the Discourse of Gender-Bending*. Bloomington: Indiana University Press, 2020.

Magliocco, Sabina. *Witching Culture: Folklore and Neo-paganism in America*. Philadelphia: University of Pennsylvania Press, 2004.

Russo, Mary. *The Female Grotesque: Risk, Excess, and Modernity*. London: Psychology Press, 1995.

Simukulwa, Nali, and Jordan Robledo. "Exclusive: The Boulet Brothers on Dragula Season 4 and How 'Queerness and Horror Go Hand in Hand.'" *Gay Times*, October 25, 2021. https://www.gaytimes.co.uk/drag/exclusive-the -boulet-brothers-on-dragula-season-4-and-how-queerness-and-horror-go -hand-in-hand/.

Sizemore-Barber, April. *Prismatic Performances: Queer South Africa and the Fragmentation of the Rainbow Nation*. Ann Arbor: University of Michigan Press, 2021.

Taylor, Verta, and Leila J. Rupp. "Chicks with Dicks, Men in Dresses: What It Means to Be a Drag Queen." *Journal of Homosexuality* 46, nos. 3–4 (2004): 113–33.

Eighteen · D FERRETT

Witching Sound in the Anthropocene (and Occultcene)

The witches' ritual chant—"She changes everything She touches, and everything She touches changes"—could surely be commented on in terms of assemblages, since it resists the dismembering attribution of agency. Does change belong to the Goddess as "agent" or to the one who changes when touched? But the first efficacy of the refrain is in the "She touches." The indeterminacy proper to assemblages is no longer conceptual. It is part of an experience that affirms the power of changing to be NOT attributed to our own selves nor reduced to something "natural." It is an experience that honors change as a creation. —ISABELLE STENGERS

When we think of touch, we think also of impact—whether physical, mental, emotional, material or immaterial, whether forever or ephemeral. Touch is the threshold of change, and sound touches—it has an impact and can *change things*. Isabelle Stengers points to the first efficacy of the witches' ritual chant ("she touches") as a sonic refrain or part of an assemblage that resists the dismembering attribution of agency—dispersing it across multiple agents and forces that "honor[s] change as a creation" within a wider project of "reclaiming animism," and with it, the unbelievable of "magic."[1] To listen to the ritual witches' chant is, therefore, to engage as a participant in the potential of sonic touch as it manifests and changes things in a series of circuitous agencies and impacts. The touch of the witches' chant, its affective alchemy, reanimates agencies beyond our selves, evokes magic, summons spiritual essences and bodily spirits from the material and immaterial world. This is a kind of touch arguably disavowed by the Enlightenment, tyrannized by Judeo-Christian religion and white supremist patriarchy, and forcefully subsumed by neoliberal capitalism into complex systems that seek to translate and appropriate the value of such potential as it manifests in and through cultural figurations of the witch. Following Stengers, the efficacy I wish to raise in this chapter is that of the "witches' ritual chant," because it recognizes the monotonous, rhythmic, repetitive ritual sound of witches as integral to touch, impact, and change wherein agents, agency, and intention operate across an active network of material and immaterial phenomena. Witches are therefore vital to the witches' ritual sound, but they are not its sole agents. Rather, instead of focusing on the agency of the witch, witches are part of an assemblage that affirms the power of "*witching* sound." *Witching sound* (instead of *witch*) refocuses attention on the activity, on the distribution of agency, power, technologies, and practices that propound the craft, the rituals, and the moments in time and space when sound touches, has an impact, and changes things.

This touch and impact is different from, and other than, that of the dominant human agent situated at the center of the distinct geological age in which we are currently living, named the Anthropocene, a geological term that names the profound environmental impact of human activities on the Earth and its climate. Listening to the witches' ritual chant offers a way of reimagining and rethinking agency, touch, and impact in an era of social-political-environmental crisis, beyond a dominant human agency and the narrative of the Anthropocene, toward other life, agency, touch, and potential. In this sense, I argue that witching sound raises and makes audible a shadow *cene* to that of the Anthropocene, an *Occultcene*, that can, like the Anthropocene, be thought of in terms of *impact*, but instead, raises other stories of touch that relate to the occult and occulted agencies. In this sense, biopolitical questions and ideologies around what constitutes agency and meaningful, valuable life oscillate between the Anthropocene and its abjected shadow: the Occultcene.

The contemporary witching sound of the band Divide and Dissolve and their album *Gas Lit* displaces Anthropos—as the ideal humanist subject—and challenges the Anthropocene "end of the world" narratives to reveal the "ongoing (settler) colonialisms [that] have been ending worlds for as long as they have been in existence."[2] Connecting the hidden, the othered, the dead, and the inert, this album's witching sound appeals to the agencies of the Occultcene as a repressed force buried in the geologics of the Anthropocene; it compels a deeper listening to the sonic geology of the Occultcene; the agencies of the subterranean and the origins, history, and structures of earth; the changing relationships with the atmosphere; and the matter of celestial bodies, extra-terrestrial materials, seismic waves, and deep time.

THE WITCH IN WITCHING SOUND

The Occultcene and witching sound, as emergent from the Western (occulted) histories and cultural conceptions of the West and the Occult, agitate a deep and chaotic political ambivalence. Despite the adoption of the witch and witchcraft as vitalizing symbolism and mobilization by feminist, queer, trans-rights, and anti-racist thinking and activism, witching sound is not necessarily politically affiliated with these intersectional movements. The fragility and potential of meaning within the semiotic-material soundings of the witch are considered by music and sound theorists as a complex negotiation between, on the one hand, harnessing the empowering sonic performative forces of the witch and, on the other hand, confirming the stereotypes and hierarchical binaries that are used to legitimate violence and oppression against women, people of color, queer, trans, and nonbinary people, animals, and nonhuman life. Karina Eileraas, in her article "Witches, Bitches and Fluids," based on the performative resistance politics of (punk/goth/Riot Grrrl) girl bands, recognizes the musical and performative invocation of the witch as a purposeful invocation of misogynistic and patriarchal genealogy that attempts to appropriate and reverse the assault on women through *ugly* aesthetics (shrieks, hisses, noise, screams, croaks, laughter, *hysterical* soundings). For Eileraas, the adoption of cultural and historically despised figures in music and performances that exaggerate the *anti-pretty* alongside what has been socially construed as the abject of the female body and sexuality is used by punk and Riot Grrrl bands as a weapon of resistance against "society's wounding inscriptions."[3] However, Eileraas also unsettles this conception of empowerment and intent by questioning whether identification with the abject truly operates as effective resistance when it is precisely the inscription of the ugly, the abject, baseness, and bestiality that have been deployed to instill fear and justify violence, slavery, domination, and genocide (Eileraas makes reference to Hitler's deployment of a "rhetoric of ugliness" and "contamination" to condemn Jewish people).[4] In his chapter "Queering the Witch," Jason Lee Oakes expresses comparable concerns in that, while he recognizes the positive queering of the hyperfeminine mystical "witchiness" of Stevie Nicks by drag queens and the queer community, he also importantly retains the question of whether it is really "possible for women, queers, or other marginalized subjects to reposition these patriarchal myths and their portrayal of femininity."[5] Similarly, Elizabeth Pérez's focus on the "witch-hop" of Azealia Banks—as incorporative of Afro-futurism, "Black-Atlantic traditions" and "Afro-Cuban religions"—critically analyses what could be considered Banks's "black conjure feminism."[6] Pérez questions the strategic and ideological essentialism of Banks's Womanism with the particular risk of reinforcing the post-Enlightenment colonial biopolitics that simultaneously establish Black people as "less and more than human"—a white superhumanization of Black people (wild, savage, close to nature, extraordinary powers) that "merely reinforces stereotypes and fosters anti-Black discrimination."[7] While the archetype of the witch and magical femme, queer, womanist practice importantly embodies both oppression and potential resistance, its sonic figures, signs, and affects are in continual flux, transforming and mutating in a system of meaning that can be hacked, short circuited, re-coded, re-wired, and re-contextualized. As such, the significance of agency and intention returns in that the *witching* craft of a musician, writer, coder, artist is critical to an assemblage of desire and political impact. In Patricia MacCormack's terms, in the current geopolitical context, the witch can be understood as nothing more than an oppressed and marginalized subject (made object) "who seeks agency over her own body and drives."[8] This agency is crucial in terms of the impact of an intersectional feminist-oriented witching sound.

While the Occultcene does not have an identifiable genesis impact moment that can be definitively located (although the Enlightenment might tentatively be referred to as its most effective suppressant), the 2016 US presidential election, in the context of the climate emergency, is a significant node with respect to the reinvigoration and reamplification of the Occultcene, intensifying variable political investments in the power of the Occult as aligned with nature and as supported by the ideals of esoteric knowledge. Post-2016, the porosity between the Anthropocene and the Occultcene continues to expand, and the social cauldron of drive, power, and desire intensifies. In such an era, the witching sound of Divide and Dissolve conjures and bears heavy genealogies in a performative practice with focused intent to "fight for Indigenous Sovereignty, Black and Indigenous Liberation, Water, Earth, and Indigenous land given back."[9]

In 2016, a month after the election, Takiaya Reed woke up from a dream in a cold sweat with an urgent feeling, thinking, "We gotta do this. It's not a time to be complacent. It's a time to turn up."[10]

HEAVY WITCHING SOUND

At the time of this writing, Divide and Dissolve were a duo based in Melbourne, Australia, made up of Takiaya Reed (saxophone, guitar, live effects) and Sylvie Nehill (drums, live effects); they released their third album *Gas Lit* in 2021 (Nehill has since left the band). The genre is described primarily as "doom metal" and frequently fused in music reviews with additions of "sludge," "drone," and "stoner rock." However, despite the affinities with slow dragging tempos, crushing low-ends, and bass-laden "heaviness," the band claims to bear no genre loyalty and in fact specifically disidentifies with (doom) metal music and the metal scene: "Aesthetically, our music is never gonna arrive at the same place a lot of other metal music does. I don't wish to pay homage to the same people that a lot of people in metal do. We want to be honouring our ancestors, the earth, and every living thing. That's what's at the forefront of our minds when we play music."[11] Drawing heaviness out of the fortitudes of metal territories (dominated by white male musicians, fans, and scene commentators) is a politicized act. Just the presence of this *heavy* band made up of two women with Indigenous heritage is arguably a subversive deterritorialization of a well-guarded semiotic arena of signs, a presence that corrodes what might be regarded as the "legitimate" ownership of heavy sonic signifiers. Despite their *heavy* and *metal* (hash)tags, Divide and Dissolve's practice has evolved within contemporary feminist queer punk and experimental music scenes rather than within metal music subcultures.

In metal music, *heavy* signs are frequently associated with the occult and its connotations of masculinized and satanic power. On a surface level, these heavy and occult signs serve to reinforce an esoteric emphasis within predominantly white brotherhood networks that significantly flirt with the Devil and its white male supremacist powers (sexual and violent power over women in particular). The difference in Divide and Dissolve's *heaviness* can be read, in part, semiotically and in relation to the band's representation of identity as repeatedly articulated through indigeneity and Reed's African American and Tsalagi (Cherokee) heritage and Nehill's Māori heritage. Where many *heavy* bands' semiotic repertoire, identity, and mythology draw from an occult palette of images that include eroticized "witches," skulls, snakes, dark cloaked lords, Baphomet, and so on, Divide and Dissolve foreground dull muted landscapes, flora and fauna with surreal color tones, merch that reads "Destroy White Supremacy" and "No Prisons, No Slaves, No Masters," and promo pictures in dresses that are pretty (sheer and coded feminine) within pastoral garden settings. Indeed, prettiness is neither extra to nor incompatible with their heavy sound but enlaced in a practice that seeks to challenge beauty standards and decolonize fashion and stylistic conventions.[12]

Heavy power in this album is wrested away from cloaked identities, God/Devil, good/evil, masculinized power dramas, satanic/occult signs, and funeral doom; nor is the sound heavy from withdrawals of weighted cultural capital, subsumed in a cool death. On the contrary, in *Gas Lit*, beauty, love, and life coexist with destruction, rage, and death in a *heavy* sound that carries the trauma of Indigenous people and the dehumanization brought by colonialism while it also serves to articulate the force of freedom, joy, and resistance, bringing into being diverse worlds in which life lives without white supremacy. Reed clarifies: "It's about hope as a practice. . . . It is so important for black and indigenous people to not have to only focus on trauma. . . . The things that black and indigenous people are forced to think about every day are heavy."[13]

GRAVITAS OF OTHER ENERGIES

Music is a great facilitator of connecting with the past. Through music and practicing art we can connect with ancestors, and engage in lines of communication centuries old. Art helps us not just imagine but create futures.
—SYLVIE NEHILL

In the droning low-end vibrations of drums and guitar, Divide and Dissolve's witching sound creates something that can be regarded as material and immaterial, conjured via their own agency and intention (continually articulated by the band as important) as well as by an agency other than themselves (figure 18.01). Reed elucidates: "It's not just us."[14] Both

FIGURE 18.1. Divide and Dissolve, 2022. Photograph by Jamie Wdziekonski.

Reed and Nehill elaborate on their heavy sound by directing attention to the depth and space that invites other energies: ancestors, water, earth.

Gas Lit (produced by Ruban Nielson) creates depth, weight, and space rather than focusing on the teleology of musical development. It opens and closes with an interplay of reverberant melodic lines from the soprano saxophone in sound unlike the expected and recognizable warmth and smokiness of the sax. A far less identifiable crystal clear, at times glacial nonhuman (but nevertheless "voice") flows through the underground cavernous album in sonic currents, surfacing, plunging, and resurfacing as a melodic stream between the rock and boulders of the album's sonic, sedimentary strata. The sax heralds and brings into being a dark, subterranean, cavernous space, repeating an unresolved melancholic melody; with theatrical anticipation, a chthonic stage is set. When drums and guitar arrive, they do so with such immediate epic intensity that the musical staging offers a glimpse of operatic and orchestrated drama before it is shaken and reduced to rubble. Their presence is sudden and seismic. Saxophone notes swirling in cold-rock space are eclipsed in an explosive, volcanic instant by beat and riff as it produces earthshaking bass and drone vibration. Looping in the circuit—bass stacks, subwoofer, distortion, fuzz, floor toms, ride cymbal, bass pedal, down-tuned kit, down-tuned guitar, pedals, effects—all acoustic and electric technologies are engaged in the service of low-end drone, sluggishly looping heaviness to a point that threatens absolute stasis. As the body is immersed in this thick and heavy circuit continuum, the stasis transforms into static that transforms into space as the body begins to perceive not only a violently felt corporeal (body-shuddering) impact but the detail and layers of incandescent tones and overtones beyond the riffs and beat expanding the sense of space and depth to conjure and reveal the occulted strata of the Earth—effectively voicing material and immaterial geology and genealogies to expand the vibrating dynamism of life and death between layers. We feel not stasis but space and transformational potential.

Calling into being the density of the earth and its stratification reveals the Anthropocene narrative about the Earth as it seeks to provide a geological account of human impact on the planet when that impact is drawn through the totalizing History of Man and Civilization in relation to an ultimate dystopic "end of the world"—that will happen at some point in the future in relation to the linear time upon which the Anthropocene is based. As Yusoff argues, the narrative of the Anthropocene is not neutral or apolitical but rather configured without recognizing the "extinctions already undergone by black and indigenous peoples" and the colonial marks within the geology of its grammar.[15] In the semiotic-material-immaterial context of Divide and Dissolve's decolonizing work, what the sound summons to account is the strata of the Anthropocene story—the layers of muted colonial violence settled between geological neutrality. Geology for Yusoff is deeply imbricated in the Western colonial inscription of race and its enslaving and extraction practices:

> The organisation and categorization of matter enact racialisation. This enactment is productive of racial logics that extend through and beyond mineralogy and the deterritorialization that accompanies extraction. Geology provides the logics to elide those attachments to geography through its classification system of value and resource. While the search for geologic resources instigated the imperative to enslave, geology quickly

established itself as an imperial science that both organised the extraction of the Americas and, in the continued context of Victorian colonialism, became a structuring priority in the colonial complex, especially in India, Canada and Australia.... The ownership of strata and surface-subsurface bifurcation in Australia and Canada by the Crown continue to unsettle native title and reservation lands. This the classificatory logics of geology have implications for ongoing colonialism.[16]

In this respect, Divide and Dissolve's sound works to sonically decompress the Anthropocene's compression of geologic time and unsettle the white supremacist colonizer beneath the given humanist subject of this discourse: Civilized Man. In other words, alongside the burden and impact of enforced labor, dispossession of land, and mining and extraction technologies the band listens for and seeks to amplify the very sound hidden in the rock. When shaken so forcefully, these layers crumble to reveal the fossilized White "geologics" and "grammar of the inhuman" at the hard core of colonization all the way to the surface of now ... a geologics which inscribes the inhuman categorization of matter (as resource) to the Earth, Indigenous people, and people of color.[17] In heavy sound, the gravity of colonization is summoned and revealed as that which compresses Indigenous people and their land into object and resource. This hitherto equilibrium is pummeled into a state of destabilizing oscillation. Relentless low vibration creates a pressure that agitates the time/space of Anthropos, orchestrating a seismic shift from within the earth as a heavy counterforce that formulates through intimacy an alliance with inhuman earth, politically charged "subterranean force that travels underneath and through colonial technologies of space and time."[18] This is a heavy witching sound that surrounds and immerses the psychological/cultural/physical body of listeners, a connective warmth of alliance for Indigenous listeners and an earth/time/space/ shattering end of the world quake for the body of Anthropos.

The band's heaviness can be interpreted through a central driving combination of politics and what could be perceived as "magic" in that they foreground a deep connection with ancestors and the earth at every stage of their songwriting and performance process. They exhibit in this respect an extraordinary sense of musical engagement with and focus on connection with human beings and nonhuman being, dead and alive—raised, touched, and touching in and through sound. This "magic" is not contingent on vocal spells, chants, or incantations—indeed, aside from the spoken word poetry at the center of *Gas Lit*—delivered by the poet Minori Sanchiz-Fung—the majority of the album is mainly instrumental, comprised of saxophone, guitar(s), drums, and effects. Magical power and meaning are not therefore primarily invested in the human voice that is here decentered despite the artists' intention to communicate profoundly political intention to destroy and decentralize white supremacy, to demand Indigenous sovereignty and liberation, and to fight for reparations and the return of water, earth, and land to Indigenous people: "The abhorrent history of colonial violence, genocide, slavery, rape, and murder is still continuing today. It is this past, and the lasting and active power structures present in our world today that has driven me to prioritize decolonization."[19] Divide and Dissolve's anti-racist politics and commitment to decolonization are central to the development of their music, but it is not words, lyrics, or the human voice that primarily address these politics or the gaslit experience of Indigenous people and people of color. It is rather an understanding of the "tethers of a circuit" (Minori Sanchiz-Fung's words) across frequencies and vibrations that the living and dead can hear. Sound, and the space created within sound to listen, is understood by the band as the potential to communicate across time and sedimentary strata, bringing into being that which was and that which will be with a focus on land, on earth, and on Indigenous people connected through electronic circuits of instruments, amplification and effects, networks of interconnected nervous systems, and genealogies and geologies: "We are tethered to a circuit that excludes nothing, a song the dead can hear."[20]

LISTENING FOR IMPACT AND CHANGE

Divide and Dissolve's connective listening may be comparable to "deep listening," as conceptualized by composer Pauline Oliveros, in that meditative attention focuses in on the interplay of sound and silence. Oliveros explains that one can expand consciousness and awareness through deep listening: "Sound is not limited to musical or speaking sounds, but is inclusive of all perceptible vibrations (sonic formations)."[21] Certainly, the band thinks in frequencies and vibration, "of tuning into frequencies" with each other and with "other realms" in sound that is understood as a continuous feedback loop that shifts and moves the body—the entire body, not just received via the ear: "We are completely invested in communicating with sonic vibrations which are received not just in the ear but the entire body."[22] They listen and play at the compositional stage and during live performances in ways that facilitate improvisation and open responsiveness—open to diverse voices, other agency, contingency, and change—connecting with indigeneity as a source of strength and power and opening up this space of connection. In this respect, Divide and Dissolve's engagement with sound, silence, and space is closer to Nina Sun Eidsheim's understanding of listening beyond established and normative paradigms of the material and multisensory dimensions of music as vibration in order to yield deeper insights into relationships of force, power, and impact, as sound works on consciousness through bodily tissue. For Eidsheim, this type of relationship to sound requires intention—a willingness to undergo change: "For a relationship with sound to take place, we must be willing to take part in, propagate, transmit, and—in some cases—transduce its vibrations. From this it follows that entropy occurs when we focus on the preconceived identity of another rather than on our own ability (or inability) to undergo change."[23] Divide and Dissolve regard their live performances as a *ritual* in which the audience's energy is an important part of the creation. The audience's listening body must be willing to take part and transmit—and this requires a certain level of vulnerability in relation to *heavy* sound. In one interview, Reed and Nehill give examples of when (white) audience members have spoken over and/or disrespected this ritual; and the band has directly challenged individuals, stopped playing, in effect calling out the event as opposed to playing on.[24] A refusal to carry on playing demonstrates Reed's and Nehill's commitment to creating and respecting a ritualistic connection while simultaneously calling out gendered and racialized dominant modes of listening that determine a hierarchy of sound, or in other words, white supremist hierarchies as they seek to establish which sounds to amplify and which to ignore/suppress.[25] Agency and intent are therefore vital to Divide and Dissolve's heavy sound since they speaks to the energy required to simultaneously bear the weight of oppression and trauma while opening up a space for other agencies and intentions to have an impact and create change. Attention therefore is drawn back to the Anthropocene in a heavy witching sound that tells us: the way to reimagine and create a "beyond the Anthropocene" is to decolonize listening itself and to think differently about how the intention of soundings mean and matter in the Occultcene.

NOTES

Epigraph 1: Stengers, "Reclaiming Animism," 6–7.

1. Stengers, "Reclaiming Animism," 8.
2. Yusoff, *A Billion Black Anthropocenes*, xiii.
3. Eileraas, "Witches, Bitches, and Fluids," 134.
4. Eileraas, "Witches, Bitches, and Fluids," 137.
5. Oakes, "Queering the Witch," 50.
6. Pérez, "The Black Atlantic Metaphysics of Azealia Banks."
7. Pérez, "The Black Atlantic Metaphysics of Azealia Banks," 537.
8. MacCormack, *The Ahuman Manifesto*, 112–13.
9. Divide and Dissolve, notes for "We Are Really Worried About You," accessed July 8, 2022, https://divideanddissolve.bandcamp.com/track/we-are-really-worried-about-you.
10. Reed, as quoted in Jackie, "Divide and Dissolve."
11. Nehill, as quoted in Clarke, "Heavy Is the Head."
12. Hernandez and Attaffuah, "Heavy Doom Duo Divide and Dissolve."
13. Reed, as quoted in Jackie, "Divide and Dissolve."
14. Reed, as quoted in Supersonic Festival, "In Conversation."
15. Yusoff, *A Billion Black Anthropocenes*, 51.
16. Yusoff, *A Billion Black Anthropocenes*, 82–83.
17. Yusoff, *A Billion Black Anthropocenes*, 18, 84.
18. Yusoff, *A Billion Black Anthropocenes*, 99.
19. Nehill, as quoted in Treppel, "Divide and Dissolve Use Drone."
20. "Did You Have Something to Do With It," spoken word by Minori Sanchiz-Fung, from Divide and Dissolve, *Gas Lit*.
21. Oliveros, *Deep Listening*, xxiv.
22. Nehill, as quoted in Fifteen Questions, "Interview with Divide and Dissolve."
23. Eidsheim, *Sensing Sound*, 25.
24. Reed and Nehill, as paraphrased from Supersonic Festival, "In Conversation."
25. Stoever, *The Sonic Color Line*, 108.

BIBLIOGRAPHY

Clarke, Patrick. "Heavy Is the Head: Divide and Dissolve Interviewed." *Quietus*, January 13, 2021. https://thequietus.com/articles/29418-divide-and-dissolve-interview-takiaya-reed-sylvie-nehill-gas-lit.

Divide and Dissolve. *Gas Lit*. [MP3]. Bristol: Invada Records, 2021.

Eidsheim, Nina Sun.. *Sensing Sound: Singing and Listening as Vibrational Practice*. Durham, NC: Duke University Press, 2015.

Eileraas, Karina. "Witches, Bitches and Fluids: Girl Bands Performing Ugliness as Resistance." TDR: *Drama review* 41, no. 3 (1997): 122–39.

Ferrett, D. *Dark Sound: Feminine Voices in Sonic Shadow*. New York: Bloomsbury, 2020.

Hernandez, Triana, and Serwah Attaffuah. "Heavy Doom Duo Divide and Dissolve on Decolonizing Fashion." May 8, 2017. Accessed January 2022. https://i-d.vice.com/en_uk/article/kzwjxe/heavy-doom-duo-divide-and-dissolve-on-decolonizing-fashion.

Jackie, Amelia. "Divide and Dissolve: Radical Punk Duo from Australia." *Tom Tom Mag*, March 21, 2018. https://tomtommag.com/2018/09/divideanddissolve_issue33/.

MacCormack, Patricia. *The Ahuman Manifesto: Activism for the End of the Anthropocene*. London: Bloomsbury, 2020.

Nehill, Sylvie. Fifteen Questions, "Interview with Divide and Dissolve." https://www.15questions.net/interview/fifteen-questions-interview-divide-and-dissolve/page-1/.

Oakes, Jason Lee. "Queering the Witch: Stevie Nicks and the Forging of Femininity at the Night of a Thousand Stevies." In *Queering the Popular Pitch*, edited by Sheila Whiteley and Jennifer Rycenga, 41–54. New York: Routledge, 2006.

Oliveros, Pauline. *Deep Listening: A Composer's Sound Practice*. New York: iUniverse, 2005.

Pérez, Elizabeth. "The Black Atlantic Metaphysics of Azealia Banks: Brujx Womanism at the Kongo Crossroads." *Hypatia* 36, no. 3 (2021): 519–46.

Stengers, Isabelle. 2012. "Reclaiming Animism." *e-flux Journal*, no. 36 (2012): 1–10. https://www.e-flux.com/journal/36/61245/reclaiming-animism/.

Stoever, Jennifer Lynn. 2016. *The Sonic Color Line: Race and the Cultural Politics of Listening*. New York: New York University Press.

Supersonic Festival. 2021. "In Conversation: Divide and Dissolve." May 6, 2021. https://supersonicfestival.com/event/divide-and-dissolve/.

Treppel, Jeff. "Divide and Dissolve Use Drone to Combat Oppression and Intolerance." *Bandcamp*, March 2, 2018. https://daily.bandcamp.com/features/divide-and-dissolve-abomination-interview.

Yusoff, Kathryn. *A Billion Black Anthropocenes or None*. Minneapolis: University of Minnesota Press, 2018.

Nineteen · SHELINA BROWN

A Witch's Guide to the Underground: Sixties Counterculture, Dianic Wicca, and the Cultural Trope of the "Witchy Diva"

A witch is a psychic female, who with magical secrets and sheer force of will, makes things happen. —LOUISE HUEBNER, *Seduction through Witchcraft*

Crow flowers, nettles I've danced along, while singing my song with my red shoes on, when I'm low, I shake a toe, and then I'm off to the fields we know.
—CAROLANNE PEGG, "A Witch's Guide to the Underground"

In her 1973 release, "A Witch's Guide to the Underground," folk artist Carolanne Pegg weaves a poetic narrative of a wistful young witch who enraptures her beloved with ritual song and dance. Challenging Hans Christian Anderson's cautionary tale of "The Red Shoes," Pegg celebrates the magical power of the scarlet slippers as a witch's seductive, ceremonial attire.[1] Dancing with abandon through darkened tunnels and fields laden with crow flowers and nettles, Pegg's witchy seductress brings to life a tantalizing underworld of archaic feminine wisdom hidden in the wilderness and beyond the reaches of a patriarchal social order. Widely celebrated for her eclectic vocal style, in "A Witch's Guide to the Underground," Pegg's vocality metaphorically evokes the contrasting Wiccan tropes of the maiden and the crone, as she repeatedly switches from a girlish, soaring head voice to a creaky, strained lower vocal fry. The shifting vocal ontology of the song's enchantress thus symbolically forges generational links between contemporary witches and those of an imagined, pre-Christian past.

The fascination with the cultural trope of the witch in midcentury Anglo-America can be attributed to a variety of sociocultural factors, primarily the rise of the 1960s counterculture and the second wave feminist movement. At a time when women sought out modes of political and spiritual empowerment, popular interest in Wiccan spellwork and how-to books proliferated across the Global North. Influential Wiccan incantation records, such as Louise Huebner's *Seduction through Witchcraft* (1969), were released on major record labels at this time due to high consumer demand. Huebner's incantations, backed by eerie, ambient electronic soundscapes, offered a guide for aspiring witches, promising them the power to achieve self-actualization by tapping into the numinous power of an archaic, divine feminine. Witch studies scholar and literary theorist Justyna Sempruch analyzes the popularization of witchcraft in the mid-twentieth century as promulgating a "herstorical fantasy" that offers a site from which to renegotiate the role of women in patriarchal society. In Sempruch's view, the figure of the witch constitutes a symbolic imagining of an archaic mother, one that is conjured to combat the nullification of "woman" in today's society as well as in past historical moments.[2]

Within popular music cultures of the long sixties,[3] primarily the folk revivalist movement and the rock 'n' roll counterculture, key female vocalists frequently conjured such "fantasies" of the witch in their musical output. Stevie Nicks's composition with Fleetwood Mac, "Rhiannon" (1976), might be considered as an anthemic work of this trend. Nicks's characteristically "witchy" stage persona as well as her rebellious, preternatural vocal stylings continue to exert a strong influence on a range of Wiccan-inspired millennial indie rock artists today. Analyzing Nicks and other figures, this chapter aims to "herstorisize" the cultural trope of what I will term the "witchy diva," as it emerged within the 1960s counterculture, and soon broke into mainstream commercial music toward the conclusion of the long sixties. Drawing upon Sempruch's assertion that assuming the symbolic position of the "witch" offers women artists a vantage point from which to critique the operations of patriarchy, I will interrogate the ways in which female vocalists of the sixties drew upon essentialist cultural constructions of a numinous feminine as a means of enacting gender-based cultural resistance within androcentric popular music cultures.

DIANIC WICCA, INCANTATION RECORDS, AND FEMINIST SPIRITUALITY

The proliferation of musical output throughout the long sixties that thematized the witch as an empowering gendered cultural trope is rooted in the rise of neo-paganism and feminist spirituality, in particular, Dianic Wicca, in midcentury Anglo-America.[4] During a historical period characterized by intensified militarization, mechanization, and industrialization of the Global North, new modes of spirituality proliferated, with practitioners seeking to attain a more harmonious relationship with the natural world and to expand their consciousness beyond hegemonic doctrines of institutionalized religion. Neo-pagan spiritual practice, emphasizing self-actualization, and the "back to the land" movement, which highlighted one's connection to the natural world, strongly resonated with the values embraced by the emerging sixties counterculture.

With the proliferation of alternative spiritual practices promoting a return to nature and a shift away from patriarchal religious institutions, women of the 1960s counterculture soon began to embrace the liberatory gendered cultural meanings offered by neo-paganism. According to historian Helen Berger, the growing popularity of neo-paganist practices such as Wicca occurred alongside the rise of the second wave feminist movement throughout the 1960s. With its egalitarian, dualistic belief system, Wicca affirmed female spiritual power that had long been suppressed by patriarchal religious institutions, offering women of the counterculture a "female face to the divine."[5] Although the concept of "feminist spirituality" was not widely accepted until the early 1970s, throughout the 1960s, radical feminist activism inspired critiques of women's treatment under patriarchal religious traditions. Feminist theologian Mary Daly's controversial work, *The Church and the Second Sex* (1968), demanded that the Catholic Church be held accountable for its misogynistic practices. In response to the widespread censorship of her work, Daly staged a public protest where she called for a mass "exodus" from organized religion. Daly's protest roused women to cultivate a "divine rage" that would bring about a deconstruction of the repressive teachings of the Catholic faith. In her later, loosely autobiographical work, *Gyn/Ecology: The Metaethics of Radical Feminism* (1978), Daly recounts her initial anger against the church, which led her to promote the worship of what she termed the "Goddess of the ancient world," a divine feminine archetype repressed by patriarchal religion.[6]

Daly's apostate feminism, blended with Wiccan practices of pre-Christian Goddess worship, came to shape popular representations of "the witch" as a rebellious feminine trope. Enacting a revolutionary cultural project of reclaiming "the witch" as an empowered feminist positionality, a radical feminist splinter group arose in 1968 under the acronym W.I.T.C.H. (Women's International Terrorist Conspiracy from Hell). Inspired by the success of the 1968 radical feminist protests against the Miss America Pageant, W.I.T.C.H. sought to gain widespread media attention for the Women's Liberation Movement by staging public protests where women, costumed as witches, would disrupt hegemonic, patriarchal institutions.

According to feminist historian Wendy Griffin, the W.I.T.C.H. protests of the late 1960s inspired a struggling actor in New York City by the name of Zsuzsanna Budapest to pursue her true calling as the first High Priestess of a feminist Wiccan coven. Upon relocating to the Venice district of Los Angeles in 1970, Budapest found herself in a cultural milieu that was rife with alternative spiritualities and countercultural political activism. Budapest soon formed the Susan B. Anthony Coven Number 1, a women-only group espousing the premise that women's liberation must be grounded in both spiritual and political liberation. The earliest incarnation of the Susan B. Anthony Coven Number 1 included seven participants, who, led by Budapest, defined a new form of Wiccan practice that accorded a much more prominent role to the Goddess as compared with her role in Gardnerian Wicca. The members of the Susan B. Anthony Coven Number 1 referred to their new feminist religion as "Dianic Wicca." Dianic Wicca references the myth of the goddess Diana, who conspires to teach the oppressed of the Earth spells to overthrow their masters. The Susan B. Anthony Coven Number 1 primarily functioned as a feminist consciousness-raising group, helping women to overcome gender-based trauma; but it soon developed into a much broader movement that sought to unite spiritual practice with political activism. Budapest first coined the term "feminist spirituality" in a Los Angeles–based monthly feminist paper, *Sister*, in 1972. In this article, Budapest makes the claim that patriarchal religion denigrates women, so women must "rewrite the script"—and create a religion based on feminist values.[7]

Spearheaded by Budapest's feminist Wicca, discourse on Goddess worship proliferated in the 1970s United States, with conferences on women's spirituality held nationwide, as well as magazines, books, and other ephemera circulating widely throughout countercultural spheres.[8] With the widespread popularization of Dianic Wicca, a series of incantation records were released in the late 1960s and early 1970s. These spoken-word LPs included narrations of rituals and spells by witches and covens, usually accompanied by ambient electronic music. Perhaps the most iconic Dianic Wic-

FIGURE 19.1 Cover of Louise Huebner's book *Witchcraft for All* (1970).

can incantation record of the era was Louise Huebner's *Seduction through Witchcraft* (1969). A psychic, palm reader, and astrologist, Louise Huebner had written several books on witchcraft and had a regular public presence on Los Angeles radio and television prior to the release of her incantation book (figure 19.1). The title of her album capitalizes on her glamorous media image as a Wiccan temptress who could wield her sexuality as an extension of her magical powers.[9]

In *Seduction through Witchcraft*, Huebner claims her status as a sixth-generation witch, asserting that a witch is "a psychic female," and that only women can access the power of her incantations. In the opening track, "Introduction—Gods," Huebner addresses her intended female audience with the emphatic claim: "I can help you become a power. With enchantments, spells and charms, you will soon be able to rearrange the law and order of all things." Her following eleven incantations provide the listener with a series of spells designed to actualize their will and wield their sexual powers to both seduce desirable men and dispel unwanted suitors. Huebner's incantations are delivered in a nasal timbre that, when projected with force, wields a fearful, threatening vocality made to sound increasingly uncanny with the use of heavy reverb effects. The electroacoustic soundscape accompanying Huebner's vocality ebbs and flows, emphasizing certain incantational phrases with terrifying intensity. In Huebner's *Seduction through Witchcraft*, the witch's voice thus functions as a conduit of female desire and power that threatens to usurp the patriarchal "order of all things."

Huebner's incantations were widely disseminated across the Global North, inspiring British folk revivalist Carolanne Pegg's 1973 song, "A Witches Guide to the Underground." Drawing upon Huebner's *Seduction through Witchcraft*, Pegg's title track features the narrative of a witch and her coven who make use of native flora to cast spells of seduction. Pegg's nasal, somewhat Huebnerian vocal timbre paints a picture of a witch foraging flora of poisonous potential—marigold, tansy, crow flowers, nettles, elder tree—and directing her thoughts toward seducing the "man she fancies." Within 1960s music cultures, Dianic Wicca was first embraced by women folk artists such as Pegg who paved the way for the emergence of the Womyn's Music movement of the mid-1970s. Eclectic, countercultural feminist music-making flourished during this time, which gave rise to women-only, "back to the land" outdoor gatherings and festivals, the longest running of which was the Michigan Womyn's Festival (1976–2015).

Celebrated singer-songwriters of the long sixties Judee Sill and Joni Mitchell produced music that heavily thematized both a "back to the land," neo-pagan aesthetic coupled with expressions of feminist spirituality. Los Angeles–based artist Judee Sill was a rising star in the music industry, known for her talents as a masterful pop songwriter and arranger. Her debut solo album, *Judee Sill* (1971), features an angelic folk vocality that Sill consciously offsets with a slight nasal twang, her pop melodies meandering through intervallic leaps that take the listener in unexpected directions. One of the most enduringly popular tracks from *Judee Sill*, "Crayon Angels," tells the story of a woman in search of an alternative spirituality after finding her own feminine experience to be out of step with the doctrines of Christianity. The enigmatic opening phrase, "Crayon Angel songs are slightly out of tune / But I'm sure I'm not to blame," conveys the affect of a conflicted singing subject who feels at odds with social conventions, yet uncertain as to whether or not this feeling of dissociation is a sin of her own doing. Sill's subtle twang lends a childlike quality to her voice, evoking a synesthetic connection to the central image of the "Crayon Angels," possibly a young girl's drawing signifying a naive acceptance of Christian iconography. As the adult singing subject scrutinizes the "Crayon Angels," however, something seems to be amiss. Sill's vocal pattern "envoices" a sense of dis-ease as she dips down to an extended, even strident ornamentation on the final word of the opening phrase, "blame," forcing a strained flattening of her otherwise flawless pitch.

The "out of tune" twang of "Crayon Angels" sets the tone for a narrative that relates a woman's loss of faith in "false Prophets" and "Holy visions disappeared from view." In search of a means of satisfying her inner spirituality, the female subject looks upward in hopes of escaping not to heaven but to an "Astral plane"—a celestial sphere of pre-Christian esotericism. A desire for connection with the supernatural realm thus underpins the longing of Sill's folk ballad, a theme that runs through many of her compositions. Sill's album cover shows her dressed in a black cloak adorned with a golden cross, her face partially concealed as she looks away from the camera. The cloaked, Occultist representation of Sill resonates with her work's central thematics of a woman's troubled search for acceptance within the Christian religion, her fears of the rapture, and her fascination with the supernatural. Her unusual use of twang and uncanny melodic twists lends her voice a Peggsian, "witchy" quality, one that would be emulated by later rock vocalists, most notably, by Stevie Nicks.

While Judee Sill's "Crayon Angels" offers a wistful lament for an escape into the "Astral plane," Joni Mitchell's "Don't Interrupt the Sorrow," a key track from her seventh studio album, *The Hissing of Summer Lawns* (1975), centers an angsty female poetic subject protesting patriarchal culture that suppresses her feminist spiritual awakening, or *anima*. A Jungian concept referring to the actualization of one's inner self, Mitchell's interpretation conflates the anima with Dianic Wiccan imagery of a "vengeful little Goddess," a purported witch rising up from the flames of a burning pyre. Composed in the mid-1970s at the height of the Women's Liberation Movement, it is no surprise that Mitchell's "Don't Interrupt the Sorrow" offers up a battle cry against the "ancient crown" and "chains" of patriarchy. The sorrow that Mitchell evokes can be interpreted as the suffering of women, which she traces back to the repression of the Goddess in prehistory, the "Queen of Queens." Laden with references to witch burnings and the plight of women under early Christianity, Mitchell's layered poetic narrative features a contemporary female protagonist asserting her independence from an abusive relationship. The protagonist's singular journey is conflated with the wider historical movement of all women toward social and spiritual emancipation. Railing against the "weakness of men" and rejecting their command to "be polite," Mitchell's singing subject openly identifies as a "rebel" who unapologetically "loves a cause." The nasal twang and the emphasis on the syncopated expletive, "darn right"—delivered as a snarling curse—conveys the rebellious spirit of Mitchell's rising feminist "Anima." She blasphemously "sends God up the chimney like a childhood Santa Claus," marking a rejection of patriarchal religion as an illusion designed to keep women in a childlike state of false consciousness. The drone-like, down-tempo folk accompaniment foregrounds Mitchell's voice, her visceral delivery rising, like her "Anima," into strident moments of unbridled vocal intensity. With suspended chords avoiding harmonic resolution and a song structure resistant to formal conventions, Mitchell's "Don't Interrupt the Sorrow" unfolds as a trance-like Dianic ritual. A consummate songwriter known for her idiosyncratic vocal stylings, Mitchell conjures the spirit of Mary Daly's "divine rage"—linking her to a tradition of feminist "Anima rising" that once inspired Zsuzsanna Budapest on her spiritual quest.

STEVIE NICKS AS "WITCHY DIVA": FEMINIST CULTURAL RESISTANCE WITHIN THE ROCK 'N' ROLL COUNTERCULTURE

By the mid-1970s, with the Women's Liberation Movement in full force, the cultural trope of the witch as a rebellious woman had gained a stronghold within mainstream popular culture of the Global North. Historian Chas S. Clifton observes that such pop cultural "witches" were often represented as hypersexualized, reinforcing Western cultural anxieties surrounding women's sexuality freed from patriarchal control. The sexy and rebellious witch was often associated with outrageous behavior threatening bourgeois social mores, and soon this tantalizing trope of the dangerous "witchy woman" took hold of popular journalism, television, and film.[10] The commercialization of the witch in Hollywood films of the day, ranging from horror classics such as *Rosemary's Baby* (1968) to more comedic representations in long-running television series, *I Dream of Jeannie*

(1965-70) and *Bewitched* (1964-72), quickly transformed the witch into a popular cultural mainstay. Historian Tanice Holtz refers to this cultural moment as the "Wiccan Influx"—marking the emergence of witchcraft from underground feminist circles into the wider sphere of mainstream popular culture. In response to this rising trend, young women adorned themselves in crystals, wide-brimmed hats, and diaphanous gowns, embracing such commodified, "witchy" fashions as symbolic of feminine sexual and cultural liberation.

Aspiring vocalist and songwriter Stevie Nicks arrived in Los Angeles in 1972, at the height of the Wiccan Influx. With her flowing gypsy robes, flaring sleeves, and unruly blond locks, Nicks emerged as a popular cultural icon of the 1970s—a "witchy diva" who was at once sexy, rebellious, and known for her outrageous antics on- and offstage. Whereas folk artists such as Sill and Mitchell incorporated Dianic imagery into their musical output, Nicks fully embraced the performative trope of the witch and transformed it into a highly marketable, uniquely feminine rock 'n' roll identity. Following Sempruch's assertion that women adopt witchlike personae as a means of resisting patriarchal culture, Nicks's penchant for all things witchy can be read as a mode of gender-based resistance. Feminist music historian Sheila Whiteley has emphasized the repressive, white androcentrism that permeated 1960s rock 'n' roll, delimiting women's participation as musicians and songwriters. Whiteley observes that women who were allowed entrée into mainstream rock 'n' roll were typically cast into the stereotype of the passive, statuesque muse, and those who resisted this role had to contend with misogynistic backlash.[11]

In response to the Wiccan Influx of rebellious young women, a barrage of reactionary, anti-witch songs were penned by male artists of the day, including Donovan's "Season of the Witch" (1966), The Rattle's "The Witch" (1970), and The Eagles' "Witchy Woman" (1972), among many others. Several years prior to Stevie Nicks's joining Fleetwood Mac, former frontman Peter Green had composed "Black Magic Woman" (1968)—later popularized by Carlos Santana—possibly the quintessential anti-witch song, thematizing a fragile male protagonist struggling to ward off the spells of a demonic female seductress. Assuming the role of Fleetwood Mac's front-woman several years after Green's departure, Stevie Nicks's "Rhiannon" offers up a formidable response to "Black Magic Woman," establishing Nicks as an unapologetically sexy and rebellious "witchy diva" and an empowered songwriter and vocalist in her own right. Nicks's composition, an ode to the Welsh goddess Rhiannon, arguably surpassed

"Black Magic Woman" as one of Fleetwood Mac's most celebrated songs of their catalog. A song of enduring popularity, "Rhiannon" was featured on *Fleetwood Mac* (1975), the band's first release with the new lineup including Stevie Nicks and her partner, guitarist and vocalist Lindsey Buckingham. Although the band originally drew its name from a shared patronymic reference to the surnames of drummer Mick Fleetwood, bassist John McVie, and vocalist and keyboardist Christine McVie, with the addition of Nicks and Buckingham, the group's dynamic shifted dramatically. The longstanding friendship and camaraderie between songwriters and vocalists Stevie Nicks and Christine McVie set an empowering model for the possibility of female collaboration within patriarchal rock music culture that often functions to divide women.

Although many stories circulate with respect to the inspiration behind "Rhiannon," in a published interview from 2004, Nicks relates her encounter with an elderly scholar of Welsh mythology that inspired her composition. According to Nicks, upon being introduced to the tale of Rhiannon through a popular novel, she sought out a reclusive scholar in Arizona, Evangeline Walton, who had dedicated her life to researching the Welsh *Mabinogion*, a medieval manuscript of stories collected in the *Matter of Britain*. Of all the mythological heroines of the twelfth-century manuscript, Walton was particularly devoted to the goddess Rhiannon. Perusing the artifacts that crowded Walton's home, Nicks felt a spiritual connection to the legend of the bird goddess who was forced to battle her male suitors for her freedom. During a conversation with Walton, Nicks mused, "all the people were going to kill [Rhiannon] because they thought she was a witch," drawing a correlation between the tale of Rhiannon and her own contemporary experience of anxious patriarchal responses to women's exertion of power and sexual autonomy.[12] Shortly after, Nicks sat down at a piano and wrote a song as an homage to the once persecuted goddess, Rhiannon. Nicks concludes her interview by suggesting a magical connection between her own work and Walton's research, observing that Walton published her last work on the same day as "Rhiannon" was released. In Nicks's imagination, a powerful herstorical lineage is thus forged between the elderly scholar and the young rock star, binding them both to a tradition of arcane feminine history.

Just as the Welsh goddess once resisted the pursuit of her male suitors, Nicks's "Rhiannon" evades the conventions of harmonic resolution common to sixties pop songwriting, alternating between the ambiguous tonal centers of A minor and F major. Separated by an interval of a sixth—an intervallic relationship that symbolically evokes the supernatural in the Western tradition—the alternating A minor and F major chords of "Rhiannon" give rise to an otherworldly sonic context. Nicks's "Rhiannon" thus conjures an eerie harmonic backdrop that sets into relief her sinuous vocal patterns that twist and turn through dissonant non-chord tones and suspensions, bearing a striking resemblance to the melodic contours of Pegg's "A Witch's Guide to the Underground." With each verse, Nicks brings to life her rendition of the legend of Rhiannon, evoking synesthetic imagery of a goddess who "rings like a bell through the night" and "takes to the sky like a bird in flight." Taunting the men who seek to conquer the goddess, Nicks's raspy vibrato reaches a strained intensity on the repeated phrase, "will you ever win?" Accompanying Nicks's retelling of the legend of "Rhiannon," Christine McVie's breathy back-up vocals provide a series of spooky "ooohs" that paint soaring gusts of wind carrying the goddess to freedom. The conclusion of each narrative verse leads to a chorus that features a repetitive incantation of the name "Rhiannon," as the women's multitracked, echo-laden voices meld into a wind-swept sonic coven summoning forth the powers of the archaic feminine.

Given that Nicks and McVie both occupy a contralto vocal range, their layered vocal harmonies draw attention to the interplay between contrasting vocal timbres. Nicks's characteristically strained, nasal timbre and her hoarse, wide vibrato offer a rebellious counterpoint to McVie's smooth delivery. An iconic live performance of "Rhiannon" from 1976 showcases the layered vocalities of Nicks and McVie, while firmly centering Stevie Nicks as a formidable "witchy diva." Twirling in a Wiccan spiral dance staged against the backdrop of an elder tree silhouetted by the full moon, Nicks moves with abandon in her black, lace-trimmed robe. Prior to commencing the first verse, Nicks grabs the microphone defiantly, and with her piercing blue eyes staring straight into the camera, she declares in a raspy snarl, "This is a song about an old Welsh witch." As the song of Rhiannon, the shape-shifting, unattainable goddess, builds to a soaring climax, Nick's wide vibrato slides through her verse melodies that refuse to align with Lindsey Buckingham's accompanying guitar.[13] The unresolved, fugue-like tension of the verse finds some relief in the repeated incantation of the chorus, summoning forth the witch, Rhiannon. During the first incantation, the camera moves to a split screen featuring close-ups of Nicks and Christine McVie. The sharp edges of Nicks's raspy vibrato are rounded out by McVie's breathier timbre—a vocal union of two women that gives rise to a powerful, shared affect. The drawn-out syllables of the goddess's name ring out like a ritual chant. As the song continues to build to an extended psychedelic "freak-out" featuring virile displays of masculine instrumental rock virtuosity, Nicks's voice is never overpowered; her strong vocal formant remains centered in the sound space. As though taken hold by a Dianic trance, Nicks chants repeatedly, "dreams unwind / her love's a state of mind"—these final words ringing out like a Huebnerian spell, a magical actualization of a dreamlike union with Nicks's conjured goddess, Rhiannon.

CONCLUSION

Just as women musicians of the 1960s folk revival and rock 'n' roll counterculture raised their voices to express a feminist spiritual politics, millennial women artists continue to evoke similar thematics at a historical moment when the dangers of a patriarchal, technocratic hegemony once again loom large in the Western cultural imaginary. At the onset of the millennial, or Y2K-era, youth were plagued by intensifying anxieties of climate change, domestic terrorism, and greater militarization and conservatism spreading across the Global North, eventually leading to the protracted Iraq War (2003–11). Millennial "witchy divas" such as Florence Welsh (Florence + the Machine), Natash Khan (Bat for Lashes), and Chelsea Wolfe exemplify a wider trend of contemporary women indie artists drawing upon the witch as a popular cultural trope associated with feminine spiritual empowerment. The early explorations into Dianic music-making spearheaded by underground folk artists such as Pegg might be long-forgotten by today's youth, just as Huebner's incantation records have faded into an obscure oddity of the past. And yet these past women's concatenated voices continue to echo in the present. A tradition fragmented across time and genre, the "witchy diva" nonetheless remains prominent in the popular cultural imaginary, promising new horizons of spiritual activism.

NOTES

Epigraph 1: Huebner, *Seduction through Witchcraft*.

Epigraph 2: Pegg, "A Witch's Guide to the Underground."

1   "The Red Shoes" is a fairy tale by Hans Christian Anderson, first published by C. A. Reitzel in his compilation, *New Fairy Tales* (1845). The supernatural

power of the red shoes is linked to the threat of unbridled, even hubristic female desire.

2. Sempruch, *Fantasies of Gender*, 11.
3. The "long sixties" refers to a period of social change in the United States and across the Global North, roughly spanning the years 1955–74. Historian Christopher B. Strain defines the long sixties as the time period from the beginnings of the Cold War shortly after World War II, through the civil rights, women's, and Chicano civil rights movements, to Watergate.
4. In this chapter, the "sixties" will be utilized as a term synonymous with the "long sixties."
5. Berger, "Witchcraft and Neopaganism," 36.
6. Although Daly's anthropological work has since been problematized, the pre-Christian Goddess remains a powerful cultural trope within new religions today.
7. Griffin, "Webs of Women," 55.
8. Following Zsuzsanna Budapest, another key figure to emerge within the feminist spirituality movement was Starhawk. Her influential text *The Spiral Dance* (1979) was a how-to book for aspiring witches. Helen Berger describes Starhawk's work as "a lyrical interweaving of feminism, theology, and Witchcraft philosophy for both men and women" (38). Offering classes in feminist Wiccan practice throughout the late 1970s, Starhawk established a national coven in 1982, The Reclaiming Collective. The Reclaiming Collective came to be an influential feminist spiritual group and often engaged in political activism. The Reclaiming Collective also established "Witch Camps" across the United States, with the aim of spreading feminist spirituality and ecofeminist awareness.
9. Another key incantation was Gundella the Green Witch's *Hour of the Witch* (1970). A Detroit-based witch, Gundella's incantation record comprises spoken-word tracks of incantations backed by ambient synthesizer music composed and performed by Gundella's son. Similar to Huebner's album, Gundella's features spells to actualize one's sexual desire and to attract desirable partners. Several years after the release of Huebner's and Gundella's incantation records on Warner Brothers, Babetta, the self-proclaimed "Sexy Witch," released *The Art of Witchcraft* (1974).
10. Clifton, "The Playboy and the Witch: Wicca and Popular Culture."
11. In "Repressive Representations: Patriarchy, Femininities and 1960s' Rock," Sheila Whiteley critiques the limitations placed upon women of the sixties rock 'n' roll counterculture, observing that there is "little to suggest . . . that in terms of musical experience, the counterculture gave serious thought to the individuality or, indeed the diversity of women" (40).
12. Nicks, as quoted in De Main, *In Their Own Words*, 110.
13. In his analysis of "Rhiannon," Jason Lee Oakes observes that Buckingham's lead guitar and Nicks's lead vocals outline the same melody, but never come into alignment. See Oakes, "Queering the Witch," 51.

BIBLIOGRAPHY

Babetta. *The Art of Witchcraft*. 1974. Selby Towers_00013, released 1974. Vinyl LP.

Bennett, Andy. "Paganism and the Counter-Culture." In *Pop Pagans: Paganism and Popular Music*, edited by Donna Weston and Andy Bennett, 13–23. Durham, UK: Acumen, 2013.

Berger, Helen. "Witchcraft and Neopaganism." In *Witchcraft and Magic: Contemporary North America*, 28–54. Philadelphia: University of Pennsylvania Press, 2005.

Clifton, Chas S. "The Playboy and the Witch: Wicca and Popular Culture." In *Her Hidden Children: The Rise of Wicca and Paganism in America*. Lanham, MD: Altamira, 2006.

Crowley, Aleister. *Magick in Theory and Practice*. London, 1929.

Daly, Mary. *The Church and the Second Sex*. Boston: Beacon Press, 1968.

Daly, Mary. *Gyn/Ecology: The Metaethics of Radical Feminism*. Boston: Beacon Press, 1978.

De Main, Bill. *In Their Own Words: Songwriters Talk about the Creative Process*. London: Praeger, 2004.

Fleetwood Mac. "Rhiannon Live: 1976." YouTube, posted November 12, 2010. https://www.youtube.comwatchv=2b9BpunsVm0.

Fleetwood Mac. "Rhiannon (Will You Ever Win)." 1976. *Fleetwood Mac*. Reprise RPS 1345, released February 4, 1976, vinyl single.

Griffin, Wendy. "Webs of Women: Feminist Spiritualities." In *Witchcraft and Magic: Contemporary North America*, edited by Helen Berger, 55–80. Philadelphia: University of Pennsylvania Press, 2005.

Huebner, Louise. *Seduction through Witchcraft*. Warner Brothers, 1969.

Mitchell, Joni. "Don't Interrupt the Sorrow." Track 4, *The Hissing of Summer Lawns*. Asylum Records 7E-1051, 1975, vinyl LP.

Oakes, Jason Lee. "Queering the Witch: Stevie Nicks and the Forging of Femininity at the Night of a Thousand Stevies." In *Queering the Popular Pitch*, edited by Sheila Whiteley and Jennifer Rycenga, 41–54. New York: Routledge, 2006.

Pegg, Carolanne. "A Witch's Guide to the Underground." Track A2, *Carolanne Pegg*. Transatlantic Records TRA 266, 1973, vinyl LP.

Sempruch, Justyna. *Fantasies of Gender and the Witch in Feminist Theory and Literature*. Lafayette, IN: Purdue University Press, 2008.

Sill, Judee. "Crayon Angel." *Judee Sill*. Asylum Records, 1971.

Whiteley, Sheila. "Repressive Representations: Patriarchy, Femininities and 1960s' Rock." In *Women and Popular Music: Sexuality, Identity and Subjectivity*, 32–43. London: Routledge, 2000.

Twenty · SAIRA CHHIBBER

A Queer Critical Analysis of Contemporary Representations of the *Churail* in Hindi Film

INTRODUCTION

Stories about witches abound in South Asia, and the *churail* is a common subtype.[1] A contemporary resurgence of this figure in Bollywood marks the subject of this chapter. Traditionally represented as malevolent figures, *churails* can be human female black magic practitioners or vengeful female ghosts. Both versions of the *churail* are misandrists who hunt men using sex as a lure. The negative import of the type of woman this figure has historically represented is so significant that in contemporary India and Pakistan, the word *churail* is frequently deployed in both Hindustani and Urdu as a misogynist slur directed against women. Films centered on the witch trope in Bollywood have historically leaned into portraying this figure as lusty and murderous—as needing to be destroyed to restore the social status quo. Given this historical context, the recent shift in representations of the Bollywood witch, from villainous sexual deviant to heroic champion of gender justice, marks a social and cultural change of some significance.

Hindi popular cinema has long deployed discursive strategies to promote the social construction of gender within the boundaries of conservative Hindu dogma. Even recent Bollywood films that have aimed to shatter this framework by embracing a "new woman" have focused upon individual victories against patriarchy rather than promoting broader social change. In contrast, new Bollywood horror films like *Stree* and *Roohi* offer ways of looking at the marginalization of women through more general social categories that move beyond the rhetoric of individualism inherent within neoliberal frameworks. These new witch films also present opportunities to read female characters through the lens of queerness, concerning not simply gender or sexual expression but also an ambiguity beyond the stringent character archetypes found in traditional Bollywood narratives.

While this is ostensibly a project centered on representations of witches in Hindi popular cinema, it is also predicated on how these representations exist (and have existed) with the limited gender paradigms Bollywood has strictly employed for decades. Additionally, offering some background on the genealogy of the witch trope in South Asian literary and folk cultures contextualizes the figure of the *churail* and how she has traditionally been deployed. This chapter, of course, includes a discussion about *churail* movies themselves. The movies in question represent four decades of Bollywood witch movies. Films that reflect the misogynistic aspects of the witch trope also demonstrate how this trope reflects contemporary social and political concerns in movies like *Veerana* and *Chudail No. 1*. Contemporary films, such as *Stree* and *Roohi*, suggest new ways of seeing the trope through critical feminist and queer readings.

CHURAILS AND THE "GOOD WOMAN/BAD WOMAN" BINARY IN BOLLYWOOD

While murder is central to her identity, the witch's reliance on sex as a weapon is most significant. The witch's bodily autonomy and the resulting (perceived) social impact of this on society is the problem. In early witch films, the emphasis is placed on how the witch and her actions challenge the moral order and how that impacts men. This impulse reflects the ongoing issue of policing women's bodies and sexuality in South Asian societies, mainly as this discourse is situated along the lines of its impact on patriarchy, which is reflected in popular cinema. This concern around women's sexuality, bodily autonomy, and desire has been a central component of the postindependence Bollywood narrative. Hindi popular cinema has promoted the social construction of gender as approved by the state and various patriarchal interests, relying on a strict gender binary organized along a "good" versus "bad" axis. In stark contrast to representations of the witch who uses sex to gain power in a challenge to patriarchy, "good" women embody virtue, self-sacrifice, and the sublimation of personal desire in service to patriarchy (i.e., the wants and needs of a husband or father).[2] Ultimately, the "good" woman can police her sexuality and desires, foregrounding her position on the "good"/"bad" gender axis. For example, the taxonomy of "bad" women does not simply include women who might be understood to be bad via criminal choices or evil actions. "Bad" women in Bollywood are situated on that end of the binary because of their sex and sexuality, with figures such as the tragic courtesan (*tawaif*), vamp, or supernatural woman from precolonial traditions. Courtesans, born or sold into performance cultures that imply prostitution, represent predominantly north Indian Mughal-era entertainment traditions. These women performed songs, dance, and music and came to be conflated with a type of high-class prostitute not dissimilar to the Japanese geisha.[3] Vamps, or "item girls," are women typically presented as gangster molls who wear Western clothes (miniskirts, jeans, pants), perform in blond wigs, and speak awkwardly in English or Hinglish.[4]

The specifically transgressive roles[5] of both courtesans and vamps have featured mixed-race women or have emphasized a connection to Islamic versus Hindu culture. This coding of race and religion along the binary also points to the effacement of the subcontinent's cultural, religious, and racial heterogeneity through the construction of an artificial "good" woman predicated upon examples from conservative Hindu dogma. Although the witch emerges from precolonial Sanskrit literature and Hindu myths/folklore, she has been used to show the negative consequences of relying upon folk beliefs or esoteric religious traditions to give women power. Ultimately, courtesans, vamps, and figures such as the *churail* are marked "bad." However, they also present modes of performing gender that exist outside of the dutiful daughter, wife, and mother framework that forms the basis of the "good" woman.

CONTEXTUALIZING THE CHURAIL—LITERARY AND FOLK TALES ABOUT SOUTH ASIAN WITCHES

We can find writing on South Asian witches as far back as early medieval stories, like the eleventh-century edition of Somadeva's *Katha Sarit Sagara* (The ocean of story). Within these tales, witches are represented explicitly as women who are deviant because of their rejection of gendered power dynamics that are predicated on a need for subservience to patriarchy. In the *Katha Sarit Sagara*, we find the story of a young woman who, on a whim, is tempted to learn witchcraft. A bored young princess, seeing a group of young women flying in the sky, becomes enamored with the prospect of having similar fun and asks them how they can do this. They respond by telling her to use the magic of witchcraft, which includes breaking social taboos, such as those against murder and cannibalism.[6] It is interesting that in this story, there is far less emphasis on moral dilemmas inherent in breaking taboos to gain power. Instead, the tale focuses much more on the amusements gained through becoming a witch, learning spells, and flying around with a coterie of like-minded female friends. These adventures ultimately end as the newly initiated witch tries to share her new powers with her husband. This results in the accidental cannibalization of their son, followed by the couple's guilt-based suicides. A strongly worded parable punctuates the story: "'The doer of good will obtain good, and the doer of evil, evil' . . . thus we, wicked ones, desiring to slay a Brahman, have brought about our own son's death, and devoured his flesh."[7] Interestingly, the moral of the story is less about witchcraft per se; instead, we can see two concurrent issues: (1) the unsettling of the new powers as a result of trying to include the husband within a female-centered compact; and (2) the attempted murder of a high caste (Brahman) man. To this second point, consider that the Brahman, more than any other figure in the story, is the closest representative of the patriarchal social order. That said, the emphatic descriptions of the young woman's fun as a witch tell us something in their representation. Given the context, even at their most didactic, these medieval stories still contain tension in their push for women to sublimate their desires.

A century later, the twelfth-century Sanskrit story collection *Sukasaptati* (Seventy tales of the parrot) offers a slightly different depiction of the witch. Here she is still described as beautiful and dangerous, but rather than the protagonist, she is a component of the morality play. Her motives and magic are not questioned—they exist within the fabric of society. In one example from this collection, a witch-maiden's father actively seeks a groom for his daughter, as would be typical for any father of an unmarried daughter.[8] He does not seek to change her, nor does he abandon her. He finally finds a man foolish enough to marry her (despite the warnings of others) because the maiden's stunning looks captivate him. However, the new husband bores his witch-wife—and it seems likely that "boredom" is synonymous with sexual dissatisfaction, as through a random encounter the couple meets another young man with whom the witch-wife has an affair. Ultimately the adulterous couple is caught, and the moral of the story is that the cuckolded husband is publicly shamed while the witch-wife is abandoned. In this story, we learn nothing about the young witch's magical abilities—all the reader understands is that she has a sexual appetite that is not satisfied by her husband and that her behavior in seeking sexual fulfillment is socially unacceptable. The story connects women to witchcraft through sex, desire, and sensuality. As with the earlier stories about witches, women who place their amusements above their husbands are depicted as amoral and worthy of punishment. Where the earlier witch story features a tragic parable, this representation of the witch is broadly comedic and tailors its moral lesson to a foolish man who ignores good advice and chooses a spouse based on looks alone. Nevertheless, this woman, crucially, is not punished with violence, and the story does not imply a great tragedy on her part. Presumably, being abandoned by a boring husband could be, in fact, a positive outcome for the witch.

Witches in folk traditions shift even farther from protagonist roles in stories that take on a more gothic import due to being situated within geographies of isolated locations and at night. This witch/*churail* is a ghost who does not speak and does not communicate beyond the affective (through the exchange of looks). In particular, the folk *churail* is said to be the specter of a woman who has died in childbirth or due to gender violence. Despite having this more nuanced and sympathetic genesis, these witches are not presented as sympathetic characters. Stories describe them as beautiful temptresses who are often identifiable only via the physical feature of their backward-turned feet (*mudiapairi churail*, literally "turned feet witch").[9] These witches are found near "unclean" or impure locations such as cremation ghats or cemeteries. In these stories, the witches are described as beautiful women wearing traditional clothes who appear alone at night, trying to seduce men whom they then kill. The sexual aspect of these figures, in depicting them as traditionally attired women who use their bodies and sexuality to kill, further emphasizes an "impurity" or "uncleanness." Here, the witch is but a terrifying night-fright. She is a "bogeyman-esque" creature who warns men to keep to conventional routines and to forgo travel to "unclean" spaces and places. However, they are also a warning to women who unsettle conventions of appearance and behavior—the witch dresses as a traditional woman. However, she walks alone at night and uses her looks to create an atmosphere of seduction. This framework emphasizes a social code that draws connections to perceptions of women based on appearance, location, and masculine authority. Why don't these women have fathers, brothers, husbands, or sons accompanying them? Why is this not an immediate flag to the foolish victim who allows himself to fall prey to the witch despite these overt warning signs? That these witches are rendered largely voiceless is also telling, as it strips them of an agency that is extant in the Sanskrit stories. The frightening and sexual aspects of this folk *churail* lend themselves to representations in film more so than the early Sanskrit stories.

HISTORICAL REPRESENTATIONS OF THE CHURAIL IN BOLLYWOOD

Historically, *churail* films have been primarily labeled as B movies, with salacious plots that conveniently play up this witch's "sexy monster" aspect. Until very recently, Bollywood representations of *churails* have emphasized this trope via its most sexual and violent aspects. Many low-budget versions of Hindi witch films from the 1980s onward have walked a fine line between what the Indian film censor board might accept as folk narrative versus softcore pornography. Filmmakers have conveniently used the figure's literary and folk antecedents to mask attempts at breaking censor codes, getting close to pornography via depictions of female nudity and sexuality. Filmmakers have leveraged the folk roots of the witch as the pretext to make money by affording audiences a conduit for seeing a "dirty" movie without explicitly saying so. Films focusing on the *churail* have relied on the "good"/"bad" framework by contrasting the witch or women possessed by the witch with women who demonstrate the moral qualities reflecting the sociocultural status quo. In the case of most *churail* films, a "good" woman's love interest will become the target of the lustful *churail*. Narrative resolution can occur only if the male protagonist breaks free from the spell of *churail* to restore the established social order by killing the villain and returning to the "good" woman (who will also be compared with the "bad" *churail* throughout the film). The evil qualities of the succubus-type figure of the witch are invariably contrasted with the "Indian values" reflected by the demure, modest, and dutiful "good" woman.

Two films that provide examples of conventional representations of the *churail* are *Veerana* (directed by Shyam Ramsay and Tulsi Ramsay [1988]) and *Chudail No.1* (directed by R. Kumar [1999]). While there is variation in *churail* films from the 1980s onward, these films serve as examples for a few reasons. First, there is a growing body of work on the Ramsay brothers' productions. Second, these films represent the trope but have slightly larger budgets and include mainstream Bollywood actors, making for ease of comparison within the frame of contemporary popular cinema.

Further, these are also relatively easy-to-access films for those interested in watching earlier iterations of the witch on film in Bollywood.

Veerana is a story about a witch called Nakita. This witch terrorizes a small village by hunting and seducing men who wander into an isolated part of the countryside, the Veerana. An ancient entity, she remains young by feeding off the blood of the men she seduces and kills. A Tantric aids her[10]—Baba and an anonymous group of male cultists, all of whom worship a masculine deity called Mahakal. Although this Mahakal is presented as a monstrous deity that does not overtly resemble anything in the Hindu pantheon, it is essential to note that there *is* a deity by that name in Hinduism. This Mahakal refers to a particularly terrifying aspect of the god Shiva, who is, perhaps most importantly, identified as the consort of the goddess Kali (Maha Kali) and connected to the worship of Shakti, a female-centered power.[11] The witch story is thus connected with the precolonial goddess traditions. The witch in *Veerana* is caught early in the film due to a local landowner's intervention, and her body is destroyed. However, the witch's powers are strong, and she survives in spirit, choosing to possess the landowner's daughter Jasmin's body and to take revenge on him for disrupting her activities. The rest of the film involves Jasmin—under Nakita's control—seducing and killing men. Even though it is Jasmin who is possessed, her father and male family members are positioned as the victims in this situation.

Given the reference to Mahakal and the female powers of Shakti, it is of note that the landowning patriarchy is ultimately responsible for the witch's downfall as these men are representative of more modern, Brahmanic Hindu traditions that position men as superior. In a final gesture, we hear a voiceover narration that speaks of good vanquishing evil, while the final shot is of Jasmin alone on a seashore, looking distressed and uneasy. It is difficult to discern whether Jasmin's unease is symptomatic of the knowledge that she is somehow "tainted" by her actions or whether there is something of Nakita left within her. The film was released during a period of significant transition in India that marked the end of the Gandhi political dynasty and ushered in the neoliberal 1990s. *Veerana* demonstrates a profound unease with women's sexual agency that perhaps reflects a social unease vis-à-vis the advent of open markets and globalization with attendant concerns about the "dilution" of traditional Indian values. The film's emphasis on the patriarchy as local landowners who need to eradicate precolonial female revenants is significant. Given the structure of the "good"/"bad" binary, it is also significant that Jasmin survives the ordeal, at least initially. She is not shown to die through the destruction of the possessing witch or by suicide (a common motif in Hindi films featuring victims of sexual violence), which is also essential. However, how we might interpret Jasmin's survival is undoubtedly open to diverse conclusions.

Released a decade after *Veerana*, the film *Chudail No. 1* focuses on a spectral *churail* revenge narrative. The movie was released three years after the Hollywood blockbuster *Scream* (directed by Wes Craven [1996]) and begins with a similar conceit—someone repeatedly crank calls a young woman, singing flirtatious song lyrics and being perverse. It turns out that she is the daughter of a police inspector and is being shaken down by a gang looking for a police file that implicates their boss. The inclusion of the *Scream* sequence can be a nod to the viewer that globalization has occurred with the sharing of pop culture trends from the United States. From the film's first sequence, the woman's affect and attire immediately gesture toward the "bad" girl trope. She answers the phone confrontationally and is seen clad in a revealing black short set that could be read as a negligee. The film's villains break into the woman's house, murder her father, and then rape and murder her. The next scene cuts to a young police inspector taking his very demure and sari-attired girlfriend to meet his family. The perceptive viewer will have gleaned that the two women, although affectively dissimilar, look very much the same.

The movie follows the framework of the spectral or ghostly *churail* from folklore in the following ways. The *churail* is created through sexual violence/murder. She presents as a beautiful woman alone on lonely roadways and seeks to murder the men who harmed her. The plot of this movie diverges from earlier film antecedents, however, through an embrace of the Todorovian fantastic.[12] Including a number of possible human actions remains plausible until the supernatural denouement. Ultimately, the murderer is revealed to be a spectral *churail* acting in concert with the ghost of her father[13]—as though the father is necessary for the 1990s witch to act on her desire for vengeance. The context of the film's release (in 1999) is vital because the decade was marked by significant social and political change in India. The advent of neoliberalism and right-wing Hindutva politics, on the one hand, celebrated free market capitalism, while, on the other hand, it promoted a conservative Hindu culture predicated on the effacement of diversity.

Of these two early examples of witch movies, *Veerana* adheres to the framework of women who use magic to gain supernatural powers through sex and violence. In keeping with its traditional paradigm, this witch is explicitly villainous with no sympathetic aspects. However, ten years later, we can observe that *Chudail No. 1* features a slight evolution in the representation of this trope. This shift can be observed through a plot emphasizing the wickedness of the men who murdered the film's *churail*. In emphasizing the vileness of the killers, the film creates a potential for reading the witch's actions as appropriate. However, the film precludes forgiveness for the witch's actions. This is made explicitly clear through the spectral witch's penitent behavior, primarily through her repeated apologies for casting aspersions on her innocent sister. The ghostly witch apologizes for causing anyone to believe that her sister could drink alcohol, dress provocatively, and frequent nightclubs, then murder or possess anyone. Crucially, the behaviors that the ghost witch apologizes for are the behaviors she exhibited before her death. Therefore, it is clear that the *churail* sister apologizes for herself and for women who choose to act outside the "good"/"bad" binary—making the issue of women's behavior and breaches of the gender binary of greater import than the murder of the criminal gang members. Given that the gang members are not representative of the patriarchal social fabric, it makes sense that the witch is offered a more sympathetic cast than Nakita in *Veerana*. However, it is clear that in both films, there is an emphasis on policing behavior per traditional gender codes.

THE CHANGING FACE OF THE CHURAIL IN BOLLYWOOD

In newer films such as *Stree* (directed by Amar Kaushik [2018]) and *Roohi* (directed by Hardik Mehta [2021]), we see a distinct reimagining of the witch as an agent of vengeance fighting for gender justice. These new witch films indicate a pro-feminist shift in register by taking up identification with this figure both as a supernatural agent of chaos *and* as a contemporary woman using violence to unsettle patriarchal social frameworks. These two films inhabit shared imagined geographies, set in small Indian towns, a space that exists in contrast to the rural settings of earlier witch films. This spatial difference also highlights liminality, a cue to reading each of these films as existing on the precipice of a change or movement.

The name *Stree* is the Hindi word for "woman," and the title cues Hindi speakers to think about women from the outset. The film's ostensible protagonist is Vicky (Rajkummar Rao), a young man who is heir to a respectable tailoring business. The early part of the film is set like a conventional

Bildungsroman as Vicky is at a pivotal moment in his youth/young adulthood. He chafes against his father's expectations and has the desire to do something more than run the tailoring business once his father retires. Vicky says that he wants to do something outside of the small-town life that he leads. Against this backdrop, the townsfolk prepare for the annual haunting of a ghostly *churail* (called *Stree* by the locals), who terrorizes local men during a Hindu religious festival. In *Stree*, the *churail* is said to be the ghost of a courtesan who was murdered by a mob of men when she decided to get married and quit her profession. Now her spirit has returned to the small town where she was murdered over a century ago to exact vengeance on the descendants of those who killed her and her fiancé.

A beautiful young woman who remains unnamed throughout the film (Shraddha Kapoor) arrives in town for the festival and, through a series of misadventures, is thought to be the *Stree*. While this misunderstanding is resolved, it slowly becomes clear that she is very likely a human witch. The motives of this witch remain opaque, but she is seen to use spells and magic to control others. This witch dresses traditionally. She seems unaware of contemporary music trends and, crucially, seems uninterested in romance. She is the fixer and the catalyst for change in the context of the haunting. However, she has her own motivations as she requires something from the Stree (although it never is clear why).

In *Stree*, gender and power are explored through explorations of the monstrous as a direct result of problematic patriarchal social frameworks. In the film, the specter's origin story overturns traditional conceptions of the witch as a sexually voracious woman who deserves punishment. The courtesan is punished for choosing to live monogamously. Further, it is explicitly through the actions and directions of the unnamed woman that the curse of the Stree is broken in a way that does not result in the destruction of the avenging female spirit, whereas traditionally, the film would seek narrative closure by removing the supernatural threat and an attendant heterosexual romantic coupling. Neither occurs here.

The film also reveals that Vicky's late mother was a prostitute, creating some doubt about whether he is the tailor's biological (versus adopted) son. This is significant within the context of a caste-obsessed society as it muddles conventions concerning how critical characters in films are situated with caste privilege. However, this does offer the interesting question of whether this might point to the lack of romantic closure in the film. This may seem ridiculous to those readers who are unaware of South Asia's significant caste prejudice that colors social relations. However, it is a point that bears some examination. We do not have a clear explanation concerning why heterosexual romance is rejected, and we do not know whether this question of parentage is part of the equation. If the human witch has some magic or supernatural identity, given what we know of literary and folkloric antecedents, it does not explain why she remains sexually and romantically unavailable. Despite a friendly tone, the unnamed woman's rejection of Vicky's romantic overtures still reflects the quashing of masculine desire. Another way that this lack of coupling can also be read is as part of a broader break with convention resulting from a rupture in the gendered social order. What does it signify when male protagonists cannot restore social or moral order, having to rely instead on a woman to do it for them? To this point, it is particularly notable that the town ends up appeasing rather than exorcising the specter by erecting a statue of the Stree. In doing so, the statue acts as a reminder of crimes against women, but it also functions to venerate the ghostly woman for her protection. Breaking with recent conventions in representing women's issues in Bollywood, the statue presents a collective social response to misogyny, whereas otherwise, films have focused on individual responses to similar situations.

The film *Roohi* is centered upon a young girl by the same name (Jahnvi Kapoor) who comes from a small town with an eccentric tradition involving bride kidnapping as a precursor to marriage. While the specific circumstances are never straightforward, Roohi is possessed by a ghostly *churail*, later self-identified as Afza.[14] Later, in a plot twist involving a local gangster and the bride-napping custom, Roohi is kidnapped by two henchmen, Bhawra Pandey (Rajkummar Rao) and Kattani Qureishi (Varun Sharma). They fall in love with human (Roohi) and ghost (Afza), respectively. Pandey/Roohi and Qureishi/Afza are read as Hindu and Muslim names, respectively, which is a curious inclusion.

The exorcism subplot within the film features a series of interactions that provide a social context for understanding the fear of the *churail*. While a meek figure, Roohi at least initially resents her situation as a victim of possession. Ultimately, despite being described as the work of Brahmin priests, it is an older woman who promises to free Roohi of her possession. This mysterious woman is mainly silent and presents with scars on her feet that indicate she was once a *muriapairi*. This is intriguing as she appears to be the first "post-witch" depicted in a *churail* film. The inclusion of this triad of Roohi, Afza, and the older woman also appears to reflect early medieval Sanskrit witch stories and the descriptions of female power as evinced through the female group dynamic. Without divulging too much plot, it is clear that these two human women also present backstories concerning gender relations that reflect complex patriarchal systems relating to women in the context of heterosexual marriage.

While *Stree* presents ambiguous scenarios that allow for diverse interpretations of gender relations, *Roohi* uniquely foregrounds its queerness and the potential power that is inherent between the love of two women. Applying a queer lens to interpreting the film's plot and character relations provides a way of understanding why Afza's spirit chooses to possess Roohi outside of these conventions, perhaps identifying something kindred in her. The film's narrative indicates a specific process for the possession that ought to occur if the groom falls asleep or neglects his bride-to-be during the very long marriage ceremony. In Roohi's case, a flashback indicates that she is possessed even before her first (heterosexual) wedding ceremony begins. In a pivotal sequence depicting a psychic and physical conflict between Roohi and Afza, the spectral voice painfully and gutturally enunciates that she has offered the otherwise meek Roohi power through this possession. This dialogue about power is further emphasized by the visual impact of Roohi's contorted body being suspended by an invisible force (Afza's power) that demonstrates an inherently physical power linking the two.

The film culminates in a wedding scene with the movie's male protagonists waiting for Roohi or Afza to choose concerning which man she (they?) will marry. However, in a startling departure from genre codes, Roohi foregrounds the queer reading of the narrative by deciding to marry the *churail*. In minute detail, the film shows Roohi going through the steps of a Hindu marriage ritual by herself—explicitly asking the spectral witch if she consents to the partnership! This sequence alone, and certainly when read alongside the various subtle nods throughout the film, all but cement a queer interpretation of Roohi and Afza's relationship. This queer interpretation seems reasonable given the film's evident contestation of India's patriarchy and heterosexual marriage relations. However, the tricky part of this analysis is that these two women can maintain only a spectral, ergo socially secret, relationship as Afza is invisible to all, including Roohi.

CONCLUDING REMARKS

It seems apparent that new witch films in Bollywood present a rupture with traditional representations of the witch and the gender binary in Hindi popular culture. In all recent media examples, the figure of the *churail* is actively represented combating patriarchal frameworks, mainly through a refusal to sublimate desire for vengeance, power, and sexual self-expression. To this point, we can certainly read these new films within a context of successful hashtag activism such as #MeTooBollywood and related social unrest in India concerning gender. However, while on the surface, the transformation of this figure might suggest that social conventions fixed upon women's power and agency are shifting, this is not necessarily a given. For example, even within the new cycle of *churail* films, the witch has been stripped of a critical characteristic of the trope to make her redemption socially acceptable. In both *Stree* and *Roohi*, neither ghost nor witch presents as a sexual threat; they are both desired by men but appear modest, both figures dressing traditionally. Even in applying the queer reading in the context of Roohi, we must remember that the spectral relationship renders it invisible. This desexualization of these figures cannot be overstated, and it would be remiss to assume that the conservative characteristics of the cinematic "good" woman have been wholly effaced through a reinterpretation of the witch in Hindi popular culture. What these new representations do indicate, however, is that there is scope for remediating problematic gender tropes that have for too long been utilized to police and control women's gender expression.

Even within new Bollywood cinema that takes up women's issues, narratives focus on female protagonists contesting personal situations, with victories lending themselves to individual growth rather than to broader social change. In this respect, Bollywood horror offers us a conduit to observing the trope of the witch as it is deployed to combat structural and systemic issues. The fact that these new *churail* films are genre films that are primarily international coproductions and easily accessible via subscription streaming services is noteworthy, given the wide breadth of reception and audience. As popular media in the context of the Indian subcontinent has historically acted as a mirror of a certain kind of moral order of society, narratives focusing on the witch acknowledge the possibilities for diverse strategies of resistance to institutional patriarchy and social constructs predicated upon the subordination of women.

NOTES

1. *Churail* means witch and is sometimes spelled *chudail*.
2. Dimitrova, "Religion and Gender in Bollywood Film," 2010.

3   A reminder of Islamophobic tales from the eighteenth and nineteenth centuries centered upon the kidnapping of Hindu girls for prostitution.
4   A mix of English and Hindustani.
5   For instance, the actors Helen or Manorama (birth names Helen Ann Richardson and Erin Issac Daniels).
6   Penzer, *Katha Sarit Sagara*, 104.
7   Penzer, *Katha Sarit Sagara*, 115.
8   Wortham, *Tales of the Parrot*, 26.
9   As with the spelling of the word *churail*—*mudiapairi* is read the same way as *muriapairi*—in translating to English, I defer to the *r* versus the *rd* sound.
10 In Bollywood, a "Tantric" is a character type that applies as a catch-all phrase for a person performing esoteric rituals often connected to ancient Hindu traditions.
11 Kinsley, *Hindu Goddesses*.
12 Todorov, *The Fantastic*, 25.
13 Although these father-daughter and twin relationships are never satisfactorily explained.
14 There is a joke to be noted here, as combining the names of these two women gestures to Rooh Afza, a popular syrup drink throughout South Asia (see Hamdard's website, https://www.hamdard.com/).

BIBLIOGRAPHY

Chatterji, Shoma A. *Subject Cinema, Object Woman: A Study of the Portrayal of Women in Indian Cinema*. Calcutta: Parumita Publications, 1998.

Dimitrova, Diana. "Religion and Gender in Bollywood Film." In *Religion in Literature and Film in South Asia*, edited by Diana Dimitrova, 69–82. New York: Palgrave Macmillan, 2010.

Govindan, Padma, and Bisakha Dutta. "From Villain to Traditional Housewife! The Politics of Globalization and Women's Sexuality in the 'New' Indian Media." In *Global Bollywood*, edited by Anandam P. Kavoori and Aswin Punathambekar, 180–202. New York: New York University Press, 2008.

Kaushik, Amar, dir. *Stree*. Maddock Films, 2018. 128 min. https://www.netflix.com/ca/title/81113921.

Kinsley, David R. *Hindu Goddesses: Visions of the Divine Feminine in the Hindu Religious Tradition*. Los Angeles: University of California Press, 1988.

Kumar, R., dir. *Chudail No. 1*. Rachne Cine Arts, 1999. VHS, 99 min.

Mehta, Hardik, dir. *Roohi*. Maddock Films, 2021. 134 min. https://www.netflix.com/ca/title/81267359.

Penzer, N. M., trans. *Somadeva's "Katha Sarit Sagara."* New Delhi: BR Publishing, 2001.

Ramaswamy, Sumathi. *The Goddess and the Nation: Mapping Mother India*. Durham, NC: Duke University Press, 2015.

Ramsay, Shyam, and Tulsi Ramsay, dirs. *Veerana*. Kanta Ramsay, 1988. VHS, 145 min.

Ray, Sangeeta. *En-Gendering India: Woman and Nation in Colonial and Postcolonial Narratives*. Durham, NC: Duke University Press, 2000.

Todorov, Tzvetan. *The Fantastic: A Structural Approach to a Literary Genre*. Ithaca, NY: Cornell University Press, 1975.

Virdi, Jyotika. *The Cinematic Imagination: Indian Popular Films as Social History*. New Brunswick, NJ: Rutgers University Press, 2003.

Viswanath, Gita. "Saffronizing the Silver Screen: The Right-Winged Nineties Film." In *Films and Feminism: Essays in Indian Cinema*, edited by Jasbir Jain and Sudha Rai, 39–51. New Delhi: Rawat Publications, 2015.

Wortham, B. Hale, trans. *The Enchanted Parrot: Being a Selection from the Suksaptati*. London: Luzac and Co., 1911.

Twenty-one · MARIA AMIR

Pakistan's *Churails*: Young Feminists Choosing "Witch" Way Is Forward

Bach
Churail! Churail!
Mera Doosra Janam
Churail Churail!
Teri Kahani Khatam

Badnaam se bad ab mein bani
Chup Thi kab tak mein
Macha di khalbali

—OSMAN KHALID BUTT, *Churails*

The closing sequence for the pilot episode of Pakistan's web series *Churails* features four women from dramatically different socioeconomic backgrounds in the sprawling metropolis of Karachi contemplating a blackboard inscribed with a dichotomy *churail/naik parveen*. *Churail* is the colloquial term for "witch" in Urdu and *naik parveen* is a euphemism for purity akin to the Virgin Mary. Both parallels confine and define the lives of Pakistani women, and it is this perilously fragile binary that separates which one of these two categories society will lump any woman into. Pakistan's piety politics confines women to an extremely rigid moral/immoral nexus, and negotiating one's way out of this framing is often impossible. For this reason, the only real way out of this binary often involves what is known in Urdu as *baghawat* (rebellion).

Baghawat is a wholesale term for a variety of resistance formations. It can be read as insurrection, mutiny, treason, revolt, uprising, and rebellion in different contexts. However, in the context of women, specifically South Asian women, *baaghi ho gayi he* (she is beyond control) typically means that a woman has "crossed over" beyond respectability and that she is now out of anyone's control. This *baaghi* condition is used to refer to women who no longer cater to societal expectations often articulated through the colloquial idiom, *Log kya kahenge?* (What will people say?). Pakistani women are labeled *churails* when they become *baaghi*. It is the initial act of defiance that frames a woman as a witch. This act of defiance is underlined by women embracing and unlocking deeply suppressed rage. As it happens, in many cases South Asian women's rebellion is termed as *Jadoo toone ka asar* (being under the influence of black magic), thereby underscoring the notion that in an ideal Muslim society no "respectable" Pakistani woman would ever rebel against men. This idea is reinforced into Pakistani collective consciousness by reiterating that Islam already gives women all the rights they could possibly need and that any form of rebellion against the established social order constitutes a revolt against religion itself. Here the *churail* is cultivated as a demon entity; her rebellion against abuse and exploitation is constructed as an insurrection against a fallacious, divinely ordained male supremacy. In "The Veiled Avengers of Pakistan's Streaming New Wave" Bilal Qureshi writes, "The term '*churails*' is Pakistan's c-word, translated literally as 'witches,' but more accurately understood as a loaded epithet for a demonic, unstable, uncontrollable species of woman, the so-called bitch/witch."[1] It is precisely this "bitch-witch" that the television series *Churails* frames as a tool for emancipation in Pakistan through its four female protagonists: young Lyari-based boxer Zubaida, sullen wedding planner Jugnu, former-lawyer-turned-model housewife Sara Khan, and ex-convict Batool Jan.

MOBILIZING RAGE

This chapter focuses on how the word *churails* serves as an emancipation tool for the show's protagonists and how it serves in a variety of scenarios where these characters are freed by reclaiming the slur for themselves and embracing the supposed "loss of respectability" that accompanies this label. Shedding the weight of societal expectations and circumventing conventional performances of Pakistani piety opens radical avenues for resistance and sisterhood for the show's protagonists. One of the central themes for the series *Churails* is its wholesale endorsement of women's rage as a legitimate and powerful emotion that is invariably neutralized and policed in patriarchal societies to uphold the prevailing social order. Here this rage is set free, and each *churail* finds her power by acknowledging and mobilizing her own anger as well as that of the women around her by channeling the generational rage of the women who came and suffered before them.

Any societal balance predicated upon women's contained rage and their continued silence is inherently unjust, but this is a deeply chilling prospect for Pakistani society to grasp because it flies in the face of tradition. The fact that each of the women in the show is depicted as accessing their repressed power by weaponizing said rage against the men in their lives is revolutionary in and of itself. This premise of embracing and mobilizing women's rage renders the show truly groundbreaking in a culture where women's tolerance, humility, and suffering are consistently glorified on-screen and in practice.

....

The pilot episode of Asim Abbasi's 2020 miniseries *Churails* is titled *"Wafa,"* which in Urdu translates to "loyalty or fidelity." This episode is a deep dive into how each of the series' protagonists is punished for her loyalty to the men in her life—the cheating husband, the bullying client, the abusive father, and a convict haunted by her past bound to the man she killed for trying to rape her daughter, her own husband. Loyalty to men punishes women in patriarchal societies like Pakistan, and the show establishes this pattern from the onset. The series opens with the sequence:

> Once upon a time,
> Aik qatil, wakeel, wedding planner aur boxer
> Mil bethe aur unhe eshsaas hua
> Keh who ab tak sirf putla ban kar ji rahe the
>
> (Once upon a time, a killer, a lawyer, a wedding planner, and a boxer met unexpectedly.
>   And they all came to the same realization—that until then, they had all been living as shadows and reflections of someone else.)

It is at this juncture that each woman acknowledges the rage bubbling within her and embraces it. This rage is all-consuming but simultaneously empowering as the youngest of the group, boxer Zubaida, voices, "*Mere andar ki jo dayan he na, shuroo se hi khiski hui he*" (My inner witch you know, she's always been crazy, clamoring to be let out).

In her book *Rage Becomes Her*, Soraya Chemaly writes, "While we experience anger internally, it is mediated culturally and externally by other people's expectations and social prohibitions. Roles and responsibilities, powers and privilege are the framers of our anger. Relationships, culture, social status, exposure to discrimination, poverty, and access to power all factor into how we think about, experience, and utilize anger."[2] The one thing that all women who are termed *churails* or *dayans* in Pakistan share is that they have shed such "expectations and social prohibitions" and have redefined the "roles and responsibilities" that have been prescribed for them. The initial *baghawat* for such women is born when they allow themselves to feel, embrace, and access their rage. Rage is the first step to power, and the witch allows herself to feel angry about the world around her that refuses her a place in it unless it is on someone else's terms. Asim Abbasi's web series expresses this metamorphosis by converging and conflating deeply satisfying daily social dichotomies in Pakistan.

THE VIGILANTE COVEN

The women in *Churails* navigate an intricate dance between performed piety and radical rebellion. They set up a boutique selling burqas called "Halal Designs," the most Islam-compliant business product and model imaginable; but instead of selling burqas, they use the shop as a front for a detective agency called Churails that investigates cheating husbands and beats up molesters and abusive spouses and family members, all under the tag line "*Mard ko dard ho ga*" (Men will suffer too). The characters in the show acknowledge themselves as witches as each comes to the simultaneous understanding that every time she expressed anger at any injustice she faced, she was labeled a *churail*—this is the moment their little vigilante coven is born. Embracing and reclaiming the name for themselves is an act of emancipation that ultimately leads to the women donning burqas and the *niquab* (face covering) and going out in the middle of the night to beat up abusive boyfriends, spouses, and fathers with hockey sticks (figure 21.1). This subversion of the burqa and *niquab*—garments that are commonly regarded as tools for Muslim women's oppression—being used as tools for acts of vigilantism against men crafts a powerful message. The idea that the very garment designed to stifle a woman's presence and identity within a patriarchal system can be reworked to provide her anonymity and cover to punish her oppressor helps recode both Muslim women's agency as well as their mobility.

In *Politics of Piety*, Saba Mahmood writes about how feminist agency operates in different Islamic spaces:

> When women's actions seem to reinscribe what appear to be "instruments of their own oppression," the social analyst can point to moments of disruption, and articulation of points of opposition to, male authority—moments that are located either in the interstices of a woman's consciousness (often read as a nascent feminist consciousness), or in the objective effects of women's actions, however unintended these may be. Agency, in this form of analysis, is understood as the capacity to realize one's own interests against the weight of custom, tradition, transcendental will, or other obstacles (whether individual or collective). Thus, the humanist desire for autonomy and self-expression constitutes the substrate, the slumbering ember that can spark to flame in the form of an act of resistance when conditions permit.[3]

It is precisely this "spark to flame" born out of a desire for autonomy that has been a defining feature of South Asian feminist vigilantism. This can be connected to the famous Indian "Bandit Queen," Phoolan Devi, a poor woman from Uttar Pradesh who joined a gang of bandits after having been raped and beaten at a young age by her husband and forced by her parents to return to him repeatedly. Phoolan Devi was sentenced to eleven years in prison for over forty-eight counts of murder, robbery, and kidnapping for ransom but was ultimately elected to parliament twice upon her release before she was murdered in 2001. In *Churails*, there are several scenes where the perpetually drunk Jugnu refers to her maid, ex-convict Batool, as Phoolan every time the latter displays her flagrant bloodlust for what she wishes to do to "certain men" if she ever gets her hands on them.

The use of the burqa and *niquab* also serve as a social equalizer for the four protagonists who come from deeply disparate class backgrounds. Pakistani society is deeply fragmented along class lines, and the gap between affluent women and poor rural and urban women often seems unbreachable. The hierarchies ever-present between women from these different worlds are impossible to dismiss as they are consistently reinforced through both socioeconomic divisions as well as through lingering colonial baggage that frames affluence having as fair skin and the ability to speak fluent English. These very divisions linger in the interactions between the four protagonists of the show. Lawyer Sara Khan is the architect of the plan to form a detective agency posing as burqa boutique and blackmails her husband with photos of his many mistresses to finance her venture with the help of her best friend Jugnu. The latter comes from an extremely wealthy business background, but Jugnu's fractious relations with her father and uncle mean she works as a wedding planner for Karachi's socialites, where she organizes events that feature swans and mineral water being poured into swimming pools in a city where water is perpetually scarce.

By contrast, young Zubaida leads a double life, hiding her passion for boxing from her abusive parents by bribing her appointed bodyguard, her eleven-year-old brother, to keep her secrets. Freshly released from prison, Batool Jan rescues Zubaida from her home after she is brutally beaten, and both take refuge in Jugnu's house. Batool works as Jugnu's maid. The scenes where all the *churails* at the agency dress in *burqas* and take up arms, fake guns, and real sticks are moments where their class and status are momentarily erased. However, such sisterhood is shaky at best as there are multiple instances where the power imbalance between Jugnu, Sara, and the other women at the agency is glaringly apparent. The very fact that the wealthier women define the agenda and the types of cases the agency will take—"bread and butter cheating husbands" rather than ones where poorer women would be rescued from abusive situations, which Zubaida pushes for from the onset, highlights a vacuum of empathy that exists between Pakistan's elite and its economically marginalized classes. It is only when the abuse happens to one of the *churails* that Jugnu and Sara become cognizant of their deeply entrenched privilege, even as they continue to pretend that their covert feminist coven is entirely egalitarian.

In "The Colonial Mythology of Feminist Witchcraft," Chris Klassen expands on this condition by reiterating that if feminist witches insist on defining themselves as equal victims of patriarchy without recognizing internal class and postcolonial ridges between women, they will never achieve lasting changes: "The merging of patriarchy with colonialism simplifies very complex social structures and historical realities in such a way as to hinder useful analysis and understanding of women's (and men's) individual and group experiences. As a result, a universalizing of women's experience (all women experience oppression, therefore all women experience the same oppression) occurs, which in essence substitutes middle-class white women's experiences for the norm, denying any other social positioning a valid identity."[4] This essentializing is repeatedly witnessed in the ways Jugnu's and Sara's characters put the lives of their other colleagues on the line to settle their personal scores. Small instances such as Jugnu needing to be convinced to join the rest of the group for a meal, a domain that deeply divides how *mem saabs* (affluent women) interact with the household help in Pakistan—no shared plates or cutlery—is a defining moment of solidarity-building, which comes off as both disingenuous and self-serving.

The sisterhood built by witches is precarious when it is split along class and colonial lines. This is something that the series negotiates effectively by refusing to shy away from the discomfiting privilege and excessive wealth of two of its protagonists, Sara and Jugnu, that is constantly shown to exist in contrast to and often at the expense of the other two leads—Batool Jan's domestic labor and Zubaida's anguish at their apathy toward helping vulnerable women. However, the resounding theme of the show works because it recognizes this chasm and shows the characters working through, rather than camouflaging, their differences in the name of a shinier, happier feminist sisterhood that is cracked down the middle. Klassen acknowledges this negotiation: "Feminist theorists who argue for recognizing that sexism and racism are not the same thing are careful not to suggest that each woman look solely to her own experience and combat her own oppression individually. They are adamant about the need for social involvement, working together in coalition to combat all sorts of oppressions."[5] This approach rejects a "politics of difference" but rather frames a feminist politics where differences are acknowledged, understood, and negotiated to empower all members of the group for a more equitable future.

The concept of embracing one's inner *churail* as a road to emancipation, while freeing, comes with more than the cost of social ostracization. The women in the show are repeatedly confronted with the fact that such subversion creates conflict not just in the individual cases they deal with but with more entrenched patriarchal structures. The latter half of the series explores this structural clash in broadly economic terms—where a whitening, cancer-causing, beauty cream becomes the inroad to unearthing deeper conspiracies including a sex-trafficking ring, an illegal abortion clinic, and the murders of several poor women who migrated from smaller towns to the big city. At each juncture, the *churails* are confronted with how deeply rooted male privilege in Pakistani society is, enough to provide social, legal, political, and sexual cover for any crime imaginable.

Here, women's bodies become the site for all forms of violence—whether from individual men, to family structures, to social policing, as well as to religious and national "honor codes." In *Caliban and the Witch*,

FIGURE 21.1 Samya Arif's promotional poster for *Churails*.

Silvia Federici underscores how women's bodies are commodified and how, once this process is complete, there are no limits to how they can be exploited. "Witches embodied what had to be destroyed: 'the heretic, the healer, the disobedient wife, the woman who dared to live alone, poisoned the master's food and inspired the slaves to revolt,'" she writes.[6] The violent response from all the existing patriarchal powers in this series is directly proportional to the *churails* claiming space in society while also achieving economic mobility as their business flourishes. According to Federici, through an "intense process of social degradation," women were constructed "in the image of capital. . . . Aiming at controlling nature, the capitalist organization of work must refuse the unpredictability implicit in the practice of magic, and the possibility of establishing a privileged relation with the natural elements, as well as the belief in the existence of powers available only to individuals, and thus not easily generalized and exploitable. Magic was also an obstacle to the rationalization of the work process, and a threat to the establishment of the principle of individual responsibility. Above all, magic seemed a form of refusal of work, of insubordination, and an instrument of grassroots resistance to power. The world had to be 'disenchanted' in order to be dominated."[7]

STRATEGIES OF REVOLT

This disenchantment is what drives women to seek work with the Churails detective agency in the first place—these recruits include a middle-aged lesbian couple that Batool Jan met while she was in prison, two young middle-class women who embrace their role as honey traps to get pictures of cheating spouses, a transgender woman (popularly known in Pakistan as *hijra*), a prostitute, and young upper-middle-class coder. Each of the women recognizes a certain magic at play in what they are achieving through their work as they flip a social script that spans centuries. Every single act, from deep dives into the social media histories and bank accounts of their marks to tailing and catching men in compromising positions, serves the purpose of reworking a social fabric that has always been used to bind women for the benefit of men. This is brilliantly captured in the third episode, titled "*Ghulami*" (Slavery [or subservience]), in which the opening monologue reads "*Danda utha lo. Qanoon likha hi mardon ne hein*" (Pick up your sticks. Men wrote these laws to lock us up and to lock us in), while the track "*Maa behen ka danda*" (Mother and sisters' stick) by the band Garam Anday echoes in the background.

Perhaps the most striking element of *Churails* is how the series explores sexuality. Pakistani dramas typically depict any framing of sexuality around men's lust and women's virtue—the latter is either kept intact or lost. These binaries are an underlying feature of how sexuality and gender roles are constructed and expressed across Pakistani society. However, *Churails* embraces gender-fluid characters in a realistic light and highlights both women's desire as well as women's sexuality as an inherent part of their autonomy. This is one of the rare Pakistani productions to show sex scenes between both heterosexual and homosexual couples. In *Eros and Power*, Hunani-Kay Trask writes, "For most, if not all, women, the reality of subjugation to men and male-dominated institutions and ideologies has been like the air women breathe or the earth they walk on—a given of the female human condition. The values and tasks, behaviors and privileges of men have taken precedence over those of women. Whatever men have thought; whatever men do and say has been valued more than what women have done and said. This is what a 'man's world' has meant and continues to mean for men and women subordinated to them."[8] This "man's world" applies in nearly absolute terms for societies like Pakistan's, where the exploration of sexuality and sexual expression has always been the domain and dominion of men over women's bodies. Sex has always been framed as an act of conquest and ownership in Pakistan's social imaginary; however, *Churails* fundamentally alters this equation by allowing each of its protagonists to choose how they interact with men and showing the women as wielding power in their relationships. Sara uses her husband's infidelity to flip the script of a "wronged, clueless wife" as she uses his indiscretions to blackmail him into financing her business. Episode nine, "*Qaboo*" (Control) shows all the women realizing that they need to affect helplessness to lull the men in their lives into a false sense of security. They simulate giving up control to get it, and this time, to keep it. The following lines from the episode sum up this duality perfectly:

Jo hamein apne aap se bacha kar
Mehfooz rakh sakein
Taaqatward mard.
Jin ke baghair hum
be bas

Kamzor aur lachaar

(Those who save us from themselves
Who keep us locked away;
These strong men
Without whom, we are helpless, weak, and destitute)

This is the expression of the ideal Pakistani woman: one that men can either overpower and conquer or save and protect. Either way, such a woman is under their complete control. Each of the *churails* has far surpassed this state of helplessness, feigned or otherwise. However, the performance serves as a sleight of hand, sorcery, and deception in which the women recognize that playing at weakness may be their only way to overpower the men in their lives and take their place. Playing to men's egos here becomes a replacement for the rage that began the *churails'* journey; at this point they are driven purely by purpose and power.

Churails is a series that explores a gamut of feminist issues in which witchcraft is viewed in symbolic terms as a way out of rigid gender binaries. The masculinity and femininity on display in the series are both viewed as toxic. Women's femininity is used against them, while masculinity is deployed to make voyeurs and predators out of men. Nearly every episode is punctuated, either at the beginning or the end, with a closing noir shot of young boys standing next to pieces of meat—skeletons or pulverized flesh. This imagery is used to highlight how little boys in Pakistani society are trained and conditioned to view girls who grow up to be women not just as mere objects but as prey. The imagery of boys as hunters quite literally preying on the bodies of women is one that director Asim Abbasi reinforces again and again in graphic, gory, and uncomfortable detail. A scene where men in animal masks are auctioning women off during a clandestine party shows the auctioneer twirling a young model for the benefit of the crowd to score her "mane, epidermis, thorax, rump, profile, and frontal form" out of ten points.

These same predators then turn on the *churails* when the women step out of line and expose the men's human trafficking ring. Exposing powerful men for crimes committed against women is viewed as a far greater "crime" than the abuse of women's bodies, which are regarded as both culturally and conventionally disposable and replaceable. In her book *Good and Mad*, Rebecca Traister touches upon this condition in the light of modern-day witch-burnings: "It was Woody Allen who first called it 'a witch hunt,' publicly at least, in a particularly ill-thought-out interview given ten days after the Weinstein allegations came to light. Professing his sadness for the women who'd accused Weinstein, the producer of several of his films, Allen had warned, 'You also don't want it to lead to a witch-hunt atmosphere, a Salem atmosphere, where every guy in an office who winks at a woman is suddenly having to call a lawyer to defend himself.'"[9] This condition would be laughable if it were not so predictable: where men deem being held accountable for their crimes against women as oppression beyond the original crime itself.

In many ways the violence the *churails* in the series face is currently being replicated in how Pakistani men treat the women who stand up to patriarchy. Currently, Pakistani women participating in the annual Aurat Marches (Women's March), held to commemorate International Women's Day on March 8, are being accused of blasphemy, and there have been calls by religious authorities to publicly stone and flog the women marching. In their own way, such reactions serve as contemporary stand-ins for medieval witch-burnings, the premise being that the women singing, dancing, and marching in the streets are corrupt she-devils that need to be punished, even purged. Rebecca Traister writes: "Witch hunts entailed agents of the state prosecuting and trying civilian women and some men for—and this part is important—a crime that was not real. Those same powerful agents of the state, magistrates, and governors, would then sentence those civilians, often to long-term imprisonment or death, based on fantasized evidence of meetings with the devil in the dark woods."[10] This conditioning is ever-present in the narrative of the *Churails* series but also in how this project was treated in Pakistan, where it was promptly banned, and where all access to the Indian network Zee5 was swiftly blocked under a paywall. In his article "The Veiled Avengers of Pakistan's Streaming New Wave," Bilal Qureshi interviews the series creator Asim Abbasi: "Abbasi describes the intoxicating freedom of having *Khulee chuttee*—playful Urdu shorthand for complete freedom that translates literally as 'open holiday.' *Churails* launched in August as a flagship Zee5 original in 190 markets, while debuting locally as a Pakistani series liberated from the country's dated operating, editorial, and aesthetic standards."[11] The series met with intense media backlash and a smear campaign in the press for promoting "obscenity" and a negative image of Pakistan.

CHURAIL SOLIDARITY

Ultimately, the strength of the *Churails* series is its brutal honesty in acknowledging that the only route to women's healing from violence and exploitation in a country like Pakistan is through an uprising. This is a message that Pakistani women have taken to heart, as seen in the Aurat Marches and in contemporary feminist discourse that shows women building solidarities across class and ethnic boundaries to protest oppressive systemic abuse. The backlash against this revolt has predictably been violent—abuse, threats, and allegations backed by all arms of a powerful state machinery against *baaghi, besharam* (shameless) women.

In the series finale, the main patriarch in the show, Jugnu's monstrous Uncle Ifti, sums up the crossroads Pakistani women find themselves at:

Aurat jo sawar jai to hamaara sab se mazboot asaasa,
aur bigar jaye to sab se bari kamzori.

(Woman, who if she is tamed is our greatest asset
but if she revolts becomes our greatest weakness.)

It is rebellion that gives a woman strength. It is strength that labels a woman a witch. And weak men will always seek to burn witches.

NOTES

Epigraph: This chorus is taken from the theme song of the Pakistani web series *Churails*, penned by Osman Khalid Butt and performed by vocal artists Taha Malik and Zoe Viccaji. The lyrics, translated, are as follows:

Hide now. The Witch! The Witch!
My story begins. Your story ends.
You called me evil but now I'll show you what that means.

I was silent for so long. Now my storm will silence you.

1. Qureshi, "Veiled Avengers," 66.
2. Chemaly, *Rage Becomes Her*, xiv.
3. Mahmood, *Politics of Piety*, 8.
4. Klassen, "Colonial Mythology of Feminist Witchcraft," 81.
5. Klassen, "Colonial Mythology of Feminist Witchcraft," 82.
6. Federici, *Caliban and the Witch*, 11.
7. Federici, *Caliban and the Witch*, 100–174.
8. Trask, *Eros and Power*, ix.
9. Traister, *Good and Mad*, 192.
10. Traister, *Good and Mad*, 193.
11. Qureshi, "Veiled Avengers," 68.

BIBLIOGRAPHY

Chemaly, Soraya. *Rage Becomes Her: The Power of Women's Anger*. New York: Atria Books, 2018.

Federici, Silvia. *Caliban and the Witch: Women, the Body and Primitive Accumulation*. New York: Autonomedia, 2014.

Klassen, Chris. "The Colonial Mythology of Feminist Witchcraft." *The Pomegranate* 6, no. 1 (2004): 70–85.

Mahmood, Saba. *Politics of Piety: The Islamic Revival and the Feminist Subject*. Princeton, NJ: Princeton University Press, 2005.

Qureshi, Bilal. "The Veiled Avengers of Pakistan's Streaming New Wave." *Film Quarterly* 74, no. 3 (2021): 66–70.

Traister, Rebecca. *Good and Mad: The Revolutionary Power of Women's Anger*. New York: Simon and Schuster, 2018.

Trask, Haunani-Kay. *Eros and Power: The Promise of Feminist Theory*. Philadelphia: University Pennsylvania Press, 1986.

Twenty-two · JAIME HARTLESS AND GABRIELLA V. SMITH

From "Born This Witch" to "Bad Bitch Witch": A History of Witch Representation in Western Pop Culture

THE TRAP OF TRADITIONAL WITCH REPRESENTATION

The witch has historically served as a "controlling image,"[1] warning young women of the devastation and loneliness that awaits them if they forgo the "protections" they are promised under patriarchy by stepping outside gender norms that mandate their docility and domesticity. According to Barbara Creed's *The Monstrous-Feminine*, the witch represents the abject nature of femininity, encapsulating horrifying disruptions of order and a disrespect for boundaries and rules.[2] She is the antithesis of the "good" woman and a cautionary tale that naturalizes gender inequality by conflating women's power with evil. However, the image of the "witch" has recently been reclaimed by feminists, who increasingly see her either as a powerful allegory for the persecution experienced by women or as an emblem of resistance.[3] But how empowering are these new witch representations? Do they resist patriarchy or reaffirm it in subtler ways? This chapter maps the evolution of the witch, following her from her "wicked witch" roots to her millennial "girl power" heyday to her recent "bad bitch" renaissance. In this chapter, we argue that every "season of the witch" reflects changes in feminist politics and highlights the challenges that real-life women face as they strive to escape the confines of patriarchy.[4]

Most witches in classic cinema and literature fit into one of two boxes— they are either a *disempowered victim* of moral authorities seeking to police their gender and sexuality or a malevolent but *empowered evil* that must be destroyed.[5] The *disempowered victim* trope is widespread in dramatizations of the real-world horrors of the witch trials in Great Britain and its colonies, with films like *The Witchfinder General* showing how racialized anxieties about white women's sexuality fed witch hysteria and made women especially vulnerable to persecution.[6] The *empowered evil* witch trope is even more ubiquitous in classic films, embodying the feminine danger that the *disempowered victim* was falsely accused of harnessing, such as in *Black Sunday*, where an executed witch returns from the grave to claim the body and soul of her descendant.[7] These women embody feminine beauty and grace, but their presence heralds doom for their communities, as we see in *The Blood on Satan's Claw* (where teenage Angel corrupts a group of peers and leads them in a spree of rape and murder). Underneath the beautiful facade of these women, there is naught but death and decay, like the reanimated corpse of the witch in *Viy* that withers into a crone when she seizes her Pyrrhic victory over the monk hired to guard her. The one constant in these stories is that witches are framed as agents of Satan who must be defeated by men who reassert patriarchy in the name of law and order.[8]

The *disempowered victim/empowered evil* dichotomy treats women as either powerful but morally bankrupt, or powerless but beyond reproach. There is no room for a witch who embraces her agency or for a sympathetic morally gray practitioner. Queer theorists have long argued that forcing individuals into either/or boxes serves the interest of those in power and leads to the marginalization of those who cannot or will not fit within them, especially when social dichotomies like queer/straight, man/woman, or white/black become interlocked with moral binaries like good/evil.[9] In this dichotomous representation, women's agency is conflated with evil in a way men's is not, even as she is harmed by passivity. In short, powerful women must be punished, good women must suffer, and both must be subjugated under patriarchal rule.

More complex representations of the witch emerged from the 1960s to the 1980s. In 1951, the UK government repealed its Witchcraft Act.[10] While claims that this "Old Religion" had existed underground for hundreds of years were untrue, Modern Pagan Witchcraft in Britain became a growing alternative religion. Spiritual seekers gravitated to a more environmentally friendly and gender-balanced belief system.[11] Meanwhile, the burgeoning second wave of the feminist movement fueled growing Wiccan interest in empowering the sacred feminine. Dianic Witchcraft especially attracted radical feminists interested in developing a religion focused solely on goddess worship.¹² Filmmakers like George Romero, who saw his *Season of the Witch* as a feminist film,¹³ created more sympathetic witch films against this backdrop. When his protagonist, Joan, is dissatisfied with her controlling husband and jealous of the sexual freedom of her daughter, she turns to witchcraft instead of *The Feminine Mystique* to solve problems many women in the 1960s were experiencing.¹⁴ In the process, she violates several taboos that would demand comeuppance in a traditional witch film, such as having an affair with her daughter's boyfriend and accidentally killing her husband. Instead of punishing her, the film ends with her tempting other dissatisfied housewives to reject their dinner parties for witchy empowerment.

Yet, *Season of the Witch*'s climax is ambivalent, striking a melancholy rather than triumphant note as Joan discovers that her empowerment does not come with the happiness or freedom she was promised. We can see similar ambivalence in the TV show *Bewitched*, which introduced the world to Samantha Stephens, a witchy suburban housewife. In Samantha and her family, we see two distinct futures for the witch. Samantha is the prototype for a breed of witch that would become inescapable by the millennium—one born with morally neutral magical powers. Unfortunately, any empowerment in Samantha's brand of witchiness is undercut by her controlling husband, Darren, who pressures her to reject her magic so they can be "normal." Even when Samantha rebels against Darren's rules, it is typically to improve her home life, which domesticates her magic to serve the patriarchal nuclear family. In Samantha's extended family, we can see the seeds of a more radical and transgressive future where witches are free from the constraints of patriarchal authority, with mother Endora calling out Samantha's bland suburban existence and her "bad girl" twin cousin Serena modeling a fun-filled magical existence. Unfortunately, the narrative silences this transformative potential, treating Endora and Serena as obstacles to Samantha's domestic bliss with Darren. Much as media queer-baits LGBTQ+ audiences with plausibly deniable homoerotic subtext,¹⁵ old-school witch media taunts feminist viewers with naughty witch characters they can subversively enjoy while the text ultimately punishes them.

THE POWER AND PROBLEMATICS OF BEING "BORN THIS WITCH"

This trend is challenged by an explosion of positive witch representation in the late twentieth century. Not only do these witches use their magic for good rather than evil, but the very source of their witchiness is different. Rather than having the mantle of "witch" thrust upon them by distrustful communities or by making a pact with the Devil, they are simply born witches. This witchiness is often a family trait, passed down intergenerationally and even written into the witches' genetic code, like *Sabrina the Teenage Witch*, whose aunts are also witches, or the *Charmed* sisters, whose magic is passed down matrilineally from mother to daughter. Even in the absence of such genetic ties, witches like *Harry Potter*'s Hermione Granger or *Buffy the Vampire Slayer*'s Willow Rosenberg have natural power that emanates from inside of them. This witchiness is no longer external to the witch—it is part of her essence. To paraphrase a quote from Michel Foucault, the traditional witch had been a "temporary aberration" (i.e., a persecuted martyr or a sinful magic practitioner); the millennial witch was "now a species."[16]

Why do we see such a boom in *witch essentialism* in the 1990s and early 2000s? These decades were the zenith of the postfeminist "girl power" movement.[17] Feminism as a social movement was a frequent target of pop cultural mockery, but corporations and media conglomerates had learned that a sanitized branding of women's empowerment was a major money-maker.[18] There was a market for witches in this social landscape.[19] Young girls wanted to be the heroes of their own stories, and who better than the witch—women's traditional taboo conduit to power—to fill that void? She just needed a bit of rehabilitation and a good PR campaign. But this tells us little about why *witch essentialism* became so common at this moment. To understand this, we must turn our attention to identity politics. Around this time, the LGBTQ+ movement was increasingly mobilizing around essentialist understandings of identity, rejecting narratives that sexuality was a sinful lifestyle choice in favor of arguing that being gay or lesbian was an innate, biologically determined identity.[20] Like millennial gay/lesbian activists, the millennial witch was not choosing to embrace evil; she was simply "born this witch." As with essentialism in the LGBTQ+ movement, there is empowerment to be found in *witch essentialism*. This strategy somewhat decouples her from the *disempowered victim/empowered evil* dichotomy she existed within before. This new witch could be both good and powerful. She was something young girls could aspire to without necessarily scandalizing their religious communities or worrying their parents. However, rather than escaping the stigma of the "evil witch," the "born this witch" became another "controlling image" that naturalized inequality, creating new limiting dichotomies and policing the femininity of women in subtler but perhaps more insidious ways.[21]

This controlling image often trapped the witch within the rigids bounds of heteronormativity. Being magically empowered did not necessarily make these millennial witches agentic in their romantic relationships or liberated from gender norms. Just as the "Final Girl" of the slasher is required to abstain from drugs and sexuality to survive, the "good (girl) witch" is expected to be feminine and orient her arc around romance rather than her own self-actualization.[22] Hermione Granger of *Harry Potter* may have been admired for her brilliance, but she largely serves as auxiliary support for Harry and an object of romance for his best friend. Hermione is allowed to be exceptional only so long as her competence does not make you wonder why she is not the protagonist. Before Harry leaves to embark on his first battle with Voldemort in the climax of *The Sorcerer's Stone* film, Hermione dismisses her power as she assures him that he's "a great wizard." When Harry bashfully says, "Not as good as you," she self-effacingly replies, "Me! Books! And cleverness! There are more important things—friendship and bravery."[23] The message here is clear: Hermione has impressive knowledge, but she lacks that ephemeral heroic essence that Harry possesses. When women in this series are allowed to be heroic, it is mostly by sacrificing themselves for their children (i.e., Lily Potter) or defending their families (i.e., Molly Weasley). By contrast, many of the series' most vilified women—gossip queen Rita Skeeter, Death Eater Bellatrix Lestrange, and Ministry toady Dolores Umbridge—are notable for their obsessions with career and distance from the family unit.

Much as career-oriented women leaders in the real world are framed as bitchy, a power-hungry "born this witch" is seen as threatening.[24] This foil for the "good (girl) witch," a holdover from the Christian-inspired "evil witch" archetype, shows what happens to women who abuse the gifts they were given. Willow Rosenberg in *Buffy* initially pursues witchcraft to help her vampire-slaying best friend fight the forces of evil. Her early misadventures with magic are mostly played for laughs. But eventually Willow turns to magic for personal gain, and her growing power takes a darker turn. When she uses magic to resurrect Buffy from the dead, she is sent into a dark magic spiral that destroys her relationships with her friends when she violates their trust and bodily autonomy with forgetfulness spells and other magical mishaps. When her girlfriend Tara is murdered, Willow transforms into the season's surprise "Big Bad," drawing on dark magic to flay Tara's killer alive before jump-starting an apocalypse that is only narrowly averted by her friend Xander's love, reigniting her humanity.

Although some argue that Dark Willow's revenge arc provides valuable catharsis for women, the narrative frames her magical power as a dangerous temptation to be resisted.[25] Willow ends the show fearful of her magic, learning that her abuse of her powers paved the way for the series' final antagonist, the First Evil. She is healed only when she uses light magic to awaken all potential slayers to wage battle against the very evil that her dark magic brought into the world.

When "good (girl) witches" like Willow go bad, they must be taught to use their magic for nobler purposes than self-interest or vengeance. When they refuse to learn these lessons, their magic might be confined or destroyed. This is the fate of the three outcasts in *The Craft* (i.e., Nancy, Bonnie, and Rochelle), who invite the new girl, Sarah, to join their coven when a popular boy, Chris, spreads rumors about her "sluttiness." Their sisterhood unravels after they complete rituals to increase their power. Sarah wishes for Chris to love her, but he becomes so dangerously obsessed that he attempts to sexually assault her. Nancy, feeling omnipotent after magically ridding herself of her abusive stepfather and demanding all their deity's power, throws Chris through a window to his death. When Sarah defeats the coven through her purity of heart and natural magical gifts, the other girls lose their powers, and Nancy is confined to a mental institution. Feminist critics have grown increasingly uncomfortable with how this film demonizes Nancy (who is poor and a survivor of abuse) and Rochelle (who experiences racist bullying) to extol the virtues of upper-class white girl Sarah.[26] Thus, the power of the "born this witch" is limited. She cannot use her magic for own benefit or to revenge herself against white supremacist patriarchy. Furthermore, the magic of any witch who is not straight, white, affluent, and conventionally feminine is suspect.

THE TRANSGRESSIVE ALLURE OF THE "BAD BITCH WITCH"

But what would a truly transformative and transgressive witch story look like? As we move deeper into the twenty-first century, two seemingly unrelated factors have converged to pave the way for a potentially more revolutionary future for the witch: growing religious disaffiliation in the West and a resurgence of feminist anger with the rise of far-right politicians like Donald Trump.[27] As organized religion becomes increasingly decentered in society, popular culture has embraced moral ambiguity. While this trend has most benefited masculine antiheroes,[28] it has also produced complicated women with axes to grind against patriarchal oppressors. This includes "bad bitch witches" who use their magic to unapologetically wreak havoc on those who wrong them without being punished for their transgressions like the evil witches of yesteryear or the "good girl" millennial witches who strayed from the path of righteousness. In *The Chilling Adventures of Sabrina*, the show's protagonists initially worship Satan before ultimately banding together to overthrow him, building a more matriarchal witch society after realizing that their subjugation to the Dark Lord and his acolytes is no different from the patriarchal constraints of Christianity. This new generation of witches subverts the archetypes of classic witch films and actualizes the subtextual empowerment critically resistant readers have long found within them, escaping the *disempowered victimhood/empowered evil* trap in a way their "born this witch" predecessors could not.

Rowena MacLeod of *Supernatural* shows how the "bad bitch witch" archetype deconstructs the *empowered evil* side of this dichotomy. At first glance, Rowena, who has damned her soul to Hell in exchange for magical powers, echoes the deeply misogynist portrayals of past witches and is treated accordingly by other characters. In one of her early episodes, "Inside Man," protagonist Dean Winchester tries to slut-shame Rowena, smugly quipping, "What's a nice girl like you doing in a place like this? I'm sorry. Did I say 'nice girl'? I meant 'evil skank.'" But Rowena, who rejects this kind of moralistic condemnation at every turn, simply replies, "You say that like it's an insult. But nice girls, they're pathetic. Here's to evil skanks."[29] As the show becomes more morally complex, an unlikely friendship develops between Rowena and the Winchesters, and she ultimately sacrifices herself to close a portal God opens to Hell. While this may seem to be a redemptive arc for Rowena, she never changes who she is. She gleefully remains "an evil skank," flirting with the men on the show and running various devious schemes. Even when she sacrifices herself, she is not doing it to altruistically "save the world" but because she believes in the power of magic and prophecy. And rather than finding her sins washed away in a blinding white light like Willow, she is still sent to Hell. Yet Hell is not a punishment for Rowena, the way incarceration was for Nancy. Rowena ends the series happily ruling the underworld. Unlike her "evil witch" ancestors, Rowena gets to win.

This new "bad bitch witch" archetype similarly deconstructs the *disempowered victimhood* of other classic witch portrayals. Thomasin from

The Witch initially appears to be a passive girl viciously persecuted by anti-witch hysteria in a patriarchal context where she is worth little more than her dowry, like the martyred women in mid-twentieth-century films, such as *The Witchfinder General*. Yet Thomasin rejects this victim status, rebuffing her God-fearing Puritan upbringing by signing the Devil's book and choosing "to live deliciously."[30] The film ends with her stripping nude and rising triumphantly into the air with the very coven of witches that had menaced her family. In this moment, religious and patriarchal oppression converge to forge the very witch they fear. The inverse happens in *The Fear Street* trilogy, which begins as a traditional "evil witch" story. Although Sarah Fier appears to be maliciously cursing the town that hanged her for witchcraft, she is revealed to have been falsely accused due to her taboo love for the minister's daughter. The curse was instead the result of a demonic pact made by a wealthy, white family seeking to preserve their power. Sarah refuses to be victimized like earlier witch-hunt targets, telling her murderer at her execution, "The truth shall be your curse. I will shadow you for eternity. I will follow you forever. And everything you take and everyone you harm, you will feel the grip of my hand. I will show them what you've done. I will never let you go."[31] Her ghostly vengeance ends this wealthy family's stranglehold on the community and brings about a more just world.

Yet not everyone finds these portrayals empowering. Some critics assert that Thomasin merely submits to a new form of patriarchy, and many real-life witches worry that associations of witches with Satan feed into negative witch stereotypes.[32] However, we argue that these portrayals have the potential to empower in a way the "born this witch" archetype does not, allowing women to embrace a more transgressive vision of liberation, leaning into their darker urges to punish agents of the systems of inequality that have wronged them.[33] These "bad bitch witches" are unapologetic about their sexuality and unafraid to get mean. Furthermore, embracing this badness does not always mean entering new forms of subjugation like Thomasin or dying like Sarah Fier. In the *Suspiria* remake, Susie Bannion is instead transformed from a coven's victim into Mother Suspiriorum—a goddess who is capable of mercy to those who are deserving but also body-exploding brutality to those who cross her.

This transgressive witch representation is not inherently utopian. *American Horror Story (AHS): Coven* demonstrates the limitations of this "bad bitch witch" archetype. The intersecting identities of the witches on the show shape who is allowed to transgress and who is punished. The race, femininity, and attractiveness of young witches like Madison and Zoe inform the show's handling of the former's gang rape. Because our society's understanding of sexual violence is mapped onto heteronormative, gendered, and racialized binaries of masculine aggression and (white) feminine victimhood, the show treats Madison's murder of her assailants as an empowering "girl boss" move while condoning Zoe's retaliatory rape and murder of Madison's surviving assailant. Meanwhile, fellow witch Queenie is "othered" due to her fatness and Blackness, the show punishing her body by turning her into a "human Voodoo doll" whose power lies in injuring others through self-harm.[34] Even when these witches transgress, the persistence of the "evil witch" framework undermines their power. Supreme Witch Fiona Goode and Voodoo Queen Marie Laveau are the ultimate "bad bitch witches"—beautiful, powerful, ruthless, and endlessly meme-able. Yet they are still punished for their excesses with damnation, and the show ends with "good (girl) witch" Cordelia folding Madison, Zoe, and Queenie into a reinvigorated witch academy with a "White feminist" conception of women's empowerment.[35] This new, sanitized version of the academy, full of "good (girl) witches," is maintained as a largely white institution despite its performative nods to diversity.[36]

We thus should not make the mistake of seeing the history of the witch as a linear and progressive narrative, moving from the regressive "evil witch" tropes of yore to the cautiously empowered "good (girl) witches" of the millennium to "bad bitch witches" out to reclaim their ancestors' dark power. As Eve Sedgwick cautions in *Epistemology of the Closet*, we seldom see clean epistemic breaks in discourse over time; instead, new and old frameworks for seeing the world coexist.[37] AHS: Coven shows how society enjoys the thrill of bad women while being uncomfortable with narratives that allow their shenanigans to go unpunished. The moral restrictions of the "born this witch" continue to haunt these stories, and it is all too easy for the "bad bitch witch" to morph back into the maligned "evil witch." We should not assume that leaning into the transgressive witch archetype will necessarily translate into inclusive and feminist representation. Too often it ignores power dynamics and reinforces other regressive binaries, like the white/Black or thin/fat dichotomies underpinning racism and fatphobia. If we want witch representation that is inclusive, we must empower women, LGBTQ+ people, and people of color to tell stories that reflect their lived experiences. Only then can the witch truly live "deliciously."

TABLE 22.1 Appendix: List of Witch Films and Television

Typology of witch representations	Referenced films and release dates
Empowered evil/ Disempowered victim	*Black Sunday* (1960), *Viy* (1967), *The Witchfinder General* (1968), *The Blood on Satan's Claw* (1971)
Proto-feminist witch	*Bewitched* (1964–72), *Season of the Witch* (1972)
Born this witch	*The Craft* (1996), *Sabrina the Teenage Witch* (1996–2003), *Buffy the Vampire Slayer* (1997–2003), *Charmed* (1998–2006), *Harry Potter* (2001–11)
Bad bitch witch	*Supernatural* (2005–20), *American Horror Story: Coven* (2013–14), *The Witch* (2015), *Suspiria* (2018), *The Chilling Adventures of Sabrina* (2018–20), *Fear Street* (2021)

NOTES

1. Collins, *Black Feminist Thought*, 77.
2. Creed, *Monstrous-Feminine*, 8.
3. Federici, *Witches, Witch-Hunting, and Women*, 24–34; Sollée, *Witches, Sluts, Feminists*, 13–19.
4. Donovan, "Season of the Witch."
5. All referenced films and television shows are listed by typology in Table 22.1.
6. De Blécourt, "Making of the Female Witch," 303–5.
7. Throughout this chapter, we use *italics* to describe the binaries that define our theoretical framework; we use double quotes to outline the "typologies" that define our genealogy.
8. Creed, *Monstrous-Feminine*, 93–96.
9. Butler, *Gender Trouble*, 17–33; Namaste, "Politics of Inside/Out," 220–31.
10. Hutton, *Triumph of the Moon*, 206.
11. Adler, *Drawing Down the Moon*, 43.
12. Griffin, "Embodied Goddess."
13. Mayo, *Horror Show Guide*, 313–14.
14. Friedan, *Feminine Mystique*, 67–78.
15. Ng, "Queerbaiting and the Contemporary Media Landscape," 1.
16. Foucault, *History of Sexuality*, 43.
17. Lazar, "Right to Be Beautiful," 38.
18. Faludi, *Backlash*; Zeisler, *We Were Feminists Once*.

19 Feasey, "'Charmed' Audience."
20 Walters, *Tolerance Trap*, 1–18.
21 Collins, *Black Sexual Politics*, 69.
22 Clover, *Men, Women, and Chainsaws*, 3–19.
23 Columbus, *Harry Potter*, 2001.
24 Heilman, "Gender Stereotypes and Workplace Bias."
25 Vetere, "The Rage of Willow," 76–88.
26 Subissati and West, "Episode 16. Toil and Trouble: Witches in Film."
27 Brauer, "Surprising Predictable Decline of Religion"; Mukhopadhyay, "'I'm a Woman Vote for Me.'"
28 Mittell, "Lengthy Interactions with Hideous Men," 74–92.
29 Green, "Inside Man," 2015.
30 Eggers, *The Witch*, 2015.
31 Janiak, *Fear Street 1666*, 2021.
32 Goff, "Witches in the South"; Sollée, *Witches, Sluts, Feminists*, 111–17.
33 Madden, "'Wouldst Thou Like to Live Deliciously?'"
34 Strings, *Fearing the Black Body*, 7.
35 Sollée, *Witches, Sluts, Feminists*, 78.
36 Ahmed, *On Being Included*, 163–71.
37 Sedgwick, *Epistemology of the Closet*, 67–90.

BIBLIOGRAPHY

Adler, Margot. *Drawing Down the Moon: Witches, Druids, Goddess-Worshipers, and Other Pagans in America*. New York: Penguin Books, 2006.

Ahmed, Sara. *On Being Included: Racism and Diversity in Institutional Life*. Durham, NC: Duke University Press, 2012.

Brauer, Simon. "The Surprising Predictable Decline of Religion in the United States." *Journal for the Scientific Study of Religion* 57, no. 4 (2018): 654–75.

Butler, Judith. *Gender Trouble: Feminism and the Subversion of Identity*. New York: Routledge, 2011.

Clover, Carol J. *Men, Women, and Chainsaws: Gender in the Modern Horror Film*. Princeton, NJ: Princeton University Press, 2015.

Collins, Patricia Hill. *Black Feminist Thought: Knowledge, Consciousness, and the Politics of Empowerment*. 2nd ed. New York: Routledge, 2000.

Collins, Patricia Hill. *Black Sexual Politics: African Americans, Gender, and the New Racism*. New York: Routledge, 2004.

Columbus, Chris, dir. *Harry Potter & the Sorcerer's Stone*. Warner Brothers Pictures, 2001.

Creed, Barbara. *The Monstrous-Feminine: Film, Feminism, Psychoanalysis*. New York: Routledge, 1993.

De Blécourt, Willem. "The Making of the Female Witch: Reflections on Witchcraft and Gender in the Early Modern Period." *Gender and History* 12, no. 2 (2000): 287–309.

Donovan, Shawn Phillips. "Season of the Witch," Recorded August 26, 1966. Track 6 on *Sunshine Superman*. Columbia Studios, 1966. CD.

Eggers, Robert, dir. *The Witch*. A24, 2015.

Faludi, Susan. *Backlash: The Undeclared War against American Women*. New York: Crown, 1991.

Feasey, Rebecca. "The 'Charmed' Audience: Gender and the Politics of Contemporary Culture." *Spectator: The University of Southern California Journal of Film and Television* 25, no. 2 (2005): 39–48.

Federici, Silivia. *Witches, Witch-Hunting, and Women*. Oakland, CA: PM Press, 2018.

Foucault, Michel. *The History of Sexuality, Volume I*. New York: Vintage, 1978.

Friedan, Betty. *The Feminine Mystique*. New York: W. W. Norton, 2001.

Goff, Daniel V. "Witches in the South: Past, Present, and in Comics." In *The Politics of Horror*, edited by Damien K. Picariello, 159–70. New York: Palgrave Macmillan, 2020.

Green, Rashaad Ernesto, director. "Inside Man," Episode 17, season 10 of *Supernatural*. Aired April 1, 2015, on The CW.

Griffin, Wendy. "The Embodied Goddess: Feminist Witchcraft and Female Divinity." *Sociology of Religion* 56, no. 1 (1995): 35–48.

Heilman, Madeline E. "Gender Stereotypes and Workplace Bias." *Research in Organizational Behavior* 32 (2012): 113–35.

Hutton, Ronald. *The Triumph of the Moon: A History of Modern Pagan Witchcraft*. New York: Oxford University Press, 2001.

Janiak, Leigh, director. *Fear Street, Part Three: 1666*. Netflix, 2021. https://www.netflix.com/watch/81334750.

Lazar, Michelle M. "The Right to Be Beautiful: Postfeminist Identity and Consumer Beauty Advertising." In *New Femininities: Postfeminism, Neoliberalism and Subjectivity*, edited by Rosalind Gill and Christina Scharff, 37–51. London: Palgrave, 2011.

Madden, Victoria. "'Wouldst Thou Like to Live Deliciously?': Gothic Feminism and the Final Girl in Robert Eggers' *The Witch*." In *Final Girls, Feminism and Popular Culture*, edited by Katarzyna Paszkiewicz and Stacy Rusnak, 135–51. New York: Palgrave Macmillan, 2020.

Mayo, Mike. *The Horror Show Guide: The Ultimate Frightfest of Movies*. Canton, MI: Visible Ink Press, 2013.

Mittell, Jason. "Lengthy Interactions with Hideous Men: Walter White and the Serial Poetics of Television Anti-heroes." In *Storytelling in the Media Convergence Age*, edited by Roberta Pearson and Anthony N. Smith, 74–92. London: Palgrave Macmillan, 2015.

Mukhopadhyay, Samhita. "'I'm a Woman Vote for Me': Why We Need Identity Politics." In *Nasty Women: Feminism, Resistance, and Revolution in Trump's*

America, edited by Samhita Mukhopadhyay and Kate Harding, 1–9. London: Picador, 2017.

Namaste, Ki. "The Politics of Inside/Out: Queer Theory, Poststructuralism, and a Sociological Approach to Sexuality." *Sociological Theory* 12, no. 4 (1994): 220–31.

Ng, Eve. "Between Text, Paratext, and Context: Queerbaiting and the Contemporary Media Landscape." *Transformative Works and Cultures* 24, no. 1 (2017). http://dx.doi.org/10.3983/twc.2017.917.

Sedgwick, Eve Kosofsky. *Epistemology of the Closet*. Berkeley: University of California Press, 1990.

Sollée, Kristen J. *Witches, Sluts, Feminists: Conjuring the Sex Positive*. Berkeley: Stone Bridge Press, 2017.

Strings, Sabrina. *Fearing the Black Body: The Racial Origins of Fat Phobia*. New York: New York University Press, 2019.

Subissati, Andrea, and Alexandra West. "Episode 16. Toil and Trouble: Witches in Film." *The Faculty of Horror* (podcast), May 23, 2014. https://www.facultyofhorror.com/2014/05/episode-16-toil-and-trouble-witches-in-film/.

Vetere, Lisa M. "The Rage of Willow: Malefic Witchcraft Fantasy in *Buffy the Vampire Slayer*." In *Buffy Conquers the Academy: Conference Papers from the 2009/2010 Popular Culture/American Culture Associations*, edited by U. Melissa Anyiwo and Karoline Szatek-Tudor, 76–88. Newcastle-upon-Tyne: Cambridge Scholars Publishing, 2013.

Walters, Suzanna Danuta. *The Tolerance Trap: How God, Genes, and Good Intentions Are Sabotaging Gay Equality*. New York: New York University Press. 2014.

Zeisler, Andi. *We Were Feminists Once: From Riot Grrrl to Covergirl, the Buying and Selling of a Political Movement*. New York: Public Affairs, 2016.

Twenty-three · ANNA ROGEL

"I Put a Spell on You and Now You're Mine": A Vulvacentric Reading of Witchcraft

INTRODUCTION

Hocus Pocus, a ready-for-TV film that was released for the 1991 Halloween season has since become an audience favorite. This comedy about the Sanderson sisters, three witches who haunt Salem on Halloween, addresses female alliance, female knowledge transmission, and female authorship through a women-centered plot. Although clearly marked as the villains of the film, the Sanderson sisters have attracted a considerable fandom through their charm, their wit, and their unapologetic otherness.

In its opening sequence, the film invites the viewer to identify with the sisters, as the camera adopts the perspective of a witch flying over Salem. As she looks down at the water beneath her, she sees the reflection of her flying broom and wild hair, the emblem for her evil nature. This image disappears as soon as she flies over the woods where she lives with her sisters. In the West, visual representations of witchcraft from the fifteenth century onward have resulted in a codified representation that identifies and categorizes the witch and her craft; witchcraft is generally visualized as a female group activity of evil plotting women whose wild rides defy the natural order. A threat to the phallocentric order, the witch is depicted as a manipulator of the phallus (represented by brooms, oven forks, and wands), while her flying hair stands for her uncontrollable sexuality. As her craft is corruptive, she is constructed as a lesbian, often in the body of an old crone who converts young women and teaches them to handle phallic objects. The witch's corruption of the young and innocent finds another visual representation in the witch as a cannibal who eats children to incorporate them into the body of the coven.

Hocus Pocus plays with these representations. Since, in the opening scene, the viewer shares the perspective of the camera, she inhabits the body of the witch on whose body culture projects the associations I've enumerated. Through its depiction of a set of projections that it shows to exist exclusively outside of the witch's own reality, the film questions the validity of its "witchcraft code" at the same time as it acknowledges this code's currency in the public narrative. From the moment the witch touches the ground, the viewer adopts the gaze of an outsider to the witch's story: the witch lands on a porch, as seen from the inside of a villager's cabin. Because she has been made aware of the bias of such a narrative, the viewer is in a position to question the narrative that is projected onto the witch's body and to read the story of the Sanderson sisters as framed by the outsider's gaze and represented by the camera's perspective. This double-framing is signaled by the depiction of two books that frame the plot at the beginning and at the end of the film. The first book contains the coven's story from an outsider's perspective, while the other is the coven's spellbook that contains the witches' spells.

In *The Appearance of Witchcraft*, Charles Zika studies the iconography of witchcraft in the Middle Ages and the Early Modern period: "The notion of witchcraft as a female group activity is fundamental to its visual representation in the sixteenth century."[1] A recurring motif in the representation of such collective activity shows a group of women around a cauldron.[2] This representation has led to a misreading of any female community-building as (potentially) witchcraft and of women talking together in the absence of men as plotting.

In contemporary comedies that depict groups of women plotting to revolt against their subjugation, these modern-day "witches" use humor to resist structural discriminations in the workplace as well as in the private sphere. Rebecca Krefting argues that "charged humor" can destabilize oppressive systems as it "tears in the fabric of our beliefs."[3] Funny women use charged humor to build new forms of community and defy societal expectations and norms as they fight those who attempt to take away their political power. The fusion of the discourse of female resistance and the discourse of witchcraft has a long-standing tradition, and it is through humor that this fusion is most effective, accessible, and marketable. When the funny witch becomes a vehicle for disseminating disruptive ideas, she reveals the limits of women's representation while she pushes its boundaries. Still confined to witchhood, she is punished, redeemed, or ridiculed.

Hocus Pocus makes charged humor accessible to a broader audience that might not necessarily indulge in an openly political form of humor. But to reach a mass PG-rated audience, the film has to recycle harmful images of witchcraft, and the viewer is challenged to see through those metaphors to find the woman behind the witch.

On the one hand, the Sanderson sisters are portrayed as cruel cannibals; on the other hand, they are shown to care deeply for each other. Although she does call them "her curse," the coven's leader Winifred protects her helpless, mentally challenged sisters, who are frequently insulted and abused. As a grown woman with the mind of a child, Sarah is sexually exploited by men although she is clearly unable to consent. When Winifred's lover Billy cheated on her with Sarah, Winifred sewed his mouth shut and killed him. Eternally loyal to her sisters, Winifred punishes men whose deeds and discourses threaten her sisters and her coven.

While many representations of witchcraft have been crafted by men and are determined by a phallocentric discourse, they still allow for a gyno-, or, as I will argue, vulvacentric re-reading. Zika, like many scholars, finds an abundance of phallic objects like wands, oven forks, and brooms in the representations of witchcraft. As he focuses on the phallus that the witches manipulate to their liking, he regards the witch only in terms of her impact on men. In a woodcut by the artist Hans Baldung Grien,[4] Zika reads that "[t]he sausages roasting over the fire ... support the link between witchcraft and female sexuality."[5] As Zika equates female sexuality with a woman's handling of the phallus, he neglects the sexuality connected with her own body. Only in cauldrons does Zika find a symbol for the witch's body, specifically, its nether parts. While the cauldron serves as a powerful symbol for the creative power of the witch as well as of her coven, visual representations of witchcraft often refer to other sites of female sexuality as well.

Because Zika reads female sexuality as "conceptualized on the basis of masculine parameters,"[6] he fails to recognize the abstract representations of vulvas I find hidden in woodcuts and paintings that depict witchcraft. Depicted as garment folds, aprons, or trees, these abstract representations appear at the center of woodcuts, drawings, and paintings, where they often inhabit the vanishing point. Bernard Salomon's woodcut of Medea (1557) illustrates a story that describes her a powerful healer, but in the image her skirt is rolled up her leg, a code for reading her as a prostitute.[7]

Her garment also forms a vulva that is half the size of her body. The wand in her hand—a phallic object Zika would recognize—falls short in comparison. I also find Medea's powerful vulva-centrism in a nineteenth-century painting by Frederick Sandys.[8] Since images of witchcraft often contain an element of inversion, the viewer has to turn the image upside down to perceive its contents: Medea's garments form a vulva that is again at the center of the image. Her tripod, a conventional variation of the cauldron, represents her womb placed above her vulva. Her sensual look is not prompted by any phallic object; instead, Medea touches herself. In addition to representations of masturbation, I find vulva-centrism in images of female witches that engage in teaching. In a 1602 woodcut,[9] an old and impaired crone is surrounded by her female apprentices and her familiars. An inversion of the image shows her strangely formed apron as a vulva at the center of her coven.

A woodcut by Erhard Schön (1533) shows a witch who is burned at the stake after having burned down a city.[10] Zika finds in this picture "no moral or theological lessons. There are also no viewers in the scene to stress the social implications of the terrible events."[11] The arsonist burns at the stake, where she is kept in place by an oven fork, the conventional phallic object that women used for their wild rides before brooms became popular representations. While the fire in the city destroys the man's community, the witch laughs in his face. Although the witch is bound to the burning stake, her community and her discourse, represented by the tree that takes center stage in the image, remain intact.

Those exemplary illustrations of witchcraft that center around abstract representations of the vulva extend the traditional reading that sees the witch and her craft as simply a threat to a male-centered discourse.[12] When the discourse is centered around a reading of the vulva, the witch appears as a sexual, political, and social being who exists beyond the discourses that try to frame her. A vulvacentric discourse allows women to read and write themselves independent from phallocentric parameters, when it shows the witch engaging in meaningful discourses with other women, as teacher, friend, and lover, instituting independent social structures, discourses, and her own truth.[13]

The witch, though framed by a phallocentric discourse, communicates through a subtext and encourages the viewer to read herself beyond the societal restrictions that frame her. As the witch is demonized, she is always two: a transgressive woman who serves as a warning as well as a promise of what the female viewer could be but should never strive for.

A vulvacentric reading of *Hocus Pocus* reveals a plot by women for women: the story of the witches Winifred, Mary, and Sarah is preserved by female elders, and the girls, Allison and Dani, are obsessed with their stories. Alluring and repelling at the same time, the witches are the driving force of the film. Their power is their knowledge, and while they are eventually killed, their story still haunts the inhabitants of Salem and still captivates the viewer. Though the film seems to confirm a phallocentric reading that divides women into good girls and evil witches, *Hocus Pocus* goes beyond this divide to explore female community-building, as the female characters challenge a phallocentric reading of their lives, stories, and bodies.

FUNNY WOMEN BUILD COVENS

As Andy Medhurst points out, "Comedy is a short cut to community."[14] *Hocus Pocus* uses humor to connect and empower the female characters. When Dani and Allison first meet in *Hocus Pocus*, Allison compliments Dani on her witch costume. Dani returns the compliment and acknowledges their shared femininity both culturally and physically: "'I couldn't wear anything like that because I don't have any ... What do you call 'em, Max? Yabos? Max likes your yabos. In fact, he loves 'em.'"[15] Dani makes fun of the desire of her older brother, Max, who has a crush on Allison, and she challenges his attempt to define a woman's body through his slang.

Allison and Dani bond through humor. They are also both "really into witches" and thus connected by their shared obsession with the story of the Sanderson sisters.[16] Alison has learned the story of the witches from her mother, who "runs the museum" in the Sanderson house that contains all their possessions, the sisters' brooms, their cauldron, their spellbook, and "the place where they slept."[17] To transmit her knowledge to the younger girl, Allison agrees to teach Dani about the witches by taking her to the museum.

FUNNY WOMEN ENCHANT

Enchantments represent the *witch*'s ability to wield power through speech, and the Sanderson sisters' performance at a Halloween party proves their power over their audience. When they arrive, a man on stage who thinks their clothes are Halloween costumes tries to flirt with them by singing, "I put a spell on you."[18] Winifred's reaction to his helpless attempt to appropriate the discourse of witchcraft to seduce her is one of the great comical moments of the film and relies exclusively on a visual discourse: she gives him The Look.

The Look is a powerful instrument of women's humor when it comments on and rejects the punchlines and narratives of men. Winifred asserts her witchdom as she mounts the stage with her sister and offers her own interpretation of the song, which results in a mass enchantment of all party guests. Winifred changes the lyrics of the original song to reassert her power: "I put a spell on you. And now you're gone. My whammy fell on you, and it was strong." She also points to her power to create a discourse with her sisters that opposes the rational perspective of Max, who also witnesses the performance: "If you don't believe, you better get superstitious. Ask my sisters."[19]

The witches are challenged to read their surroundings in light of their seventeenth-century knowledge, and the sisters' reading of modern society is both funny and insightful as it reveals aspects of womanhood that have been normalized in modern days but are actually instruments of oppression. For the Sanderson sisters, women's confinement to the private sphere and societal expectations concerning their appearance are modern-day atrocities. Insulted because of their looks, they are challenged to find new creative comical responses. Two teenage boys who complain that "it's only the ugly chicks that stay out late"[20] find themselves in cages hanging from the Sanderson house's ceiling.

The witches' critique of modern times extends into spaces that are traditionally associated with witchcraft. Cooking is a central motif in the representation of female witchcraft, and the site of cooking defines the space that is assigned to the witch. Winfred calls the modern kitchen with all its confusing appliances and instruments a "torture chamber"[21] to which the woman of the house is confined. Such rooms are signs of supposed progress, and the torture chamber stands in stark contrast to the Sanderson's house, where the cooking place is located in the middle of the room, and cooking ingredients are spread all over the house.

Though the witches are charming and entertaining, their powers are limited. Winifred's spell allows them to return to Salem for solely twenty-four hours that coincide with Halloween, the only day of the year during which they will visually blend in in Salem. The witches operate within spatial and temporal restrictions, and their threat is minimized through ridicule. The simple-minded younger sisters roam aimlessly as they are easily distracted by smells (Mary) and libidinous temptation (Sarah). The powerful leader of the coven, Winifred, fails to make herself conventionally pretty, as her buck teeth resist her magic.

FUNNY WOMEN CONVERT

In literature, the witch traditionally functions as a villain who teaches girls to regard older women as enemies, thus calling into question the transmission of stories along maternal lines. In the visual arts, representations such as those of Hans Baldung Grien suggest that female-to-female teaching is a lesbian experience.[22] The witch as teacher is often represented as an ugly hag who corrupts a beautiful girl by teaching her to control a phallic object, often a broom. The image can be found in Francisco de Goya's *Linda maestra!* (Pretty teacher!) and persists to this day.[23]

As a Disney movie designed to appeal to a wide audience, *Hocus Pocus* also evokes the fear of female-to-female teaching. Dani appears in a Halloween witch costume throughout the movie and copies the witches' speech ("thou") to greet the Sanderson sisters when they reappear after 300 years: "I thought thou would never come, sisters."[24] As she politely addresses the Sandersons with their title ("Sisters"), she also positions herself as one of them: they are her sisters. When the Sandersons form a circle around the little girl, she looks more like an apprentice than a victim as all of them wear similar clothes and Dani blends in well with the house's spooky atmosphere. The girl believes the witches to be part of her coven and laughs with them. But instead of bonding with the witches through laughter, as she did with Alison, she is suddenly scared when she learns that the witches are hungry and want her to "stay for supper" (Winifred).[25] The break with the Sanderson sisters illustrates how traditional notions concerning witchcraft endanger female-to-female teaching. Dani, who idolizes the witches and commemorates them through her costume, is suddenly scared of women whom she naturally understands to be, like Allison, part of her coven.

The viewer is supposed to believe that the Sanderson sisters stay alive because they eat children. But the viewer is also given access to a counterreading of their motives, one that sees through the phallocentric metaphors through which the film presents them. As Allison teaches Max: "*Legend* has it that the bones of a hundred children were buried within these walls."[26] While other information about the Sanderson sisters is presented as a fact, Allison attributes this information about the Sanderson house to a mythical reading of the witch's home.

While the house preserves the witches' legacy through objects, the coven's spiritual legacy is carried on by the generations that followed them. The multilayered plot of the film allows for a different reading of the witches' cannibalism and their supposed victims, the children they enchant to follow them to their house. Those children, I argue, have been incorporated into the coven through alliances, storytelling, and female-to-female-teaching. The Sanderson sisters brew a potion that is then drunk by the child so they can incorporate the child's lifeforce into their own bodies. As the cauldron traditionally represents the witch's body, the Sandersons engage in an exchange that is a myth of magical birth and child raising: they feed the child from their bodily vessel and expose her to the coven's spells. Through the incorporation of the child who is ready to learn and who answers the witches' call to become part of their heritage, the witch receives immortality, and the coven stays alive.

Sexually connotated depictions prevail in the representations of the witch's apprenticeship, though Zika points to an exception as early as 1514–16.[27] A woodcut by Hans Burgkmair presents the teaching witch with a man rather than a young girl; both try to sell their arts to a king.[28] The witch is described by Zika as follows: "The crone's money bag, an allusion to her avarice, is contrasted with a monk's life governed by the scripture; while her stick, possibly symbolic of a local, vernacular knowledge, is set against the vows of the monastic rule signified by the knots of the monk's cord. The choice facing the young king is represented by the two books that hang from stars in the firmament above him."[29] But Zika ignores the fact that the image also represents the "black arts" as comparable in scope to the Christian canon: the witches "vernacular knowledge" is contained in a book that is as thick as the monk's Bible that faces the viewer as if to control her. Though not a typical visual representation of witchcraft, the image shows how the figure of the witch allows for a complex representation of womanhood. While her teaching is framed as "black art," this witch teaches her viewer a lesson about the potential of female teaching, craftsmanship, and women's economic independence. Among the people, the frail witch is the only one whose gaze engages the viewer: she enters into a kind of a visual dialogue with the world outside the frame of the image as she addresses the viewer with her modest posture and pitiful look. While the monk's book observes the viewer, the witch's book guards the monk. Although not communicated through sexual metaphors, the witch's teaching challenges the phallocentric order represented in the monk and king. Lesbianism is not portrayed in the picture. Instead, the witch connects with her female viewer as she meets her gaze.

While the killing of the witches is promoted as the central quest to the viewer of *Hocus Pocus*, Winifred follows her own plot as she tries to retrieve her book, which she guards as a mother would a child: "Book. Come to Mummy!" (Winifred).[30] When she meets a man dressed in a devil costume at a Halloween party, the sisters and the man engage in a comical variation of a witches' sabbath. The scene serves two conflicting functions within the film. It confirms a reading of the Sanderson sisters as real witches, since they perform the five demonic acts that allowed a conviction for witchcraft in the seventeenth century: participation in a witch's sabbath, sex with the devil, wild rides through the sky, *maleficium*, and a contract with the devil usually by signing his book.[31] But the scene also rejects this historical discourse that categorizes the witch as the devil's minion who hails the devil during the sabbath, since Winifred soon realizes that the man "is not our master."[32] Winifred is guided by her quest for knowledge, not by a desire for servitude. As the book contains her legacy, she does not lament her sisters, nor does she call on her own mother in the moment of her death. Her last word is "Book."[33]

CONCLUSION

The witches' death is a necessary conclusion to a mainstream family film bound by the conventions of a patriarchal discourse. But the powers coded as evil are not overcome by the powers coded as good. The witches in *Hocus Pocus* survive all conventional attempts to silence them: they are hanged and burned, but each time Winifred's power saves the coven. The sisters have already prepared their potion, and all children in Salem have answered their call. Due to their powers of enchantment and their knowledge, they can extend their mortal lives and therefore the life of the coven. The witches are eventually defeated because they allow the projections on their body to control their actions. The demise of the coven is intertwined with the betrayal of the young witch, Dani, who fails to respect the crone, Winifred: "You're the ugliest thing that's ever lived" (Dani).[34] Deprecating jokes about the witches' looks function as a running gag during the film as punchlines meant to confine the witches to their place,[35] but Winifred always finds creative retorts. Rejected by Dani, whom I read as a prospective apprentice, Winifred falls victim to a plot that judges her worth based on her looks. Distracted from her initial plan, Winifred cannot resist killing Dani because "she really hurt my feelings."[36] *Hocus Pocus* retells the story of the Sanderson sisters but also of the plot that has been imposed on their story. Dani, who used to idolize the witches, now rejects the coven. "She's jealous,"[37] Mary tries to reassure Winifred. But the crone finds Dani's rejection rooted in her ignorance of her female heritage, which results in her mistaking female-to-female teaching for cannibalism: "She doesn't even know me! You know, I always wanted a child."[38]

A PG-rated movie would not allow the cannibalistic witches to survive. The last scene of the movie shows Winifred's book, the source and keeper of her knowledge. After the eye suddenly opens to address the viewer, followed by a reprise of the sisters singing "I put a spell on you," the story of the Sanderson sisters and their reading of the world are now preserved through every viewer who has let herself be enchanted by the film. The allure of the Sanderson sisters prevails; and as they have been punished and ridiculed, yet never redeemed, their specter returned after thirty years in the long-awaited 2022 sequel.

NOTES

1 Zika, *Appearance of Witchcraft*, 26.
2 See the images *Two Witches Cooking Up a Storm* and *Female Witches Eating Together*, both reproduced in Zika, *Appearance of Witchcraft*, 19, 26.
3 Krefting, *All Joking Aside*, 2.
4 See Hans Baldung Grien's *A Group of Female Witches* (1510), as reproduced in Zika, *Appearance of Witchcraft*, 10.
5 Zika, *Appearance of Witchcraft*, 12.
6 Irigaray, *Sex Which Is Not One*, 23.
7 See Bernard Salomon's *Medea Rejuvenates Jason's Father Aeson*, as reproduced in Zika, *Appearance of Witchcraft*, 154.
8 See Frederick Sandys's *Medea* (1868).
9 *The Wonderful Discouerie of the Witchcrafts*, title page.
10 See Erhard Schön, *Burning of a Witch at Oberndorf* (1533), especially the upper left corner of the image, as reproduced in Zika, *Appearance of Witchcraft*, 183.
11 Zika, *Appearance of Witchcraft*, 182.
12 See Moira Smith for an extensive analysis of castration anxiety expressed through witchcraft in the *Malleus Maleficarum* (Smith, "Flying Phallus and

the Laughing Inquisitor"). For an exemplary visual illustration, see the woodcut *Castration Sorcery*, as reproduced in Zika, *Appearance of Witchcraft*, 41.
13   Hélène Cixous imagines such a woman to live in abstraction: "the woman who would hold out against oppression and constitute herself as a superb, equal, hence 'impossible' subject, untenable in a real social framework" (Cixous, "Laugh of the Medusa," 879).
14   Medhurst, *National Joke*, 21.
15   Ortega, *Hocus Pocus*, 00:24:09–26.
16   Ortega, *Hocus Pocus*, 00:24:29.
17   While their bodies slept in the house in the seventeenth century, their spirits slept in the house for 300 years after their physical bodies were hanged.
18   Ortega, *Hocus Pocus*, 00:54:10–11.
19   Ortega, *Hocus Pocus*, 00:56:46–52.
20   Ortega, *Hocus Pocus*, 01:04:01–04.
21   Ortega, *Hocus Pocus*, 00:50:17–18.
22   Hans Baldung Grien, *A Group of Witches* (ca. 1514), as reproduced in Zika, *Appearance of Witchcraft*, 14.
23   See Francisco de Goya's *Linda maestra!* (1799).
24   Ortega, *Hocus Pocus*, 00:30:52–54.
25   Ortega, *Hocus Pocus*, 00:31:43–44.
26   Ortega, *Hocus Pocus*, 00:25:40–44, my emphasis.
27   Zika, *Appearance of Witchcraft*, 68.
28   See Hans Burgkmair, *The Weißkunig Learns the Black Arts* (1514–16), as reproduced in Zika, *Appearance of Witchcraft*, 69.
29   Zika, *Appearance of Witchcraft*, 68.
30   Ortega, *Hocus Pocus*, 00:38:55–58.
31   Known in German scholarly discourse as *Hexenlehre*. Behringer, *Hexen*, 35.
32   Ortega, *Hocus Pocus*, 00:51:38–39.
33   Ortega, *Hocus Pocus*, 01:24:50–54.
34   Ortega, *Hocus Pocus*, 01:14:10.
35   Just like the oven fork in Erhard Schön's woodcut (1533).
36   Ortega, *Hocus Pocus*, 01:17:17–19.
37   Ortega, *Hocus Pocus*, 01:17:19.
38   Ortega, *Hocus Pocus*, 01:17:19–25.

BIBLIOGRAPHY

Behringer, Wolfgang. *Hexen: Glaube, Verfolgung, Vermarktung*. Munich: Beck, 2002.

Cixous, Hélène. "The Laugh of the Medusa," translated by Keith Cohen and Paula Cohen. *Signs* 1, no. 4 (1976): 875–93.

Irigary, Luce. *This Sex Which Is Not One*. Ithaca, NY: Cornell University Press, 1985.

Krefting, Rebecca. *All Joking Aside—American Humor and Its Discontents*. Baltimore, MD: Johns Hopkins University Press, 2014.

Medhurst, Andy. *A National Joke: Popular Comedy and English Cultural Identities*. London: Routledge, 2007.

Ortega, Kenny, dir. *Hocus Pocus*. Walt Disney Pictures, Touchwood Pacific Partners 1, 1993.

Smith, Moira. "The Flying Phallus and the Laughing Inquisitor: Penis Theft in the 'Malleus Maleficarum.'" *Journal of Folklore Research* 39, no. 1 (2002): 85–117.

Zika, Charles. *The Appearance of Witchcraft: Print and Visual Culture in Sixteenth-Century Europe*. Abingdon, UK: Routledge, 2007.

IMAGES

Baldung Grien, Hans. *A Group of Female Witches* (1510). Chiaroscuro woodcut. Museum of Fine Arts, Boston, W. G. Russel Allen Bequest, 69.1064. Reproduced in Zika, *The Appearance of Witchcraft*, 10.

Baldung Grien, Hans. *A Group of Witches* (ca. 1514). Pen and ink, heightened with white on red-brown tinted paper. Albertina, Vienna. Reproduced in Zika, *The Appearance of Witchcraft*, 14.

Burgkmair, Hans. *The Weißkunig Learns the Black Arts*, 1514–16. Woodcut from Marx Treitzsaurwein, *Der Weißkunig* (Vienna: Kurzböck, 1775). Reproduced in Zika, *The Appearance of Witchcraft*, 69.

Castration Sorcery; A Spell against Earwig; The Use of Axe Magic to Steal Wine. Woodcut. From Hans Vintler, *Buch der Tugend* (Augsburg: Johannn Blaubirer, 1486), fol. 161v. Reproduced in Zika, *The Appearance of Witchcraft*, 41.

Female Witches Eating Together. Woodcut. From Ulrich Molitor, *De laniis et phitonicis mulieribus* (Cologne: Cornelius von Zierickzee, ca. 1496–1500), fol. D2r. Reproduced in Zika, *The Appearance of Witchcraft*, 26.

Goya, Francisco de. *Linda maestra!* (1799). Etching, burnished aquatint, and drypoint on cream laid paper. Philadelphia Museum of Art. Currently not on view.

Salomon, Bernard. *Medea Rejuvenates Jason's Father Aeson*. Woodcut. From Ovid, *La Metamorphose d'Ovide* (Lyon: J. de Tournes, 1557), 78. Reproduced in Zika, *The Appearance of Witchcraft*, 154.

Sandys, Frederick. *Medea* (1868). Oil on canvas. Birmingham Museum and Art Gallery, Birmingham, UK.

Schön, Erhard. *Burning of a Witch at Oberndorf in 1533, and Her Arson in the Town of Schiltach*. Woodcut. From broadsheet, "Ein erschröcklich Geschicht . . . beschehen zu Schilta bey Rotweil, Nuermberg" (Stefan Hamer, 1533). Reproduced in Zika, *The Appearance of Witchcraft*, 183.

Two Witches Cooking Up a Storm. Woodcut. From Ulrich Molitor, *De laniis et phitonicis mulieribus* (Cologne: Cornelius von Ziericksee, ca. 1496–1500), title page. Reproduced in Zika, *The Appearance of Witchcraft*, 19.

The Wonderful Discouerie of the Witchcrafts of Margaret and Phillip Flower, Daughters of Ioan Flower Neere Beuer Castle: Executed at Lincolne, March 11. 1618 . . . Together with the Seuerall Examinations and Confessions of Anne Baker, Ioan Willimot, and Ellen Greene, Witches in Leicestershire. [London], 1619.

PROTEST AND RECLAIMING

Twenty-four · CAROLYN CHERNOFF

Hexing the Patriarchy: The Revolutionary Aesthetics of W.I.T.C.H.

INTRODUCTION

Formed in 1968, with roots in second-wave US radical feminism, W.I.T.C.H. reemerged as a series of autonomous cells after Donald Trump's election in 2016. Originally the initials stood for the Women's International Terrorist Conspiracy from Hell. The current group says the initials stand for Witches' International Troublemaker Conspiracy from Hell, moving away from the fraught terms *woman* and *terrorist*; but both twentieth- and twenty-first-century versions of the group maintain that the initials can have multiple and changing meanings. Flux is a tactic here, and a refusal to fit one static definition. Like its earlier iteration, the twenty-first-century W.I.T.C.H. employs the strategies of public *hexes*[1] and *zaps*[2] to challenge patriarchal power. Unlike the twentieth-century group, which was associated with the second-wave white feminism of the time, the twenty-first-century W.I.T.C.H. operates under the aegis of intersectional, trans-affirming feminism and centers sex work among other issues that the twentieth-century feminist movement generally portrayed as among the problems of patriarchy. The politics of both groups are radical (for their respective times), although they differ dramatically in terms of representation and focus. Both the original and contemporary modern W.I.T.C.H. employ political theater and socially engaged art, using tropes of the monstrous to challenge patriarchal power. Their revolutionary aesthetic: monstrous femme meets Black Bloc, disseminated through clever control of social media.

In this chapter, I address the concept of *monstrous femme* as a revolutionary aesthetic for the newest incarnation of W.I.T.C.H. Focusing on the Instagram account of the inaugural Portland, Oregon, W.I.T.C.H. revival group (@WITCHPDX),[3] I look at how the group represents itself and its politics while maintaining control of their collective image as a form of socially engaged art. I focus on the revolutionary aesthetic of W.I.T.C.H. through the lens of forbidden identity and forbidden acts, particularly the hex and curse that many practicing witches generally disavow except as a means of last resort. In hexing the patriarchy, W.I.T.C.H. deploys strategies of media control and playing with identity to challenge oppressive systems of power.

Let me be clear from the start of this chapter: I am not now, nor have I ever been, a member of W.I.T.C.H., although if I am or were, I would have to deny it. The Portland W.I.T.C.H values statement specifies, "Anyone publicly claiming to be one of us is not one of us—we are anonymous." In an age of branded identity and social media cult following, W.I.T.C.H.'s insistence on anonymity is jarring as well as practical (anonymity acts as protection against *doxxing*, or the public revealing of private identity including legal name, address, and means of contact—information that political enemies often employ to threaten or harass individuals). The twenty-first-century W.I.T.C.H. uses social media the same way it uses magic: in contradictory and challenging ways.

Until recently, even the most public or publicly accepted witches have been uncanny and subject to social censure up to and including death. With that in mind, the socialist-feminists Robin Morgan, Peggy Dobbins, Judy Duffett, Cynthia Funk, Naomi Jaffe, and Florika formed the first W.I.T.C.H. (Women's International Terrorist Conspiracy from Hell) in New York City in October 1968. Rather than focus exclusively on challenging patriarchy, W.I.T.C.H. broke from other radical feminists in their desire to support a broader range of social issues, including challenging capitalism. Their first public action was the Halloween 1968 zap (theatrical ritual and protest) of Wall Street. Dressed in black garb (cloaks, pointy hats, and the like), a coven of thirteen feminist activists, armed with a fake pig's head, marched down Wall Street to curse the financial district.[4] One of the organizers, Robin Morgan, claimed that the action was responsible for the decline of the Dow Jones average the day after the event.[5]

In the twentieth-century W.I.T.C.H., we see a set of tactics emerge: disruption, visibility, anonymity, and strategic use of media coverage. But the twenty-first-century W.I.T.C.H. occupies an unusual position: it demands

FIGURE 24.1 W.I.T.C.H. protest, 1968.

anonymity of its members, yet exists on public platforms, primarily Instagram, known for their visual appeal and public reach. I argue that the twenty-first-century W.I.T.C.H. demonstrates the ways in which social media have changed the possibility of socially engaged art, allowing protest groups to harness the power of art along with public messaging (as sociologist Dustin Kidd argues in his work on social media, "'Art' refers to the creative dimension of all human action"[6] and is inherently part of social media). At the same time, twenty-first-century W.I.T.C.H. groups claim solidarity with the original W.I.T.C.H. groups and continue to deploy tactics of causing a scene and disrupting mainstream narratives. Twenty-first-century W.I.T.C.H. draws on feminist history while simultaneously challenging binary notions of gender along with what is truly monstrous about patriarchal violence.

WHICH W.I.T.C.H./THE ETERNAL W.I.T.C.H.

The election of Donald Trump in 2016 brought a new level of visibility to the age-old specter of the witch as monstrous/powerful woman.[7] Even before the November election, many cities saw anonymous signs on the street and on social media inviting people to join in an international curse to remove Trump from office, or to hex Trump alongside the patriarchy.[8] Similar actions spread rhizomatically,[9] or in nonhierarchical, nonlinear ways, through social media. To bring down a monster like Trump, the logic went, we needed ancient powers.

In Portland, Oregon, W.I.T.C.H. PDX emerged as the first of the post-Trump witch groups to claim a particular name and to connect specifically to the second-wave group. In an interview with anonymous members, W.I.T.C.H. PDX explains why and how the group's geographic location makes sense and shapes its goals and actions: "The Pacific Northwest has long been a hotbed of activism and radical thought, but also of racism. We're so close, geographically, to the birthplace of the Riot Grrrl movement, plus Portland has a vibrant queer community that's ahead of the curve in many ways on gender and other forms of social justice."[10] At the same time, W.I.T.C.H. PDX acknowledges, "Our city has a history of marginalizing and displacing people of color and Oregon as a whole has a violently racist past and a large population of white supremacists. There are a lot of things to work on right here. We're hoping to help effect change in our own community and inspire people to do the same nationwide."[11]

In this statement and observation, we see the shifting dynamics and politics of W.I.T.C.H.: both explicitly connected to second-wave feminism while at the same time articulating group values that contemporary progressive and radical activists see as missing from so much second-wave organizing: race-critical, gender-expansive, sex-work-positive perspectives, while still specifically pointing to white imperialist capitalist patriarchy as the enemy.

The Portland W.I.T.C.H. manifesto, however, makes it clear that W.I.T.C.H. is not a trend, but eternal, proclaiming, "For centuries, the dominant culture has persecuted anyone who dares to be different," arguing that "a single witch is a dangerous outlier. A coven is a force to be reckoned with. An international circle of witches is unstoppable. Together, we are W.I.T.C.H. (Witches' International Troublemaker Conspiracy from Hell), reviving the spirit and intentions of the 1960s organization of the same name. We aim to use our power to fight injustice in all its intersectional forms, and help dismantle the white supremacist patriarchal system that perpetrates it. The new generation of W.I.T.C.H conjures our collective rage, joy, grief, strength, determination and ferocity into a force for change." The all-caps statement in white letters on a black background, posted on the now-defunct Portland W.I.T.C.H. chapter's website, makes it clear that the current iteration of the group is both a continuation as well as an updated version of the work of witches throughout history as well as the first, 1960s, W.I.T.C.H.

Whether in-person or online, across the span of fifty years, W.I.T.C.H. has prioritized using the figure of the witch to directly challenge injustice and oppression. The development of social media, however, has enabled current W.I.T.C.H. chapters to use the media directly in a way that earlier W.I.T.C.H. members could not. Whereas second-wave W.I.T.C.H. actions included in-person disruptions of ongoing events, like the "Up against Wall Street" action of Halloween 1968, Instagram W.I.T.C.H. focuses on clever documentation and branding, on circulating photos and images, as well as on public participation in protest and ritual. The Instagram images follow a basic aesthetic of all-caps white lettering in a basic font on a black background, a strict insistence on anonymity, and the image of the witch in situ at protests and demonstrations in garb (pointy hats, figure-obscuring black gowns and capes, faces obscured by veils) with homemade cardboard signs invoking the very techniques that mainstream witches and Wiccans often disavow: curses and hexes. HEX THE PATRIARCHY, HEX BACK ALLEY ABORTIONS, HEX WHITE SUPREMACY, read signs painted in black on corrugated cardboard cut from the sides of large boxes, or in white lettering on black backgrounds.

REVOLUTIONARY AESTHETICS AND THE MONSTROUS FEMME

Many theorists work with the concept of *woman as monster*. While Barbara Creed's concept of the *monstrous-feminine* argues that the female reproductive body is at the root of what is monstrous (in film),[12] I argue that *monstrous femme* is a revolutionary aesthetic that builds on historical patriarchal fear of woman as castrator and villain—but that also decentralizes a binary-gendered body. Inspired by Creed's monstrous-feminine, monstrous femme is a gloss, an inversion, and a way to talk about the witch as gendered but decoupled from a binary-gendered body. Femme, not feminine; femme, not female. Femme puts the emphasis on power relations and roles rather than on a physical body or way of comportment. Femme can also be understood as the link between beauty and terror, where what is "feminine" is what is looked at (an object), but also is powerful and frightening because of what the object reveals about the fears and insecurities of those looking.[13]

How can we talk about the monstrous femme as a revolutionary aesthetic without mentioning Hélène Cixous's beautiful, laughing Medusa? Gender essentialist and TERF[14] arguments aside, the revelation that Medusa is beautiful, that her power is beauty, is another way of seeing the power of the monstrous femme as something constructed beyond biological notions of gender and identity. Other modern and contemporary artists and critics working with what I am terming the revolutionary aesthetic of monstrous femme include film theorist Carol Clover's Final Girl (when she lives to tell the tale);[15] French artist Orlan's 1977 project "Medusa" and "The Reincarnation of Saint-Orlan," a series begun in 1990;[16] queer beauty writer Arabella Sicardi's Girl Monster Methodology and the 2013 "Most Important Ugly" photo series (with collaborator Tayler Smith);[17] and French sex worker, author, and auteur Virginie Despentes's essay "A Gun for Every Girl" in *King Kong Theory*. In these collected theories, reflections, and artworks, we see what Durga Chew-Bose argued about 1990s teen movies writ large: "Monsters trump the binary of smart and pretty and instead adopt power as the ultimate makeover."[18]

If the historical figure of woman is monstrous because of her genitals, whether seen as castrated or as holding the power to castrate (Cixious, Creed), the revolutionary aesthetic of the monstrous femme is not connected to biology but rather to power, history, and representation. Femme is a queer way to talk about gender, just as W.I.T.C.H. is a queer way to invoke power from the margins. Key aspects of monstrous femme as revolutionary aesthetic include the following:

1. intentional self-representation
2. use of marginalized media
3. invocation of the monster

The current example of twenty-first-century W.I.T.C.H. employs Instagram and selfies but also other types of stigmatized or marginalized media, "vain" or trivial self-representation, and the invocation of weapons of the weak to summon power.[19] The immediacy of the smart phone and social media enable the monstrous femme to a new degree—images can be made in the moment and circulated worldwide in a click.

As of August 19, 2020, the W.I.T.C.H. Tumblr account @witchblr names nineteen active chapters in North American (Canada, the United States, and Mexico), though there have been dozens of active chapters worldwide since 2017, including in at least eight countries.[20] By my loose count there have been at least fifty-three active chapters with Instagram accounts between January 2017 and August 2020.

In the W.I.T.C.H. PDX manifesto, no longer available at its original URL because the group has deactivated their web presence, all-cap white letters on a black background stated the following: "For centuries, the dominant culture has persecuted anyone who dares to be different. The gentle healers, the midwives, the queers, the loners, the wise elders, the pagans, the foreigners, the wild women. Dissent is threatening to the status quo, especially when it is shrouded in unfamiliar customs and the mysterious sacred feminine. Those who seek to oppress and suppress us have always called us 'witches' to silence us. Now, we step out of the shadows, embracing this word and all it stands for."

A few paragraphs down, the manifesto clarified: "Together, we are W.I.T.C.H. (Witches' International Troublemaker Conspiracy from Hell), reviving the spirit and intentions of the 1960s organization of the same name. We aim to use our power to fight injustice in all its intersectional forms and help dismantle the white supremacist patriarchal system that perpetrates it. The new generation of W.I.T.C.H. conjures our collective rage, joy, grief, strength, and ferocity into a force for change."

Manifestos themselves are a revolutionary aesthetic, in both form and content. For both W.I.T.C.H. groups, or W.I.T.C.H. across the decades, the written manifesto is a statement of collective identity and action. While the manifesto may appear to be "just" a text, it is an object of power and protest, publicly proclaiming the group, calling it into existence, naming the enemy, and inviting others to join the resistance, even if only tacitly. Viewed through the lens of the monstrous femme, a manifesto is also a spell: words with power.

W.I.T.C.H. uses aspects of traditional or historical magic to do its political work (spells and rituals) as well as more contested or feared aspects of witchcraft (binding, hexing, and cursing). The optics of W.I.T.C.H. include recognizable symbols (the black-clad witch in dress and cape and pointy hat with a broom), "weird" or "unrecognizable" symbols (sigils), and the pentagram. I argue that making these distinctions visible, literally, is part of the radical aesthetics and work of the contemporary W.I.T.C.H. Along with their use of social media, clear identity politics and conscious anonymity while invoking the specter of the monstrous femme are all part of what makes W.I.T.C.H. a powerful political project.

Twenty-first-century W.I.T.C.H. is media savvy. Different chapters have a presence across social media as well as coverage in print journalism. Instagram, however, is a place for W.I.T.C.H. to shine. It is true that Snapchat is even more heavily used by the eighteen- to twenty-four-year-old demographic (often more likely to be outspoken activists with the energy of new converts)—but on Snapchat, messages and images disappear after a limited amount of time. That is part of Snapchat's appeal, that it is ephemeral. So, while W.I.T.C.H. may make use of Snapchat or other media platforms like Facebook and Twitter and whatever new options springing up each day, it is Instagram that is the primary vehicle.[21]

Why Instagram? Because it is heavily used. Because it is a visual medium. Because it is excellent for the "curating" and "aesthetic" concerns that drive a lot of social media. But above all, it is anonymous. One can certainly use a legal name with Instagram and link to personal websites, but Instagram is a place where one can create a persona, carefully support that persona with an aesthetic and curated posts (original and re-blogged), control who can see the feed, and generally communicate with the world in ways of one's own choosing. W.I.T.C.H. uses Instagram to continue a type of media blackout associated with the 1990s and Riot Grrrl.[22] It is ironic, certainly, to claim that a group is enacting a media blackout via social media—but it is a strategy of unidirectional communication (like the communiqués of past radical groups)—that uses the contemporary channels of social interaction that dominate so many of our days. W.I.T.C.H. posts, W.I.T.C.H. shares, but only under the cloak of anonymity.

It is powerful. It is meant to be a bit scary, to destabilize the audiences' certainty of who might be speaking. It is also smart: as organizations and people get doxxed, anonymity and media control protect private identities. Anonymity via social media is a tactic.

REVOLUTIONARY AESTHETICS ONLINE

Like the advertising-influenced art of ACT UP and their graphic design collective Gran Fury or the feminist art of Barbara Kruger or Jenny Holzer, the "art" of W.I.T.C.H. is text-reliant, with clear, repeated symbols. The images are confrontational: a coven of black-clad witches with pointy hats and veiled faces, even gloved hands, marches in a picket line formation—a circle in front of the department store Nordstrom. They carry protest signs. If not for the garb (and the messages on the signs), this could be any union action. The Nordstrom action, though, was a protest and ritual all in one, as seen in a video clip posted on January 24, 2017, to the now-defunct Instagram account of the Portland group's full moon invocation and banishment ritual held at the department store in December 2016. There are thirteen signs and thirteen witches, using the classic number of a coven. White capital letters on large black picket signs read: EQUALITY. PROGRESS. WITCH. ANGRY. EARTHLY. IMMORTAL. UNTAMED. HEALER. WILD. DARK. PEACE. FEMININE. JOYOUS. Around and around the witches march, the signs flash, with no end or beginning, just the eternal circle.

The W.I.T.C.H. PDX Instagram feed began on January 21, 2017, the day of the International Women's Marches in protest of Donald Trump's inauguration. Social media, and particularly a visual forum like Instagram, coupled with the ability to share images in real time from around the world, is a particularly useful tool for social movements worldwide. There were eleven posts on the W.I.T.C.H. PDX account, mostly photos of the W.I.T.C.H. PDX coven in action, often reposted images from other accounts. There's a video from the action of that day, with the coven in garb and armed with signs (NO FASCIST WITCH HUNT; TRANS WOMEN ARE WOMEN; WE SHALL NOT SUFFER THE PATRIARCHY TO LIVE; WHITE SILENCE IS VIOLENCE; WITCHCRAFT IS REBELLION; A TIME TO BUILD A TIME TO BURN), and a screenshot of a headline announcing the inauguration protests as the biggest protest in American history.

The day after the Women's March, the W.I.T.C.H. PDX Instagram account produced four posts. Two were photos of the group in action; two were memes, reposted images of other people's text posts, both calling for centering trans women and women of color while decrying white supremacy. It is the carefully curated posts and re-blogged words and images as much as the cleverly composed photos of W.I.T.C.H. in action that demonstrate the group's tactics and revolutionary aesthetic in the form of digital linkage and appeals to solidarity. These are invisible webs woven across the internet. Again, we see the monstrous femme tactics (media control, memes, images) and the monstrous femme aesthetic (the cyber-savvy witch, anonymous and dreadful, aligned with others across time and space).

Outside of the initial posts I describe, the Instagram account featured images of crystals, calls to support survivor of sexual violence Cyntoia Brown and to punish the rapist Brock Turner, a Guerrilla Girls re-blog, protest information, memes supporting sex workers and trans rights and decrying police brutality and the PIC. There were images of rituals, protests, Captain Cook being murdered with emojis over faces (heart eyes/hearts), all accompanied by motifs including roses, hearts, and pastel pink, with mostly black and white texts, interspersed with quotes from Ursula K. LeGuin, Venus of Willendorf images, political graphics from the leftist artist Micah Bazant, reminders of sabbats and other important celebrations, and calls for support for Puerto Rico and Mexico in the wake of catastrophic earthquakes. These are contemporary W.I.T.C.H. concerns: trans-affirming, pro sex-work and sex workers, broadly political in the sense of punishing evildoers, and exhausting or overwhelming in volume, scope, and imagery.

So, alongside the triple moon, broom, pentagram, and sigils, we also see trans symbols, graphics, and memes and the post–Riot Grrrl aesthetic of cuteness plus rage. The revolutionary aesthetic uses contemporaneous internet culture alongside the social movements of the 1980s and 1990s to capture a kind of zeitgeist. These online aesthetics reinforce the idea that all women, trans, cis, and gender-nonconforming people are already witches and could hex the patriarchy at any moment. A key difference between second-wave W.I.T.C.H. and contemporary W.I.T.C.H., however, is that while capitalism and patriarchy are shared enemies, contemporary W.I.T.C.H. was galvanized by the election of Donald Trump and the estimated 47 to 52 percent of white women voters who helped elect him.[23] So the contemporary W.I.T.C.H. protest is raced and gendered but attempts consciously to center white supremacy as the real enemy, even as other issues matter too.

CONCLUSION

W.I.T.C.H. is a political project with revolutionary aesthetics that also demonstrates the power of the internet and the ways in which social movements grow and change over time. Twenty-first-century W.I.T.C.H. demonstrates the ways in which social media have changed the possibilities of socially engaged art, allowing protest groups to harness the power of art and continue the original W.I.T.C.H. tactics of causing a scene and disrupting mainstream narratives while also challenging binary notions of gender along with what is truly monstrous about patriarchal violence. At the same time, twentieth-century W.I.T.C.H. emerged out of second-wave white US feminist organizing, which activists of color at the time and progressive and radical activists today rightly critique for its failure to engage with the politics of race, a type of gender essentialism, trans-exclusion, whore-phobia, and failure to include sex work. One of the benefits of working in a movement over time is that sometimes movements win; when movements win, categories often change. So it might be seen as a victory that contemporary feminist-affiliated projects are able to explicitly state an identity that is anti-racist, trans-affirming, and sex-work positive when those three categories were all conceptualized in different terms—and seen as threatening to mainstream second-wave feminist causes—for the founders of the twentieth-century W.I.T.C.H.

The twenty-first-century iteration of W.I.T.C.H. is media-literate and relies, in particular, on social media. Its aesthetic both is intentionally generic—the most basic of white fonts on black backgrounds, mostly text-based, with occasional black-and-white photos of anonymous witches in witch-garb with signs at actions—and invokes equally the specters of the monstrous femme (of which the witch is a critical example) and the Black Bloc. Particularly after the 2016 US presidential election, social media saw plenty of posts advertising free-floating magic, ritual, and witchcraft specifically focused on neutralizing Trump and fighting fascism—witchcraft, though not necessarily W.I.T.C.H.-craft. I focus specifically on the revolutionary aesthetic of Instagram W.I.T.C.H., but there is some slippage, which is part of lower- and uppercase witch magic.

Let me end, however, as I began: I am not now, nor have I ever been, a member of W.I.T.C.H., although if I am or were, I would have to deny it. For identity-based movements, the protection of a collective identity over individual authority or fame remains a challenge, a curse, and a form of binding. It is the work of playing with representation and identity that gives W.I.T.C.H. much of its power. Through using and subverting tropes of social media, W.I.T.C.H. reminds us that social movements and social protest spread rhizomatically, in unexpected ways, adapting to technology as it changes. Anonymous, yet on social media, W.I.T.C.H. also reminds us of the power of a leaderless movement: You can't decapitate a leader if you can't find a head.

NOTES

1. The political theater of W.I.T.C.H. deliberately plays with some of the rules and agreements of historical witchcraft. While there are as many ways to be a witch as there are witches, most witches generally avoid hexes and especially curses, except as an absolute final resort. This is because of the rule of three: whatever you do will come back to you three times; and because of the Wiccan Rede, a version of the Golden Rule (and it harm none/do what thou wilt). So, if you curse someone or something, be prepared for your own life to be impacted. Again, while W.I.T.C.H. invokes the specter of the witch (and many W.I.T.C.H. participants are also witches), it is a deliberate or conscious invocation and one that intentionally destabilizes identity and power. So just as twentieth-century W.I.T.C.H. pioneered the public hex or zap, performing a type of curse against powerful agents of patriarchal oppression, so too does the twenty-first-century W.I.T.C.H. generally intentionally perform the fraught acts of hexing, cursing, and binding (restricting another to prevent them from causing harm).
2. A *zap* can be a kind of spontaneous public action or a coordinated attempt to flood email and voicemail of decision-makers around a particular issue. Some political groups coordinate zaps at a particular time of day to flood or overwhelm their target with calls, emails, social media posts, etc.
3. The handle @witchpdx is the Instagram account name for W.I.T.C.H., of Portland, Oregon. PDX is the call sign for the Portland International Airport. I focus on @witchpdx partly because they were the first, and perhaps most highly influential, of the twenty-first-century W.I.T.C.H. revival groups.
4. Echols, *Daring to Be Bad*, 97.
5. Brownmiller, *In Our Time*, 49.
6. Kidd, *Social Media Freaks*, 5.
7. It's tricky but must be noted that while most witches, historically, have been women or female, there were and are witches of all sexes and genders. Because so much of feminist politics has a shared past investment in centering women and female bodies, the term "woman" is often used, although as the twenty-first-century W.I.T.C.H. tries to specify, trans women, trans men, nonbinary people, and those outside a strict gender binary tied to sex as assigned at birth are included in the figure of the witch and the actions of W.I.T.C.H.
8. See, for example, Ephrat Livni, "Feminist Witches Are Casting Hexes on Donald Trump," Quartz, October 29, 2016, https://qz.com/822080/feminist-witches-are-casting-hexes-on-donald-trump/; BBC News, "Witches Cast 'Mass Spell' against Donald Trump," February 25, 2017, https://www.bbc.com/news/world-us-canada-39090334.
9. See Deleuze and Guattari, *A Thousand Plateaus*.
10. Haute Macabre, "W.I.T.C.H. PDX."

11   Haute Macabre, "W.I.T.C.H. PDX."
12   Creed, *The Monstrous-Feminine*.
13   On the link between beauty and terror, see, for example, George Menz, "Beauty and Terror," *Gadfly Magazine*, October 17, [no year], accessed April 9, 2024, https://www.thegadflymagazine.org/home-1/beauty-and-terror.
14   Trans-exclusionary radical feminist.
15   Clover, *Men, Women, and Chainsaws*.
16   See Hugues Marchal, "Orlan," AWARE, 2017, accessed April 9, 2024, https://awarewomenartists.com/en/artiste/orlan/ (in general); and Rudolf Frieling, "Orlan, 'The Reincarnation of Saint Orlan, (1990–1993)," Media Art Net, accessed April 9, 2024, http://www.medienkunstnetz.de/works/reincarnation/ (specifically).
17   See Arabelle Sicardi, "Girl Monster Methodology," https://www.instagram.com/p/e2TNftiN7j/?hl=en, accessed June 4, 2024, and "Most Important Ugly" project at http://www.fashionpirate.net/2014/04/most-important-ugly_22.html, accessed June 4, 2024.
18   Chew-Bose, as quoted in cléo journal, "'90s Teen Party Movies."
19   Portraits by Cindy Sherman and Orlan, for example, fit this revolutionary aesthetic, as did Poly Styrene's invocation of "little girls" in the introduction to the 1977 punk rock song by X-Ray Spex, "Oh Bondage! Up Yours!"; 1990s Riot Grrrl also serves as inspiration and touchstone in "reclaiming" girl culture and weaponizing femme image.
20   Tumblr site: http://witchpdx.tumblr.com/chapters.
21   Auxier and Anderson, "Social Media Use in 2021."
22   Upon receiving unwanted media attention in the early days of widespread Internet usage, Riot Grrrl made public calls for a media blackout—for Riot Grrrls to boycott [or grrrlcott] press.
23   See Amanda Becker, "White Women Had Doubts: They Voted for Trump Anyway," The 19th News, November 7, 2020, https://19thnews.org/2020/11/white-women-had-doubts-they-voted-for-trump-anyway/.

BIBLIOGRAPHY

Auxier, Brooke, and Monica Anderson. "Social Media Use in 2021." Pew Research Center, April 7, 2021. https://www.pewresearch.org/internet/2021/04/07/social-media-use-in-2021/.

Brownmiller, Susan. *In Our Time: Memoir of a Revolution*. New York: Dial Press, 1999.

Cixous, Hélène. "The Laugh of the Medusa," *Signs* 1, no. 4 (1976): 875–93.

cléo journal. "'90s Teen Party Movies and the Golden Age™ of Feminist Film?," December 3, 2014. https://cleojournal.com/2014/12/03/90s-teen-party-movies-and-the-golden-age-of-feminist-film/.

Clover, Carol J. *Men, Women, and Chainsaws: Gender in the Modern Horror Film*. Princeton, NJ: Princeton University Press, 1992.

Creed, Barbara. *The Monstrous-Feminine: Film, Feminism, Psychoanalysis*. London: Routledge, 1993.

Deleuze, Gilles, and Felix Guattari. *A Thousand Plateaus: Capitalism and Schizophrenia*. Minneapolis: University of Minnesota Press, 1987.

Despentes, Virginie. "A Gun for Every Girl." In *King Kong Theory*. New York: The Feminist Press, 2010.

Echols, Alice. *Daring to Be Bad: Radical Feminism in America 1967–1975*. Minneapolis: University of Minnesota Press, 1989.

Haute Macabre. "W.I.T.C.H. PDX: Portland Brings Back the Women's International Terrorist Conspiracy from Hell." Last accessed January 27, 2017. http://hautemacabre.com/2017/01/ w-i-t-c-h-pdx-portland-brings-back-the-womens-international-terroristconspiracy-from-hell/.

Kidd, Dustin. *Social Media Freaks: Digital Identity in the Network Society*. London: Taylor and Francis, 2017.

Twenty-five · TINA ESCAJA AND LAURIE ESSIG

Witch-Ins and Other Feminist Acts

INTRODUCTION

Days before the presidential election in 2020, two middle-aged professors of gender studies and the authors of this article were scraping smashed pumpkin off the steps of Burlington, Vermont's, city hall. We were carefully placing the stringy bits of orange flesh into a shopping bag because we did not want to leave a mess in a public place that is also a space that many unhoused people call home. We were in the last moments of our fifth and final Trumpkin Smashing, a feminist "witch-in" that for five subsequent Octobers attracted young and old alike. We would parade down the street holding pumpkins carved in the image of the great Orange Evil himself, inviting unsuspecting pedestrians to recite incantations in English and Spanish, playful spells to dismantle the misogynistic, racist, and xenophobic rhetoric of Trump and his followers. The performance culminated with throwing the Trumpkins from the balcony of Burlington's city hall (figure 25.1). We played with the carnival and gothic iconography of Halloween while connecting with aspects of other secular and religious traditions, such as the Day of the Dead in Latinx cultures. We yelled and cackled and laughed at ourselves a lot. We knew we were ridiculous. We were using the absurdity of our acts to say something about the impossibility of this moment, part of a long tradition of feminist activism that has utilized the figure of the witch, at times ironically, at times sincerely.

In what follows, we attempt to assemble a messy feminist archive of five years of embracing not just the witch but also other forms of embodied and debased femininity, including the hysteric, the failed mother, and the vulva itself.[1] Our messy feminist archive is building from Martin F.

FIGURE 25.1 Activists smashing Trumpkins, 2020. Photograph by Rachel Elizabeth Jones. Courtesy of the authors.

Manalansan's queer archive as something that is a "trashy, dirty, disgusting and untidy disorganization of bodies, things, and emotions."[2] In what follows we try to find meaning in our own untidy and trashy mix of stuff and feelings that accumulated during five years of anti-fascist activism as part of Feminists Against Bullshit (FABS). FABS primarily utilized the figure of the witch as a way of honoring our foremothers but also to expand this gendered figure into a more capacious space of feminist rage that included not just foremothers but fore-queers and fore-agenders and anyone else who ever was brave enough to fight patriarchy with sublimely absurdist acts.

INSUBORDINATES/INSUMISXS RESIST

The feminist Trumpkin Smashing was born in September of 2016 when a group of *insumisxs*[3]/insubordinates belonging mainly to the academic field of gender studies met to discuss how we could resist the growing white-supremacist and masculinist movement of Donald Trump. In an email from Laurie Essig on June 28, 2016, participants were invited to a "strategy session disguised as a cocktail party." This meeting was the germ of a new movement and feminist performance re-action conceived by Tina Escaja and Laurie Essig, both directing gender studies programs in Vermont. The *insumisxs* began a feminist protest and performance group, initially called "Feminists Against Trump" (FAT) but, in an effort not to give Trump extra energy, soon transformed into FABS.

Given that Halloween was on the horizon, we decided to start with the figure of the witch. Rather than having a sit-in, we would create a witch-in and replace pumpkin-smashing with Trumpkin Smashing. We knew the long tradition of feminist activism that has utilized the figure of the witch. Our witch-ins were inspired by the 1960s activism of W.I.T.C.H., the Women's International Terrorist Conspiracy from Hell, and their curses on members of Congress and bridal expos and Wall Street. Like W.I.T.C.H., whose members saw themselves as allied with a larger progressive agenda, we too wanted to fight against more than just patriarchy. We cursed capitalism and xenophobia and white supremacy. And like W.I.T.C.H., we were stunned by the true evil of it all, and so we responded with affective rather than effective protests, what the W.I.T.C.H. witches called *zaps*. We created a lot of zaps, a series of messy acts from Trumpkin Smashings to a Vulva Detox Tent to a public Panic Attack that are all part of our archive.

In order to archive these acts, we sat down with one of the other founding FABS witches, Lindsay/Lou London, and collected our memories and emotions about these events. We also conducted a survey of past participants. The survey, which was distributed through a Facebook ad on the FABS Facebook page, received sixteen responses from participants in FABS events between 2016 and 2020. The survey asked participants to describe which events they participated in as well as how they *felt* about those events. The survey participants were between the ages of eighteen and sixty-five, about half identified as female, four as male, and four genderqueer, nonbinary, or gender-nonconforming. Eleven of the sixteen participants identified as some version of white.

THE ARCHIVE

Feminist Witch-Ins and Trumpkin Smashings

On October 29, 2016, we put on black clothes, dyed our hair purple, and donned our witch hats. We gathered at the top of Burlington's Church Street. We had advertised the event in a local alternative paper, and when we arrived, we were relieved to see about fifteen other witches there.[4] We were scared. Scared that Donald Trump would win the election. Scared that there could be some sort of violence against people in our group. Scared that practicing Wiccans might be insulted by our use of the witch for political rather than for spiritual purposes. And yet we also felt powerful. Escaja remembers:

I have my cheap witch hat filled with buttons and memorabilia from past and ongoing protests: a $1 bill painted in red: "corporations are not people"; Don't downsize education at UVM; . . . In my hand, a wand with the question "Witch way to the election?" It is Halloween 2016. Women have gathered at the top of Church Street, getting ready to chant spells against patriarchy and Donald Trump. It is our first Trumpkin Smashing and I am a warrior. My improvised outfit is my shield and my weapon. I feel empowered.

Another founding witch, London, a nurse who showed up with her then infant strapped to her chest and her toddler held by the hand, remembers how surprised she was, coming from West Texas, that it was all so easy. She could not believe that we could stage this event on the main commercial street in town. "I was like 'What? We can do this down the main street?' Coming from a highly conservative space, you would be burned at the stake. Not really but kinda. For me, too, tapping into this ancient lineage and this ancient opportunity for alchemy. And we did. Even if the only alchemy we made was within ourselves. Those four years were such dark times." Several of our participants in that first witch-in also felt fear buoyed by a sense of feminist camaraderie and joy. A few of them remember the collective action of chanting as particularly important, more important than costuming oneself as a witch. One person who participated in several Trumpkin Smashings stated, "[I was] disappointed that I never got it together to costume/present myself in an overtly witch fashion" but still felt it was "extremely cathartic to parade down Church St. with other angry, bad-ass witches." The chants inspired another participant who remembered: "I was unsure the first time, but then it was exciting and empowering. . . . I remember bringing the feminist chants home for my elderly feminist mother because they made me happy and I knew they'd make her happy." Another participant remembered that they were "tentative to participate in group chants/'hexes' but found that the absurdity and intense feeling of community overtook my hesitancy. There were many voyeurs who were simultaneously confused by and supportive of the 'hexes.' As we marched down the street, I felt an intense connection to other members of the collective, many of whom I had never met previously." The chants themselves were both ridiculous and deeply feminist. The witches said things like: "Abracadabra, here's a spell. Donald Trump, go to hell!" Trump's name was then replaced with other names or words like Steve Bannon, Stephen Miller, patriarchy, transphobia, and white supremacy. We also shouted in Spanish

"We believe you/Te creemos/Believe Survivors/¡Cree en ellas!" Some of our chants, like the talk between us, mixed the two languages together: ¡Somos malas y está bien! Patriarcado, go to hell! Trump grabs coños. Y nosotras feministas tambien votan." These mixed chants often devolved into just English as we chanted "Trump grabs pussies, but pussies grab back!"

Despite Escaja being a celebrated poet, the chants we wrote were not particularly poetic. Yet the very act of chanting—even screaming—them together in a public place, dressed as the degraded figure of the witch, was, as many of our participants pointed out, powerful and cathartic. The point of these chants was to collectivize our rage into one primal scream. Moving from protest to performance, these chants served to unify a disparate group of feminists to make anger not just visible but collective. As William Mazzarella puts it, affect is understanding that "society is inscribed in our nervous system," and by manifesting social power in the debased yet also feared figure of the witchy feminist and smashing Trumpkins, we displayed a kind of bodily intolerance for fascism.[5] For Mel Chen, there is a "link between tension and agitation . . . [like that] between a sedimented rigidity and the movement that is dubbed insurgency."[6]

A PUBLIC PANIC ATTACK

It was this sort of bodily intolerance that inspired us a few months later to embrace another debased feminized figure: the hysteric. On January 14, 2017, we traded our witch costumes for the costumes of domesticated women—aprons and rubber dishwashing gloves—and gathered again on Church Street for what we billed as a public Panic Attack. We advertised by asking, "Does the thought of Donald Trump becoming president of the United States give you the SCREAMING MEEMIES!?!" And we then suggested that we could resist "Trumpism with absurdism." We held signs that said "Panic" and "Fight Back!" Through a bullhorn, we announced to passersby the days, hours, minutes, and seconds until Trump was inaugurated. Then we played a siren and encouraged everyone around us to run in circles screaming. FABS participants even fell onto the cold ground kicking their legs. Looking at photos there might have been ten or so participants on that frigid day, but many more people shopping and working downtown joined us in our panic attack. On Facebook, we received some criticism over our use of "panic" for not taking mental illness seriously, but we were working through the feminist theory of Jackie Orr, who in *Panic Diaries* reframes panic not as pathology but as the most rational response to the death drive of phallogocentric patriarchy, or as she calls it, "Daddy."[7] We embraced panic and hysteria as highly feminized forms of distress. The panic attack and the witch-ins felt like a way to make visible our very real anxiety and panic over growing fascism. According to one participant, "It felt like an act of visiblizing amidst contexts of being invisibilized." Somehow, by embracing our sense of terror in the form of the abject hysteric, we created a small oxygen bubble in which to breathe as we faced the inevitable despair of the Trump years.

FAILED MOTHERS AND A HEX ON THE NRA

The third sort of debased female figure we used was the failed mother. We used the mourning, bereaved mother to hex the NRA. London created a beautifully disturbing sculpture of a child riddled with bullets, and on June 2, 2018, FABS gathered. We dressed as mourning mothers and publicly wailed and beat our chests and also danced and blew bubbles and told bystanders that we were "making feminist magic and putting a hex on the NRA." The Hex on the NRA event was held in response to the Santa Fe school shooting that had occurred two weeks earlier; but it was also conceived in response to the explosion of toxic masculinity that has resulted in so many mass shootings and a government that can offer only thoughts and prayers or (mistakenly) talk about mental illness in response to such tragedies.[8] We were building on the power of mourning mothers in movements like Madres de Plaza de Mayo in Argentina and also on the power of naming dead children as demanding a form of public mourning and public grief. As Judith Butler says in an interview with George Yancy (speaking about the COVID-19 pandemic rather than about the pandemic of mass shootings), it is "[a] difficult question: How to mourn mass death? . . . The internet has more fully claimed its place as the new public sphere, but it can never fully substitute for the gatherings, both private and public, that allow losses to be fathomed and lived through with others. A purely private form of mourning is possible but cannot assuage the cry that wants the world to bear witness to the loss."[9] By publicizing our grief over more dead children and more mourning parents and families, we momentarily stopped the business of "shopping" and encouraged bystanders to publicly grieve.

A VULVA DETOX TENT

In October 2018, the EcoCulture Lab at the University of Vermont hosted the Feverish World symposium and invited people to make some sort of structures in response to global climate collapse.[10] FABS decided to create a Vulva Detox. We constructed a large pink and red tent and inside placed London's sculpture "the glitoris" (a nongendered rendering of what the clitoris is and can be) and created an altar to various feminist icons like Ida B. Wells, Clara Campoamor, Angela Davis, and Kate Bornstein. We also created a feminist zine-making space in which participants were invited to use their "imaginations and feminist rage" to make their own feminist zines (nearly thirty of which were left in our archive). Looking at them now, the zines evidence both feminist rage and feminist imagination. "Born 2 die, gender is a fuck," but also "I love being a lesbian. Lesbians r strong! Womyn r strong! You r powerful!" and "I am female and trans male, I shouldn't have to jump through hoops to feel like I deserve feminism. I am 100% real. Feminism is real. . . . I love you. I love myself. I love my vagina."

We dressed in bright yellow hazmat suits and gas masks and ushered people into the tent. We told them that by entering the sacred and debased space of the vulva, participants would rid themselves of the toxicity of misogyny and discover their feminist selves. We moved beeping red wands over the participants telling them we were detoxing them not just of woman-hating but also of white supremacy, transphobia, climate-change denial, fascism, toxic masculinity, and more. The Vulva Detox Tent was a response to misogynistic hatred of the pussy and the feminine, as exemplified by Trump's brag, "grab 'em by the pussy," and by the lack of impact his boasting about sexual assault had on his election. We also wanted to speak to the progressive critique of the centering of the vagina in the Women's March, especially in the pussy hats, as excluding women who do not have vaginas. As Brittney Cooper wrote in "Pussy Don't Fail Me Now," we owe it to ourselves to think about the place of the pussy in both gendered violence and in feminist organizing. In her article, Cooper is "struggling with the attempt to displace vaginas from feminist conversations," but, like us, she is also deeply aware that cis women are privileged in ways that trans women, and especially trans Black women, are not.[11] Acknowledging our mostly white privilege (for this action/performance it was three cis women), we wanted to create the possibility of the vulva as a deeply expansive metaphor that could, in some ways, envelop all of us. We acknowledged that not all of us are born from women's bodies and that some prefer to call that which we call the vulva by other names, but we also wanted to acknowledge the relationship between hating and destroying women/female bodies and the destruction of the earth. For Verónica Gago, theorizing the body as territory "de-liberalizes the notion of the body as individual property . . . the relationship between patriarchy and accumulation on the global scale [and] the subjugation of women, nature, and the colonies with 'civilization' . . . inaugurates capitalist accumulation with the sexual and colonial division of labor as its foundation."[12]

We wanted to reclaim the vulva not as the site of feminist organizing but as the site at which we learn to stop hating the feminized, including the feminized figure of Mother Earth, who was the subject of the conference. We were trying to think of the feminized body as colonized territory, as Gago does, territory that is exploited, raped, degraded, and ultimately must be reclaimed in order to survive. To do so with the tools of Black feminist thought that Cooper offers is to acknowledge that white supremacy makes a universal feminist vulva/pussy an impossibility. But to imagine the world anew, as Gago does, is to hold onto the vulva as a metaphorical space in which we could imagine being cleansed of both white supremacy and a deep and abiding hatred of the feminine/women. Our Vulva Detox Tent offered the feminine body/women as a site not of violence but of possibility and pleasure.

WHAT'S THE USE AND OTHER CONCLUSIONS

And so, we arrive back at our fifth and final Trumpkin Smashing with two professors scraping pumpkin off the ground. We are reappropriating a historical icon, the witch, reduced in popular culture to an expressionist image used to scare children and adults, despicable and old, with marks that conflate old age with evil and "ugliness" in women; the fairy godmother is her opposite: "beautiful," blond, and young. We are redefining a figure into which misogyny and sadism have been poured, and we embrace the witch from a place of solidarity and global connection. As the bumper sticker says: "We are the daughters of the witches you couldn't burn."

Witches/women were and continue to be tortured and destroyed as scapegoats, regardless of whether they had or have a relationship with wisdom, the occult, *la sabiduría*. We embraced the witch as a stand-in for how women/feminized people were and are left behind under capitalism. According to Silvia Federici, witches are the women who have no means to survive under conditions of nascent *and* late capitalism. When the commons became private property in the thirteenth century in England, older women with no husbands to protect them and no land on which to farm became "useless" to the new order. "Land privatization produces a persecution of 'witches.' There seems to be . . . a peculiar relationship between the dismantling of communitarian regimes and the demonization of members of the affected communities that makes witch-hunting an effective instrument of economic and social privatization."[13]

We too are standing at a time when the collective public good has been nearly thoroughly dismantled, when greed and rapaciousness threaten our very existence, when patriarchy is out to destroy all that is feminized, and when witches are being blamed. As Sadie Doyle puts it,

> The backlash years of the early 21st century revealed to many women something we had always suspected: we had never belonged to that daylight world. We had tried; we had worked; we had been loyal to the rules and values of society as we knew it. But no matter how far we thought we had come, or how often our mothers told us we could do anything, we still lived within a system that used female bodies as grist to maintain male rule. In the story that patriarchy told about itself, we were always going to be the villains. And if that was the case, we might as well make some magic out of it.[14]

We made magic by embracing abject feminized forms not just as resistance but as change. This is what Gago calls feminist *potencia*, a form of counterpower that is "the force that drives what is perceived as possible, collectively and in each body."[15] Feminist *potencia*, according to Gago, is how we change everything.

This is an archive of the *potencia* of our witch-ins and other feminist acts. We embraced the abject and feminized figures because there are certain historical moments in which these figures gain a sort of power. Here, in what are probably the end days of global capitalism (and perhaps the world), embracing the witch and other demonized figures of the feminine, our acts become an instrument for the critique of capitalism, white supremacy, and heteropatriarchy. We might ask, à la Sara Ahmed, "What's the use" of this feminist *potencia*, this desire to change everything? Having read through the archive of our useless political acts, even our readers must have already come to the exasperating conclusion that there is no obvious use, and yet, in the uselessness of our acts, we found power—not in the located power of the state, what Gago calls *poder*, but in the resistance and solidarity of feminist *potencia*. Ironically, *potencia* might in fact be more useful than *poder*. As Erica Chenoweth's work shows, peaceful resistance has done more to change the world than violent acts have. But patriarchal cultures teach us that war is the only effective way to fight back.[16] FABS offers a different and ultimately more effective path: undermine power with humor, critique, and solidarity. ¡Viva la bruja! ¡Viva la revolución!

NOTES

1. Feminists Against Bullshit (FABS), of which we are members, organized a variety of actions, but in this chapter we focus on actions that were centered on abject and feminized figures such as the witch.
2. Manalansan, "The 'Stuff' of Archives," 94.
3. From the Spanish *insumisas*, with an inclusive suffix, "x," meaning "rebellious," "defiant."
4. The entire first Trumpkin Smashing and Witch-In was made into a short film by Eva Sollberger and can be viewed here: Eva Sollberger, "A 'Witch-In' Targets Trump," *Seven Days*, November 3, 2016, https://www.sevendaysvt.com/vermont/a-witch-in-targets-trump-siv465/Content?oid=3796540.
5. Mazzarella, "Affect," 292.
6. Chen, "Agitation," 560–61.
7. Orr, *Panic Diaries*.
8. For more on the relationship between masculinity, especially white masculinity, and school shootings, see the Kaiser Health News report by Phillip Reese, "When Masculinity Turns 'Toxic': A Gender Profile of Mass Shootings," KFF Health News, October 3, 2019, https://khn.org/news/when-masculinity-turns-toxic-a-gender-profile-of-mass-shootings/. For more about how mental illness is *not* the cause of mass shootings, see Jaimie Ducharme, "Doctors Say Mental Health Is Not to Blame for Mass Shootings," *Time*, August 5, 2019, https://time.com/5644147/mass-shootings-mental-health/.
9. Yancy, "Judith Butler."
10. For more about the structures at the conference, see "Tentworks," EcoCulture Lab, accessed April 9, 2024, https://ecoculturelab.net/tentcity.
11. Cooper, "Pussy Don't Fail Me Now."
12. Gago, *Feminist International*, 92.
13. Frederici, *Witches, Witch-Hunting and Women*, 15.
14. Doyle, "Monsters, Men and Magic."
15. Gago, *Feminist International*, 16.
16. Chenoweth, *Civil Resistance*.

BIBLIOGRAPHY

Chen, Mel. "Agitation." *South Atlantic Quarterly* 117, no. 3 (2018): 551–66.

Chenoweth, Erica. *Civil Resistance: What Everyone Needs to Know*. New York: Oxford University Press, 2021.

Cooper, Brittney. "Pussy Don't Fail Me Now: The Place of Vaginas in Black Feminist Theory and Organizing." *The Crunk Feminist Collective*, January 23, 2017. Accessed January 25, 2022. http://www.crunkfeministcollective.com/2017/01/23/pussy-dont-fail-me-now-the-place-of-vaginas-in-black-feminist-theory-organizing/.

Doyle, Sadie. "Monsters, Men and Magic: Why Feminists Turned to Witchcraft to Oppose Trump." *Guardian*, August 7, 2019. https://www.theguardian.com/lifeandstyle/2019/aug/07/monsters-men-magic-trump-awoke-angry-feminist-witches.

Federici, Silvia. *Witches, Witch-Hunting and Women*. Oakland, CA: PM Press, 2018.

Feminists Against Trump. "Public Panic Attack: Feminist Protest." Video by Meghan O'Rourke. Town Meeting TV, January, 2017. https://www.cctv.org/watch-tv/programs/public-panic-attack-feminist-protest.

Gago, Verónica. *Feminist International: How to Change Everything*. Translated by Liz Mason-Deese. London: Verso Books, 2020.

Jones, Rachel Elizabeth. "Don't Panic: In Advance of Trump Inauguration, Burlington Activists Perform Hysteria." *Seven Days*, January 16, 2017. https://www.sevendaysvt.com/LiveCulture/archives/2017/01/15/dont-panic-in-advance-of-trump-inauguration-burlington-activists-perform-hysteria.

Manalansan, Martin F., IV. "The 'Stuff' of Archives: Mess, Migration, and Queer Lives." *Radical History Review* 120 (Fall 2014): 94–107.

Mazzarella, William. 2020. "Affect: What Is It Good For?" In *Enchantments of Modernity: Empire, Nation, Globalization*, edited by Saurabh Dube, 291–309. London: Routledge Taylor and Francis Group.

Orr, Jackie. 2006. *Panic Diaries: A Genealogy of Panic Disorder*. Durham, NC: Duke University Press.

Yancy, George. "Judith Butler: Mourning Is a Political Act amid the Pandemic and Its Disparities." *Truthout*, April 30, 2020. https://truthout.org/articles/judith-butler-mourning-is-a-political-act-amid-the-pandemic-and-its-disparities/.

Twenty-six · JACQUELYN MARIE SHANNON

Disappearing Acts: Attending "Witch School" in Brooklyn, New York

In October 2020, I enrolled in "Witch School," an eight-week intensive course in "modern Western syncretic" or "ethical traditional" witchcraft, hosted online (due to the pandemic) by Catland Books, a small witch-owned business in Brooklyn, New York.[1] Joining me were over three hundred witches from across the United States and beyond, seeking practical tools for practical magic. Many later expressed that practicing witchcraft in the context of a global pandemic helped them find "ways to cope," "recharge," "get through this," and "bear it all," something "worth doing," and "something to look forward to."[2] Their words suggest a mobilizing vitality that speaks to the significance of these specific rituals for individuals grappling with death and loss.

Witch School was created and led by Dakota St. Clare, self-described queer nonbinary "witch, diviner, spirit worker" and charismatic and outspoken co-owner of Catland Books.[3] Dakota has enjoyed international recognition for events like Hex Trump and Hex Brett Kavanaugh and has been interviewed and featured in major media publishing outlets, including the *New York Times*, *Vogue*, *Newsweek*, and *Time*.[4] Dakota conceives of Witch School as a "bootcamp" with "zero bandwidth for bullshit."[5] Rather than promising "all the answers," Witch School makes available "the most complete picture possible of what is out there" so that people are empowered to make their own choices.[6]

Most of the witches who found their way to Witch School in 2020 identified as solitary practitioners, united largely by the shared context of a global pandemic and a gravitation toward Catland's "modern Western syncretic" or "ethical traditional" approach to the craft.[7] "Western syncretic witchcraft" refers to the integration of various eclectic elements from diverse Western occult traditions, emphasizing individualized spiritual practices and personal exploration. "Ethical witchcraft" prioritizes principles such as consent, cultural respect, and personal responsibility in one's practice, and insists on critical awareness of and just action in response to such issues as the ethical sourcing and use of sacred herbs, open and closed traditions, and the colonial legacies of racialized magical discourses. "Traditional witchcraft" generally refers to pre-modern practices rooted in folklore and oral traditions, often characterized by animistic beliefs, ancestral veneration, and an emphasis on elements and the natural world.[8] In the context of Witch School, traditional witchcraft is understood more broadly as the embracing of aspects of magical practice for which there is efficacious precedent through experimentation and documentation over time.

This chapter joins a growing body of ethnographic research on modern Western witchcraft as it is understood and practiced in the field.[9] There is much more to be said about the ways in which Witch School, in particular, and modern Western witchcraft, in general, negotiates its relationship to syncretic source material for its rituals, particularly with regard to its critical stance on issues of cultural appropriation and other questions of ethical practice. One can also say more about witchcraft and queer culture and spirituality, including the significant role queer witches like Dakota have played in the social politics of witchcraft, in both leading critical conversations around questions of ethics and access as well as their use of ritual, privately and publicly, as a vehicle for social and political change. These discussions, while both worthy of attention, lie beyond the scope of this chapter.

The following discussion is instead motivated by questions of form—what these witchcraft ritual forms are, how they work, and what they make possible. Approaching my analysis of its rituals through a dramaturgical lens, I hope to explain something about how modern Western witchcraft works in and as performance, what these performances *do* with the complexity of both magic and this historic moment, and *how*. In order to do this, I draw upon participant observation from Catland's Witch School as a site of modern witchcraft ritual performance realized through a queer feminist politics of transformation and self-determination.[10] Over the course of eight weeks, I communed with hundreds of witches synchronously via Zoom for three-hour classes led by Dakota each Saturday night, and asynchronously every day for discussions and community on the private "Witch School 2020" Discord server.[11] The content covered by the course ranged from astrology and divination to curse work and protection magic to working with deities and the dead. Exchanges on Discord included everything from clarifying questions for more "seasoned witches" and narrative reflections on ritual homework to photographs of private ritual tools and altars, before and after rites selfies, sigils, tarot spreads, and portraits of animal familiars. While Saturday sessions were mostly lecture-based, Witch School followed an experiential learning model, supported in part by the weekly assignment of ritual homework.

Catland's Witch School offers an impressively thorough and comprehensive survey of the modern Western witchcraft landscape while remaining rooted, unapologetically, in a particular queer feminist politics emphasizing autonomy, liberation, and non-normative self-determination that, for myself and many others in the group, was a key motivating factor for our enrollment in this particular course over an increasing number of alternative avenues for studying witchcraft online.[12] The content of questions and comments during Q&A sessions and across Discord discussion channels suggest that the demographics of Witch School participants reflected that of the shop's local clientele with relatively diverse representation across the gender and racial spectrum—the result, perhaps, of the shop's public alignment with intersectional inclusivity and social justice, as well as its stated mission to create a secure and inclusive environment where people from diverse backgrounds and varying levels of experience can engage in a journey of spiritual exploration, learning, and personal growth.[13]

Witch School takes a dramaturgical approach to the teaching of modern witchcraft. It describes its goal as offering inspiration, resources, means, and the foundations that enable people to form their own individual practice, path, or tradition: "the Witch's Arsenal," a constellation of tools and techniques through which one may feel empowered to *do* witchcraft.[14] Witchcraft is presented as an explicitly active practice, not a passive state of being. There is no *witch* without the *craft*. Witchcraft is not about what one is but *what one does*. It is about taking action and doing something. This active, dramaturgical approach to modern witchcraft—in its insistence on magic as being not a question of belief, but of access—conditions the possibility for a queer feminist witchcraft practice through which practitioners can access power and take control of their lives. "Being a witch is being autonomous," Dakota insists. "That's the whole point. That's how we draw power. We are defying the patriarchy, we are defying the submissive norm."[15]

DISAPPEARING ACTS: PURIFICATION AND PROTECTION RITES

Modern Western witchcraft seeks as its goal the alteration of one's circumstance in accordance with one's will. Witches manifest this goal through ritual, using particular dramaturgical structures and techniques to provide immateriality with presence. Somewhat paradoxically, witchcraft's ritual dramaturgies are predicated on absence and loss. In this chapter, I investigate purification and protection rites specifically as examples of witchcraft ritual practice located, always, in action at the crossroads of exposure and loss—in order to explain something about the act of performatively conjuring presence into being in the particular context of witchcraft and magic. I then conclude with a brief discussion about modern witchcraft in the context of the pandemic, reflecting upon its significance as a set of dramaturgical techniques and structures that offer people motivation and means of living and acting in these still-unfolding, strange times.

In practice, modern Western witchcraft may take a number of forms, but a co-constitutive dynamic of absence and presence, secrecy and exposure, is key to its efficacy. The example I focus on here—purification and protection rites—belongs to a category of performance I call *disappearing acts*: ritual practices that engage magic through structures and techniques predicated on loss and absence but performed as/through rites of exposure. Operating at the crossroads of exposure and loss, these practices illustrate witchcraft's dramaturgical capacities for "keeping hidden things hidden while at the same time revealing them, [and for] keeping secret things secret while displaying them."[16] Because the essential material with which witchcraft deals is indeed *im*material, invisible matters that are thus always to an extent secret matters, always hidden, one can experience witchcraft's magic through some form of mimetic simulation, a "skilled revelation of skilled concealment."[17]

Witch School presents purification as "any process of rendering something pure, i.e., clean of foreign elements and/or pollution."[18] In witchcraft, purification is often encountered with regard to spiritual hygiene. Purification rites are used in both the maintenance and protection of one's own spiritual health, as well as prior to undergoing major rituals and before and/or after certain forms of spellwork. The ritual homework assignment for performing purification and protection rites took the form of corporeal cleansing. Preparation included first using astrological correspondences to determine timing and the appropriate herbs to use. A purification herb is brewed into a ritual bath and floor wash, and the protection herb is ground and powdered using a mortar and pestle.[19] The performance of the ritual unfolds through several steps, customized to one's taste, creativity, and circumstance, including the dressing and lighting of a candle, the recitation of incantation or prayers, the application of the brew, and the drying and anointing of the body. This process is repeated for three nights, incorporating the floor wash to cleanse one's space and passing the smoke of protective herbs over the body at its end.

As a practice of spiritual hygiene, purification is a matter of maintenance and must be performed regularly ("One does not shower once and then never again"). Further, it "*always* carries some sort of upheaval, flux, and fallout. It's messy, it hurts, and it's not to be trifled with."[20] It is "never a cure-all" and must never be done as a solitary act. As Dakota explained it, "Nature hates a vacuum, and one is at their most tender and most vulnerable after purification." Every time one performs a purification rite, one must also follow it up with protection rites. Dakota stressed that "protection takes time and energy—*it is work*! And it is work which must be renewed regularly." Continuing their discussion, they added additional gravitas to the concept of protection with a dark-humored reminder that "if you're looking for one abiding truth in the universe, it is chaos, entropy, disease, you know, degradation and death. These are eternal, they will always be true, they will always be there." They continued:

> Even as we speak . . . our universe is flying apart at faster and faster rates . . . we're hurdling closer to solar death which will spell out oblivion for everything in our galaxy . . . before that happens, the Andromeda galaxy might collide with ours. If you go out to a place without light pollution and you look up into the night sky on most nights . . . you can actually see the Andromeda galaxy hurdling toward us on a crash-course that will absolutely destroy the evidence that we ever existed. So if you're looking for like "The Divine Plan" and all of it and everything being ordered and you know, surefooted, and making you feel nice and snug, you know comfy and snug, there's really not a lot of evidence there for that so, the point is that we age, we die, *and that's just how magic works as well, you know, there's no spell that lasts forever. Everything falls apart eventually. So you are going to have to make sure that when it comes to magic, uh, protection, that you re-up on it, okay?*[21]

The gravity around which purification and protection rites were introduced seemed to garner significant enthusiasm from participants who were especially active in discussion over the following week, checking in with each other and sharing their processes. It was also the first ritual homework assignment with explicit instructions, presented with a sense of urgency and seriousness that bred anticipation for what would happen as well as a feeling of risk for what *could* happen. Dakota's mentions of "how not to fuck yourself up," imminent "solar death," and the "world burning," amid other ambiguous references to danger and harm, produced an ambiance of risk that, coupled with an alertness to minute sensations in the body, could generate an awareness of presence in the affect of anticipation. In this highly charged context that ritual produces, experiences of the immaterial take on a palpable immediacy; its presence becomes viscerally articulated and accessible.

Through the ritual's sculpted silence, the thrill of fear arises, generated by a sense of stakes attached to one's choices when partaking in the risky business of forbidden knowledge. This fear is accompanied by a state of hyper-attuned alertness in the practitioner through which the presence of the immaterial, of active, invisible, magical forces at work becomes perceptible. Its presence is realized not by any particular content of the rituals themselves, not through words written or chanted, nor through the particular herbs or candles used, but through the dramatic moment it induces, the experience itself of engaging in witchcraft through the labor of working incantation, herbs, and candles. The magical reality evoked when practicing witchcraft derives not from following a prescriptive and sacrosanct ritual structure but from the experiential process of interaction between the practitioner and their material and immaterial interlocutors within an elevated, affectively charged, and activated ritual context.

Within the ritual context of corporeal cleansing, certain dramaturgical techniques produce particular effects that register in and through practitioners' bodies. The body serves as an interactive locus for magic that provides a sensitive, enfleshed interface between material and immaterial worlds. The skin itself, Michel Serres writes, "is a variety of contingency: in it, through it, with it, the world and my body touch each other, the feeling and the felt, it defines their common edge. Contingency means common tangency: in it the world and the body intersect and caress each other. . . . Skin intervenes between several things in the world and makes them mingle."[22] The body mediates in these rituals, but it is not itself a medium. It serves instead as an activated environment for interaction, for a tangled comingling of material and immaterial sensations that register as spatialized affect and directional, ephemeral movement: letting go, releasing, lessening, and losing.

As it enacts rites, the body becomes an instrument for attuning and attending to ephemeral sensations that evidence magic at work as a moving-through/from/out. Many participants, for example, reported physically experiencing either a shifting of weight and energy (heavy to light, lethargy to vigor) or a displacement (through biological processes that involve the excretion of bodily fluids, such as sweating and crying).[23] They describe a sense of "heaviness lifted," of being "less weighed down," "darkness away," "feeling lighter, like light itself," or, as one participant put it, "a sparky zip feeling," accompanied by "abnormal elation." Others expressed a sense of exhaustion as evidence of work (physical and spiritual), of feeling "drained," as if having undergone a "spiritual purging," "purging the dead weight," "purging spiritual gunk."[24] Someone shared that during the rites they "felt so exhausted, at times near crying, at times nauseous/heavy in the body but lightheaded, like releasing toxins, in a way." Another admitted to having "sobbed like a child . . . literally like a child . . . flooded." Others described "bawling in the tub," "howling tears," "so much sweating," "drenched sheets." Dakota affirmed these experiences as especially common at the beginning of purification rites, offering the reasoning that "you're shaking a lot of shit loose."[25]

Purification rites perform transformation as a disappearing act through the material actions of corporeal cleansing in which the body itself becomes a site for the experience of magic. It operates from the presumption of excess "spiritual gunk" or "pollution" attached to the body, what Mary Douglas would describe as "dirt out of place," that can be "purged" through ritual cleansing.[26] Douglas argues that this idea of pollution "is a reaction to protect cherished principles and categories of contradiction."[27] One way that we respond when confronted with the unclear or uncertain is to address it directly, with intention, and to attempt to establish a new framework of reality capable of accommodating it. Purification rites are one such way modern witchcraft attempts to construct and enact new frames and patterns in order to work with(in) the uncertainty of immaterial matters.

The process of disappearance as a method of elimination that structures purification rites locates magic's "something happening" as a performance of movement across the borders of the flesh, from the inside out, "downward and outward." Biological processes like excessive sweating and crying, of bodily fluids being expelled from the body, conjure up discourses of the grotesque, a poetic category that, according to Kenneth Burke, "focuses in mysticism" and often emerges in contexts of confusion, ambiguity, and oxymorons. Burke explains that the grotesque reflects instances in which "confusion in the forensic pattern gives more prominence to the subjective elements of imagery than to the objective, or public, elements."[28] As practitioners use the imagery of purging and excess within these private rituals to designate evidence of release and cleansing, we can recognize the way in which the grotesque functions discursively to structure experience through "the symbolizing of parallels, 'correspondences,' whereby simple notions of identity become confused, as one thing is seen in terms of *something else*."[29] These rituals of spiritual cleansing are seen in terms of physical cleansing; the spirit is cleansed in terms of the body. Attunement to sensations of weight and shifting mass assign a kind of material locatability and particularity to the ambiguous, complex, inarticulate notion of spiritual toxicity that practitioners are then rendered capable of "working through" and "releasing."

Purification rites operate as a process of letting go, of loss and release, but always with the presumption that one must and will "begin again." It is a practice of spiritual hygiene that requires maintenance by return. We might consider what Dakota describes as necessary "re-upping" of such spellwork as evidence for how these rituals operate as "restored behavior," or what Richard Schechner describes as performances that "offer to both individuals and groups the chance to become someone else 'for the time being,' or the chance to become what they once were. Or even, and most often, to re-become what they never were."[30] Through the lens of restored behavior, we might argue that the purification rite "becomes the text" in the present moment, becomes itself the transformation. Following Walter Benjamin's logic, the rite-as-text operates as a language-itself, not by what it contains, but by its capacity; not by the specific (im)material it transforms but by its ability to transform.

Purification rites are a performance of transformation itself, "actualized" through the body around a myth of spiritual pollution, one that is presented ambiguously, shrouded in secretism, while remaining generally uncontested.[31] The ritual restored behavior of the sweating, crying, exhausting, draining, excessive, expelling grotesque body is an actualization of transformation that must operate according to its own constructed pattern of reality and maintain its own conditions for perpetuation, re-evidencing belief in an always already spiritually toxic body through restored behavior as "a means of collecting behavior and 'keeping' it for the performance-to-be."[32] Further, because the rituals always already necessitate simulation of some kind, they contain within them, structurally and dramaturgically, some aspect of loss, of absence, of failure, of incommensurable excess. This loss at the center of witchcraft's workings feeds into its own futurity as a queer modality of striving.[33] *"Never underestimate cumulative magic,"* Dakota insisted in the final session; *"Do not settle for the devil you know. Ambition is key."*[34]

SUMMONING SOMETHING TO BE DONE AND MAKING DO

Driving this chapter has been an interest in looking at specific rituals not for their content or meaning per se, but for how it is that rituals work and what it is that they do. What do certain ritual practices, their dramaturgical techniques and frameworks, afford, make opportune, make doable, make possible? Writing about and within this current historic moment also means extending this line of thinking further to speculate on why it is that so many people are seeking out witchcraft right now. What feelings of potentiality and hope might these ritual techniques offer people in the midst of so much darkness, loss, grief, and despair? In his writing about performances with/of/from loss, André Lepecki asks: "How does one *access* loss, how does one act in the face and fact of loss, how does one respond to endless events of violence, of untimely deaths, of fear, of passion, of the mundane in the human?"[35] How do we deal when "fear and loss loom"? The answer for many—far more than we will ever know—in 2020 was witchcraft. Magic, I'll incant once more, is not a question of belief but of access.[36] My analysis of disappearance in modern witchcraft ritual suggests that one both produces and accesses magic (a performative of potentiality and hope) by way of actively acknowledging and accessing loss—of *doing something* with and to it.

We return again to the very first day of Witch School and the opening topic: "What Is Witchcraft?" As Dakota began presenting, they were interrupted by what sounded like waves of wailing emergency vehicle sirens outside their window. The scene went something like this:

DAKOTA: *(with a confident but pleasant tone, as if reading a storybook to a kindergarten classroom)* Let's get started. What is witchcraft? Well to make it plain and simple, there are as many ways to be a witch as there are people in the world. Witchcraft is . . .

(*Sound of loud sirens blare outside, interrupting.*)

(*Off-script shouting*) This is New York. You hear this? This is New York.

Ohhhhh here we go . . .

(*The sirens grow louder.*)

(*A large sigh, then*) Mmmhmm, right? Yes. Okay, umm, witchcraft is so unbelievably complex in its various interpretations that it is profoundly simple. Witchcraft is a practice, not a belief.

(*An underscore of sirens continues, irregular and unpredictable, as they continue*)

More than anything, it's a term used to indicate what one does, not why they do it. The only shared belief or ideology among all practitioners of witchcraft is that their actions, their spells, their methods will result in some tangible effect.

(*Siren volume increases, as if its source has multiplied. Interrupting*)

(*Shouting*) THAT IT IS WORTH DOING!

Are you fucking kidding me with this right now? Not a peep in Bushwick until I start this class.

(*Sirens plus honking. Mars energy emerges. Fury.*)

Oh my GOD! Somethin' better burn down if it's going to be this much noise.

(*Quieting down*)

With that being said, for the modern witch, it is perhaps best to address witchcraft as possibly the highest manifestation of one's autonomy, agency, and personhood. What does that mean?

(*Sirens returning with a vengeance.*)

Here we go again! Is Brooklyn on fucking fire? What the fuck is going on tonight?

Anyway . . . To be Witch says I'm in the driver's seat.

(*Struggles to shout above sirens against which Dakota's voice seems to wage war, resiliently and insistently, with each word.*)

I. DICTATE. MY. OWN. FATE.

I'm going to shape MY LIFE according to MY DESIRES, my WANTS, my needs.

Having been a solitary practitioner for many years, I confess that I initially decided to enroll in Witch School in search of some kind of distraction or escape, a distancing from the pandemic's dark, relentless, forbidding reality that left me and those I love still grieving, fearful, debilitated, with shades of compounded grief and anxiety, both specific and abstract; worn down by the unrelenting threat and unknowing that seem to have rendered everything feeling quite impossible. We are all still exhausted. Understanding dramaturgy as a conceptual and aesthetic response to need, "a fusion between action and work that operates in a specifically catalytic mode," I remain intrigued by how people are *doing* right now.[37] How they are feeling, but also, how they are living, functioning, *making do*. It is clear that the exigencies of this moment in history continue to beg for dramaturgical intervention. Some kind of how. In early 2020, I wondered about what dramaturgies might emerge in response to these unprecedented times; I was curious about what contemporary performances of life (and death) in this moment would look like. Magic and witchcraft need to be part of this conversation.

From the very first day of Witch School, as the scene above captures, the reality of the specter of the pandemic was kept unrelentingly in view. And yet hundreds of witches across the United States and beyond, a great majority of them healers and artists, teachers, EMTs, and other frontline workers alike, managed to successfully carry forth with its ritual teachings and workings, each trying to cope, trying to "summon a fuck to give" so they could keep going.[38] The force of modern witchcraft begins with what its practitioners are bringing into it—the expectations, desires, fears, and anxieties of everyday life—and develops by creating with and among these concerns its own dramaturgically generated tensions and ambiguities around fear, death, and loss. But it is how these rituals come to *matter* to people right now, I would argue, that makes them most compelling. Indeed, what matters has less to do with any symbolic meaning or content rituals contain, and far more to do with the ways in which they formally catalyze movement, producing for people a much needed "spark." "It's really just rewarding to go through the motions," one person shared, and to "feel . . . motivated to do anything these days."

The particular practice of modern Western witchcraft I encountered as a participant in Catland's Witch School is worthy of attention as an archive of performances of life amid loss in 2020. The extensive ephemeral evidence I drew from in my analysis of what I called "disappearing acts" testifies to actual ritual techniques that people are increasingly seeking and actively practicing in these times as a means of coping. These rituals provide means for people to "bear it all," while also bearing witness to this moment. Bearing witness, Derrida argues, is not about proving the nature of something so much as evidencing that something is happening, is being lived through. It gives testament to life itself, proclaiming, "I swear that I saw, I heard, I touched, I felt, I was present."[39] As Michel Serres writes, "I carry, therefore I am."[40]

Many described their practice as having "rekindled" or as having "lit a fire" under them, of feeling "enlivened . . . in such a magical way," finding "a spark of energy and vigor [that is] seeping into all other areas of my life." I believe that witchcraft, in its tangle with reality, its offering of structure, of motivation, its refusal to concede in the face of death, danger, failure, in its capacity for doing and dreaming in the dark, allows people to access a sense of magic through loss; and by doing so, it capacitates them to act, somehow, in service of a life worth living. "It gives me life," one practitioner confessed, "one of the best things to happen to me during this horrible time we are living in."

NOTES

1. The terms *witchcraft*, *witch*, *magic*, and *ritual* are complex, multivalent, and ambiguous terms whose formations of meaning are highly conditioned and produced by their usage. For the purposes of this chapter, I employ them according to their emic value as used and defined by practitioners in the specific context of Catland's Witch School in 2020. "Modern Western witchcraft" is a similarly complex and contested designation that I employ similarly throughout this chapter as it is used and variously understood and defined (or left ambiguous and undefined) by practitioners in this specific context. While there was a clear articulation of Witch School's approach to modern Western witchcraft as being decidedly non-Wiccan in focus, it did not exclude Wiccan practices and beliefs from its purview. That there is no official and definitive specification of or within this broader category in the context of Witch School is a reflection of its necessary capaciousness for including a wide variety of solitary practitioners with vastly differing identities, understandings, and approaches to their personal practice under its umbrella.
2. Quotes taken from a sample of comments posted to the private Discord server forum discussion. "Witch School 2020," Discord, October 2020.
3. Catland Books has closed since the time of writing. During its operation it was co-owned by Dakota St. Claire and author and occultist Melissa Jayne Madara. Dakota has since started Apokrypha (co-founded and operated with Bee Sampson), where they continue to offer Witch School online. Melissa has since developed Moon Cult, where they offer digital resources and classes on magic, traditional witchcraft, and botanical arts.

4   For a description of Dakota's public hexing ritual performances Hex Trump and Hex Brett Kavanaugh, see Goldberg, "Season of the Witch"; Fink, "Witches Hosting Hex on Brett Kavanaugh, Rapists, Patriarchy"; Donovan, "How Witchcraft Is Empowering Queer and Trans Young People."

5   St. Clare, "Week I: The Basics."

6   Which Dakota stresses is "not the same thing as an endorsement." St. Clare, "Witch School 2020," Discord, November 3, 2020.

7   The designations of "modern Western syncretic" and "ethical traditional" reflect participants' understanding of Witch School curriculum as drawing upon a wide range of traditions, practices, and beliefs but with an emphasis on cultural context and ethical responsibility. This involved, for instance, discussion regarding the ethical sourcing and dispersal of herbs and ritual accoutrements, open and closed practices, trans-inclusive frameworks for ancestor veneration, colonial legacies of racialized magical discourses and more.

8   Chas Clifton categorizes as "traditional witchcraft" the practices of self-styled practitioners who draw inspiration from early modern historical materials, including witch trial narratives in their ritual practice such as the idea of witches' sabbaths, notions of pacts, flying, and communication with the dead. Both Dakota and Witch School participants mostly disagree with this categorization. Rather, traditional witchcraft is understood as the embracing of aspects of magical practice for which there is efficacious precedent through experimentation and documentation over time. See Clifton, "Witches Still Fly: Or Do They?"

9   See, for example, Pike, *Earthly Bodies, Magical Selves*; Salomonsen, *Enchanted Feminism*; Magliocco, *Witching Culture*; Ezzy, *Sex, Death and Witchcraft*. Up until this point, such work has tended to focus on specific communities within the broader category of neo-paganism rather than on witchcraft as a heterogenous community of practitioners. Recent scholarship has signaled an interdisciplinary turn toward the study of non-Wiccan witchcraft identities, communities, and practices. Notably lacking in the literature is qualitative attention to witchcraft performed by a growing number of solitary practitioners who do not undergo initiation rites into any particular tradition but who "create their own path."

10 In its shift online due to the pandemic, Catland's Witch School provides a rare opportunity to research modern witches gathering together in large numbers to learn and practice ritual. The participant group is not only large (more than three hundred) but also very mixed in terms of location (well distributed across the United States, with some international representation as well), experience, motivation, and orientation to the practice, factors that may lend my analysis broader significance for discussions of modern witchcraft and the reenchantment of public culture.

11   Discord is a popular online social media platform application built for community gathering with video, voice, and group and direct messaging exchange capabilities. It uses the term "servers" to designate independent digital spaces for conversation and exchange that it hosts.

12   St. Clare, "Week I: The Basics."

13   The Witch School curriculum was not explicitly targeted toward any particular demographic and provided cultural context, ethical frameworks, and resources for a wide variety of practices. Lessons touched upon everything from Hellenic polytheism and Catholic saintcraft to Haitian Voudo and Mexican *brujería*, while critically framed through an understanding that certain practices, for a plethora of historical and cultural reasons, are either "open" or "closed" to certain individuals or may require a process of initiation. Ritual homework was assigned in such a way that allowed individual practitioners to make it their own (for example, by creating personal correspondence tables for ritual spellcrafting, or propitiating deities or ancestral spirits from one's own culture and traditions). Catland Books, "About," accessed October 18, 2020, http://www.catlandbooks.com/pages/about. This page is no longer available.

14   Catland Books, "WITCH SCHOOL ONLINE," event description, accessed October 18, 2020, http://www.catlandbooks.com/events-calendar/2020/10/3/witch-school-online. This page is no longer available.

15   Donovan, "How Witchcraft Is Empowering Queer and Trans Young People."

16   Taussig, "Viscerality, Faith, and Skepticism," 474.

17   Goldman, *The Mouth of Heaven*, 102, as cited in Taussig, "Viscerality, Faith, and Skepticism," 474.

18   St. Clare, "Week I: The Basics."

19   In my field notes, I reflected on the process of grinding herbs with a mortar and pestle as a technique for "powering" magic: "The effort and labor, the physical action, the sensory experience of the smells as they release, the circular rhythm and even the pain of the repetition. Some things are way harder to grind of course, but the sweat and toil feeds into the work. It's kind of a sacrificial exchange for me. The work makes it work, even if it doesn't completely work. There's always bits that don't grind and hold out."

20   St. Clare, "What Is Purification Magik?" (slide), "Week I: The Basics."

21   St. Clare, off-script speech, "Week I: The Basics" (emphasis added).

22   Serres, *The Five Senses*, 80.

23   These effects are reflected in hundreds of comments made from across a wide sample (more than fifty) of participants on the Witch School Discord discussion channels as well as in live chat exchanges during class sessions. My own physical experience of these rituals supports these general patterns of experience as communicated by the community.

24   "More than just physical exhaustion, [but] a spiritual purge, draining away of the negative to bring forth the positive." "Witch School 2020," Discord, October 17, 2020.

25 St. Clare, "Witch School 2020," Discord, October 20, 2020.
26 Douglas, *Purity and Danger*.
27 Douglas, *Purity and Danger*, 38.
28 Burke, *Attitudes toward History*, 60.
29 Burke, *Attitudes toward History*, 62.
30 Schechner, "Restoration of Behavior," 2–45.
31 Schechner reminds us that "myths are word-versions of rituals"; the two dialectically inform one another (Schechner, "Restoration of Behavior," 5).
32 Schechner, "Restoration of Behavior," 3.
33 One can further theorize these practices more explicitly through the lens of queer futurity and a politics of hope.
34 St. Clare, "Week V: Divination and Where We Go from Here."
35 Lepecki, "Testimony for the Living (Or, Metabolic Theater)."
36 St. Clare, "Week I: The Basics."
37 Georgelou, Protopapa, and Theodoridou, "Why Dramaturgy Today," 18–20.
38 Quoted from a meme shared on Discord on the last day of Witch School.
39 Derrida, *Sovereignties in Question*, 75–76.
40 Serres, *The Five Senses*, 320.

BIBLIOGRAPHY

Primary Sources

St. Clare, Dakota. "Week I: The Basics." Catland Books Witch School Online, October 3, 2020. Zoom. 3 hours. Jottings from synchronous live class and transcribed recording.

St. Clare, Dakota. "Week II: The Building Blocks." Catland Books Witch School Online, October 10, 2020. Zoom. 3 hours. Jottings from synchronous live class and transcribed recording.

St. Clare, Dakota. "Week V: Divination and Where We Go from Here." Catland Books Witch School Online, November 28, 2020. Zoom. 3 hours. Jottings from synchronous live class and transcribed recording.

Secondary Sources

Burke, Kenneth. *Attitudes toward History*. Boston: Beacon, 1937.

Clifton, Chas S. "Witches Still Fly: Or Do They? Traditional Witches, Wiccans, and Flying Ointment." In *Magic and Witchery in the Modern West*, edited by Shai Feraro and Ethan Doyle White, 223–44. London: Palgrave Macmillan, 2019.

Derrida, Jacques. *Sovereignties in Question: The Poetics of Paul Celan*. Edited by Thomas Dutoit and Outi Pasanen. New York: Fordham University Press, 2005.

Donovan, Moira. "How Witchcraft Is Empowering Queer and Trans Young People." *Vice*, August 14, 2015. https://www.vice.com/en_us/article/zngyv9/queer-trans-people-take-aim-at-the-patriarchy-through-witchcraft.

Douglas, Mary. *Purity and Danger: An Analysis of Concepts of Pollution and Taboo*. New York: Praeger, 1966.

Ezzy, Douglas. *Sex, Death and Witchcraft: A Contemporary Pagan Festival*. London: Bloomsbury, 2014.

Fink, Jenni. "Witches Hosting Hex on Brett Kavanaugh, Rapists, Patriarchy at New York Ritual." *Newsweek*, October 12, 2018. https://www.newsweek.com/witches-hosting-hex-brett-kavanaugh-rapists-patriarchy-new-york-ritual-1167843.

Georgelou, Konstantina, Efrosini Protopapa, and Danae Theodoridou. "Why Dramaturgy Today." In *The Practice of Dramaturgy: Working on Actions in Performance*, edited by Konstantina Georgelou, Efrosini Protopapa, and Danae Theodoridou, 11–24. Amsterdam: Antennae Valiz, 2017.

Goldberg, Michelle. "Season of the Witch." *New York Times*. November 3, 2017. https://www.nytimes.com/2017/11/03/opinion/witches-occult-comeback.html.

Goldman, Irving. *The Mouth of Heaven: An Introduction to Kwakiutl Religious Thought*. New York: John Wiley, 1975.

Lepecki, André. "Testimony for the Living (Or, Metabolic Theater): André Lepecki on Rabih Mroué." Walker Art Center, March 25, 2019. https://walkerart.org/magazine/andre-lepecki-rabih-mroue.

Magliocco, Sabina. *Witching Culture: Folklore and Neo-Paganism in America*. Philadelphia: University of Pennsylvania Press, 2004.

Pike, Sarah M. *Earthly Bodies, Magical Selves: Contemporary Pagans and the Search for Community*. Berkeley: University of California Press, 2000.

Salomonsen, Jone. *Enchanted Feminism: The Reclaiming Witches of San Francisco*. London: Routledge, 2002.

Schechner, Richard. "Restoration of Behavior." *Studies in Visual Communication* 7, no. 3 (1981): 2–45.

Serres, Michel. *The Five Senses: A Philosophy of Mingled Bodies*. Translated by Margaret Sankey and Peter Cowley. London: Continuum, 2008.

Taussig, Michael. "Viscerality, Faith, and Skepticism: Another Theory of Magic." *Hau: Journal of Ethnographic Theory* 6, no. 3 (2016): 453–83.

Twenty-seven · BERNADETTE BARTON

We Are All Witches: My Pagan Journey

It was 2008, and I was meeting a good friend's new guy, "Edgar," at a coffee shop in Kentucky. Edgar was visiting from Colorado, where he was enrolled at Naropa University in Boulder, a Buddhist-inspired institution of higher education that fascinated me. We quickly began talking about religion like old friends. As we discussed the main belief systems characterizing Eastern and Western religious paradigms, Edgar asked me, "Which one do you identify with?" I blinked, took a moment to consider, and broke into a big smile, "Neither," I said, "I am a Wiccan." I had had an unusual religious upbringing mixing equal parts immersion in Catholicism and a Hindu-esque spiritual path, complements of each parent, but I had found and embraced paganism on my own during my journey toward becoming a feminist. I had created an altar in every living space I had had since I was twenty-one, had gone on a retreat led by Starhawk on the Big Island of Hawaiʻi, had participated in many Wiccan circles, had sported goddess jewelry, had read tarot cards, had adorned my home in goddess art and symbols, and had read many texts of feminist spirituality; but this pivotal conversation with Edgar was the first time I perceived paganism as its *own* religious framework, as big and juicy and important as Christianity or Judaism or Hinduism, and not just as my little spiritual hobby that I rarely discussed.

Reflecting on this conversation, I realized that Christian messaging—dating back centuries—that witchcraft and paganism were something to fear and shun had taught me to keep quiet about my Wiccan practices and inclinations. While increasing numbers of people identify as pagan and Wiccan, witchcraft is largely misunderstood, and some still cast witches as the spawn of Satan, especially in the US Bible Belt, where I live. The word *witch* conjures an ancient hag stirring a cauldron, a one-dimensional storybook stereotype invoking an ugly, secluded, dangerous, female "other." Like many stereotypes generated by majority groups to control members, the trope of "witch" muddies our perception of lived experience. It also renders invisible our daily pagan practices, denies paganism the reverence and respect given other religious paradigms, and thus undermines our ability to deliberately practice it to enhance our lives. It is an especially egregious example of brainwashing: even I, a feminist witch, did not accord paganism the reverence it deserves; and I am not the only one. Paganism is hiding in everyone's plain sight because, as I will demonstrate in the following pages, *we are all witches*. By this I mean that most humans daily engage in a lengthy list of pagan practices, in other words, undertaking actions made with the intent to manifest something in one's life.

Since this pivotal conversation with Edgar, I have written a book exploring the consequences of conservative Christianity on queer people in the Bible Belt and taught classes on religion, sexuality, and mysticism. I regularly teach a unit on paganism in my religion class, and I lecture on "Why We Need the Goddess" in gender classes. I find over and over again that a significant minority of students (usually 5 to 10 percent) also identify as pagan, and almost everyone enjoys learning about it. In this autobiographical chapter, I briefly describe the origins and characteristics of paganism (and its most popular branch, Wicca), and I share details of my spiritual journey toward uncovering my inner pagan. Mine is just one such tale of awakening, and I offer it here in hopes that it may serve as a model to others. From shaking hands to blessing someone when they sneeze, wearing the colors of one's sports team at a game, giving a toast, sending flowers, making a home altar, and wild dancing at a club, this speculative essay shows how you and I *already* engage in a rich variety of Wiccan rituals in daily life.

WHAT IS PAGANISM?

A 2014 Pew study found that 1 to 1.5 million Americans identify as Wiccan or pagan.[1] As some of the chapters in this volume explore, modern paganism blends historical, nature-based practices and reimagined rituals in a polytheistic framework. Paganism is an umbrella term sheltering a range of geographically distinct earth-based traditions like Shamanism, Druidism, Santeria, Wicca, and melded beliefs like Christo-paganism that draw on ancient symbolism pre-dating all the world's religions. For example, Venus figurines found throughout Europe date as far back as 20,000 BC,[2] whereas Hinduism, the earth's oldest religion, originated approximately in the fifteenth century BC. Wicca is the branch of paganism that British writer Gerald Gardner introduced in the United Kingdom in the mid-twentieth century and that Starhawk, a US ecofeminist, further developed; it spread mostly throughout the West.[3] Wicca is a twentieth-century new religious movement blending ancient practices with new elements.[4] Of pagans, 50 percent identify as Wiccan. Much like Baptist churches are a denomination within Christianity, Wicca is a branch of paganism.

I found feminism and Wicca at the same time—in the late 1980s—through the writings of Starhawk and those of passionate second-wave feminists.[5] I had always felt alienated as a girl, and later as a woman, from the embedded sexism in Western and Eastern religious frameworks. In the Christian and Hindu paths I had explored as an adolescent and young adult, both faiths continually ranked men over women, linking maleness with the Divine (Jesus and God in Christianity) or tracing male lineages spanning centuries (Masters and Gurus in Hinduism). I longed for the sacred feminine before I had words to explain what was missing in my experience of religion. I looked for it as a teen at my Catholic high school, attending a Legion of Mary after-school meeting with a friend. This is an international organization of people who serve God under the banner of Mary; but, at my school, the Legion of Mary was a girls' club only. Upon seeing me, the club's faculty sponsor, Sister Dennisita, a tiny nun in her eighties wearing a full habit, pointed at me and said, "Mary has chosen you." After this pronouncement, I felt I really had no choice but to return; who was I to argue with Mary? We met once a week as a group, lit candles, shared good deeds we had done, and prayed the rosary. While I enjoyed worshipping Mary, I could not help but be aware she wielded little to no influence over matters of church leadership and theology.

When I questioned the absence of the feminine divine in religious dogma at my Catholic church and high school, or when I questioned the adults practicing Catholicism and Radha Soami (the Hindu path my father followed), most simply gaslit me, implying that I was silly and immature to ask such questions. They said that with more years and acquired wisdom, the "truth" would reveal itself. Of course, there are pockets of egalitarianism in every faith. Catholics can pray to Mary (as I did) and to a host of female saints, while Hinduism is polytheistic, with both gods and goddesses. I also knew of feminists working to reimagine Christianity and Judaism to affirm women,[6] but this did not appeal to me. After trying and failing to find a female-affirming path through patriarchal religiosity, I suspended my engagement in any religious paradigm until I found Wicca.

Wicca is itself *inherently* feminist, which is to say that feminism—the political, social, and personal perspective to respect all persons, while working toward equality and bodily autonomy—well aligns with the foundational pagan belief that everything is sacred. In other words, a faith that perceives all living things as sacred must include the feminine divine. Wicca is also a set of practices that women are as or more likely than men to lead. Moreover, there is no hierarchy, no sin, and no damnation in Wicca. As I will shortly elaborate, Wicca is a belief system prescribing actions that revere the natural world, do no harm, and empower people. Finding Wicca felt like coming home.

While pagan practices and beliefs are as diverse as the people who engage in them, pagans share the following common features:[7] One, paganism includes most characteristics people typically associate with a religion. It has a theology that answers questions about life and death, and participants gather for rituals and observe a sacred year. Two, paganism has no central hierarchy or dogma. As such, pagans are spiritually diverse and syncretic (they blend ideas from two or more spiritual paradigms). Indeed, many pagans deliberately incorporate scientific, metaphysical, and mystical insights and worldviews in their practice. Three, paganism stresses personal responsibility for one's beliefs and behaviors. This means that modern paganism encourages adherents to develop their individual understanding of and relationship with the Divine while thoughtfully aligning their pagan beliefs with worldly actions. Four, pagans see all parts of the universe as sacred and as having some form of consciousness. In this way, pagans prefer pantheistic (the idea that all the world together makes up the Divine) and animistic (every part of creation is sacred) understandings of the Divine over theistic (the belief that a god or gods created the universe) ones, though elements of nature are often represented in monotheistic (the Great Goddess), duotheistic (a goddess and a god) and polytheistic forms (mother earth, father sky, the ocean goddess, Diana, et al.). Five, pagans believe that everything living has an energetic signature one can access through intent and ritual, and that all parts of the living universe can communicate with itself. Making magic entails encouraging parts of the living world to cooperate to manifest certain outcomes. Pagans believe anyone can guide universal energies or, in other words, do magic through specific rituals that raise energy and focus attention.

EVERYDAY MAGIC

It is October of 2023, and I am beginning a new research project on the nature of alignment. I find myself floundering as I conceptualize the work, struggling to corral my ideas so that data collection is efficient and illuminating. Remembering a similar situation from twenty or more years earlier, when I was interpreting and writing up my dissertation, I decide to do a little magic, that is, engage cosmic energies with intention and attention.[8] I shuffle through a decades-old tarot deck and pull out the major arcana cards of the Magician and the Hanged Man. These I place on my altar in a prominent place. The Magician is a card of creation, and the Hanged Man, to me, represents an ability to change one's perception, to see multiple angles of something, to look afresh upon a phenomenon. In other words, I believe if I metaphorically hang upside down, something new will present itself. Perhaps it was only a coincidence or the placebo effect, but within hours of activating the Magician and Hanged Man, I decide on a path forward with my work, write up and release a call for participants, and begin scheduling interviews.

As explained, pagans believe the living universe can communicate with all parts of itself, and when parts choose to cooperate, this is magic. Starhawk, feminist witch, progressive activist, and one of the mothers of twentieth-century Wicca, defines magic as "the art of changing consciousness at will."[9] Gerald Gardner described magic as "the art of getting results."[10] What might a ritual look like? To do magic one starts with an intent, something that one wishes to create. Pagans then raise energy by casting a circle, dancing, drumming, honoring the four elements in the corresponding four directions (East, West, South, North), and by representing the intent in some symbolic form for the sacred universe to manifest. For example, my wife and I regularly host a raucous winter solstice party, on the longest night of the year, to celebrate the returning light and to burn off that which those gathered no longer need. In addition to dancing and karaoke, we also have a fire, and I supply the guests with small slips of paper and encourage those interested to write down elements of their lives they would like to release and to place the slips in the fire. During the 2018 midterm election, we hosted a watch party and offered guests a place to write their most hopeful visions for the future, seeking to draw on some sacred energy to create change.

It is likely you also have a place where you store things that are important to you—keys, photos of loved ones, money, jewelry—or where they naturally gather, both inside and outside. Pagans deliberately create such places: surfaces on which one arranges meaningful objects that honor one's life and focus one's energy. We call these altars. I purposely built my first altar in my early twenties, when I was teaching English as a second language in Tokyo, Japan. Unmoored in a country where I did not speak the language, my altar helped anchor me as me. Since then, whenever I move to a new home, my first act of unpacking is to set up my altar. The longer I live in a home, the more altars spring up throughout the space. Not only do I have a primary altar on my bedroom dresser; I also create little sacred spaces in every room as well as in my front and backyards. Altars concentrate divine energy, value that which is important to me, and are a way to express creative spiritually. On my altar, I place spiritual symbols, jewelry, shells, crystals, angel cards, candles, goddess figurines, and other meaningful memorabilia. For example, one such item is a battered rubber cow my mother saved for me, the first-ever gift I received as a newborn from my Aunt Janet.

My wife, Anna, and I also use my altar as a vehicle for attracting specific desires. When we were first dating, Anna painted a tree of life on a bottle and gave it to me as a gift. We keep it on my altar. When we want to manifest something in our lives—to get a new job, solve a problem, find a place to live, make new friends, whatever—we write down the wishes on a piece of paper, roll it up, and place it in the bottle to let the magical universe do its part, or not. Important to the art of manifesting is that there be no ill intent, no "power over," as Starhawk theorizes. Magic is a process of bringing forth power from within to encourage patterns in energy.

Here I described my pagan altar. Members of Buddhist, Shinto, Christian, Hindu, and Yoruba faiths may also have home altars. In many parts of the United States, one will see memorials on the side of the road marking the place someone died. It may include flowers, religious symbols, statues, and messages remembering a loved one. While pagans engage in rituals like building altars knowingly and deliberately, in the pages below I argue that the act of manifesting in pagan ritual is so deeply intuitive and natural to humans that both secular and religious people engage in it with and without conscious recognition.

"KNOCKING ON WOOD"

Have you ever "knocked on wood" after saying something positive to avoid tempting fate? For example, you comment to a friend, "Wow, my car's running great" or "I'm so glad I haven't caught that bad cold" or "The weather has been perfect on our vacation," and then quickly added, "knock on wood," while tapping something wooden with your knuckles. Pagan Celts and Germans believed trees housed fairies and that one might request good luck from them, or prevent bad luck, by knocking on a tree. You have also likely blown out candles on a cake for your birthday while making a wish. Candles contain the element of fire, and the act of blowing out a flame demonstrates your intent to manifest a desire by activating the element of air. Both of these contemporary common actions, like many, many others, have pagan origins.

In our daily lives, we wear special clothes and jewelry to feel powerful and to protect ourselves; we play certain kinds of music to raise our energy if we are sleepy or to calm ourselves when agitated; and we bless our food before we eat. We relax around a fire and bring food to loved ones suffering a loss. We light candles before a meal, take off our shoes when entering certain spaces, bring flowers to mark a special occasion, hang water feeders to draw birds and bees to our backyards, get tattoos to mark meaningful life events, decorate ourselves with glamorous makeup to attract a romantic partner, watch fireworks, sing in a chorus, and kiss under the mistletoe. We shake hands and hug in greeting, wear ceremonial clothes at graduations, make New Year's resolutions, and join flames in a candle ceremony at a wedding. In doing so, we are making magic. Or, in other words, we are making a small request of universal energies to bless us with good fortune and/or to support our desired creations. Consider the following.

HOME ADVANTAGE

In Western society, a sports game is an almost entirely secular event. Yes, a team may pray before a game, and Christian players may cross themselves as they enter the field (as well as engage in many other religious rituals); but for the most part, people perceive a sporting event as materialistic, not spiritual. Let's explore the pagan elements embedded in the everyday experience of a football game (either the American or British version) to illustrate routine and ordinary pagan expressions. A live game takes place outside in a large arena. Fans dress in the colors of the team they are rooting for, many with specific signage, to show solidarity with the players and raise power for their victory. Fans also concentrate energy before a game in activities like tailgating in a parking lot or gathering at someone's home or backyard. Fans connect with old friends and make new ones, share drinks, laugh, and occasionally sing and dance. Some make small fires to stay warm. At the game, whole arenas of people come together in what sociologist Emile Durkheim calls "collective effervescence," chanting for the players. Sometimes a "wave" will erupt in a stadium: friends and strangers join and raise their hands in a synchronized action sweeping through hundreds, perhaps thousands of people in an energy transfer.

Of course, there is an element of power in a sports game—as one team must lose for the other to win—so one might consider this a compromised kind of magic, and the "dirtier" the play if fans heckle, the more negative the energy. Still, most players and fans agree to an ethics of the game that honor all, at least in theory. Viewed through the lens of paganism, one sees fans engage in a collective magic, manifesting the wish that their team win. Indeed, one finds the "magic" of the communal work of fans to be so powerful it has a name in contemporary society: home advantage.

CHOOSE YOUR OWN PATH

Paganism, like most religious paradigms, offers believers guidance on how to live well in the material world; and it offers a framework for exploring what part of us persists after physical death. Like members of Eastern religions, pagans believe life reincarnates. In contrast, the Western faiths preach that we each live a single life ending in a transfer to heaven, purgatory, or hell. I find it helpful to envision each religious paradigm—Christianity, Hinduism, Paganism, Judaism, Buddhism, and so on—as a path to the Divine. Sometimes I imagine the churches and temples and mosques and synagogues as different pieces of clothing one might wear (evening gowns and pajamas), or vehicles one might take (trains and trucks). We choose the clothes and drive the vehicle that best connects us to the sacred. For me, paganism has the best-fitting clothes, the most sustainable transportation, and the most "right-feeling" way of accessing the spiritual in everyday life.

In early childhood I learned that witchcraft was done by crazy old unmarried women petitioning dark forces with spells and hexes; and I did not register my own regular acts of crossing myself with holy water, kissing under mistletoe, and lighting candles to remember someone who has passed as equally suspect. By making visible some aspects of paganism threaded through my life and yours, I hope I have dispelled stereotypes about magic and witchcraft, to help legitimate paganism as a religious paradigm, and to showcase our deep and intuitive pagan spirituality. Naming and honoring our everyday pagan rituals, or learning to *perceive* the magic we continually weave, has the potential to both improve our lives and dismantle intersecting systems of domination (fundamentalism, racism, poverty, sexism, and so on), which to me is a win-win! This is because Wicca empowers adherents to take responsibility for their spiritual development, to follow their inner guidance, and to favor syncretism over a single set of beliefs.

NOTES

1. Pew Research Center, "The Changing Religious Composition of the U.S.," in *America's Changing Religious Landscape,* May 12, 2015, https://www.pewresearch.org/religion/2015/05/12/chapter-1-the-changing-religious-composition-of-the-u-s/.
2. Knight, *Stolen Images*.
3. Gardner, *Witchcraft Today*; and Starhawk, *The Spiral Dance*.
4. White, *Wicca*.
5. Walker, *The Skeptical Feminist*.
6. Christ and Plaskow, *Womanspirit Rising*.
7. Higginbotham and Higginbotham, *Paganism*.
8. Radin, *Real Magic*.
9. Starhawk, *Dreaming the Dark*, 13.
10. Gardner, *Witchcraft Today*, 29.

BIBLIOGRAPHY

Christ, Carol P., and Judith Plaskow. *Womanspirit Rising: A Feminist Reader in Religion*. San Francisco: Harper and Row, 1979.

Gardner, Gerald B. *Witchcraft Today*. New York: Citadel Press, 2004.

Higginbotham, Joyce, and River Higginbotham. *Paganism: An Introduction to Earth-Centered Religions*. Woodbury, MN: Llewellyn Publications, 2016.

Knight, Peter. *Stolen Images: Pagan Symbolism and Christianity*. Wiltshire, UK: Stone Seeker Publishing, 2015.

Lerner, Gerda. *The Creation of Patriarchy*. New York: Oxford University Press, 1986.

Radin, Dean. *Real Magic: Ancient Wisdom, Modern Science, and a Guide to the Secret Power of the Universe*. New York: Harmony Books, 2018.

Starhawk. *Dreaming the Dark: Magic, Sex and Politics*. Boston: Beacon Press, 1988.
Starhawk. *The Spiral Dance*. New York: Harper and Row, 1979.
Walker, Barbara G. *The Skeptical Feminist: Discovering the Virgin, Mother and Crone*. San Francisco: Harper, 1987.
White, Ethan Doyle. *Wicca: History, Belief, and Community of Modern Pagan Witchcraft*. East Sussex, UK: Sussex Academic Press, 2015.

WITCH EPISTEMOLOGIES

VI

Twenty-eight · RUTH CHARNOCK AND KAREN SCHALLER

Witching the Institution: Academia and Feminist Witchcraft

We call on:

    Our ancestors. A mother who would jokingly tell her students she was a witch as a form of discipline but whose own witchcraft was pushed to the edges of domestic life—divination classes snuck in; tarot when her husband wasn't home; body squashed down in hours and hours of homework. A father who grew up dowsing on his grandfather's farm. Great-aunts and uncles: she who died with no bread in her mouth but the words to name a genocide—Holodomor. He who would not leave the university even with a gun at his head, shot at his desk on the charge of "Professor." Those forbidden from the knowledge of their own mother tongues, daughters of enclosure, displacement, extermination: Thigibh. Приходь. Mnu. קומץ. Ἔλλα. COME.

All the witches who have been forced out of institutions or who are forced to hide within them: Dubravka Ugrešić, whose antinationalist stance and critique of war branded her a "public enemy," a "traitor," a "witch"; the woman walking into a union meeting with obsidian in her bra; those whose unruly bodies undermine their epistemic status, their knowledge reduced to "mouthy" voices, "strident" and "too loud"; the ones who do not charm their colleagues or keep them "sweet." Those women who, as Clarissa Pinkola Estés puts it, "swagger-stagger" to work in professional wear of all kinds, only for their "fabulous tails" to fall below their hemlines.[1] *The women who came up spellbound by words and ideas and wanted to weave spells with others from these things but who now find themselves bound differently by the institution: tangled up in policy documents; hands tied by guidelines.*

We call on "convocation"; we call on "lecture-casting"; we call on "burning ambition." We call on "what's at stake." We invite you to bear witness to the language of the witch: congealed and concealed and bound within the institution.

We cite academic witches emerging into, or already out in, the open. We re-cite Araby Smyth, Jess Linz, and Lauren Hudson, the graduate students whose collaboration conjures a network of rebels, what they call a "backlash to the catastrophe of the neoliberal university" in the form of a feminist coven.[2] Rebecca Tamás, the poet investigating the figure of the witch, spelling her out against history's occlusions, bringing her agency to life through the ritual of words.[3] Susan Greenwood, the anthropologist researching London's pagan subcultures through a participatory methodology animating reflexive dialogue between witchcraft and academic training.[4] Alexis Pauline Gumbs, the queer Black feminist materializing critical embodiments that reshape the relationship between the intellectual, creative, and oracular, whose meditations with marine animals ask us to encounter through an ontology of wonder.[5] Vanessa Machado de Oliveira, who provides us with spells for the hospicing of modernity.[6] Marie-Andrée Godin, the artist whose doctoral research is asking how magic and postcapitalism can manifest new futures.[7] Sarah Amsler, queer thinker and feeler imagining Sycorax differently.[8] Linda Stupart, the artist whose spell and sigil for binding all-male conference panels, art collectors, and gallerists casts critical attention on the murderous effects of heteropatriarchal institutions.[9]

In citing, we summon.

Come, we call on you too. Listen for a spell: university. Univercyté, universeté, universitee, universitei, universiteit, universitat, universidad, universidade, università, universitēte, universitēt, universitet. Whichever tongue speaks it, studies this: the whole of creation, sum of things, the state of everything. Universitas: the body of masters and scholars, guild, the whole of creation.[10] The body of masters and scholars. The whole of creation. It is an invocation: Do you hear the magic there?

We set this down; we spell this out.

....

When we think about the academic institution, where is the witch? Equally, when we think about the witch, where is the academic institution? And why is it that, although cultural representations of witches coming into their witching frequently imagine this happening in the classroom, scholarly study of witches rarely acknowledges a relationship between the academic institution and becoming witch?[11]

Written collaboratively, this piece takes the form of a series of spells and rituals to counteract the knowledge-industrial complex and how it has positioned the witch. Part of this work will be to reclaim academic witches who have been excluded from the academy's account of itself and, sometimes, excluded in subtle ways from the academy itself. We are also interested in our own makings and unmakings as academic witches, in a longer genealogy.

This chapter is an altar. We place onto it our first object.

In Deborah Harkness's 2011 novel, *A Discovery of Witches*, Diana Bishop is a reluctant witch and avid academic, having "renounced [her] family's heritage and created a life that depended on reason and scholarly abilities, not inexplicable hunches and spells."[12] The novel enjoys Diana's struggles to renounce her magic in favor of her academic training, writ largest in her encounter with an enchanted manuscript, "Ashmole 782," that she calls up as part of her research into the history of science: "I had made my decision: to behave as a serious scholar and treat Ashmole 782 like an ordinary manuscript. I'd ignore my burning fingertips, the book's strange smell, and simply describe its contents. Then I'd decide—with professional detachment—whether it was promising enough for a longer look."[13] To be a witch within the institution, *A Discovery of Witches* tells us, is always to be performing "*as* a serious scholar" [emphasis added], rather than just being one. It is to always be dissembling, ignoring, deciding, detaching, disavowing, and dispelling. It means ignoring "*burning fingertips*" or, as Diana says elsewhere about her hunt for the right research field, "looking for a field so rational that it would never yield a square inch to magic."[14] For Diana, academia is the spell that binds her magic both because the academy does not "yield" to witchcraft and, paradoxically, because she will not let herself yield to magic to game the academy: "It's a slippery slope. . . . I protect myself from a vampire in the library today, and tomorrow I protect myself from a hard question at a lecture. Soon I'll be picking research topics based on knowing how they'll turn out and applying for grants that I'm sure to win. It's important to me that I've made my reputation on my own. If I start using magic, nothing would belong entirely to me. I don't want to be the next Bishop witch."[15] We know in this moment (although Diana does not) that her attempts to repress her magic in favor of her critical faculties will fail. In fact, it is one of the book's pleasures that Diana's academic attachments wane as her connection with her powers and her desire for vampire/academic Matthew Clairmont wax.

Yet although Diana initially sees herself as an academic rather than a witch, witchcraft is indivisible from her life as an academic. Even as her rejection of magic positions criticality as the witches' opposite, their relation is more intimate than that rejection imagines. While Diana defines academia against witchcraft, her success as an academic is also defined by this relationality—her desire to *not* be a witch is the condition for her academic life. When we find out that her parents were witches and anthropologists, we realize that Diana's feelings about magic are genealogical, bound up in her family history. But her family personal history is, eventually, articulated as the genealogy of contemporary academia itself: "'You're trying to push your magic aside, just as you believe your scientists did hundreds of years ago. The problem is . . . it didn't work. Not even the humans among them could push the magic out of their world entirely.'"[16] Harkness's novel is enchanting; but it is as much a product of her scholarship on the history of science as it is creative writing.[17]

....

Here is a knot: the witch and academia are tied in an intimate relation not reducible to a difference between university knowledge-making and witchcraft. In Harkness's figure of the spellbound Diana, we can locate a cultural imaginary that fantasizes the witch and academia together: it is a pattern that repeats. The witch and academic institution are entangled—that is, bound together. But Harkness's figure also indexes the affects at work when we imagine that binding: these belong as much to our critical as to our cultural imaginations.

Consider the Oxford's Ashmolean Museum's 2018–19 exhibition *Spellbound*,[18] a collection of English artifacts from the twelfth century to the present.[19] The exhibit website describes it as an exploration of "the inner lives of our ancestors, offering an insight into how people in the past actually felt and what they did to cope with the world they lived in."[20] Witchcraft, magic, and ritual are situated as a means for coping with precarity: the website tells us that in a "world where mass disease, death in childbirth and warfare were features of everyday life, magical interventions offered people a sense of control over their fate and a means of relieving anxieties."[21] While recognizing the possibility of a relationship between agency and witchcraft, that is, of witchcraft, ritual, and magic as practices that respond to the socioeconomic and political ecologies in which these took (or take) place, this etiology simultaneously constructs that agency as mere fantasy or, as the exhibit materials state, "magical thinking." Indeed, in the exhibition catalog, Marina Wallace describes this false agency as a form of alarming nescience: "Magic describes not only a way of thinking, but also the use of words and sounds, rituals and actions to manipulate or extract information from the natural world, so as to affect our environment. With magic we move from the irrational into the absurd."[22]

Spellbound breaks the spell of these artifacts: they are not magical. Our fascination with these objects is thus constructed as an uninformed attraction, in the contemporary, to the irrationality of the past and to the material record its objects provide of how recently enthralled by irrational belief we were, and indeed, may still be: "Looking at human hopes, fears and passions and asking visitors questions about their own beliefs and rituals, the exhibition aims to show how, even in this sceptical age, we still use magical thinking."[23] This message, circulated on the exhibition's website and in its signage, is notable for the way it orients the exhibit's visitors who, in coming into contact with these objects, can encounter their own proximity in the "sceptical" present to magical belief. Fascination works here as a threshold effect: visitors are invited to experience how compelling magical thinking is and recognize its lingering in the twenty-first-century psyche, yet also recognize that fascination itself as a border zone between the irrationality of that magical thinking and the rationality with which one should view it. In doing so, the exhibit enacts its own kind of border-making, a ritual of distinction drawn between the irrational past and the skeptical present, between those who believe and those who know. *Spellbound* asks of its visitors: Will they be transformed into objects themselves, subject to the same kind of scrutiny academics apply to the materials gathered, or will they leave knowing, no longer under these artifacts' spell? In doing so there is another presence on display: the transformative ability of the academic, whose critical interest maintains the boundary between these relics and the academic institutions that make knowledge about them. Rationality works here to maintain these objects as subject to the epistemic authority of the academic.

The *Spellbound* exhibition is itself an artifact, materializing the academic study of witchcraft as the practice of breaking spells. Not only are the objects of witchcraft dispelled into remnants of magical thinking, but so too are the witches themselves reconfigured into bodies that do not know better, unable to cope with a world beyond their knowledge. Here is history repeating itself. As Isabelle Stengers remarks, "Our pride in our critical power to 'know better' than both the witches and the witch hunters makes us the heirs of witch hunting."[24]

....

Yet knowing better, historically, is not as opposed to magic as we might like to think. Jason Josephson-Storm demonstrates that modernity takes shape through a myth of disenchantment that relegates superstition, ritual, witchcraft, and magical belief to the distant past and, according to the colonizing logics of the Western knowledge project, the "distant" present. But that loss of enchantment, he argues, never actually took place. Not only are accounts of European modernity disrupted by the "survival" of magical belief within Europe, but the institutional production of that modernity— the emergence of the university as we know it—is indebted to the project of magical knowledge. As Josephson-Storm points out, those figures who emblematize the scientific revolution saw themselves as magicians, and the early enlightenment project was, itself, a "quest for divine science."[25] Academia is founded on a distinction not between magic and science, then, but between whose magic is aligned with the project of knowledge-making and whose magic is dispelled—which magic is divine and which is cast out and criminalized. In this way the witch is subordinated to the knowledge project: subject to and the object of the study of demonology.

Universities did not simply produce knowledge about the witch; they were also, as Andreas Corcoran observes, involved in trials themselves. Corcoran's study of three professors of law in Northern Germany shows how those teaching at universities were also involved in judicial matters, called on to judge and speak justice in witch trials.[26] Indeed, the witch *as* a subject of and for investigation put under pressure questions for the law about the nature of proof, truth, and evidence: the study of demonology and the prosecution of suspected witches helps us to see how the science of knowledge is imbricated with the legal question of the witch. In his work on evidence in early modern witch trials, Malcolm Gaskill contends that "like the law, science relied on conviction and testimony, and was profoundly influenced by legal language and principles."[27] Notably, however, the shift toward a science of proof also involved a change in the credibility of witchcraft itself. Gaskill points out that in the early modern period, "the concept of witchcraft was not on trial: suspected witches were."[28] Yet prosecuting witchcraft "became an increasingly taxing exercise in persuasion and proof."[29]

The notion of academic expertise consolidated itself, in part, around the body of the witch it was authorized to prove and judge. That consolidation involved the disavowal of women as knowledge-makers and as seekers of divine science, too. Reducing witchcraft to magical thinking marks an eruption of that disavowal in the present by erasing the history of women's contributions to knowledge and reanimating bifurcations between the knowledge-making legitimated by the academy and those methods devised and practiced by women in other spheres. Giulia Smith observes that feminist scholarship on the history of knowledge has increasingly "stressed the contribution of female inventors in the transition from the alchemical to the scientific age [who] devised a practical empirical method within the domestic realms of horticulture and herbalism well before the onset of the 'official' scientific revolution."[30] Indeed, in her work on women's contributions to alchemy and scientific culture in sixteenth- and seventeenth-century Italy, Meredith Kay demonstrates how historians' tendency to focus on those domains available to men—the "public" spaces of universities, laboratories, and anatomy theaters—as sites for the scientific revolution has occluded how invested in empirical culture women were, practicing natural inquiry in contexts that were "more hospitable" to them, such as the home, salons, and epistolary correspondence.[31] Not only were women actively engaging medicinal and alchemical techniques to care for their families, their households, and themselves; they were also consulting earlier texts by women that accorded their own empirical authority to their gender.[32] Kay points out that women's writing in the period "collapses boundaries between natural history, astronomy, and astrology, and between the 'old' Aristotelian science and the 'new' empiricism," and she notes that historians of science are increasingly recognizing the significance of both "natural knowledge" and "natural philosophy" to scientific cultures at that time.[33] But Kay also observes (albeit in a footnote) that women's knowledge of the natural world held a long association with witchcraft.[34] She points to textual cultures from the period that represent knowledge-making as a "divine act" and construe the woman who "seeks to know" as stealing from God.[35] Witch, here, marks the delegitimizing of women's knowledge-making about the very matters that elevated others to become "Fathers" of science. In the witch hunts, that delegitimization took the form of violent erasure; as Barbara Ehrenreich and Deirdre English argue in their history of women healers, the "witch-healer's methods were as great a threat . . . as her results, for the witch was an empiricist."[36]

Isabelle Stengers writes that we are all "the heirs of an operation of cultural and social eradication."[37] That eradication contracts around the epistemic status of the witch, whose shifting legal constructions can help us to see how criminalizing the witch involved first demonization and, later, the disavowal of her credibility as a knowing subject and, indeed, the disavowal of her existence itself. As Josephson-Storm points out: "In the early eighteenth century, many Western European law codes redefined witchcraft as an issue of pretense, fraud, or deception rather than blasphemy or dangerous *maleficia* (as it had been primary understood), but like the changing notions of witches' 'superstition,' this did not necessarily mean that the law completely denied that witches had powers. Rather, it meant that witches' powers (as those of the devil in general) were increasingly understood as diabolical illusions and only later as delusional."[38] At stake here is the witch's ability to discern the false origin of her power and, later, to know the difference between power and illusion. At stake is the witch as reality or delusion. The witch herself is never sovereign.

We notice too that within the humanities, witchcraft tends to be studied predominantly by historians and literature departments (as we have already seen in *Discovery of Witches*). In the context of the former, this is because witchcraft belongs to the past; in the latter, because it belongs to the imaginary world of fiction. Elsewhere in the academy, witchcraft in the contemporary is positioned as a question for anthropology and sociology and, more recently, geography. But as Randall Styers points out, the principal evidence for contemporary witchcraft is still drawn predominantly from non-Western contexts—as Styers puts it, although "discourses on the 'primitive' are, in the contemporary, intellectually untenable, contemporary theories of magic still evoke this and consign magic to 'primitive,' 'folk,' 'traditional,' and 'indigenous.'"[39] Scholarly discourse on witchcraft functions, in this way, as an "ideological tool in aid of European and American imperialism and colonialism," and it is used to affirm that some cultures or groups "require and beseech domination."[40] In her critique of how these ideologies inflect geography studies' approach to studying witchcraft, Amber Murrey argues that, in order to understand the violent risks of our own scholarly practices when we study witchcraft within academia, "we must unpack the situated-ness of scholars within a larger implicit framework."[41] It is our contention that the university itself is dense with the bodies of witches, disavowed and dismembered in the emergence of our profession. It is a disavowal that persists when the witch remains a foreign subject, over there, back then, and never *right here.*

We can see this, too, even in the academic work on witches that seems to be the most sympathetic to them—Federici moves between positing witches as "witches" and sometimes just as witches (as in, unmarked by quotation marks).[42] Every time we see the putative quotation marks around the category of witch, we experience an erasure, a disavowal, an attempt to dispel. This felt sense of erasure is all the keener when the person writing seems witch-sympathetic or, even more, when it comes from someone we thought identified as a witch.

....

We place this object: The witch's ladder.

This is an artifact the curators of *Spellbound* cannot place: a length of rope, knotted eighteen times around clutches of feathers at even intervals.[43] Is this malevolent magic, or a metaphorical ladder? There is no way of unraveling its mystery, but, in the face of this undecidability, the object is given a rational explanation. The exhibit catalog tells us: "Historians are more inclined to view the mysterious object as a sewel: a tool for driving deer."[44] Like the academic's "inclination," a ladder is a leaning.[45] But it is also an unraveling, its fabrication revealed in its construction.

Perhaps it is not an object but a making, a method. Patricia McCormack reminds us that occulture is about "producing affects which alter modes of behaviour and thought in the practitioner."[46] What if it was never knowable, always, according to McCormack's description of witchcraft, an object made in the practice of "non-verifiable acts of change"?[47] Stengers refers to witchcraft as an "art of immanent attention."[48] To what might the witch's ladder ask us to attend? Perhaps unknowability here marks the very survival of witchcraft—of, as Stengers writes, the witches' challenge to us to accept "the possibility of giving up criteria that claim to transcend assemblages and that reinforce again and again the epic of critical reason."[49] We retrieve it as a magical object: see how it manifests a contact point, a disturbance, between the witches' entanglement with nonverifiability and the taxonomic project that disavows and erases what it cannot place.

....

What kind of spell are we under?

A dispellment. The university is constituted via the destruction of the witch and the dispelling of her forms of knowledge. As Federici tells us, the "'rationalization'" of the natural world—the precondition for a more regimented work discipline and for the scientific revolution—passed through the destruction of the "'witch.'"[50] The university's appearance, in its contemporary form, is predicated on the witch's disappearance.

....

What kind of spell are we under?

A dispellment. The university, as part of the knowledge-industrial complex, has disavowed, and continues to disavow, witching as an epistemology and ontology: "At the stakes not only were the bodies of the 'witches' destroyed, so was a whole world of social relations that had been the basis of women's social power and a vast body of knowledge that women had transmitted from mother to daughter over the generations—knowledge of herbs, of the means of contraception or abortion, of what magic to use to obtain the love of men."[51] For the university, the witch's knowing is not epistemologically recognizable as knowledge. We have felt this disavowal of our knowledge within the university; we have felt our powers dispelled. We have felt our networks of knowledge-making with other women dispersed by the institution's systematic misogyny. The university as boy's club, set up to exclude women's talk with its citational fetish, its closed circles, its andrognosis. Federici tells us how the word "gossip" once referred to "women friends, with no necessary derogatory connotations."[52] During the Middle Ages it came to signal a "woman engaging in idle talk."[53] The term's shift corresponds with the witch trials and with the destruction of women's social worlds that Federici tracks above.

....

What kind of spell are we under?

A dispellment. Our talking is part of our making, but the university does not value our talking. This piece was made from talking, from running off at the mouth. We make through our gossiping; our gossiping is our making.

....

What kind of spell are we under?

A dispellment. The university is constituted against the gossip.

....

What kind of spell are we under?

A dispellment. We need to grieve for all the things we never made, for all the time we kept our magic away from the institution and, in so doing, lost our thread, felt unraveled by work.

....

All the things we never made: an incantation for manifesting the unmade.

> We call on Brigid, we call on Athena, we call on Boann, we call on Mara, we call on Mokosh
> We call on all the metabolisms of the earth, its makings and compostings
> We call on spider, weaver of life
>
> We grieve what has yet been unsaid
> What was undone can now be made
> Our knowledge is our own

You might make a witch's ladder while you chant this invocation; or some other object that is unknowable by the university and cannot be incorporated by it. Let it lean and unravel.

....

What kind of spell are we under?

A dispellment. But we might let ourselves imagine otherwise. Invoking Sycorax, the denigrated yet powerful witch in *The Tempest*, Sarah Amsler tells us how:

> The enclosure of education belongs to the long history of enclosing knowledge, the body and/as the earth that has turned so many women and other counterproductive subjects into voiceless memories.... [W]itchy learning does not happen as abstract concept or imagination but through embodied, relational and sensorial experiences that intervene in living reality. By attuning to the Sycoraxes in our needs and desires, we may sharpen our sensitivity to trashed and exiled possibilities that, while real, are unintelligible from within prevailing critical educational identities, paradigms, imaginaries and horizons of hope.[54]

We want to be witchy learners and to hold space for other witchy learners. We want to witch education otherwise; to *delight in* our unintelligibility within and for the institution.

We need counterspells, stories of women who take back their witching, who attune to their inner Sycoraxes.

....

We place this object on the altar:

In Sylvia Townsend-Warner's 1926 novel *Lolly Willowes*, an unmarried woman, Laura (Lolly) Willowes, moves in with her brother and his family in London following the death of her father. Feeling herself to be "an inmate" of this new life, Lolly longs for her "potting-shed, earthy and warm, with bunches of poppy heads hanging from the ceiling, and sunflower seeds in a wooden box, and bulbs in thick paper bags, and hanks of tarred string, and lavender drying on a tea-tray."[55] Lolly, in case it is not already clear, is a plant witch in disguise. Lolly also reads Joseph Glanvill as a child.[56]

Lolly is deeply uneasy in the city. She dreams, restlessly, of something else: "A something that was shadowy and menacing, and yet in some way congenial; a something that lurked in waste places, that was hinted at by the sound of water gurgling through deep channels and by the voices of birds of ill-omen. Loneliness, dreariness, aptness for arousing a sense of fear, a kind of ungodly hallowedness—these were the things that called her thoughts away from the comfortable fireside."[57] Spurred by these, and other visions, Lolly decides to leave her family in London (much to their opprobrium) and move to the countryside, to live on her own. Therein, she proceeds by taking naps in beech woods, drinking dandelion wine, and throwing the guidebook and map she had bought to orient herself in her new village down the well.[58]

All seems well, until Lolly's well-meaning but oppressive nephew Titus decides he will also move to the village. Maddened by this unexpected yet familiar stymying of her only-just-won freedom, Lolly casts out into the woods, entreating them for support: "'No! You shan't get me. I won't go back. I won't . . . Oh! Is there *no* help?' . . . She stood in the middle of the field, waiting for an answer to her cry. There was no answer. And yet the silence that followed it had been so intent, so deliberate, that it was like a pledge. . . . As she came to the edge of the wood she heard the mutter of heavy foliage. 'No!' the woods seemed to say, 'No! We will not let you go!'"[59] When she gets home, a kitten has taken up residence. In the moment of it biting her, Lolly realizes that she has "entered into a compact with the Devil" and that the cat is her familiar.[60] At this point, the novel swerves into an exultant unfurling of Lolly's "new witch life."[61] She goes to her first Sabbath. She has a queer awakening when she dances with another witch from the village.[62] She meets with Satan and he licks her cheek.[63] The novel closes with her wandering off into the night, in search of a wood to sleep in: "She had never done such a thing before, and yet it seemed most natural."[64]

To read *Lolly Willowes* is to trace our own desires to witch as we will. Lolly's travails remind us that the patriarchy's spellbinding is reiterative; we will need to free ourselves from it over and over again, just as it will seek to trap us repeatedly, in different forms. There is a kinship, here, between Lolly and the speaker in Rebecca Tamás's 2019 poem "/penis hex/"—both realize that the patriarchy must be constantly banished, if we are to get back to the woods:

> maybe I'm not actually bothered by the logical
> summation of things
> their soft and sweet calculation and steadfast rationale
> maybe I like it out here in the dark cold wood
> with all my bits hanging down and fiery creatures
> perching on every surface shaking their claws[65]

....

What's at stake?

What's at stake here is not only an abstraction but our own bodies: as witches, as women, in the academy, and looking back at it. We do not want to reproduce the treatment of the witch as an object in the academy. We are/have been academics; we are witches.

What's at stake?

The question of whether our own witching has been or is being dispelled by the academy and how we might gather it back to ourselves.

What's at stake?

The stake was not a question. Any questions that led up to the stake had foreclosed answers.

What's at stake?

I left academia in 2019, newly pregnant and feeling that my body would not thrive in the strip-lit, coffee-stained, no-green environs of my former workplace. Having left, though, I still feel the pull back—some kind of binding to the academy. I do not feel myself to be under its spell so much as charged with the responsibility for breaking it for others or helping them to break it for themselves.

I set up workshops for female academics who are unhappy within academia or have just left it. My intention for these workshops is that they will be a space for somatic exploration, for ritualizing, for grieving, for creating paths out of academia, for holding a mirror up to the institution. Before every session, I cast a circle, I call in my guides.

What's at stake?

My ability to disenchant or to enchant, differently.

What's at stake?

I think of the workshops as gentle invitations to women to stop disavowing their bodies. I lead breathing and visualization exercises. I suggest working with guides, from this life or another, to help the group feel supported in their academic travails. But frequently I meet with hard resistance from individual women in these sessions. The somatic and spirit work that I view as essential—to my being, to my feminist praxis—is reflected back to me as a luxury of my position outside the academy. I can spend time in dream states because I am not an adjunct, I have not been summarily jettisoned from the system, I am not overworked. I am not disenchanted.

What's at stake?

I had this dream once, when I was thinking about leaving academia, that I had been "gifted" with a silver tongue, but that when I opened my mouth to speak, it turned into a chain that filled my mouth. It unspooled into the seminar room, tethered to someone in there.

What's at stake?

I feel my offering retreat in shame—both threatening and threatened.

What's at stake?

Maybe I want all female academics to come out as witches; to be witches.

What's at stake?

My body inflamed, swimming with leukocytosis. I am alive with rage. What would I be if it weren't for this? So, Baba Yaga, Grandmother whisperer, you have a place here too. Hold me in your little house with chicken legs that churn things up, even in piles of dirt. Where do I turn, when even my best knowledge is thrown out? I lack the charm and charisma to perform the alchemy my male colleagues are so good at. Instead, I have sick lumps in my throat: words, aspirations, what I have had to swallow. All the little pricks: these add up.

CLOSURE CHARM

We refuse the charms of institutional knowledge-making. We echo Jamie Sutcliffe in his resistance to the opposition between critical and magical thinking: "Magic possesses its own form of criticality, and we needn't always input the critical as an additional drive to lend reflexive value to it. Magical thinking implies illusion—but thinking magically is a form of politically engaged and aesthetically tempered investigation."[66]

We will not wrap this up. We will not "abjure" our "rough magic," like Prospero, or drown our books.[67] To conclude is to foreclose and the institution wants to foreclose on the witch.

This is an opening.

NOTES

1. Pinkola Estés, *Women Who Run with the Wolves*, 4.
2. Smyth, Linz, and Hudson, "Coven," 855. At the time they published their article, Smyth and Linz were PhD candidates at the University of Kentucky; Hudson was at CUNY Graduate Center. Their project conjures "the caring and threatening energy of witches" (856) to subvert the affective geographies of the neoliberal university; their article works as a "tour through the feminist coven's rituals and spaces" (856).
3. Tamás is Lecturer in Creative Writing at City University of London. In addition to her poetry collection *Witch*, Tamás also coedited, with Sarah Shin, *Spells: 21st Century Occult Poetry* (London: Ignota Press, 2018).
4. Greenwood researches the anthropology of magic, witchcraft, and magical consciousness. Now an independent scholar, she has lectured at the University of Sussex, Goldsmiths, and the University of London.
5. Gumbs is an independent scholar. After she received her PhD from Duke University, Gumbs held the visiting Winton Chair at the University of Minnesota, was a National Humanities Center Fellow, and was a 2022 National Endowment of the Arts Creative Writing Fellow.
6. Machado de Oliveira is a Canada Research Chair in Race, Inequalities and Global Change at the University of British Columbia.

7   Godin is a Canadian artist who, at the time of this writing, is a doctoral researcher at Aalto University in Finland funded by the Social Sciences and Humanities Research Council of Canada. She conducts her research under the title www³ (World Wide Web/Wild Wo.Men Witches/World Without Work). See her page at the university, https://www.aalto.fi/en/department-of-art/doctoral-candidate-marie-andree-godin-impossible-labor-www3-world-wide-web-wild.

8   Now an independent scholar, Amsler was an associate professor at the University of Nottingham at the time of writing.

9   Stupart is a lecturer in Fine Art at Birmingham City Institute of Creative Arts.

10 Etymology for "university" (noun) from *Oxford English Dictionary Online*, s.v. "university," accessed June 4, 2024, https://www.oed.com/dictionary/university_n?tab=etymology#16692711.

11 In addition to Diana in *A Discovery of Witches* (which we go on to discuss), we are thinking of the witching imbricated with academic institutions in the *Harry Potter* series, Sabrina in Netflix's 2018 series *Chilling Adventures of Sabrina*, Willow's emergence as a witch in Twentieth-Century Fox's *Buffy the Vampire Slayer*, and the school as site for the completion of the coven in Columbia Pictures' 1996 film *The Craft*. In Mary Stewart's novel *Thornyhold* (London: Hodder and Stoughton, 1998), Gilly first meets her witch aunt and experiences her own first rising of magic while at boarding school. In Dario Argento's 1977 horror movie *Suspiria* (and Luca Guadagnino's 2018 remake) a prestigious dance academy is actually run by a coven of witches. A more recent example is A. L. Hawkes's Hawthorne University Witch series of novels (published by Dresnin Media of Mission Viejo, CA).

12 Harkness, *Discovery of Witches*, 5.

13 Harkness, *Discovery of Witches*, 12.

14 Harkness, *Discovery of Witches*, 10.

15 Harkness, *Discovery of Witches*, 30.

16 Harkness, *Discovery of Witches*, 104.

17 Harkness is a historian at the University of Southern California researching the history of science and medicine, the scientific revolution, magic, and alchemy. See Deborah E. Harkness, *The Jewel House: Elizabethan London and the Scientific Revolution* (New Haven, CT: Yale University Press, 2007); and Deborah E. Harkness, *John Dee's Conversations with Angels: Cabala, Alchemy and the End of Nature* (Cambridge: Cambridge University Press, 1999).

18 *Spellbound: Magic, Ritual and Witchcraft*, exhibit, Ashmolean Museum Oxford, August 31, 2018–January 6, 2019.

19 Notably, when Sky One launched its adaptation of *Discovery of Witches*, they held its preview in Oxford to coincide with the exhibition; it featured a tour of the exhibit *Spellbound: Magic, Ritual and Witchcraft*, at the Ashmolean Museum Oxford, led by Harkness.

20 "Spellbound: Magic, Ritual, and Witchcraft," press release, Ashmolean Museum Oxford, accessed October 23, 2023, https://www.ashmolean.org/press/spellbound-exhibition-press-release.
21 "Spellbound," press release, Ashmolean Museum Oxford.
22 Page et al., *Spellbound*, 166.
23 "Spellbound," press release, Ashmolean Museum Oxford.
24 Stengers, "Reclaiming Animism," 42.
25 Josephson-Storm, *Myth of Disenchantment*, 309.
26 Corcoran, "Demons in the Classroom."
27 Gaskill, "Witchcraft and Evidence," 66.
28 Gaskill, "Witchcraft and Evidence," 41.
29 Gaskill, "Witchcraft and Evidence," 38.
30 Smith, "Streamed through the Veins of Leaves," 140.
31 Kay, *Daughters of Alchemy*, 3.
32 Kay, *Daughters of Alchemy*, 3.
33 Kay, *Daughters of Alchemy*, 4.
34 Kay, *Daughters of Alchemy*, 203.
35 Kay, *Daughters of Alchemy*, 203.
36 Ehrenreich and English, *Witches, Midwives, and Nurses*, 17.
37 Stengers, "Reclaiming Animism," 42.
38 Josephson-Storm, *Myth of Disenchantment*, 56.
39 Styers, "Magic and Social Control," 34.
40 Styers, "Magic and Social Control," 35.
41 Murrey, "Decolonising the Imagined Geographies," 157.
42 See, for example, Federici, *Caliban and the Witch*, 15. We understand here that Federici employs the quotation marks around "witches" when she means to signal that these were women *accused* of witchcraft, under a violent patriarchal agenda, who did not necessarily practice witchcraft (as distinct from those who did practice, where Federici does not employ quotation marks). Nevertheless, we still feel this marking out as a form of ontological violence.
43 Images of the artifact can be seen on the exhibit website or in Page et al., *Spellbound*, 86.
44 Page et al., *Spellbound*, 87.
45 Etymology from *Oxford English Dictionary Online*, s.v. "ladder," accessed June 4, 2024, https://www.oed.com/dictionary/ladder_n?tab=etymology#39873282.
46 MacCormack, "Occulture," 59.
47 MacCormack, "Occulture," 59.
48 Stengers, "Reclaiming Animism," 45.
49 Stengers, "Reclaiming Animism," 45.
50 Federici, *Witches, Witch-Hunting and Women*, 28.
51 Federici, *Witches, Witch-Hunting and Women*, 33.
52 Federici, *Witches, Witch-Hunting and Women*, 36.

53 Federici, *Witches, Witch-Hunting and Women*, 38.
54 Amsler, "Learn like Witches," 8.
55 Townsend-Warner, *Lolly Willowes*, 8.
56 Joseph Glanvill was the seventeenth-century author of *Saducismus Triumphatus*, which petitioned for a recognition of the real existence of witches and witchcraft (as a malign force in society).
57 Townsend-Warner, *Lolly Willowes*, 67.
58 Townsend-Warner, *Lolly Willowes*, 95–107.
59 Townsend-Warner, *Lolly Willowes*, 138.
60 Townsend-Warner, *Lolly Willowes*, 142.
61 Townsend-Warner, *Lolly Willowes*, 145.
62 Townsend-Warner, *Lolly Willowes*, 160.
63 Townsend-Warner, *Lolly Willowes*, 166.
64 Townsend-Warner, *Lolly Willowes*, 202.
65 Tamás, *Witch*, 15.
66 Sutcliffe, *Magic*, 17.
67 Shakespeare, *The Tempest*, 115. Citations refer to the Shakespeare Arden edition. The play was first published by Thomas Nelson and Sons in Surrey in 1623.

BIBLIOGRAPHY

Amsler, Sarah. "Learn like Witches: Gesturing towards Further Education Otherwise." In *Caliban's Dance: Further Education after the Tempest*, edited by Maire Daley, Kevin Orr, and Joel Petrie, 59–96. London: Trentham Books, Institute of Education Press, 2020.

Corcoran, Andreas. "Demons in the Classroom: Academic Discourses and Practices Concerning Witchcraft at the Protestant Universities of Rinteln and Halle." PhD diss., European University Institute, Florence, 2012.

Ehrenreich, Barbara, and Deirdre English. *Witches, Midwives, and Nurses: A History of Women Healers*. 2nd ed. New York: Feminist Press, 2010.

Federici, Silvia. *Caliban and the Witch: Women, the Body and Primitive Accumulation*. London: Penguin, 2004.

Federici, Silvia. *Witches, Witch-Hunting and Women*. Oakland, CA: PM Press, 2018.

Gaskill, Malcolm. "Witchcraft and Evidence in Early Modern England." *Past and Present* 198, no. 1 (2008): 33–70.

Greenwood, Susan. *Magic, Witchcraft and the Otherworld: An Anthropology*. London: Routledge, 2020.

Gumbs, Alexis Pauline. *Dub: Finding Ceremony*. Durham, NC: Duke University Press, 2020.

Gumbs, Alexis Pauline. *M Archive: After the End of the World*. Durham, NC: Duke University Press, 2018.

Gumbs, Alexis Pauline. *Spill: Scenes of Black Feminist Fugitivity*. Durham, NC: Duke University Press, 2016.

Gumbs, Alexis Pauline. *Undrowned: Black Feminist Lessons from Marine Animals*. Chico, CA: AK Press, 2020.

Harkness, Deborah. *A Discovery of Witches*. London: Penguin, 2011.

Josephson-Storm, Jason Ananda. *The Myth of Disenchantment: Magic, Modernity, and the Birth of the Human Sciences*. Chicago: University of Chicago Press, 2017.

Kay, Meredith. *Daughters of Alchemy: Women and Scientific Culture in Early Modern Italy*. Cambridge, MA: Harvard University Press, 2015.

MacCormack, Patricia. "Occulture: Secular Spirituality." In *Magic*, edited by Jamie Sutcliffe, 57–63. London: Whitechapel Gallery; Cambridge, MA: MIT Press, 2021.

Machado de Oliveira, Vanessa. *Hospicing Modernity: Facing Humanity's Wrongs and the Implications for Social Activism*. Berkeley, CA: North Atlantic Books, 2021.

Murrey, Amber. "Decolonising the Imagined Geographies of 'Witchcraft.'" *Third World Thematics: A TWQ Journal* 2, nos. 2–3 (2017): 157–79.

Page, Sophie; Marina Wallace, Owen Davies, Malcolm Gaskill, and Ceri Houlbrook. *Spellbound: Magic, Ritual and Witchcraft*. Oxford: Ashmolean Museum, University of Oxford, 2018. Exhibition catalog.

Pinkola Estés, Clarissa. *Women Who Run with the Wolves: Contacting the Power of the Wild Woman*. London: Random House, 1992.

Shakespeare, William. *The Tempest*. Edited by Frank Kermode. Surrey: Arden Shakespeare, 1992.

Smith, Giulia. "Streamed through the Veins of Leaves: Elizabeth Mputu and Faith Wilding's Remedial Plants." In *Magic*, edited by Jamie Sutcliffe, 138–43. London: Whitechapel Gallery; Cambridge, MA: MIT Press, 2021.

Smyth, Araby, Jess Linz, and Lauren Hudson. "A Feminist Coven in the University." *Gender, Place and Culture* 27, no. 6 (2020): 854–80.

Stengers, Isabelle. "Reclaiming Animism." In *Magic*, edited by Jamie Sutcliffe, 42–46. London: Whitechapel Gallery; Cambridge, MA: MIT Press, 2021.

Stupart, Linda. "Spell for Binding All-Male Conference Panels" and "Sigil for Binding Murderous Art Collectors and Gallerists." 2016. Accessed October 23, 2023. http://lindastupart.net/Spells.php.

Styers, Randall. "Magic and Social Control." In *Magic*, edited by Jamie Sutcliffe, 34–37. London: Whitechapel Gallery; Cambridge, MA: MIT Press, 2021

Sutcliffe, Jamie, ed. *Magic*. London: Whitechapel Gallery; Cambridge, MA: MIT Press, 2021.

Tamás, Rebecca. *Witch*. London: Penned in the Margins, 2019.

Townsend-Warner, Sylvia. *Lolly Willowes*. London: Virago, 2013.

Twenty-nine · MARGARETHA HAUGHWOUT AND OLIVER KELLHAMMER

A Ruderal Witchcraft Manifesto

INTRODUCTION

Ruderal witchcraft is a set of practices for anti-capitalist organizers and those with whom they organize: the cast out, the old, the squatters, the abolitionists, the revolutionaries, the healers, the facilitators, the survivors, the anarchists, and the commoners. Ruderal witchcraft enables sabotage, sanctuary, and the disruption of capitalist futures through work with invasive species, weeds, and other living beings ostracized by bourgeois society.

Historically, witches are witches because they are accursed, landless, creeping through the vestiges of the commons, betwixt and between the binary of public and private property: haunting, rejected, old. Like witches, weeds are tossed to the edges of property, making use of boundaries and fence lines. They persist, just outside of view. The categories of witches and weeds are categories of accusation and part of a process of erasure for the purpose of appropriating land and labor to create the commodity form.[1] The burning of the witch is enacted through the erasure and perversion of cultural memory; the power of the witch is forgotten. The ruderal witch comes back into their power by embracing all those practices that invite accusation. Care work, sex work, healing work, the work of remembrance, cultivation of the commons—the work of reproduction—the work, in short, of the femitariat,[2] is enacted through engagement with the untamed plants and critters that crawl around their feet. Along with their nonhuman kin, witches move in and out of wild and cultivated realms, healing and poisoning, conjuring and conspiring, testing and permeating the boundaries between public and private, nature and society, to create secret sanctuaries for dangerous becoming. Witchy power returns with

FIGURE 29.1 "Rubble, Riot, Gate."

monstrous ferocity through this entanglement with other ruderal and cast-out species that together nurture and defend a new world while unraveling the old. They push at demarcations of property through new territorial occupations of the empty lot, the old canal, the crack in the sidewalk; suddenly there are new resources, shared alliances, a new world in the midst of the old.

Ruderal ecologies are, by definition, composed of plant species that thrive in spaces of disturbance. The root meaning of "ruderal" is rubble, ruins; as such, these are species that make their home in debris fields, landfills, abandoned mines: wherever the earth or pavement has been broken. Ruderal species adapt to changing environments quickly, and they rapidly reproduce themselves; they are itinerant travelers, making use of all the means of transportation modernity has to offer.

Ruderal ecologies are a heresy, an apostasy, defying tidy notions of "natural" or pristine, thriving in spite of—*because of*—the wavefront of accumulation. The colonial frontier arrives, cheapens, then exploits the labor of both humans and nonhumans, contaminates, and continues on.[3] Ruderal species, along with cattle and sugarcane, for example, are on the edge of accumulation projects, threatening valuable and complex Indigenous kinship networks, creating cheap, simpler ecologies, thus setting up the conditions for multispecies exhaustion and unleashed pathogens.[4] It is a misperception, however, that ruderal species are always a threat. As Indigenous scholars Nicholas Reo, Kyle Whyte, and Darren Ranco remind us, Indigenous vulnerability is an imperial construct that enables invasion (not dissimilar, we note, to the colonial notion of a prelapsarian nature).

One form of resistance to the cheapening process engendered by the frontier that Reo, Whyte, and Ranco acknowledge is to get to know the ruderal ecologies as they emerge, in all their stages of succession.[5] What larger structures of exploitation are ruderal ecologies supporting or resisting? In getting to know them—their shifts and claims, their collaborations over time—can they help us ruderal witches learn to better adapt to the emerging conditions of what Jason W. Moore calls the Capitalocene?

As eco-interventionist artists based in North America, we, the conjurers of this text, are invested in the power of the radical imagination. Through the *Ruderal Witchcraft Manifesto*, we insist that the potential for collective resistance and renewal exists all around us; we just need to know how to summon ruderal powers.

RITES OF RUDERAL WITCHCRAFT

The ruderal witch's practices are material and stand in opposition to the exoticized figure of the witch that is packaged for us in the market. The market sells an image of the witch whose powers are accessed through commodities such as gems blasted off the sides of mountains, or white sage unethically harvested from Indigenous lands. This docile image offers no resistance to modernity's structures of exploitation.

The immanence of the wasteland is often forgotten, but it lies in wait to generate new realities. The wastelands are a power that conjure witches into being; thinking otherwise is how the power is forgotten. To craft with feral species found here, at the tangled edges of private property, is an act of conjure that ushers forth once-dormant powers that refuse while simultaneously healing, dreaming, and claiming another modernity where revolutionaries can resist systemic violence and thrive.

We inaugurate nine entanglements with ruderal ecologies that conjure the power of ruderal witchcraft. These entanglements must be enacted all together for new worlds to take hold:

HEAL
REMEDIATE
POISON
SHAPESHIFT WITH HYPERECOLOGIES
SHAPESHIFT WITH HYPERORGANISMS
ENACT FUGITIVE COMMONS
GRIEVE
PRACTICE NECROMANCY
LOVE SPELLS OF SIMULTANEOUS SABOTAGE AND RETREAT

Working with, amid, and through ruderal ecologies in these nine ways will turn you into a ruderal witch.

1 HEAL: We wander through vacant lots and urban meadows, we inspect the edges of sprayed suburban lawns, the compacted soil of construction sites where the little plantain weed (*Plantago major* and *Plantago lanceolata*) is always poking through.

Environmental scientist Robin Wall Kimmerer cites the Potawatomi who call plantain "White Man's Footsteps." She generously writes that "it arrived with the first settlers and followed them everywhere they went," and that "this wise and faithful plant, faithfully following the people, became an honored member of the plant community,"[6] thriving in disturbance, acting as a scab on the land and on human skin: the leaves of plantain are used externally as a poultice to draw out toxins and venom from bites and stings. Plantain heals wounds with extraordinary sureness. Use the leaves internally for ulcers (it heals the tissue of the digestive tract), and the seeds internally as a bulking agent (the marketed psyllium is made from a cousin, *Plantain ovata*).

Plantain is polymorphous in adapting to footsteps of any scale: bare ground, runoff, rubble. The wide leaves of *Plantago major* hug dirt and tar, mimicking its relationship to disrupted surfaces. Plantain breaks up clay, and draws out toxins in blighted soil, healing its own multispecies territory. Like many ruderal herbs, plantain exceeds the notion of individual healing in favor of "contingent healing" of one's neighborhood, community, kinship network. Working with herbs such as little plantain is the healing work of the ruderal witch.

Healing individual bodies one by one continues the necessary, but often unpaid or precarious, labor of the femitariat. Modes of collectivity must also be enacted with those unfaithful weeds that refuse to be put to work for regimes of exploitation.

> 2   REMEDIATE: Often occupying zones of contamination, ruderal ecologies contain the threat of hidden poison but also, due to the regrowth of healing, toxin-absorbing herbs; these zones contain within themselves the seeds of their own recovery. Plants that grow here not only produce some of our strongest poisons and strongest medicines,[7] but also recuperate the soils, reassembling ecological conditions that are beneficial for humans and their more-than-human kin.

The common reed, for example, can be used for the project of bioremediation. Ruderal witchcraft lets the common reed (*Phragmites australis subspecies australis*) proliferate. Given how it commingles with the native *Phragmites*, it is a shapeshifting hyperorganism, which we define below. A companion of the muskrat, who is a caretaker of waterways, the common reed can stabilize eroded banks and shores. Importantly, the common reed can filter sewage once the solid waste is allowed to settle out, and it filters other kinds of domestic wastewater (from kitchens, for example). A constructed wetland of reeds can filter water and facilitate the breakdown of polluting nutrients via the bacteria living on the reeds' roots. The filtered water can be used for irrigation or groundwater recharge, or it can be released more safely into waterways. Consider *Phragmites'* advantages in highly toxic sites near water where it can grow densely.[8] From our ruderal witch's pouch, we introduce the common reed for remediation.

Our understanding of bioremediation needs to be reassessed, however, when ecological processes are put to work under the job title of "ecosystem services" to restore properties for the market. For these reasons, ruderal ecologies and ruderal witches must be at times tactically poisonous, ugly, unreadable, or dangerous in order to elude gentrification, land grabs, real estate development, and other forms of accumulation and extraction.

3 POISON: We understand that accumulation and extraction projects, whether they are luxury condominium developments, gas pipelines, or mining, require violence against women, Indigenous genocide, and exploitation that work along a global color line.[9] We understand that increasingly, in the name of so-called green capitalism, a planetary biotariat (in league with the femitariat) is put to work to clean up pollution and restore environments, and this work is usually unpaid.

When poisons stay in the mix, there is a persistent threat of rashes, hallucinations, and shock to human systems. Poisons can function as the threat of costly economic damage to those buying and selling land.

Herbalists know that what differentiates plant medicine from a poison is always about dosage; a small dose might be a remedy while a large dose might be an injury. Take poison ivy, for instance. In material doses it is dangerous, but in doses where it is diluted to the hundredth degree it cures what it causes, clearing rashes and inflammation.

Poison ivy loves spaces of disturbance. It is also a master of disguise. It travels as a vine, but can also be a deceptively small sprout, or an elusive bush. Its vines will wrap around trees, but it is hard to spot when leafless. Its leaves can be differently shaped, and it hides among lookalike plants. Put the seeds in seed balls with small chunks of Japanese knotweed rhizomes to bring property value down.[10] Use it to deter those who would impede territorial defense.[11] Use poison ivy with other ruderal plants, like the thorny Himalayan blackberry, to stir caution and keep renegade spaces from view.

The practice of ruderal witchcraft is a tactical practice that braids together healing, remediating, and poisoning in a way that welcomes those who can read the landscape, while eluding notice by those who cannot.

4 SHAPESHIFT WITH HYPERECOLOGIES: Ruderal witchcraft prioritizes relationships through a participation with shapeshifting superpowers of hyperecologies. The term *hyperecology* describes the renegotiations that occur as native and non-native biota bump up against each other in the niches afforded by rubble and heaved-up earth.[12]

Introduced species that have, for example, traveled on the hooves of livestock on the frontier or in the ballast of slave ships, or that have hitchhiked along on so-called ornamental plants (uprooted from cultures of use elsewhere) find themselves in the midst of fractured ecologies, in conditions where depleted soil, erosion, and new and excessive amounts of nutrients are at play. Disturbed ditches beside roadsides typify the kind of site where runoff, invasive species, and native species commingle. The ruderal witch is familiar with these conditions too, walking along the edge of the pavement and gravel, helping to organize new forest solidarities. The ruderal witch divines these new, resilient relationships, their interstitial and disregarded wisdom, and helps them along.

The resilient and changeable qualities of ruderal species can afford protection, structure, and nutrients or function as insectary for other species within a hyperecology. In Central New York, new combinations of invasive purple loosestrife, garlic mustard, and box elder combine with native bloodroot, viburnum, and sumac. Bloodroot has suffered extreme habitat loss and has not returned to new growth forests;[13] instead, it emerges along roadsides that butt up against feed corn crops with its impetuous accomplices. Purple loosestrife removes excess nitrogen and phosphorus, and leaves of garlic mustard enrich soil, which the bloodroot appreciates as much as it does the slope of the ditch and the dappled shade of viburnum, box elder, and sumac.[14] Combinations such as these may prove to be more resilient to the emerging climate catastrophe, with introduced species collaborating with indigenously present ones.

The ruderal witchcraft that comes through engagement with hyperecologies is particularly pertinent as we navigate new challenges of the capitalogenic climate crisis. Our changing environments often look hostile, and sometimes they are; the loss of wolves leads to overabundant populations of deer and ticks, or the absence of bog turtles and the advance of invasive purple loosestrife and common reed are bound up in one another. There is much to grieve.

5   SHAPESHIFT WITH HYPERORGANISMS: The term *hyperorganism* describes the hybridity that emerges within an organism as native and non-native species commingle.[15]

What might initially appear to be a discrete organism might turn out to be a shifting amalgam of selves cohabiting within a common body. Some of the most recognizable entities encroaching on the indeterminate spaces of the American Northeast are not discrete species at all, but hybrids: self-assembling comings-together of multiple organisms combining into single, yet contingent, wholes.[16] The vacuum left behind by the capitalist extinction machine soon plays host to a strange new hybridity—the ruderal witch's familiars—like the shapeshifting canids who combine the gene pools of coyotes, abandoned farmyard dogs, and the ghost of the eastern wolf, long exterminated, now reassembled into this dog-like being that lopes along abandoned railway sidings scavenging trash.[17] Rampant, so-called Oriental bittersweet vines (*Celastrus orbiculatus*) pour into the catastrophe left behind by progress, smothering power poles and crumbling warehouse walls and erupting into a ruderal future with unstoppable hybrid vigor (noting that so-called invasives from Asia are always indicated as such, reflecting centuries-long racism, and century-old US terror of economic dominance by China and Japan). They are a hyperorganism, an amalgam created when a once insignificant American vine genetically fused with a later arrival from China, resulting in new botanical superpowers.

The phenotypic expression of hyperorganisms responds to shifting environmental conditions. The mutating conditions of the hyperecology shape its constituent hyperorganisms. Relationships precede individuals. Ruderal witches shift along with these contingent, hybrid beings, deeply sensitive to how hyperorganisms evolve within their ruderal worlds to live within them, in turn replicating these international solidarities.

6   ENACT FUGITIVE COMMONS: A witch's alignment with the shapeshifting superpowers of hyperecologies and hyperorganisms affords new opportunities to exceed enclosure, exceed nationalist categorizations of more-than-human life, and create positive models of international, extra-human resilience that can be understood as ungovernable spaces, spaces that are not entirely enclosed. Commons, what Peter Linebaugh describes as spaces of "cooperative labor, common resources, and communal distribution,"[18] are yet waiting, hidden in the weeds: inscrutable, contingent, entirely, or partially fugitive.

Commons are spaces where usufruct practices are the norm, where relationship creates abundance rather than scarcity. The landscapes of the Americas, prior to European colonization, were mostly cultivated as commons by Indigenous peoples, and active commons still can be found from Oakland, California, to Chiapas to the Amazon. Linebaugh reminds us we can find linked examples from the Mississippi Delta to the upper Nile to Ireland. Examples of recent temporary commons are Tahrir Square, Occupy Wall Street, and Standing Rock,[19] but they are also always under threat. Commons in the Americas these days often begin as ruderal, neglected spaces—what Fred Moten and Stefano Harney call the undercommons, or fugitive spaces.[20] They often persevere when initiated as tactical interventions such as guerrilla gardens.

The end of feudalism in Europe was precipitated by the climate event of the Little Ice Age, the Black Death, and by persistent peasant organizing within the commons across Europe.[21] The commons were shared spaces for lateral organizing, community care, the reproduction of life, and the reproduction of culture, where viable alternatives to feudalism were put into effect. People who were accused of witchery within the European commons were skilled in the use of plants and worked with natural cycles to help shape harvests and celebrations. Older women often held the memory of negotiations around the use of land and resources within the commons.[22] For capitalism to take hold, witches, with their abilities to reproduce life, culture, and community, would need to be removed.[23] Commoning would collapse as a result. The demonization and extermination of witches in Europe not only produced the docile, white woman but became the template for the demonization, oppression, and extermination of colonized subjects across the European colonies and the ongoing neocolonial conquests that continue to the present day in the Global South.[24]

Colonized subjects, queer folx, and older people, those historically feminized by science, state, and the market, have been central to negotiations and facilitation of shared agreements in the commons. They are living repositories of agreements, betrayals, customs, and histories of use.[25]

In seizing the term *witch*, we recognize these histories. In seizing the term *witch*, we recognize that the ongoing femicide in the Global South is necessary to erase memories of mediations and agreements, cultures of care, and practices of resistance—so that capitalist markets can take hold. In seizing the term *witch* and working with ruderal plants (and each other) to produce food, medicine, and other materials for each other, we cultivate what Michael Taussig calls "breathing space" at the margins.[26]

Ruderal alliances afford opportunities for new aggregations of mutuality, care, cooperation, and reciprocity. Because, as Moten and Harney argue, most commons now have an excess of administrative politics, we insist on cultivating their fugitivity.[27] In these ruderal, fugitive, undercommons, activists, friends, artists, comrades, and runaway weeds negotiate, study, and plan escape.[28]

7 GRIEVE: The "marmosets, the spider monkeys, the tamarin, the jaguars, the sloths, frogs, lizards, parakeets, mahogany, ironwood, brazil nuts, cocoa, passiflora vines, orchids, bromeliads" burn in the Amazon to make way for soybeans and cows.[29] The ruderal is a graveyard, a charnel ground, always ruined. Senna, mimosa, dandelion, and tiririca grow first in the roads and then in the burnt lands, and then in the new monocrop plantations in the Brazilian forests. Knowing how to read these plants and the ruins they are connected to leads to moments of pause. Our grief opposes temporalities where the future eclipses the past.

The ruderal landscapes we are concerned with in this manifesto are produced from bourgeois notions of progress that imagine endless growth and techno-utopianism; bourgeois temporalities are temporalities that prevent grieving, prevent the acknowledgment that the past exists in the present.

In *Theses on the Philosophy of History*, Walter Benjamin describes the Angel of History, driven by the storm of progress that blows into the future, yearning to tend to the expanding tragedy in its wake.[30] Collective grief alters the direction of time, and multispecies, relational temporalities tied to grief delay extinction events because of the refusal to endlessly work, the refusal to look ahead.

Grief is not sadness or despair. Thom Van Dooren describes grief as part of a "becoming-together inside rich histories of biosocial inheritance and relationship."[31] Vinciane Despret states, "It is through the grief one undergoes that life comes to matter; it is by accepting this grief that it counts."[32]

Grieving happens collectively; it happens in *common*. "You don't need love to withstand it, you need shoulders," says the moon witch Sogolon.[33]

In a time where the future is closed, unimaginable, and unlivable for most of the life on this planet, the stakes are high. For ruderal witches, doing the future well means listening to the ghosts of the past.

8 PRACTICE NECROMANCY: Our cascading catastrophe is born of denial: denial of difference, of reciprocity, of the moral claims of the past.[34] Denial that the dead (who may only be sleeping) dream.[35]

With mugwort and ailanthus, that grow in the dust of corpses, we must "seize on these things, awaken them from the dead," evoke tensions between labor as use value and as exchange value in the zones where what we do and for whom isn't entirely commodified.[36]

Ruderal witchcraft is a practice of conjuring the dead. Ruderal ecologies already perform necromancy, and when we learn to heed the wreckage with them, our powers multiply. Plants like kudzu, Japanese knotweed, and ice plant haunt the edges of private property with stories of the Transcontinental Railroad, US settler colonialism, and Chinese migrant labor; as soils and native ecologies crumbled with the laying of train tracks, the life worlds of the Cherokee, Pawnee, and Sioux, too, were exterminated.[37] Itchgrass, a weed in Gulf Coast sugarcane plantations, travels by train.[38] With these plants, we divine the future, reckon with the past, reveal hidden knowledge; we weaponize the dead.

9   LOVE SPELLS OF SIMULTANEOUS SABOTAGE AND RETREAT: Ruderal witchcraft evades capture. Late-stage capitalism is cybernetic capitalism, a process of integration and dissolution of difference, where large-scale systems combine both human and nonhuman agents in mutual communication and control. Its power is driven by the assumption that biological, physical, and social patterns can be adjusted through algorithms.[39] Conceptions of self-governance, autopoiesis, and emergence as well as the notions of homeostasis in nature, and of nature as a system (ecosystem), give us a problematic lens with which to see nature as a system that can be in balance—a concept that holds significant sway in the liberal imagination and visions of "planetary management."[40]

Ruderal witchcraft disrupts planetary management strategies by adding life and by rapidly changing epigenetic forms. Weeds shapeshift and morph, outbreed, respond to changing environmental conditions; they do the unexpected, making them difficult to surveil and predict. We flood vacant spaces with scotch broom and mallow, which eventually evolve into complex forest ecosystems, creating environments for retreat. We employ temporal strategies to slow down the system,[41] retreating into ruderal sanctuaries for the reproduction of the self and of kin . . . for a spell.

Does capitalism recover from ruderal sabotage and assimilate new processes of life and relationship? Weedy sabotage must be crafty in order not to facilitate recommodification or resubsumption of the bioremediated lot into the space of the market. The practice of ruderal witchcraft can create useful illusions of abandonment and waste, while the important work—organizing, healing, remediating—is happening just beyond the tangled brambles of Himalayan blackberry and Japanese honeysuckle. The sabotage is not total; it is one strategy for resisting reduction into the realm of abstract information, real estate, or other market forms. So every time we toss a seedball, help Callery pear to seed itself, or root some *Robinia*, we make a small step away from biometric regimes toward the allure and magic of covert sanctuaries.

SIGNS PROPHECIES AND SPELLS AT THE MARGINS

Magic, what Michael Taussig describes as taking "language, symbols, and intelligibility to their outermost limits, to explore life and thereby change its destination," appears in transition zones, where land and labor becomes property, where beings and materials are consigned when they are deemed disposable, where the border walls do not hold, where the cement buckles.[42] In recollecting the train tracks that divided whites from Blacks in her Kentucky hometown, bell hooks argues that "margins have been both sites of repression and sites of resistance."[43] While there is danger in idealizing the margins, they enable critical distance from the structures of labor and property that would otherwise seem natural.[44] Nothing is settled in these zones; witches and ruderal species emerge as signs of insecurity, between use value and exchange value, a challenge to the idea and practice of land as property. Ruderal witchcraft continues the project of unsettling.

The margins are closing in. It has been speculated that we are, or soon will be, living on a "planet of weeds."[45] Ruderal witchcraft is a planetary response to the planetary conditions of the Capitalocene, practices that sabotage, heal, dream, conjure, haunt, seduce. They are planetary and always contingent. In the neoliberal condition of the United States, through the production of the complicit, heteronormative, white woman, witchcraft has been rendered unthreatening enough to be commodified, while in the Global South, accusations of witchcraft continue to fly about where the extraction and accumulation projects penetrate Indigenous lands, and the implications are dire. Where extraction projects take hold, there is always more violence against women and racialized and feminized bodies.[46] While the term "ruderal witchcraft" cannot be claimed everywhere, the practices can be. In embracing the ruderal, we resist commodification—at once ugly and hidden.

Ghosts, weeds, and other fugitives exist in the margins, in a *terrain vague*, as you grab a coffee in between sessions, walk quickly through the homeless encampment under the freeway, drive between the city and the suburbs, take the train through Connecticut, cross abandoned railways. Next time you pass through, consider collecting some mugwort leaves for a topical application, shaking some fennel seeds to encourage their spread, ducking behind a paulownia for a consultation with the dead.

NOTES

1. Federici, *Witches, Witch-Hunting, and Women*, 3–4, 21.
2. Moore, Gann, and sparrow, "Comrades in Arms with the Web of Life."
3. Patel and Moore, *A History of the World in Seven Cheap Things*, 22.
4. Mittman, "Reflections on the Plantationocene."
5. Reo et al., "Invasive Species, Indigenous Stewards."
6. Kimmerer, *Braiding Sweetgrass*, 213–14.
7. Buhner, *Herbal Antivirals*, 90–92.
8. Scott, *Invasive Plant Medicine*, 261–67.
9. Tagle et al., "Asking, We Walk," 42–45.
10. Angeloni, "Japanese Knotweed."
11. We are inspired by the work of Max Haiven and Cassie Thornton, who made seed bombs with Japanese knotweed to bring property values down in an intervention against luxury real estate ventures. Haiven and Thornton, "2 Talks, 2 Ways 2 Prophet."
12. Kellhammer, "Nature 2.0."
13. Kimmerer, *Braiding Sweetgrass*, 200.
14. Del Tredici, *Wild Urban Plants*, 40, 80, 238.
15. Kellhammer, "Hyperorganisms."
16. Walker, "Study Warns of Hybrid Invasive Weeds."
17. *Economist*, "Greater than the Sum of Its Parts."
18. Linebaugh, *Stop, Thief!*, 25.
19. Linebaugh, *Stop, Thief!*, 24–25.
20. Harney and Moten, *Undercommons*, 42–43.
21. Stafford, "'Cheap Nature."
22. Federici, *Caliban and the Witch*, 20–50.
23. Federici, *Caliban and the Witch*, 170.
24. Federici, *Caliban and the Witch*, 198–200, 219–38.
25. Federici, *Witches Witch-Hunting, and Women*, 32.
26. Taussig, *The Devil and Commodity Fetishism*, 92.

27   Harney and Moten, *Undercommons*, 77.
28   Harney and Moten, *Undercommons*, 74, 110.
29   Haughwout, "AMAZON IS BURNING," *empyre* (listserv), September 16, 2019, http://lists.artdesign.unsw.edu.au/pipermail/empyre/2019-September/010713.html.
30   Benjamin, *Illuminations*, 257–58.
31   Van Dooren, *Flight Ways*, 140.
32   Despret, *What Would Animals Say*, 87.
33   James, *Moon Witch Spider King*, 338.
34   Rose, *Reports from a Wild Country*, 13.
35   Farley, "When the Stars Begin to Fall," 229.
36   Marx, *Capital*, 289.
37   Karuka, *Empire's Tracks*, 58–59, 102–3.
38   Westbrooks, "Invasive Plants."
39   Galloway, "The Cybernetic Hypothesis," 111.
40   Moore, "Opiates of the Environmentalists?"
41   Tiqqun [Collective], *The Cybernetic Hypothesis*, 146.
42   Taussig, *The Devil and Commodity Fetishism*, 15.
43   hooks, "Marginality as a Site of Resistance," 341.
44   Taussig, *The Devil and Commodity Fetishism*, 92.
45   Quammen, "Planet of Weeds."
46   Tagle et al., "Asking, We Walk," 42.

BIBLIOGRAPHY

Angeloni, Christian. "Japanese Knotweed Knocks £20bn off Value of UK Property Market." *Independent*, September 28, 2018.

Benjamin, Walter. *Illuminations*. New York: Schocken Books, 1968.

Buhner, Stephen. *Herbal Antivirals: Natural Remedies for Emerging and Resistant Viral Infections*. North Adams, MA: Storey Publishing, 2013.

Davis, Mike. *Dead Cities*. New York: New Press, 2002.

Del Tredici, Peter. *Wild Urban Plants of the Northeast: A Field Guide*. Ithaca, NY: Cornell University Press, 2020.

Despret, Vinciane. *What Would Animals Say if We Asked the Right Questions?* Minneapolis: University of Minnesota Press, 2016.

The Economist. "Greater than the Sum of Its Parts." October 31, 2015.

Estes, Nick, and Roxanne Dunbar Ortiz. "Examining the Wreckage." *Monthly Review* 72, no. 3 (2020). https://monthlyreview.org/2020/07/01/examining-the-wreckage/.

Farley, Anthony Paul. "When the Stars Begin to Fall: Introduction to Critical Race Theory and Marxism." *Columbia Journal of Race and Law* 1, no. 3 (2011): 226–46. https://doi.org/10.7916/cjrl.v1i3.2263.

Federal Interagency Committee for the Management of Noxious and Exotic Weeds and Randy G. Westbrooks. "Invasive Plants: Changing the Landscape of America." All U.S. Government Documents (Utah Regional Depository), Paper 490, 1998. https://digitalcommons.usu.edu/govdocs/490/.

Federici, Silvia. *Caliban and the Witch: Women, the Body and Primitive Accumulation*. Brooklyn, NY: Autonomedia, 2014.

Federici, Silvia. *Re-enchanting the World: Feminism and the Politics of the Commons*. Oakland: PM Press, 2019.

Federici, Silvia. *Witches, Witch-Hunting, and Women*. Oakland: PM Press, 2018.

Galloway, Alex. "The Cybernetic Hypothesis." *Differences* 25, no. 1 (2014): 107–31. https://doi.org/10.1215/10407391-2432538.

Gan, Elaine. "An Unintended Race: Miracle Rice and the Green Revolution." *Environmental Philosophy* 14, no. 1 (2017): 61–81. https://doi.org/10.5840/envirophil20174648.

Haiven, Max, and Cassie Thornton. "2 Talks, 2 Ways 2 Prophet: University of the Phoenix + Luxury SF Real Estate Jewelry." Talk presented at RTS Talks, San Francisco, CA, April 25, 2017.

Harney, Stefano, and Fred Moten. *The Undercommons: Fugitive Planning and Black Study*. New York: Autonomedia, 2017.

hooks, bell. "Marginality as a Site of Resistance." In *Out There: Marginalization and Contemporary Cultures*, edited by Russell Ferguson, Martha Gever, Trinh T. Minh-ha, and Cornel West, 341–43. Cambridge, MA: MIT Press, 1990.

James, Marlon. *Moon Witch Spider King*. New York: Riverhead Books, 2022.

Karuka, Manu. *Empire's Tracks: Indigenous Nations, Chinese Workers, and the Transcontinental Railroad*. Oakland: University of California Press, 2019.

Kellhammer, Oliver. "Hyperorganisms." Accessed January 31, 2022. http://www.oliverk.org/art-projects/research/hyperorganisms.

Kellhammer, Oliver. "Nature 2.0: Post Industrial Ecologies of the Hudson River Estuary." Accessed January 31, 2022. http://www.oliverk.org/myevents/nature-20-post-industrial-ecologies-of-the-hudson-river-estuary.

Kimmerer, Robin Wall. *Braiding Sweetgrass: Indigenous Wisdom, Scientific Knowledge, and the Teachings of Plants*. Minneapolis MN: Milkweed Editions, 2013.

Linebaugh, Peter. *Stop Thief! The Commons, Enclosures, and Resistance*. Oakland, CA: PM Press, 2014.

Marx, Karl. *Capital, Volume One*. London: Pelican Books, 1976.

Mittman, Greg. "Reflections on the Plantationocene: A Conversation with Donna Haraway and Anna Tsing." *Edge Effects*, June 18, 2019.

Moore, Jason W. *Capitalism in the Web of Life: Ecology and the Accumulation of Capital*. New York: Verso, 2015.

Moore, Jason W. "Opiates of the Environmentalists? Anthropocene Illusions, Planetary Management and the Capitalocene Alternative." *Polen Ekoloji*, December 9, 2021.

Moore, Jason W., Tom Gann, and josie sparrow. "Comrades in Arms with the Web of Life: A Conversation with Jason W. Moore." *New Socialist*, October 16, 2021.

Patel, Raj, and Jason W. Moore. *A History of the World in Seven Cheap Things: A Guide to Capitalism, Nature, and the Future of the Planet*. Oakland: University of California Press, 2017.

Quammen, David. "Planet of Weeds." In *Natural Acts: A Sidelong View of Science and Nature*, 161–88. New York: W. W. Norton, 2008.

Reo, Nicholas J., Kyle Whyte, Darren Ranco, Jodi Brandt, Emily Blackmer, and Braden Elliott. "Invasive Species, Indigenous Stewards, and Vulnerability Discourse." *American Indian Quarterly* 41, no. 3 (2017): 201–23. https://doi.org/10.5250/amerindiquar.41.3.0201.

Rose, Deborah Bird. *Reports from a Wild Country: Ethics for Decolonization*. South Sydney: University of New South Wales Press, 2004.

Scott, Timothy Lee. *Invasive Plant Medicine: The Ecological Benefits and Healing Abilities of Invasives*. Rochester, VT: Healing Arts Press, 2010.

Stafford, Richard Todd. "'Cheap Nature, or, the Cultural Logic of Historical Capitalism' with Jason Moore." Podcast *Capitalism, Climate, and Culture*, March 13, 2019. Accessed June 19, 2024. https://culturalstudies.gmu.edu/articles/13020.

Tagle, Thea Quiray, Lorraine Affourtit, Mirna Boyadjian, Margaretha Haughwout, Beverly Naidus, and Laurencia Strauss. "Asking, We Walk: Challenging *Zapaturismo* in International 'Activist Art' Residencies toward a Praxis of Radical Hope." *Ethnic Studies Review* 44, no. 3 (2021): 31–48.

Taussig, Michael T. *The Devil and Commodity Fetishism in South America*. Chapel Hill: University of North Carolina Press, 2010.

Tiqqun [Collective]. *The Cybernetic Hypothesis*. South Pasadena CA: Semiotext(e), 2020.

Van Dooren, Thom. *Flight Ways: Life and Loss at the Edge of Extinction*. New York: Columbia University Press, 2014.

Randy D. Westbrooks. "Invasive Plants: Changing the Landscape of America." Federal Interagency Committee for the Management of Noxious and Exotic Weeds Report, 1998.

Walker, Haley. "Study Warns of Hybrid Invasive Weeds." *Great Lakes Echo*, November 23, 2010.

Thirty · NICOLE TRIGG

Feminism as a Demon, or, The Difference Witches Make: Chiara Fumai with Carla Lonzi

Radical means roots: Italian art writer and feminist Carla Lonzi (1931–1982)—an inspiration to Italian multimedia artist Chiara Fumai (1978–2017)—sought out the roots of injustice and the roots of embodied knowledge in her struggle for the end of "a man's world." Radical feminism in this key willfully dwells in a nonconformist network of interstices repressed by that world, occult lifeways that shirk and are shirked by normative representation.

Lonzi and radical feminists like her revolt against the disciplinary processes that make us all "the same" under the law. They do not dismiss nor are they placated by piecemeal protections that reduce harm while continuing to fight for freedom of thought and action for every person against alienating and dehumanizing social conditions and categories. Radical feminists fight for an epistemological shift that "empties of meaning the goal of seizing power."[1] In Lonzi's vocabulary, as reanimated by Fumai, being different is no longer a pejorative but signals a world other than this one. This other world contains multitudes and is continually becoming itself, exceeding the purported boundaries of the individual and every other categorical construct. *Being between, neither this nor that,* difference means change: a potential destruction of established norms and values and a proliferation of alternatives. This betweenness is therefore very dear to radical feminists and to witches.

Together with other feminists since the 1960s, I reclaim the misogynist epithet "witch" on the grounds that "the witch burning in early modern

Europe is still regarded as the climax of an ongoing war between a patriarchal Church and nonpatriarchal indigenous beliefs, and the witch-hunt itself is made into a model that can explain the brutality of later European colonizations or, more recently, the holocaust of the Jews."[2] The act of reclaiming thus serves to remember the unrelieved history of intersecting forms of imperialist, white supremacist, capitalist patriarchal violence and to mark a site of resistance. Self-proclaimed witches also take recourse in the etymology of the word *witch*, as derived from the Old English *wicca*, tracing the latter through "the Indo-European *wic*, *weik* or the Norse *vikja*, meaning 'to shape, bend or twist.'"[3] Accordingly, a witch is a person "skilled in the craft of shaping, bending and changing reality."[4] I adhere to this definition as I explore the charged relationship between Fumai and Lonzi, a pair of would-be witches. I surmise that Fumai cultivated the craft of altering reality by appropriating and reanimating the words and personas of deceased, deviant women. Witches insist that other worlds are not only possible, they are already present. For Fumai, the ecstatic double movement of the ritual of possession awakens the transformative potential that exists always and everywhere between beings. Meanwhile, Lonzi approached both art writing and feminism as vehicles for changing the known world that—like Witchcraft, but unlike other political projects—departs from the transformation of oneself. In her words: "I believe that when a person does art criticism, they ought to examine themselves, have an experience, absorb themselves in that sector of activity, in other words conduct an initiation—the word came to me and I'm keeping it—because an initiation means you go into a thing, drop down into it, it absorbs you, you transform yourself and in the meantime you live, no?"[5]

Indeed, according to both Lonzi and Fumai, ripping holes in the established order to clear access to other, marginalized realms or in which to invent nonproprietary modes of knowing and relating, begins by making and sustaining contact with the void where self-certainty should be. Here I mean a person's secure sense of self, because their cultural milieu reflects and affirms their identity. For radical feminists and witches who refuse to assimilate to a dominant culture that refuses their differences, such a void is close at hand. Carla Lonzi affirmed its feminist potential in 1977, writing, "This 'I' as cultural void ... constitutes the prerequisite for a rediscovery of our body, that is, of a culture of our own.... But every woman confronts and measures this emptiness alone: it is hardly bearable, [in it] is the risk of the loss of sense ... a risk with which I am assured that I can live, now that I know I share it: feminism gave me this."[6] It follows that

Fumai's performances of possession by the presences, voices, and words of radical women—countercultural thinkers of the postwar period including Lonzi, Ulrike Meinhof, and Valerie Solanas as well as nineteenth-century sideshow performer Annie Jones, a.k.a. "the bearded woman," and psychic medium Eusapia Palladino—do not turn on the artist's presence (in keeping with a canonical definition of performance art), but rely instead on her absence.[7] Fumai withdraws her own will and subjectivity to make dis/possession possible. A door is cracked open here that is normally locked and bolted in a world ordered by the ideology of proprietary personhood. "It wasn't easy for me to recognize that the absence of identity, which I had always experienced as distinctively my own, which brought me both satisfaction and desperation, *was* myself, it was the sole possibility of being myself," Lonzi asserts.[8] Because the established order historically and currently misidentifies women and other others as less than human, they find themselves in its negative spaces.

Fumai created performance scores by appropriating, remixing, and reanimating others' words. Curator duo Francesco Urbano Ragazzi describes her way of working as "one long echo": the material and immaterial traces of the life of Lonzi among others are exhumed, then made to travel and resound across media, including the artist's own body and voice. Urbano Ragazzi suggests that Fumai's work of appropriation is tied to and reclaims the antisocial, deviant, thieving figure of "the criminal woman," classified as such by the Italian eugenicist and criminal anthropologist Cesare Lombroso in 1893.[9] Lombroso's spurious contribution to the social sciences picks up where the persecution of women as witches leaves off: by identifying as menaces to society those women and girls who fail to fulfill, or indeed actively sabotage, their assignment as sexual and reproductive operatives, thus undermining the sacred, conjoined institutions of family and nation. Such "criminal women" ought to be contained if not eliminated, warns Lombroso, and in any case segregated from the stock of "normal women," those best equipped to perpetuate the "superior" (read: white) Italian race. In her appropriative performances of feminist dis/possession, Fumai deliberately provokes the enduring fear of the unattached woman, of female sexuality, and of female disobedience in Western modernity, inviting all "criminal women" to show themselves.

Introducing her 2013 performance "Shut Up, Actually Talk" as part of a process of "unworking," Fumai cites one criminal woman in particular: Valerie Solanas (1936–88).[10] Solanas had envisioned a radical feminist future in which "SCUM will become members of the unwork force, the fuck-up force; they will get jobs of various kinds and unwork. For example, SCUM salesgirls will not charge for merchandise; SCUM telephone operators will not charge for calls; SCUM office and factory workers, in addition to fucking up their work, will secretly destroy equipment. SCUM will unwork at a job until fired, then get a new job to unwork at."[11]

At a glance, the SCUM of the title of Solanas's manifesto suggests a slur on men, as in "men are scum"; whereas Solanas applies the name to herself and her feminist legion. Like Fumai, Solanas tests the potential of affirming the negative epithet, with the idea of torquing the present system of signification and valuation into new shapes, with new openings. Unworking means willfully violating the interlocking cultural codes on which human, animal, and environmental exploitation and expropriation depend, including the law of private property, the ideology of individualism, and of course, the ethic of work. Accordingly, unworkers prefer appropriation before authorship. Together with Solanas, Fumai gestures at a deconstructive process of unpacking and reanimating what and who have been wrapped up and discarded by the hegemonic order, suggesting that the return of the repressed can and will change everything.

The title, "Shut Up, Actually Talk" is a translation of *Taci, anzi parla*, Lonzi's 1978 publication comprising over one thousand pages of mixed-genre diary entries. The performance text consists of the translation of a lineated manifesto from 1977, "Io dico io" (I say I), also written by Lonzi under the banner of the Italian feminist writing and publishing collective, Rivolta Femminile (Female Revolt).[12] By ventriloquizing Lonzi and Solanas, Fumai conjures two women who made a practice of thinking and writing through their gender assignment. Neither sought to erase or reverse their inferior social status as women; rather, each sought to examine the creative and critical potentialities of the negativity of their differentiation. I refer to them as radical feminists of difference, feminists calling on and from an elsewhere, animating an uncanny other who does not meld with the status quo once concessions are won, whose relationship to space, place, and time marks a fugue and a clearing from the dominant paradigm. It is in this sense that Fumai practices "feminism as a demon."[13]

Katherine McKittrick writes that in addition to its religious valences, the demonic signals "a non-deterministic schema . . . a process . . . hinged on uncertainty and non-linearity," and it "acts to identify a system (social, geographic, technological) that can only unfold and produce an outcome if uncertainty, or (dis)organization, or something supernaturally demonic, is integral to the methodology."[14] She specifies, glossing Sylvia Wynter, that

FIGURE 30.1 Advertisement for Chiara Fumai's "Shut Up, Actually Talk!," 2013.

the demonic "makes possible a different unfolding, one that does not *replace* or override or remain subordinate to the vantage point of 'Man' but instead parallels his constitution and his master narratives of humanness."[15] In other words, the demonic accounts for a level of difference that fails to be encompassed by history's "progress," devised as a unilinear, vertical succession of "syntheses." It does not relate to the dominant term, "Man," dialectically, but is instead—to borrow some of Lonzi's key words—unhitched and unexpected.[16] The "Unexpected Subject"[17] of feminism is demonic because it arises through encounters between socially differentiated others that are normally preempted by hegemonic power structures. Lonzi felt dogged by the logic of superiority and inferiority, or "absolute difference" disguised as "absolute dual."[18] She was primarily concerned with the social inferiorization of women, their monstrous *not-A* to men's *A*, hiding in plain sight behind the screen of naturalized gender, and as a consequence, women's absence from history. In the essay "Beyond Miranda's Meanings," Sylvia Wynter addresses Caliban's absent Native or Black woman-companion and mate in Shakespeare's *The Tempest*, unthinkable on account of her double difference;[19] she is therefore silenced in advance, relegated to the "demonic grounds" of repressed human content. Indeed, the demonic threatens the integrity of the established order and its regulatory and reproductive systems as the uncannily animate, composite outside of that order. Anything can and does happen here.[20] Depending on a person's attachments or detachments to or from the world-as-we-know-it, the threat of the demonic stirs an entire range of excited feelings—as Fumai conspired to do, performing her possession both of and by other witches.

In her preamble to the performance, Fumai explains that a third *unexpected subject* besides Lonzi and Solanas will make an appearance: Zalumma Agra, "The Circassian Girl" or "'Star of the East,'"[21] a sideshow performer from P. T. Barnum's American Museum. Barnum employed women of various actual origins to incarnate Zalumma, emblem of the "purest white race,"[22] whose signature attribute was nonetheless associated with racial difference: voluminously styled and crimped hair.[23] Whether such a combination of racial signifiers denotes a positive, negative, or other fantasy of miscegenation around the time of abolition and the subsequent spread of scientific racism,[24] Zalumma typified Orientalism as "raw" white female beauty, at the ready for Western refinement, yet with a residue of sexual slavery. Her story arc vindicated both imperialism and paternalism in relation to cultural and gender differences. Indeed, generations of Black and other radical feminists have articulated that it was in this context of post-Enlightenment, racist science and entertainment, that racial differences as well as gender differences—reserved for white, middle-class women of European descent—were secured. Zalumma was fashioned as the living-but-silent display of these categories interacting, a mix of the familiar and unfamiliar but about-to-be-erased. Insofar as her appearance aroused a safe, self-assuring Orientalist fantasy for white male target audiences, it was a comfort *and* a titillation that advanced the installation of such social norms as white Western male supremacy; white womanhood as passive, compliant, and full of sexual promise; and Black womanhood as dangerous, if not invisible and illegible.

Fumai injects her voice and Lonzi's words into and back out of Zalumma, as she meanwhile makes way for Zalumma's players to be resurrected with a new script—no longer silent. The social hierarchies fortified by the myth of the "Circassian Girl" are blown apart by Fumai's Zalumma/Zalumma's Fumai: the available identities of proper white men and white women are no longer validated but explicitly refused in the course of the performance. In her preface, Fumai observes that "culture perceives an idea as contradictory, but it's not contradictory, it's a thought from the double—a non-logocentric presence"; she then goes on: "like, who are you / and the answer / usually the devil answer(s) / never says who she is, she says / YOU KNOW WHO I AM, DON'T YOU."[25] She pronounces the last line in a guttural voice between hiss, rasp, and growl.

Carla Lonzi wrote in 1970: "Woman does not relate to the male world dialectically. The demands she brings to light do not imply an antithesis, but action on another level."[26] The demonic feminist-of-difference witch wears at least two faces: one that snarls and grimaces, keeping at bay the sameness that would absorb it ("I distance myself"[27]), and another that is less legible and more changeable. This other face is looking at something invisible, already occupied with encountering and inhabiting the world differently. Flipping between the faces of despised derivative and strategic separatist—spinning her head around as necessary, or for fun—the witch labors with her back turned, hissing over her shoulder, guarding the commodious threshold between worlds. The witch is associated with three modalities: victimhood, vindication, and initiation. From harmed, to harming, to unhitching from the harmful loop altogether and beginning unprecedented action/s. The first two modes *are* dialectically related to the patriarchal order that produces witches and other feminine monsters to sustain itself; the mode of initiation is not, but it may coincide with unfinished business. Talking back to the patriarchs and "Daddy's Girls" who would silence her is the witch's prerogative as she processes her waning attachments.[28]

In an epistolary essay addressed to Fumai after her death, Federico Campagna expounds on the labyrinth as a figure for reality apprehended as a continuous rather than separable formation. Through this lens, "built originally as a prison—according to the myth [of the Minotaur]—the labyrinth soon revealed its nature as a path of initiation."[29] Lonzi and Fumai agree, pronouncing, "I am my own adventure," and "Losing my way is my proof."[30] Common sense dictates that the *outside* of patriarchal subjectivity and propriety is a maze of bondage and confusion, but witches see (to) it otherwise: as a lifeway of radical hospitality, an initiation into unassimilable human experience "from the double," and an opportunity to attend to one another's "non-logocentric presence" as human beings, to which human language—deployed unilaterally—is always inadequate. Among witches, language, gesture, and attentiveness to the manifestations of all others, including what one does not yet know or expect of oneself, mingle in every direction; such encounters boost the emergence of radical alterity between beings who, unhitched from the usual ideological enclosure, recognize and value their interdependence. "You fear that I will be the interlocutor with the world that you could never be."[31] Fumai chooses to possess and be possessed by Zalumma Agra, not because Zalumma Agra and her story waver at a tipping point into racial and sexual assimilation, but because—viewed otherwise—she marks and holds the place of indeterminate and defamiliarized difference, because she resides on the threshold of knowability and is nevertheless present. Zalumma "doesn't belong to *no thing*," Fumai announces, since she "is not the wife, is not the mother, is not the lover, is not the prostitute";[32] in other words, no category of normative femininity envelops her. She is a just figure to incorporate, therefore, as the echo portends: "You will come to envy my *no thing*."[33]

Recalling Fumai's note that "the devil never says who," I look to Hannah Arendt to shed light on the nexus of identity, difference, and the "path of initiation." In *The Human Condition*, Arendt outlines that *what* a person is may be readily established in words—a list of qualities that solidify their social and personal identities, signifiers of belonging or unbelonging "necessarily share[d] with others like [them]"—whereas "the manifestation of *who* the speaker and doer unexchangeably is, though it is plainly visible, retains a curious intangibility that confounds all efforts toward unequivocal verbal expression."[34] This "who" shirks description and at the same time constitutes a person's non-substitutable "difference" or "uniqueness," which she exhibits to everyone and has in common with no one.[35] The "who" is action—performance—without any name, and the "what" are the fixed meanings of words. In a logocentric culture, the "what" that rolls easily off the tongue is privileged, the "who" is devalued, and the catalog of recognizable qualities comes to answer for a person's ineffability, as if in apology. Saying who, then, when the "who" resists saying, is in actuality saying "what." "You don't know who I am, and you make yourself my mediator,"[36] Fumai delivers the line in a hoarse crescendo. You, the patriarchal subject of whichever gender, attempt to speak for my unspeakable "who," finding the indeterminacy unbearable.

"The devil never says who she is, she says, YOU KNOW WHO I AM, DON'T YOU."[37] If the only substance of the "who" is live action and speech, it leaves nothing behind outside of the impressions left with spectators—"like the *daimōn* in Greek religion which accompanies each [person] throughout [their] life, always looking over [their] shoulder from behind and thus visible only to those [they] encounter."[38] This *daimōn* of everyone living—or dead—counts on YOU to receive it, to sense its "non-logocentric presence" without substitutes. *Daimōnic*/demonic elements stack together in Fumai's work: spiritual residues of the actual dead—the un-bodied "who"—on top of the byproducts of cultural repression, of the "who" while it lives. "The point is that the manifestation of the 'who' comes to pass in the same manner as the notoriously unreliable manifestations of ancient oracles, which, according to Heraclitus, 'neither reveal nor hide in words, but give manifest signs.'"[39] As many spectators as actors are needed to receive and hold these wordless signs that introduce a "character of startling unexpectedness" into the world.[40] Extending Arendt's thought, Adriana Cavarero describes such a scene more precisely, as "an interactive theater in which every person is both actor and spectator at the same time."[41] This point cannot be overemphasized: the "who" that constitutes each person's radical distinctness and that therefore holds vital political potential, does not exist except in relation; we receive one another's "who" in a reciprocal exchange of keen, open-minded attention and fearless self-exhibition. Goading the audience, Lonzi and Fumai ask: "Do you know what exposing yourself means?"[42]

Fumai's performance of demonic feminist possession reclaims and cultivates attentiveness to the "who" rather than to the "what," and it goes further by basing her act—the exhibition of *her* "who"—on the invocation of spirits, which is to say, by assembling more than one "who" together with her own. Fumai calls upon Lonzi and other members of Rivolta Femminile, as well as Zalumma Agra or the anonymous women who portrayed her; and she offers her voice to all the silenced women whom Zalumma's appearance brought to mind, or banished from it, too. In demonic feminist unworking, the "who" is multiplied exponentially, and to Cavarero's point, every attendee at the gathering is both actor and spectator at the same time. The audience of "Shut Up, Actually Talk" senses that inasmuch as Fumai speaks, she is also being spoken.

By extension, if viewers of Fumai and readers of this essay require something more substantial to hold on to, we can pivot from the person

(Fumai) as medium, to the medium of the text, and to the activity and experience of *reading*. Witnessing Fumai witnessing Lonzi and Zalumma Agra, we encounter a model of reading and engaging with the dead that is participatory to an extreme. Arendt describes the relationship between writers and readers, or artists and spectators, by evoking the supernatural:

> We mentioned before that this reification and materialization [of thought into art], without which no thought can become a tangible thing, is always paid for, and that the price is life itself: it is always the "dead letter" in which the "living spirit" must survive, a deadness from which it can be rescued only when the dead letter comes again into contact with a life willing to resurrect it, although this resurrection of the dead shares with all living things that it, too, will die again.[43]

The text or other art form is the dead remnant of the life poured into its creation, a life that can however be temporarily reanimated by a willing, even willful recipient: the reader or viewer prepared to devote full attention to this "reified thought," and in so doing, to de-reify it. In the act of reading, the reader not only returns the art or text back into thought and life; they also allow this thought to travel through them, to such an extent that it changes them. Peggy Phelan writes, after Roland Barthes, that "the reader, in becoming writing's destination, inhabits an identity-less-ness that is crucial to becoming something other than who or what we are; it is fundamental to the transformation of subjectivity that we seek in reading. To read is to long to return to ourselves from a different angle than the one we possessed at our departure point."[44] Phelan's "who or what we are" should not be mistaken for the *who* spelled out above via Arendt; rather, these are Phelan's words for the *what* of fixable, qualifiable identity. *Who* is a state of dynamism, associated here with a demonic feminist subject—an actor and a spectator, a reader and a writer—actively desiring change through close encounters with texts and the spirits they deliver. In this light, text and reader interrelate through an ethics of hospitality: each plays host *and* guest to the other, and so the reality-altering magic of intersubjective transformation persists and is cultivated across the gulfs between people, living and dead.

How might we bewitch—make lost or abandoned—those modes of our thinking and doing that reproduce harm? Unhitching from the dominant frame, witches turn to each other, and the possibilities for doing differently proliferate between them. Fumai chooses to reanimate Lonzi's scathing rejection of deeply entrenched patterns of patriarchal logic, to draw strength from her utter determination as she backs away into the unknown, spitting, and insisting—against all odds and admonishments—that other worlds are possible and immanent.

NOTES

1. Lonzi, *Sputiamo su Hegel*, 20. Unless otherwise noted, all translations are my own.
2. Salomonsen, *Enchanted Feminism*, 7.
3. Salomonsen, *Enchanted Feminism*, 7.
4. Adler, *Drawing Down the Moon*, 11.
5. Lonzi, *Autoritratto*, 62.
6. Lonzi, "Itinerario di riflessioni," 22.
7. Ragazzi, "Roundtable Dedicated to Chiara Fumai," 29:40.
8. Lonzi, "Itinerario di riflessioni," 25 (emphasis added).
9. Ragazzi, "Roundtable Dedicated to Chiara Fumai," 53:15.
10. Fumai, "Shut Up, Actually Talk," 00:50. Valerie Solanas was a US-born radical feminist best known for penning her *SCUM* (Society for Cutting Up Men) *Manifesto*, in 1967. She advocated for the revolutionary feminist overthrow of society, and for the elimination of men. Importantly, for Solanas, men are not men on (strictly) biological terms, but insofar as their masculinity hinges on dominating women and emasculated others; similarly, women could also be "Daddy's Girls," and therefore just as culpable as macho men.
11. Solanas, *SCUM Manifesto*, 42.
12. Rivolta Femminile was founded in Rome in 1970 by Lonzi, the artist Carla Accardi, and the writer Elvira Banotti.
13. Fumai offered this qualification in the preamble to her 2013 performance of "Shut Up, Actually Talk," 01:50.
14. McKittrick, *Demonic Grounds*, xxiv.
15. McKittrick, *Demonic Grounds*, xxv.
16. Lonzi repeatedly employs the metaphor of the hook or hitch. She writes, for instance: "There is a moment in a girl's life that passes like a meteor: the moment *she unhitches herself* from her paternal home and, alone, perceives in confusion the entire potentiality of her being." Lonzi, *Sputiamo su Hegel*, 87 (my emphasis).
17. "Whoever is outside of the master-slave dialectic becomes conscious and introduces the Unexpected Subject into the world." Lonzi, *Sputiamo su Hegel*, 47.
18. Spackman, "Monstrous Knowledge," 297.
19. Wynter, "Beyond Miranda's Meanings," 360.
20. Denise Ferreira da Silva concludes her article, "Hacking the Subject: Black Feminism and Refusal Beyond the Limits of Critique," with these encouraging words: "Because, as my experiment with hacking the patriarch-form

indicates, I am convinced that what lies outside the equations, in which the sexual black (and native) female body means nothing, is a Nothing by which I mean Everything and Anything else than the World as we know it today." Ferreira da Silva, 38.

21 See *Circassian Girl*.
22 See *Circassian Girl*.
23 Martin, *White African American Body*, 104.
24 Frost, *Never One Nation*, 57.
25 Fumai, "Shut Up, Actually Talk," 02:05–02:22.
26 Lonzi and Rivolta Femminile, *Sputiamo su Hegel*, 42.
27 Lonzi, "Io dico io"; and Fumai, "Shut Up, Actually Talk."
28 Solanas, *SCUM Manifesto*, 13.
29 Campagna, "Tunnel, Axe, Quarry, Hare," 141.
30 Lonzi and Rivolta Femminile, "Io dico io"; and Fumai, "Shut Up, Actually Talk."
31 The line reflects Lonzi's struggle to untether from the same old, same old, and re-tether to the unexpected. The feminine noun *interlocutrice* implies that another woman is the antagonist, having failed to break with patriarchal logic. Lonzi battles to separate from what harms her—even if it goes by the name "feminism"—while holding on to the possibility of a richly diverse, worldly existence *not* grounded in hierarchy and war. Rivolta, "Io dico io"; and Fumai, "Shut Up, Actually Talk."
32 Fumai, "Shut Up, Actually Talk."
33 Lonzi and Rivolta Femminile, "Io dico io"; and Fumai, "Shut Up, Actually Talk."
34 Arendt, *Human Condition*, 181 (emphasis added).
35 Arendt, *Human Condition*, 181.
36 Lonzi and Rivolta Femminile, "Io dico io"; and Fumai, "Shut Up, Actually Talk."
37 Fumai, "Shut Up, Actually Talk."
38 Arendt, *Human Condition*, 179–80.
39 Arendt, *Human Condition*, 182.
40 Arendt's word for this process of exchange is *politics*. Arendt, *Human Condition*, 178.
41 Cavarero, *Tu che mi guardi*, 34.
42 Lonzi and Rivolta Femminile, "Io dico io"; and Fumai, "Shut Up, Actually Talk."
43 Arendt, *Human Condition*, 169.
44 Phelan, "Not Surviving Reading," 78.

BIBLIOGRAPHY

Adler, Margot. *Drawing Down the Moon: Witches, Druids, Goddess-Worshippers, and Other Pagans in American Today*. Boston: Beacon Press, 1986.

Arendt, Hannah. *The Human Condition*. Chicago: University of Chicago Press, 2018.

Campagna, Federico. "Tunnel, Axe, Quarry, Hare: A Labyrinth for Chiara Fumai." In *Poems I Will Never Release: Chiara Fumai 2007–2017*, edited by Francesco Urbano Ragazzi, Milovan Farronato, and Andrea Bellini, 138–47. Milan: Nero Editions, 2021.

Cavarero, Adriana. *Tu che mi guardi, tu che mi racconti: Filosofia della narrazione*. Milano: Feltrinelli, 1997.

The Circassian Girl, Zalumma Agra, "Star of the East." Philadelphia: Jas. B. Rogers, 1873. http://hdl.handle.net/11134/110002:2330.

Ferreira da Silva, Denise. "Hacking the Subject: Black Feminism and Refusal beyond the Limits of Critique." *philoSOPHIA* 8, no. 1 (2018): 19–41.

Frost, Linda. *Never One Nation: Freaks, Savages, and Whiteness in U.S. Popular Culture, 1850–1877*. Minneapolis: University of Minnesota Press, 2005.

Fumai, Chiara. "Shut Up, Actually Talk." Filmed Jauary 11, 2013, La Maison Rouge, Paris, France. Daily Motion video, 18:27. https://www.dailymotion.com/video/xziqcy.

Lonzi, Carla. *Autoritratto: Accardi, Alviani, Castellani, Consagra, Fabro, Fontana, Kounellis, Nigro, Paolini, Pascali, Rotella, Scarpitta, Turcato, Twombly*. Milano: Et al., 2011.

Lonzi, Carla. "Itinerario di riflessioni." In *É già politica*, 13–50. Milano: Scritti di Rivolta Femminile, 1977.

Lonzi, Carla. *Sputiamo su Hegel e altri scritti*. Milano: Et al., 2010.

Lonzi, Carla, and Rivolta Femminile. "Io dico io." In *La presenza dell'uomo nel femminismo*. Milano: Scritti di Rivolta Femminile, 1978.

Phelan, Peggy. "Not Surviving Reading." *Narrative* 5, no. 1 (1997): 77–87.

Martin, Charles. *The White African American Body: A Cultural and Literary Exploration*. New Brunswick, NJ: Rutgers University Press, 2002.

McKittrick, Katherine. *Demonic Grounds: Black Women and the Cartographies of Struggle*. Minneapolis: University of Minnesota Press, 2006.

Ragazzi, Francesco Urbano. "Roundtable Dedicated to Chiara Fumai with Francesco Urbano Ragazzi, Milovan Farronato, Andrea Bellini, and Cristiana Perrella." Produced by Centro per l'Arte Contemporanea Luigi Pecci and Centre d'Art Contemporain Genève. Recorded February 2021. Video, 74:05. https://5e.centre.ch/en/words/table-ronde-dediee-a-chiara-fumai/.

Salomonsen, Jone. *Enchanted Feminism: Ritual, Gender and Divinity among the Reclaiming Witches of San Francisco*. London: Routledge, 2002.

Solanas, Valerie. *SCUM Manifesto*. London: Verso, 2015.

Spackman, Barbara. "Monstrous Knowledge." In *Monsters in the Literary Imagination*, edited by Keala Jewell, 297–310. Detroit: Wayne State University Press, 2001.

Wynter, Sylvia. "Beyond Miranda's Meanings: Un/silencing the 'Demonic Ground' of Caliban's 'Woman.'" In *Out of the Kumbla: Caribbean Women and Literature*, edited by Carole Boyce Davies and Elaine Savory Fido, 355–72. Trenton, NJ: Africa World Press, 1990.

Thirty-one · MARY JO NEITZ AND MARION S. GOLDMAN

Religion and Magic through Feminist Lenses

Tales of secularization are among the most influential narratives shaping the discourse about religion in North America and Western Europe. As sociologists of religion, we have heard, read, and participated in innumerable debates about the ongoing process of disappearing religiosity in our complex global world. Encounters with vernacular religious practices we observed in Finland stimulated our thinking about secularism in Northern Europe. We argue that magic is alive in the vernacular practices (paganism) we observed in Finland and in practices associated with the diffuse Human Potential Movement in the United States.[1] This preliminary research led us to consider how magic and vernacular religions have been marginalized and sometimes legally defined as illegitimate social practices.

The Peace of Westphalia in 1648 formally cemented the interdependence of congregational religions and the governing machinery of European nation states.[2] From the nineteenth century onward, missionaries and anthropologists sent to newly occupied or annexed territories carried these binary assumptions that shaped the contours of "real" legitimate religion. Almost unanimously, these travelers defined magical practices as primitive superstition.[3] This chapter explores different approaches to secularization and religion by acknowledging the personal and social impacts of witchcraft, local celebrations, household rituals, astrology, tarot, and other forms of divination.

In the twenty-first century, an increasing number of people in Western Europe and North America report that they have no religion or that they are spiritual rather than religious.[4] However, there is growing evidence that many respondents are by no means atheistic, irreligious, or secular. They describe engagement with centuries-old practices and vernacular traditions both within and outside of formally institutionalized religions.[5] Assumptions that contemporary institutionalized religion and vernacular spirituality have a binary relation obscure how magic shapes both cosmology and practice within and outside of formally recognized religions.

Many liberal twentieth-century second-wave feminists were influenced by Simone de Beauvoir's discussion of secularization as a sign of progress and gender equality.[6] However, scholars, activists, and popular writers have questioned assumptions about pervasive secularization or its importance in facilitating social equality. Donna Haraway's groundbreaking work confronts the dualistic thinking that frames binaries such as nature/culture, purity/pollution, self/other, male/female, and civilized/primitive. Her analyses of cyborgs and primate science challenge the ontology of thought that reflects divisions between humans and animals and humans and machines.[7]

Along with other transnational feminists, Vietnamese writer and filmmaker Trinh T. Minh-ha renounced the progress narrative.[8] In her 1989 book *Woman, Native, Other*, the Enlightenment was reframed as an "endarkenment." Feminist critiques of colonialist discourse developed a logic that challenged binaries and could be extended to magic/religion. We bring this critical conversation within feminism to bear on widespread academic assumptions and the marginalization of magic.

We will provide a heuristic definition of magic and review evidence of pervasive magical practices described in contemporary survey research about magical practices and worldviews. We will then turn to a brief discussion of how Western social scientists and religious studies scholars separated magic from religion and dismissed magic. We critique these binaries and then discuss the work of three queer feminists of color from different generations who break down the walls between religion and magic. Magic is central to Gloria Anzaldúa's foundational work. M. Jacqui Alexander builds on Anzaldúa's discussions of magic in ways that are more assertive and direct. Finally, we discuss the expansive, future-oriented work of Omise'eke Natasha Tinsley. These three related feminist approaches ground our consideration of the religion/magic binary and the foundational Western scholarship that has reified it. However, placing magic as a central element in conceptions of all religion disrupts the religion/secular binary and adds nuanced perspectives about religion, race, gender, and power.

MAGIC

Magic, religion, and spirituality are all contested concepts. Dominant religious and political organizations valorized their own practices and marginalized and often prohibited practices that contested their power and authority. In the European context, state churches exerted political and cultural power that shaped public attitudes and formal laws toward less entrenched religious groups that did not conform to their teachings. As Talal Asad reminds us, "Religion is not a transhistorical, transcultural phenomenon. Its definition inevitably reflects discursive processes that are temporally and culturally specific."[9] Hillary Waterman defines magic in ways that inform the cultural and historical fluidity that is central to our perspective in this chapter.[10] Important elements common to all kinds of magic are as follows:

1. Actors are practitioners, a subject and an agent similar to a spirit or energy source.
2. Magic is both located within and decontextualized from everyday life.
3. Magic has a special-purpose language, speech register, and music.
4. Magic has rituals and taboos.
5. Magic uses amulets, herbs, and talismans.
6. Magic often involves altered states of consciousness induced by chanting, fasting, or herbal draught.

Assumptions that magic is separate from religion have grounded the discourses supporting the denigration, marginalization, and suppression of witches. Social scientists rarely treat magic as central to religious experience and expression, although it is acknowledged in biblical miracles, revelations, and varied magical practices within formally recognized faiths. All magic is not part of witchcraft, but magic is critical to witchcraft in all cultures.

EVIDENCE FOR THE PERSISTENCE AND GROWTH OF MAGIC

Survey research that asks questions about practice indicates that many "religious 'nones'"—individuals who respond to survey questions and closed-ended interviews by saying that they have no religion—routinely engage with astrology, practice divination, and perform various other magical practices. Major research organizations such as the Pew Research Center have begun to grapple with ways to incorporate magical beliefs and practices into typologies of religion instead of lodging them outside of it. Their evidence supports new frames where religion, secularity, and the practice of magic are not exclusive.

A 2018 Pew study of a representative sample of Americans differs from most current research because it included questions about spiritual beliefs outside the standard measures of religion.[11] Findings indicated that 42 percent of their sample believed that "spiritual energy is energy located in physical things like mountains, trees, crystals." Belief that material things are imbued with spiritual energy or power is basic to most magical thought because spells produce the transfer of power from one object to another to effect desired changes. Of the respondents, 29 percent affirmed belief in astrology. More revealing was the demographic distribution of responses. Individuals who responded positively to questions about magical beliefs and practices were disproportionately younger, female, and more educated, with some college attendance or college degrees.

Part of this Pew project involved constructing classifications of Americans' religiosity that were not based on denominational affiliation or formally recognized religious traditions. Pew researchers asked about a wide variety of beliefs and practices and divided the sample into groups according to how the responses clustered. There were seven categories of respondents separated into three groups: the highly religious, somewhat religious, and nonreligious. New Age believers were distributed across all three, but within the groups, the belief that "spiritual power is located in physical things" sharply separated the categories. Among the highly religious, none of the most conservative "God and Country Believers" identified physical manifestations of spiritual power, unlike 85 percent of the "Diversely Devout," who did. It is hard to know if these findings represent a major change in American religiosity. It is possible that the belief in material containers of spiritual energies has been widespread for centuries, but with the contemporary decline of formally institutionalized faiths, these beliefs and practices are now more visible.

Declines in church attendance, belief in one true God, and denominational membership have been interpreted as providing evidence for secularization. In Max Weber's classic interpretation, they point to our disenchanted world.[12] However, when the Pew survey included questions about belief that "spiritual power is located in physical things," almost half the respondents said yes. These survey results do not offer a full profile of respondents' cosmologies, but they suggest something other than a purely secular perspective. The bestselling writings of Indigenous authors like Robin Wall Kimmerer speak to a desire for healthier ways to live on the earth and for understanding of the connections of spirit between all beings.[13]

WESTERN TREATMENTS OF MAGIC

Because they believed that salvation came through faith alone, leaders of the sixteenth- and seventeenth-century Protestant Reformations in Northern Europe attempted to destroy the magical symbols and devotions that were part of medieval Roman Catholicism. Protestants questioned the efficacy of objects such as relics or holy water as means to honor God or effect change, and they also diminished and feared magical practices outside the church. Some Protestant reformers, moreover, drew from biblical passages that associated magic with demons or the devil. The efforts to separate magic and religion and erase magic from social life involved two different rhetorical strategies.

Some accepted practitioners' basic claims about the power of magic to effect change. However, they asserted that the sources of that power were evil. Religious and secular authorities accused women of witchcraft when they participated in rituals and operated within imaginary worlds where the devil was real and sexual congress with him was possible. Another, later rhetorical strategy dismissed magic as ineffectual pseudoscience operating with faulty assumptions.[14] Magic was simply deemed empirically wrong.

Over time, traditional rituals and practices were pushed out from the center of society in Europe and North America, although they were retained as household practices by women who preserved them. Women wove magical practices into daily life, enacted them in seasonal celebrations, and passed them on to their daughters.[15] Although elaborate cosmologies spelled out correspondences and causal relationships, these were less important than practice. People who sought the help of witches, conjurers, and diviners and who participated in rituals and utilized charms and divinatory tools trusted that witches had power to protect and to effect changes and transformations.

In the nineteenth century, emerging academic disciplines of sociology and anthropology affirmed Christianity's binary definitions that entirely separated magic and religion. The idea of Christianity as the one true religion permeated scholarship in religious studies, theology, history, anthropology, and sociology. Scholars disparaged magical religions as superstitions or folk practices. They developed perspectives where religion was not just different from but superior to magic. Both academics and colonizers extended these binary definitions and hierarchical categories to non-Western societies. In some cases, such as Buddhism and Hinduism, Western scholars focused on texts and disregarded their magical aspects. Protestant understandings of what constituted religions also undermined attempts to establish more pluralistic views, as was the case at the 1893 Parliament of the World's Religions.[16]

As they developed scholarly definitions of religion, nineteenth-century British academics delegitimated magic.[17] Their biases were built into legitimations of Western colonization of Asia, and the Global South brought opportunities to extend their academic and political biases. E. B. Tylor, founder of cultural anthropology, presented an evolutionary model, wherein magic—defined as manipulative practices—was positioned at a primitive level, lower than the system of abstract beliefs that characterized real religion.[18] In contrast to his earlier flexibility, Émile Durkheim subsequently affirmed the magic/religion binary. Following Durkheim, later sociologists contended that religion is superior to magic because it creates a moral community through a church in contrast to magic, which is an individual act.[19] Moreover, magic could not answer questions about the meaning of life, offer otherworldly rewards, or sanctify a definitive moral order. Others suggest that religion is superior to magic because it affirms the unique relationship between humans and a powerful God who rewards and punishes their actions.[20] These widely shared distinctions between magic and religion fail to capture the dynamics of paganism or other vernacular religions. Since antiquity, Western philosophers and social theorists have also separated magic and science. Victorian anthropologist Sir James Frazer, for example, described magic as failed science because it involved arcane systems of thought that ignored reality.[21] Frazer believed that magical systems of ideas were incorrect and should be entirely dismissed.

Some twentieth-century cultural anthropologists developed less ethnocentric understandings of non-Western magical practices. E. E. Evans-Pritchard explored the rationality of Azande witchcraft, and others studied theatrical qualities of magical rituals.[22] However, sociologists and religious studies scholars who focused on Western societies sustained earlier scholars' negative biases and continued to emphasize the magic-religion binary.[23] Folklorist Sabina Magliocco argues that this binary is "grounded in a concept of religion as an analytic category that privileges Christian monotheism as the norm and views religions that deviate from it as deficient. Magic is used as a foil against which to define legitimate religious practice, perpetuating a pattern going back to classical time."[24] Critics of magic tend to reduce it to mere acts adrift from coherent cosmology. However, magic involves recognition of power/energy/spirit located in the material world, possibilities for manifesting that power, and codes of ethics or morality that shape the acceptable uses of that power.

The essentially pragmatic quality of magical practices oriented toward the experiential seems particularly suited to twenty-first-century spirituality. What made magic insufficient for Durkheim and other academics fits well with the current, more fluid organization of religion throughout most of the world. Vernacular traditions are accessible to individual practitioners since there are no tests or required professions of faith to enter into practice. Instead, the emphasis is on doing and on relationships with other practitioners. Moreover, where state churches and institutionalized faiths have lost their hegemonic status,[25] the importance of suppressing marginal religions and the legal apparatuses for doing so have diminished.

It is important to move away from old definitions of magic as evil, bad science, or primitive religion and to examine it as part of *all* religions. A central issue in contemporary sociology of religion in Europe and North America involves documenting and interpreting the rise of "religious 'nones.'" Saying that one has no religion has no obvious meaning. It is clear that the majority of respondents are not atheists,[26] although they may not believe in God or go to church or identify with a particular denomination. Questions about belief, congregational commitment, and religious identification remain social scientists' common measures of religiosity.[27] However, these measures fail to capture the many ways that people engage with spirit. As sociologists turn toward the study of "nonreligion," it is important that they avoid assuming that magic is separate from religion. Individuals who do not identify with world religions are not necessarily secular.

FEMINISM AND MAGIC

In the twentieth century, some feminists embraced witchcraft as a source of power. In 1968 some second-wave feminists in New York City called themselves witches and cursed Wall Street capitalists.[28] Some American branches of neo-paganism that emerged in the witchcraft revival of the 1970s, such as Dianic Wicca and Reclaiming, explicitly embraced feminism.[29] At the same time, however, from the mid-twentieth century through the first decades of the twenty-first century, other feminists disdained every kind of spirituality and religion.[30]

Most academic feminists who ignored or critiqued all religions affirmed the sacred/secular binary and embraced secularity as essential to feminist agendas. Nevertheless, some feminists considered the concept of secularization as a gendered phenomenon.[31] Moreover, some contemporary feminists suggest that the sacred/secular binary supports an exclusive, primarily white feminism that devalues the experiences of many women of color and working-class women as well.[32]

Poet and independent scholar Gloria Anzaldúa was among the few second-wave feminist theorists who underscored the importance of magic. Anzaldúa spent her life working toward a theory of spiritual activism. That aspect of her work was largely overlooked during her lifetime. Anzaldúa wrote in English, Spanish, Spanglish, and other languages of the Texas/Mexico border region where she grew up. She experienced many borders in her life as a lesbian queer woman of mixed race and dark skin. In *Borderlands* she called for a "mestiza consciousness" to break down subject/object dualism. Anzaldúa described feeling deviant when she was growing up because of social responses to her Indian heritage and her sexuality. Yet she also felt that she was a two-spirit person who possessed magical powers.[33] As someone existing in multiple social realities, she had to learn to live in the interface, switching modes, practicing magic, and experiencing magical realities: "I look for omens everywhere [in nature].... We are not supposed to remember such otherworldly events.... We have been taught that the spirit is inside our bodies or above our heads someplace in the sky with God. We are supposed to forget that every cell in our bodies, every bone and bird and worm has spirit in it."[34] Anzaldúa describes her trance experiences as transformative states of consciousness necessary to her writing process.[35] In this mode she experienced the sacred and secular as integral and recognized the interconnections of all beings.[36]

According to AnaLouise Keating, Anzaldúa's literary trustee, most feminist scholars ignored Anzaldúa's politics of spirit: "Although [feminist scholars] celebrate her groundbreaking contributions to feminist theory and her innovative formulations of the Borderlands and the new mestiza, they rarely examine the important roles Anzaldúa's spiritual activism plays in developing these theories."[37] Since Anzaldúa's death in 2004, Keating has continued to advance a holistic interpretation of Anzaldúa's contributions to feminist spirituality. Anzaldúa framed her own spiritual activism as an epistemology that later feminist scholars have expanded. M. Jacqui Alexander, an Afro Caribbean lesbian scholar and activist, has worked to preserve and disseminate knowledge of the material and spiritual practices from the African diaspora. Her book *Pedagogies of Crossing* includes a tribute to Anzaldúa.[38]

Alexander describes working collectively with others from 1997 through 2000 in order to understand the role of spirit and sex in their lives. She reports that many of the feminist activists in their group found it difficult to "come out spiritually," something she characterizes as the "subtle internalization of dominance."[39] She describes the process within her collective: members came to understand colonialism as "linked to dualistic and hierarchical thinking: divisions among the mind, body, and spirit; between sacred and secular, male and female, heterosexual and homosexual; . . . between the erotic and the divine."[40] Undoing the pain of colonialism therefore requires a movement toward wholeness, to reunite the erotic and the divine.[41]

Alexander opens her chapter "Pedagogies of the Sacred" with an invocation—an invitation to remember the shared past of the descendants of enslaved Africans who were taken across the Atlantic. Their spirituality is both "changing and changeless," coming from many African localities and continuing to transform in the Americas.[42] Alexander argues that spirit knowing is a way of making the world intelligible for many women who share this heritage.

Alexander references her own training and participation in African diasporic spiritual traditions. For her, it is spiritualized labor in which the body becomes a medium for the divine and a pathway to knowledge. Like Anzaldúa, Alexander emphasizes the spiritual as an epistemology, an embodied way of knowing and a pathway to healing. She also cautions that the critique of patriarchal religion has "kept us [feminists] away from the search for spirit."[43]

Anzaldúa and Alexander share the understanding that dismantling binary thinking is central to liberation. Transnational feminists attuned to colonial dislocations and fragmentation of identities have critiqued many aspects of Western thinking, including the idea of progress. Writers like Alexander prompt feminists to take the sacred seriously and stimulate twenty-first-century scholars to take the project into the future. One example of this future-orientation is Omise'eke Natasha Tinsley's creative exploration of

Vodun in *Ezili's Mirrors*. Tinsley writes in three voices (each represented by a different font) that express her academic voice, the voice of spirit knowledge, and the voice of the ancestors. Tinsley shows how witchcraft can be a way of knowing. Trance work creates access to ancestors' knowledge.[44] Although she describes her own participation in diasporic circles, including Vodun and Santeria, much of Tinsley's text analyzes contemporary performance traditions, where she finds many manifestations of Ezili—as the black femme, as a worker, as Party Queen, and as embodied rage. In Vodun, one can also explore possibilities of gender fluidity where "any person has the potential to be inhabited by different genders."[45] Tinsley finds words that evoke nonbinary ways of thinking and being. She celebrates the polyvocality of the African diaspora and describes the process of writing as a process of engaging with "theoretical polyamory."[46] Like Anzaldúa and Alexander, Tinsley describes finding commonality through working together in ritual and emphasizing the importance of healing. She affirms queerness and quotes José Esteban Muñoz: "Queerness is a longing that propels us onward, beyond romances of the negative. Queerness is that thing that lets us feel that this world is not enough."[47]

All three of these feminist scholars and activists reimagined how magic works in the contemporary world. Thinking about magic as a vital and transformative force in people's lives is a radical departure from mainstream Western thought.

CONCLUSION

Magical practices must be recognized as part of the contemporary religious landscape. For centuries Western academics have placed magic in binary opposition to religion and have delegitimated its religious impacts. This binary is part of the same package as other binaries in Western thought, including culture/nature, male/female, and civilized/ primitive. While the practice of magic can entail esoteric knowledge or specific ritual actions, it can also be accessible and profoundly antihierarchical. These qualities may help explain why men and, more specifically, white Euro-Americans are more likely to be atheists, and why women, Indigenous people, and people of color are more likely to be "spiritually awake."

There is a great deal of research attempting to explain why women are more religious than men by most quantitative measures. Explanations of this phenomenon range from hypotheses that women are more risk-averse than men to discussions of how women experienced modernization differently than men.[48] Returning to Anzaldúa, Alexander, and Tinsley and their different encounters with magic, we see the impact of multiple experiences of being othered. These three women were on the devalued sides of the binaries of race, gender, and sexuality. Reclaiming magic was part of their processes of reclaiming all parts of themselves. Magic's epistemologies and cosmologies may provide healing relationships with other humans and with the natural world.

Not everyone doing tarot or astrology fully embraces magic as a cosmology. But engagement in such practices is one of many indications that secularization is not the linear and progressive force theorized by Western social scientists and many second-wave feminists. There is much to be gained in leaving behind sacred/secular and magic/religion binaries. Fluid and queer perspectives are necessary for understanding the multiple manifestations of religion/spirit/magic in the twenty-first-century West.

NOTES

1. Neitz and Goldman, "The Pagan Canopy in Finland"; Goldman, *The American Soul Rush.*
2. Beyer, "Socially Engaged Religion."
3. Stark, "Reconceptualizing Religion, Magic, and Science."
4. Wilkins-Laflamme, "A Tale of Decline or Change?"
5. McGuire, *Lived Religion*; Ammerman, *Studying Lived Religion*; Luhrmann, *How God Becomes Real.*
6. Beauvoir, *Second Sex.*
7. Haraway, "Manifesto for Cyborgs"; Haraway, *Primate Visons.*
8. See Grewal and Kaplan, *Scattered Hegemonies*; Alexander and Mohanty, *Feminist Genealogies, Colonial Legacies, Democratic Futures*; Tsing, *Friction.*
9. Asad, *Genealogies of Religion,* 28–29.
10. Waterman, "Herbs and Verbs."
11. Data was collected as part of the American Trends Panel conducted December 4–18, 2018. The analysis is based on 4,729 responses, with a response rate of 86 percent. See Pew Research Center, *The Religious Typology.*
12. Weber, "Science as a Vocation."
13. Kimmerer, *Braiding Sweetgrass.*
14. Edmonds, *Drawing Down the Moon.*
15. Moser, "Submerged Spirituality in the Italian Alps."
16. The first Parliament of the World's Religions, an interfaith meeting of religious leaders from all over the world, coincided with the 1893 World's Co-

lumbian Exposition in Chicago. Tomoko Masuzawa, in *The Invention of World Religions*, argues that the pluralistic logic of the category of "world religion" provided a continuation of the universalistic destiny of European modernity.

17   Tambiah, *Magic, Science, Religion*.
18   Tylor, *Primitive Culture*.
19   Durkheim, *Elementary Forms of Religious Life*, 57–63.
20   Stark, *One True God*, 115
21   Frazer, *The Golden Bough*.
22   Tambiah, *Magic, Science, Religion*.
23   Stark, *One True God*.
24   Magliocco, "New Age and Neopagan Magic," 635.
25   Brown and Woodhead, *That Was the Church That Was*.
26   Smith and Cragun, "Mapping Religion's Other."
27   The National Opinion Research Center (NORC) has used these basic questions for decades, as have other major survey organizations such as the Pew Research Center. A counterexample is discussed below (Pew Research Center, *The Religious Typology*). Because such studies provide data about long-term trends, the same questions get replicated.
28   Jones, "Women's International Terrorist Conspiracy from Hell."
29   Budapest, *The Holy Book of Women's Mysteries*; Starhawk, *The Spiral Dance*; Neitz, "In Goddess We Trust."
30   Neitz, "In Goddess We Trust,"168.
31   Braude, *Sisters and Saints*; Woodhead, "Gendering Secularization Theory."
32   Mamood, *Politics of Piety*; Keating, "I'm a Citizen of the Universe"; Phillips, *The Womanist Reader*; Nyhagen, "Contestations of Feminism."
33   Anzaldúa, *Borderlands*, 41.
34   Anzaldúa, *Borderlands*, 58.
35   Anzaldúa, *Borderlands*, 68–72.
36   Anzaldúa, *Borderlands*, 80.
37   Keating, "I'm a Citizen of the Universe," 54.
38   Alexander, *Pedagogies of Crossing*, 283–86.
39   Alexander, *Pedagogies of Crossing*, 280, 281.
40   Alexander, *Pedagogies of Crossing*, 281.
41   Alexander, *Pedagogies of Crossing*, 282.
42   Alexander, *Pedagogies of Crossing*, 290–91.
43   Alexander, *Pedagogies of Crossing*, 325.
44   Tinsley, *Ezili's Mirrors*, 24.
45   Tinsley, *Ezili's Mirrors*, 43.
46   Tinsley, *Ezili's Mirrors*, 172.
47   José Muñoz, as quoted in Tinsley, *Ezili's Mirrors*, 188.
48   Edgell et al., "From Existential to Social Understandings of Risk"; Li et al., "Why Are Women More Religious than Men?"; Woodhead, "Gendering Secularization Theory."

BIBLIOGRAPHY

Alexander, M. Jacqui. *Pedagogies of Crossing: Meditations on Feminism, Sexual Politics, Memory, and the Sacred*. Durham, NC: Duke University Press, 2006.

Alexander, M. Jacqui, and Chandra Mohanty, eds. *Feminist Genealogies, Colonial Legacies, Democratic Futures*. New York: Routledge, 1997.

Ammerman, Nancy. *Studying Lived Religion: Contexts and Practices*. New York: NYU Press, 2021.

Anzaldúa, Gloria. *Borderlands =La frontera: The New Mestiza*. San Francisco: Spinsters/Aunt Lute, 1987.

Asad, Talal. *Genealogies of Religion: Discipline and Reasons of Power in Christianity and Islam*. Baltimore, MD: Johns Hopkins University Press, 1993.

Beauvoir, Simone de. *The Second Sex*. Translated by Howard M. Parshley. 1949. New York: Knopf, 1953.

Beyer, Peter. "Socially Engaged Religion in a Post-Westphalian Global Context: Remodeling the Secular/Religious Distinction." *Sociology of Religion* 73, no. 22 (2012): 109–29.

Braude, Ann. *Sisters and Saints: Women and American Religion*. New York: Oxford University Press, 2007.

Brown, Andrew, and Linda Woodhead. *That Was the Church That Was: How the Church of England Lost the English People*. London: Bloomsbury, 2016.

Budapest, Zsuzsanna. *The Holy Book of Women's Mysteries*. 1979. Boston: Red Wheel/Weiser, 2007.

Durkheim, Émile. *The Elementary Forms of Religious Life*. Translated by Joeseph Swain. 1912. London: George Allen and Unwin, 1915.

Edgell, Penny, Jacqui Frost, and Evan Stewart. 2017. "From Existential to Social Understandings of Risk: Examining Gender Differences in Nonreligion." *Social Currents* 4, no. 6 (2017): 556–74.

Edmonds, Radcliffe G. *Drawing Down the Moon: Magic in the Ancient Greco-Roman World*. Princeton, NJ: Princeton University Press, 2019.

Frazer, James. *The Golden Bough: A Study in Magic and Religion*. 1890. New York: Macmillan, 1935.

Haraway, Donna. "Manifesto for Cyborgs: Science, Technology, and Socialist Feminism in the 1980s." *Socialist Review* 80 (1985): 65–108.

Haraway, Donna. *Primate Visions: Gender, Race and Nature*. New York: Routledge, 1989.

Goldman, M. *The American Soul Rush: Esalen and the Rise of Spiritual Privilege*. New York: New York University Press, 2012.

Grewal, Inderpal, and Caren Kaplan, eds. *Scattered Hegemonies: Postmodernity and Transnational Feminist Practices*. Minneapolis: University of Minnesota Press, 1994.

Jones, Marian. "Women's International Terrorist Conspiracy from Hell: What to Know." *Teen Vogue*, October 28, 2021. https://www.teenvogue.com/story/womens-international-terrorist-conspiracy-from-hell.

Keating, AnaLouise. "'I'm a Citizen of the Universe'": Gloria Anzaldúa's Spiritual Activism as Catalyst for Social Change." *Feminist Studies* 34, nos. 1–2 (2008): 53–69.

Kimmerer, Robin Wall. *Braiding Sweetgrass: Indigenous Wisdom, Scientific Knowledge, and the Teachings of Plants*. Minneapolis MN: Milkweed Editions, 2015.

Li, Yi, Robert Woodberry, Hexuan Liu, and Guang Guo. "Why Are Women More Religious than Men? Do Risk Preferences and Genetic Risk Predispositions Explain the Gender Gap?" *Journal for the Scientific Study of Religion* 59, no. 2 (2020): 289–310.

Luhrmann, Tanya. *How God Becomes Real: Kindling the Presence of Invisible Others*. Princeton, NJ: Princeton University Press, 2020.

Magliocco, Sabina. "New Age and Neopagan Magic." In *The Cambridge History of Magic and Witchcraft in the West*, edited by David J. Collins, 635–65. Cambridge: Cambridge University Press, 2018.

Mamood, Saba. *Politics of Piety: The Islamic Revival and the Feminist Subject*. Princeton, NJ: Princeton University Press, 2004.

Masuzawa, Tomoko. *The Invention of World Religions: Or, How European Universalism Was Preserved in the Language of Pluralism*. Chicago: University of Chicago Press, 2005.

McGuire, Meredith B. *Lived Religion: Faith and Practice in Everyday Life*. New York: Oxford University Press, 2008.

Moser, Mary Beth. "Submerged Spirituality in the Italian Alps: Goddesses, Ancestresses, and Women's Ritual in the Archaeological Record." In *The Land Remembers Us: Women, Myth and Nature*, edited by Mary Jo Neitz and Sid Reger, 159–90. Brooklyn, NY: Women and Myth Press, 2020.

Neitz, Mary Jo. "In Goddess We Trust." In *In Gods We Trust: New Patterns of Religious Pluralism in America*, edited by Thomas Robbins and Dick Anthony, 353–72. New Brunswick, NJ: Transaction Press, 1990.

Neitz, Mary Jo, and Marion S. Goldman. "The Pagan Canopy in Finland." Paper presented at the annual meeting of the International Society for the Sociology of Religion, Turku, Finland, June 22–24, 2013.

Nyhagen, Line, 2019. "Contestations of Feminism, Secularism and Religion in the West: The Discursive Othering of Religious and Secular Women." *Nordic Journal of Religion and Society* 32, no. 1 (2019): 4–21.

Pew Research Center. *The Religious Typology: A New Way to Categorize Americans by Religion*. August 29, 2018. https://www.pewforum.org/2018/08/29/the-religious-typology/.

Phillips, Layli. *The Womanist Reader: The First Quarter Century of Womanist Thought*. New York: Routledge, 2007.

Smith, Jesse M., and Ryan T. Cragun. "Mapping Religion's Other: A Review of the Study of Nonreligion and Secularity." *Journal for the Scientific Study of Religion* 58, no. 2 (2019): 319–35.

Starhawk. *The Spiral Dance*. San Francisco: Harper, 1979.

Stark, Rodney. *One True God: Historical Consequences of Monotheism*. Princeton, NJ: Princeton University Press, 2001.

Stark, Rodney. "Reconceptualizing Religion, Magic, and Science." *Review of Religious Research* 43, no. 2 (2001): 101–20.

Stark, Rodney, and William Sims Bainbridge. *The Future of Religion: Secularization, Revival, and Cult Formation*. Berkeley: University of California Press, 1987.

Tambiah, Stanley Jeyaraja. *Magic, Science, Religion, and the Scope of Rationality*. Cambridge: Cambridge University Press, 1990.

Tinsley, Omise'eke Natasha. *Ezili's Mirrors: Imagining Black Queer Genders*. Durham, NC: Duke University Press 2018.

Trinh T. Minh-ha. *Women, Native, Other: Writing Postcoloniality and Feminism*. Bloomington: Indiana University Press, 1989.

Tsing, Anna Lowenhaupt. *Friction: An Ethnography of Global Connection*. Princeton, NJ: Princeton University Press, 2005.

Tylor, Edward. *Primitive Culture*. 1871. New York: J. P. Putnam's Sons, 1920.

Waterman, Hillary. "Herbs and Verbs: How to Do Witchcraft for Real." JSTOR Daily, October 25, 2017. https://daily.jstor.org/herbs-verbs-how-to-do-witchcraft-for-real/.

Weber, Max. "Science as a Vocation" (1917). In *From Max Weber: Essays in Sociology*, translated and edited by Hans Gerth and C Wright Mills, 129–56. New York: Oxford University Press, 1949.

Wilkins-Laflamme, Sarah. "A Tale of Decline or Change? Working towards a Complementary Understanding of Secular Transition and Individual Spiritualization Theories." *Journal for the Scientific Study of Religion* 60, no. 1 (2021): 516–39.

Woodhead, Linda. "Gendering Secularization Theory." *Social Compass* 55, no. 2 (2008): 187–93.

Thirty-two · KATIE VON WALD AND AP PIERCE

Crafting against Capitalism: Queer Longings for Witch Futures

The witch has persevered through time as a symbol of embodied rebellion, resistance, and survival for contemporary feminist and queer struggles. It is the witch's historical resistance to capitalist structures that has made her simultaneously fascinating and reviled. Whether in her ability to heal, bring babes into the world, commune, soothe, or imagine, those deemed witches were and are those closely tied to the communal, the wild, and the erotic. This chapter argues that, at its core, witchcrafting involves an intentional and revolutionary attention to care through pleasure. It is in caring for those made most vulnerable by capitalist exploitation, in reveling in pleasure, and nourishing her[1] relationships that the witch rebels against the alienation of the senses, body, and community under racial capitalism. Maintaining the rebellious core of witchcrafting is made difficult under neoliberalism. Taking resistance to capitalist and neoliberal violence as central to radical witchcraft, this chapter aims to envision witchy futures against and beyond capitalism. Our queer longing for the witch is a rupture from hegemonic iterations of care and pleasure that have been relegated to private and commodified spaces where feminized and racialized subjects' labor is exploited. Instead, we consider how the erotic, expressed as care and pleasure, is a force for energetic anti-capitalist manifestations. Informed by Black feminist frameworks and in dialogue with queer theories, we see witchcraft as a form of praxis toward reorganizing the violent hierarchies of gender, race, and sexuality that are at the foundation of capitalist domination. At the heart of this chapter, we ask: What can queerness do for the witch and her crafting? And what can the witch do for queer networks, communities, and covens? We argue that in practicing queerly, we craft radically anti-capitalist futures. The witch or, rather, networks of witches become what is queer and unruly: an intentional misrecognition, the fluid cresting of self-abandoning pleasure, and the making of substantial methods for survival.

HISTORICAL CONTEXT

The disparaging accusation of being a witch, or of participation in witchcrafting, has long been a tactic of capitalist organizations to confine the movements, knowledge, and rebellions of the dispossessed. In her critical expansion of Marxist history, Silvia Federici points to the "primitive accumulation" of women's reproductive capacities as central to the formations and successes of capitalist organization.[2] For Federici, it is the violent transition from laboring serf to (unpaid) domestic laborer that granted the capitalist order access to women's reproductive labor to (re)produce the workforce physically, emotionally, and sexually. Federici asserts that rather than capitalism being the oppositional force that destroyed feudalism, capitalism was a response to the rebellions of the laboring classes, a means of containing the rage and revolt of the exploited. Federici reads the witch hunts of the fifteenth and sixteenth century within this context as a direct war against women, forcing them into the defining roles of exclusionary domesticity while confining their sexual activity and surveilling their reproductive technologies. It is for these reasons that many of those accused of witchcraft were often healers, midwives, elders, and gossips. For Federici, the witch symbolizes that "the degradation of women [is a] necessary [condition] for the existence of capitalism in all times," and women have long-standing genealogies of anti-capitalist movement and resistance.[3]

While Federici briefly contends with the roles of colonization and enslavement in these processes, her analysis focuses heavily on the communities and experiences of European women and their confining roles as defined by capitalist heteropatriarchal order. While it is true that the degradation of women is fundamental to capitalist organization, we also turn to Cedric Robinson's argument that capitalism has always been (and will always be) "racial capitalism."[4] Robinson demonstrates how categories of race allowed for the sixteenth-century bourgeoisie to consolidate power, "seizing every occasion to divide peoples for the purpose of their domination."[5]

Racial capitalism is the economic system of domination whereby ethnic and racial traits serve as a basis for exploitation and state-building.

Further, the very binary categories of gender as man *or* woman are themselves an instrument of capitalist and colonial domination.[6] Capitalist expansion demands the violent othering of deviant organizations of gender and sexuality for the accumulation of bodies and labor. Omise'eke Natasha Tinsley's *Ezili's Mirrors* explores the imaginaries of genders and sexualities outside of Western colonial domination, as she recenters both the spiritual and same-sex-loving crosscurrents of revolutionary Haitian Vodou practitioners.[7] She asks, "What would it mean . . . if we took seriously that the Haitian Revolution was launched not by a man or even a woman, but by the spirit of women who love women?"[8] With this call, Tinsley brings together the complicated terrain of the supernatural, spiritual, and magical as sites of Black queer revolution, care, and love that counter the assumptions and prescriptions of capitalist organizations both historically and currently. We are particularly interested in Tinsley's theorization of a Vodou epistemology that seeks knowledge outside of "Enlightenment rationality" and capitalist logics.[9] For Tinsley, these Vodou practices have historically resisted coherent organizations and have preserved "stories of gender and sexual creativity that are also mythistoric records of slavery and revolution."[10] It is not our intention to collapse Vodou and witchcraft but rather to put them in conversation, to insist on a way of knowing, being, loving, and resisting that takes seriously the spiritual, the supernatural, and the erotic. We, like Tinsley, aim to challenge the very structures that enforce gender binaries as the only possibility and look to histories of the deviant as resisting such capitalist genderings.

The accusation of and violence against so-called witches across capitalist empires is a racializing project as much as it is a gendering project. Capitalism defines orders of race, gender, and sexuality, and at every turn, it is witches who are intent on dis-ordering these structures. The violence imposed on witches is a tactic to manage gendered, sexed, and raced transgressions as evidenced by the fact that the first person accused of witchcraft in colonial New England was an enslaved woman from Barbados, Tituba.[11] In her novel, *I, Tituba: Black Witch of Salem*, Maryse Condé practices a critical imagining of Tituba's story in order to offer Tituba "her revenge."[12] Condé's work seems to be an act of care or witchcrafting itself, breathing dimensionality into a historic subject otherwise lost to (or, rather, disappeared from) the archive. Condé's Tituba is characterized by her intense connection to magic and sexuality, linkages for which she is eventually punished. Thus, in Condé's work we see again the figure of the witch emerge, through tragedy, as one resisting the gendered, sexual, and racial violence of capitalist organization through her commitments to community, sexuality, and care. Tituba reflects this ethos, commenting that as a witch she could only feel a "tenderness and compassion for the disinherited and a sense of revolt against injustice."[13]

It is from this historical and literary context that the witch is revived as a symbol of feminist and queer struggle. While Federici may not have been concerned with whether those killed for "witchcraft" were in fact "real" witches, we, inspired by this Black feminist intellectual genealogy, are. It is through this history and tradition that current bewitching practices find their footing and demand ongoing invocations against capitalist heteropatriarchal regimes. We must be wary of the ways the witch's rebellious legacy is tamed by the very capitalist organizations that her existence threatens.

NEOLIBERAL CAPITALISM AND THE ENTREPRENEURIAL WITCH

The figure of the witch as a scapegoat in gendering, racializing, and state-building projects has continued alongside the expansion of capitalism and colonialism; power, though, continues to remodel itself so that it stifles rebellion. Neoliberalism has risen as the dominant economic and political regime of our contemporary moment: the impetus to privatize has moved beyond goods and services, beyond the privatization of social services and into the compulsory marketization of the self.[14] The ever-adaptive neoliberal regime squashes resistance in its absorption of difference—that which is othered can be recast in ways that further benefit "market winners."[15] Imani Perry describes the feminization of the figure of the "entrepreneurial man," who "inevitably does that by which he may obtain the greatest amount of necessaries, conveniences, and luxuries, with the smallest quantity of labour."[16] The "entrepreneurial woman" of this neoliberal era is proudly a feminist, insofar as this identity can aid her self-maximization and marketability.[17] Depoliticized and consumer-based white feminism loves a rebel—as long as all she does is buys the clothes to match.

We point to the "entrepreneurial witch" as a figure who represents neoliberal capitalism's absorption of witches' difference, otherness, and transgression into market logics. The mainstream consumerism of "witchy" self-identity strategically divorces the witch and her crafting from care, pleasure, and resistance. In other words, the making of witchcraft into a lifestyle or brand is a specific tactic for neoliberal capitalism to both neutralize the witch as a threat to structures of power and to sow division among witch subjects. The entrepreneurial witch is steeped in normative white womanhood, and she picks and chooses parts of Black, Indigenous, or Latinx magics as they suit or benefit her witchy self-brand.[18] The marketable identity of "witch" is achieved through purchase, and it is furthered through the commodification of this identity and its associated normative practices. Lakeesha Harris describes how historical and contemporary constructions of witches erase the ways in which Black women witches "have always faced death for conjuring," while white witching enjoys its newfound home in the marketplace.[19]

Further, Lisa Aldred describes the New Age movement's romanticization of different Indigenous spiritual practices in its efforts to "save [New Age practitioners] from their own sense of malaise" and then commercialize their newfound knowledge for profit.[20] Such "malaise" is evocative of Susan Buck-Morss's "anaesthetic" regimes of capitalism that produce sense-dead subjects through the simultaneous overstimulation and numbing of the working class.[21] As the opposite of the aesthetic (that which is "sensed"),[22] capitalism's anesthesia reduces subjects' ability to experience their environment and resist unjust social formations. Efforts to revive the ability to sense, then, are also absorbed into market logics; if you want to feel, purchase these items. The brand of the entrepreneurial witch requires a whitewashed, racist re-packaging of the spiritual practices of Black and Indigenous people with a fetishistic, colonial perspective that problematically imagines racialized others as more "in touch" with the senses or as "closer" to nature. Further, the entrepreneurial witch's incorporation into neoliberalism contributes to the construction of people and practices as deviant. The subjugated and persecuted knowledges of *brujas*, Vodou practitioners, Hoodoo spiritualists, Black conjurers, and other people of color working in this space are made to be "outside" of the marketable because of the ways they threaten white supremacy and capitalist relations or because of their function in and through liberation efforts.[23]

We outline the entrepreneurial witch to contrast her with resistive witchcrafting, in which collectivity conjures magic. If the witch, in all her chaos and undoing, is to continue to do anti-capitalist praxis, she must resist the individualizing commodification of witchcrafting that, for white witches, insists on racist appropriation. Resistive (witch)crafting is not a product to be bought and sold—it is a relation, one that connects bodies through pleasure and care. Such a witchcraft not only understands the specificity of spiritual practices to their different racial and cultural communities and histories; it is also informed by the political and theoretical work of past witches to create resistive, queer, and communal presents. Thus, we are interested in distinguishing between production and (witch) crafting—wherein production signals accumulation and exploitation, and crafting involves processes of commoning. George Caffentzis and Silvia Federici discuss *commoning* as community care work, a "commitment to the creation of collective subjects" and "a means to construct a non-capitalist world."[24] They argue that spaces of commons have always existed as part of the struggle against capitalism. Today these may take the form of mutual aid efforts or community gardens[25]—to us, these processes of commoning constitute forms of (witch)crafting against capitalism. As Sarah Jaffe writes, "all organizing is magic," attending to a future that does not yet exist.[26] The entrepreneurial witch produces and consumes as it benefits her; queer witchcrafting resists such commodification and individuation through practices of care and pleasure, informed by the erotic, that work to build anti-capitalist futures in the present.

QUEER EROTIC AS CARE

Now, we enter the playful and imaginative space of what witchcraft *could* be with and through queerness, acknowledging that such resistance is not a luxury but a necessity for those relegated to the margins of power. We do so with the knowledge that "queer" itself emerges with complicated tensions. Who is queer, who has access to queerness, and how knowledge is produced about queer subjects often resides within institutions, with theorists, where whiteness goes unmarked as universal. As we engage in queer theory and Black feminisms here, we recall Tinsley's work. She points out that white queer scholars have "denaturalized conventional gender and sexuality while renaturalizing global northernness and unmarked whiteness" and prefer "to wait (figuratively) for queers of color to arrive . . . in the hopes that they will join the sexuality centered signifying games already set up."[27] We push off from these shores, informed by and intellectually indebted to queer of color and Black feminist critique, and we understand that the very foundation of all anti-capitalist queer praxis must consider how gender and sexuality are always already racialized.

Expansive (and sometimes vague) interpretations of queerness provide us with the opportunity to dig into the concept's intellectual usefulness for the witch and her crafting practices. As such, we engage with the understanding of queer not as a category of static sexual identity but as a political and epistemological perspective from which to understand a relation to power and deviance. Queerness is not to be claimed as a possession, but it may be wielded, as Cathy Cohen notes, to "transform the basic fabric and hierarchies that allow systems of oppression to persist."[28] Queer subjects are those made deviant or rebellious by violent capitalist orderings. If we are to craft queerly, we must recognize the various matrices of power that divide and organize bodies and craft with strategic misrecognition, refusal, and illegibility. We must redirect witching toward revolutionary potentials. We must queer (witch)crafting for new futures.

This is not the only gift queer perspectives give to the witch. José Esteban Muñoz theorizes queerness as always at the horizon, as a "longing . . . that lets us feel that this world is not enough, that indeed something is missing."[29] This queer horizon, however, is felt and found in the tender moments of queer intimacies in the present that signal to us how we might make utopian worlds. These queer collisions invoke a radical and liberatory future. Taken together, queerness as relationships to power and to time indicates the capacities of transgression, dreaming, loving, and desiring differently. Such queer entanglements—with both power and futurity—speak deeply to the intentions of witchcraft as a transformative practice for resistive community-building. It can inform how anti-capitalist commoning may be understood as queer utopian world-making. Witchcrafting informed by such queer longings becomes a critical practice in forming ephemeral intimacies that direct us toward a liberatory, anti-capitalist future.

Queer frameworks orient us to these relations; but we believe that they come to life when considered alongside Audre Lorde's understanding of the erotic. Lorde's work, too, is concerned with liberatory world-making and understands pleasure as an energetic resource for doing such work. Lorde's "erotic" refers to processes of feeling deeply and acutely for oneself and others, demanding fullness in experience, and providing a stance from which to face the structures intent on exploiting the life forces of the dispossessed.[30] These anesthetizing regimes of power, Lorde argues, transform the erotic into "plasticized sensation."[31] She writes of "the principal horror" of capitalist systems as that which profits off human need and connection, robbing the erotic of its value.[32]

Such alienation from the senses is a disconnection from one's spiritual, creative, and pleasurable powers. Lorde's erotic is yet another queer relation, one that points to the power of connection through pleasure: "The sharing of joy, whether physical, emotional, psychic, or intellectual, forms a bridge between the sharers which can be the basis for understanding much of what is not shared between them."[33] In other words, through these queer erotic relations of pleasure, not only do we revive the senses and provide an invitation to dislocate oneself from anesthetizing and individualizing logics of capital and neoliberalism, but we care for one another. It is because of this commitment to dealing in erotic energy that we create opportunities to care against dehumanizing capitalist structures. Tim Dean theorizes this potential, describing the ways that pleasure can resist "formations of power that depend on—and, indeed, produce—identit[y]," categorizations such as gender or race.[34] Such categorizations allow for further exploitation by unevenly managing bodies and life chances. Dean identifies "self-dislocating pleasures," or processes of pleasurable communion, as dissolving the individualized body that is targeted by violence and discipline and defined by binary gender, normative sexual desire, and racialization.[35] Pleasure, then, can "dislocate" one from the self-maximalizing logics of the entrepreneurial witch. Queer resistive witchcraft invests in navigating, nurturing, and expanding queer eroticism and pleasure, always care-fully in community. We emphasize these dimensions of queer care, pleasure, and the erotic together as actions through which crafting against capitalism takes place.

This is how we, the witchcrafting queers, intentionally center a radical commitment to anti-capitalist praxis. Witchcrafting is an erotic, fully embodied, ritualist doing in communion with others, whether they are present on this plane or the next. Through the nurturing of and reveling in the pleasures of caring for oneself and one's community, witchcrafting is a conjuration of change for a more pleasurable future. Our queer longing for the witch is an embrace of erotic invocation as a method for anti-capitalist world-making, and a utilization of queer erotics *as* care, *as* crafting.

CONCLUSION: THE WITCH AS QUEER, UNRULY SUBJECT

We are not interested in recouping the entrepreneurial witch—we see witchcrafting as processes of commoning, caring, communion, and resistance. Like Cohen, we bring focus to formations of power and parastatal racial capitalism; like Lorde, we understand the potential of the erotic as a creative force that nourishes our communities and relations with one another; like Muñoz, we emphasize the creation of future worlds through the possibilities of the present. Recentering the witch as a queer, unruly figure who favors "self-dismissal" over self-maximalization orients her politically against dominant power and in favor of processes of commoning pleasure and care. Such self-dismissal does not mean she succumbs to the sense-dead anesthetic regime; rather, it is a process of sens*ing* (her environment, her relationships, her pleasures) so much that the witch cannot be contained as a so-called autonomous, rational individual and she exceeds "the body's limits."[36] Queer witchcrafting takes seriously the intention of what La Marr Jurelle Bruce outlines as "radical compassion," or the "will to care for, a commitment to feel with, a striving to learn from, and an openness to be vulnerable before a precarious other, though they may be drastically dissimilar to yourself."[37] It is the call to *be*, deeply, with others. Thus, queer and unruly witchcraft forges networks of solidarity (between humans, nonhumans, land, plants) through the communal and the magical.

As there have "always been commons 'outside' of capitalism,"[38] there has always been queer and unruly witchcrafting—or, rather, in her resistance, the witch has always been crafting queerly. This is a tradition, a genealogy, and a practice that must continue to inform the shapes crafting takes today. Here we have worked to unravel some of the various intellectual and political threads that weave the contemporary witch through the present and into the future. In approaching the witch queerly, we begin our care-ful resistance to capitalist structures. We begin making unruly queer futures.

NOTES

1. We use the pronouns "she" and "her" when referring abstractly to the figure of the witch as a way of pointing to the feminized history and construction of witchcraft. We understand that those performing witchcraft may engage with or occupy many diverse gendered experiences and desires, and we aim to draw attention to the ways in which patriarchal, racist, capitalist regimes dually demonize femininity and feminize witchcrafting.
2. Federici, *Caliban and the Witch*.
3. Federici, *Caliban and the Witch*, 13.
4. Robinson, *Black Marxism*.
5. Robinson, *Black Marxism*, 28.
6. Lugones, "Toward a Decolonial Feminism."
7. Tinsley, *Ezili's Mirrors*.
8. Tinsley, *Ezili's Mirrors*, 11.

9   Tinsley, *Ezili's Mirrors*, 22.
10 Tinsley, *Ezili's Mirrors*, 24.
11 Condé, *I, Tituba*.
12 Jones, "The Best Witch Novel Is One Nobody Talks About."
13 Condé, *I, Tituba*, 151.
14 Perry, *Vexy Thing*.
15 Perry, *Vexy Thing*, 103.
16 Perry, *Vexy Thing*, 100–101.
17 Perry, *Vexy Thing*, 104.
18 Aldred, "Plastic Shamans and Astroturf Sun Dances"; Harris, "Healing through (Re)membering and (Re)claiming"; Stewart, "Work the Root."
19 Harris, "Healing through (Re)membering and (Re)claiming," 255.
20 Aldred, "Plastic Shamans and Astroturf Sun Dances," 329.
21 Buck-Morss, "Aesthetics and Anaesthetics."
22 Buck-Morss, "Aesthetics and Anaesthetics," 6.
23 Harris, "Healing through (Re)membering and (Re)claiming"; Tinsley, *Ezili's Mirrors*; Stewart, "Work the Root."
24 Caffentzis and Federici, "Commons against and beyond Capitalism," i103.
25 Caffentzis and Federici, "Commons against and beyond Capitalism," i95.
26 Jaffe, "All Organizing Is Magic." This quote from Jaffe is an adaptation of a quote from adrienne maree brown and Walidah Imarisha that "all organizing is science fiction."
27 Tinsley, *Ezili's Mirrors*, 204–6.
28 Cohen, "Punks, Bulldaggers, and Welfare Queens," 437.
29 Muñoz, *Cruising Utopia*, 1.
30 Lorde, "Uses of the Erotic."
31 Lorde, "Uses of the Erotic," 54.
32 Lorde, "Uses of the Erotic," 55.
33 Lorde, "Uses of the Erotic," 56.
34 Dean, "Biopolitics of Pleasure," 487.
35 Dean, "Biopolitics of Pleasure," 487.
36 Buck-Morss, "Aesthetics and Anaesthetics," 12.
37 Bruce, *How to Go Mad without Losing Your Mind*, 23.
38 Caffentzis and Federici, "Commons against and beyond Capitalism," i95.

BIBLIOGRAPHY

Aldred, Lisa. "Plastic Shamans and Astroturf Sun Dances: New Age Commercialization of Native American Spirituality." *American Indian Quarterly* 24, no. 3 (2000): 329–52. https://doi.org/10.1353/aiq.2000.0001.

Bruce, La Marr Jurelle. *How to Go Mad without Losing Your Mind: Madness and Black Radical Creativity*. Durham, NC: Duke University Press, 2021.

Buck-Morss, Susan. "Aesthetics and Anaesthetics: Walter Benjamin's Artwork Essay Reconsidered." *October* 62 (1992): 3–41. https://doi.org/10.2307/778700.

Caffentzis, George, and Silvia Federici. "Commons against and beyond Capitalism." *Community Development Journal* 49, no. S1 (2014): i92–i105. https://doi.org/10.1093/cdj/bsu006.

Cohen, C. J. "Punks, Bulldaggers, and Welfare Queens: The Radical Potential of Queer Politics?" GLQ: *A Journal of Lesbian and Gay Studies* 3, no. 4 (1997): 437–65. https://doi.org/10.1215/10642684-3-4-437.

Condé, Maryse. *I, Tituba, Black Witch of Salem*. Charlottesville: University Press of Virginia, 2009.

Dean, Tim. "The Biopolitics of Pleasure." *South Atlantic Quarterly* 111, no. 3 (2012): 477–96. https://doi.org/10.1215/00382876-1596245.

Federici, Silvia. *Caliban and the Witch: Women, the Body and Primitive Accumulation*. New York: Autonomedia, 2004.

Harris, Lakeesha J. "Healing through (Re)membering and (Re)claiming Ancestral Knowledge about Black Witch Magic." In *Black Women's Liberatory Pedagogies: Resistance, Transformation, and Healing within and beyond the Academy*, edited by Olivia N. Perlow, Durene I. Wheeler, Sharon L. Bethea, and Barbara M. Scott, 245–63. Cham: Springer International Publishing, 2018. https://doi.org/10.1007/978-3-319-65789-9_14.

Jaffe, Sarah. "All Organizing Is Magic." *Verso Books* (blog), October 25, 2019. https://www.versobooks.com/blogs/4465-all-organizing-is-magic.

Jones, J. Nicole. "The Best Witch Novel Is One Nobody Talks About." *Paris Review* (blog), October 28, 2020. https://www.theparisreview.org/blog/2020/10/28/the-best-witch-novel-is-one-nobody-talks-about/.

Lara, Irene. "Bruja Positionalities: Toward a Chicana/Latina Spiritual Activism." *Chicana/Latina Studies* 4, no. 2 (2005): 10–45.

Lorde, Audre. "Uses of the Erotic: The Erotic as Power." In *Sister Outsider: Essays and Speeches*, 53–59. Berkeley CA: Crossing Press, 2007.

Lugones, Marià. "Toward a Decolonial Feminism." *Hypatia* 25, no. 4 (2010): 742–59.

Muñoz, José Esteban. *Cruising Utopia: The Then and There of Queer Futurity*. 10th anniv. ed. New York: New York University Press, 2019.

Perry, Imani. *Vexy Thing: On Gender and Liberation*. Durham, NC: Duke University Press, 2018.

Robinson, Cedric J. *Black Marxism: The Making of the Black Radical Tradition*. 3rd ed. Chapel Hill: University of North Carolina Press, 2021.

Stewart, Lindsey. "Work the Root: Black Feminism, Hoodoo Love Rituals, and Practices of Freedom." *Hypatia* 32, no. 1 (2017): 103–18. https://doi.org/10.1111/hypa.12309.

Tinsley, Omise'eke Natasha. *Ezili's Mirrors: Imagining Black Queer Genders*. Durham, NC: Duke University Press, 2018.

Contributors

MARIA AMIR is a teaching fellow at Lahore University of Management Sciences (LUMS), Lahore, Pakistan. Amir's work focuses on South Asian postcolonial feminist identities, feminist folklore, and women's movements. She is a former human rights journalist who has worked primarily in Pakistan on issues concerning gender and minority rights. She currently teaches courses in Gender Studies at the Mushtaq Ahmad Gurmani School of Humanities and Social Sciences at LUMS, where she wholly embraces the framework of a feminist coven-classroom space to foster and further the power of female rebellion against all restrictive cultural norms and frames of piety policing.

RUTH ASIIMWE is the founder and Strategy, Partnerships and Fundraising Director of Youth Line Forum. She is the author of *My Heart Is Your Shelter* and *Another Woman*.

BERNADETTE BARTON is Professor of Sociology and Director of Gender Studies at Morehead State University. She is the author of *The Pornification of America: How Raunch Culture Is Ruining Our Society* (2021), *Stripped: More Stories from Exotic Dancers* (2017), and *Pray the Gay Away: The Extraordinary Lives of Bible Belt Gays* (2012). Barton writes and lectures on contemporary issues of gender, sexuality, religion, culture, happiness, alignment, and the sex industry. Her book projects in progress include *Rural Queer Resistance*, an exploration of marriage equality mobilization in Rowan County, Kentucky; *Sex Work Today: Erotic Labor in the Twenty-First Century*, an anthology of new research on the sex industry she coedited; and *Alignment: What It Is and Why It Matters*.

ETHEL BROOKS is Chair of Women's, Gender, and Sexuality Studies and Associate Professor of Women's, Gender, and Sexuality Studies and Sociology at Rutgers University. She is Chair of the Board of the European Roma Rights Centre and member of the Bavarlipe Academy of the European Roma Institute for Arts and Culture, the RomaMoMA Think Tank, and the US Delegation to the International Holocaust Remembrance Alliance (IHRA) and its Roma Genocide Working Group. In 2022, Brooks curated for One Day We Shall Celebrate Again, the RomaMoMA/OFF-Biennale contribution to Documenta 15. She contributed art and performance to Documenta 15 and to the 2022 and 2019 Venice Biennales. From 2022 to 2023, Brooks was editorial consultant for the *Los Angeles Times* podcast *Foretold*. Since 2007, she has directed the Feminist Critical Analysis course in Dubrovnik. She is the author of the award-winning *Unraveling the Garment Industry: Transnational Organizing and Women's Work* (2007). Her current book focuses on encampment, claim-staking, and Romani futures.

SHELINA BROWN is Assistant Professor of Musicology at the College-Conservatory of Music at the University of Cincinnati. Her research centers on counterhegemonic vocal practices in women's repertoire from the avant-garde of the 1960s to contemporary punk and underground scenes. A Canadian national raised in Kyoto, Japan, Brown is bilingual in Japanese, and has a lifelong fascination with spiritual practices in both Japan and Anglo-America. She is currently developing her dissertation on Yoko Ono's music and feminist spirituality into a book project. Brown also researches Japanese popular music, particularly the genres of *enka* and Vocaloid pop.

RUTH CHARNOCK is a queer writer, storyworker, creative mentor, tarot reader, and lapsed academic, based in the United Kingdom. She is the author and editor of *Joni Mitchell: New Critical Readings* (2019), and she writes about sex, music, witching, tarot, nonmonogamy, bodies, motherhood, feelings, and literature. Her latest piece, "3 tarot cards for the new mother," was included in the edited collection *Blood and Cord: Writers on Early Parenthood* (2023).

SOMA CHAUDHURI is Associate Professor of Sociology at Michigan State University, where she co-directs the Center for Gender in Global Context. Her research lies at the intersection of gender, violence, social movements, and development, with a special focus on violence against women. She started her academic career studying the contemporary witch hunts targeting women workers in the tea plantations of Jalpaiguri, India. A qualitative researcher by training and practice, her research has been funded by several grants from major institutions, including the National Science Foundation and Social Science Research Council.

CAROLYN CHERNOFF is a public scholar and cultural worker in Philadelphia. She has worked as a professor, a puppeteer, and a performance artist, among other things. Her research and writing examine the role of everyday culture in creating and interrupting social inequality.

SAIRA CHHIBBER is a PhD candidate in the Cultural Studies program at Queen's University. Her research on contemporary media representations of female supernatural figures emerging from Hindu myth and folklore—*churail, nagin,* and *vishkanya* (witches, snake women, and poison damsels)—examines the intersections of horror, gender, and national identity in Hindi-language popular media.

SIMON CLAY is a postdoctoral research fellow at University of New South Wales, Sydney, Australia. Clay has a background in gender studies and sociology with a research focus on the health-related practices of marginalized individuals and the way these practices can be forms of radical emancipation and self-care. He is currently working on a project focused on the history of Lilith, her genealogies, and the various ways she has been conceptualized over time. He has a forthcoming publication on the Lilith as a "monster feminist" icon that explores how Lilith's monstrous aspects have been mobilized by feminists as tools of empowerment and resistance.

KRYSTAL CLEARY is Senior Professor of Practice in the Department of Communication and Program of Gender and Sexuality Studies at Tulane University. Her research and teaching cross-pollinate intersectional feminist and queer theories, critical disability studies, and cultural studies of media. Her work has appeared in *Disability Studies Quarterly, Feminist Media Histories, Feminist Pedagogy,* and the edited collection *Disability Media Studies* (2017).

ADRIANNA L. ERNSTBERGER is Assistant Professor of History and Chair of the Department of History and Global Studies at Marian University in Indianapolis, Indiana. Her research explores the social, political and institutional history of transnational women's movements, specifically focusing on the disciplinary development of women's and gender studies programs in universities throughout the Global South. She is coeditor of a special issue of *Women's Studies Quarterly* (Spring/Summer 2024), which focuses on global threats to women's, gender, and sexuality studies over the last five years. Ernstberger teaches thematic interdisciplinary courses on global women's movements, global slave systems, comparative genocide studies, and, of course, global witch histories.

TINA ESCAJA is a destructivist/cyberpoet, digital artist, and scholar based in Burlington, Vermont. She is Distinguished Professor of Spanish and Gender and Women's Studies, and the Director of the Gender, Sexuality and Women's Studies Program at the University of Vermont. As a literary critic, she has published extensively on gender and contemporary Latin American and Spanish poetry and technology. Considered a pioneer in electronic literature in Spanish, her creative work transcends the traditional book form, leaping into digital art, robotics, augmented reality, and multimedia projects exhibited in museums and galleries internationally. Escaja has received numerous awards, and her work has been translated into multiple languages. She is member of the North American Academy of the Spanish Language (ANLE) and a Corresponding Member of the Royal Spanish Academy (RAE). A selection from her literary and digital projects can be experienced at www.tinaescaja.com.

LAURIE ESSIG is Director and Professor of Gender, Sexuality and Feminist Studies at Middlebury College. She is the author of several books, including her most recent *Love, Inc.: Dating Apps, the Big White Wedding, and Chasing the Happily Neverafter* (2019). *Love, Inc.* argues that romance as an ideology became even more powerful in the last few decades even as actual marriage rates declined. Romance promises us a safe and secure future as a private love affair, even as our future is more and more precarious. Rather than demanding the necessary political and structural changes today for a secure tomorrow, we are too busy reading romance novels, obsessing over royal weddings, or swiping through our dating apps to pay much attention to the world around us. Essig has written for a variety of publications including *Boston Globe, Chronicle of Higher Education, The Conversation, New York Times,* and *Washington Post.* She is now at work on a podcast on the global anti-gender-ideology movement, titled *Feminism, Fascism, and the Future.* The podcast can be found on Spotify.

MARCELITTE FAILLA is Visiting Assistant Professor of African American Studies and Women's, Gender, and Sexuality Studies at Emory University. Her interests lie at the intersection of Africana studies, gender and sexuality studies, and Black religion. Marcelitte's current book project investigates how Black women and femmes employ African-heritage religions for material manifestation, healing, and protection from anti-Blackness. As a Black witch and practitioner of Isese Ifá and Hoodoo, she often holds ceremonial space in academic and community settings. Failla lives in Atlanta, Georgia, with her partner and four familiars. To find out more, visit www.MarcelitteTheThird.com.

D FERRETT is a writer, singer, and academic. She is Associate Professor of Music, Sound and Culture at Falmouth University and the author of *Dark Sound: Feminine Voices in Sonic Shadow* (2020).

MARION S. GOLDMAN is Professor Emeritus of Sociology and Religious Studies at the University of Oregon. Her books have included nineteenth-century women prostitutes in Virginia City, Nevada; male spiritual entrepreneurs in the Human Potential movement; and nuns who worked for social justice. Most of her research deals with women, including the high achievers who gave up hard-won careers to follow Bhagwan Shree Rajneesh to Central Oregon. Her recent work focuses on the vernacular religious practices of women and men in Northern Europe and the United States. Her honors include the Hamilton Prize (1980) and a Fulbright Specialist Award (2021).

JAIME HARTLESS is Assistant Professor of Sociology at Farmingdale State College, State University of New York. Hartless received her PhD in Sociology from the University of Virginia in 2019. Her research broadly focuses on cultural boundary–drawing within the context of LGBTQI+ and feminist movements. She has previously written about the contested place of men within feminism, how the changing dimensions of queer spaces impact women's experiences therein, and the utility of using horror films to teach about gender and sexuality. Her work has been published in *Compass*; *Gender, Place and Culture*; *Journal of Homosexuality*; *Sociology*; and *Teaching Sociology*. Her current book project explores the politics of allyship in LGBTQI+ and feminist movements, examining how activist decisions to center or decenter identity shape who feels ownership of social movements. She currently lives in Queens, New York, with her two wizard cats.

MARGARETHA HAUGHWOUT creates ecological interventions, participatory events, walking tours, experimental pedagogies, installations, and biological processes in order to cultivate a radical imagination that antagonizes proprietary regimes and capitalist forms of labor. Haughwout's active collaborations include the Coven Intelligence Program, with efrén cruz cortés, a coven that uncovers "revolutionary ecologies of work" between witches, plants, and machines; and the Guerrilla Grafters, who graft fruit-bearing branches onto ornamental street trees in the urban environment. Her personal and collaborative artwork is found nationally and internationally, most recently at the Stadtwerkstatt in Linz, Austria; and at the Yerba Buena Center for the Arts in San Francisco. Her living installations can be found at Bennington College and at NATURE Lab in Troy, New York. She writes and lectures widely, most recently at the World-Ecology Research Network conference in Bonn, Germany, and at the National College of Art and Design in Dublin. Haughwout is Associate Professor of Art at Colgate University.

PATRICIA HUMURA works as a global human rights practitioner and a policy advocate coordinator at Irise Institute East Africa, coordinating ninety organizations in Uganda, Kenya, Tanzania, and Burundi. Humura's work centers feminist intersectional analysis.

APOORVAA JOSHI is a PhD student in Sociology at Rutgers University. Her work spans culture and cognition, decoloniality, and feminist inquiry and investigates the relationship between imagination and materiality as well as the role of the social in that relationship. Her previous research focused on how contemporary witchcraft practitioners interact with the cultural symbol of "the Witch." Currently, she is exploring decolonial imaginations of the present and future. She has an MSc in Human Rights from the London School of Economics (2012) and an MA in Sociology from Rutgers University (2022).

GOVIND KELKAR is Visiting Professor at the Council for Social Development and Institute for Human Development, India, and Gender and Community Advisor to UNOPS S31, Copenhagen. She is Executive Director of GenDev Centre for Research and Innovation, India, and was Senior Adviser at Landesa, in Seattle (May 2013–March 2020). In her concurrent assignments, Kelkar was International Research Coordinator of ENERGIA International, The Netherlands; and the research lead on Gender and Energy at Swaminathan Research Foundation, Chennai. She is also Distinguished Adjunct Faculty of the Asian Institute of Technology, Bangkok, Thailand. Kelkar also holds the position of Honorary Professor at the Institute of

Ethnology, Yunnan Academy of Social Sciences, China; and Honorary Senior Fellow at the Institute of Chinese Studies, Delhi. She has authored sixteen books and numerous scholarly publications.

OLIVER KELLHAMMER is an ecological artist, educator, activist, and writer. Through his botanical interventions and public art projects, he seeks to demonstrate nature's surprising ability to recover from damage. His work facilitates processes of environmental regeneration by engaging the botanical and sociopolitical underpinnings of the landscape. His work continues to evolve, and he has recently investigated psychosocial effects of climate change, decontaminating polluted soil, reintroducing prehistoric trees to industrially logged landscapes, and cataloging brownfield biodiversity. He is based in New York, where he is a part-time Assistant Professor in Sustainable Systems at Parsons School of Design. Kellhammer's land-based works are included in Vancouver's public art collection and parks. Recent exhibitions took place in Trondheim, Melbourne, Dublin, and Malmö. He has lectured widely, including at Aalto University, Bainbridge Graduate Institute, Colgate University, Emily Carr University, New York University, OTIS, Rensselaer Polytechnic, Smith College, Tohoku University, University of British Columbia, University of Oregon, and University of Windsor.

AYÇA KURTOĞLU is Professor at Acıbadem Mehmet Ali Aydınlar University in Turkey. Prior to her current appointment, she worked as a research assistant (1987–1992) at Marmara University, an instructor at Bilkent University (1999–2007), and a volunteer in women's NGOs and as a part-time lecturer at the Gender and Women's Studies Program at Middle East Technical University (2007–16). She earned her PhD in Sociology from Middle East Technical University. She was at the University of Warwick (1993–1994) as a visiting PhD student, and at Peace Research Institute in Oslo (1994) as visiting researcher. She published single-authored, coauthored, and edited books on hometown relations, peace culture, gender sensitive rights-based monitoring, and gender and women's studies. She is also author of articles on women's strikes, violence against women, and sexual citizenship. Her current research areas include visual sociology, gender studies, and migration.

HELEN MACDONALD is a social anthropologist with a PhD from the School of Oriental and African Studies, London. She is currently Associate Professor of Anthropology at the University of Cape Town, South Africa. Her long-standing research on witchcraft accusations in Chhattisgarh, central India, culminated in her book *Witchcraft Accusations from Central India: The Fragmented Urn* (2020). She is a founding member of the International Alliance to End Witch Hunts. Macdonald's other research projects include studies of tuberculosis in India and South Africa, and studies of parents of trans children. She serves as treasurer for Anthropology Southern Africa and three world bodies—the World Council of Anthropological Associations (WCAA), the International Union for Anthropological and Ethnological Sciences (IUAES), and the World Anthropological Union (WAU).

ISABEL MACHADO is a cultural historian who specializes in the fields of Gender and Sexuality Studies and Celebration Studies. She is currently a lecturer at the University of British Columbia's Institute for Gender, Race, Sexuality, and Social Justice. For the ongoing oral history project, Queens of the South(s), she is interviewing performers from different parts of the globe who defy gender normativity. She is the author of *Carnival in Alabama: Marked Bodies and Invented Traditions in Mobile* (2023), and she serves as coeditor-in-chief for the *Journal of Festival Studies*.

BRANDY RENEE MCCANN is a writer and researcher at the Center for Gerontology at Virginia Tech. She writes about life in Appalachia from an interdisciplinary perspective. McCann is at work on a memoir/grimoire documenting her history in Appalachian folk magic. Her literary work can be found in *Dead Mule, Reckon Review, Still: The Journal*, and most recently in Barbara Kingsolver's edited collection, *Anthology of Appalachian Writers* (2023). McCann's scientific work on aging in Appalachia can be found in a variety of academic journals. Follow her on Instagram @appalbrandy.

DEV NATHAN is with the Southern Centre for Inequality Studies, Johannesburg; the Institute for Human Development, Delhi and Ranchi; The New School for Social Research, New York; and the GenDev Centre for Research and Innovation, Gurgaon. He is also the coeditor of the Cambridge University Press series Development Trajectories in Global Value Chains. In addition to economics, he also works on gender analysis of Indigenous societies. He coauthored *Witch Hunts: Culture, Patriarchy and Structural Transformation* (2020). Some recent publications include "Knowledge Economy and Gender Inequality: Indigenous Peoples and the Caste System," in *Gender, Technology and Development* (2022); and *Reverse Subsidies in Global Monopsony Capitalism* (2022). His forthcoming books are *Knowledge and Global Inequality: 1800 to the Present* and the co-authored *Gender Regimes in Net Zero Transitions*.

MARY JO NEITZ is Professor Emerita in Women's and Gender Studies at the University of Missouri in Columbia, Missouri. She conducted comparative multisite ethnographic studies of pagan and Dianic Wiccan groups in the Midwest and Rocky Mountain West. She has a PhD in Sociology from the University of Chicago. She taught courses in feminist theories and methods, sociology of religion, intersectionality, and race, religion, gender, and sexuality. She is currently Vice President and Board member of the Association for the Study of Women and Myth, an organization whose mission it is to support scholarly and creative endeavors that elucidate aspects of the sacred feminine, women, and mythology. She lives with her two cats in Boone County, not far from the Missouri River, where she enjoys watching the seasons change.

AMY NICHOLS-BELO is Associate Professor of Anthropology and Global Health Studies and Chair of International and Global Studies at Mercer University in Macon, Georgia. Her research explores anti-witchcraft practices and witchcraft belief in Mwanza, Tanzania, and has been published in *Medical Anthropology* and in the edited volume *Gender, Supernatural Beings, and the Liminality of Death: Monstrous Males/Fatal Females* (2021).

ALLISON (OR AP) PIERCE is a PhD candidate in Feminist Studies at the University of California, Santa Barbara. Their research lies at the intersection of digital media studies, feminist theory, queer and affect studies, and antiwork politics—specifically, they are interested in the resistive circulation of unproductivity in digital space. Their dissertation examines the discursive construction of AI and its implications for labor, pedagogy, and queer futurity. Their research generally engages absurd, unlikely, or ironic digital objects and their impact on the affective circuits of digital sociality.

EMMA QUILTY is a postdoctoral research fellow at Monash University, Victoria, Australia. Quilty is a social anthropologist and has been practicing witchcraft for over fifteen years. She is currently working on the book project *Witchy Feminism*, which will speak from both her ethnographic and personal experiences to illuminate the world of contemporary witchcraft. Her research stands at the crossroads of feminist and queer studies, as shown through her past publications exploring witchcraft rituals as well as through the role of social media in the spread and development of modern witchcraft.

ANNA ROGEL graduated in comparative studies with a thesis on cinematic representations of darkness. She holds a position as a researcher and lecturer at the department of Yiddish Culture, Language, and Literature at the Heinrich-Heine University, Düsseldorf, where she specializes in folkloric and fantastic literature from the late medieval period to the present. Her current project, "Magical Mayse Bukh," investigates different concepts of magic according to their literary and cultural function in medieval and early modern Yiddish fairy tales. She is a member of the Arbeitskreis Interdisziplinäre Hexenforschung, and her research focuses on the symbolic representations of witchcraft and magic in popular secular culture.

KAREN SCHALLER is a lecturer in Literature at the University of East Anglia in the United Kingdom. She is a multimodal and interdisciplinary feminist researcher specializing in theories of affect, feeling, emotion, and embodiment. Her work tracks economies of feeling in twentieth- and twenty-first-century literary and critical cultures; materializes the biopolitics of academia and distributions of vitality across domestic and institutional scenes; and performs tactics of feminist resistance.

JACQUELYN MARIE SHANNON is a ritual artist and PhD candidate in Theater and Performance at The Graduate Center, CUNY, in New York City. She is interested in magic, witchcraft, and ritual; death, haunting, and mourning; queer and feminist performance; affect, sensuality, and dramaturgies of the body. Her work gravitates toward questions of presence, enchantment, and the supernatural, exploring how performance conjures, catalyzes, and transforms. She also investigates artistic processes that engage marginal registers of performance extending beyond bounded notions of body, space, and time and that cultivate and operate as and through liminal and altered states, alternative temporalities, synesthesia, hypnosis, visions, and dreams. Shannon also holds an MA from Indiana University in Communication and Culture, an MA from NYU in Educational Theater, and an MPhil from The Graduate Center, CUNY, in Theater and Performance.

SHASHANK SHEKHAR SINHA is an independent researcher. He has worked as Publishing Director of Routledge (South Asia) since 2012. Earlier, he taught history at undergraduate colleges in the University of Delhi for almost a decade (1994–2004) and worked with Oxford University Press from 2004 to 2012. Sinha works at the intersections of history and cultural anthropology and publishes regularly in academic journals and books on areas related to tribes, gender, witch-hunting, and heritage and culture. To address the gap between academic and popular understandings of history, he regularly writes for popular media platforms and for features in television programs. He is the author of *Restless Mothers and Turbulent Daughters: Situating Tribes in Gender Studies* (2006); and *Delhi, Agra, Fatehpur Sikri: Monuments, Cities and Connected Histories* (2021). He has also coedited *Gender in Modern India: History, Culture, Marginality* (forthcoming 2024).

GABRIELLA V. SMITH is Adjunct Professor of Sociology at Radford University. Her research centers on expressions of gender and race in various cultural milieus. She is particularly interested in gender and race within material culture and media and has written on gender dynamics in modern witchcraft self-help books and on how colors are gendered and racialized through garden plant names. Smith received her PhD in Sociology from the University of Virginia in 2019 and founded her company, Gabriella the Garden Sage, in 2021. She currently lives, writes, teaches, and gardens in the heart of Appalachia—Virginia's magical New River Valley.

NATHAN SNAZA directs the Humanities Center at the University of Richmond, where he teaches English literature and gender studies. He is the author of *Tendings: Feminist Esoterisms and the Abolition of Man* (Duke University Press, 2024) and *Animate Literacies: Literature, Affect, and the Politics of Humanism* (2019); his essays have been published in *Curriculum Inquiry*, *Feminist Formations*, *Feminist Studies*, *Parallax*, *Social Text*, and *Studies in Gender and Sexuality*.

SHANNON HUGHES SPENCE is a PhD student in Sociology at the Southeast Technological University (SETU), Ireland. Spence's doctoral thesis, titled "Out in the Club—Young Women's Experiences of the Night-Time Economy in Ireland," explores the liminality and appeal of the nighttime economy for young women, while simultaneously examining the risk and safety aspect that is present. Spence also works part-time as a research assistant in health science at the University College Dublin (UCD). Her research interests include themes of power, gender equality, women's lived experiences, health, sexual violence, historic witch trials, and the occult.

ERIC STEINHART grew up on a farm in Lancaster County, Pennsylvania, in a Pennsylvania German (Deitsch) family with roots going all the way back to William Penn. He was immersed in Deitsch magical culture from childhood on. He has degrees in computer science and in philosophy and is Professor of Philosophy at William Paterson University. He has long worked on alternative and new religious movements in the United States. He uses analytic metaphysics to work out naturalistic foundations for contemporary pagan practices. He has written about, and participated in, a variety of nature-based magical practices.

MORENA TARTARI is currently a research fellow and Principal Investigator of the EU-funded research project WHoSGreen in the Department of Sociology and Social Work, Babeș-Bolyai University (Romania). Previously, Morena was a STARS-Grant awardee (Supporting Talent in Research Programme) at the University of Padua (Italy); a Research Fellow at the Department of Sociology, Social Policy and Criminology, University of Southampton (UK); and a Marie Sklodowska-Curie Research Fellow at the University of Antwerp (Belgium). Her early research focused on the emergence of moral panics centered on satanic ritual abuse in contemporary Italy. Then, during her Marie Sklodowska-Curie Fellowship, she studied the processes of stigmatization of single mothers and their practices of resistance against familism in institutional contexts. Her current research focuses on nonreligious identities, practices, and values, and emergent forms of spirituality in contemporary atheism and agnosticism in Europe. Her research interests include institutional ethnography and feminist standpoint theory.

NICOLE TRIGG is a writer, translator, and transdisciplinary scholar of feminist, queer, and decolonial methodologies, currently pursuing their PhD in Italian Studies and Gender and Women's Studies at UC Berkeley. Their primary area of inquiry is experimental cultural and intellectual production in postwar Italy, with a special emphasis on the oeuvre of Carla Lonzi. Their research themes include the politics of difference and disidentification; creative practices and decolonization; and intersubjectivity and/as difficulty. Their recent writing is published in *ASAP Journal*; *California Italian Studies*; *Women and Performance: A Journal of Feminist Theory*; and the Documenta 15 publication *Jimmie Durham and a Stick in the Forest by the Side of the Road* (2022). Nicole is also the translator from Italian of *Total*

Memory, a science-fiction short story authored by Gilda Musa in 1968, published in 2021.

TUSHABE WA TUSHABE is Associate Professor in the Center for Human Sexuality Studies at Widener University. Tushabe's research centers decolonial practices with a focus on African epistemologies, feminist theory, and LGBTQI+ sexualities.

KATIE VON WALD is a PhD candidate in Feminist Studies at the University of California, Santa Barbara. Her work looks at the construction of femininity and feminine sexualities through madness, medicine, and performance. Her dissertation, "Chasing Auras: The Afterlives of 19th Century Hysterical Pathologies on Feminine Subjects and Unruly Queer Futures," offers a queered history of hysteria to investigate discourses of feminine madness as they relate to the movements of feminized subjects across boundaries of reality, resistance, and confinement. She is the cofounder of the Queer Arts Collective, an autonomous organization at UCSB exploring queer politics through arts and aesthetics.

JANE WARD is Professor and Chair of Feminist Studies at the University of California, Santa Barbara. She writes about gender and sexual cultures and is the author of multiple books, including *The Tragedy of Heterosexuality* (2020) and *Not Gay: Sex between Straight White Men* (2015). Her work has been featured in the *Guardian*, *New York Magazine*, *New York Times*, and the *Washington Post*, and broadcast on the BBC and NPR. Ward is also an amateur witch, a community organizer, and a parent to one cat, two chickens, and one human.

Index

2016 US presidential election, 135, 249–50, 265–66, 347, 349, 357

abachwezi, 29
Abbasi, Asim, 306–7, 314–15
abjection, 11, 119, 122, 260, 263–64, 366, 369, 370n1
abolitionism, 6, 39, 109, 420, 441
Aboriginal people, 25
abortion, 49, 52, 54–55, 67, 119, 310, 351, 410
academia, 401–15
academic witches, 402–3
accusations of witchcraft, 94, 233, 325, 417n42, 420, 428, 431, 453; and colonialism, 240; as community-based, 181, 183–84, 194, 196, 221–30; and flying ointments, 118–20, 124; and legal recourse, 17, 192, 197, 200n8, 215–16, 241–42; as misogynist violence, 2–5, 7–8, 10–12, 176–77, 190, 192–94, 205–16, 219–30, 241–43; racialized, 466; and resource scarcity, 7–8, 183–84, 465; Salem Witch Trials, 34–35, 40–42, 179; targeting men, 238–39, 243; and women's power, 118–20, 177–78. *See also* witch hunts
ActionAid India, 226
activism, 11, 82, 102n26, 219, 429, 450; feminist, 18, 46–56, 150, 234, 264, 277–78, 287n8, 301, 347–59, 363, 392, 457–58; human rights, 198; Indigenous, 13, 97; magical, 6; queer, 234, 321; racial justice, 109; spiritual, 286, 287n8, 456–57; and tarot, 111, 113–15
adivasi people, 2–4, 10, 19n1, 206, 221, 223–29, 230n16
Affrilachian, 97, 102n22

Africa, 91; and Indigeneity, 43, 178, 182; and racist witchcraft accusations, 12, 15, 17; witches in, 23–32, 85n4; witch hunts in, 5, 7, 175–84, 190–201. *See also individual countries*
African Americans, 36, 92, 95–96, 102n22, 267
Africana religious traditions, 5, 15, 24, 65, 75–85, 86n7, 94–97, 457
African diaspora, 9, 13, 65, 82, 457–58
agency, 63, 243, 294, 301, 381, 402, 405; feminist, 11, 49, 52–53, 308, 319; sexual, 295; and witching sound, 262–63, 265, 267, 272
Agra, Zalumma, 441–45
Ahmed, Sara, 114, 369
Ahmed, Waseem, 61, 69n5
Akalatunde, Iyalosa Osunyemi, 83–84
Aldred, Lisa, 468
Alexander, Courtney, 109. *See also* Dust II Onyx
Alexander, M. Jacqui, 12–13, 35, 450, 457–59
Allen, Paula Gunn, 235
Allen, Woody, 314
altars, 19, 98, 367, 374, 388–89, 392–93, 403, 412
altered states of consciousness, 16, 121, 126, 451. *See also* ecstasy/ekstasis; possession; trance
Amazon (region), 175–76, 427, 429
American goddess movement, 46, 121
American Horror Story: Coven, 254, 325–26
American Indians, 92, 101n3. *See also* Indigenous Peoples; Native Americans
Amir, Maria, 17
Amsler, Sarah, 402, 411, 416n8
amulets, 97, 133, 451

Anastasia (@anastasiamoongirl), 62
ancestors, 82, 85, 91–92, 192, 267–68, 270, 324, 401, 404; ancestor mediumship, 79; ancestor veneration, 80, 83, 98, 191, 266, 384n7; ancestral healing, 4; ancestral trauma, 79–80; and witch lineages, 3–4, 13, 64, 94, 97–98, 115n7, 137, 326, 385n13, 458
Ancient Greece, 8
Anderson, Hans Christian, 275, 286n1
androgyny, divine, 131–32, 138
Anger, Kenneth: *Inauguration of the Pleasure Dome*, 255
Anglo-American witchcraft, 16
animals, non-human, 27, 31, 94, 99, 133, 222, 228, 252, 264, 402, 439, 450; animal-based magic, 8; witch association with, 4, 10, 13, 119, 124, 374
Anthropocene, 17, 262–72
anthropology, 12, 287n6, 402, 404, 438, 449, 453–54; study of witchcraft, 1, 5, 37, 85n4, 193, 196, 408, 415n4
anti-capitalism, 76, 80, 82, 84, 420, 464–65, 468–71
anti-racism, 4, 6, 82, 109, 264, 271, 357
Anti-Witchcraft Allegation Campaign Coalition–Ghana, 240
Anzaldúa, Gloria, 450, 456–59
Aos Sí, 51
Apokrypha, 383n3
apostate feminism, 277
Appalachian folk magic, 15–16, 90–101
Arendt, Hannah, 443–45
Argentina, 6, 234, 366
Arif, Samya, 311
Arvin, Maile, 7
Asad, Talal, 451
Ásatrú, 137, 139
Ashanti people, 177
Ashmolean Museum: *Spellbound*, 404–5, 416n19
Asia, 427, 454; witches in, 289–301, 304–16; witch hunts in, 2–3, 5, 7–8, 10–12, 17, 175–84, 194, 205–16, 219–30, 240–42. *See also individual countries*

Asian American Literary Review: Open in Emergency (special issue), 111
Asian Americans, 110–13
Asian American Tarot, 111–13
Asiimwe, Ruth, 14, 24, 29–30
Asparagus (@aquaichor), 62
astrology, 19, 70n16, 79, 90, 138, 150, 258, 279, 407, 449, 451–52, 459; and agricultural planting, 94–95; at Catland Witch School, 374, 376; and social justice, 6
aswangs, 8
Athena, 139, 411
Atwood, Margaret, 150
Aune, Kristen, 47
Aurat Marches, 315–16
Austen, Ralph, 179, 181
Australia, 123, 266, 270
Azande witchcraft, 454

Baba Yaga, 8, 414
Babetta, 287n9
bad bitch witch, 18, 323–27
Bai, Santu, 227
Bailer, Sophia (Leninger), 134
Baker, Diane, 121
Bakiga people, 24, 26
Ballard, H. Byron, 99–100
baneful witches, 94
Banks, Azealia, 265
Banotti, Elvira, 446n12
Barbados, 36, 38
Barnum, P. T., 441
Baroja, Julio, 162
Barthes, Roland, 69n13, 445
Bartlett, Katharine, 216
Barton, Bernadette, 18
Batooro people, 24
Bazant, Micah, 356
BDSM, 16, 118, 122–23, 125. *See also* kink
Bean Sí, 50
Beauvoir, Simone de, 450
Beissel, Conrad, 131, 138
Benjamin, Tom, 110
Benjamin, Walter, 379, 429

Berger, Helen, 277, 287n8
Berger, John, 150
Berkley, 201n44
Berman, Marshall, 146
Bernstein, Elizabeth, 212
Bewitched, 148, 283, 320, 327
Beyer, Rebecca, 95, 97, 99
Bhangi and Another v. The State of Chhattisgarh, 209, 211, 217. See also Yadav, Bhangi
Bible, 65, 93–96, 99, 134, 251, 338, 451, 453
binding, 132, 134–36, 153, 353, 357, 358n1, 402, 403–4, 414; of Donald Trump, 6
bioremediation, 424, 431
Bishnoi people, 229
Black Bloc, 347, 357
Black Death (bubonic plague), 178, 428
Black feminism, 15, 19, 35, 76–85, 86n7, 86n15, 265, 368, 402, 441, 464, 467, 469. See also womanism
Blackfoot people, 86n15
Black Forest Clan, 137
Black Lives Matter, 100
black magic, 29, 37, 180, 229, 242, 289, 305. See also dark magic
Black Sunday, 319, 327
Black witches, 5–6, 15, 65, 75–85, 86n7, 86n20
The Blair Witch Project, 8
Blavasky, Morgana, 257
The *Blitch* Fund, 81–82
The Blood on Satan's Claw, 319, 327
Bloody Mary, 9
Bloody May Day, 145
Boann, 411
Bobolizan, 177
Bodin, Jean, 178
Bodos, 223
Boehme, Jacob, 131–32, 134, 137–39
Bollywood, 17, 19, 289–91, 294–95, 299–302
Bongmba, Elias Kifon, 240
Boo Hag, 8
Bornstein, Kate, 367
born this witch, 320–27

Boserup, Ester, 182
Boulet Brothers, 255
Bourdieu, Pierre, 152
The Bower, 123, 127n39
Bradbury, Ray, 233
brauchers, 134–36, 138
Briggs, Robin, 181, 183
Brigid, 411
British Empire, 50, 180, 319; in India, 225; in Ireland, 15, 47–52; in Tanzania, 192, 196–97; in Uganda, 23. See also Great Britain
Brooks, Ethel, 15
brooms, 148, 331, 333–35, 337, 353, 356
brown, adrienne maree, 112, 114, 473n26
Brown, Cyntoia, 356
Bruce, La Marr Jurelle, 472
brujas/brujos/brujxs, 5–6, 8, 249, 254, 256, 370, 468
Brujas del Mar, 6
brujería, 37, 385n13
Brut33, 254
Bryceson, Deborah Fahy, 195
Buckingham, Lindsey, 284–85, 287n13
Buck-Morss, Susan, 468
Budapest, Zsuzsanna, 278, 282, 287n8
Buddhism, 66, 388, 393, 395, 454
Buffy the Vampire Slayer, 321–22, 327, 416n11
Burgess, Charlie Claire, 112. See also Fifth Spirit Tarot
Burgkmair, Hans, 338
Burke, Kenneth, 379
Butler, Frederick (@drunk_on_decay), 64
Butler, Judith, 366
Butt, Osman Klalid, 304
Byrd, William, 91

Cabot, Laurie, 254
Caffentzis, George, 469
Cahana, Jonathan, 122
Cailleach, 9
Çakın, Ayhan Kerem, 153
Caliban, 441

California, 123–24; Los Angeles, 81, 278–80, 283
Cameroon, 7, 179
Campagna, Federico, 442
Campoamor, Clara, 367
Campus Witches (Kampüs Cadıları), 144–45, 149–50, 154
candles, 6, 77, 83, 101, 376–77, 390, 393–95
Candomblé, 37–38, 68
cannibalism, 18, 292; eating children trope, 8, 10, 118–19, 259, 332, 337–40
capitalism, 7, 18, 28, 139, 146, 149, 296, 312, 368, 428, 430; capitalist realism, 69n13; and colonialism, 43n16, 66–67, 79, 105, 234–36, 350, 437, 466–67; global, 7–8, 66, 234–35, 369; racial, 464–66, 471; resistance to, 15, 61, 63, 76–85, 348, 350, 356, 420, 425, 437, 455, 464–72; and witch hunts, 182, 196, 224–25, 369. *See also* anti-capitalism; commodification; neoliberalism
Capitalocene, 422, 431
carceral feminism, 212
Caribbean, 12–13, 34, 36, 82, 457
Carrie, 9
cartomancy, 107, 160. *See also* fortune-telling; tarot
caste, 2, 19n1, 183, 221, 225–26, 228–30, 292, 298
Catholic Church, 15, 38, 160–61, 169, 237, 249, 257, 277, 385n13, 388, 390, 453; and witchcraft, 47–56
Catland Books, 6, 372, 383n3
Catland Witch School, 18, 372–86
Catta Coven, 137
cauldrons, 9, 54, 332–33, 335, 338, 389; digital, 110
Cavarero, Adriana, 444
Celtic paganism, 9, 50–52, 56, 394
Chanda, Triveni, 229
Chapman, Justin, 23–24
Charmed, 19n3, 321, 327
charms, 95–97, 132–33, 136, 280, 453
Charnock, Ruth, 18
Chaudhuri, Soma, 224

Chemaly, Soraya, 307
Chen, Mel, 365
Chenowith, Erica, 370
Chernoff, Carolyn, 18
Cherokee Nation, 91, 101n3, 267, 430
Chesapeake Conjure Society, 77
Chew-Bose, Durga, 352
Chhattisgarh Witchcraft Atrocities Prevention Act, 17, 206, 211–12, 216, 228
Chhibber, Saira, 17
children, 9, 11, 29, 49, 97, 133, 136, 149, 151, 153, 162–64, 205, 227, 241, 368, 412; anti-witch killings of, 194, 200nn20–21, 222; care of, 78, 84, 196; eating/killing of, 8, 10, 118–19, 259, 332, 337–40; maternal sacrifice for, 322; and public grief, 366; witnessing violence against women, 207–8, 210
The Chilling Adventures of Sabrina, 324, 327, 416n11
China, 176–78, 182, 427
#Christian, 61
Christianity, 40, 50, 77, 122, 161, 238, 263, 276, 277, 281–82, 338, 389–90, 394–95, 453–55; and Appalachian folk magic, 16, 90, 95, 98–100; Christian nationalism, 137; Christian supremacy, 80; Christo-fascism, 135–36; and colonialism, 14, 23–24, 235; and Deitsch spirituality, 132, 134–35, 137, 139; evangelical, 76, 96, 191, 193, 198; feminist critiques of, 47; patriarchy in, 324; and tarot, 107; views on witchcraft, 23–28, 191, 322, 388; and witch hunts, 198, 225; and womanism, 86n20. *See also* Bible; Catholic Church; Congregationalism; Gnostics; Pentecostalism; prosperity gospel messaging; Protestantism; Puritans
Chudail No.1, 290, 294, 296–97
churails, 8, 17, 289–301, 304–16
Churails (TV show), 17, 304–16
Circe, 60
Cixous, Hélène, 341n13, 352
Clau, Simon, 16

Cleary, Krystal, 16
Clifton, Chas S., 282, 384
climate crisis, 6, 265, 286, 367, 426
closed *vs.* open practices, 15, 60–69, 107, 115n7, 373, 384n7, 385n13
Clover, Carol, 353
Cockettes, 255
cocreation, 15, 75–85, 120
Cohen, Cathy, 470–71
Cohen, Stephen, 255
Cold War, 287n3
Collins, Patricia Hill, 78
colonialism/imperialism, 1, 38, 79–80, 182, 267, 310, 373, 384n7, 422, 465; in Africa, 23–26, 31, 192–97; in Asia, 221, 223, 454; British, 15, 23, 47–52, 180, 192, 196, 225, 319; and capitalism, 43n16, 66–67, 79, 105, 234–36, 350, 437, 466–67; in Europe, 47–48, 56; European, 64, 68, 91, 94–96, 234, 327–28, 408, 427–28, 437; feminist resistance to, 12, 67–69, 350, 437, 450, 457; and gender, 234–36, 240, 368; and *I, Tituba, Black Witch of Salem,* 34–42; and Indigenous Peoples, 422; neo-, 105, 428; in North America, 34, 47, 91, 94, 100, 101n3; Ottoman, 146; and patriarchy, 1–7, 79, 350; and race, 234–36, 237, 265, 269–70, 441, 468; settler colonialism, 4–5, 8, 13, 34, 91, 96, 263, 423, 430; US, 408, 430; and witchcraft, 10, 12, 14–15, 23–26, 31, 63–64, 66–67, 192–97, 408; and witch hunts, 2–3, 7–8, 179, 319. *See also* decoloniality; postcolonialism
coloniality of power, 234–35
colonial/modern gender system, 235
Combahee River Collective Statement, 40, 78–79
Committee on the Elimination of Discrimination against Women (CEDAW), 148
commodification, 4, 158, 312, 430; of divination, 158–69; of witchcraft, 6, 19, 60–61, 66–69, 283. *See also* capitalism

commoning, 428, 469–72
Concern for the Elderly (COEL), 193
Condé, Maryse: *I, Tituba: Black Witch of Salem,* 15, 34–44, 466–67
Congo, 7
Congregationalism, 34
conjure, 77, 93, 95, 99, 265, 468
container spells, 97, 99
controlling images, 318, 321–22
Coomaraswamy, Radhika, 212
Cooper, Brittney, 367–68
Corcoran, Andreas, 406
Cory, Hans, 196–97
Couldry, Nick, 69
counterculture, 17, 275–87, 438
covens, 54, 256–57, 280, 285, 402, 465; and Appalachian folk magic, 100; Black Forest Clan, 137; Catta Coven, 137; in *Churails,* 17, 307, 309; in *The Craft,* 323, 416; in *Hocus Pocus,* 325–40; Reclaiming Witchcraft, 5, 121–24, 127n30, 287n8, 456; Susan B. Anthony Coven Number 1, 278; and W.I.T.C.H., 348, 350, 355; Wolfa Coven, 137
COVID-19 pandemic, 6, 18, 366, 372, 375, 381–82, 384n10
Cox, Laverne, 261n11
Coyle, T. Thorne, 252
The Craft (film), 323, 327, 416n11
Creed, Barbara, 318, 351–52
crones, 4, 7, 9, 92, 258–60, 276, 319, 331, 334, 338–40
Crowley, Aleister, 121, 255
Crowley, Karlyn, 107
crystals, 3, 52, 66, 68, 268, 283, 356, 393, 452
cultural accessibility, 106, 109–10, 113
cultural appropriation, 3, 60–61, 63–64, 68–69, 100, 102, 108, 373, 468
cunning, 93, 95, 99–100, 135
Cunningham, Scott, 138, 252

daini, 2–3, 11
Dalits, 221, 225–26, 229

INDEX *493*

Daly, Mary, 277, 282, 287n6
dark magic, 10, 322–23. See also black magic
Daughters of the Moon Tarot, 108
Davidson, Ellis, 136
Davis, Angela Y., 36, 78, 367
Dawtas of the Moon, 76
dayans, 221, 228, 307
Day of the Dead, 361
Dean, Tim, 471
decolonial feminism, 1, 7, 15, 234
decoloniality, 12, 17, 39, 42, 61, 112, 237, 269, 271–72; decolonial feminism, 7, 15, 68–69, 234; decolonial love, 15, 68
Decoration Day, 97–98
deep listening, 271
Deitsch (Pennsylvania Germans), 16, 131–39
demonic feminism, 439–45
demonic grounds, 441
demonology, 178, 238, 406
demons, 118–19, 124, 283, 305, 325, 339, 453
Derrida, Jacques, 382
deservedness, 76, 79, 81–85
Despentes, Virginie, 352
Despret, Vinciane, 429
Detroit Hoodoo Festival, 79
Devi, Bholi, 229
Devi, Chhutni, 184
Devi, Phoolan, 308
Devi, Sushila, 228
devil, 34, 119, 125, 180, 259, 266–67, 315, 321, 325, 339, 408, 412, 442–44, 453; "devil worship" discourse, 63. See also Satan
Diana, 278, 391
Dianic Wicca, 277–82, 456
Dior, 108
disability, 26, 109, 113
Discord, 374, 385n11
disempowered victim trope, 318–19, 321, 324, 327
Divide and Dissolve, 17, 263, 265–72
Dobbins, Peggy, 348
Do Lodo, Alejo (@itsalexsiwa), 65

domestic violence, 52–53, 133, 212, 282, 306–7, 309, 314, 323
Donmoyer, Patrick, 133–34
Donovan: "Season of the Witch," 283
doom metal, 17, 266. See also Divide and Dissolve
Douglas, Mary, 378
Douglass, Alexis, 79–80
Doyle, Sadie, 369
Dracmorda, 255
drag, 17, 249–59, 265
Dragula, 257
Druidism, 389
Duffett, Judy, 348
Durkheim, Émile, 395, 454–55
Dust II Onyx, 109

The Eagles: "Witchy Woman," 283
early modern period, 16, 63, 66, 118–19, 125–26, 132, 175–84, 233, 237–39, 332, 384n8, 406, 436
ecofeminism, 121, 287n8, 390
ecstasy/ekstasis, 256, 258, 437; and BDSM, 118–26; ecstatic dance, 16. See also altered states of consciousness
Egyptians Act of 1530, 70n19
The Egyptian Secrets, 132–34
Ehrenreich, Barbara, 178, 407
Eidsheim, Nina Sun, 272
Eileraas, Karina, 264
Ellcessor, Elizabeth, 109
El Salvador, 8
emergent strategy, 106, 112–14
empowered evil trope, 319, 324, 327
England, 15, 91, 131, 137, 239, 369, 404; Medieval, 9; witch hunts in, 183–85. See also Great Britain; United Kingdom
English, Dierdre, 178, 407
Enlightenment, 13, 37–38, 147, 263, 265, 406, 441, 450, 466
Ephrata Cloister, 130
Ernstberger, Adrianna L., 17
eroticism, 40–41, 120–25, 267, 320, 457, 464, 466, 469–71

Escaja, Tina, 18, 362–65
essentialism, 51, 265, 276, 321, 352, 357
Essig, Laurie, 18, 362
Estés, Clarissa Pinkola, 401
ethical traditional witchcraft, 372–73, 384n7
Etsy, 68, 124
Europe, 3, 6, 8–9, 63, 85n4, 97, 118–20, 131, 158, 191, 254, 390, 406, 408, 441; European colonialism, 64, 68, 91, 94–96, 234, 327–28, 408, 427–28, 437; religion in, 451, 453, 455; secularism in, 449; and tarot, 106–7, 110; witch hunts in, 4, 16, 47, 63, 66–67, 124–25, 175–85, 233, 237–39, 437, 465. See also individual countries
Evans, Arthur, 252
Evans-Pritchard, E. E., 181, 454
Eylül'ün Kadın Yüzleri, 148
Ezili, 13, 458

Facebook, 94, 100, 257, 354, 363, 365; Magically Spiritual Black Women group, 75
Failla, Marcelitte, 15
fakelore, 137
Fear Street, 325, 327
Federici, Silvia, 4, 66, 150, 194–95, 259, 312, 368, 409–10, 417n42, 465, 467, 469
feitiçaraia, 37
femicide, 6, 50, 144, 150, 428. See also gender-based violence
feminist killjoy, 114–15
Feminists Against Bullshit (FABS), 18, 362–70, 370n1
feminist spirituality, 47, 108, 277–82, 286, 287n8, 388, 457
feminist studies/theory, 3, 35, 40, 310, 366, 456
feminist witchcraft/witches, 5–6, 46–56, 100, 122, 126n2, 136, 139, 309, 374, 389, 392; and academia, 401–15. See also proto-feminist witch; Reclaiming Witchcraft; W.I.T.C.H.
feminist witch studies, 1, 4, 14

femmes, 265, 359n19; Black, 15, 75, 78–79, 82–84, 458; definition, 85n3; monstrous, 17–18, 347–48, 351–57
Ferret, D, 17
Feverish World symposium, 367
Few, Martha, 240
Fifth Spirit Tarot, 112
Final Girl, 322, 353
Finland, 238–39, 449
First Merseburg Charm, 132–33, 136
Fisher, Mark, 69
Fleetwood Mac: "Rhiannon," 276, 283–86, 287n13
Florika, 348
Flowers, Thomas, 240
Flying Broom, 148–50
flying ointments, 118, 124–25
folklore, 1, 8–9, 15, 125, 239, 291, 296, 373
folk magic, 63; Appalachian, 90–101
fortune-telling, 147; in Italy, 16, 158–69; Romani, 63, 68, 107, 115n7; in Turkey, 16, 150–53. See also cartomancy
Foucault, Michel, 321
Foxfire series, 99
Frazer, James, 454
Freya, 136
Fumai, Chiara, 436–45
Funk, Cynthia, 348
funny witches, 18, 332

Gago, Verónica, 368–69
Ganim, Carole, 92
Gardner, Gerald, 135, 137–38, 278, 390, 392
Garza, Alejandro (Alex Garza/Mista Alex/Mista Boo), 249–60
Gaskill, Malcolm, 406
gatekeeping, 62–63
Gates, Racquel J., 111
Gaur, Karishma, 228
Gaur, Naina, 228
Gawain, Shakti, 79
gay people, 19n3, 251, 252, 253, 260n1, 321. See also homosexuality; lesbians

gender-based violence, 7–8, 195, 199, 212, 241, 276, 278; and witchcraft accusations, 2. *See also* accusations of witchcraft; domestic violence; femicide; misogyny; witch hunts
gender studies, 239, 361–62
Gen Z, 18
German people, 8, 91, 94, 131–32, 394. *See also* Deitsch (Pennsylvania Germans)
German pietists, 131–32, 134
Germany, 8, 132, 137, 183, 406
Geschiere, Peter, 181, 195
Ghana, 7, 177, 183, 240–42
Gharavi, Lance, 139
ghosts, 9–10, 13, 289, 293, 296–99, 301, 427, 429, 432
Giberson, Tess, 105
Ginzburg, Carlo, 180
girl power, 318, 321
Global North, 4–7, 16–17, 66, 159, 191, 198, 240, 276–77, 280, 282, 286–87
Global South, 3, 5, 7, 12, 16–17, 66, 233–36, 239–40, 242, 428, 431, 454
Gnostics, 122–23
goddesses, 9–10, 127n39, 131–32, 138–39, 252, 256, 262, 277–78, 281–82, 283–86, 287n6, 295, 325, 388–91, 393
goddess movement/spirituality, 6, 46, 100, 108, 121–22, 136, 277–78, 320
Godin, Marie-Andrée, 402
Goldman, Marion S., 18
Gonds, 225
Gordon, Avery, 13, 35
Gottlieb, Kathryn, 64
Goya, Francisco de, 337
Gran Fury, 354
grannies, 15–16, 90–101
Great Britain, 23, 51–52, 180, 192, 196–97, 225, 280, 319, 390, 454. *See also* British Empire; England; United Kingdom
Great Rite, 138
Greece, 146; Ancient, 8
Greek mythology, 126n3, 444
Greek people, 145

Green, Peter: "Black Magic Woman," 283–84
Greenwood, Susan, 152, 402, 415n4
Grey, Peter, 118
Grien, Hans Baldung, 333, 337
Griffin, Wendy, 46, 278
Grimm's Fairy Tales, 8
grimoires, 124, 132–33
Grossman, Pam, 68
Guatemala, 10, 240
Guerrilla Girls, 356
Gullah Jack, 65
Gumbs, Alexis Pauline, 402, 415n5
Gundella the Green Witch, 287n9
Güner, Halime, 148

Hafez, Sherine, 4
Hagen, Rune Blix, 239
hags, 8–9, 337, 339
Haitian Vodou, 13, 75, 385n13, 466
Haitian voodoo, 62
Haiven, Max, 432n11
Halloween, 253, 255, 331, 335–37, 339, 348, 351, 361, 363–64
Hamraie, Aimi, 113. *See also* Society of Disabled Oracles
Hanako-san, 9
Haraway, Donna, 450
Harding, Rachel, 38
Harkness, Deborah: *A Discovery of Witches*, 403–4, 408, 416n11, 416n19
Harmony Society, 131, 138
Harney, Stefano, 428
Harris, Lakeesha, 468
Harry Potter, 5, 321–22, 327, 416n11
Hartless, Jaime, 17
Hartman, Saidiya, 13, 35
Hartmann, Franz, 138
Hatfield family, 92
Haughwout, Margaretha, 18
Haus of Boo, 257–58
Hawai'i, 388
Hawkes, A. L., 416n11
Hawthorne, Nathaniel, 40
healing justice, 106, 111–12

heathenry, 132, 136–38
heavy sound, 267–68, 270, 272
Hegel, G. W. F., 139
Helfenstein, Dr.: *Secrets of Sympathy*, 133
Hellenic polytheism, 385n13
Heller, Meredith, 255
Heraclitus, 444
herbalism, 3–4, 6, 23–27, 30–32, 91, 96–99, 124–25, 138, 192, 239, 407, 425
Hermanas Vampiro drag collective, 255
heteronormativity, 16, 105, 119, 147, 251, 322, 326, 431
heteropatriarchy, 9, 34, 118–19, 122, 369, 402, 465, 467
Hex Brett Kavanaugh, 372
hexing, 12, 395, 413; Deitsch, 133–36; as feminist resistance, 6, 131, 347–59, 364, 366–68, 372
Hex on the NRA, 366
Hex Trump, 372
High John the Conqueror, 65
hillbilly Hoodoo, 93
Hinduism, 17, 66, 226–27, 289, 291, 295–300, 302n3, 302n10, 388, 390, 393, 395, 454
Hindu Succession (Amendment) Act, 226
Hindutva politics, 296
Hinton, Alexander, 198
Hip House, 251
Hirau and Others v. The State of Madhya Pradesh, 209, 211
Hitler, Adolf, 265
Hocus Pocus, 18, 331–40
Hohman, John: *The Long Lost Friend*, 133
Hollywood, 4, 282, 296
Holtz, Tanice, 283
Holzer, Jenny, 354
Homer, 60
homophobia, 3, 26–27, 137
homosexuality, 26, 48, 251–52, 313; decriminalization of, 48. *See also* gay people; lesbians
homosocial relationalities, 16, 26, 151

Hoodoo, 35, 63–65, 68, 75, 77–78, 80–81, 86n7, 93–95, 468
hooks, bell, 75, 78, 82–83, 100, 102n27, 431
horned god, 252
horror genre, 9, 254–57, 282, 289, 301, 416n11
Howell, Rebecca Gayle, 93
Hudson, Lauren, 402
Huebner, Louise, 275–76, 279–280, 286, 287n9
Human Potential Movement, 449
Hume, Lynne, 123
hyperecologies, 423, 425–27
hyperorganisms, 423–24, 426–27
hysteria, 18, 164, 264, 319, 325, 361, 365–66

Iceland, 158, 238–39
idisi, 132–33, 135–36, 138
I Dream of Jeannie, 282–83
Ifá, 75, 80, 83, 86n7
#IHaveFeministRebellionInMe, 150
Illouz, Eva, 162
Imarisha, Walidah, 473n26
India, 270, 289, 291, 294–97, 300–301, 308, 315; witch hunts in, 2–3, 7–8, 11, 17, 176–84, 194, 205–16, 219–30, 240–42
Indian Penal Code, 208
Indian Supreme Court, 206, 209, 211, 214
Indigeneity, 184, 267, 272
Indigenous Latin American spiritualities, 67
Indigenous Peoples, 2–3, 5, 13, 43n1, 68, 79, 168, 408, 437, 453, 458; in Appalachia, 91, 94, 96–97, 101; and colonialism, 10, 37–38; and commons, 427; and crystals, 66; and Divide and Dissolve, 266–72; genocide of, 425; and New Age culture, 107, 468; and palo santo, 67; and white sage, 102n28, 422; and witchcraft, 63, 431; and witch hunts, 7, 12, 175–76, 178–84, 221, 223–24. *See also* American Indians; Native Americans; *individual nations and tribes*

INDEX *497*

Indonesia, 7
Instagram, 2, 5, 61, 68, 75, 348, 349, 351, 352, 353–57, 358n3
interdisciplinarity, 1, 12, 106, 240, 384n9
International Women's Day, 144, 148, 315
International Women's March, 355, 367
International Women's Suffrage Alliance, 147
International Women's Union, 147
intersectional feminism, 106, 114, 265
intersectionality, 2, 7, 42, 105–6, 114, 158, 264–65, 347, 353, 374
intersex people, 26–27
Iraq War, 144, 286
Ireland, 94; Irish witches, 15, 46–56
Irish Constitution, 50
Irish Free State, 15, 48–52, 53, 56
Irish High Court, 49
isangoma, 24
Isis, 139
Islam, 147, 192, 225, 228–29, 291, 299, 305, 307–8
Istanbul Convention, 150
Italy, 407, 436, 438–39; fortune-telling in, 16, 158–69

Jaffe, Naomi, 348
Jaffe, Sarah, 469
Jakes, T. D., 77
Japan, 9, 291, 427; Tokyo, 393
Jesus Christ, 99, 193, 258, 390
Jim Crow, 78
Johnston, Sarah, 119
Jones, Annie, 438
Josephson-Storm, Jason, 406, 408
Joshi, Apoorva, 15
joy, 114, 123, 127n39, 260, 267, 350, 353, 355, 364, 471; rebellious, 144–54
Judaism, 65, 265, 391, 395; Kabbalah, 63–64

Kali, 295
Kapoor, Jahnvi, 299
Kapoor, Shraddha, 298

Karnataka Prevention and Eradication of Inhuman Evil Practices and Black Magic Act, 242
Kat, 19n3
Kavanaugh, Brett, 6, 372
Kay, Meredith, 407
Keating, AnaLouise, 456
Kelkar, Govind, 16, 241
Kellhammer, Oliver, 18
Kentucky, 102n27, 388, 431
Kenya, 7
Khan, Natash, 286
Khasi people, 181
Khúc, Mimi, 111–12. *See also* Asian American Tarot
Kidd, Dustin, 349
Kifaro, 29
Kimmerer, Robin Wall, 13, 97, 423, 453
kink, 110, 122, 125. *See also* BDSM
Kissman, Kriss, 158
Kitsimba, 12
Kivelson, Valerie, 238
Klassen, Chris, 309–10
Kramer, Heinrich, 119. See also *Malleus Maleficarum*
Krefting, Rebecca, 332
Kriebel, David, 134, 137
Kruger, Barbara, 354
Kubrick, Stanley, 9
Kumar, R., 294
Kurnaz, Işıl, 149
Kurtoğlu, Ayça, 16

Lady Speech (@ladyspeechsankofa), 64
La Llorona (figure), 9–10
La Llorona (film), 10
La Malinche, 10
La Masacre, 257
La Más Draga, 258
Lamia, 8
Larner, Cristina, 178
La Siguanaba, 8
Latifah, Daizy October, 81–82, 84
Latinx people, 361, 468
Latinx witches, 5

law and order feminism, 212
Law on Demonstrations and Marches (Turkey), 145
Law on the Abolition of Lodges, Zawiyahs and Tombs, 147
Leek, Sybil, 137
Legal and Human Rights Centre (LHRC), 192, 194, 198–99
Legion of Mary, 390
Le Guin, Ursula K., 356
Leonard, Zoe, 105
Lepecki, André, 380
lesbians, 19n3, 108, 234, 312, 321, 331, 337, 367, 456–57. *See also* homosexuality
Les Ghouls, 255
Lewis, David, 139
LGBTQ+ communities, 27, 47–48, 50, 100, 110, 252–53, 320–21, 326
Linebaugh, Peter, 427
Linz, Jess, 402
Lombroso, Cesare, 438
London, Lindsay/Lou, 363
Lonzi, Carla, 436–45, 446n12, 446n16, 447n31
Lorde, Audre, 78, 114–15, 470–71
Love, Hess, 77–78, 84
Lovett, Ann, 49
Lua people, 177
Lugones, María, 234–36
Luja, Sado, 197
Luna, Bri (@thehoodwitch), 75

Mabinogion, 284
MacCormack, Patricia, 265
Macdonald, Helen, 17, 221, 225
Machado, Isabel, 17
Machado de Oliveira, Vanessa, 403
Madara, Melissa Jayne, 383n3
Maddox, Kelly-Ann, 110
Madhya Pradesh High Court, 206, 209–211, 213, 215–16
Madhya Pradesh Police Commission, 208
Madres de Plaza de Mayo, 366
Magdalene laundries/asylums, 53–54, 56

Magical Resistance, 6
Magliocco, Sabina, 252, 256, 454–55
Mahanubhavpanth, 227
Mahmood, Saba, 308
Malawi, 183
Malaysia, 177
Malleus Maleficarum, 119, 239, 340n12
Mama Bree (Carlos Briano), 253
Manalansan, Martin F., IV, 361–62
Manda, Lucida Domoko, 24
Māori people, 25, 267
Mara, 411
Marwaris, 223
Marx, Karl, 183
Marxism, 465
Maryland: Baltimore, 76–77, 80, 83
masculinism, 132, 145, 146, 151, 154
masculinity: toxic, 366–67
Massachusetts: Salem, 34–35, 40–42, 134, 179, 234, 315, 331, 335–36, 339, 466
Massey, Carissa, 93
Mather, Cotton, 34, 41–42
Mather, Increase, 41
Matres/Matronae, 132
May, Rollo, 151
Mazzarella, William, 365
Mbiti, John S., 24
McCann, Brandy Renee, 15–16
McCormack, Patricia, 409
McKittrick, Katherine, 439
McVie, Christine, 284–85
McVie, John, 284
Medea, 333–34
Medhurst, Andy, 335
media studies, 106
Medicaid, 77
Medicare, 77
Medusa, 352
Meimaridi, Mara, 145–46
Meinhof, Ulrike, 438
Mejias, Ulises A., 69n7
Mercantile Doctrine of Accumulation, 178
Mesopotamia, 118
Messi, 6
mestizo spiritualities, 67

#MeTooBollywood, 301
Mexican feminists, 6
Mexican people, 17
Mexican witches, 8, 385n13
Mexico, 8, 9, 249, 258, 353, 356, 456; Monterrey, 252–53, 255–57
Michigan, 6; Detroit, 79, 86, 287n9
Michigan Womyn's Music Festival, 280
Middle Ages, 149, 177, 332, 410
Middle Passage, 12–13
midwives, 92–93, 149, 178–79, 353, 465
Miguel, Edward, 196, 201n30
millennials, 17, 276, 286, 318
millennial witches, 286, 321–22, 324
Minotaur, 442
misogyny, 10, 46, 114, 119–20, 264, 277, 283, 289–90, 299, 324, 361, 367–68, 410, 436. *See also* femicide; gender-based violence; sexism
Mista Boo, 17, 249–60
Mitchell, Joni, 280–83
mob violence, 17, 197–99. *See also* witch-hunts
Modern Pagan Witchcraft, 319
modern Western syncretic witchcraft, 372–73
Modern Witches, 150
mojo bags, 77, 97
Mokosh, 411
Molina, Lorenza de, 240
Monabarie Tea Estate, 228
Mongela Commission, 193
monotheism, 391, 455
monstrosity, 255, 257, 294–95, 298, 316, 318, 349–50, 441–42; monstrous femme, 17–18, 347–48, 351–57
Moon Cult, 383n3
Moore, Jason W., 422
Moravians, 130–32, 138
More Other Backward Classes (MOBCs/OBCs), 221, 223, 226, 229
Morgan, Ffiona, 108. *See also* Daughters of the Moon Tarot
Morgan, Robin, 348
Morrill, Angie, 7

Moten, Fred, 428
Motherpeace Tarot, 108, 115
Mountain Mary (Anna Maria Jung), 134–35
Moura, Ann, 252
Moye, Jayme, 138
Mozambique, 7
Mullick, Sanjay Bosu, 229
Muñoz, José Esteban, 458, 470–71
Murrey, Amber, 408
mutual aid, 76, 79, 81–82, 85, 469

Naropa University, 388
Nath, Debarshi Prasad, 223
Nathan, Dev, 16, 241
National Crime Records Bureau (NCRB), 219–20
Native Americans, 36, 86, 235. *See also* American Indians; Indigenous Peoples
Needles, Sharon, 257
Nehill, Sylvie, 266–68, 272. *See also* Divide and Dissolve
Neitz, Mary Jo, 18
neo-heathenry, 137
neoliberalism, 106–7, 114, 148, 153, 195, 263, 290, 295–96, 402, 415n2, 431, 464, 467–68, 471
neo-paganism, 135, 137, 252, 256, 258, 277, 280, 384n9, 456
Nepal, 7
Netherlands, 179, 183
New Age spiritualities, 64, 66–67, 70n16, 76–79, 106–10, 114, 452, 468
New England (US), 47, 179, 238, 466
New York City, 6, 86n7, 278, 348, 455; Brooklyn, 372–83
Next World Tarot, 105, 113, 115
Ngere tribe, 108
Nguyen, Lani, 112. *See also* These Small Mysteries
Nichols-Belo, Amy, 17
Nicholson, Jack, 9
Nicks, Stevie, 265, 281, 287n13; "Rhiannon," 276, 283–86, 287n13

Nielson, Ruban, 268
Nigeria, 7, 181, 198
Night March, 144–45
Nishad, Amar Singh, 209–11
Nishad, Dhruv, 207, 211
Nishad, Hirau, 208–11, 214
Nishad, Kulwantin Bai, 205–16
Nishad, Mangan, 210
Nishad, Mannu, 207–11, 213
Nita, Nita Kebo, 257
Njals Saga, 136
Nordic witches, 239
Norns, 132
Norse mythology, 132
Norse/Viking magic, 64, 132
North Carolina, 97
Norton, Rosaleen, 121
Norway, 179–80
Nyabingyi, 26

Oakes, Jason Lee, 265, 287n13
obeah witch, 9
Occultcene, 17, 263–65, 272
occult violence, 190–99
Occupy Wall Street, 428
Odin, 136
okubanda, 26
Old Christmas, 98–99
old heathenry, 132, 138
Oliveros, Pauline, 271
Olodumare, 84
Omilana (@divinepriestess), 65
omufumu, 25, 27
open practices. *See* closed *vs.* open practices
oracle decks, 110, 113, 116n29
Orang, Purni, 227
Order of Nine Angles, 137
An Ordinance to Provide for the Punishment of Persons Practicing or Making Use of So Called Witchcraft, 192
Ordo Templi Orientis, 138
Oregon: Portland, 348, 350–51, 355, 358n3
Orientalism, 441
Orisa Osun, 83

Orlan, 353
Orr, Jackie, 366
Osteen, Joel, 79
Osunfunmilola (Juji Bae), 81, 83; *A Little Juju Podcast*, 80
Ottoman Empire, 145–46
Our Bodies, Ourselves, 109
Our Tarot, 105, 109
Oyewùmí, Oyéronké, 235

paganism, 18, 169, 353, 402, 449, 454; and Deitsch magic, 135–39; neo-, 135, 137, 252, 256, 258, 277, 280, 384n9, 456; and witchcraft, 3–4, 50–52, 56, 64, 95, 127n39, 169, 277, 319, 388–96, 456
Pakistan, 17, 289, 304–16
Palladino, Eusapia, 438
Palmié, Stephan, 37
Papua New Guinea, 7, 179, 181
Parés, Luis Nicolau, 36
Parish, Jane, 183
Parliament of the World's Religions, 459m1
Parris, Samuel, 34
Partners for Law in Development, 212; *Contemporary Practices of Witch-Hunting*, 225
Patidars, 229
Pawnee Nation, 430
Peace of Westphalia, 449
Pegg, Carolanne, 281, 286; "A Witch's Guide to the Underground," 275, 280, 285
Peirce, Charles Sanders, 139
Penn, William, 130
Pennsylvania, 131–39
Pennsylvania Dutch people. *See* Deitsch (Pennsylvania Germans)
Pentecostalism, 90
Pérez, Elizabeth, 265
Perry, Anne, 36
Perry, Imani, 43n1, 467
persons with albinism (PWA), 190–92, 194, 198–99
phallocentrism, 331, 333–35, 337, 339

INDEX 501

phallogocentrism, 366
Phelan, Peggy, 445
Philippines, 8
Piepzna-Samarasinha, Leah Lakshmi, 114
Pierce, AP, 19
Pinrose, 68
Poetic Edda, 132
Poland, 150
polytheism, 385n13, 389–91
popular culture, 111, 257; witch representations in, 17–18, 60, 92–93, 282–83, 286, 289–301, 304–16, 318–27, 331–40, 368. *See also* Bollywood; Hollywood
possession, 7, 18, 26, 228, 295–97, 299–300, 437–38, 441, 443–44
postcolonialism, 48, 56, 182, 192, 195–98, 221, 235, 240, 309
postfeminism, 321
post-witch, 299
Potawatomi people, 13, 423
potencia, 369–70
powwow. *See* brauchers
The Prevention of Witch (Dain) Practices Act, 241
Progressive Women's Association (PWA), 148
Prohibition of Tomb Keeping and Certain Titles, 147
Proietti, Silvana, 257
property, 35, 67, 368, 420–21, 423, 425, 430–32, 439; gendered, 147, 177, 179, 195, 223, 226, 227–28, 369; and witchcraft accusations, 8, 177, 179, 195, 223, 226–27
prosperity gospel messaging, 76–79, 85
Protestantism, 99, 131, 137, 453–54
proto-feminist witch, 327
Punjabis, 223
purification, 18, 193, 229, 375–80
Puritans, 36, 42, 134, 325
pussy hats, 367
Pyles, Loretta, 111

QTBIPOC, 105
Quakers, 130

queer studies, 3
queer theory, 19, 319, 464, 469
queer world-making, 261n10, 470–71
Quijano, Aníbal, 234
Quilty, Emma, 16, 122–23
Qureshi, Bilal, 305, 315

Rabha, Biru Bala, 184
Rabhas, 223
racialization, 85n4, 234, 272, 326, 384n7, 431, 464; of witchcraft, 15, 60, 64, 68, 319, 373, 466–69
racism, 3, 35, 36, 75, 168, 237, 310, 326, 441, 468, 472n1; anti-adivasi, 19n1; in *The Craft*, 323; of Donald Trump, 361; and hate crimes, 48; internalized, 83; and "invasive species" discourse, 427; resistance to, 12, 84, 350, 396. *See also* anti-racism; cultural appropriation; white supremacy
radical feminism, 277–78, 319, 347–48, 436–39, 441
rage, 10, 17, 267, 314, 414, 465; divine, 277, 282; feminist, 17, 56, 277, 282, 305–7, 350, 353, 356, 362, 365, 367, 458; patriarchal, 42
Ralushai Commission, 180
Ramani, 10–12
Ramon's calendar, 94
Ramsay, Shyam and Tulsi, 294
Ranco, Darren, 422
Ranger, Terence, 194
Rao, Rajkummar, 297, 299
The Rattle: "The Witch," 283
RavenWolf, Silver, 137
Rawat women, 225
Reclaiming Witchcraft, 121, 456; Witch-Camps, 5, 122–24, 127n30, 287n8
Reed, Takiaya, 266–67, 272. *See also* Divide and Dissolve
Regias del Drag, 254, 256–57
Rehmeyer, Nelson, 134
Reis, João José, 38
Reo, Nicholas, 422
Repeal the 8th movement, 49, 54–55

Republican Laws (Turkey), 148, 153
Republican Party (US), 6
resistive witchcrafting, 19, 468, 471
resource scarcity: and witchcraft accusations, 7–8, 224
revenge, 17, 36, 295–96, 323, 466
Rhiannon (goddess), 283–86
Richards, Jake, 95, 99–100
Richter, Roxane, 240
Rider-Waite-Smith Tarot, 107
Riot Grrrl, 264, 350, 354, 356, 359n19, 359n22
Rivolta Femminile, 439, 444, 446n12
Road, Cristy C., 113. *See also* Next World Tarot
Robinson, Cedric, 465
The Rocky Horror Picture Show, 255
Rogel, Anna, 18
Romani people, 63, 68, 70nn19–20, 107, 115n7
Romero, George, 320
Roohi, 289–90, 297, 299–301
root doctors, 92, 96, 99
root work, 93
rootworkers, 62
Rosemary's Baby, 282
Rountree, Kathryn, 139
Rowlands, Alison, 237–38
Rude, Mey, 120
ruderal ecologies, 18, 421–25, 430
ruderal witchcraft, 420–32
Rungus, 177
RuPaul's Drag Race, 254, 257
Rupp, Leila J., 260n5
Russia, 8, 239; Muscovy, 238
Russo, Mary J., 260

sabbaths, 124, 180, 258, 339, 356, 384n8
Sabrina the Teenage Witch, 19n4, 60, 321, 327
Safety Access Zones, 54
saining, 53, 97
Salem (TV show), 254
Salem, MA, 34–35, 40–42, 134, 179, 234, 315, 331, 335–36, 339, 466

Salem Witchcraft Papers, 34
Salem Witch Trials, 34–35, 40–42, 179
Salomon, Bernard, 333
Sampson, Bee, 383n3
Sanchiz-Fung, Minori, 271
Sandoval, Chela, 15, 68
Sandys, Frederick, 334
Sansi, Roger, 37
Santa, Carlos: "Black Magic Woman," 283–84
Santa Inéz, María de, 240
Santería, 68, 389, 458
Santhals, 177, 180
Satan, 134, 236, 251, 266–67, 319, 324–25, 327, 388, 413. *See also* devil
Satnamis, 225
savage slot, 190, 192, 194, 198–99, 200n4
Savransky, Martin, 43n16
scapegoating, 2, 4, 10, 194, 196, 368, 467
Schaller, Karen, 18
Schechner, Richard, 379, 386n31
Scheduled Tribes, 221, 223, 226
Schelling, F. W. J., 139
Schön, Erhard, 334
Scotland, 178–79
Scottish people, 94, 97
Scream, 296
SCUM, 438–39, 446n10
Season of the Witch (film), 320, 327
second-wave feminism, 277, 347, 350–51, 357, 390, 450, 455–56, 459
Secrets of Sympathy, 133
secularism, 17, 19, 80, 147, 361, 393–94, 449–50, 452–53, 455–67, 469
Sedgwick, Eve Kosofsky, 326
Seizemore-Barber, April, 255
Self, Kathleen, 136
self-care, 52–53, 106, 111, 114, 158
Sempruch, Justyna, 276, 283
Sephora, 68
Serra, Piper, 112. *See also* These Small Mysteries
Serres, Michel, 377, 383
settler colonialism, 4–5, 8, 13, 34, 91, 96, 263, 423, 430

sexism, 49, 84, 310, 390, 396. *See also* misogyny
sex magic, 121
sexualization, 92, 93, 239, 282, 301
sexual violence, 9, 49–50, 52–54, 200n12, 212, 271, 296, 306, 308, 319, 323, 326, 356, 368; by Donald Trump, 367; by Harvey Weinstein, 314–15; rape crisis centers, 47; rape culture, 112; under slavery, 34; and witchcraft accusations, 2–4, 225, 227–30. *See also* #MeTooBollywood
sex work, 79, 291, 298, 302n3, 312, 333, 347, 352, 356–57, 420, 443
Shakespeare, William, 9; *Macbeth*, 9; *The Tempest*, 411, 441
shamanism, 122, 135, 168, 389
Shamita, 11
Shannon, Jacquelyn Marie, 18
shapeshifting, 8, 423–27, 430
Sharma, Varun, 299
Shawnee people, 91
The Shining, 9
Shipman, Sarah, 109. *See also* Our Tarot
Shiva, 295
Shrivastev, R. K., 208, 210
Sicardi, Arabella, 352
Sierra Leone, 184
Sill, Judee, 280–81, 283
Sindhis, 223
Sinha, Shashank Shekhar, 17, 224–25
Sioux people, 430
Sirene, Morgan, 110. *See also* Slutist Tarot
The Sixth and Seventh Books of Moses, 133–34
Skelton, Robin, 252
Slow Holler Tarot, 110
Slutist Tarot, 110
Smith, Dorothy, 159
Smith, Gabriella V., 17
Smith, Giulia, 407
Smith, Linda Tuhiwai, 25
Smith, Tayler, 352
smudging, 97
Smyrna, 145–46

Smyth, Araby, 402
Snapchat, 354
Snaza, Nathan, 15
Socialist Feminist Collective (SFC): *Kitchen Witches*, 149–50
social justice, 6, 78, 105, 139, 350, 374
Society of Disabled Oracles, 113
sociology, 47, 158–59, 169, 212, 224, 349, 408, 449, 453–55
Sogolon, 429
Solanas, Valerie, 438
solidarity, 7, 12, 18, 54, 148, 154, 310, 315–16, 349, 355, 368, 370, 394, 426–27, 472
Solidarity Against Beating, 148
Sollberger, Eva, 370n3
Somadeva: *Katha Sarit Sagara*, 291–92
Sophia, 131, 133, 138–39
sorcery, 10, 12, 26, 37, 119, 149, 153, 197, 200n8, 222, 227, 237, 240, 314
South Africa, 7, 24, 180, 194, 198, 200n20, 255
South African Law Commission, 180
South Asia, 5
Spade, Dean, 82, 87n25
Spain, 10, 240
species loneliness, 13
Spence, Shannon Hughes, 15
Spillers, Hortense, 35
spiritual co-creation, 15, 75–85
Sprenger, Jacob, 119. *See also Malleus Maleficarum*
Standing Rock protests, 428
Starhawk, 121, 138, 252, 254, 287n8, 388, 390, 393
starter witch-kits, 68
The State of Madhya Pradesh vs. Dhirpal Nishad and 25 Others, 208–9
St. Clare, Dakota, 372–74, 376–81, 383n3, 384n6, 384n8
Stein, Diane, 139
Steinhart, Eric, 16
Stengers, Isabelle, 262–63, 406, 408–9
Stewart, Mary, 416n11
stigma, 3, 15–16, 115n7, 163–66, 228, 240, 253, 321, 352

Strain, Christopher B., 287n3
Strauss, Jake, 134
Stree, 289–90, 297–98, 300–301
Stroeken, Koen, 191, 200n14, 201n44
Stupart, Linda, 402
Styers, Randall, 408
Sukuma people, 190–97, 199n1, 201n44
Sungusungu people, 197
Supernatural, 324
Susan B. Anthony Coven Number 1, 278
Suspiria, 325, 327, 416n11
Susquehannock people, 91
Sutcliffe, Jamie, 70n16, 415
Sweden: Dalarna, 178
sweet jars, 97
Sycorax, 402, 411–12
syncretism, 14, 60–64, 372–73, 384n7, 391, 396

talismans, 64, 97, 451
Tamás, Rebecca, 402, 413, 415n3
Tanner, Ralph, 197
Tanzania, 7; witch hunts in, 17, 190–201
tarot, 6, 19, 68, 70n16, 76, 150, 154, 158–63, 166, 168, 249, 252–53, 256–57, 374, 388, 392, 401, 449, 459; justice-centered decks, 16, 105–16; *vs.* oracle decks, 116n29. *See also* cartomancy
#TarotSoWhite, 110
Tatari, Morena, 16
Taussig, Michael, 428, 431
Thailand, 177
Thelema, 255
These Small Mysteries, 112
thiefing sugar, 40
Thing'o, Ngũgĩ wa, 24
third space, 16, 151, 153
Thlen, 181
Thomas, Keith, 179, 183
Thornton, Cassie, 432n11
Thule Society, 137
Tiff, 122
TikTok, 5, 61–62, 64–65, 67–68, 69n5, 69n7

Tinsley, Omise'eke Natasha, 13, 40, 450–51, 459, 466, 469
Toivo, Raisa Maria, 233, 239
Townsend-Warner, Sylvia: *Lolly Willowes*, 412–13
Traister, Rebecca, 314–15
trance, 122, 125, 138, 282, 286, 456, 458. *See also* altered states of consciousness
trans-exclusionary radical feminism (TERF), 352
transgender people, 5–6, 53, 126, 242, 261n11, 312, 355–56, 358, 367
Trask, Hunani-Kay, 313
trauma, 11, 15, 46–56, 79–80, 111, 115, 216, 228, 267, 272, 278
travesti, 253, 255
Trigg, Nicole, 18
Trinh T. Minh-ha, 450
Trinidad, 12
Triple Goddess, 132, 138, 356
Trouillot, Michel-Rolph, 190
Trump, Donald, 6, 323, 347, 349–50, 355–57, 361–68, 370n4, 372
Trumpkin Smashings, 361–65, 368, 370n4
Tuck, Eve, 7
Tulane University, 112
Tumblr, 64, 353
&tunderdotonhī, 205
Turkey: fortune-telling in, 16, 150–53; Gezi Park protests, 144–45; Istanbul, 144, 146; witches in, 144–54
Turkish Civil Code, 147
Turkish Communist Party, 148
Turner, Brock, 356
Turner, Nat, 65
Tushabe, Tushabe wa, 14
Twitter/X, 68, 354
Tylor, E. B., 454

uchawi, 191–92, 199
Uganda, 7, 14, 23–25, 28, 198
Uganda Constitution, 23, 28
uganga, 191–92
Ugrešić, Dubravka, 401
undercommons, 428–29

United Kingdom, 47, 49, 319, 390. *See also* England; Great Britain; Scotland
United Nations Human Rights Council, 241
University of California, Riverside, 4
University of Vermont: EcoCulture Lab, 367
UN World Women's Congress, 148
Urbano Ragazzi, Francesco, 438
Urban Outfitters, 68
Urglaawe, 137
US Civil War, 97–98

valkyries, 132, 135–36, 138
vamps, 291
Van Dooren, Thom, 429
Veerana, 290, 294–97
Venus of Willendorf, 356
Vermont, 18, 361–62, 367
Verta, Taylor, 260n5
Virgin Mary, 49, 304
Viy, 319, 327
Vodun, 458
Vogel, Karen, 108, 115n12. *See also* Motherpeace Tarot
Volund, 132
Von Wald, Katie, 19
Voodoo, 60, 62–65, 68, 326
vulvacentrism, 331–40

Walker, Alice, 86n20
Wallace, Marina, 405
Walton, Evangeline, 284
Warlis, 227
Washington, Teresa N., 85n4
Waterman, Hillary, 451
Way of Sophia, 138–39
Weber, Brenda R., 107
Weber, Max, 452
Weinstein, Harvey, 314–15
Weiser, Ron, 6
Wells, Ida B., 367
Welsh, Florence, 286
Welsh goddesses, 283–85

Welsh people, 91, 94, 98
Wen, Benebell, 110. *See also* Asian American Tarot
wheel of the year, 138
white feminism, 5, 326, 347, 357, 456, 467
White-Johnson, Jen, 113. *See also* Society of Disabled Oracles
Whiteley, Sheila, 283, 287n11
white magic, 37
white sage, 68, 102n28, 422
white supremacy, 4, 14, 17, 137, 266, 267, 270–71, 368, 442; in Christianity, 137; of Donald Trump, 362; tarot challenges to, 105, 112; witch challenges to, 1, 6–7, 10, 15, 61, 323, 350–51, 353, 356, 362–64, 367, 437, 468; in witch communities, 64
white witches, 5, 60, 64, 161, 468
Whyte, Kyle, 422
Wicca, 3, 64, 100, 252, 259, 275–76, 319, 351, 363, 383n1, 384n9, 388–92, 396; and Deitsch magic, 137–39; Dianic, 277–82, 456; Gardnerian, 137–38, 278, 390; spiral dance, 285; Wiccan Rede, 358n1
Wiccan Influx, 283
Wilkinson, Crystal, 97
W.I.T.C.H., 18, 278, 347–59, 363
#Witch, 61
The Witch (film), 9, 324–25
witch accusations. *See* accusations of witchcraft
witch bottles, 97
#Witchcraft, 61
Witchcraft Act (1957, Uganda), 23
Witchcraft Act (UK), 319
Witchcraft Ordinance (British colonial Tanzania), 197
The Witchcraft Sourcebook, 35–36
witch doctors, 23
witches' ritual chant, 262
the Witchfinder General, 319
Witchfoot (@witchfoot_incorporated), 67
witch-hop, 265

witch hunts, 1, 9, 145, 154, 236, 258–59, 325, 355, 369, 406–7; in Africa, 5, 7, 175–84, 190–99; in Asia, 5, 7, 175–82, 241; and Christianity, 198, 225; and colonialism/imperialism, 2–3, 7–8, 179, 319; in England, 183–85; in Europe, 4, 16, 47, 63, 66–67, 124–25, 175–85, 233, 237–39, 437, 465; feminist theory of, 175–85; in Iceland, 238; in India, 2–3, 7–8, 10–12, 17, 176–84, 194, 205–16, 219–30, 240–42; and Indigenous Peoples, 7, 12, 175–76, 178–84, 221, 223–24; as metaphor, 314–15; in New England, 34–35, 40–42, 179; in Tanzania, 17, 190–99. *See also* accusations of witchcraft
witchiness, term, 68
witching sound, 263
witch-ins, 361, 370n4
witchy, term, 68
witchy diva, 276, 283, 285–86
Wolfa Coven, 137
Wolfe, Chelsea, 286
womanism, 86n20, 265
women's liberation movement, 278, 281–82
Women's Path, 147

Women's People Party, 146
Women's Union, 147
Women's Voice, 148
womyn's music movement, 280
Wong, Alice, 113. *See also* Society of Disabled Oracles
World Cup (2022), 6
World War I, 146
World War II, 136, 287n3
Wynter, Sylvia, 34, 439–40

X. *See* Twitter/X

Yadav, Bhangi, 209–11
Yancy, George, 366
Yao, Xine, 114
Yıldız, Burçak, 152
Yoruba people, 12, 75, 83–84, 85n4, 235, 393
YouTube, 84, 110, 258
Yusoff, Kathryn, 269

Zambia, 7, 179
Zarillo, Dominick, 238
Zee5, 315
Zika, Charles, 332–34, 338
Zoom, 47, 373

www.ingramcontent.com/pod-product-compliance
Lightning Source LLC
Chambersburg PA
CBHW030344290525
27268CB00001BB/1